Teaching Civic Engagement Across the Disciplines

Elizabeth C. Matto
Alison Rios Millett McCartney
Elizabeth A. Bennion
Dick Simpson
EDITORS

AMERICAN
POLITICAL
SCIENCE
ASSOCIATION

AMERICAN POLITICAL SCIENCE ASSOCIATION

Designed by Drew Meadows

Photo Credits
Eagleton Institute: page 1
University of Illinois, Chicago, Political Science Week: page 97
2016 National Student Convention, Liz Monge: pages 209 and 375

ISBN (Hard Cover) 978-1-878147-55-4
ISBN (Soft Cover) 978-1-878147-56-1
ISBN (ePUB Fixed Layout) 978-1-878147-57-8
ISBN (ePUB Reflowable) 978-1-878147-58-5

*For teacher-scholars of all disciplines seeking
to prepare informed and engaged citizens*

Contents

Section I. Foundations of Civic Engagement Education

Section II. Civic Engagement Education: Purpose and Practice

Section III. Connecting Civic Engagement Education Across the Disciplines

Conclusion

Tables and Figures

Tables

Figures

Foreword

I n 2013, the American Political Science Association (APSA) was proud to support the publication of *Teaching Civic Engagement: From Student to Active Citizen* as a key element of our renewed and expanding commitment to both civic engagement education and political science education more broadly. At the beginning of the twentieth century, education for civic engagement and responsive governance were founding objectives of the political science profession. These goals remain essential for the twenty-first century, as citizens continue to seek productive ways to engage in their community and the political process.

The first book has been a very valuable resource for both exploring the role of civic engagement education in political science as well as identifying effective strategies for incorporating civic and political engagement in the political science classroom. These important efforts stand alongside diverse and expanding efforts in civic engagement and political science teaching and learning. Indeed, civic engagement and education in civics have been an important theme throughout the history of APSA and will continue to be a high priority for the association in the coming years. The work contained in this new book *Teaching Civic Engagement Across the Disciplines*—and the resources in the book's online companion website—builds on the first volume by providing further insight into the important place that civic engagement education holds in political science. Furthermore, the book illuminates resources for expanding civic engagement education into other disciplines and into schools, universities, and communities.

APSA's civic engagement efforts seek to parallel this expansion. The association has worked to integrate civic engagement into publishing, public engagement, and the annual research conference, along with more traditional political science education and teaching and learning venues. Research on strategies for effectively teaching civic engagement has formed a core theme of APSA's Teaching and Learning Conference since its inception in 2005. The association has also initiated more recent efforts to expand APSA's online syllabi collection and more generally to improve online teaching resources (particularly in civic education). APSA recently assumed official sponsorship of the *Journal of Political Science Education*, affirming the enduring value of research on teaching and civic engagement for the discipline of political science. Teaching and pedagogical resources have been integrated across the association's programming, including the introduction of pedagogy workshops at the APSA Annual Meeting and the Centennial Center at APSA headquarters as well as a pedagogy webinar as part of our professional development resources. These efforts underscore the conviction that political science education and teaching civic engagement should be of fundamental concern to the discipline as a whole. Finally, APSA has also officially endorsed the Campus Compact initiative asking universities to develop a civic action plan that would promote more civic engagement by students, faculty, and staff. As APSA intensifies its efforts pertaining to teaching civic engagement we hope to encourage the discipline to enhance the role of the classroom as a training ground for citizens.

As this new volume recognizes, though, teaching civic engagement and providing resources for a better informed and prepared citizenry cannot be confined to the political science classroom. Indeed, APSA's public engagement efforts are fundamentally concerned with exposing people outside the discipline to political science expertise and research that is relevant to their lives, thereby encouraging informed, engaged citizenship. By working to connect journalists to subject experts and supporting scholars in promoting their work and research, we hope to assist political scientists to communicate effective ways that citizens can influence government; to share strategies for increasing engagement; to illuminate issues to help citizens make more informed choices; and to challenge citizens to think critically and examine alternative viewpoints.

Taking full advantage of these opportunities requires recognizing that the scholarly and educational missions of political science are intertwined and complementary. Civic education efforts are most promising and effective when grounded in strong scholarship, not only in pedagogy but also in the purpose of citizenship and the origins of effective citizens and government. Similarly, the purpose and mission of political science as a scholarly discipline becomes clearest when we situate our research within larger questions of what good governance is and how it can be achieved, how democracy is created and sustained, and what good citizenship is and how it can be attained.

The questions addressed in this volume, then, are not simply about civics and citizenship in our universities and communities, though the importance of those issues in and of themselves should not be understated. The authors of the chapters in this volume engage core questions about the role and purpose of political science itself, and what the discipline of political science can offer. As the authors observe, political science is uniquely suited to supporting and encouraging civic education efforts spanning universities, disciplines, and the wider world; in the process, citizenship and the discipline will both gain.

The scholars represented in this volume have contributed their own significant acts of civic engagement by providing this substantial resource that will support the continued emergence of informed and engaged citizens. For their initiative and their contributions to our understanding of the role and importance of political science as a discipline, they deserve our gratitude. ∎

STEVEN RATHGEB SMITH, EXECUTIVE DIRECTOR
AMERICAN POLITICAL SCIENCE ASSOCIATION
JULY 2017

Acknowledgments

The editors would like to acknowledge and thank all those who contributed to the completion of this book and its companion website. Steven Rathgeb Smith, Executive Director for the American Political Science Association (APSA), offered key support at every stage for which the editors are grateful. Barbara Walthall, APSA's Director of Publishing, and Drew Meadows, editorial and publications associate, were invaluable partners in publishing and launching this book and its companion website. Meghan McConaughey applied her research and writing proficiency to preparing the front matter of the book. Maureen Heffern Ponicki skillfully organized and prepared the text's references. Xander Laughlin assisted in editing draft manuscripts. Brendan L. Keating assisted with preparing components of the website. Mackenzie Rice and Michele Calderon helped in many other ways, such as proofreading and compiling the bibliography.

The editors also thank the Eagleton Institute of Politics at Rutgers, The State University of New Jersey; the Towson University Faculty Development and Research Committee, Office of the Provost, College of Liberal Arts, and Office of Student Affairs; Indiana University South Bend's Research & Development Committee; and the University of Illinois at Chicago's Political Science Department for support of the research and writing of this volume. Our colleagues at the APSA Teaching and Learning Conference and the APSA Annual Meeting provided so many thoughtful comments to help us refine chapters in the book and overall manuscript.

Finally, we thank our families for their unending patience throughout this effort. ∎

SECTION I

Foundations of Civic Engagement Education

Introduction

Alison Rios Millett McCartney

"Democracy needs to be born anew every generation, and education is the midwife."
—John Dewey[1]

The 2016 American elections ignited fierce debates about the goals of our democracy, who this government works for, what our institutions should be doing, and what it means for citizens to participate in those decisions. These questions revealed deep divides within the citizenry beyond geographic, demographic, professional, or generational differences. The elections exposed that while Americans want a healthy, sustainable democracy that can effectively address twenty-first century problems, many Americans do not understand how their government works and how to access their government to solve common problems. A large number of our fellow citizens have become too frustrated by policy outcomes or disillusioned by partisan bickering to participate.[2] Only 50%–57% of the adult voting age population has been turning out to vote in national presidential elections. An even lower percentage, about one-third, voted in midterm elections.[3] Among developed countries, the United States ranks 27 out of 35 in voter turnout.[4]

Nonparticipation is not limited to only national voting; state and local elections usually have even lower turnout. These results suggest a massive free-rider problem, as Mansbridge explains in the opening chapter, "Why Do We Need Government? The Role of Civic Education in the Face of the Free-Rider Problem." If we look at other measures of citizen participation, such as volunteering, the numbers are even more alarming. In 2015, the US Bureau of Labor Statistics estimated that about 25% of Americans were volunteering in their communities.[5] In a study just before the 2012 elections, the Pew Research Center showed that only about 48% of Americans participated at least once in a civic group or activity, such as working with other citizens to solve a community problem or attending a political meeting on local, town, or school affairs, during the preceding year. However, these numbers were much higher for those with higher income levels.[6] Collectively, these statistics paint a picture in which only one-quarter to one-half of Americans—and a potentially unrepresentative set of citizens—participate in decision making in their communities.

An effective democracy cannot continue to fulfill its goal of taking care of the needs of all of its citizens if its citizens do not participate. At the very least, we need a sizeable, sustainable, and diverse majority to be involved in significant ways.[7] With so many citizens sitting on the sidelines, we cannot succeed.

We need, as Dewey indicates, quality civic education to foster the redevelopment of a knowledgeable, capable, and engaged citizenry. Americans can no longer live and work in their isolated silos. Instead, we need to build our democracy with geographically, demographically, professionally, and politically diverse people who hold a wide variety of viewpoints and experiences and who are educated in how government works, how problems can be peacefully confronted, and how we can work together to find mutually beneficial solutions. Civically educated citizens, who are willing and capable of pursuing the mutual gains through cooperation within society and government, are the future that this country must have to survive and thrive in the twenty-first century. However, as Butin writes, "…none of us are born with the skills, knowledge, and disposition to be thoughtful, engaged, and active citizens."[8]

Since the end of the Cold War, education policy has failed to invest in this foundation of our democracy. As researchers recently noted, "The majority of states do not include civics, social studies or citizenship in their education accountability systems."[9] Meanwhile, as Rogers explains, political science as a discipline is the natural place for education about government, but it has long "abandoned its role in teaching the practice of politics by leaders and average citizens, perhaps out of fears of partisanship or others concerns, such as securing our place in the academy."[10] With the publication of *Teaching Civic Engagement: From Student to Active Citizen* in 2013, the American Political Science Association (APSA) has reasserted political science's commitment to quality civic education, civic engagement education, and political engagement education and its commitment to working with all disciplines to provide quality civic learning opportunities for all students at all levels.

We are not alone in this goal. As section I of this book indicates, key actors in higher education also seek a rejuvenation of quality civic education and engagement. In her chapter, Musil summarizes the call to action on civic engagement education launched in 2012 through the joint publication, *A Crucible Moment: College Learning and Democracy's Future*, by the US Department of Education and the Association of American Colleges and Universities (AAC&U). In their chapter, Seligsohn and Grove of Campus Compact, a coalition more than 1,000 colleges and universities, explain that Campus Compact was founded in 1985 because college presidents were concerned that higher education was not fulfilling its role of helping to sustain a healthy democracy. Today, Campus Compact promotes civic action plans to further civic engagement on all its member campuses. The bipartisan Council of State Governments' report, written by state government leaders, proposes that "…educating on how state and local government touches the lives of citizens is a key foundational element" to "boosting the next generation's ability to participate in our democracy, and the need is urgent." Barrett and Greene then bluntly warn that, with the decline of civic education and the low levels of citizens' trust in government, "How, indeed, can anyone trust a powerful entity that they do not understand?" Political scientists, as the knowledge experts on government, should work with these actors, with educators in other disciplines, and on the K–12 level to expand understanding of the powerful and necessary entity of government.

DEFINITIONS AND PARAMETERS

As we bring these actors together for this important conversation, we should distinguish between civic education, civic engagement education, and political engagement education, although all are important. *Civic education*, or *civic learning*, centers on developing knowledge about political processes, governmental institutions, and power relationships at all levels. It includes, for example, learning about history, state and federal constitutions, decision-making and policy-making processes, duties of government agencies, roles of key actors within government and society, how levels of governance relate to one another, and how decisions at various levels of government impact citizens. It seeks to foster the values of democracy, such as freedom of speech, respect for difference of opinions, respect for the rule of law, equal participation, and responsibility for regular, informed participation. Civic education explores messy issues, such as the free-rider problem and free-use goods debates discussed by Mansbridge, and is not limited to just one issue (e.g., the environment, abortion, corruption) or level of government. Finally, civic education includes developing skills for democracy, such as how to contact representatives and how to register to vote. This civic education—not just rote memorization of facts—is the bedrock of democracy, without which democracy crumbles due to citizens' distrust in government and one another, anger and frustration about how to enact change, and the ability of well-placed societal actors to manipulate the system to achieve their own goals rather than the mutual goals of the community.

Civic engagement education is an evidence-based pedagogy that includes civic learning and emphasizes building civic skills, knowledge, experience, and a sense of efficacy to develop citizens who regularly and productively participate in their communities throughout their lives. It is not the same as offering volunteer opportunities because volunteering can be a one-time event that does not necessarily connect to civic learning, require examining the ideas, structures, or relationships that bring the volunteer to act, or include reflection, the lack of which Elizabeth Minnich aptly termed a "disaster of thoughtlessness."[11] Volunteering activities are worthwhile contributions to the community and can help to increase students' tolerance and understanding of others' viewpoints and experiences. But, as Smith, Nowacek, and Bernstein recently wrote in the *Chronicle of Higher Education*, "they are not a substitute for participation in politics [because]... the political world is the battlefield on which we all must engage."[12] Civic engagement education is also not the same as an internship because the internship is not necessarily connected to civic learning or the community.[13]

Civic engagement education also usually includes an active-learning component. Chapters in section II of this book and in *Teaching Civic Engagement: From Student to Active Citizen* give many useful examples which can be incorporated into any level course at any type of institution. Research across disciplines shows that active learning increases knowledge gains of traditional content as well as providing an increase in a sense of efficacy and empowerment, which are instrumental in putting knowledge into practice. These gains can be particularly noticeable for female students in male-dominated fields and students from disadvantaged backgrounds.[14]

Further, civic engagement education encourages deep and substantial participation in democracy, rather than leaving youth comfortable in insulating, limited, and risk-averse forms, or what Harward and Shea have termed "drive-by" participation. While drive-by participation, such as signing petitions and making online posts, does engage one in collective problems, it does not require reflection on actions or even follow-through to ensure that representatives took appropriate actions. Harward and Shea explain that deeper or "vertical" participation requires citizens to reflect, follow-up on choices, and apply information in substantial and continual engagement activities. This type of participation, which is embedded in quality civic engagement education, is essential for a well-functioning democracy because while elections may select government representatives, they do not determine the longer process of actual policy development.[15]

Finally, civic engagement education is a global endeavor.[16] The United Nations (UN) held a youth conference in November 2016 in which civic engagement was a primary theme. The conference summary proposed that states should invest in quality civic engagement education at all school levels and in all types of educational institutions and develop benchmarks and measures to ensure that all young people have the opportunity to learn how to access their political systems and guarantee their rights.[17] Adrian Vierita, Ambassador to the Permanent Mission of Romania to the UN and a leading voice in this area, stated shortly before the conference that, "youth have a unique voice, vision, and energy. If they are involved to a bigger extent in the process of decision making, we can have a better society with a better standard of living and better systems."[18] When asked why the UN is moving to this area, one of the conference organizers, Hernán Vales, commented that there is a "critical mass of interest at all levels of government and in the international community and the youth are the ones who will bear the brunt of today's decisions and should therefore be involved in decision making."[19]

Political engagement education is part of and grows from civic engagement education. While political engagement "refers to explicitly politically oriented activities that seek a direct impact on political issues, system, relationships, and structures,"[20] civic engagement education seeks to prepare students for a wide range of activities in the community and the political system by providing active-learning components to build a skill set (e.g., planning, organizing people and events, and interacting with government structures), a track record of concrete experience, and the confidence required to be an effective citizen. Civic engagement education *always* has a community goal and action, such as working with a recycling program or youth group.[21] Whereas civic engagement *may* have a direct or indirect political goal, political engagement education *always* has political (although not necessarily partisan) goals.

In sum, civic engagement education is a multidiscipline, evidence-based, and active-learning pedagogy that should and can be pursued at all types of educational institutions. It is a valuable form of experiential learning, well documented for its high impact on student learning.[22] Its goals are to impart knowledge about our democratic systems, skills to peacefully and constructively access those systems, values of responsibility for democracy, and experience for empowerment of our citizens. A global need as democracy advances across the world and societal problems become increasingly complex, civic engagement education should be available for all youth in all areas of study.

HINDRANCES, CHALLENGES, AND SOLUTIONS

As several chapters in this book explain, we face many hindrances and challenges as we pursue the goal of bringing civic engagement education to all students. One is a lack of resources. As discussed by Barrett and Greene in "Civic Education: A Key to Trust in Government," state governments are one of the gatekeepers of resources for civic engagement education. With the support of the federal government and collaborations, such as those described by Musil in her chapter with excerpts from *A Crucible Moment* and *Civic Prompts*, state governments can set meaningful requirements to ensure that students are exposed to more civic learning. As former Supreme Court Justice Sandra Day O'Connor and former Congressman Lee Hamilton propose, we need to take concrete steps toward "bringing a high-quality civic education to every American student [which] requires more than individual programs and curricula....It requires a systematic approach that is only possible through public policy."[23]

Other resources include teacher training and curricular development. Programs such as those studied by Owen and Riddle, in "Active Learning and the Acquisition of Political Knowledge in High School," in section II,[24] and offered by organizations such as the Lenore Annenberg Institute for Civics at the University of Pennsylvania,[25] the Mikva Challenge, and iCivics[26] seek to provide K–12 teachers with tools to bring civic engagement education into the classroom. But colleges and universities need to do more. As Surak, Jensen, McCartney, and Pope explain in "Teaching Faculty to Teach Civic Engagement: Interdisciplinary Models to Facilitate Pedagogical Success," in section III, the lack of updates to promotion, tenure, retention, and merit (PTRM) policies mean that the current systems in most universities actively discourage faculty involvement in civic engagement education. Higher education institutions must invest resources and remove barriers to developing and sustaining civic engagement education by reevaluating PTRM and workload policies to encourage, support, and reward this type of pedagogy.[27] In addition, higher education institutions should invest in instituting best practices in civic engagement education, as Bennion discusses in "Moving Forward with Assessment: Important Tips and Resources," to ensure that resources are properly and efficiently used.

Colleges and universities should also invest resources in extending the reach of civic engagement education; currently most civic engagement education is isolated to a few disciplines.[28] If all students are to be citizens, then they should all learn how they can interact with social and political systems to address common problems utilizing their disciplinary knowledge while also learning how to work with those who are trained in other disciplines. The key to achieving this goal, as Seligsohn and Grove explain in "The Essential Role of Campus Planning in Student Civic Education," is for higher education institutions to carefully plan how they use their limited resources.

One option is to develop innovative and comprehensive interdisciplinary programs and courses, as Matto and McHugh discuss in "Civic Engagement Centers and Institutes: Promising Routes for Teaching Lessons in Citizenship to Students of All Disciplines" and illustrated in the freshman learning communities which McTague explores in "Politically Themed Residential Learning Communities as Incubators of Interest in Government and Politics." The programs and courses explored in section II of this book demonstrate how effective civic engagement education is possible in any discipline. A second means is to connect curricular and cocurricular experiences to provide deeper learning opportunities, as Strachan and Bennion propose in "New Resources for Civic Engagement: The National Survey of Student Leaders, Campus Association-al Life, and the Consortium for Inter-campus SoTL Research." Still further, we must learn how higher education institutions can foster their own civic engagement education goals by working directly with the community, as Forren demonstrates in "Partnering with Campus and Communi-ty to Promote Civic Engagement: Miami University's Citizenship and Democracy Week;" Crigler, Goodnight, Armstrong, and Ramesh in "Collaborative Civic Engagement: A Multidisciplinary Approach to Teaching Democracy with Elementary and University Students;" and Simeone, Sikora, and Halperin in "Unscripted Learning: Cultivating Engaged Catalysts."

We also need to teach students how to engage in effective deliberation. As Thomas and Brower argue in "The Politically Engaged Classroom," campus climates that nurture political learning and democratic practices and that include more interactive and discussion-based teach-ing lay the groundwork for achieving civic engagement education goals. Strachan further explores a key aspect of that campus climate in "Deliberative Pedagogy's Feminist Potential: Teaching Our Students to Cultivate a More Inclusive Public Sphere" by explaining that deliberation pedagogy that is inclusive of women and minorities is integral to creating this foundation. Despite what some may claim,[29] this type of campus climate is not partisan. It is ideological only in the most general sense that it supports democratic governance, the rule of law, the equal participation of all citizens, and peaceful resolutions to common problems.

MOVING FORWARD

As Senator Barbara Mikulski recently said, "We have to go from outcry to outcomes."[30] Research-er Peter Levine echoes this call by stating that citizens' good intentions to participate are simply not enough.[31] We need citizens who have the knowledge of how government works; the skills to access, work within, and change the system; the values of regular, responsible participation; ex-perience with the government system and leaders; and a sense that they can be effective. By more thoughtfully focusing our resources to work toward these outcomes, we can provide quality civic engagement education for all students. We can give them the opportunity to become better work-ers, better leaders, and better members of their communities. We can build resilient communities and diminish the free-rider problem as we confront the challenges that the twenty-first century brings. We can have a better government that works to fulfill the needs of all of its citizens.

The chapters in this book outline the path to achieving these goals. Civic engagement education is a comprehensive pedagogy that, properly constructed, provides students with the knowledge, skills, values, experiences, and confidence that they need to be successful citizens. Political scientists, as the information experts on government, public policy, political systems, and institutional processes, must be central to a cross-disciplinary effort wherein teacher-scholars work together to bring civic engagement education opportunities to all students at all levels of education.[32] Civic engagement education is an accessible and valuable tool for every discipline, and advancing effective civic engagement education is critical to ensure a vibrant, fruitful democracy. ∎

ENDNOTES

1. John Dewey, *The Need of an Industrial Education in an Industrial Society* (1916).

2. Jonathan Gould, Kathleen Hall Jamieson, Peter Levine, Ted McConnell, David B. Smith, Mabel McKinney-Browning, and Kristen Cambell, *Guardian of Democracy: The Civic Mission of Schools* (Philadelphia: The Leonore Annenberg Institute for Civics of the Annenberg Public Policy Center at the University of Pennsylvania and the Campaign for the Civic Mission of Schools, 2003), http://civicmission.s3.amazonaws.com/118/f0/5/171/1/Guardian-of-Democracy-report.pdf.

3. Michael McDonald, *United States Election Project* (2017), http://www.electproject.org, Accessed April 2, 2017.

4. Drew DeSilver, "US Voter Turnout Trails Most Developed Countries" (Washington, DC: Pew Research Center), http://www.pewresearch.org/fact-tank/2016/08/02/u-s-voter-turnout-trails-most-developed-countries/. Accessed April 2, 2017.

5. US Bureau of Labor Statistics, "Volunteering in the United States, 2015," February 25, 2016. https://www.bls.gov/news.release/volun.nr0.htm. Accessed April 2, 2017.

6. Aaron Smith, "Civic Engagement in the Digital Age" (Washington, DC: Pew Research Center, 2013), http://www.pewinternet.org/2013/04/25/civic-engagement-in-the-digital-age/, Accessed April 2, 2017. Peter Levine explores indicators of civic engagement in Peter Levine, *The Future of Democracy: Developing the Next Generation of American Citizens* (Lebanon, NH: University Press of New England, 2007).

7. For discussion of this point, see Theda Skocpol, *Diminished Democracy: From Membership to Management in American Civic Life* (Norman: University of Oklahoma Press, 2003); Robert D. Putnam, *Bowling Alone: The Collapse and Revival of American Community* (New York: Simon and Schuster, 2000); Stephen Macedo, *Democracy at Risk: How Political Choices Undermine Citizen Participation and What We Can Do About It* (Washington, DC: Brookings Institution Press, 2005); William E. Hudson, *American Democracy in Peril: Eight Challenges to America's Future* (Washington, DC: CQ Press, 2010).

8. Dan W. Butin, "Introduction," in *The Engaged Campus: Certificates, Minors, and Majors as the New Community Engagement*, edited by Dan W. Butin and Scott Seider (New York: Palgrave Macmillan, 2012), 2.

9. Hunter Railey and Jan Brennan, "50-State Comparison: Civic Education" (Education Commission of the States, 2016), http://www.ecs.org/ec-content/uploads/Companion_Report_-_50-State_Comparison_-_Civic_Education.pdf, Accessed April 2, 2017. Note that after the Soviet Union dissolved, Americans' trust in their government plummeted, briefly peaked above 50% after the September 11 attacks, and, since 2007, has stayed even lower than after the Watergate scandals. Heading into the 2016 elections, only 19% of Americans believed that the government nearly always or most of the time does "the right thing." While trust in government is not necessarily the goal of civic engagement education, the lack of civically engaged citizens can increase distrust of government and one another. Pew Research Center, "Beyond Distrust: How American View Their Government (Washington, DC: Pew Research Center, 2015), http://www.people-press.org/2015/11/23/1-trust-in-government-1958-2015/, Accessed April 5, 2017.

10. Michael Rogers, "The History of Civic Education in Political Science: The Story of a Discipline's Failure to be a Leader over Its Own Jurisdiction," this volume.

11. Alison Rios Millett McCartney, "Teaching Civic Engagement: Debates, Definitions, Benefits, and Challenges" in *Teaching Civic Engagement: From Student to Active Citizen*, eds. Alison Rios Millett McCartney, Elizabeth A. Bennion, and Dick Simpson, (Washington, DC: American Political Science Association, 2013), 13. For Minnich's quote, see Elizabeth Minnich, Foreword to *The Engaged Campus: Certification, Minors, and Majors as the New Community Engagement*, eds. Dan Butin and Scott Seider (New York: Palgrave MacMillan, 2012), xi.

12. Michael B. Smith, Rebecca S. Nowacek, and Jeffrey L. Bernstein, "Don't Retreat. Teach Citizenship," *Chronicle of Higher Education* 63 (2017): 21, http://www.chronicle.com/article/Don-t-Retreat-Teach/238923, Accessed on February 28, 2017.

13. McCartney, "Debates, Definitions," 13.

14. See, for example, Levine, *The Future of Democracy*; Meira Levinson, "The Civic Empowerment Gap: Defining the Problem and Locating Solutions" in *Handbook of Research on Civic Engagement in Youth*, eds. Lonnie R. Sherrod, Judith Torney-Purta, and Constance A. Flanagan, (Hoboken, NJ: John Wiley and Sons, 2010), 331–61; J. Cherie Strachan, "Student and Civic Engagement: Cultivating the Skills, Efficacy, and Identities That Increase Student Involvement in Learning and Public Life," in *Handbook on Teaching and Learning in Political Science and International Relations*, eds. John Ishiyama, William J. Miller, and Eszter Simon (Clenthenham, UK: Edward Elgar Publishing, 2015): 60–73; Scott Freeman, Sarah L. Eddy, Miles McDonough, Michelle K. Smith, Nnadozie Okoroafor, Hannah Jordt, and Mary Pat

Wenderoth, "Active Learning and Student Performance in Science, Engineering, and Mathematics," *Proceedings of the National Academy of Sciences of the United States of America* 111 (2014): 8410–415; Michael Prince, "Does Active Learning Work? A Review of the Research," *Journal of Engineering Education* 93 (2014): 223–31; Mary M. Hoke and Leslie K. Robbins, "The Impact of Active Learning on Nursing Students' Clinical Success," *Journal of Holistic Nursing* 23 (2016): 348–53; Donald M. Gooch and Michael T. Rogers, "Dude, Where's the Civic Engagement? The Paradoxical Effect of Civic Education on the Probability of Civic Participation," in *Civic Education in the Twenty-First Century: A Multidimensional Inquiry*, eds. Michael T. Rogers and Donald M. Gooch (Lanham, MD: Lexington Books, 2015), 295–344. See also regular entries in the Active Learning in Political Science blog, available at http://activelearningps.com. This site was reviewed by Joseph W. Roberts, "Review of Active Learning in Political Science Blog," *Journal of Political Science Education* 13 (2017): 109–111; Debra L. DeLaet, "A Pedagogy of Civic Engagement for the Undergraduate Political Science Classroom," *Journal of Political Science Education* 12 (2015): 72–84; Matthijs Bogaards and Franziska Deutsch, "Deliberation by, with, and for University Students," *Journal of Political Science Education* 11 (2015): 221–32.

15. Brian M. Harward and Daniel M. Shea, "Higher Education and the Multiple Modes of Engagement," in *Teaching Civic Engagement*, eds. McCartney et al., 21–40.

16. For more information, particularly on the "Talloires Declaration on the Civic Roles and Social Responsibilities of Higher Education," see David Watson, Robert M. Hollister, Susan E. Stroud, and Elizabeth Babcock, *The Engaged University: International Perspectives on Civic Engagement* (New York: Routledge, 2011).

17. Human Rights Council of the United Nations, "First Session of the Forum on Human Rights, Democracy and the Rule of Law: Report of the Co-Chairs," (United Nations General Assembly A/HRC/34/46\, 2017). Podcasts of the conference, "Widening the Democratic Space: the Role of Youth in Public Decision-Making" can be viewed at http://www.ohchr.org/EN/HRBodies/HRC/Democracy/Pages/ForumDemocracy.aspx.

18. Ambassador of Romania to the United Nations Adrian Vierta: Interview with the author, October 21, 2016. Embassy of Romania to the United Nations: Geneva, Switzerland.

19. Hernán Vales, Human Rights Officer, Office of the United Nations Commissioner for Human Rights: Interview with the author, October 20, 2016. Office of the United Nations High Commissioner for Human Rights: Geneva, Switzerland.

20. McCartney, "Debates, Definitions," 14.

21. These distinctions are meant as parameters, not stark absolutes. See the more extensive definition in McCartney, "Debates, Definitions," 14. See also Anne Colby, Elizabeth Beaumont, Thomas Ehrlich, and Josh Corngold. *Educating Citizens: Preparing America's Undergraduates for Lives of Moral and Civic Responsibility* (San Francisco: Jossey-Bass and the Carnegie Foundation for Teaching, 2003); Barbara Jacoby and Associates. *Civic Engagement in Higher Education: Concepts and Practices* (San Francisco: Jossey-Bass, 2009); 2009; Peter Levine. *The Future of Democracy: Developing the Next Generation of American Citizens* (Boston: Tufts University Press, 2007); Scott London. The Civic Mission of Higher Education: From Outreach to Engagement (Washington, D.C.: Kettering Foundation, 2002); Macedo et al 2005; Cliff Zukin, Scott Keeter, Molly Andolina, Krista Jenkins, and Michael X. Delli Carpini, A New Engagement: Political Participation, Civic Life, and the Changing American Citizen (Oxford: Oxford University Press, 2006); Donn Worgs, "Public Education and the Coproduction of Public Education," in Public Engagement for Public Education: Joining Forces to Revitalize and Equalize Schools, eds. Marion Orr and John Rogers (Stanford, CA: Stanford University Press, 2011): 89–116; and McCartney 2006, 113–28.

22. Elizabeth A. Bennion, "Experiential Education in Political Science and International Relations," in Ishiyama et al., 351–68; Arthur W. Chickering and Zelda F. Gamson, 1987. "Seven Principles for Good Practice in Undergraduate Education," *American Association of Higher Education Bulletin* 39 (1987): 3–7; Linda H. Lewis and Carol J. Williams, "Experiential Learning: Past and Present, New Directions for Adult and Continuing Education," in *Experiential Learning: A New Approach*, eds. Lewis Jackson and Rosemary S. Caffarella (San Francisco: Jossey-Bass, 1994), 5–16; David A. Kolb, *Experiential Learning: Experience as the Source of Learning and Development* (Englewood Cliffs, NJ: Prentice Hall, 1984); Barbara Jacoby et al., *Civic Engagement in Higher Education: Concepts and Practices* (San Francisco: John Wiley, 2009); Richard M. Battistoni and William E. Hudson, eds. *Experiencing Citizenship: Concepts and Models for Service-Learning in Political Science*, (Washington, DC: American Association for Higher Education, 1997).

23. Sandra Day O'Connor and Lee Hamilton, in Gould et al., *Guardians of Democracy*, 5.

24. Center for Information and Research on Civic Learning and Engagement can be found at www.civicyouth.org.

25. Lenore Annenberg Institute for Civics at www.AnnenbergClassroom.org.

26. See Betty O'Shaughnessy, "High School Students as Election Judges and Campaign Workers: Does the Experience Stick?" in *Teaching Civic Engagement*, eds. McCartney et al., 297–312.

27. See also Lorilee R. Sandmann, "Community Engagement: Second Generation Promotion and Tenure Issues and Challenges" in *The Future of Service-Learning: New Solutions for Sustaining and Improving Practice*, eds. Jean R. Strait and Marybeth Lima (Sterling, VA: Stylus Publishing, 2009), 67–89; KerryAnn O'Meara, "Faculty Civic Engagement: New Training, Assumptions, and Markets Needed for the Engaged American Scholar," in *"To Serve a Larger Purpose:" Engagement for Democracy and the Transformation of Higher Education*, eds. John Saltmarsh and Matthew Hartley (Philadelphia: Temple University Press, 2011), 177–98.

28. In addition to this volume, see Michael B. Smith, Elizabeth S. Nowacek, and Jeffrey L. Bernstein, *Citizenship Across the Curriculum* (Indianapolis: Indiana University Press, 2010).

29. See, for example, David Randall, "Making Citizens: How American Universities Teach Civics," National Association of Scholars (2017). Retrieved from https://www.nas.org/images/documents/NAS_makingCitizens_fullReport.pdf.

30. Barbara Mikulski, "Civic Education, Civic Engagement, and Civic Responsibility: Foundations of a Democratic Society," Langenberg Lecture and Symposium, University of Maryland, Baltimore, April 10, 2017.

31. Peter Levine, *We Are the Ones We Have Been Waiting For: The Promise of Civic Renewal in America* (Oxford, UK: Oxford University Press, 2013), 14–21.

32. For more discussion on this point, see John Saltmarsh, Matthew Hartley, and Patti Clayton, Democratic Engagement White Paper, *New England Resource Center for Higher Education* (2009), retrieved from http://repository.upenn.edu/gse_pubs/274.

Why Do We Need Government? The Role of Civic Education in the Face of the Free-Rider Problem

JANE MANSBRIDGE

We face a future of growing interdependence, as well as one in which previously plentiful goods like clean air and water once available to all must now be provided by human effort. As a consequence, human beings will now have to produce for one another many more "free-use goods"—goods that, once brought into being, can be used by anyone without paying. (Examples range from toll-free roads to a stable climate.) Free-use goods create a "free-rider problem" because people expect to use the good without paying and thus do not contribute to producing it. Along with the core motivations of duty and solidarity that often lead people to contribute, societies usually need to impose on themselves some external coercion, in the sense of a threat of sanction or force, to generate the taxes or the compliance to produce the required free-use goods. In large, relatively anonymous societies, that coercion usually must be state coercion. As we become more and more interdependent and use up more and more of the free-use goods that "nature" previously provided, we will need more and more state coercion to produce the free-use goods that we will increasingly need. Democracy is our way of legitimating that state coercion. Engaged citizens can help design the required coercion so that it is minimal, does not crowd out the intrinsic motivations of solidarity and duty, and is sensitive to local needs and culture. Even more importantly, they must help monitor that needed state coercion and resist its overreach.

Many students, and many citizens, have never asked themselves the question: what is government for, anyway? The answer seems obvious: you only have to look around you to see all the things that governments provide: the school building the students are in, the teachers, the busses, the janitors; outside, the roads, the traffic lights, the road maintenance, the ports and airports, the armed forces, and the police. What do they have in common? This is a good question to ask students. The answer, they might be interested to learn, was not discovered until 1950–1965—within the lifetime of some of their parents. That answer is: all of these things are *free-use goods*.[1] Once this kind of good is produced, anyone can use it freely, without paying.

Yet free-use goods create *free-rider problems*. When anyone can "free-ride" on others' contributions by using a good without paying for it (because the good is intrinsically a free-use good), many people are naturally tempted not to pay. If people do not pay to produce the good, it often does not come into being, or it may be produced at much lower levels than people would be willing to pay for if the only way to get the good were to pay for it.

In a highly stylized example, imagine that there were only two ways of producing clean air in a community of 1,000 people. Either each person could buy a gas mask for $5, or each could contribute $5 to a community effort to buy a filter for the smokestack causing the bad air. A filter seems obviously the better solution. But if my not contributing $5 would make the filter that the community could buy only one thousandth less effective, I would be tempted not to contribute. Then I could keep my money and breathe the relatively clean air that others' contributions to the filter produced. I *would* be willing to pay $5 for a gas mask if that were the only way I could breathe good air. But I may *not* be willing to pay $5 if the good air produced by the filtered chimney were a free-use good, which I could use without paying. Solving this free-rider problem is the main reason for government. By voting to tax ourselves $5 for the filter and punishing those who did not pay, we can buy a filter good enough to produce 100% clean air. Because in this example we would each be willing to pay $5 for a gas mask, we can without any economic loss vote to tax ourselves $5 to produce the same result more efficiently with a filter. Any time a group of people wants to produce something that is most efficiently a *free-use good*, we see the most important reason for government: the production of legitimate coercion.

I use the word "coercion" instead of a more innocuous word like "regulation" to make vividly the point that when free-use goods are involved we need to use something we do not like to get something we need. No one wants to be coerced. Coercion takes away our freedom. Even a small fine, like a parking ticket, is essentially a piece of state coercion. It reduces our freedom to park where we want. Collectively, we have created that coercion to produce a free-use good, such as a space in front of a fire hydrant in case there is a fire. Because coercion is in itself what ethical philosophers call a "bad," in the best world every use of coercion would be legitimated to and by the coerced themselves, in terms that they could understand and accept. Democracy is, so far, humanity's best way of legitimating that coercion.

The role of citizens in this process is to figure out for themselves what ends require government coercion as a means and then to participate in any processes that will make this coercion more legitimate and better suited to the ends for which it is a means. These processes include voting for what the citizens think are the best policies. They include acting as watchdogs to see when the means of coercion may be being used for illegitimate ends. They also include helping design better, and perhaps lesser, means of coercion that will produce the same end at less cost. Citizens themselves, who know "where the shoe pinches," are often as good guides as any expert to how programs should be designed. Understanding the end that government coercion is designed to produce and coming up with good or better ways of producing that coercion is as much the job of a citizen as watching to make sure that the coercion is used in the right way to produce the ends that citizens want and protesting publicly when the coercion is not correctly used.

Returning now to the larger question of what is a free-use good, one might ask oneself and one's students to consider the school, its building, teachers, and janitors, and all that makes the school work. Right after the American Revolution, all education was private. What would happen if all education in this country were private today? What would happen to the workforce? An educated workforce is a free-use good. Once someone educates a child, anyone can hire that child. Once almost all of the people in a country are literate (most Americans have a high school education, and many have a college education), an employer can be guaranteed that anyone that employer hires will be able to read, write, and probably do a lot more. But the employer does not have to pay for that person's education. An employer would want to pay for the education only of someone who would stay long enough for the cost of the education to be repaid.

Consider the roads, their lights, and their maintenance. What would happen if all roads were toll roads? Nontoll roads are a free-use good. The defense of the country? Law and order? What would it be like if each of us had our own private security force? Public security is a free-use good. Pressed to think of other examples of free-use goods, students might come up with clean air, rivers, ponds, and oceans, and even a stable climate. These examples bring us back to the free-rider problem, which free-use goods create, and which, by slowing or halting the production of free-use goods, can lead to halting commerce and travel, increased insecurity and war, rising crime, the collapse of the criminal justice system, and rising seas and other dangerous changes to the habitat.

One important solution to the free-rider problem is simply to turn the free-use good into a private, pay-for-use good. Breaking the commons into private lots, for example, gives each owner of the now private property an incentive to cultivate it efficiently and sustainably. But for many free-use goods, such as all those listed previously, this solution is not workable. In those instances, we often need state coercion to collect the money to pay for the free-access good or to prevent abuses that will benefit one person at the expense of others. We need to tax people to pay for roads or the military, have a military draft when we do not want a paid army, create a police system to produce law and order, and prevent dumping of toxic substances in the rivers. Each of these moves requires state coercion. The means of state coercion in a democracy are decided by the citizens who participate in government.

AN EXPERIMENT

Students and anyone else can grasp the logic of the free-rider problem experientially by participating in a "common pool" exercise. When I conduct this exercise, I "endow" each participant with an imaginary $100. I then ask everyone to give me either $0 or the whole $100 (nothing in between, for simplicity) for a common pool, which I then double and return to all the participants equally. After everyone has had a chance to ask questions about the exercise, it becomes clear that each person individually will benefit from giving $0, but the more people who give only $0, the more the whole society wastes the doubling resource. Optimally, everyone would give $100; then everyone would leave the room with twice what they had before—$200. If everyone gives only $0, everyone leaves the room with no more than what they had before, and the doubling resource is completely wasted. The product of the doubling is a "free-use good" in the sense that once it is produced, everyone can benefit from it.

After all the participants have made their choices, writing $0 or $100 on a piece of paper and handing it to me, the exercise prompts discussion about the percentage of people who may have contributed as well as who might have contributed and why. It can get the participants thinking about the differential success of societies where higher and lower percentages contribute. It can prompt questions of how common such "doubling" situations are—with analogies to fish in the ocean or ponds and to law and order in society.

On the question of motivation, one can tease out at least three ways—solidarity, duty, and coercion—of getting people to contribute to the provision of free-use goods. Each of these three incentives has its own costs and benefits, particularly in different contexts. Almost everyone lives in very small contexts like the family, where everyone knows almost everything about everyone else and social sanctions are easily available. Somewhat larger contexts include schools or churches, where many people still are able to know others by reputation and so some social sanctions are still available. In the largest and most anonymous contexts, where no one knows the others' past reputations and cannot easily exercise informal forms of social coercion, state coercion is often the most efficient way of producing free-access goods. For most of us, this is not a welcome conclusion, as most people do not like to be coerced. Coercion is inherently a bad. So the coercion we produce should be the minimal amount needed to do the job, and in a democracy, the means of coercion are in the hands of participating citizens.

INTERDEPENDENCE

Because no one likes coercion, it is even more problematic that, because our social and economic worlds are getting more and more interdependent every day, over time we have come to need, and are going to need, more and more free-use goods and therefore more and more state coercion. This is the reality we, our students, and our fellow citizens need to face squarely.

Consider the blueberries I can now put on my table in winter. When I was a child, I could eat blueberries for a couple of weeks a year—maybe a month. Now I can get blueberries from a supermarket at any time of year. Think of the free-use goods required to achieve this small miracle. In January, more than half of blueberries in US markets come from Chile. Even before they are planted, the Chilean Agricultural Ministry gives farmers information about the crop, such as weather and market conditions. This expert advice is a free-use good for every farmer. Citizens who are not farmers pay the taxes that produce the money to pay the experts who give that advice. They pay those taxes partly out of a sense of duty ("I should pay taxes because what would happen if everyone did not pay their taxes?") and solidarity ("I should pay taxes because it is good for the country"). They also pay taxes in part because if they did not pay taxes they would first get a fine, and then, if they continued not to pay, go to prison. The threat of fines and prison is state coercion.

The Chilean Plant and Animal Health Policy, which is one of the strictest in the world, helps to keep dangerous organisms out of the agricultural system. This guarantee of food safety is a big factor in the US stores buying those blueberries. The guarantee of food safety is a free-use good. It benefits everyone, whether they have paid for it or not. To guarantee the safety of that food, the Chilean government again has to pay experts to develop the standards and pay inspectors to check the crops while they are growing and after they are harvested. Again, they need taxes to pay these people (and those taxes come in part from state coercion). Most importantly, they impose fines on farmers who produce unsafe fruit. Those fines (and in the worst cases, prison sentences) are direct examples of state coercion. This system also requires courts to try the cases in court and make sure fines are imposed fairly. The costs of building and maintaining the court buildings and paying the janitors, judges, secretaries, and clerks to make the court system run are paid by taxes, which come in part from state coercion approved by participating citizens.

As people have children, those children grow up to be adults, and more people fill the planet. As we use up our resources and invent and use technologies that produce pollution, many free-use goods that "nature" provided for earlier generations—such as clean air and clean water (or any water)—now have to be provided by human beings. When forests are plentiful, we do not need restrictions on cutting trees. The forest can be a free-use good with no need for human action. When there are ample fish in the sea, we do not need restrictions on taking them out so the fish that are left can reproduce. The ocean and the fish can be free-use goods with no need for human action. On the desert or on tops of mountains, where there are no sources of pollution, we can breathe the clean air as a free-use good with no need for human action. It is only when the ample supply of all these things begins to give out that human beings need to take positive action to make walking in the forest, fishing, and clean breathing possible again. Whenever we want to make these things available as free-use goods, we will probably have to use and approve state coercion.

Short of the absence of nuclear war, climate stability is the biggest free-use good we need. It is also a good that all the people of the earth are the most interdependent in producing. We all affect the climate, and we all benefit from its stability. But it is difficult to arrange things so that only those who pay benefit. Climate stability is the big daddy of all free-use goods. The problem is that we do not have a global government, and at this moment in history, few people want one. So it is difficult to use state coercion to help produce this free-use good. We have to rely in larger part than we usually do on people's individual commitments to duty and feelings of solidarity. And to produce the necessary state coercion, we need to cobble together treaties among governments that essentially promise, "If you will use your state coercion to help produce this, we'll use ours." This situation reasonably makes most of us a bit uneasy.

THINKING ABOUT COERCION

Although we do not always need coercion, let alone state coercion, to produce free-use goods that we cannot efficiently make private, in large relatively anonymous societies much of the time state coercion is the most efficient way of solving the free-rider problem. That is why it is so important to design state coercion to be 1) minimal; 2) structured not to drive out intrinsic motivation; and, 3) most importantly, legitimate.

Let me unpack some of the pieces in that paragraph. To begin, we do not need coercion all the time to produce free-use goods. Donations, for example, are a major source of free-use goods. People donate to support help for the needy, the local Little League, the Public Broadcasting System, and many other free-use goods. Museums usually charge an entrance fee, so they are not fully free-use, but the entrance fees are not usually enough to pay for their full upkeep, so they are partial free-use goods, supported in part by donations. Voluntary citizen donations help create many free-use goods, reducing the need for state coercion.

When people give to support a free-use good, they usually do so out of a sense of duty (or conscience) or else out of a feeling of solidarity (or community). Consider the simple example of taking dishes to the sink after eating. You have the option of leaving those dirty dishes in the sink. Then they get in the way of others who need to use the sink. Also, when the next person goes to get a clean plate, the cupboard is empty. If you wash your plates and put them back in the cupboard, you are providing the others with two free-use goods: an unobstructed sink and clean plates in the cupboard. Leaving aside coercion (mild punishment from the irritated looks or comments of the others), why would you wash the dishes? As mentioned earlier, usually you provide the free-use good because you are motivated by some form of duty or conscience ("What if everyone did this? I don't want to set a bad example") or some form of solidarity or love ("I don't want to let the others down" or "I want to make life easier for Jenny").

Many free-use goods can be provided by citizens' voluntary acts, prompted by duty or solidarity. Voluntary acts of civic engagement, such as going door to door to get out the vote, often produce free-access goods, such as a community in which the voters are more informed and the elected representatives more responsive. In general, what we call "civic engagement" consists of voluntary acts generated by some combination of duty and solidarity. Voting itself is one of those acts. The act of voting produces the overall free-use good of a more legitimate government. In general, poorer and less educated people are less likely to vote than richer and more educated people. So some countries introduce a small fine, sometimes the amount of a parking ticket, for not voting, to produce the overall good of a more equal turnout and a more legitimate subsequent government. In countries like the United States, where there is no such fine, we appeal to citizens' sense of duty and solidarity by, for example, giving out stickers to voters that say, "I voted!" The sticker honors the voluntary act for the good of all and also inspires others who see it on someone's lapel in the course of the voting day. The United States ranks highest among all measured countries on volunteering, with 41.9% saying in 2004 that they had either "donated money to an organization in the last month" or "given time to an organization in the last month." New Zealand had almost as high a percent (41.5%). Norway had 39%, and Canada had 38%.[2]

Because coercion is, in general, a bad thing, when we do have to institute coercion to get a free-use good produced, that coercion should be, in the first place, minimal—no more than needed to get the job done. Sometimes the needed coercion is more efficient and perhaps more friendly when the coercion is local. In a small enough group, the coercion can even be informal, such as the scowl aimed at the person who left their dishes in the sink. In a small group where everyone knows everyone's business, people will "do the right thing" and contribute to the free-use good because they know that their failure to contribute will be known and will follow them. They will rightly fear that when later they need others to contribute to a free-use good that particularly benefits them, the others might shrug and retaliate by holding back their contributions at that point. "Tit-for-tat" retaliation, an informal form of coercion and a great way of solving free-rider problems, requires known reputations.

Yet it is not easy to make coercion minimal. When people create a regulation, they should do so, for fairness, in general terms. Not "Sally should clean her dishes and put them in the cupboard; if not, she won't get supper tomorrow," but "All members of this family should clean their dishes and put them in the cupboard; if not, they won't get supper the next day." But when people make rules general, those rules sometimes do not work well. What about the children in the family too young to wash their dishes? Or the moment when there was not time to do it? Rules intended to be fair by being general also will sometimes apply to situations that do not or should not require coercion. The greater and more diverse the constituency that a rule covers, the more likely such over-application becomes.

Local political control—having towns and cities make and enforce the rules instead of the state governments or having state governments make the rules and enforce them instead of the federal government—is one way of making it more likely that the rules make sense to those who have to obey them. With growing interdependence, however, local control becomes more difficult. Letting each state place barriers on its borders and exact a tariff for each of the goods coming in would result in a massive decline in interstate commerce, causing harm to all. Relying on each local community to maintain its section of an interstate highway through its own local taxes would result in highly uneven patches in the highway. Letting each town decide whether or not to let people dump their effluent directly into a common river would result in some towns taking advantage of (free-riding on) the antipollution efforts of others. The more we each experience the effects of others' actions—the more interdependent we are—the more local control evolves into a problem of local free riding. The question of how to keep the regulations that produce free-use goods sensitive to local conditions and needs is going to take a lot of thinking in the twenty-first century. Citizens have a major role in that thinking, working with elected and appointed officials to try to tailor regulations to what the local, state, and national polity really needs.

Another major problem in keeping state coercion minimal is that government agencies can be overzealous in expanding their reach, sometimes from their top administrators' crass desire for more power and perhaps higher salary, but often from the earnest convictions of many people in the agency about the importance of their own good work. Experts are also inclined both to overestimate their own intelligence and intuitions in comparison to those of the citizens affected and to downplay the costs of adhering to a regulation. Designing coercion to be minimal requires a lot of innovative thinking and a lot of trial and error to find ways of curbing the unnecessary applications of state power. Voluntary action on the part of citizen "watch dogs" can help curb the unnecessary growth of coercion.

One recent idea is, whenever possible, to substitute "nudges"—the conscious use of preconscious biases—for coercion. A clean restroom is a free-use good. Everyone benefits from the clean restroom whether they pay for it (by cleaning it themselves or paying through taxes to have it cleaned) or not. Mostly, we rely on people's commitment to duty and feelings of solidarity to keep public restrooms clean. In places where these two motives are not enough, sometimes we bring in state coercion ($20 fine for littering). In one airport in The Netherlands, however, they decided to enlist instead people's preconscious sense of fun and painted a picture of a fly on the back of the men's room urinals. Amused, the men aimed at the fly, and the cost of cleaning the restrooms plummeted.[3] It is not that easy, however, to find nudges that can substitute for most coercion.

Coercion should be designed not only to be minimal but also not to drive out the duty and solidarity that help solve many free-rider problems. Since the early 1970s, psychologists have shown that extrinsic motivation tends to drive out intrinsic motivation. In the classic early study, the students who were subjects in the study were given interesting puzzles to work on. In the next session, half the group was paid to do the puzzles. In the third and final session, the experimenter left the room for eight minutes, saying "You may do whatever you like while I am gone." The students who had been paid to do the puzzles spent significantly less time on them than those who had never been paid. Those who had been paid to do the puzzles seem to have conceptually reassigned the activity in their minds as "work to be paid for" rather than "fun thing to do." The extrinsic motivation of the pay had driven out the intrinsic motivation of doing the puzzles for fun.[4] We can see the same dynamic in a recent study of an Israeli day-care center that instituted fines for picking up one's children late. They found that instituting the fines actually increased the number of late pickups, not decreasing them as they had hoped. It seems that the parents implicitly saw the fines as a kind of pay for the extra time the staff had to stay at the center, so they no longer felt guilty at the inconvenience they were imposing.[5] The extrinsic motivation of fee-for-service had driven out the intrinsic motivations of duty and solidarity. State coercion is an extrinsic motivation. It can easily drive out the intrinsic motivations of solidarity or duty that a free-rider problem sometimes generates in those who want to solve it.

Extrinsic motivations need not always drive out intrinsic motivations, however. When extrinsic motivations are designed properly, they can even reinforce intrinsic motivation. So in many systems, pay or other extrinsic incentives may be framed as a reward for good performance. In this case, the message of positive feedback may outweigh the negative effects of extrinsic rewards.[6] If universities paid professors by the word for each article they wrote, this form of pay would almost certainly reduce the professors' internal motivation to write. But when universities give professors higher salaries in recognition of their contributions to scholarship, this form of pay probably increases the professors' internal motivation. In the pay-per-word case, the pay acts as a substitute for internal motivation; in the pay-as-honor case, the pay acts as a social signal of approval for the internal motivation. Looking at state coercion through this lens would encourage us to ask how coercion can be designed to appeal to citizens' sense of duty and solidarity, not to undermine it. We do not know, for example, whether having a fine for not voting, an extrinsic motivation, drives out the intrinsic incentive to vote. It may well do that. In all these problems of designing coercion, citizen ingenuity—pooling all of our minds to get a better collective result—can be extremely helpful.

To accentuate internal motivation and reduce external coercion, some citizens can model duty and solidarity for others. People are far more likely to pay their taxes voluntarily, in part out of duty and solidarity, when they know that most others are paying theirs fully and voluntarily as well. Over the millennia, human beings have created increasingly comfortable lives for themselves, on average, by using their well-developed social antennae. Humans as well as deer and other animals often find it a useful shortcut to take signals on appropriate behavior from others around them. Such conformity can be overdone and must be guarded against, but in many ways this often unconscious habit serves us well. If most people are recycling, not littering, paying their taxes, volunteering for the common defense, and in other ways contributing to the goods that are free-use for all, the rest of us will often do the same thing, especially if when we think about it we realize that it is the right thing to do.

In contrast to driving out the intrinsic motivations of duty and solidarity, coercion can also reinforce those motivations. When some people pay taxes but see others getting away with not paying taxes, they can feel like suckers, taken advantage of, and the next time cheat a little on their taxes themselves. The same dynamic appears with any voluntary contribution to producing or maintaining a free-use good. In our free-rider experiment using donations of $100 or $0, a second round of the experiment will typically produce a smaller percentage giving than in the first round, and a third round will produce a smaller percentage still. In game-theoretic terms, the norm of giving will "unravel," sometimes quite quickly, to an "equilibrium" where no one gives anything at all. In each case, the people who have given look afterward at the people who did not give and think, "Why should *they* get away with that?" Instituting a little coercion "around the edges," just enough to get the potential "defectors" to do their bit, can sustain the motivations of duty and solidarity among the givers. When this dynamic is in play, we can think of the coercion as providing an ecological niche for the motivations of duty and solidarity to survive and thrive.

Finally, of all the requirements for instituting good state coercion, the most important is that the coercion be legitimate. This essential need for legitimacy in state coercion is the central reason for democracy.

Rousseau began his *Social Contract* with the words, "Man is born free; and everywhere he is in chains. ... How did this change come about? I do not know. What can make it legitimate? That question I think I can answer."[7] Unlike Rousseau, we *do* now know the answer to his first question. The logic of the free-rider problem, discovered between 1950 and 1965, reveals the cause of our "chains"—the reason we have laws that limit our freedom. The "chains" are all the laws that limit our freedom, enforced by state coercion. Yet we need those laws/coercion/chains, as discussed earlier, to produce the free-use goods we need.

Once we recognize the logic of the free-rider problem, based on our need for free-use goods, then we must immediately ask Rousseau's second question: what can make that coercion legitimate? Rousseau argued that legitimacy could come only from a social contract—an agreement of each with each, each counting equally. For Rousseau, the act of giving the law to ourselves transforms us and makes us moral beings and citizens, the authors of the constraints that bind us. It activates the moral requirements of duty and solidarity to obey the law.

Whether we buy all the details of Rousseau's analysis or not, it seems quite possible historically that, at least so far, democracy is the best way that humans have devised for making state coercion legitimate. The word of God may have been sufficient in earlier eras and in some places today, but overall, humanity has not found a way of producing sufficient agreement on the meanings and applications of the word of God to avoid the tragedy and human waste of extensive warfare over those meanings. The authority of a monarch may have had significant weight in earlier eras and in some places today, but in the context of increased mobility and exposure to other systems, this mode of legitimation has tended to wither over time. Democracy, by contrast, has sustained and increased its legitimacy. Almost all of the states of the world today at least claim to be democracies.

Democracies have survived and thrived primarily because the people coerced by the laws perceive the process that generated those laws to be fair. They perceive the process as fair because the ideal behind the process *is* fair, in the sense that it stands up to critical scrutiny. In the democratic ideal, no one counts for more than anyone else. In what some have called the "liberal" democratic ideal, the participants all have the procedural human rights that have evolved over the years, including preeminently the rights of free speech and political organization.

The equality ideal, at least among adult men, seems to have been part of our heritage from the longest segment of the Environment of Evolutionary Adaptedness, the 98% of human history when we were hunter-gatherers. Although most primates have strong hierarchies, bonobos do not. Early humans also seemed to be organized on the basis of male equality, although we adapt easily to hierarchy. After human beings settled into agriculture, we became more hierarchical because hierarchy is an easy way to organize on a large scale. Even within a hierarchy, however, the egalitarian ideal was likely to prevail among members of the same caste or class. The ideal of the equal underlying dignity of all humans is there, in embryo, in many religions. When representative government of the modern form began to arise in Europe in the fifteenth century, the ideal of the equal right of each citizen to participate in government had a foothold in existing practices within the same level of a hierarchy. As early as the eleventh century, for example, within the Roman Catholic Church, cardinals voted for the pope as equals, with each vote counting equally, at least as a default position.

In practice, no democracy achieves the ideal of each vote counting absolutely equally. Therefore, no democracy is fully legitimate on the criterion of political equality. Indeed, for *all* of our political ideals, all regimes fall on a spectrum between more and less legitimate, rather than into a dichotomy of legitimate versus not legitimate. The ideals of democracy (like equality and freedom) are aspirational, the goal being to come as close to the ideal as possible, given the constraints in other values, including other ideals. Failure to achieve the ideal in all its fullness should thus be no reason for despair, although it should prompt a willingness to examine why the practice is falling short and, in the right circumstances, to try harder. Here again, citizen ingenuity and experimentation can often come up with better ways of achieving more equality and more freedom without significant losses in other values. Our progress comes from trying and often failing, then trying again.

One source of perceived legitimacy is good outcomes—peace, safety, or a rising economy. Democracies often, over time, produce relatively good outcomes, in part simply because they are perceived as legitimate and therefore people obey the law for reasons of duty and solidarity, not needing much coercion. Another reason is that the processes of inclusion built into democracies tend to generate more dispersed and accurate information and therefore more good ideas. Yet democracies also have a base in the fairness of their decision processes. Some other forms of government (most importantly the Chinese government) derive their legitimacy almost entirely from their relatively good outcomes. But when a government also derives its legitimacy from fair processes, that government can remain legitimate even when output falters. Thus, once solidly established, democracies tend to be more stable than other forms of government.

The stability and the efficacy of state coercion thus depend on the perception of legitimacy. Yet perceptions can be manipulated. A good polity will rest not only on perceived legitimacy but also on forms of legitimacy that can stand up to critical scrutiny.

Because the legitimacy of democracies depends on their fair procedures, democracies lose legitimacy when their procedures become less fair. When democratic procedures become less fair, the necessary state coercion loses legitimacy, and society tends to become less efficient. Democracies obviously lose legitimacy when they rest on systems of illegal corruption, but they can also lose legitimacy when they rest on systems of "institutional" or legal corruption such as that produced by massively unequal amounts of money in the political system, with a consequent loss of trust in representatives and eventually the loss of mutual trust among citizens. Conversely, democracies gain legitimacy when illegal corruption is reduced or eliminated (difficult to accomplish because illegal corruption tends to create its own equilibrium), when institutional corruption is reduced, when well-designed institutions and the selection of representatives of integrity increase constituents' trust in their representatives, and when well-designed institutions, good civic education, and civic engagement increase mutual trust among citizens.

Citizens have a major role to play in establishing fair procedures in a democracy and keeping them fair. Often when a new issue arises in a locality or the country, the question also arises of how to deal with it. Sometimes the elected body of a town, state, or country will establish a commission to investigate the problem and suggest solutions. Citizens can volunteer their expertise or volunteer to help collect other citizens' views. They can monitor the process to see that representatives of all groups affected are consulted and taken seriously. If the process goes to a referendum, citizens can try to become informed and help others become informed. If the process is decided by a legislative vote, citizens can monitor that vote to make sure that the legislators are not being unduly influenced by considerations other than the common good. They can communicate with their representatives directly or through interest groups and the media. They can organize to support or oppose the legislators' votes in the next election. The legitimacy of the laws is precious. In a democracy, that legitimacy is in the hands of the citizens, for better and for worse.

Finally, the legitimacy of state coercion also depends on the legitimacy of enforcement of the laws. At the "street level," the people who enforce the laws need to do so sensitively and minimally, in ways that respond to local as well as universal norms of fairness. "Descriptive representation," such as the deployment of African American police officers in an African American area or officers with a hunting or mining background in a hunting or mining area, can help promote the perception of legitimacy among those who are coerced. This situation works, however, only when descriptive representation is accompanied by actual substantive fairness, not by decisions that favor some unfairly and disfavor others. Explanation also helps increase perceived legitimacy. It might help, for example, if when officers stopped someone for speeding on a freeway, they produced the ticket along with a one-page explanation of why the speed limit had been set at the level it was on that stretch of the highway. Finally, what I call "recursive deliberation" greatly increases perceived legitimacy. If the coerced can explain their perspectives, the enforcers can explain theirs, and eventually the laws themselves can change in response to what both learn in that interaction, the coercion will begin to approach more closely the ideal of citizens giving a law to themselves. The law, and the coercion produced by that law, will become more legitimate.

In making the enforcement of the laws more legitimate, citizens also have a vital role to play. If the law has a legitimate goal, then citizens should obey that law voluntarily and should model compliance to others, so that state coercion need not enter the picture. When a law is enforced, citizens should monitor that enforcement for fairness and for sensitivity to local conditions. Each insensitively enforced law, whether taking away a hunting license, a stop-and-frisk, or even a rude clerk at the motor vehicles office, reduces the legitimacy of the law and its enforcement. At the street level, a citizen's or group of citizens' sensitive responses to an insensitively enforced law—whether through contact with the enforcer, the enforcer's superior, or the political system ultimately responsible for enforcement—can make a great difference not only to the tenor of future enforcement efforts but also to the larger respect for law in that community.

CONCLUSION

Most college students today grasp the logic of supply and demand. Even among political science students, however, few grasp the more recently discovered logic of the free-rider problem. Yet, for reasons I have tried to set out in this chapter, this logic rivals in its importance the logic of supply and demand. Failure to understand this logic generates a failure to understand why today we need so many "regulations." Failure to understand that we are increasingly doomed to more regulation and greater state power generates a failure to understand how urgent it is to guard against state power while creating it, how urgent it is to design regulation minimally and well, and how urgent it is to enforce state coercion minimally and with sensitivity.

Civic education and the lifelong civic engagement that it brings can help ensure that coercion is well constructed and that citizens have the knowledge to monitor and help shape state power. The chapters in this book explain how and why we can prepare all citizens for this role. Without citizens educated in how our democracy works and prepared to engage in our institutions both to provide guidance when they work well and to step in when they falter, our democracy cannot survive and thrive in this era of increasingly complex problems. ∎

ENDNOTES

1. The most frequently used terms are "public goods" and "non-excludable goods," but these terms are technically incorrect for the phenomenon I describe. The economists' use of the term "public goods" includes the requirement that such goods be "non-rival," in that the use by one individual does not reduce availability to others, and "non-excludable," but neither condition applies to free-use goods. (Once such goods are used up, some are excluded from use.) See Jane Mansbridge, "What Is Political Science For?" 2012–13 APSA Presidential Address, *Perspectives in Politics* 12 (2014): 8–17.
2. Gallup World Poll, 2004, as reported in http://www.nationmaster.com/country-info/stats/Lifestyle/Society/Volunteering-and-social-support/Volunteering/Volunteered-your-time, accessed March 2, 2017.
3. Richard H. Thaler and Cass R. Sunstein, *Nudge: Improving Decisions about Health, Wealth, and Happiness* (New Haven, CT: Yale University Press, 2008).
4. Edward L. Deci, "Effects of Externally Motivated Rewards on Intrinsic Motivation," *Journal of Personality and Social Psychology* 18 (1971): 105–15.
5. Uri Gneezy and Aldo Rustichini, "A Fine Is a Price," *Journal of Legal Studies* 29 (2000): 1–17.
6. Edward L. Deci and Richard M. Ryan, *Intrinsic Motivation and Self-Determination in Human Behavior* (New York: Plenum, 1985), 52, 77, 300.
7. Jean-Jacques Rousseau, *On the Social Contract* [1762], ed. Roger D. Masters, trans. Judith R. Masters (New York: St. Martin's Press), 46.

The Politically Engaged Classroom 2

Nancy Thomas and Margaret Brower

Although college and university professors utilize many different styles of teaching, pedagogies, and approaches to learning in the classroom, some are ideal for fostering student political interest, knowledge, and agency. This chapter focuses on discussion-based teaching as a pedagogical approach for faculty members to create political learning opportunities for their students across disciplines. The chapter draws from five qualitative case studies of colleges and universities with higher levels of student political participation, a research project from Tufts University's Institute for Democracy and Higher Education. These case studies provide a deeper understanding of how faculty members from across different disciplinary fields can integrate political learning into their classrooms through discussions on controversial social and political issues among students with diverse social identities, ideological perspectives, and lived experiences.

Over the past few decades, colleges and universities have revitalized their efforts to advance student civic engagement. Unfortunately, other than in particular disciplines, these initiatives are usually apolitical in nature. As a result, students graduate lacking the skills in political discourse, critical thinking, problem solving, and collective action that they need to address complex and divisive public issues and events in American democracy. For this study, five institutions were identified because of their unusually high levels of political and electoral student engagement across disciplines. Through qualitative case studies at these five institutions, researchers at Tufts University's Institute for Democracy and Higher Education examined their campus climates for political learning and engagement in democracy and identified structural, human, political, and cultural characteristics common to the five campuses.

This chapter examines one of those characteristics: discussion-based teaching using matters of political consequence as content, embedded across disciplines, which emerged as a dominant theme in our research.[1] Faculty members and students who participated in our focus groups and interviews often mentioned these types of experiences. In our research, controversial issue discussions in the classroom emerged as a predominant attribute of highly politically and electorally engaged colleges and universities. The faculty members at these institutions took their role seriously by learning to facilitate dialogue across differences effectively, and their institutions provided these faculty members with the opportunity to learn these pedagogical skills. Specifically, they sought personal and professional development training in discussion-group teaching; established inclusive classroom dynamics; invited student perspectives based on the students' diverse backgrounds, lived experiences, and opinions; and introduced challenges for students to consider new perspectives on an issue.

HIGHER EDUCATION'S INCONSISTENT CIVIC COMMITMENT

Higher education serves complementary purposes in American society. Ideally, individual students pursue learning to advance their careers and quality of life while simultaneously developing as socially responsible, engaged citizens. Collectively, educated Americans provide the foundation for US economic prosperity and for public problem solving and policy making guided by principles of freedom, equal opportunity, and concern for the common good. This civic mission has been affirmed repeatedly since the establishment of early institutions of higher education, perhaps most clearly by President Truman's Commission on Higher Education, which identified higher education as democracy's necessity.[2] The report identifies the goals of higher education as a means to "bring to all people of the Nation ... Education for a fuller realization of democracy in every phase of living ... and for the application of the creative imagination and trained intelligence to the solution of social problems and to the administration of public affairs." More recently, the US Department of Education, the White House, civic leaders, and scholars in both higher education and political science have challenged the academy to recommit to learning that strengthens and ensures the future of democracy.[3]

Historically, higher education's commitment to student civic learning has fluctuated. The most recent wave of interest in civic learning surged over 20 years ago in response to concerns over declines in social capital and the nation's civic health, a problem vividly captured in the shifting behaviors of Americans choosing to bowl alone rather than in leagues.[4] Colleges and universities admirably responded to this problem by bolstering student civic experiences such as volunteerism, service-learning, public interest internships, and student community-based research. They also pursued new institutional strategies, such as the creation of civic offices and support for community-university partnerships for local problem solving.

While valuable, these efforts have fallen short of educating for democracy. Civic engagement experiences are typically designed to be apolitical, and indeed, students are cautioned to avoid political conversations in their field placements.[5] Political learning generally engages small groups of students in particular majors or with specific interests. As a result, students gain a sense of empathy for others and a duty to serve but not necessarily the knowledge, skills, and commitment to tackle social and policy problems.

Some institutions, however, can demonstrate high levels of student political engagement. Seeking a purposeful sample for this study, we conducted a quantitative analysis using the National Study for Learning, Voting, and Engagement (NSLVE) database. By calculating both actual and predicted aggregate student voting rates for each college and university participating in NSLVE, we could identify institutions with higher-than-predicted student voting rates. Over the past two years, we visited nine of these institutions and conducted qualitative case studies to observe and understand their campus climates for political learning and engagement in democracy. This chapter is based on an analysis of the first five of the nine institutions.

We found that these uniquely politically engaged campuses manifest particular attributes and characteristics including a student-centered mission; a demonstrated commitment among faculty, staff, and students to building campus community, a culture of caring, and high levels of social connectivity; a commitment to diversity and intergroup relationships as well as a strong equity purpose; collaborative governance and decision-making that included students; and robust student activism and other forms of political action. These are reviewed in our other chapter in this book, "Politics 365: Fostering Campus Climates for Student Political Learning and Engagement." In this chapter, we share findings on ways that the classroom experience supported students in developing knowledge, skills, and interest in public affairs, problem solving, and policy making. On the campuses we studied, teaching political issues and democratic engagement skills is not relegated to courses in political science or interdisciplinary programs. Every discipline recognizes and teaches its relevance to public life. We dedicated the entire chapter to this particular attribute because it was pervasive across all of the campuses we visited and because both faculty and students were remarkably consistent in reporting on the role that classroom discussion-based teaching using public issues as content played in student political learning and development.

THEORETICAL FRAMEWORK

Research on organizational climate grew substantially in the late 1960s and 1970s.[6] In the late 1990s researchers started examining "common patterns of important dimensions of organizational life or its members' perceptions of the attitudes toward those dimensions"[7] in higher education.[8] While the term "climate" has been defined a number of ways, Ryder and Mitchell describe it as, "people's attitudes about, perceptions of, and experiences within a specified environment."[9] Hurtado et al. suggests that campus climate studies can be used to "identify areas for improvement [so that institutions can] achieve educational goals."[10]

Assessing campus climate is a complex task requiring attention to a broad range of factors. Examining campus climate for diversity, Hurtado, Clayton-Pederson, and Allen considered four institutional characteristics: history, structures and compositional diversity, psychological climate (perceptions, attitudes, and beliefs about diversity), and interactions among diverse members of the campus community.[11] Other scholars study campus climate in relation to perceptions, behaviors, and expectations.[12] Campus climate can also be studied from an institutional leader perspective, focusing on cultural assumptions and institutional practices.[13] Bolman and Deal study complex organizations by examining them from four perspectives: structural, human resource, symbolic, and political.[14]

None of these scholars specifically examined an institution's climate for student political learning and engagement in democracy. Addressing this gap in the literature, we augmented the Bolman and Deal framework[15] and constructed a conceptual framework for campus political learning and engagement with some distinctions: we supplanted the "symbolic" frame with a "cultural" frame to reflect other literature identifying an organization's culture as critical to institutional climate. Our framework also distinguishes between political forces internal to the organization and those that are external, an important difference given the role that public officials, state election laws, and local civic health might play. The framework also included dimensional subcategories that illustrate the complexity of colleges and universities (see figure 2.1). This framework informed the design of our mixed-method study to examine campus climate for student political learning and engagement in democracy.

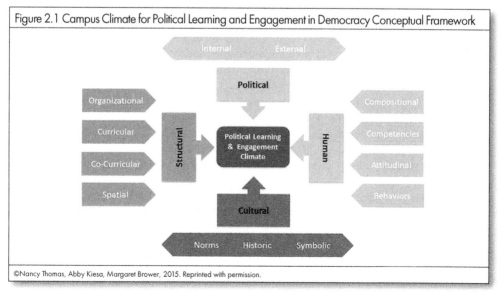

Figure 2.1 Campus Climate for Political Learning and Engagement in Democracy Conceptual Framework

METHODS AND SAMPLE

We selected the case study institutions based on a quantitative analysis of institutional student voting rates. While voting may not be the only form of political participation, it is a fundamental civic act and arguably a gauge of student interest in public affairs. Being able to measure empirically a civic act and then reconstruct the student experiences that may explain that act is a unique research opportunity. Indeed, most studies of student civic learning measure the effects of a particular experience (e.g., service) on individual student development. Having actual individual level voting data provided a compelling basis for this research. Further, by visiting multiple institutions, we could observe different student experiences and explore the extent to which these institutions shared attributes.

The National Study of Learning, Voting, and Engagement (NSLVE) at Tufts University is a large dataset of student voter registration and voting records. Launched in 2013, NSLVE now has data for more than 900 American colleges and universities nationwide, representing a proportionate number of four-year public and private colleges and universities as well as a significant number of community colleges. The NSLVE dataset includes nearly 8.5 million de-identified student records obtained with permission from each institution. These enrollment records are housed at the National Student Clearinghouse, a nonprofit organization that serves as a national repository for 96% of students enrolled in accredited, degree-granting US colleges and universities. The NSLVE dataset also contains publicly available individual registration and voting data provided by Catalist, an organization that collects all publically available voting records and makes them available for academic research. The process of matching enrollment and voting records was completed by the National Student Clearinghouse, which then removed all student identifiers and sent the de-identified records to us for analysis. With these data, we calculated an actual student voter registration and voting rate for each participating college and university, broken down by demographic factors such as age, field of study, and voting location.

When this study began, the dataset contained approximately 2.3 million college student records from 219 participating colleges and universities. We conducted a quantitative analysis to select the first four colleges and universities for these climate studies (n=219). By the time we completed those visits, the dataset had nearly doubled to 4.4 million students and 473 campuses. We used the same method to select a fifth campus from the larger dataset (n=473).

To voting and enrollment records, we added institution-level variables available through the Integrated Postsecondary Education Data System (IPEDS) as well as civic data collected by the US Census Bureau and analyzed by the Center for Information and Research on Civic Learning and Engagement (CIRCLE). We then ran a multiregression analysis to predict voting rates for NSLVE colleges and universities (n=219) using three variable types: individual student variables (e.g., gender), institutional variables (e.g., institution size), and civic variables (e.g., social cohesion at the state level, restriction on voter registration). We used voting as a proxy for political engagement. Based on this regression model, we calculated a predicted voting rate for each institution. Comparing the actual and predicted voting rates for all campuses in the study, we identified campuses with positive residuals of at least five percentage points—campuses we called "positive outliers." To select from among the institutions with high residuals and identify a diverse set of institutions, we considered factors such as campus size, geographic location, populations served, and Carnegie classification. The names of the positive outlier institutions are confidential, but they include

- A four-year public located in a suburb of a large city in the Northeast; enrollment 4,000; residual 13.3 percentage points above the predicted voting rate,
- A four-year private located in a small city in the East; enrollment of 2,200; residual 5.5 percentage points above the predicted voting rate,
- A two-year public located in a midsized city in the Midwest; enrollment 19,500; residual 7.9 percentage points above the predicted voting rate,

- A four-year public located in a large city in the Southwest; enrollment 13,000; residual 5.2 percentage points above the predicted voting rate, and
- A four-year public located in a suburb of a midsized city in the Southeast; enrollment 5,500; residual 10.2 percentage points above the predicted voting rate.

As the database has grown, we have run the regression repeatedly, and the five institutions we selected remain positive outliers.

CASE STUDIES

Visiting five institutions between April 2014 and April 2015, we collected the data through semistructured interviews and focus groups with students, faculty, and staff. On each campus, a minimum of six interviews were conducted with no fewer than two senior administrators, three staff members, and one dean of students or vice president of student affairs. We held a minimum of six focus groups on each campus with no fewer than 15 faculty members and 15 students. At larger institutions, we increased the number of students and faculty by adding focus groups. We worked with each institution to ensure that the focus groups consisted of a diverse group of students and faculty representing a broad range of disciplinary and cocurricular interests.

The semistructured interviews and focus groups were open-ended and developed according to our conceptual framework. In total, 74 interviews and focus groups were conducted with 237 participants. All interviews and focus groups were audio-taped and transcribed verbatim. Our conceptual framework also informed the codebook for analyzing these data[16] and a hierarchical "coding scheme" was used to organize the codebook.[17] This structure allowed us to synthesize the data into broader categories before using cross-case axial coding to identify relevant themes emerging from these codes.[18] To analyze the data, we conducted a repeated review of all interview and focus group transcripts and selected co-occurring pairs of codes with higher-than-average frequencies that aligned with the each section of the conceptual framework.

DEFINITIONS

We use the following definitions to frame our research. *Civic engagement* refers to individual and collective action to identify and address social needs and problems. Civic engagement (sometimes used interchangeably with "community engagement") reflects a broad range of actions, including volunteering, voting, donating money or goods to charity, organizing fund drives for a cause, helping neighbors solve community problems, community organizing, and social entrepreneurship.

Political participation is often envisioned as engagement with government. We view political participation as involvement with democratic systems and practices, which would include citizen-driven action, with or without formal government structures. Political engagement can include a broad range of activities including engaging in the electoral process (voting, campaigning, running for office, registering, and voting), community organizing (mobilizing others to act together to address a public problem), advocating (writing and publishing commentary and speaking publicly on matters of public concern), and convening (protesting or organizing deliberative forums to facilitate change).

Political learning refers to classroom and cocurricular experiences that increase student understanding of and ability to navigate and shape systems and structures of power, particularly political (just systems for policy making) and economic (how resources are distributed) in the context of a pluralistic society across differences of social identity, ideology, or life experiences.

Drawing in part from Gutmann and Thompson,[19] we define *democracy* as a form of government in which free people have an equal opportunity to participate in and shape the social, political, and economic systems that affect their lives. Democratic learning and engagement involve examining the tensions around the practical application of democratic principles of liberty, equality, individual prosperity, diversity and inclusion, and shared responsibility for the common good. While *educating for democracy* has no partisan leaning or ideology, the process and goals are clearly political.

FINDINGS

As indicated, this chapter concerns only the "structural" frame and the "curricular" dimension in our conceptual framework. All five of the case study institutions manifested pervasive habits, embedded across disciplines, of classroom discussions about current events, policy disputes, cultural and ideological diversity, and controversial political issues, and for this reason we chose to focus on this finding in depth. At these institutions, we observed faculty members discussing how they often integrated current events and policy debates into their teaching approaches. In particular, four major themes emerged as core characteristics of these teaching approaches:

- *Training and preparation:* Faculty using discussion-based teaching actively sought training to develop their discussion teaching skills.
- *Establishing classroom dynamics:* Faculty established classroom dynamics conducive to successful discussion by building relationships and trust among students. Some techniques included establishing classroom ground rules, encouraging dissent, and fostering an inclusive atmosphere for learning and effectively managing conflict.
- *Diversity as a pedagogical asset:* Social and ideological diversity among the students in the class was used as a pedagogical asset.
- *Introducing dissenting viewpoints:* The professors introduced missing and dissenting perspectives and played "devil's advocate" to press students to think critically and broaden their own perspectives. This was particularly true when classes lacked compositional diversity.

TRAINING AND PREPARATION

We found that faculty members using discussion-based teaching actively sought support for facilitating discussions on controversial or intercultural topics. In particular, faculty sought professional development opportunities to improve their intergroup facilitation skills. How they developed these skills varied.

At one of our case study institutions, a small group of professors shared the concern that they felt unprepared to work with the increasingly diverse student populations attending the college. They brought civic organizations to campus to conduct trainings in public deliberation. They attended two diversity trainings, including a "trust building" workshop. They also formed an informal community of practice in which participants shared readings and experiences. Over time, they actively held themselves out as people who were attendant to student social identity in both the classroom and in their faculty advising roles. They named themselves "Agents of Change" (pseudonym) and identified themselves publicly as part of this group by posting a notice on their office doors. Soon, others at the college sought the same training, which eventually became associated with the faculty development center on campus. More faculty members sought the training, and at the time of our research, over 85 professors had become Agents of Change. In addition to continued workshops and trainings, they also gather six times each academic year to discuss challenges and opportunities for people of color on campus. The original Agents of Change now run internal trainings for other faculty. Whenever a task force or committee is formed, the administrator convening the group ensures that at least one or two Agents of Change are involved. Faculty explained that while Agents of Change began as a unique, grass-roots faculty initiative with no institution financial support, the group feels otherwise supported across campus, including by the administration.

At another institution, the office of civic engagement served as a resource for faculty by hiring external consultants to conduct trainings on how to incorporate diversity and civic issues into the classroom. That office was a well-known place for running workshops on white privilege. Numerous faculty and students mentioned participating in these workshops and explained how this experience changed the way they thought about privilege and power in and beyond the classroom.

ESTABLISHING CLASSROOM DYNAMICS

Faculty members at our case-study institutions actively sought opportunities to make classroom discussions political and socially relevant by challenging their students to consider diverse perspectives, and they viewed the management of these discussions as an important skill, while also recognizing that their students were uncomfortable with conflict or emotional about a topic. Instead of avoiding these interactions, they relied on skills and strategies, such as pausing and taking some time to encourage students to "check their temperatures" and reenter the discussion. Faculty members then proceeded to manage the classroom and create opportunities so students could respectfully disagree with another and grow from these challenges.

Successful discussions were carefully planned. One faculty member shared, "you want [students] to feel that they can say something that not everybody's going to agree with, and that's a challenge sometimes." Creating that open classroom environment requires that faculty lay the groundwork by building relationships and trust among the students, establishing classroom guidelines, encouraging dissent, and managing conflict. By establishing the right classroom dynamic, faculty members could encourage tangents, sometimes serving as reflective moments, without losing control of the learning.

At one institution, a unique first-year composition course was used to teach students how to engage in political or controversial issue discussions. Rather than study literature, as is commonly the practice, students in this course examined controversial public issues. They then learned how to frame the issues, take the perspectives of others, argue and debate, present written positions, and reflect on the process. One student said, "She had a different opinion, and I had a different opinion, but even though we had different opinions, we still could come to some kind of compromise." Because most students took this elective, faculty members teaching other courses could rely on a certain level of understanding among students about respect, perspective taking, argument, and finding common ground.

Faculty members also established a tone of civility and respect. One student explained:

> We were able to have a legitimate discussion. Yes, people disagreed, but we were able to do it in a calm manner and respect each other's opinions. It really made the class that much more worthwhile and informative because you were able to get differing opinions and maybe even question your own perspective, whereas in the beginning, it was everyone was so cut throat, my opinion is the only one that matters, and yours is wrong. But it was all about the environment that [the professor] fostered for our debates.

When necessary, the professor might intervene and pause the conversation to manage incivility: "Sometimes it's necessary to just stop the conversation or the dissent[er] and then just say, 'Let's step back for a moment and watch what's happening here. Is there a better way for us to process this than calling each other names?'" This professor did not stop the conversation. Rather, he managed conflict by creating a pause during which students could reflect on their emotions and words. One student who had experienced this type of classroom management explained:

> We had a lot of controversial debates in class but only once did [the professor] have to shut it down. But for the most part he managed it very, very well, with people being able to voice

their different opinions. And he made you stand up for what you believe because, regardless of whether you agreed with what he said, he would always play the devil's advocate and he wouldn't let you answer "just because" or "because of this."

Discussion can be intimidating for some students, and one faculty member explained how he draws out reticent participants or students who have not yet fully formed their arguments. He spoke of knowing his students well enough so that he could "just tell" when someone wants to speak but is not confident enough to "chime in." Creating an inclusive classroom means encouraging all students to share contrasting yet sometimes underdeveloped arguments.

DIVERSITY AS A PEDAGOGICAL ASSET

Compositional diversity at the institutional level: Most of the institutions we visited served diverse groups of students, and on those campuses, faculty and students emphasized how diversity enriched student learning. At one institution, the students were both socially and ideological diverse. Another institution served a student population with a significant number of veterans and students over 30, and many faculty talked about how age diversity improved the learning experiences of younger students. One is designated by the Department of Education as a Hispanic-serving institution. One faculty member described typical interactions in her class: "We had anti-choice, pro-choice, we had gun control, no gun control. All these kids from different points of view, they all respected and enjoyed each other's company and had a group hug in the end."

At its most basic level, cultural diversity enriches the student experience by facilitating intergroup interactions and relationships. This is particularly significant in a country in which Americans self-sort into homogeneous communities where they talk and work with people of the same culture, ideology, and values.[20] One faculty member explained that one white student had never spoken to a black person before taking her class, and by interacting with black students and even engaging in heated and controversial debates, the white student developed an appreciation for her peers' different perspectives. Another focused on age diversity and shared a story involving a Spanish class in which an older student explained how speaking Spanish had increased the effectiveness of her hospital work because she could communicate with Spanish-speaking patients.

Religious diversity can be used to increase learning for democracy. At another institution, there was a large Christian student population on campus. Yet, faculty members would challenge their students to be critical of religion by creating dissenting discussions in the classroom. These conversations were difficult. One student met with her professor after a contentious class debate and asked her why she constantly critiqued her religion. After realizing her professor also identified with the Christian religion but was trying to challenge the class to consider different perspectives, she realized the value of perspective-taking on developing her beliefs. She shared:

> [My professor] said sometimes she goes against the gradient with Christianity because half the class at the beginning raises their hands and says they're Christians anyway. So she has seen a lot of people have their faith deepened even though she's going against them because, I kid you not, she would say stuff and I'd be like, "I have never heard that in the Bible before." I would literally go home, and I would open my Bible and try to find that, or I would talk to somebody I knew who knew something like that and it caused me to dig deeper into it. Even though she wasn't gung ho for it, she was saying things against it; it caused me to look harder.

At these particular institutions, faculty drew from and integrated the students' individual life experiences, ideological perspectives, and social diversity to make the course materials accessible and relevant and to provide students with opportunities to practice democratic engagement. For example, one of the institutions had a large health sciences department with a significant portion of students from low-income backgrounds. A faculty member there described how he taught the subject matter by exploring the implications of the Affordable Care Act for his students personally. He asked, for example, whether or not people should be required to pay a fine if they could not afford health insurance. He described the experience to us: "When it relates to their own bodies and their own lives, they're very motivated to talk about it. ... Obamacare matters because it's happening to them."

Although faculty members provided opportunities for students to incorporate their own diversity into the classroom experience, this approach should not be confused with tokenism. Faculty members do not call on low-income students or veterans and ask for their perspective on political topics. Instead, they integrate content into the classroom curriculum that creates spaces for students to share their diversity of experiences as assets to the discussion.

INTRODUCING DISSENTING VIEWPOINTS

When compositional diversity is lacking, faculty introduce dissenting views: For institutions in our study with less compositional diversity in the student body or for classes at diverse institutions that, for some reason, draw a less diverse set of students, authentic political discussions required the intentional introduction of perspectives "not in the room." This approach was particularly relevant to students with more politically conservative views who were on campuses where students are perceived as predominantly liberal. These conservative students felt that they could not share their dissenting points of view in the classroom. Therefore, this approach was particularly important for these select students who felt their perspectives could not be voiced more freely and naturally.

Many professors address this problem by playing "devil's advocate" to introduce dissent among ideological homogenous groups of students. Although all of our institutional case studies supported this approach, institutions with more homogenous student populations explained the utility of inquiry and constructing learning experiences and environments among like-minded students. At one institution, faculty members ignited political conversations by using controversial reading assignments, films, and news media clips. A faculty member from this institution explained, "I think it's more to get them knowledge about what's going on, as opposed to, of course, trying to get them to pick a side or maybe think about what side they are on. It's more about knowing how to deal with people in a political environment." Another strategy used by faculty members from another institution included using course texts for constructing dissent in the classroom. One faculty member explained how students engaged with this exercise, stating that students will "say flat out, 'I disagree with you and here's why,' and I find that as long as it's rooted in the text some way then it doesn't feel personal and they're always coming back to the claims and the arguments which makes it a little easier to disagree."

Do effective discussion teachers share their own political perspectives? This question arose repeatedly in our study, and there was no consensus on this subject. One faculty member explained:

> I keep my views out of it but simply ask questions, be the devil's advocate, regardless of the way the class tends to go, and try to take the other point of view. I find that students are very willing to look at the other side of it and maybe not agree with it, but at least understand where [other] people are coming from.

Others, however, felt that being "authentic" meant that they disclosed their viewpoints to students but also assured them that the class would be balanced and representative of all viewpoints. The goal is to present all perspectives, but insist they are based on evidence, not just opinion.

Another way to present multiple and opposing points of view is to have the students play devil's advocate with each other. One faculty member pairs students and asks them to defend opposing sides of an issue and then share with the class not only the positions on the issue, but also their experience as "opponents." She explained, "I am just trying to teach the whole picture." Students also recognized the value of participating in these discussions in which multiple perspectives were considered.

The professors invited expression about diverse lived experiences and perspectives drawing from the students in the class. When that diversity of perspectives was introduced into the classroom—whether it was by leveraging the existing diversity or constructing dissenting spaces for students to consider viewpoints not present in the classroom—students learn important lessons about democracy.

DISCUSSION-BASED TEACHING INFLUENCES BOTH STUDENT AND INSTITUTIONAL CIVIC IDENTITY

The ways in which students experienced discussion-based teaching on matters of political consequence reinforced this finding. Repeatedly, students across these institutions confessed that their favorite courses involved discussions and debates in the classroom. One student described her experience as "practicing" politics:

> It was a good class because we had one central thing that we could be talking about and different viewpoints made the conversation so energetic. I may feel one thing, and you feel the exact opposite on every point that I presented, and then after a while you started to see that the people who did not agree started to come together and defend each other as well as expand on what they were talking about. By the end of the class you'd have two different sides when everybody started off disagreeing and they're just doing back and forth. There's no real winner because in politics and philosophy, a question is always open-ended and so it's open to interpretation. So I loved that class. It blew my mind.

Students said that this approach encouraged their development as critical thinkers and civic leaders. Indeed, one student shared his experience:

> [The professor] would keep on pushing you to kind of make you get to the bottom of what you believed [and that] really make you think. And he made everyone speak. You couldn't just be passive because a lot of times people want to just be passive and just, "Yeah, I agree with what you said" or "Pretty much what she said" and [the professor] was like, "Okay, well, why?" And so I really, really appreciated that class. It made me think about a lot of things differently and find out why I believed [particular ideas] because sometimes I would start saying why I thought I believed it and [realized] maybe I didn't really know.

Other students from across institutions and disciplines echoed similar sentiments as students discussing issues such as prostitution or affirmative action. These topics are political in nature, but these classrooms themselves were described as places where students not only engaged with the political dimensions of issues but also practiced politics by perspective-taking, debating, reframing issues, and questioning one another. These are higher-order skills associated with critical thinking and democratic practices. A diversity of perspectives and experiences was commonly referenced as an important piece of these discussions. Engaging in discussions of political consequence in the classroom, students learned to challenge their personal beliefs and to question rules in society.

One faculty member explained that his students are "allowed to find their voice here. Once they find their voice they become dangerous, they become protestors, they become activists. ... [They] already had that in them but now they can fully express that. Well guess what? What I just told you about the mission of the college fits that perfectly." This faculty member described student political engagement as aligned with the institution's identity.

Students also shared this perspective explaining that they left the classroom thinking about their civic roles differently. As students reflected on their experiences with political learning in the classroom through discussion-based practices, they shared how their sense of agency changed. Some students explained that the classroom experience provoked them to redefine their ideas of democracy and reconsider their campus as a democratic space. One student reflected, "I think that you can be politically involved without necessarily having to participate in voting or democracy at a national or even state level. You can be politically involved even on campus or within special interest groups." Other students echoed this change in perspective as they described their involvement in leadership activities on campus. Some students referred to their campus as its own democracy.

Although most of the data suggests students at these case-study institutions thrive in classroom political discussions, some expressed a different experience. Not all students feel comfortable with dissent in the classroom. For example, one faculty member explained some of his students' experiences with caution and shared, "But I think there's a lot of hesitancy and nervousness in classrooms still. You know: 'Am I going to say the right thing? Do I talk about these issues? Am I smart enough?'" Students do not gain critical thinking and civic skills from these discussions if they do not participate in them. Therefore, while most students on these campuses are benefiting from participating in discussion-based learning, strategies are still needed to engage students with lower confidence levels in the classroom to ensure all students are gaining these skills.

CONCLUSION

On all five case study campuses, faculty across the curriculum employed skilled, discussion-based teaching with current events, policy debates, and controversial issues as content. While we were surprised at the consistency across campuses, we know from other studies that students develop political interest and efficacy when they have opportunities to express their opinions and discuss controversial issues.[21] Studies have also demonstrated that deliberation among socially diverse students has long-term impact—they are more engaged in the political process than their peers who did not experience deliberative practices either inside or beyond the classroom.[22] Further, more conventional pedagogies—teaching through lectures, memorization of facts, and assessment through recall—have been criticized as less effective.[23] Students forget what they learn in a lecture,[24] but when they engage in the process of coconstructing knowledge through inquiry, discourse, and problem solving, they learn and remember what they have learned.[25] In contrast to lectures and textbooks without corresponding interactive teaching methods, discussion-based teaching helps students develop advanced skills in reasoning, intergroup understanding, critical thinking, and the transference of knowledge to problem solving.[26]

Discussion-based teaching using public issues was an attribute common to all five of the campuses we visited, and students repeatedly reported the transformational effect of those experiences as having improved their learning and shaped their political interest. Nonetheless, as with most qualitative research, our study cannot confirm a direct causal relationship between teaching method and voting. Student interest in voting may be affected by other factors, such as external political influences (e.g., candidate visits or voter mobilization efforts). Pedagogical practices and political content in the classroom are one component of a campus climate, as discussed in our other chapter in this book, "Politics 365: Fostering Campus Climates for Student Political Learning and Engagement." Additional research is needed to understand better the value of political classroom conversation to creating a robust campus climate for political learning and how this attribute works alongside the others identified in our study.

The political landscape in the United States has changed dramatically over the past 30 years, and arguably, during the 2016 election season. These changes include growing political and economic inequality, increasing partisanship and polarization among politicians and Americans more broadly, and public distrust of and disengagement from government systems and institutions. The next generation of citizens needs to do better. Since the burst of energy associated with higher education's civic movement over the past few decades, US colleges and universities have been focusing on *individual* civic engagement and mostly apolitical learning experiences. The shift needs to be toward the collective, educating students to explore new perspectives both critically and respectfully, to participate in difficult dialogues on matters of political consequence, to compromise and collaborate, and to engage in processes for building a stronger democracy. The classroom is the ideal place to *practice* these arts of democracy. ∎

ENDNOTES

1. The National Study of Learning, Voting, and Engagement (NSLVE) data includes a breakdown of 2012 voting rates by disciplines. Among the 900 colleges and universities currently participating in NSLVE, education majors, for example, vote at the highest rate (56%) while students in the physical sciences, mathematics, and computer technology voted at rates of 41%, 37%, and 41% respectively. The average voting rates for these disciplines among the five institutions in this study, however, were as follows: physical sciences: 59%, mathematics: 53%, and computer technology: 45%.

2. G. F. Zook, *Higher Education for American Democracy: A Report*, vol. 1 (US Government Printing Office, 1947).

3. H. C. Boyte, ed., *Democracy's Education: Public Work, Citizenship & the Future of Colleges and Universities* (Nashville, TN: Vanderbilt University Press, 2015), 8; National Task Force on Civic Learning and Democratic Engagement, 2012; J. Saltmarsh and M. Hartley eds., *"To Serve a Larger Purpose": Engagement for Democracy and the Transformation of Higher Education* (Philadelphia: Temple University Press, 2011); B.R. Barber and R.M. Battistoni, *Education for Democracy* (Dubuque, IA: Kendall Hunt Publishing, 2011); A. Gutmann and D. Thompson, *Democratic Disagreement: Why Moral Conflict Cannot Be Avoided in Politics and What Should Be Done About It* (Cambridge, MA: Belknap Press, 1999).

4. R. Putnam, *Bowling Alone: The Collapse and Revival of Civic America* (New York: Simon & Schuster, 2000).

5. E. Hartman, "No Values, No Democracy: The Essential Partisanship of a Civic Engagement Movement," *Michigan Journal of Community Service Learning* 19 (2013): 58–72; A. Colby, E. Beaumont, T. Ehrlich, and J. Corngold, *Educating for Democracy: Preparing Undergraduates for Responsible Political Engagement* (San Francisco: Jossey-Bass, 2007).

6. M. W. Peterson and M. G. Spencer, "Understanding Academic Culture and Climate," in W. G. Tierney ed., *Assessing Academic Climates and Cultures* (San Francisco: Jossey-Bass, 1990).

7. Peterson and Spencer, *Assessing Academic Climates and Cultures*, 173.

8. S. Hurtado, K. A. Griffin, L. Arellano, and M. Cuellar, "Assessing the Value of Climate Assessments: Progress and Future Directions," *Journal of Diversity in Higher Education* 1 (2008): 204–21.

9. A. J. Ryder and J. J. Mitchell, "Measuring Campus Climate for Personal and Social Responsibility," *New Directions for Higher Education*, (2013): 31–48.

10. Hurtado et al., "Assessing the Value of Climate Assessments," 204.

11. S. Hurtado, J. F. Milem, A. R. Clayton-Pedersen, and W. R. Allen, "Enhancing Campus Climates for Racial/Ethnic Diversity: Educational Policy and Practice," *The Review of Higher Education* 21 (1998): 279–302.

12. A. R. D'Augelli and S. L. Hershberger, "Lesbian, Gay, and Bisexual Youth in Community Settings: Personal Challenges and Mental Health Problems," *American Journal of Community Psychology* 21 (1993): 421–48; S. R. Rankin and R. D. Reason, "Differing Perceptions: How Students of Color and White Students Perceive Campus Climate for Underrepresented Groups," *Journal of College Student Development* 45 (2005): 43–61; S. C. Brown, "Learning across the Campus: How College Facilitates the Development of Wisdom," *Journal of College Student Development* (2004): 134–48; U. M. Jayakumar, T. C. Howard, W. R. Allen, and J. C. Han, "Racial Privilege in the Professoriate: An Exploration of Campus Climate, Retention, and Satisfaction," *The Journal of Higher Education* 80 (2009): 538–63; G. P. Morrow, D. Burris-Kitchen, and A. Der-Karabetian, "Assessing Campus Climate of Cultural Diversity: A Focus on Focus Groups," *College Student Journal* 34 (2000): 589.

13. G. D. Kuh, "Organizational Theory," in *Student Services: A Handbook for the Profession*, fourth edition, ed. Susan R. Komives and Dudley B. Woodard, Jr. (Hoboken, NJ: Wiley, 2003), 269–96; E. H. Schein, "Culture: The Missing Concept in Organization Studies," *Administrative Science Quarterly*, (1996): 229–40.

14. L. G. Bolman and T. E. Deal, *Reframing Organizations: Artistry, Choice, and Leadership*, third edition (San Francisco: Jossey Bass, 2003).

15. Bolman and Deal, *Reframing Organizations*.

16. D. Layder, "The Reality of Social Domains: Implications for Theory and Method," in *Knowing the Social World* (New York: Open University Press, 1998).

17. A. Lewins and C. Silver, *Using Software for Qualitative Data Analysis: A Step-by-Step Guide* (London: Sage Publications, Ltd., 2007).

18. S. B. Merriam, *Qualitative Research: A Guide to Design and Implementation: Revised and Expanded From Qualitative Research and Case Study Applications in Education* (San Francisco: Jossey-Bass, 2009).

19. Gutmann and Thompson, *Democracy and Disagreement*.

20. B. Bishop, *The Big Sort: Why the Clustering of Like-Minded America Is Tearing Us Apart* (New York: Houghton Mifflin, 2008).

21. E. Colby, "Political Agency and Empowerment: Pathways for Developing a Sense of Political Efficacy in Young Adults," in *Handbook of Research on Civic Engagement in Youth* (Hoboken, NJ: Wiley, 2010), 525–58; D. E. Hess, *Controversy in the Classroom: The Democratic Power of Discussion* (New York: Routledge, 2009).

22. K. Harriger, J. J. McMillan, Ch.M. Buchanan, and S. Gusler, "The Long-Term Impact of Learning to Deliberate," *Diversity & Democracy* (2015): 27–28.

23. D. K. Cohen, *Teaching for Understanding: Challenges for Policy and Practice* (San Francisco: Jossey-Bass, 1993).

24. D. L. Finkel, *Teaching with Your Mouth Shut* (Portsmouth, NH: Heinemann-Boynton/Cook, 2000).

25. R. F. Elmore, "Teaching, Learning, and Organization: School Restructuring and the Recurring Dilemmas of Reform," Paper from Annual Meeting of the American Educational Research Association, Chicago (1991, April).

26. W. J. McKeachie, *Teaching Tips: Strategies, Research, and Theory for College and University Teachers*, ninth edition (Lexington, MA: DC Heath, 1994), 56.

Deliberative Pedagogy's Feminist Potential: Teaching Our Students to Cultivate a More Inclusive Public Sphere

3

J. Cherie Strachan

Many political theorists and social scientists argue that deliberation is the key to cultivating healthy civic identity. As opportunities to engage in deliberative decision making in natural settings decline, incorporating deliberative pedagogy in formal civic education has become an increasingly important tool for promoting civic and political engagement. Yet patriarchal prejudices that once justified restricting women's access to the public sphere still affect female students' abilities to participate effectively in deliberative processes, especially when deliberation is explicitly linked to political participation. Hoping to draw attention to the hierarchical structures and norms used to marginalize women as well as minorities, this chapter examines factors contributing to women's disenfranchisement. It also recommends a number of approaches for improving women and minority students' learning experiences when civic engagement endeavors rely on deliberative pedagogy.

A liberal arts education is intended to cultivate a students' capacity for reasoned deliberation, critical thinking, and good judgment. While these goals for student development have long been associated with Americans' understanding of an appropriate college education, the task of achieving such outcomes has become increasingly difficult over the past several decades.[1] Professors at US institutions are now tasked not simply with honing these skills, but often with introducing them to students. This shift can be tracked to declining opportunities for people to engage in reasoned deliberation in the public sphere—a loss that has had dramatic consequences for the youngest generations of Americans who are most likely to have come of age without participating in such deliberative activities. The current and upcoming classes of US college students are far less likely to have experienced deliberation as an integral component of their political socialization because the vibrant infrastructure of voluntary associations that once provided such experiences no longer exists.[2] In many ways, instructors in all disciplines at US institutions now face the same task as our colleagues working in countries that have historically lacked a well-developed civil society—acquainting students with the basic features of deliberation and collective decision making in a democracy. As such, it has become necessary to teach our students these highly valued skills through formal civic education experiences that are explicitly designed to address the weakening of our public sphere.

As professors attempt to remedy the most recent shortcomings of our public sphere, it is important that our pedagogy not reinforce its most egregious, long-standing flaws. For many decades, patriarchal prejudices against women and members of marginalized demographic groups were used to justify restricting full and equal participation in all aspects of public life, and these prejudices still affect the ability to persuade others in deliberative settings.[3] If academics intend to play a proactive role in cultivating civic leaders who will rebuild deliberative civil society and promote democracy, we must take care to do so in a way that avoids reintroducing these same biases back into our public sphere.

This chapter seeks to inform deliberative pedagogy across the disciplines by exploring the experiences of women in Western culture and how these experiences affect women's ability to participate effectively in civic and political life. This focus is applicable to many other cultures as well because patriarchal societies spread across the world thousands of years ago and women's exclusion from the public sphere continues to cut across many current cultures and societies. A critical approach to teaching deliberation may help identify and dismantle the structures and norms used to prevent women and other marginalized people from fully participating in deliberative decision making, which is central to a healthy democracy.

In addition to examining the factors that have kept women on the margins of public life in America, this chapter describes a number of approaches that may be used by instructors in any discipline to confront and reduce barriers to women's acceptance as political agents. For even though women now achieve visible political roles—as evidenced by former Secretary of State Hillary Clinton's unsuccessful 2008 and 2016 presidential campaigns and by female justices, governors, senators, representatives, and state legislators—it is important to note that aside from voting, women self-report lower rates of political participation on a wide array of measures ranging from the low-intensity activity of discussing political issues with others to the high-intensity activity of running for office.[4] Hence the approaches described in this chapter, which admittedly may undermine each other's effects in practice, include strategies for helping women achieve success within current patriarchal systems as well as strategies designed to provide longer-term solutions by changing these systems from within. Exploring these approaches offers a unique opportunity to use deliberative pedagogy to bring women and other underrepresented voices into the public sphere in a way that will benefit all of society and strengthen democratic institutions.

INSIGHT FROM DELIBERATIVE DEMOCRACY SCHOLARS

While mainstream political scientists typically assess formal, institutionalized processes (such as voting rights, electoral integrity, and majority rule) to determine the health of a democracy, deliberative democracy scholars, dismayed by the decline in opportunities for public deliberation, emphasize the role that public deliberation plays in authentic, democratic governance. This definition of democracy shifts attention to the type of interactions that must take place among citizens and public officials to facilitate reasoned decision making and informed judgment. These types of interactions, theorists argue, help move political participation beyond an adversarial (and likely ill-informed) process that pits citizens against one another and toward an exchange characterized by inclusiveness, mutual respect, and reason-giving.

Several early theorists in this subfield of deliberative democracy attempted to identify and explain all of the essential elements of authentic deliberation required for a democratic society to claim legitimacy. While criteria vary somewhat from scholar to scholar, most would likely acknowledge that deliberation includes discursive efforts to identify solutions for shared, public problems in a process characterized by open, inclusive exchanges. Further, the participants in this process should engage in reason-giving, consider one another's perspectives, and treat each other as equals.[5] Deliberative pedagogy builds on this work, turning to formal instruction rather than natural political socialization, to prepare students for participation in democracy's underpinning deliberative processes.

INSIGHT FROM RADICAL FEMINISM

While mainstream feminism is often associated with concern for women's status within society as it currently exists, radical feminism recognizes that patriarchal cultures succeed in oppressing women because they are organized around the principles of domination and control. Hence the same rigid social hierarchies that evolved to create submissive roles for women are the root cause of all forms of oppression, including those based on race, class, ethnicity, sexual orientation, ability, and religion.[6] At its core, radical feminism requires overturning oppressive organizing structures that are the antithesis of deliberation. As Johnson states: "Whether we begin with race or gender or disability status or class, if we name the problem correctly, we will wind up going in the same direction."[7]

Biases about which types of people are most qualified to resolve public problems accompany students into the classroom. We must find a way to make deliberative pedagogy effective for all of our students, not simply for those most likely to be comfortable and well received in deliberative settings. Work in the tradition of deliberative democracy and radical feminism can be combined with that of the scholarship of teaching and learning to assess our efforts and to identify best practices for deliberative pedagogy that help to build inclusive, rather than exclusive, definitions of citizenship and community.

PATRIARCHY AND WOMEN'S PARTICIPATION IN THE PUBLIC SPHERE

Within traditional patriarchy in America's colonial and founding era, the law of coverture eclipsed the possibility of women's unchaperoned presence, let alone participation, in the public sphere. Women had no legal identity aside from their position within a household headed by a male relative. As such, they were officially represented in all public proceedings—economic, political, civic, and religious—by a male head of household. Women were excluded from participation in the social contract that the American founders believed shaped their relationship with their newly established government—whereby men are born free with inalienable rights and must voluntarily agree to be governed—for two reasons: first, because women were deemed inherently unqualified for such participation, and second, because most thought such participation would undermine society's stability. These conclusions were based on assumptions about women's natural ability and character. Women's inability to engage in reason and their overly passionate natures justified somber male guidance, while their physical weakness necessitated male provision and protection.[8]

Beyond their inability to meet the criteria for citizenship, women were also associated with an uncontrollable craving for all forms of self-gratification, so much so that their participation in the public sphere would result in chaos and corruption. Women who attempted to be active in public life were not only considered to be reaching beyond their limited abilities but perceived as a threat that could undermine society's fragile stability with their demands. Such unfortunate outcomes could be avoided if women were guided into their natural role as submissive helpmates within the domestic sphere, where they would focus on fulfilling the needs of their families rather than their own overreaching ambitions. Indeed, patriarchy defines masculinity, in large part, as the ability to control women, with men responsible for ensuring that their wives and daughters conform to these gender-appropriate roles.[9]

Despite the success of the first two waves of the US women's movement, which relied on social protest to gain the vote in 1920 and to gain more complete access to education, the workplace, and politics in the 1960s, women's ability to participate fully in deliberation—in public life, on college campuses, and in our classrooms—is still affected by the legacies of this patriarchal system. The following sections explore some of the more damaging legacies that deliberative democratic instruction can both explore and help to eliminate.

WOMEN'S CONSENT, BENEVOLENT SEXISM, AND (LACK OF) GENDER CONSCIOUSNESS

Throughout much of American history, women's consent to playing a limited role in society has been used to justify confining women to the domestic sphere. But social constructionists are quick to point out that individuals are quite capable of embracing identities that relegate people like themselves to an inferior position in society.[10] The benevolent nature of many of the prescriptive stereotypes used to constrain women has made this tendency a particularly troublesome gender trap for women. The ideal "communal female" is supportive, other-oriented, and nurturing—qualities that many find difficult to argue against. More tellingly, this ideal woman serves as a resource for others' aspirations rather than pursuing her own ambitions. Even now, many people (both men and women) expect women to exemplify these idealized traits, allowing them to claim that they love and admire (appropriately behaved) women while harshly sanctioning those who reject traditional gender roles.[11]

To the extent that women themselves co-opt their own empowerment by internalizing such identities, it will be difficult for them to advocate for their own best interests in the public sphere.[12] Some feminist scholars fear this pattern prevents women from even identifying, let alone voicing, their legitimate political concerns, in part because women are socialized to be more polite than men.[13] According to Robin Lakoff, in her seminal work on gender and politeness, "Little girls were indeed taught to talk like little ladies, in that their speech is in many ways more polite than that of boys or men, and the reason for this is that politeness involves an absence of strong statement, and women's speech is devised to prevent the expression of strong statements."[14] Of course, not all women modify their speech accordingly, but as benevolent sexism predicts, those who do not are often disliked and are subject to social sanction as a result.

Not only do many women avoid making strong arguments themselves, they are more prone than others to prioritize social harmony over political participation, often choosing to avoid face-to-face conflict and political disagreement within their interpersonal networks altogether.[15] Given that people discussing public affairs will almost inevitably disagree with one another at some point over some issues, perhaps it should not be surprising that women—and to a lesser degree, minorities—are also far less likely than white men to participate in political discourse that requires them to be persuasive. Even controlling for experiences that bolster political and social capital fails to eliminate these demographic patterns completely.[16]

One final piece of evidence that many women continue to embrace the role of the communal female is their lack of group, or gender, consciousness. Unlike members of other demographic groups that have been the subject of discrimination (including the elderly as well as ethnic/racial and religious minorities), women are often far less likely to notice unfair treatment or to attribute it to their shared gender status. Hence they are less apt to mobilize to air these grievances in the public sphere.[17]

In short, one legacy of patriarchy in Western culture is that even now, women quite often do not see themselves as the type of people who should participate fully in the public sphere, especially when that participation requires them to address contested political views or to help resolve divisive issues in their communities.[18] Internalizing the traditional, communal feminine roles advocated by benevolent sexism further undermines women's ability to see themselves as political actors.

One approach to countering this particular remnant of patriarchy is to combine deliberative pedagogy with diversity education intended to bolster the political identities and gender consciousness of female students. These efforts might include diversity programming that focuses on the accomplishments of the two waves of the women's movement, as well as on the ways contemporary community and political issues specifically affect women and other marginalized groups. This approach can help to transform female students into political actors by developing their ability to recognize and voice concerns in a way that has heretofore been fully available only to white men of means in our society.

A second approach to this particular remnant of patriarchy is to make women as comfortable as possible in the public sphere by holding *all* participants to high standards of politeness and civility. Such efforts not only provide a more welcoming space for women but also will likely yield better outcomes. Studies of interpersonal communication reveal the role of politeness in facilitating "exploratory talk," where people construct shared meanings as they develop ideas. Polite interactions involve soliciting others' opinions, qualifying one's claims, providing supportive feedback, acknowledging others' contributions, and avoiding confrontation. All of these conversational patterns encourage collaboration—and are especially useful when assessing future undertakings. By contrast, interactions characterized by challenges, disagreements, and interruptions lead to entrenched positions, especially when these tactics are used in public. As Holmes notes, "Those attacked often respond defensively, and little progress is made in exploring the issues and ideas proposed."[19]

Thus, women's learned, polite communication patterns—or what some might more broadly describe as a distinct women's culture—provide a valuable resource for deliberative pedagogy.[20] Many have long argued that modeling feminine interaction patterns would result in "better working relationships, better understanding of complex issues, and better decision making."[21] Indeed, recent research suggests that more inclusive processes and more empathetic policy recommendations result when women deliberate within gender-exclusive enclaves or even when group composition substantially favors women.[22] It seems feminine modes of discourse and value preferences flourish when women's participation reaches a threshold, at which point they are numerous enough to influence group norms of appropriate behavior.

We need not wait for large numbers of female participants to transform traditionally masculine public spaces, however. We can purposefully create "feminized settings," as has occurred in deliberative public issue forums organized in the United States such as those organized by the National Issues Forum or AmericaSpeaks—which are (and were in the case of AmericaSpeaks) associations dedicated to improving democracy by facilitating small- and large-scale deliberative forums throughout the country. In doing so, however, we run the risk of undermining the ability to influence political decisions as the preferences that emerge from such forums are often not perceived as political demands.[23] Yet it is worth noting that a similar type of socialization used to take place within American versions of civil society, where countless Americans, including both average people and, notably, ambitious political elites, learned to manage conflict in public settings via parliamentary procedure.[24] Formal rules required turn-taking, minimized interruptions, eliminated the need to "fight" for the floor, and discouraged ad hominem attacks, all of which may have formally "feminized" public interactions (even—or perhaps especially—in male enclaves) to promote social harmony and to sustain working relationships among members of a deliberative community. Teaching our students how to perform exaggerated versions of civility and politeness may help to combat examples of aggressive, rude behavior modeled daily by media pundits and politicians, while simultaneously creating a more inviting environment for our female and minority students.

THE EFFECTS OF GENDERED DIVISION OF LABOR ON PERCEPTIONS OF LIKEABILITY AND EXPERTISE

Even if women come to think of themselves as appropriate participants in deliberative decision making and are not alienated by egregious examples of incivility in what remains of our public sphere, they face additional barriers to achieving persuasive influence in such settings. As Sanders argues:

> Some Americans are apparently less likely than others to be listened to; even when their arguments are stated according to conventions of reason, they are more likely to be disregarded. Although deliberators will always choose to disregard some arguments, when this disregard is systematically associated with the arguments made by those we know already to be systematically disadvantaged, we should at least reevaluate our assumptions about deliberation's democratic potential.[25]

If scholars committed to deliberative pedagogy intend to help remedy historical prejudices in the public sphere, such systemic inequality must be overcome. Empirical research on gender and social influence provides insight into the cause of the difficulties women experience achieving influence in such settings.

As noted earlier, patriarchy, until quite recently, resulted in a gendered division of labor in the United States, with women working primarily in the home and men assuming prominent roles in the workplace and in political institutions. Men have historically held more high-status positions in society than women, thus reinforcing gendered stereotypes about competency, status, and appropriate behavior. Men's assumption of leadership and efforts to influence others in deliberative settings are deemed both appropriate and laudable. Women, generally associated with low-status domestic positions, are expected to be communal and self-sacrificing rather than commanding.[26]

These expectations pose a conundrum for women. Unlike their male counterparts, when they attempt to wield influence in a group setting, they must first work to establish their competency. Yet women who engage in displays of competence—or even who exhibit assertiveness through means such as eye contact—are less well-liked and wield less influence than other women.[27] Men and boys are particularly prone to dislike and sanction these women (although other women also often object), because such behaviors are linked to efforts to gain status or to promote narrow agendas, which violate expectations grounded in the traditional ideal of the communal female. This aversion is overcome only when women combine high levels of perceived competence with a warm, communal style of communication that focuses on helping others. In short, traditional femininity is linked to women's likability—and both trump expertise and competence as prerequisites for influencing others.[28]

Men face far fewer hurdles in their attempts to influence others in group settings, as the success of their efforts is not predicated on displays of competence or communality. Men are already assumed to be competent and not expected to be communal. Women, however, must undertake a careful balancing act, conforming to traditional feminine norms to establish likability *and* proving their competency before achieving influence over others. Simply put, "As influence agents, males seem to have greater behavioral latitude than their female counterparts."[29] Given the difficulty of balancing these expectations, it is possible that women avoid engaging in civic and political discourse not only because they do not think of themselves as overtly political actors, but also because it is apt to be frustrating.

Teaching students about these patterns before having them participate in deliberative discussions in class or on campus may alleviate the effects of this patriarchal legacy. When students are aware of how implicit gender biases affect their reaction to men's and women's persuasive efforts, they may be able to begin consciously checking these reactions and altering their behavior. This approach may help create more egalitarian deliberative forums, but unless such training is systematically included on college campuses across the country, women will still face gendered barriers to persuasion and influence as soon as they enter a new deliberative setting.

To address this issue, a second approach is to provide targeted training for female students to make them aware of how their contributions to deliberative decision making will be perceived and teach them tactics to side-step the barriers these perceptions raise. Carli, for example, suggests that women purposefully combine a warm, communal communication style (to establish likability) with high levels of competence.[30] Similar strategies, focused on effectiveness rather than eliminating biases, have been developed to help women successfully navigate workplace negotiations and leadership roles.[31] It is important to recognize that these strategies are designed specifically to teach women how to achieve influence while appearing to conform to gender stereotypes. They may be quite useful in helping individual women, but they do little to break down—and may even help to reinforce—gendered expectations that negatively affect women in the first place.

A third approach involves taking into consideration how different features of deliberative forums will affect female students' experiences. For example, women's influence wanes when forums are framed as political discussions because politics is still largely perceived as a masculine endeavor in American society. Women fare much better when forums are framed as community problem-solving efforts, as the community is one aspect of the public sphere where women have historically been far more active and welcome. The types of issues discussed also affect women's experiences in deliberative forums, with their influence increasing when traditional "women's issues" such as child care, education, elder care, and social welfare are on the agenda. Women are already perceived as experts on such issues, allowing them to avoid the difficult task of establishing competence. Just as important, such concerns are more readily linked to women's roles as nurturers and caregivers, making it easier to frame their preferences as part of a communal rather than a self-serving agenda.[32] The makeup of participants may also influence women's participation in forums, as being in a numerical minority not only reduces women's status and authority but also results in more competitive and assertive communication styles that further reduce their likelihood of contributing. Finally, decision rules appear to affect women's participation, with majority rule prone to suppressing women (especially when they are in the minority) and unanimous agreement often empowering them.[33]

It is one thing to know what factors make deliberative forums more comfortable spaces for women and another to act on this knowledge. Questions remain about whether structuring classroom and campus forums specifically to facilitate female students' participation is the most effective way to meet the learning objectives associated with deliberative pedagogy. If we frame deliberative forums as community rather than political events to facilitate our female students' participation, will they still learn to think of themselves as political actors who are obligated to participate in the public sphere? If we wish to cultivate political identities among our female students, should we prepare them for the reality they are likely to face beyond our campuses—where women will probably constitute a minority of the decision makers in the room, where unanimous agreement is rarely required, and where feminine modes of discourse are not apt to be the norm?

If we throw female students into deliberative settings that they will inevitably find frustrating, we may well diminish the likelihood that they will seek out participation in the deliberative public sphere in the future. Yet if we do not prepare them for the realities they are likely to face when we cannot manipulate decision rules and group composition, they will be in for a rather rude awakening after graduation. Given these concerns, would it would be more effective to sequence female students' experiences in deliberative forums, from the most inviting settings to the least, as a way of building their identities and skills over time? These are choices that feminist scholars and teachers must grapple with as we make choices that will affect the lessons both women and men learn as we more purposefully implement deliberative pedagogy in our classrooms and on our campuses.

RESOURCES AND PROPOSED PRACTICES FOR DELIBERATIVE PEDAGOGY

Those who wish to promote civic engagement through deliberative pedagogy now have a wide array of resources to support their endeavors. Many teacher-scholars have adapted experiences designed by deliberative democracy advocates for the classroom or for campus-community projects. They have, for example, used a modified version of deliberative polling—developed by James S. Fishkin at Stanford University's Center for Deliberative Democracy—to not only improve students' substantive learning, but also their anticipated civic and political engagement.[34] This approach relies on trained moderators to guide citizens' through an in-depth deliberative dialogue on policy issues, with the goal of producing more informed preferences. Others have adapted Fishkin's and Ackerman's recommendation for a national holiday called Deliberation Day into a student-organized campus event,[35] or have implemented practices from AmericaSpeaks' large-scale deliberative town hall format to improve student understanding of the federal budget process.[36] (AmericaSpeaks, one of the most prominent organizations facilitating deliberative forums across the country, closed in 2014.)

Meanwhile, Wabash College has purposefully embedded deliberative modules into science courses, helping students learn to grapple with the types of "wicked" public policy issues facing contemporary scientists. These deliberative modules, including facilitated discussion of climate change in a biology course and of energy policy in a chemistry course, were led by trained moderators and encouraged students to consider multiple viewpoints and to grapple with the trade-offs and alternative values associated with different policy preferences.[37] Several other campuses have moved beyond one-shot deliberative experiences in the classroom, developing more comprehensive campus-community programming and long-term experiences for select students.[38]

Those teachers seeking to replicate such projects will find an array of resources ranging from assessment tools to moderator guides at The National Coalition for Dialogue and Deliberation, which serves as a network and clearing house for those engaged in the applied work of deliberative and participatory democracy. The Kettering Foundation, dedicated to cultivating engaged citizenship through deliberation, provides additional resources, along with professional development opportunities for academics and practitioners. A ready source of issue guides to facilitate student deliberation can be found at the National Issues Forum, while Public Agenda specializes in providing in-depth nonpartisan research and reports on issues of concern.

Yet few of the published SoTL pieces on deliberative pedagogy purposefully provide assessment designed to determine whether they facilitate the participation of women and minorities in these curricular and co-curricular experiences. Scholars interested in doing so can draw insights for best practices from recent empirical work on gender and deliberation, such as Karpowitz' and Mendelberg's *The Silent Sex*,[39] or from the theoretical, empirical, and applied work published in *The Journal of Public Deliberation*—where a recent special edition was entirely dedicated to concerns about equality and equity.

Despite the lack of SoTL research, one approach is to implement features intended to promote equity in classroom and campus activities. To promote students' civic engagement, for example, the department of political science and public administration at Central Michigan University (CMU) voted to embed a deliberative collective action simulation into every introduction to American government course offered on campus. This project, which exposes approximately 700 students each academic year to deliberative pedagogy, attempts to incorporate best practices for promoting equity among participants. Students meet in moderator-facilitated small groups four times throughout the semester. They use this class time to develop a series of resolutions where they not only recommend a policy position on a current, contested public issue, but also recommend a collective action strategy for promoting adoption of these preferences. Several features of this activity are designed to promote equitable participation in deliberation. Given the female advantage in CMU's student body and introductory classes, women typically constitute at least half of the small group participants, which should help women's norms shape communication patterns and provide them with voice. Given that CMU is approximately 85% white, additional safeguards are implemented to facilitate minority students' inclusion. These features are embedded in the grading rubric, as students are evaluated based on whether they create a deliberative environment where listening to understand is valued just as highly as providing persuasive reason-based arguments and where an egalitarian exchange of ideas enhances the quality of the solutions proposed. Project instructions also strongly encourage students to make decisions through consensus-building rather than majority rule, which is another feature that should enhance equitable participation for women and minorities. In short, students are explicitly encouraged to think of political participation as the deliberative pursuit of the common good, rather than a zero-sum game with winners and losers.

These features are appropriate for an introductory class, where the goal of incorporating deliberative pedagogy is to promote civic and political engagement to a wide swathe of freshmen and sophomores. More comprehensive programs targeting advanced students may find additional ways to enhance female and minority participation in deliberative learning. One option may be to create enclaves, where students with similar demographic traits deliberate with one another first, before engaging with others in a broader setting. Another may be to embed deliberative modules into courses specific to particular demographic groups—such as Women in Politics or African American Politics—where students overtly discuss whether it is worth adopting stereotypical communication patterns to bolster persuasive ends. Female students can discuss, for example, whether they should purposefully perform traditional femininity to bolster their likeability and, thus, their effectiveness in deliberative settings or whether they should focus on undermining those stereotyped expectations instead. Another simple step may be to require diversity courses as a prerequisite for participation in high-visibility campus or campus-community deliberative endeavors. Although incomplete, this list provides a starting point for incorporating recent research on equitable participation and deliberative pedagogy, with hopes that careful attention to distinct student experiences will drive creative interventions and assessment to identify best practices.

CONCLUSION

This overview is intended to emphasize that there is no single approach to promoting a gender-neutral and equitable public sphere. It is also intended to highlight the tensions that exist among these choices. Radical feminism clearly recommends embracing the long-term goal of feminizing the public sphere so that women's culture, and the feminine modes of discourse associated with it, comes to shape norms of appropriate behavior in deliberative settings. Both empirical social science and critical feminist theory indicate the result would be more inclusive with less aggressive interactions, resulting in more empathetic, and ultimately more effective, policy recommendations. This transformation would help to dismantle the social hierarchies that prevent all marginalized people from participating in public deliberation—and would also yield reflective decision-making processes that produce the innovative solutions to common problems prized by advocates of both deliberative democracy and educational reform.

Unfortunately, creating feminized deliberative spaces appears to enervate participants' ability to influence political decisions.[40] Clearly, far more work must be done to encourage participants in deliberative forums to recognize the inherently political nature of their endeavors, to recognize that they are political actors, to view their collective recommendations as policy solutions, and to hold public officials accountable for implementing them. Yet this task confronts the long reach of patriarchy's influence over Western culture. Not only were American women long confined to the domestic sphere, the very traits associated with femininity were used to justify the claim that women were unfit for citizenship. Hence, successfully reframing politics as a feminine endeavor (exploratory talk that produces a common good), rather than a masculine endeavor (an adversarial zero-sum game with winners and losers), will inevitably be an uphill battle and a long-term goal.

An effective short-term or interim strategy, then, may be to adopt more mainstream feminist tactics by preparing female students to wield influence in the public sphere the way that it currently exists. This approach may serve not only to empower individual women in the short-term but also to feminize deliberative institutions from the inside out. Yet this short-term strategy comes with risk. If we prepare young women to participate in masculinized institutional settings to help them wield influence now, our efforts could result in assimilating them into male culture and promoting male norms of appropriate behavior. The goal of radical feminism is not to help women succeed because they have learned to establish their own version of privilege in patriarchal social hierarchies. The goal is to help women succeed despite the differences their historic marginalization has produced so that the sheer weight of their numbers will eventually feminize the public sphere. Yet successful women sometimes reject the goals of radical feminism because they benefit from the status quo. "Having achieved acceptance by the patriarchal system, they risk losing power, rewards, and recognition if they challenge that same system."[41] Herein lies the dilemma. If we do not teach young women how to participate effectively in current public forums, it seems unlikely that they will take part in civic, and especially in political, life at high enough rates to transform deliberative institutions and settings. Yet teaching them to participate effectively could simply reify a gender-neutral version of the hierarchical status quo, where other types of people are marginalized instead of women.

Pursuing short-term goals for women's increased participation without undermining long-term goals for a more egalitarian public sphere will require a careful balancing act as we move forward. Moreover, at these early stages in the development of deliberative pedagogy as a distinct teaching method, we cannot claim which, if any, of the approaches described throughout this chapter are most effective for each discipline. As such, we should take inspiration from the turn toward empirical social science in the subfield of deliberative democracy, as well as from the scholarship of teaching and learning, to begin identifying which of these approaches, or combination of approaches, are effective, and which are unexpectedly counterproductive.

This work must be an integral part of deliberative pedagogy's development in every discipline, for if we make no effort "to correct for the deliberative disempowerment of women in mixed groups, women are likely to continue to be less frequent and influential contributors."[42] Given the array of options for addressing women's "deliberative disempowerment," failing to make any effort to address women's historic exclusion from deliberative decision making is not only irresponsible, but a lost opportunity to help our students become the type of citizens who will help build a key facet of an effective democracy in the twenty-first century—a more inclusive and egalitarian public sphere for everyone. ■

ACKNOWLEDGMENTS

A previous version of this chapter was published in *Deliberative Pedagogy and Democratic Engagement: Making Teaching and Learning in Higher Education Relevant to the Adaptive Challenges of our Communities*, edited by Nicholas V. Longo, Timothy J. Schaffer, and Maxine M. Thomas (East Lansing, MI: Michigan State University Press). The work included in this edited collection was undertaken by members of a Kettering Foundation working group on deliberative pedagogy.

ENDNOTES

1. Matthew Hartley, "Idealism and Compromise and the Civic Engagement Movement," in *To Serve a Larger Purpose: Engagement for Democracy and the Transformation of Higher Education*, ed. John Saltmarsh and Matthew Hartley (Philadelphia: Temple University Press, 2011), 27–48.

2. Robert D. Putnam, *Bowling Alone: The Collapse and Revival of American Community* (New York: Simon & Schuster, 2000); Theda Skocpol, *Diminished Democracy, From Membership to Management in American Civic Life* (Norman: The University of Oklahoma Press, 2003).

3. Seyla Benhabib, *Democracy and Difference: Contesting the Boundaries of the Political* (Princeton, NJ: Princeton University Press, 1996); Lynn M. Sanders, "Against Deliberation," *Political Theory* 25 (1997): 347–76; Iris Marion Young, *Inclusion and Democracy* (Oxford: Oxford University Press, 2000).

4. Lonna Rae Atkeson and Ronald B. Rapoport, "The More Things Change the More They Stay the Same: Examining Gender Differences in Political Attitude Expression, 1952–2000," *Public Opinion Quarterly* 67 (2003): 495–521; Lawrence R. Jacobs, Fay Lomax Cook, and Michael X. Delli-Carpini, *Talking Together, Public Deliberation, and Political Participation in America* (Chicago: University of Chicago Press, 2003); Jennifer L. Lawless and Richard L. Fox, *Men Rule: The Continued Under-Representation of Women in US Politics* (Washington, DC: Women & Politics Institute, 2012); Jennifer L. Lawless and Richard L. Fox, *Not a "Year of the Woman"…and 2036 Doesn't Look So Good Either* (Washington, DC: Brookings Institute, November 2014); Jennifer Wolak and Michael McDevitt, "The Roots of the Gender Gap in Political Knowledge in Adolescence." *Political Behavior* 33 (2014): 505–533.

5. J. Cherie Strachan, "Deliberative Democracy," in *American Governance*, ed. Stephen Schechter (New York: Macmillan Reference USA, 2016).

6. Allen G. Johnson, *The Gender Knot: Unraveling our Patriarchal Legacy, 3rd ed.* (Philadelphia: Temple University Press, 2014).

7. Ibid., 244.

8. Mark E. Kann, *The Gendering of American Politics: Founding Mothers, Founding Fathers, and Political Patriarchy* (Westport, CT: Greenwood, 1999).

9. Ibid.

10. Paul L. Berger and Thomas Luckman, *The Social Construction of Reality: A Treatise in the Sociology of Knowledge* (New York: Doubleday, 1966).

11. Peter Glick and Susan T. Fiske, "An Ambivalent Alliance: Hostile and Benevolent Sexism as Complementary Justifications for Gender Inequality," *American Psychologist* 56 no. 2 (2001): 109–118.

12. Julia C. Becker and Stephen C. Wright, "Yet Another Dark Side of Chivalry: Benevolent Sexism Undermines and Hostile Sexism Motivates Collective Action for Social Change," *Journal of Personality and Social Psychology* 101 (2011): 62–77.

13. Janet Holmes, *Women, Men, and Politeness* (New York: Longman, 1995); Robin T. Lakoff, *Language and Women's Place* (New York: Harper & Row, 1975); Robin T. Lakoff, *Talking Power* (New York: Basic Books, 1990); Virginia Sapiro, *The Political Integration of Women: Role, Socialization, and Politics* (Chicago: University of Illinois Press, 1983).

14. Lakoff, *Talking Power*, 51.

15. Diana C. Mutz, *Hearing the Other Side: Deliberative versus Participatory Democracy* (New York: Cambridge University Press, 2006).

16. Jacobs, Cook, and Delli-Carpini, *Talking Together, Public Deliberation, and Political Participation in America*.

17. Patricia Gurin, "Women's Gender Consciousness," *Public Opinion Quarterly* 49 (1985): 143–163.

18. Francesca Polletta and Pang Ching Bobby Chen, "Gender and Public Talk: Accounting for Women's Variable Participation in the Public Sphere," *Sociological Theory* 31 (2014): 291–317.

19. Holmes, 212.

20. Ibid.; Mutz.

21. Holmes, *Women, Men, and Politeness*, 198; 213.

22. Christopher F. Karpowitz and Tali Mendelberg, *The Silent Sex: Gender, Deliberation and Institutions* (Princeton, NJ: Princeton University Press, 2014).

23. Polletta and Chen, "Gender and Public Talk."

24. Skocpol, *Diminished Democracy*.

25. Sanders, "Against Deliberation," 349.

26. Linda L. Carli, "Gender Effects on Social Influence," in *Perspectives on Persuasion, Social Influence, and Compliance Gaining*, eds. John S. Seiter and Robert H. Gass (San Francisco: Jossey-Bass, 2004), 133–148.

27. Stephen L. Ellyson, John F. Dovidio, and Clifford E. Brown, "The Look of Power: Gender Differences in Visual Dominance Behavior," in *Gender, Interaction, and Inequality*, ed. C. L. Ridgeway (New York: Springer-Verlag, 1992), 50–80.

28. Carli, "Gender Effects on Social Influence."

29. Ibid, 144.

30. Ibid.

31. Linda Babcock and Sara Laschever, *Women Don't Ask: The High Cost of Avoiding Negotiation—and Positive Strategies for Change* (Princeton, NJ: Princeton University Press, 2003); Joan C. Williams and Rachel Dempsey, *What Works for Women at Work: Four Patterns that Working Women Need to Know* (New York: New York University Press, 2014).

32. Carli, "Gender Effects on Social Influence."

33. Karpowitz and Mendelberg, *The Silent Sex*.

34. Christopher Larimer and Karen M. Hempson, "Using Deliberation in the Classroom: A Teaching Pedagogy to Enhance Student Knowledge, Opinion Formation, and Civic Engagement," *Journal of Political Science Education* 8 (2012): 372–388.

35. Bruce Ackerman and James S. Fishkin, *Deliberation Day* (New Haven, CT: Yale University Press, 2004); Matthew Bogaards and Fraziska Deutsch, "Deliberation By, With, and For University Students," *Journal of Political Science Education* 11 (2015): 221–232.

36. Dena Levy and Susan Orr, "Balancing the Books: Analyzing the Impact of a Federal Budget Deliberative Simulation on Student Learning and Opinion," *Journal of Political Science Education* 10 (2014): 62–80.

37. Sarah A. Mehltretter Drury, "Deliberation as Communication Instruction: A Study of Climate Change Deliberation in an Introductory Biology Course," *Journal on Excellence in College Teaching* 26 (2015): 51–72; Sarah A. Mehltretter Drury et al., "Using Deliberation of Energy Policy as an Educational Tool in a Nonmajors Chemistry Course," *Journal of Chemical Education* 93 (2016): 1879–85.

38. For a review of these projects, see Nicholas V. Longo, "Deliberative Pedagogy in the Community: Connecting Deliberative Dialogue, Community Engagement, and Democratic Education," *Journal of Public Deliberation* 9 (2013): 1–18.

39. Karpowitz and Mendelberg, *The Silent Sex*.

40. Polletta and Chen, "Gender and Public Talk."

41. Johnson, *The Gender Knot*, 43.

42. Christopher F. Karpowitz and Chad Raphael, *Deliberation, Democracy, and Civic Forums: Improving Equality and Publicity* (New York: Cambridge University Press, 2014), 133.

The Essential Role of Campus Planning in Student Civic Education

4

Andrew J. Seligsohn and Maggie Grove

The authors argue for the necessity of campus planning for the achievement of student civic and democratic learning and development through two central contentions. The first is that a campus climate characterized by a thoroughgoing commitment to the public good is essential for effective student civic education and development. The second is that colleges and universities must develop comprehensive plans to create such a climate. Through a review of Campus Compact's 30th Anniversary Action Statement and the Civic Action Planning it initiates, the chapter illuminates the key elements of a public good commitment, aspects of planning to put the commitment into practice, and the evidence showing that a campus climate manifesting the commitment is necessary for the attainment of civic learning and development outcomes for students.

When we think about student civic education, we are likely to focus on curriculum or pedagogy. If we focus on curriculum, we ask *what* students should learn. If we focus on pedagogy, we ask *how* students should learn. In the context of civic education, a curricular focus leads us to ask what students should learn about history, public policy, law, sociology, economics, media studies, and other disciplines to acquire the knowledge and skills that will enable them to exercise their rights and undertake their responsibilities as citizens of a democratic republic. A pedagogical focus leads us to ask what mix of traditional classroom learning, simulations, and experiential learning will facilitate the development not only of knowledge and skills but also of the dispositions suitable for citizenship.

In the context of US colleges and universities, both the curricular and the pedagogical lenses call attention to the roles of faculty members in student civic education. Faculty members act collectively, through structures that vary across institutions, to shape the curriculum, and they act individually (for the most part) to shape the pedagogical practices within individual courses. Much of our thinking, therefore, about student civic education involves thinking about what decisions faculty should make in their roles as curricular policymakers and pedagogical practitioners.

This chapter approaches student civic education from a different angle. Rather than asking what policies faculties should enact or what practices professors should adopt, it asks how institutions can create environments maximally conducive to student civic learning and development. To explore that question, we examine a specific initiative, the Campus Compact *30th Anniversary Action Statement of Presidents and Chancellors*, through which colleges and universities across the United States are engaged in the development of Campus Civic Action Plans intended to achieve a variety of goals, among which is the preparation of students for lives of engaged citizenship.

We begin by providing background on Campus Compact, its Action Statement, and the substantive commitments included therein. We then describe the Campus Civic Action Planning process that follows from the Action Statement. Finally, we show why campus planning is essential if goals for student civic education are to be achieved. Faculty action, whether individual or collective, is necessary but not sufficient for the forms of institutional change required to foster student civic learning and development.

CAMPUS COMPACT AND THE 30TH ANNIVERSARY ACTION STATEMENT

Campus Compact is a national coalition of more than 1,000 colleges and universities committed to the public purposes of higher education. Founded during the 1985–1986 academic year by a group of college presidents concerned about higher education's role in sustaining a healthy democracy, the organization comprises a national office in Boston, Massachusetts, and a network of 33 state and regional Compacts across the country. Campus Compact member institutions represent the diversity of higher education including two-year and four-year colleges, graduate-only institutions, and all forms of institutions from the public, private, and faith-based sectors.[1]

While the activities of Campus Compact have evolved consistent with its founding mission of supporting higher education's role in advancing democracy, its current work encompasses a wide range of efforts aimed at deepening higher education engagement. Illustrative examples include developing and disseminating digital and print resources for students, faculty, and staff; providing professional development for faculty and community engagement professionals; leading multicampus initiatives to develop and test promising practices; and convening a wide range of constituencies to advance the public purposes of higher education.

In January 2015, as Campus Compact's 30th anniversary approached, its board of directors deliberated over the best way to mark that milestone. Rather than focus exclusively on a review of Campus Compact's accomplishments, board members were unanimous in the view that the anniversary represented an opportunity to identify what Campus Compact and its member institutions must do to continue progress toward its founding goals. In keeping with the democratic values and participatory traditions of the Campus Compact network, the board called for an engaged process through which students, faculty, staff, and community partners articulated the commitments they would like to see colleges and universities make in service of public and community goals. That wide-ranging set of ideas formed the core of the first draft of the *30th Anniversary Action Statement*. The Action Statement went through several iterations, with the key work unfolding over two days at Augsburg College in Minneapolis at Campus Compact's 2015 annual Network Leadership Meeting, a gathering of the Compact's national staff, national board, state and regional executive directors, and state board chairs.

In discussions facilitated by leading civic engagement scholars and practitioners Rick Battistoni and Tania Mitchell, the key elements of the Action Statement took shape. Rather than create a document around a set of specific directives to campuses, the group reached consensus that the Action Statement should articulate a set of principles and goals embraced by the presidents and chancellors who became its signatories. The single practical commitment contained in the Action Statement is therefore a commitment to build a Campus Civic Action Plan that makes public how each college or university will put the principles of the Action Statement into practice.[2]

The principles and goals of the Action Statement are best understood against the contextual backdrop described in the initial paragraphs of the document.[3] While the movement for the public purposes of higher education has achieved a great deal over the 30 years since the founding of Campus Compact, the Action Statement argues, it is also the case that the challenge of sustaining the health and strength of democracy has grown more difficult. The dramatic increases in the degree both of political polarization[4] and of economic inequality[5]—factors that separate citizens from each other—mean that colleges and universities must do more to effect positive change in supporting the capacity for citizens to work together to solve public problems and seize public opportunities.

Recognizing the deep challenges posed by polarization and inequality, the Action Statement articulates five core commitments affirmed by signatories as representing both their present values and the focus of efforts to deepen the public impact of their work. Here are the five commitments:

1. We empower our students, faculty, staff, and community partners to cocreate mutually respectful partnerships in pursuit of a just, equitable, and sustainable future for communities beyond the campus—nearby and around the world.
2. We prepare our students for lives of engaged citizenship, with the motivation and capacity to deliberate, act, and lead in pursuit of the public good.
3. We embrace our responsibilities as place-based institutions, contributing to the health and strength of our communities—economically, socially, environmentally, educationally, and politically.
4. We harness the capacity of our institutions—through research, teaching, partnerships, and institutional practice—to challenge the prevailing social and economic inequalities that threaten our democratic future.
5. We foster an environment that consistently affirms the centrality of the public purposes of higher education by setting high expectations for members of the campus community to contribute to their achievement.

Following these five statements of principle comes a practical pledge, as each signatory "makes a commitment to develop a Campus Civic Action Plan within one year." The plans, which will be publicly shared, constitute a statement to members of the campus community and the broader public of how the institution will put the five commitments into practice.

Just one of the five commitments, commitment #2, speaks directly to the civic education of students. Commitments #1 and #5 emphasize the extent to which everyone on a campus, including students, is responsible for pursuing public aims, but they do not speak about educational practices specifically. Our argument, however, is that the entirety of the Campus Civic Action Plan following from the Action Statement commitment is crucial to the civic and democratic education of students because it shapes the environment in which student civic education takes place. Before presenting a defense of the role of Civic Action Planning in student civic learning and development, we turn to planning itself to provide a clearer sense of the process and focus of Civic Action Planning.

BUILDING CAMPUS CIVIC ACTION PLANS

As part of the campaign connected with the 30th Anniversary Action Statement, Campus Compact has provided support for campuses building Campus Civic Action Plans through in-person institutes and workshops, virtual meetings, online resources, and publications. The goal of these efforts is to help leaders of Civic Action Planning efforts build processes that will be maximally effective in advancing progress on the five central commitments in the Action Statement. Campus Compact resources provide direction on conceptual approaches for planning, composition of planning teams, planning timelines, and other practical matters.

Campus Compact's substantive guidance for institutions building Campus Civic Action Plans focuses on three forms of change:

1. systems and policy change,
2. culture change, and
3. capacity building.[6]

To achieve the goals articulated in the five commitments, change in all three forms will be necessary. Consider the example of what it would take for a typical institution to move from where it is now to a real guarantee that all students are prepared for democratic participation in keeping with commitment #2.

To begin with, most institutions would require curricular revision to ensure that all students acquire the knowledge, skills, and dispositions required for effective participation as citizens. Currently, in most institutions the curriculum makes it possible for some students to achieve civic learning outcome while leaving many students with pathways to graduation that do not involve civic learning. Because the curriculum is the most important policy of a college or university—the policy that most directly affects the substance of student learning—curricular change is a crucial form of policy change. That policy change will bring with it systems changes, as courses that enable civic and democratic learning must be developed, identified, and supported.

For those policy and systems changes to be effective, culture change will be required. When opportunities arise to design or redesign courses to achieve civic learning outcomes, faculty members will need to step forward. When new courses are proposed as meeting curricular requirements for civic education, faculty committees will review them. Whether or not those opportunities and responsibilities are seized and undertaken with the effort and attention required depends in significant part on whether civic education itself is viewed as essential for students and as an element of the role of faculty members both individually and collectively. Were it so viewed now, civic education would already be an expected element of a college education; as it stands, that is not the case.[7]

For curricular change to have the desired impact on student civic learning, these changes in policy, systems, and culture must be joined by increased faculty (and possibly staff) capacity. Even when they are eager to do so, many faculty members will need to learn how to design courses that achieve civic learning outcomes. Because developing civic skills requires access to experiential learning, opportunities for professional development in experiential pedagogies will be essential, such as those described in "Teaching Faculty to Teach Civic Engagement" in this book. In addition, these changes in policy, systems, culture, and capacity aimed at curricular redesign will be maximally effective only if they are matched by parallel changes in the areas of tenure, promotion, and merit-based compensation. When community-engaged research and teaching, along with the scholarship of teaching and learning, are valued in formal policies and institutional culture, faculty members are far more likely to invest time and resources in building their capacity to undertake them.

A similar logic applies to other policy changes that are necessary to achieve the five commitments in the Action Statement. Consider the implications of commitments #3 and #4, "contributing to the health and strength of our communities—economically, socially, environmentally, educationally, and politically," and challenging "the prevailing social and economic inequalities that threaten our democratic future." One of the most effective ways a college or university can contribute to the economic strength of adjacent communities is by focusing its purchasing power on small businesses, and such an approach can be effective in challenging inequalities when there is special effort placed on engaging small businesses owned by and employing members of disadvantaged groups.

Here again, changes in policy or systems may be necessary to enable small businesses to engage successfully with complex purchasing processes designed with corporate suppliers in mind. Even when those changes are made, staff members responsible for purchasing will need to reach out to communities with which they may not be familiar and overcome the skepticism of community members for whom the university campus has long felt like alien territory. That requires both a change in culture so that breaking out of familiar patterns is valued and encouraged and the development of new skills so that university staff members understand and know how to overcome the challenges of working with less-experienced suppliers.

This change framework—with its interlocking emphases on systems and policy, culture, and capacity—can be applied to all of the commitments and nearly every dimension of the university. Tenure and promotion, admissions and financial aid, research support, and real estate development—all represent opportunities for advancing the public good by attending to these forms of change.

The greatest public impact can be achieved when efforts across these varied domains are thoughtfully integrated. For example, many institutions build partnerships with primary and secondary schools to support improved educational attainment for students from underserved communities. Such partnerships are frequently focused on tutoring and mentoring of primary and secondary students by college students through service-learning and volunteerism. If those partnerships are developed with attention to systems and policy, culture, and capacity, they have the potential to succeed. They can help the younger students make academic progress while introducing college students to the realities of education in low-wealth communities and the policy environments that produce those realities.

But consider how much more impact can be achieved when the relationships that constitute a university-school partnership are leveraged to make the school a site of opportunity not only for children but for their parents. When community engagement offices and academic departments invite into partnerships staff members from human resources, purchasing, and other units that create economic opportunity, universities can work with community members to create mutually reinforcing positive dynamics for children, families, and neighborhoods. This integrated approach is, at its core, asset-based as it seeks to identify and mobilize all of the elements of the university and of the community that can contribute to stronger, safer, more equitable, and prosperous communities.

Thus, Campus Compact's approach to Civic Action Planning seeks to catalyze thoroughgoing campus change that moves the college or university forward in pursuit of its public mission through teaching, research, and institutional conduct across a wide range of domains. Much of the activity called for in this approach may seem distant from the education of students. Our argument is that the overall conduct of institutions of higher education has an impact on the civic development of students. In the next section, we provide evidence for that argument.

CAMPUS CLIMATE AND STUDENT CIVIC DEVELOPMENT

Several streams of evidence point to the conclusion that student civic development is strongly affected by the degree to which the institution evidences in its conduct a substantive commitment to the public good. While different elements of institutional climate and conduct are emphasized in each cluster of evidence, taken together they strongly suggest that institutions wishing to achieve the goal of preparing their students for lives of engaged citizenship must commit to building a campus climate of engagement for the public good.

The first body of evidence comes from the realm of primary and secondary education. A series of studies has addressed the question of how best to cultivate in students prosocial behaviors and habits, including moral and ethical reasoning as a guide to interaction with others. The research shows that the school climate has a decisive impact on the behavior of students and that the school climate is itself driven primarily by the behavior of the adults in the school. When students witness caring, ethical conduct by teachers and school leaders, they will tend to emulate that behavior.[8] This empirical conclusion is consistent with a view of ethical development as old as Aristotle that emphasizes the role of habituation in moral development and the role of exemplars in guiding the development of habits.[9]

The second body of evidence comes from analyses of data from the Personal and Social Responsibility Inventory, a survey of students on a large number of college campuses. These analyses build a strong case for the proposition that campus climate affects students' civic and social development and that the conduct of institutional leaders and faculty members contributes significantly to the climate. Reason found a strong positive relationship between students' perceptions of institutional commitment to positive social values and their own development with respect to those values.[10] Subsequent analysis has shown that the impact of experiential civic education and service-learning is magnified when students perceive that the institution is committed to the values relevant to the course.[11] Ryder et al. have shown the key role faculty play through their own conduct in establishing the climate perceived by students.[12] And Mitchell et al. have shown that a climate of campus engagement has a positive effect on student mental health, even for those students who are not themselves engaged in the community.[13]

The last stream of evidence focuses on the drivers of college student voting behavior. The evidence is grounded in the National Study of Learning Voting and Engagement (NSLVE). By linking publicly available voting records with student registration data from the 1,000 participating colleges and universities, the NSLVE researchers have identified actual voting rates for each campus. They have also built a predictive model to establish an expected voting rate for each campus, which allows them to identify overperforming and underperforming campuses. Qualitative research on over- and underperforming campuses has provided a basis for drawing conclusions about what factors lead to high levels of student voting participation, a key form of civic participation.

The central finding of the NSLVE team is that a campus climate of engagement is the primary predictor of voting by college students. When students are engaged in discussions of community and broader public issues in all aspects of their daily lives, they will understand why it is important to vote and will choose to do so. Such a climate is encouraged by a high level of permeability between the campus and surrounding communities. When campuses are isolated from community and public issues, students will not see participating in elections as worthwhile and will abstain.[14] Thus, students abstain from participation in elections that shape the world they will inherit, and, at the same time, a profound opportunity to build the democratic capacity of our citizenry is lost.

CAMPUS CLIMATE AND CIVIC ACTION PLANNING

The Campus Compact Civic Action Planning process engages institutions in broad and deep thinking about how they can orient every aspect of their action toward public goods. There are many good reasons for engaging in this work, among which are the many benefits to be realized by members of communities beyond the campus. But the benefits of such an integrated approach to campus civic action do not stop at the boundaries of the campus. By exemplifying a commitment to the public good and saturating the student experience with evidence of it, campus leaders and faculty members can cultivate in their students dispositions that are supportive of civic and democratic participation. Such participation itself reinforces the campus climate of engagement and magnifies the effect of leadership actions.

The 450 presidents and chancellors who have signed Campus Compact's *30th Anniversary Action Statement* affirm the proposition that education for democracy is a central purpose of colleges and universities relevant to the experiences of all students, not just those who happen to choose a particular course or major. Transforming that commitment into practical changes in student civic learning and development requires institutions to engage in a broad reconsideration of policies and practices that may, on their face, seem quite distant from student learning. If we envision a series of concentric circles with civic and democratic learning at the center, curricular policies and pedagogical practices will be the smallest circles. Faculty tenure, promotion, and merit-compensation policies will be in the next ring, as they directly affect the incentives for faculty to make curricular and pedagogical changes. Policies for the support of community-engaged research will be further out from the center, and further still are policies and systems governing admissions, financial aid, purchasing, and real estate development. But each of these areas has an effect on civic learning and development by contributing to the campus climate in which students are immersed during the crucial years of college. We have shown that students receive strong signals from the institutions to which they have entrusted their education. If those institutions manifest in everything they do commitments to the public good and to democratic values, along with a willingness to allocate resources commensurate with those commitments, colleges and universities can fulfill their obligation to cultivate citizen graduates prepared to ensure the health and strength of our democracy into the future. ∎

ENDNOTES

1. Campus Compact, "Campus Compact Overview," (2016) http://compact.org/actionstatement/.
2. Campus Compact, *Campus Compact 30th Anniversary Action Statement of Presidents and Chancellors* (2015) http://compact.org/actionstatement/.
3. Campus Compact, *30th Anniversary Action Statement.*
4. Shanto Iyengar and Sean J. Westwood, "Fear and Loathing across Party Lines: New Evidence on Group Polarization," *American Journal of Political Science* 59 (2015): 690–707.
5. Joseph E. Stiglitz, "Inequality and Economic Growth," *Political Quarterly* (Supplement, 2015): 134–155.
6. Campus Compact, *Creating a Great Campus Civic Action Plan* (2016b) http://compact.org/Campus-Compact-Action-Plan.pdf.
7. National Task Force on Civic Learning and Democratic Engagement, *A Crucible Moment: College Learning & Democracy's Future* (Washington, DC: Association of American Colleges and Universities, 2012), 8.
8. Stephanie M. Jones and Suzanne M. Bouffard, "Social and Emotional Learning in Schools: From Programs to Strategies," *Social Policy Report* 26 (2012); Stephanie M. Jones, Suzanne M. Bouffard, and Richard Weissbourd, "Educators' Social and Emotional Skills Vital to Learning," *Phi Delta Kappan*, 94 (2012); Richard Weissbourd, Suzanne M. Bouffard, and Stephanie M. Jones, "School Climate and Moral and Social Development," in *School Climate: Practices for Implementation and Sustainability*, ed. Teri Dary and Terry Pickeral (New York: National School Climate Center, 2013).
9. Andrew Seligsohn, "Colleges and Universities as Exemplars in the Development of Citizens," *Journal of College and Character* (2016), 17.
10. Robert Reason, "Creating and Assessing Campus Climates that Support Personal and Social Responsibility," *Liberal Education* 99 (2013).
11. Seligsohn, "College and Universities."
12. Andrew J. Ryder, Robert D. Reason, Joshua J. Mitchell, Kathleen Gillon, and Kevin M. Hemer, "Climate for Learning and Students' Openness to Diversity and Challenge: A Critical Role for Faculty," *Journal of Diversity in Higher Education* 9 (2016).
13. Joshua J. Mitchell, Robert D. Reason, Kevin M. Hemer, and Ashley Finley, "Perceptions of Campus Climates for Civic Learning as Predictors of College Students' Mental Health," *Journal of College and Character* 17 (2016).
14. Nancy Thomas and Margaret Brower, "Politics 365: Fostering Campus Climates for Student Political Learning and Engagement" in *Teaching Civic Engagement Across the Disciplines*, ed. Elizabeth Matto, Alison Rios Millett McCartney, Elizabeth Bennion, and Dick Simpson (Washington, DC: American Political Science Association, 2017).

Excerpts from A Crucible Moment and Civic Prompts

5

Caryn McTighe Musil

This watershed APSA book is going to print as *A Crucible Moment: College Learning and Democracy's Future* marks the fifth anniversary since it was released at the White House. What appropriate timing. There had already been an earlier portentous convergence when *A Crucible Moment* (2012) came out just as APSA's book *Teaching Civic Engagement: From Student to Active Citizen* (2013) was making its final manuscript edits before sending everything to the printer. Part of what *A Crucible Moment* sought to capture was the dynamic, emerging movement arising in multiple quarters, practiced in many different arenas, and drawing on earlier scholarly and political movements that had strived for full democratic inclusion in learning and in everyday life. Created after a series of five national roundtables composed of a diverse set of stakeholders inside and outside of the academy who informed its framing and recommendations, *A Crucible Moment* was determined to both document the progress made while also calling for evermore comprehensive actions. The stakes for the nation and the world were too high if we dared to leave so many students untouched and untaught, their talents untapped to grapple with the problems that threatened their futures. The excerpts here capture these goals.[1]

The vice president for outreach at Auburn University said in a public meeting a year after *A Crucible Moment* was released, "Not since Ernest Boyer's *Scholarship Reconsidered* has a national report received such buzz and had such impact." One measure of that impact is APSA's second volume which forges into untilled territory recommended in *A Crucible Moment*: the major, where students spend the greater part of their academic life while in college. The Association of American Colleges and Universities (AAC&U), with its focus on making civic learning an expected rather than an optional outcome for every college graduate, is once again in lockstep with APSA. We published *Civic Prompts: Making Civic Learning Routine across the Disciplines* in 2015. An excerpt from that publication is included in this chapter as well. Its lever for educating students to be more informed, responsible, and active citizens in their workplaces as well as their personal lives is the *design* of the departmental major, not just the choice of how an individual faculty member teaches a course. The invitation in *Civic Prompts*, therefore, is to the faculty as part of those disparate disciplines to grapple with what civic learning and practices look like from where they sit—and act. Faculty within the contexts of their departments are asked to define and describe all of this on their own terms, considering their disciplinary modes of inquiry, pedagogies, and hands-on applications in real-world settings. And then, they are asked to reconfigure the structure of their department to be sure such learning and practice are common across all student majors. AAC&U is wagering that the results could transform higher education, even as it concurrently activates a new generation of citizens to be agents who "promote the general welfare" and "establish justice" as the Preamble to the Constitution pledged we would do as a democratic nation.

FROM A CRUCIBLE MOMENT: COLLEGE LEARNING AND DEMOCRACY'S FUTURE

Why must the United States require its educational system to educate for citizenship as well as careers? Public schooling and ever-expanding access to postsecondary education have been distinguishing characteristics of our democratic nation. Higher education in a robust, diverse, and democratic country needs to cultivate in each of its graduates an open and curious mind, critical acumen, public voice, ethical and moral judgment, and the commitment to act collectively in public to achieve shared purposes. In stark contrast, higher education in a restrictive, undemocratic country needs only to cultivate obedient and productive workers. As *A Nation of Spectators* astutely asserted, "We believe that economic productivity is important but must not be confused with civic health."[2]

The National Task Force wants to stress that educating students for purposeful work in a dynamic, complex economy is more than ever an essential goal of higher education. However, we reject a zero-sum choice between the fullest preparation for economic success and education for citizenship. *A Crucible Moment* outlines a path that prepares students for both knowledgeable citizenship and economic opportunity. As employers themselves make clear, the United States should not be forced to choose between preparing students for informed democratic citizenship and preparing students for successful college completion and career opportunities.

Public leaders who believe that the "economic agenda" of higher education is reducible to workforce training also fail to understand that there is a civic dimension to every field of study, including career and technical fields, as well as to every workplace. Industries and services have ethical and social responsibilities of their own, and, in a democracy, citizens and community partners routinely weigh in on such questions. Workers at all levels need to anticipate the civic implications of their choices and actions. The nation—and the world—have experienced disastrous results when civic consequences are ignored and only economic profit is considered, as the subprime mortgage crisis and the bundling of toxic loans have dramatically illustrated. ...

Even if they are not commonplace, in colleges today there are some nascent models that embed questions about civic responsibilities within career preparation and that therefore point to the next level needed in campus civic work. California State University, Monterey Bay (CSUMB), for example, defines civic literacy as the "knowledge, skills, and attitudes that students need to work effectively in a diverse society to create more just and equitable workplaces, communities, and social institutions."[3] In addition to a general service-learning course, CSUMB students must complete a second such course rooted in their major. Every business student, for example, takes a Community Economic Development course that includes 50 hours of service to a community organization. Importantly, the overriding question that these students explore is, "How can businesses balance the 'triple bottom lines' of profit, people, and planet?"[4] Similarly, for students in the School of Information Technology and Communications Design, the service-learning course is constructed around the guiding questions, "How has digital technology accentuated or alleviated historical inequalities in our community, and what is my responsibility for addressing the digital divide as a future IT professional?"[5] To strip out such probing civic questions from *either* higher education *or* the workplace is to contribute to the creation of the citizenless democracy. ... A healthy democracy demands that civic dimensions in thinking and in working be cultivated, not ignored or suppressed. In addition to serving as an engine of economic development, higher education is a crucial incubator for fostering democratic voice, thought, and action. The shared capacities needed both in the modern workplace and in diverse democratic societies include effective listening and oral communication, creative/critical thinking and problem solving, the ability to work effectively in diverse groups, agency and collaborative decision making, ethical analyses of complex issues, and intercultural understanding and perspective taking. ...

Despite the cited clear evidence that civic learning in college is compatible with preparation for the modern workforce and improved graduation rates, the dominant external policy discourse about higher education "reform" is silent on education for democracy. Does the civic mission of higher education in our increasingly multicultural democracy need to be scuttled to achieve better jobs for students or higher graduation rates? It does not. And it must not.

It is time to bring two national priorities—career preparation and increased access and completion rates—together in a more comprehensive vision with *a third national priority*: fostering informed, engaged, responsible citizens. Higher education is a space where that triad of priorities can cohere and flourish.

A Crucible Moment argues that a socially cohesive and economically vibrant US democracy and a viable, just global community require informed, engaged, open-minded, and socially responsible people committed to the common good and practiced in "doing" democracy. In a divided and unequal world, education—from K–12 through college and beyond—can open up opportunities to develop each person's full talents, equip graduates to contribute to economic recovery and innovation, and cultivate responsibility to a larger common good. Achieving that goal will require that civic learning and democratic engagement be not sidelined but central. Civic learning needs to be an integral component of every level of education, from grade school through graduate school, across all fields of study.

We are not suggesting that colleges implement a single required civics course. That would hardly be sufficient. Rather, we are calling on colleges and universities to adopt far more ambitious standards that can be measured over time to indicate whether institutions and their students are becoming more civic-minded. This report therefore urges every college and university to foster *a civic ethos* that governs campus life, make *civic literacy* a goal for every graduate, integrate *civic inquiry* within majors and general education, and advance *civic action* as lifelong practice (see the online companion for specific indicators in each of the four areas). In so doing, we seek a more comprehensive vision to guide the twenty-first-century formulation of education for democratic citizenship on college and university campuses. As this report suggests, investing in this broader vision promises to cultivate more informed, engaged, and responsible citizens while also contributing to economic vitality, more equitable and flourishing communities, and the overall civic health of the nation. ...

Reordering current educational priorities and building new levels of civic knowledge and engagement will require unprecedented, widely coordinated, and collective commitments to action. No single entity can effect change at the level and scale required. Leadership will be essential from multiple groups, including K–20 educators, educational associations, civic associations, religious organizations, business, community members, nonprofits, government agencies, unions, and youth. The first step for all concerned is to recognize the erosion of the national investment in civic learning and democratic engagement—and the dire consequences of that disinvestment. The second step is to mobilize the will and the commitment to reverse the downward spiral.

To reframe the way we prepare Americans for civic responsibility, the National Call to Action presented in this chapter presents five overarching actions aimed at addressing the current civic deficit and ensuring that we provide all students with the kind of education that will prepare them to take active responsibility both for the quality of our communities and for the future—US and global—of our democracy.

These five essential actions need to be held as shared commitments across multiple sectors and actors:

1. Reclaim and reinvest in the fundamental civic and democratic mission of schools and of all sectors within higher education.
2. Enlarge the current national narrative that erases civic aims and civic literacy as educational priorities contributing to social, intellectual, and economic capital.
3. Advance a contemporary, comprehensive framework for civic learning—embracing US and global interdependence—that includes historic and modern understandings of democratic values, capacities to engage diverse perspectives and people, and commitment to collective civic problem solving.

4. Capitalize upon the interdependent responsibilities of K–12 and higher education to foster progressively higher levels of civic knowledge, skills, examined values, and action as expectations for every student.
5. Expand the number of robust, generative civic partnerships and alliances locally, nationally, and globally to address common problems, empower people to act, strengthen communities and nations, and generate new frontiers of knowledge.

In order to achieve a systemic realignment both within an institution and across sectors, the National Call to Action requires leadership from—and offers specific recommendation for—four primary constituent groups:

1. two-year and four-year colleges and universities;
2. policy and educational leaders responsible for educational quality;
3. federal, state, and local governments; and
4. a broad coalition of communities with a key stake in democracy's future.

If these multiple stakeholders take action in a collective and coordinated way, US democracy will be strengthened through a reinvigoration of the quality of learning, the commitment to the well-being of others, and civic responsibilities exercised in workplaces.

The central work of advancing civic learning and democratic engagement in higher education must, of course, be done by faculty members across disciplines, by student affairs professionals across divisions, and by administrators in every school and at every level. The fourth prominent group of actors are the students themselves. The collective work of these groups should be guided by a shared sense that civic knowledge and democratic engagement, in concert with others and in the face of contestation, are absolutely vital to the quality of intellectual inquiry itself, to this nation's future, and to preparation for life in a diverse world.

Higher education has particular contributions to make—and corresponding obligations—in terms of understanding the depth, complexity, and competing versions of what "civic" actually means and entails. Specifically, higher education must in this next generation of civic learning investments build a broader theory of knowledge about democracy and democratic principles for an age marked as it is by multiplicity and division. Colleges and universities need to provide far more enabling environments than are now in place through which students can expand their critical abilities to make judgments about issues and actions, their powers to investigate and analyze, and their wisdom and passion to seek justice with keener insight into how to determine what is just, for whom, and under what circumstances.

To prevent civic learning and democratic engagement from being sidelined by contending forces that consider it discretionary, we call on community colleges, four-year colleges, and universities to assume creative and courageous leadership as they continue to build civic-minded institutions. We recommend four defined areas of endeavor (ethos, literacy, inquiry, and action) to ensure all students and the public benefit from higher education's civic investment.

1. Foster a civic ethos across all parts of campus and educational culture.[6]
2. Make civic literacy a core expectation for all students.
3. Practice civic inquiry across all fields of study.
4. Advance civic action through transformative partnerships at home and abroad.

Multiple incentives may be employed for embracing the public purpose and civic involvement of an institution; we encourage each college and university to construct its own Civic Investment Plan to fully articulate how its institutional strategies will reinforce its civic mission. Learning outcomes can and should be explicitly defined by how they contribute to civic capacities. Student affairs professionals can provide more arenas for students to develop their public-oriented leadership. Students already deeply enmeshed in social justice and civic transformational activities can be publicly upheld as contributing to a campus civic ethos, just as athletes are praised for sustaining school spirit. Faculty can be offered reduced course loads when designing community-intensive collaborative projects around which to build courses and research.

Similarly, students can make a civic commitments portfolio part of their culminating project before graduation in which they reflect on what they have learned and how they aspire to carry civic literacy and civic action into their workplaces and communities. Alumni offices and institutional researchers can track students at selected intervals to learn more about the impact of college on students' civic and political participation. Alumni events can feature civic issues when graduates reconvene, and alumni can be tied into ongoing civic networks in the cities and towns where they live.

All sectors within higher education can and should make education for democratic citizenship a shared enterprise for the twenty-first century, but colleges and universities cannot and should not presume to do it alone. Higher education will need to create strategic civic partnerships with a range of other entities: community and civic organizations; businesses; hospitals; K–12 schools; policy leaders; local, state, and federal governments; and global partners. Such partnerships, if taken seriously, will likely reconfigure academic inquiry, pedagogy, and scholarship. ...

It is time to make education for democracy a core quality commitment, clearly and explicitly. We therefore call on policy and educational leaders responsible for quality at all levels to ensure institutional commitment, capacity, and effectiveness in preparing students as knowledgeable citizens ready to contribute to a democratic and globally engaged polity.

1. **Make civic learning for democratic engagement an expected component of program integrity and quality standards at all levels.**
   - Review and strengthen the federal standards that govern accreditation to ensure that preparation for democratic citizenship becomes integral rather than optional in educational institutions.
   - Review state and/or state system learning outcomes and program standards for postsecondary study to ensure all students will be prepared for democratic participation and for knowledgeable involvement in the global community.
   - Review academic standards for regional, national, and specialized accreditation to ensure they address preparation for democratic participation and global community, in ways appropriate to educational mission.
   - Review educational goals and learning outcomes at the campus and program levels to ensure students are prepared for informed democratic participation and global community in ways appropriate to institutional mission and particular subjects of study.
   - Monitor educational practice across the curriculum and cocurriculum to ensure every program provides meaningful opportunities for students to advance in civic learning and global engagement.

2. **Make demonstrated achievement in civic learning—US and global—an integral part of quality assurance and public accountability at all levels.**
   - Engage scholars and educational leaders in developing indicators and reporting frameworks for student achievement that include civic learning.
   - Include civic learning in US and global contexts as expected student learning outcomes in public reporting frameworks—national, state or state system, and campus-specific.
   - Create and support an ongoing, integrated research program—involving scholars from different disciplines and views—to build deeper understanding of practices and policies that foster civic learning and democratic engagement in US and global contexts.
   - Disaggregate the data on participation in civic learning programs and pedagogies to ensure students from all backgrounds are participating.
   - Make national reporting on students' gains in civic knowledge, skills, and engagement a signature for US education and a point of widely shared pride. ...

PRIORITIES FOR FUTURE RESEARCH

1. Disseminate more widely existing assessment tools for measuring students' civic learning and effective practices in democratic engagement
2. Amass and publicize evidence that shows how civic learning, civic agency, and democratic engagement result in increased retention and college success; design additional studies to probe this linkage.
3. Support scholars doing research on civic learning and engage students in the process.
4. Use the Civic Investment Plan matrix to identify specific research projects that could be initiated at one's own institution.
5. Establish standards in civic learning to serve as guidelines for measuring and reporting progress.
6. Sponsor and support further research on the impact of programs and partnerships that foster civic learning and democratic engagement on learning outcomes and student development.
7. Include additional research questions in routinely administered higher education surveys to explore how learning environments can enhance key civic competencies.
8. Develop national civic indicators and report on levels of civic and democratic knowledge, skills, values, and action achieved by high school and college graduates. ...

Virtually in chorus, the many civic educators and leaders who joined in this analysis through national roundtables affirmed that federal, state, and local governments can and should play a key role in moving civic learning from being incidental to being expected of all college graduates. It takes a community to sustain a democracy. It is important to engage government at multiple levels and multiple agencies to work in concerted partnership with each other and with educators, campus leaders, students, policy makers, and local, state, and regional business and community leaders. In this important public role, the thrust should be to create a far more supportive and enabling public climate for revitalizing and reaffirming higher education's civic mission.

In this spirit, we recommend that the US Department of Education and other federal agencies—such as the National Endowments for the Arts and for the Humanities; the National Science Foundation; the US Departments of Labor, Justice, State, Health and Human Services, and Housing and Urban Development; and the Corporation for National and Community Service, to name only a few—work together with the higher education community and civic organizations, state and local governments and other state systems, and with other policy leaders and influencers, to assume leadership at all levels in the following five key arenas:

1. Champion civic learning explicitly and repeatedly as a fundamental US priority and a component of all educational programs.
2. Strategically refocus existing funding streams to spur civic learning and practice.
3. Create financial incentives for students to facilitate their access to college while expanding their civic capacities.
4. Tie funding for educational reform and research initiatives to evidence that the funded initiatives will build civic learning and democratic engagement.
5. Report on the levels of civic and democratic learning, set national and state goals for student achievement in civic learning, and make such outcomes a measurable expectation of school and degree-granting institutions. ...

The national roundtables that shaped this report included key people representing other entities that interact with, influence, and in some cases are the intellectual lifeblood of colleges and universities. All attendees eagerly participated in formulating the National Call to Action, both as a whole and with respect to the part their own groups, could play in elevating education for democracy and civic responsibility as a priority for every college student.[7] ...

It is through the collective power of multiple entities inside and outside higher education that there is hope of achieving a more capacious and transformative expression and practice of civic learning and democratic engagement. John Dewey understood the connection ..., [a]nd former congresswoman Barbara Jordan understood that democracy is not simply sustained by a set of eloquent aspirations but requires as well a capacity for generating collective action: "What the people want is very simple. They want an America as good as its promise."[8] Together we can make it so.

FROM *CIVIC PROMPTS: MAKING CIVIC LEARNING ROUTINE ACROSS THE DISCIPLINES*

...World War II shattered economies, eviscerated democratic nations, destroyed life and landscape at a scale heretofore unimaginable, and revealed grisly horrors when few moral compasses governed individuals or nation-states. President Harry Truman understood that the world needed more than just an economic revival represented in part by the ambitious Marshall Plan. Convinced that colleges and universities should play a vital role in creating a different global future, he appointed a Commission on Higher Education, chaired by American Council on Education president George F. Zook. The commission mapped a modern mission for the academy in a series of reports in 1947. Many of the commission's recommendations have been followed: from ending the academy's racial segregation, to the expansion of access to four-year institutions, to the establishment of community colleges. Driving all of the recommendations, however, was the commission's reaffirmation of the civic mission of higher education.

Nowhere is that more emphatically stated than in the commission's summary statement about what the overall goals for higher education should be:

- Education for a fuller realization of democracy in every phase of living.
- Education directly and explicitly for international understanding and cooperation.
- Education for the application of creative imagination and trained intelligence to the solution of social problems and to the administration of public affairs.[9]

A Crucible Moment, organized through a joint project with the US Department of Education, The Global Perspectives Inventory, Inc., and the Association of American Colleges and Universities, picks up the baton of these three cornerstone goals for higher education. The national report is grounded in the teaching experience of faculty, the research about the impact of civic learning and democratic engagement on students and the community, and a deep conviction that without higher education embracing fully its critical civic mission, US democracy will be put at risk.

A key recommendation in *A Crucible Moment* states: "Expect students to map their capacity to make civic inquires a part of their intellectual biography over the course of their studies and to reflect on and demonstrate their cumulative learning through general education, their majors, and their out-of-class experiences."[10] *Civic Prompts* tackles one of those frontiers: the major. Identifying the expected levels of civic achievement within fields, the report argues, would influence the boundaries of the subjects studied, the pedagogies adopted, and how students prepared themselves for their professional lives as well as for their participation in the civic life of their local and global communities. The major is, after all, where students devote the greatest portion of their academic studies. In turn, those studies often determine the course of their professional lives. ...

Despite the evidence of increased opportunities for students to expand their civic knowledge and skills while in college, especially through community-based engagement, *A Crucible Moment* found that these opportunities were for the most part random, unconnected, uneven, optional, and available only to some students. With its recommendations formulated by a broad and varied constituency within and beyond higher education and by a National Advisory Task Force, *A Crucible Moment* mapped how civic learning and democratic engagement could become more pervasive, integrative, and intentional. The report set a high bar: make such learning expected for every college student. But how can the academy move civic learning from niches to norms? ...

The questions that follow are designed to be used within a single disciplinary department or program on your campus or across multiple departments and programs where some cross disciplinary comparisons and fertilizations might occur. One might also opt for orchestrating the conversation serially. That is, begin within a single department but plan to follow up with a gathering in which those departments that also used the *Civic Prompts* can discuss their findings and brainstorm how to make civic learning more commonplace across majors. To generate the most fruitful discussions, we encourage participants to resist thinking about the barriers to infusing civic learning across the disciplines and instead think creatively about what they might do if there were no rules or limits.

For our first disciplinary cluster meeting in our AAC&U project, we asked each participant to write a short civic bio in order to jumpstart the conversation. We then shared the civic bios with everyone both within and beyond each person's disciplinary cluster group. We think doing the same for your campus departmental discussions would be a productive exercise before you gather to respond to the questions in the following *Civic Prompts*. The people at AAC&U's Chicago meeting[11] were faculty members who had already incorporated differing levels of civic learning and democratic engagement into their courses. Our directions simply asked participants to compose a short, two-to-three paragraph snapshot describing how they came to raise civic questions about public issues in their classes. Some questions we suggested they might elaborate on included: Why do you organize the study of your discipline this way? How did you come to such a point? And why in some cases do you opt to encourage students to be engaged in hands-on collaborative work with others to achieve shared public ends? How do your personal commitments intersect with your work?

The civic bio exercise would, however, also be a revealing exercise for faculty who may not yet have incorporated civic questions intentionally into their courses. By amending the questions slightly, one could invite faculty members to explore their own identity as an engaged citizen in their society, the kind of knowledge they need to do so responsibly and in an informed way, and then pose a query about where students might best learn how to do the same.

The *Civic Prompts* that follow are designed to be used in smaller group settings of eight to 12 people. The small number allows for richer exchanges through self-reflection, dyads, triads, and table work, but the size also ensures there are opportunities for sharing key insights as a whole group. Very likely action items will flow from these investigations at a personal, departmental, and even possibly institutional level. It is helpful, then, to capture the essential content of the conversation so everyone can have sufficient time to reflect on and consider the unexpected discoveries and specific embodiments of civic learning and democratic engagement in a course as they take shape over time. Having some kind of record of the exchanges also allows the group to ask, so what? Does the conversation suggest the department as a whole as well as individual faculty within the department might want to make any changes in how the major is organized or its pedagogies and assignments adopted? Do the findings imply that more recognition should be given for the faculty whose scholarship is shaped by public engagement? If so, how?

In the last section of *Civic Prompts*, a list of seven questions, which are described in greater detail, formulate different ways to uncover existing civic dimensions already taught and perhaps not named as such as well as provoke fresh approaches that might be adopted in departmental designs. The prompts are:

1. Which. . . [civic learning] capabilities does your disciplinary domain especially embrace?
2. What are some lines of civic inquiry especially amenable to your disciplinary domain?
3. What are some big issues that are common to your disciplinary domain that lend themselves to civic inquiries and/or actions?
4. What are some civic pedagogies suited to your disciplinary domain?

5. What kinds of assignments generate a line of questioning or civic actions within the context of your disciplinary or interdisciplinary courses?

6. What are some forms of civic action that are appropriate to your disciplinary domain and which you could incorporate more intentionally in your courses as selected points and levels?

7. In what ways does your disciplinary society currently invest in civic learning and democratic engagement as a component of the discipline and how else might it offer leadership and resources? ■

ENDNOTES

1. With thanks to Mackenzie Rice, Towson University, for her work on selecting and arranging the excerpts. The only changes made to the original text, unless otherwise noted, are adapting citations to endnotes.

2. National Commission on Civic Renewal, *A Nation of Spectators: How Civic Disengagement Weakens America and What We Can Do About It* (College Park, MD: National Commission on Civic Renewal, 1998), 7.

3. Seth Pollack, "Civic Literacy across the Curriculum," *Diversity & Democracy* (2011): 8.

4. Pollack "Civic Literacy," 8.

5. Pollack "Civic Literacy," 9.

6. For expansion on each point, see *A Crucible Moment: College Learning and Democracy's Future* (Washington, DC: Association American of Colleges & Universities, 2012), 31–33.

7. Included K–12 systems, higher education association, disciplinary associations, civic organizations and community leaders, employers, and foundations and philanthropic entities. For details and action recommendations for each group, see *A Crucible Moment*, 38–40.

8. Barbara Jordan, "Harvard University Commencement Address, June 16, 2011," The Barbara Jordan Forum, Accessed October 1, http://www.utexas.edu/lbj/barbarajordanforum/quotes.php.

9. President's Commission on Higher Education, "Higher Education for American Democracy, Vol. I, Establishing the Goals" (Washington, DC: Government Printing Office, 1947).

10. *A Crucible Moment*, 32.

11. Immediately after the release of *A Crucible Moment*, The Robert R. McCormick Foundation was quick to step up to support proposals by AAC&U to initiate engagement with Chicago area two- and four-year colleges and universities in response to *A Crucible Moment*'s recommendations. For this specific McCormick-funded project, "Civic Inquiry and Action across the Disciplines," and for McCormick's overall leadership, AAC&U extends its special gratitude for the Foundation's unwavering support of cultivating informed and engaged citizens.

Civic Education: A Key to Trust in Government

6

KATHERINE BARRETT AND RICHARD GREENE

The Council of State Governments (CSG)[1] recently released a report on the critical role civic engagement plays in education. This recognition by leaders of state government is a step forward at an important time in history when the public's trust in both national and state government is weak as is their belief in their own ability to influence policy. While civic education is at the core of equipping citizens with the knowledge and experience needed to actively participate in our democracy, it is in poor shape in America. Attention to state and local government has been particularly neglected.

The report recognizes that there is no one-size-fits-all formula for civic engagement, but educating on how state and local government touches the lives of citizens is a key foundational element. The report highlights various state programs that have been effective tools for boosting civic engagement.

CSG reminds us that schools are uniquely situated to model effective political discussions in an era of political division and that teacher training and development should be prioritized to help build this capacity. In summary, teaching civic engagement in schools is key to boosting the next generation's ability to participate in our democracy, and the need is urgent.

The public's sense that government is not serving them efficiently and effectively is particularly strong when it comes to their understanding of the federal government. But that does not mean that states are free of a similar phenomenon; they are similarly targets of widespread mistrust. According to a September 2016 Gallup poll, some 37% of Americans surveyed had little trust or confidence in their states.[2] There are a number of reasons why this is true, including the kind of vicious electioneering that fills the television airwaves and the growth of various movements dedicated to attacking, rather than improving, the very existence of government. But one more factor that is particularly troublesome, given the fact that it can be resolved, has been the decline in civic education, particularly that which focuses on the states and localities. How, indeed, can people trust a powerful entity that they do not understand? It is a basic element of human nature that ignorance leads inexorably to mistrust.

The experts agree. As Gerald Wright, professor and chair of the department of political science at Indiana University states, "students are overly cynical now. To be effective citizens they need to understand how the system operates, and there is too much of a tendency just to say 'Aw, they're all corrupt.' And they won't participate and it takes them out of the game and then it leaves the space open for those who want to get in the game for their own self-interest."[3] Randall Reid, director of performance initiatives at the International City/County Management Association, points out that "becoming a better civic creature helps you understand the place you're in."[4]

THE STATE OF THE ART

Despite its importance, the quality of civic education in America, in many states, is abysmal. Although there have been a number of initiatives to bolster the field, the most recent results from the National Assessment of Educational Progress, or NAEP, show only 23% of eighth graders attaining "proficient" status in civics. Of eight subject areas, only US history showed worse results—with 18% of eighth graders showing proficiency.[5] In 2014, the Annenberg Public Policy Center released a survey that tells a particularly gloomy tale of the state of knowledge about government in the United States. Of the 1,416 respondents, only 36% could name all three branches of government, and 35% were unable to name any branch of government.[6] At least 40 states have a requirement for a course in American government or civics.[7] The remaining 10 have no requirements for any civic education. But even the states with a requirement do not guarantee that young people are getting the necessary background they should. Requirements for coursework have minimal impact unless they are accompanied by strong teacher development, rigorous standards, active learning, and a broad-based civic curriculum.

One of the significant problems in civic education today is that the attention to state and local government has been squeezed. Most civics/political science courses in K–12 schools and colleges are focused on the federal government—not state and local government, said Dick Simpson, professor of political science at the University of Illinois at Chicago.[8] They are also focused on government structure—the number of Supreme Court justices, the different branches of government, the two houses of Congress, and so on. "You learn about the federal government and not about things you can actually affect like the city council and your state legislature," Simpson said.

In a 2013 survey of teachers, the Center for Information and Research on Civic Learning and Engagement, or CIRCLE, overseen by Peter Levine, associate dean of research at Tufts University's Jonathan Tisch College of Civic Life, found that 86% said the major emphasis or entire focus of the civic courses they taught was the US Constitution.[9] This has not always been the case. Until the early 1970s, the vast majority of public schools devoted a reasonable chunk of time to state and local government. But that has waned. California, for example, used to have a half-semester course in high school devoted to the study of state government. "But that went away a long time ago," said Ted McConnell, executive director of the Campaign for the Civic Mission of Schools.

"Presidents are visible and big international and national events make the front page of the newspaper," said Tom Carsey, professor of political science at the University of North Carolina at Chapel Hill. "But if you explain to students and their parents that most of their daily lives are shaped by policies at the state and local level, then that becomes more relevant and exciting." He said that making the connection to the impact of state and local government on students' lives is easy, given a K–12 or college setting and the fact that students likely get to school on state or local roads and that their parents pay state and local taxes.[10] "States have enormous power," said Indiana University's Wright. "They control so much of our day-to-day lives—health care, education, welfare, licensing of all the professions.... Most of the things that affect our lives are the result of state law, not federal law." But, he said, students do not get the news about state government and politics.[11] At the university level, most colleges have an introduction to American government class as part of the course menu. But just as in K–12, texts for these courses are focused on the national government.

WHAT SHOULD CIVIC EDUCATION INCLUDE?

Obviously, there is no good, one-size-fits-all formula for a complete and thorough civic education program in K–12 or higher education. But experts cite at least four common elements that should be included for the curriculum to be complete and to help foster a better understanding of and trust in government:

1. an overview of the broad role of state and local governments;
2. the role of state and local governments as they relate to the federal system;
3. key aspects of state policy making—outlining the importance of budgets, state-local relations, and major areas of state spending such as K–12 education, Medicaid, transportation, corrections, and higher education—and the role of the executive branch, legislature, and the courts; and
4. (perhaps most important) how state and local government touches the lives of citizens, including students themselves.

Teenagers may tend to think that government is remote, that governmental decision making is carried out by a group of older adults they have never met making decisions that may or may not have a direct—or, at least, a perceived—impact on their lives. Sue Crawford, a political science professor at Creighton University and a Nebraska state legislator, makes a point of teaching her students how legislative decisions may affect their careers and professional choices. "I'm communicating how critical the state government is in determining who gets to be in a profession, where the boundaries of the profession are, scope of practice fights," she said. She said it is important to engage students, particularly at the college level, and help them "in understanding what's involved in being in their (planned) profession. The state has a key role in (occupational) requirements and licenses. That's one piece that people don't know."[12]

HOPE FOR A CHANGE IN MOMENTUM

Although the status quo for civic education is still worrisome, there has been recognition during the last decade or so that civic education is of critical value. As a result, there has been a growing focus on increasing the attention paid to educating America's young people in the ways their government works. But these shifts are coming slowly and could take years or decades to lead to significant change. At the top of the list of initiatives has been an effort to step up attention to social studies. This focus has been encouraged through the Common Core State Standards initiative and through the development of the C3 social studies framework, which includes civics, economics, geography, and history. The underlying notion is that simply learning how the government works and how politics works is one step, but to make it interesting and memorable, you also need action. "Just a dry set of facts is not sufficient," said Simpson.[13]

The Campaign for the Civic Mission of Schools has identified a group of practices that can improve the civic understanding of young people. This includes student-centered participatory classroom activities rather than reading and memorizing information from a textbook, participation and discussion about student government, and involvement in community or political projects such as working through the city council and neighborhood organizations to turn a vacant lot into a neighborhood garden.[14] Also recommended are the kinds of games and simulations that are available through iCivics, which was founded by former Supreme Court Justice Sandra Day O'Connor in 2009 "to restore civic education in our nation's schools."[15]

Project-based learning and action civics ensure that students get a real laboratory experience of being able to attack a problem and effect change. There are many opportunities at the local level to practice the skills to do that, said Marshall Croddy, president of the Constitutional Rights Foundation in California.[16] So, for example, creating a class project aimed at persuading a city council to put up a stop sign at a busy intersection can be far more useful than studying a flow chart that shows the way public meetings can influence action and policy. The emphasis in lower grades and high school is on simulations, speakers, and internships. "It has a more active component," said Simpson. It is not just learning about how laws are passed in the abstract sense. "If we can get a student interested in passing a law, they'll learn the rules of the legislative body."[16] Despite a growing emphasis on active learning, it is still rare. In CIRCLE's 2013 survey of teachers, only 13% included community service in their civics curriculum and a smaller percentage included participation in a political campaign or "nonpartisan election-related activities."[18]

A 2015 effort by Campus Compact, a national coalition of 1,100 college and universities, promotes more civic education and engagement at the college level. University presidents attending a meeting in Boston in 2015 signed a pledge to review the civic engagement programs of their campuses and create civic action plans. The Higher Learning Commission, which accredits colleges, also is reinforcing attention to civics as a priority. The idea of Campus Compact, said Andrew Seligsohn, its president, is to facilitate higher education's role in supporting a healthy democracy. It started many years ago with a commitment to promoting volunteerism. In recent years, there has been a much clearer intention to build the student experience beyond a service ethic to a citizenship ethic. Otherwise, students do not fully grasp how the issues they are interested in—helping the homeless, for example—connect to public policy.[19]

With a great deal of competition for student time, one of the stickiest questions for legislators and other state decision makers is how to promote the adoption of civics as a core part of the curriculum. The question is also how to set standards that provide flexibility and freedom to teachers while ensuring that the topic is taken seriously throughout the school system.

SOME BRIGHT SPOTS

Illinois was one of the states that most recently passed a requirement to teach civics in high school. In August 2015, governor Bruce Rauner signed HB 4025 (Public Act 99-0434) into law. Notably, the law did not just require a civics course; it embedded best practice elements, as well. "They have to engage in conversations on current and controversial issues in class, service-learning, and simulation of democratic processes," said the McCormick Foundation's Shawn Healy. "That's written into the statute. That's a huge win. That's what I'm most proud about."[20]

New York State education law requires instruction in citizenship and patriotism and the State Social Studies Learning Standards include an understanding of "the governmental systems of the United States and other nations; the United States Constitution; the basic civic values of American constitutional democracy; and the roles, rights, and responsibilities of citizenship, including avenues of participation."[21] In addition, the New York State Board of Regents has required the passage of a one-semester class, Participation in Government, for high school graduation. This class has six units covering government structures, obligations of citizenship, voting, running for office, public policy, and civic rights.

"Our state has always recognized the importance of having a knowledgeable citizenry," said New York State senator Carl L. Marcellino, chair of the Senate Education Committee and past chair of The Council of State Governments. "Our Participation in government classes provide our seniors with the information and skills to understand our local, state, and national governments, and to make informed decisions. As our media outlets become more diverse, a strong background and understanding in our government and public policy is all that more important."[22]

Perhaps the state that has gone furthest in embracing civic education is Florida. Its effort got off the ground with a 2007 meeting convened by former US senator Bob Graham, who also served as governor of Florida, and former US representative Louis Frey. Together, they released a white paper, which made the case that the state's below-average voting participation and civic engagement could be addressed through a greater focus on civic learning in schools. A 2009 speech to a joint session of the state legislature by former Supreme Court justice Sandra Day O'Connor helped to build enthusiasm, and in 2010, the justice Sandra Day O'Connor Civics Education

Act (CHAPTER 2010-48 Committee Substitute for House Bill No. 105) was passed.[23] The act required civics content to be integrated into English and language arts standards in every grade from kindergarten through high school and includes a full-year course in seventh grade.

CHALLENGES AND POTENTIAL SOLUTIONS

While there is strong momentum for improving civics education, a number of obstacles stand in the way.

THE NEED FOR HIGH-QUALITY PROFESSIONAL DEVELOPMENT

One of the biggest gaps in civic education is teacher training and development. While teacher-education programs often include a required course in American government and politics, these courses are almost always focused on the national level.[24] Crawford noted that this basic American government course is often "the only political science or government course that people who teach get." The federal/national focus of this course reinforces the idea that only the federal government is important. "This is what our teachers are learning," she said.[25] Providing more training, however, requires resources, which are scarce. "The amount that has been spent for teacher professional development has been minimal," said Croddy. "Something at the state level which would provide funding either through the state budget or the state education budget for support of that kind of teacher professional development or evaluation is really needed."[26]

At the federal level, for a long time programs in support of civics received enthusiastic verbal support but little financial support. The situation has brightened recently with the signing of the Every Student Succeeds Act in 2015. The act authorizes a limited amount of grant funding for teacher-development programs, as well as for efforts to expand evidence-based practices, to innovate and to assess what is working.[27] The availability of grants through the American History & Civics Academics Grants Program was announced in the spring with applications due during the summer of 2016.[28]

Even with funding, getting teachers trained statewide is a challenge that requires multiple partnerships, creative thinking, and considerable effort. For example, in Washington, the state legislature found a way to enhance teacher training through a legislative scholar program. The five-day summer workshop in Olympia provides information to teachers about the legislative process and how the legislature and the courts work with each other. According to the website description, the program gives teachers resources and ideas for their classroom teaching.[29]

SHARP POLITICAL DIVISIONS

The intensely partisan environment nationwide has led some teachers to avoid talking about political issues with their students. While most teachers say they are supported by their principals or other administrators in discussing controversial topics, in the 2013 CIRCLE survey of teachers, 25% said they believed that parents or other adults would object to political discussions in the classroom.[30] The key here is not to avoid controversial subjects but to make sure presentations on controversial subjects are balanced and that teachers are not ideologues who sway the conversation. It is also important to help students learn how to discuss public issues with civility and how to sort fact from fiction. In CIRCLE's 2013 survey of teachers, only 42% of respondents "practiced how to discuss public issues with civility on a regular basis," and only 39% knew how to find the resources they needed "to teach students how to sort fact from fiction in a digital age."[31]

While intense partisanship may have cut off political dialogue in some schools, it also underlines the need to have such discussions in the first place. "What teachers do with respect to discussing politics is even more critical because of polarization," said Healy. "Research tells us that schools are some of the most heterogeneous environments we ever will occupy. On top of that, you have trained professionals with expertise in facilitating the conversations."[32]

CIVIC EDUCATION WITHOUT THE TEACHERS

Not all routes to improved civics are founded in the traditional teacher-student relationship. For example, a number of states and local governments have budget simulation tools on their websites. These have the potential to teach people of all ages how a budget is formed in a hands-on way. On California's budget simulation website, a headline asks: "How Will You Balance California's Budget?"[33] The opening text likely would resonate with legislators all over the United States. "What should California do to plan for long-term pension and retiree health care costs? How much should be invested in programs that were cut during the recession? What can the state do to make revenues more stable?"[34] Many legislative websites also offer pages designed to engage young people, explain how decisions are made, and provide some entertainment in the process. Iowa, for example, has a prominent tab on the main page of the legislature's website that offers "Resources & Civic Education."[35] Resources include short pieces on how a bill becomes a law and what legislators do, a few educational games, a map of the week, and a good deal of information about visiting the Iowa Capitol, including a virtual tour.

In Nebraska, a section of the website for students and teachers offers a history of the unicameral legislature, information on lawmaking, and a list of specific student-oriented programs.[36] In addition, there is a unicameral kids program designed for fourth graders, information about the state's Unicameral Youth Legislature, a policy development exercise, and simulations of committee hearings and floor debates.

Many civic education organizations encourage legislators to visit K–12 classrooms or campuses that have civic courses so they can speak, in first person, about how their government really works from their perspective. For example, the National Conference of State Legislators provides resources on its website to help legislators who are visiting classrooms.[37] Unfortunately, the funding for that program has dwindled over time.[38] "If citizens can see an elected official in the flesh, (they can see) that they're not corrupt and they're not monsters," said Wright.[39] Research in Florida shows the impact of visits by local or state officials. The greatest impact comes from participating in a community-service project. But even one visit from a local or state official has a significant impact, based on test-score data collected by the Florida Joint Center for Citizenship.

University of North Carolina's Carsey suggested that institutes that help train new legislators could also provide lectures to legislators about how to communicate what they do to young people. "These are skills that can be learned," said Carsey. "A little bit of training might not just give legislators some tips but also a little more confidence."[40]

Another way to involve legislators is through civic-action projects. The Constitutional Rights Foundation showcases ways in which young people have engaged in their communities. "What we found very helpful is to bring politicians and legislators and government officials into the process [of] helping the students understand how to make change in a positive, proactive way," said Croddy. "We have the showcases and we invite politicians and legislators and work with the groups, critique the approaches, and offer suggestions." A collection of 53 civic-action projects from the foundation is available on YouTube. These projects cover student work on topics such as gentrification, body cameras for police, underage drinking, and animal rights.[41] Students "are required to reach out to public officials," said Croddy. "There's a whole web of opportunities for young people to interact. You can't do high-quality civic action unless you interact with the people who are charged with the public-policy function. You learn through that process."[42]

CONCLUSION

The quiver of approaches to improving civic education in America—particularly as it pertains to states and localities—is full of options. The good news is that the nation appears to be on the edge of recognizing the importance of this kind of action. Will such education dramatically elevate trust in government? That is yet to be seen. But it is clear that this is a very important starting point. ■

ENDNOTES

1. Founded in 1933, The Council of State Governments (CSG) is our nation's only organization serving all three branches of state government. CSG is a region-based forum that fosters the exchange of insights and ideas to help state officials shape public policy. This offers unparalleled regional, national, and international opportunities to network, develop leaders, collaborate, and create problem-solving partnerships.

   The 56 US states and territories are members of The Council of State Governments, and six Canadian provinces also partner with CSG. State leaders from all three branches of government guide the organization. CSG serves the nation through offices in Lexington, Kentucky, that house the headquarters and affiliated organizations; the CSG Justice Center headquartered in New York; and four regional offices in Atlanta, Chicago, New York, and Sacramento, California. The CSG Associates program allows representatives of the private sector to offer their perspectives to public-sector members.

2. Gallup. Trust in Government, 2016 (http://www.gallup.com/poll/5392/trust-government.aspx).

3. Gerald Wright, interview by Barrett and Greene, April 13, 2016.

4. Randall Reid, interview by Barrett and Greene, July 7, 2016.

5. National Center for Education Statistics, The National Assessment of Educational Progress, The Nation's Report Card, 2014 (http://www.nationsreportcard.gov/#civics).

6. Annenberg Public Policy Center. Americans Know Surprisingly Little About Their Government, September 17, 2014 (http://www.annenbergpublicpolicycenter.org/americans-know-surprisingly-little-about-their-government-survey-finds/).

7. Surbhi Godsay, Whitney Henderson, Peter Levine, and Josh Littenberg-Tobias, State Civic Education Requirements, The Center for Education & Research on Civic Learning & Engagement, Jonathan Tisch School of Citizenship and Public Service, Tufts University, updated October 19, 2012 (http://civicyouth.org/wp-content/uploads/2012/10/State-Civic-Ed-Requirements-Fact-Sheet-2012-Oct-19.pdf).

8. Dick Simpson, interview by Barrett and Greene, April 5, 2016.

9. Surbhi Godsay and Felicia M. Sullivan, A National Survey of Civics and U.S. Government Teachers, The Center for Education & Research on Civic Learning & Engagement, June 3, 2014, (http://civicyouth.org/wp-content/uploads/2014/06/CIRCLE_FS2014_TeacherSurvey.pdf).

10. Tom Carsey, interview by Barrett and Greene, April 7, 2016.

11. Wright interview.

12. Sue Crawford, interview by Barrett and Greene, March 10, 2016.

13. Simpson interview.

14. The Civic Mission of Schools is a seminal work that was produced by the Campaign for the Civic Mission of Schools in 2003 and includes promising programs, approaches, and recommendations. (http://civicmission.s3.amazonaws.com/118/f7/1/172/2003_Civic_Mission_of_Schools_Report.pdf). A follow-up report, called Guardian of Democracy: The Civic Mission of Schools (2011), updates and adds to the proven practices, program ideas, and recommendations (http://civicmission.s3.amazonaws.com/118/f0/5/171/1/Guardian-of-Democracy-report.pdf).

15. A wide variety of civic resources are available from iCivics at https://www.icivics.org/; other activities can be found in the resources section at the end of this chapter.

16. Marshall Croddy, interview by Barrett and Greene, July 11, 2016.

17. Simpson interview.

18. A National Survey of Civics and U.S. Government Teachers, 3.

19. Andrew Seligsohn, president, Campus Compact, interview by Barrett and Greene, June 27, 2016.

20. Shawn Healy, interview by Barrett and Greene, July 7, 2016.

21. Social Studies Standard 5 Civics, Citizenship, and Government, Office of Curriculum and Instruction, New York State Education Department, http://www.p12.nysed.gov/ciai/socst/socstand/ssa5.html.

22. Debbie Peck Kelleher, committee director, New York State Senate Education Committee e-mail message to Barrett and Greene, October 20, 2016.

23. Stephen Masyada, director of the Florida Joint Center for Citizenship, and Doug Dobson, executive director of The Lou Frey Institute of Politics and Government, interview with Barrett and Greene, September 15, 2016.

24. Levine interview.

25. Crawford interview.

26. Croddy interview.

27. The National Coalition for History, President Signs "Every Student Succeeds Act," with New Funding for History & Civics Programs, December 3, 2015, http://historycoalition.org/2015/12/03/history-related-provisions-in-the-every-student-succeeds-act/.

28. The National Coalition for History, American History & Civics Academies Grants Availability, June 2, 2016 (http://historycoalition.org/2016/06/02/american-history-civics-academies-grants-availability/).

29. Legislative Scholar Program, Washington State Legislature (http://leg.wa.gov/ScholarProgram/Pages/default.aspx).

30. A National Survey of Civics and US Government Teachers, 8.

31. A National Survey of Civics and US Government Teachers, 4.

32. Healy interview.

33. "How Will You Balance California's Budget," Next 10, https://www.budgetchallenge.org/pages/home.

34. The California Budget Challenge is produced by an organization called Next 10, which uses "The Budget Challenge" for interactive sessions in classrooms and for adult audiences around the state. In its in-person appearances, Next 10 uses clickers to get audiences to weigh in on policy options and see budget impacts (https://www.budgetchallenge.org/pages/about).

35. Resources & Civic Education, The Iowa Legislature (https://www.legis.iowa.gov/resources).

36. For Students and Teachers, Nebraska Legislature (http://nebraskalegislature.gov/feature/teach.php).

37. "America's Legislators Back-To-School Program," National Conference of State Legislatures (http://www.ncsl.org/legislators-staff/legislators/legislators-back-to-school/legislator-in-the-classroom-legislative-appropria.aspx).

38. Angele Andrews, program principal, National Conference of State Legislatures, interview by Barrett and Greene, July 14, 2016.

39. Wright interview.

40. Carsey interview.

41. Student Created Videos, Civic Action Project, Constitutional Rights Foundation (https://www.youtube.com/playlist?list=PLOicNIzZMkHR_7ZM-WKjgnzD1dcSIsUW2).

42. Croddy interview.

The History of Civic Education in Political Science: The Story of a Discipline's Failure to Lead

Michael T. Rogers

Today, there is growing concern in the United States over the decline in civic engagement, particularly among youth. This alarm is accompanied by disquiet about America's formal civic education, particularly at the high school and collegiate levels. Combined, these developments raise doubt about the health of American democracy. One academic discipline that has the potential to have a significant impact on both civic education and engagement of Americans is political science. Thus, it is worth asking: Have the actions by political scientists generally and the American Political Science Association (APSA) in particular significantly promoted civic education and engagement in America?

To answer this question, Part I of this chapter provides the history of civic education and engagement for the discipline of political science and its national organization, APSA, since its founding in 1903. Although many in the discipline espoused a civic mission at its origins, the history of political science and APSA shows it has had minimal influence on and has not been an outspoken advocate for civic education and engagement for much of the twentieth century. Other disciplines (education, history, psychology, and sociology) were more important in shaping America's formal civic education through social studies programs. That said, some recent initiatives by APSA and political scientists show renewed interest in and leave the discipline well-poised to make a positive impact on civic education and engagement in the twenty-first century.

To give some direction to this renewed interest, Part II of this chapter provides a summary of what scholars know and what we still need to learn about civic education and engagement. While various academic disciplines (education, history, psychology, sociology, and political science) have contributed to the rapidly growing civic education and engagement literatures, there are some significant gaps political scientists can help address. In fact, Part II will suggest how, rather than reinvent the civic education and engagement wheels, political scientists are best served through interdisciplinary collaborations and research that integrates the significant contributions of our sister disciplines. Then, the chapter concludes by arguing that APSA and political scientists should follow the model of influential interest groups. By positioning ourselves as information experts and coalition builders for democratic education, APSA and political scientists can best meet our recent commitment to a civic mission and emerge as key advocates for and principle agents in civic education and engagement policy formation.

If the Association [APSA] is to be encouraged to give civic education another try, then it must do so in light of the history that is uniquely ours, from which we have much more to learn and for which we bear some responsibility.

—James Farr[1]

As the turn of the twenty-first century loomed on the horizon, a movement for civic revival began in political science. The president of the American Political Science Association (APSA) at that time was Elinor Ostrom. She was at the forefront of this undertaking, as Ostrom formed a task force to address concerns about civic education and engagement in the United States.[2] Her decision was fueled by the research of political scientists at the end of the twentieth century that painted a bleak picture of civics in the United States. On one hand, seminal studies of civic literacy highlighted the low, stagnant political knowledge of Americans over the past 50 years.[3] On the other hand, the social capital literature spawned by Putnam documented a pronounced decline in civic engagement of Americans during this same time.[4] Collectively, these and other developments in academia led many to question whether political science was giving sufficient attention to civic education of citizens for all levels of education, especially because the study and understanding of politics is a core feature of our discipline.

To explore this debate and to offer insight on where political science as a discipline might direct its energies, this chapter is divided into two parts. Part I begins with our past. It examines the history of political science and APSA's relationship with civic education and engagement from 1903 to today. The evolution of this relationship between civics and the discipline of political science parallels the fluctuations I previously documented in a more general meta-history of formal civic education in the United States during the twentieth century.[5] Political scientists' interest, or lack thereof, in promoting civic education and engagement through the twentieth into the twenty-first century follows almost lockstep with America's interest in the issue. There was intense focus on civics at the beginning of the twentieth century and again with the start of the twenty-first century, but for the bulk of this time Americans showed general disinterest, leaving civics stagnant or in a state of decline.[6] Part II explores different pedagogical and research approaches that are helping political scientists to understand and address the growing civics problem, while noting where additional, interdisciplinary research is needed to enhance the scholarly knowledge of civic education and engagement. Overall, it is argued that political science is well poised today to contribute significantly to holes in civic literacy and engagement research and practice, especially through interdisciplinary collaborations.

PART I: THE PAST AND PRESENT OF CIVICS IN POLITICAL SCIENCE

In "A Meta-history of Formal Civic Education," I demonstrated how the United States has struggled with building durable civic education processes. Civic instruction, whether informal or formal, seems as susceptible to experience stagnation and decay as it is to result in civic growth and engagement. Whether one looks at the more informal civic education process of the 1700s or the more formalized civic education program developed in the 1800s and reinvigorated in the early 1900s, the long view of the history of civics in the United States reveals a country as likely to be characterized by a stagnating or declining civic life as it is to see civic revival. Democracy is only possible in societies that instill the civic knowledge, skills, and values necessary to produce a vibrant democratic citizenry capable of self-government. America needs to reinvigorate its civic education program once again, developing one adequate to promoting a politically informed, active, and engaged citizenry in the twenty-first century.[7]

What is needed is a civic ecology composed of groups—both public and private—that serve as leaders, advocating and empowering Americans to live civic lives. Arguably, no group has more reason to be such a leader in the fight for civics than political scientists, as its subject of study is politics. In fact, the very origins of this academic discipline are tied to its founders' general sense of civic duty to fulfill Progressive Movement ideals through being civic instructors, trainers, and leaders.[8]

Next, the history of civic education is provided for the discipline of political science and its seminal professional organization, APSA. When Iftikhar Ahmad observes that "research on political scientists' education ideas and activities about curriculum and instruction in social studies is disparate,"[9] he demonstrates the need for such a history for the discipline. While his work somewhat addresses this gap, the following history gives a more comprehensive and complete picture. For one, Ahmad's claim needs qualification. The problem is not so much that the research is disparate; it is just piecemeal and needs to be reconstructed into one comprehensive history.

By weaving together the various articles on the subject from leading political science journals (primarily the *American Political Science Review*, *PS: Political Science & Politics*, and *Perspectives on Politics*), this chapter assembles a complete history of civics in the discipline. It is worth noting this history covers civics specifically, not the more general educational program of social studies. If political science and APSA are judged solely by their activities in the twentieth century, the discipline might well be judged a failure on the civics front. As Richard Battistoni argues, even recent efforts in the discipline have left it having an impact on civics that is "marginal at best."[10] However, recent activities in political science, especially of an interdisciplinary nature, give reason to believe political science will have a more meaningful impact on citizenship training in this century.

EARLY 1900s: APSA DECLARES CIVIC GOALS, BUT NOT A MISSION

In "Meta-history of Formal Civic Education," I showed that the Progressive Movement in the early 1900s led to America's second civic revival.[11] Progressive ideals also played a central role in the emergence of the discipline of political science as a new, distinct academic field in the research university.[12] Political science was a byproduct of the Progressive Movement's reformation of municipal government. Claire Snyder notes that APSA, the national association for political scientists in the United States, formed in the first decade of the 1900s and readily assumed "a program of civic education and social reform."[13] More specifically, Ahmad explains that APSA formed in 1903 offering "three goals: the study of the government and its organs, the use of empirical methods, and the preparation of good citizens." He adds that the latter goal was not without its critics, citing Henry Jones Ford who "questioned the epistemological foundation of political science for promoting good citizens."[14] Ford questioned the compatibility of those who study government through objective empirical methods also taking such a normative action as to define and act to create the citizens of their subject matter. Hand in hand with this, Ford espouses a skepticism common in political science that such endeavors tend to fail to come to fruition. The history provided here will show the concern at the origins of APSA that Ford espouses—about the legitimacy and/or viability of political scientists deciding what good citizens are and then creating them through its curriculum—persists today among many in the discipline. In fact, it remains pervasive in the discipline even as APSA recently took steps to make civic education a central feature of its mission.

Still, let us not get too far ahead in the story. As James Farr explains, civic advocates in the discipline initially won the day as APSA embraced the "community civics movement" and, by extension, "the social center movement" in its 1916 committee report, *The Teaching of Government*.[15] He claims, "For political scientists at the turn of the century, civic education was crucial for stabilizing and moderating the American experiment in democracy. In an era marked by industrialization, immigration, class conflict, and other forces of rapid change—not to mention corrupt politicians and ineffective bureaucrats, as the Progressive Era judged—citizens, whether young or old, native or newly arrived, needed to learn (more) about their duties, rights, and privileges, as well as about government, party, and administration." He concludes, "The political scientists' worldview thus connected civic education to rights and duties by way of understanding practical arts, social analysis, and history. These connections were tied to professional associations, as well as pedagogical convictions."[16] Although the APSA never formally went so far as to declare a civic mission, the discipline had clearly set citizenship education as a goal for the profession.

Given these sentiments, Sheilah Mann unsurprisingly finds political scientists actively contributed to civics education through public schools in the early 1900s. Early APSA members routinely participated in "projects for secondary school instruction and teachers" and even had a standing committee on teaching political science in 1903 that morphed into a section on instruction in political science by 1904.[17] Ahmad concludes that "during the first few decades of the twentieth century political scientists' traditionalist vision was canonized into the social studies curriculum." As he explains, this traditionalist vision is not without its problems (e.g., it excluded women and was culturally insensitive), but it was an "integral part of the curriculum."[18] Yet, for all this civic mindedness and participation in training civics teachers and shaping the civics curriculum, it should be noted that in the 1900s APSA failed to turn its goals of citizen preparation formally into a mission of the association. Thus, it was easy for the discipline to turn away from such activities, which it began to do in the 1930s. By the beginning of World War II, APSA and its members had begun to shun involvement in public schools, preferring instead to focus internally on legitimating its discipline as a scholarly and scientific activity in higher education.[19]

What produced such a dramatic change? Hindy Schacter and Stephen Leonard help give an answer in their articles debating if APSA had a civic mission in the early 1900s. Schacter documents how APSA and political scientists tried to address civic literacy in its early committees. Much like the service-learning movement today, early political scientists sought to produce better, more active citizens through Deweyian experiential learning programs that relied on service projects and not simple rote memorization of governmental operations and structures.[20] However, Leonard emphasizes that such activities did not last long. In fact, he finds a host of political scientists shared Ford's sentiments previously discussed, arguing the discipline's civic education endeavors were "pure futility and waste."[21] Such observations became pervasive in the discipline after a decade or so of the infant academic discipline's rudimentary stabs at citizenship training appeared to have little to no effect on public civic literacy and engagement. Thus, Leonard finds by the 1930s leading members of APSA had begun questioning if the association ever had or should have had a civic mission. Such pessimism about civics quickly spread in the discipline, and the organization quickly forsook its early civic education emphasis. Therefore, while admitting that APSA initially espoused a "tripartite" set of disciplinary goals—(1) to educate "citizens and future political leaders;" (2) to produce qualified civil servants for the newly instituted merit bureaucracy; and (3) to build a cadre of graduate students to be future political scientists—Leonard explains how in less than two decades the two most civic-oriented legs of the APSA agenda had dissolved. Sure, the first committee—the 1908 Committee of Five—emphasized civic education and the dissemination of political science research knowledge to educate "citizens *qua* citizens." However, the second APSA committee in 1914, the Committee of Seven, already shifted away from this focus to one of training career civil servants for the bureaucracy. Then, the third APSA committee, the Munro Committee in 1922, took a completely less politicized path. The 1914 committee had already dropped the citizenship training goal, and the Munro Committee followed suit by dropping the civil service training goal. The new focus was on self-aggrandizement of the discipline, as the 1922 committee chose to emphasize recruiting graduate students to political science to ensure the profession's health in the academy.[22]

MID-1900S: ESTABLISHING THE DISCIPLINE AS A LEGITIMATE SCIENCE DISPLACES THE FOCUS ON CIVICS

By mid-century, America seemed to have achieved a golden age for civics, but it was a hollow golden age. At this time, a three-semester program of civics had crystalized in formal civic education at the secondary level, something not achieved before or since. However, beneath this robust curricular surface civic education had begun to stagnate. A couple of developments combined to undo America's civic revival in the early twentieth century. Pluralism and multiculturalism politicized civic education. As the narrative of civic education became more controversial, the growing popularity of the German research university model was the perfect distraction and outlet for higher education to avoid entering the politicized civic fray.[23] Interestingly, the history of political science and APSA reveals that the discipline is a quintessential example of the consequences of the politicization of civic education in America—academia forsook civic education in favor of recruiting PhD students to the academy.

Overall, Leonard demonstrates that as early as 1914 the APSA began truncating its tripartite set of goals, turning its focus increasingly to one leg—recruiting future political scientists. Why? First, there was the skepticism of some political scientists about the effectiveness of the discipline's civic activities as previously discussed. Simply put, political scientists rapidly learned that enhancing the civic competency of citizens is difficult. This was all the fuel the political scientists who were civic naysayers needed. Leonard highlights the quick spread of this view in APSA, as there was a growing frustration among political scientists with their apparent inability to improve civic literacy.[24] In fact, the ensuing decades would give rise to a conventional view that persists in the discipline today that civic courses do not improve civic literacy.[25]

Given the growing frustration in the discipline with its inability to positively impact civic education, APSA and political scientists adopted a passive approach to civic education, the formal approach of teaching facts through textbooks. Through reviewing the proceedings of the APSA Committee on Instruction in Political Science in the mid-1900s, one can see this preference for textbook-based instruction on national government materializing in the discipline. Such a preference drove the committee's criticisms of what, to this day, remains an unprecedented civic instruction program for secondary education in America. In the mid-1900s, it was common to find a three-course regiment in civic education in high schools that included a civics course in 9th grade along with another civics or government course and a "Problems of Democracy" course.[26] Examining this curriculum, the committee members first lament that in the early 1900s Deweyian experiential field work and field trips had displaced classroom textbook-based instruction in national government. Then, the committee was concerned by the fact that civic instructors favored their own local textbooks, which the members again believed neglected the role of national government.[27] Finally, the real tragedy in the committee's criticisms was its effect on the three-course civic education norm. By attacking the "Problems of Democracy" course in this sequence for displacing traditional civics instruction in the structure and operation of national government, it made the three-course regiment vulnerable to reform and reduction at the very time when other social science disciplines were demanding they also be covered in the secondary curriculum.[28]

Whether intended or not, the decision by the APSA Committee on Instruction in Political Science to emphasize a reduction in the civics emphasis by the discipline to teaching the sterile facts of national government made courses like "Problems of Democracy" easy targets for removal from secondary education. In the remainder of the century, this is what ensues as the three-course regiment civics norm becomes reduced on average to one course in civics, American national government. When secondary schools where faced with new curricular demands, should it come as any surprise that "Problems of Democracy" disappeared from the curriculum? If the scholarly discipline associated with the study of politics had vocalized its own discontent with the course, why should secondary schools keep it? Neither APSA nor its committee struck the course from the school ledger, but the discipline's reduction in its civic emphasis is commiserate in this decline. In fact, the history of citizenship training in political science for the remainder of the twentieth century is one where the discipline is content to only teach the sterile facts of national government through general education classes at the higher education level. Not surprisingly, political scientists' passivity on civics did nothing to preserve the three-course regiment of civics in secondary education. The discipline was content to watch it be reduced to only one course in national government at the secondary education level as well.[29]

Still, political scientists' frustration with the difficulty of meaningful civic education is only one part of this history of civic education in the discipline. Such frustration may have resulted in the discipline reducing its civic expectations to primarily instruction in national government for most citizens, but the turn away from a civic mission was fueled by more than this. There was a second development in the discipline, what Gunnell argues is the only true paradigmatic shift in the discipline of political science, the change from German statism to pluralism in the 1920s. This paradigm shift set the stage for political scientists to abandon their civic education activities because such endeavors are too politicized.[30] In its infancy, the discipline of political science was dominated by German statism, which meant that political scientists believed democracy needed a "homogeneous 'people.'" By the 1920s, pluralism was gaining popularity within the discipline and challenging German statism as the hegemonic view. As pluralism became the new paradigmatic view of political scientists, it led to a revolution in democratic thinking. Pluralists argued that the "democratic dogma" of the statists must be replaced by "democratic realities," that is, democratic theory must accept and embrace the fact that democratic societies are inevitably heterogeneous, that the "people" are a diverse series of associations of different groups of people.[31] While this revolution in the democratic thought of political scientists may seem inevitable today given our indoctrination into pluralism and multiculturalism arguments, it is important not to miss the subtle implications of this significant reorientation in thinking. Global events like industrialization, immigration, and urbanization—not to mention World War I and II— made the world much smaller in the mid-1900s. Pluralism, or the widespread interaction and mixing of cultures, became a growing reality of life in the twentieth century. This newfound appreciation of diversity had profound effects, such as politicizing previously apolitical and marginally political arenas. In some areas (e.g., the identity and difference literature over race, gender, and sexuality issues), these effects are readily evident. However, in other areas like formal civic education, they have not been so readily noticed.

Civic Education in the Twenty-First Century highlights how pluralism politicized civic education. For example, there is the debate between Robert Maranto, who advocates a more rigorous, government-sanctioned civic education program, and Jeffrey Hilmer, who adamantly believes civic education must be free of government influence.[32] Then, Gary Bugh creates a spectrum of pedagogies based on patterns in the ways faculty advocate teaching civic education. While he identifies four pedagogies (formal, political participation, minority dissent, and civic engagement), his spectrum emphasizes pluralism. Bugh admits there are likely more than four pedagogies and that these pedagogies can often be at odds with each other.[33] For example, minority dissenters who tell stories of resistance to power and struggles for equality are sometimes depicted as radicals promoting political disruption or revolution by formalists who prefer teaching facts and content. Yet, majority dissenters criticize formalists for reinforcing a content often determined by and conducive to the power of the dominant majority. Notice the politicization of pedagogy and civic education developing here.

In the nineteenth century, civic education largely avoided such politicization. As I demonstrated in "A Meta-history of Formal Civic Education," at that time formal civic education experienced substantial growth through the common school movement, at least until the Civil War consumed the focus and energy of the country. A similar growth began in the twentieth century, but this time it was pluralism in perspectives on the issue that politicized civic education in America.[34] Such mixed reviews, both outside and within the discipline, made it easy for APSA and political scientists to turn away from their pursuit of civic education initiatives in favor of focusing on the academic endeavor of political science. While a mature, twenty-first century approach to this politicization of civic education might be to embrace all the pedagogies on the spectrum and promote civic education and engagement in a multiplicity of ways, at the infancy of this debate in the mid-twentieth century the all-too-common response was to see civic education as a toxic enterprise better avoided. Ironically, this response became the dominant reaction in the very discipline whose subject matter is politics and whose relevance to society remains inextricably attached to its ability to promote a politically capable and civically competent citizenry.

Thus, the final piece in this twentieth century history of APSA and political scientists shunning civics is a development in academia that comes to consume APSA and political scientists for the remainder of the century. As the discipline struggled with the reality that producing better citizens is exceedingly difficult, frustrating, and politically controversial, it found an alternative purpose and less contentious means by which to establish and promote its identity. As Leonard (among others) explains, a transformation sweeping American universities was leading them to leave the civic university model a la Jefferson behind to pursue the German science and research-oriented one.[35] If the Jeffersonian civic university model of higher education had persisted into the twentieth century, political science might have had more incentive to maintain its civic orientation. However, the scientific- and research-oriented German university model popularized the pursuit of producing politically neutral, expert information in one's field. Wither civic education in political science.

Becoming popular in the mid-twentieth century, the timing of the adoption of the German research university model in America could not have provided a better out for APSA and many political scientists. They were frustrated with their early efforts to dramatically raise the civic literacy of citizens and that civic education had become overly problematized by pluralism, which raised concern that civics was a veiled indoctrination that was culturally insensitive. In such an environment, an internal focus on enhancing one's intellectual knowledge and prowess, as the German model of higher education suggested, was an easy sell in the discipline. APSA's civic goal was displaced by its newfound scientism; the discipline became consumed with recruiting and producing PhDs, not cultivating better citizens. One can see this turn developing in APSA as early as the 1930 Committee on Policy. In it APSA elevated its research and publication priorities and downgraded citizenship and public service.[36] The civic goal of political science was not completely abandoned by APSA (Ishiyama et al. find some continued advocacy of civic education in the discipline in the 1940s and again in a 1951 APSA committee report), but Leonard's claim that it is scarce seems apt.[37] Mann arrives at the same conclusion, noting occasional civic reports (e.g., *Goals for Political Science* in 1951) and actions by APSA and its members as late as the 1960s and 1970s. Yet, political science's general civics trajectory for the remainder of the twentieth century was a sterilized, fact-based civic education primarily in national government. Beyond that, the discipline focused energy and initiatives on enhancing the "science" in political science.

By 1971, the profession defined its "mission in terms of providing guidelines and resources about the analytical skills and subjects of political science" not "normative goals associated with citizenship education."[38] Ahmad probably best captures the hollowness of our discipline's interest in civic education in the twentieth century. He observes, "the APSA's numerous committees, which were formed in various decades of the twentieth century—for example, the Committee of Five in 1908, Committee on Instruction in 1916, Committee on Instruction in Political Science in 1922, Committee for the Advancement of Teaching in 1951, and Committee on Precollegiate Education in 1971—hardly mentioned the requisite skills for civic participation in a participatory democracy."[39] While some political scientists (Stephen Bennett offers Merriam and Jennings) suggested the possibility of a successful political science career that included a civic education orientation,[40] the overwhelming norm is generating a textbook-based, factual, and scientific knowledge of politics and political structures, not an engaging and experiential civic education that produces a more politically literate and civically competent citizenry.

LATE 1900S: CIVIC DECAY

By the end of the twentieth century, a civic orientation is rather absent in the discipline of political science. As Niemi and Smith observe:

> For 30 years political scientists largely ignored high school education in civics and government. There are two explanations for this neglect. First, the prevailing view was that students learned nothing from civic courses. Second, social scientists increasingly saw themselves as members of scientific disciplines, so whatever interest they had in precollege education was devoted to augmenting disciplinary knowledge.[41]

Their first observation exhibits the widespread skepticism in the discipline that civic courses matter. Instead, many scholars believed such courses make little difference in the civic literacy and competency of Americans.[42] In their second remark, Niemi and Smith demonstrate the extent to which political science had completely embraced the German university model of higher education at the expense of its earlier civic orientation. Given these developments in the discipline, political science failed to be a significant force and advocate for civic education in the latter half of the twentieth century. This failure is particularly glaring at the primary and secondary level, where college education and history departments played the primary role in determining both the content and training of social studies teachers. Ahmad finds this lack of involvement by political scientists perplexing given its substantial influence on civic education in social studies at the beginning of the twentieth century. He notes also that the discipline has greatly diversified its subfields over this time and observes, "It is puzzling, however, that political scientists did not promote their subfields to social studies education, even though materials from those subjects are appropriate for citizenship education in high schools."[43]

Like Ahmad, Mary Hepburn also sees the behavior of political scientists as "puzzling." Writing in the late 1980s, she critiqued political science for its lack of participation in secondary civic education. She began by noting that most academics outside the discipline of education were aloof to secondary school reforms, and observed, "Political scientists as a group appear no less distant" from such developments. Yet, she adds, "Given the public policy interests of much of political science, the distance is especially puzzling."[44] In particular, Hepburn laments the decline in political socialization research within the discipline because "there is less reflection on the total process of political education within the political science discipline."[45] Like Bennett, she notes there are individual exceptions in the discipline (she offers Gerald Pomper as an example). However, her last words are that "few political scientists get involved in researching or changing the school educational process" and that "the gulf between political science research and instruction in colleges and universities, on the one hand, and the teaching of 'government,' 'civics,' and 'citizenship' in the schools, on the other, is a good example of the distance between" universities and secondary schools overall.[46]

If political scientists desire some recommendations on how our discipline could become more involved in primary and secondary civic education in the next century, Hepburn has some good ideas. For example, she recommends political scientists be more involved in developing and evaluating textbooks and other curricular materials used at the secondary level, even offering the interdisciplinary collaboration at Indiana University between its schools of education and political science in the 1970s as a model. In addition, she recommends the discipline be more active in teacher education programs, as well as curriculum changes.[47] Collegiate education departments throughout the country are routinely involved in such activities, but the collaboration of political science departments in these areas is rare. Often other disciplines—most notably history, but also psychology and sociology—are involved, but it remains uncommon for the discipline of political science to participate beyond the occasional political scientist (or political science department) who seeks out such opportunities.

As Mann points out, APSA likewise remained aloof in public schooling through the end of the twentieth century. It did scrutinize the emerging K–12 education policy of the Clinton administration's *Goals 2000: The Educate America Act*. Yet, APSA ultimately "decided not to participate *as an association*." She gives a number of reasons for our discipline's absence: that (a) APSA had avoided endorsing a particular curriculum or textbook since 1975; (b) it is assumed the discipline's diversity of interests and views would make a consensus on textbooks difficult; and (c) political scientists generally see civics and government in K–12 as not "synonymous" with political science. She concludes by criticizing APSA for being too content with leaving it to its members to voluntarily get involved in the creation of national and state civic standards. While APSA claims to support such activities, it has done little to encourage them.[48]

Unfortunately, Hepburn's plea in 1987 (as well as Ahmad's and Mann's more recently) that "the time seems right for political scientists to get involved in improving political education in schools" largely went unheeded by the discipline.[49] For almost a decade, no significant action was taken. In the interim, the extent of APSA activities in this area was to form a Committee on Education in the early 1990s. Its primary product, the "APSA Guidelines for Teacher Training," amounted to no more than passive recommendations by political scientists for government teachers.[50] APSA and political scientists only began to seriously respond to the critiques of academics like Hepburn, Mann, Snyder, and Ahmad in the waning years of the twentieth century. In 1996, under the leadership of the association's president Elinor Ostrum, APSA formed a task force on civic education and engagement. The organization and discipline finally took steps to revive its civic goal and orientation.[51]

Yet, these steps to explore a greater role for political science in citizenship training were less a result of internal critiques by its members and more a result of the sounding of the alarm about the civic state in the United States by a number of scholars—most notably Putnam with his declining social capital argument—and mainstream media.[52] By the turn of the twenty-first century, the damage to formal civic education was done. Various studies document the decline in the civics curriculum at the secondary education level from three semesters to one during this time period.[53] In fact, Niemi and Smith find that by 1980 only about six in 10 high school students were even taking a one-semester course on American government, a development that only slightly improved by the end of the twentieth century.[54] Compounding this decline, numerous works criticize the sterile way American government is taught (especially to nonmajors), the poor education of social studies teachers in politics, and the poor quality of government textbooks.[55] All indicators are that civic education had significantly regressed by the close of the twentieth century.

Turn of the Century: Civic Revival in the Twenty-First Century

With the dawn of the twenty-first century, three educational movements—service-learning, the Scholarship of Teaching and Learning (SoTL), and the Civic Mission of Schools—materialized that collectively have shown great promise to address the civic decline of the previous century.[56] In particular, the service-learning and SoTL movements combined to produce a profound transformation in higher education that trickled down to the discipline of political science.

First, a revival of Deweyian experiential learning through the service-learning movement has given rise to a number of service-learning centers at colleges and universities across the country (see the chapter by Matto and McHugh in this volume). One central reason for our discipline's interest in service-learning is tied to its ability to promote greater civic engagement, particularly among youth, by moving political scientists beyond using traditional, lecture-oriented instruction.

Thus, a growing number of political scientists exist among the ranks of the service-learning practitioners. Battistoni provides a good list of some of the significant contributions by our discipline to this movement. In 1997, again under Elinor Ostrom's presidency, APSA produced an edited volume titled *Experiencing Citizenship: Concepts and Models for Service-Learning in Political Science*, launched its own service-learning webpage, dedicated an issue of *PS: Political Science & Politics* to the pedagogy, and routinely included panels and workshops on service-learning at its disciplinary conferences.[57] Some political scientists and their departments again began to require their students to become engaged in their surrounding communities. Service-learning (re)emerged as an important pedagogical practice in the discipline and continues to be recognized as such today.[58]

Next, the SoTL movement had just as transformative an effect on political science. Cherie Strachan and Elizabeth Bennion explain how the SoTL movement promoted the founding of the APSA Political Science Education Section (PSE) in 1993. Also, during this time the SoTL research articles became a staple feature of *PS* in "The Teacher" section. Strachan and Bennion also note that in 2005 the PSE section launched the peer-reviewed *Journal of Political Science Education*, which followed on the heels of the initiation in 2004 of the APSA Teaching and Learning Conference, a conference dedicated exclusively to sharing SoTL research.[59] The ultimate validation of SoTL in the discipline recently occurred as APSA has now become the official sponsor of the *Journal of Political Science Education*. This elevates the SoTL research in the discipline and further legitimates the *Journal of Political Science Education*, putting it on par with APSA's other journals that are oriented toward more traditional scientific research.[60]

While the overall effect of the SoTL movement in political science is striking, Strachan and Bennion's point that "SoTL has made *slow* and steady inroads" in the discipline is well-made.[61] Still, political science is late to the SoTL movement. Other disciplines in the social sciences have a much longer history of studying how to best teach their disciplines and often provide more outlets for publishing such research. To prove this point, one need only analyze the University of Central Florida's SoTL website, as it provides a convenient list of SoTL journals by discipline.[62] One finds journals dedicated to publishing SoTL research are much more common in other social studies disciplines and have been so for much longer. This is especially the case if one's criteria is that the disciplinary journal *solely* publish SoTL research (see table 7.1).[63] Political science (and sociology) is at the bottom end of the spectrum of social sciences supporting SoTL research. Our discipline (like sociology) only has one journal dedicated to such research. Then, sociology and political science each have only a few other journals that occasionally publish SoTL research. History and psychology are at the other end of the spectrum, the high end of support; both dedicate multiple journals to such research.

More importantly, history and psychology have been supporting the SoTL research much longer than political science or sociology. For example, although the publication is not by the American Historical Association, the discipline of history has *The History Teacher* as a journal for publishing such research. This journal has been in publication since 1967 and its publisher—the Society for History Education, Inc.—traces its origins to the 1940 Teachers' History Club.[64] Still, it should be noted that the discipline's HistorySOTL society did not form until 2006.[65] Psychology has just as long a record with supporting research on how to teach its subject. Its *Teaching of Psychology* journal dates back to the 1950s when the *Teaching of Psychology Newsletter* morphed into a journal.[66] Finally, the American Sociological Association (ASA) sponsors the journal *Teaching Sociology*. ASA has been publishing it since 1986, when (like psychology) ASA turned its teaching newsletter into a journal.[67]

Still, service-learning and SoTL have made significant inroads in political science, transforming the discipline by encouraging more than simply sterile, traditional lecture of scientific facts on politics. Both are fueling innovations by political scientists (and other disciplines) in civic education that should have a positive impact on civic literacy and engagement over the course of the next few decades.

Table 7.1 SoTL Journals by Social Studies Discipline			
POLITICAL SCIENCE	**HISTORY**	**PSYCHOLOGY**	**SOCIOLOGY**
Journal of Political Science Education [PS: Political Science & Politics] [Perspectives on Political Science]	The History Teacher Teaching History: A Journal of Methods Teaching History [London Historical Association]	Teaching of Psychology Psychology Learning & Teaching [Journal of Educational Psychology] [Contemporary Educational Psychology] [Educational Psychologist] [Cognition and Instruction]	Teaching Sociology [Sociology of Education]
1 solely SoTL **3 publish SoTL**	**3 solely SoTL**	**2 solely SoTL** **7 publish SoTL**	**1 solely SoTL** **2 publish SoTL**

Table created from the University of Central Florida's "SoTL Journals" website found at: http://www.fctl.ucf.edu/ResearchAndScholarship/SoTL/journals/.

Brackets added to journals that are not solely SoTL journals.

Then, the Civic Mission of Schools movement, particularly in higher education, has been no less significant to political science. For example, it was not long after the Wingspread Declaration on Renewing the Civic Mission of the American Research University in the late 1990s that APSA took a step toward integrating a civic mission into its mission statement.[68] One of the glaring omissions of the founding of political science is that—for a discipline that had grown out of the civically minded Progressive movement—its professional association, APSA, never formally adopted a civic mission. As shown previously, it did espouse a civic goal of citizenship training. However, it was not until the twenty-first century that APSA formed a strategic planning committee that recommended the association adopt a mission statement that included a civic mission. The last bullet of their proposed mission statement, which APSA did adopt, establishes the following civic goal: "Serving the public, including disseminating research and preparing citizens to be effective citizens and political participants."[69]

Although some scholars question if the APSA Task Force on Civic Education in the 21st Century (formed at the behest of then-president Elinor Ostrom) produced any concrete outputs, at least the ripple effects from the task force were significant in the discipline.[70] As important as any concrete outputs, the task force and APSA's forming and backing of it legitimated disciplinary activity in the realms of civic education and engagement. While the task force did experience a rather quiet demise in 2002, it was replaced by the APSA's first-ever Standing Committee on Civic Education and Engagement.[71] This committee has continued to legitimate the civic mission of APSA. Most notably, it produced the highly collaborative work, *Democracy at Risk: How Political Choices Undermine Citizen Participation, and What We Can Do About It.* APSA has even undertaken publishing SoTL books, most notably the 2013 edited volume *Teaching Civic Engagement: From Student to Active Citizen,* edited by McCartney et al. It truly appears a new civic age is dawning in the discipline of political science.

Still, Farr best captures the reality of political science's relationship with civic education, arguing the "Association's [APSA's] identification with public pedagogy" has been "fitful and episodic."[72] Ishiyama et al. explain why this is the case, noting "The structure of incentives in the discipline mitigates against pursuit of educational issues in the APSA."[73] With political science's complete buy in to the German university model where career advancement is driven almost exclusively by scientific research, civic education has little traction.

In the area of civic education and engagement, the history of APSA and political science closely parallels the ups and downs in formal civic education in the United States. In the early

1900s APSA clearly espoused an interest in civics just as was common in the country. This led to innovative curricular and experiential learning in schools at all levels that enhanced formal civic education. However, by the 1930s this civic orientation began to wane in APSA and the United States. Because of the increasingly politicized nature of civic education by the mid-1900s and the growing popularity of the German research model in higher education, most political scientists (as well as other academic disciplines) readily turned their focus to scholarship, not citizenship training, to secure their legitimacy and authority. While the political apathy, illiteracy, and disengagement of the late twentieth century cannot solely be attributed to political science's inward turn, political scientists have not done their part to counter such developments. The question is this: Will political scientists learn from their past and choose to be a force advocating and promoting a robust civic ecology in the twenty-first century, or are political scientists going to repeat the past failures in this area?

PART II: CIVIC EDUCATION—A COMPLEX INTERPLAY OF CIVIC LITERACY AND CIVIC ENGAGEMENT

Political theorists have long posited the importance of civic education and civic engagement. In fact, in the Western tradition such arguments are at least as old as Plato, who advocated a rigorous civic instruction of the guardian class.[74] Plato's student, Aristotle, equally valued civic education but added an emphasis on the importance of civic participation.[75] It was inevitable that these arguments for civic education and civic engagement would merge. Yet, too few scholars have explored their interplay directly.[76]

When exploring the interplay of civic education and engagement, three political thinkers stand out in the history of Western political thought. French theorists Jean-Jacques Rousseau and Alexis de Tocqueville and the English philosopher John Stuart Mill all suggest an interaction between civic education and engagement, arguing one can lead to the other and that increases in one can strengthen or promote the other.[77] Combined, the arguments of such political thinkers provide a rich formulation of the dynamics of civic education that begs for empirical verification. For example, Plato and Aristotle suggest an important role for a formal civic curriculum in laying the foundation.[78] Their emphasis on a rigorous civic education posits a basic level of civic literacy or knowledge is needed for effective participation (or leadership in Plato's case) in the regime.[79] Then, while Plato's and Aristotle's curriculum seems primarily instruction based, Rousseau encourages a similar formalized civic education with his work *Emile*, although one important qualification is needed. Rousseau's formalized civic education was as much experiential as it was instructional or bookish.[80] Rousseau's innovation is picked up by both Tocqueville and Mill. Tocqueville suggests political engagement may be what first draws citizens into the civic education dynamic and then can lead to more diverse forms of civic engagement.[81] Mill adds that civic engagement is itself civically educational.[82] Combining these works in a theoretical formulation of civic education shows the complex interplay of cross-cutting and reinforcing tendencies between civic literacy or political knowledge and civic engagement or political participation.

Does empirical research confirm or refute this theoretical formulation? Empirical research confirms the complexity of the civic education dynamic. For example, not all civic education leads to civic or political participation, just as not all civic engagement leads to increased knowledge of politics.[83] To date, academics have been assembling a fair understanding of civic education, civic literacy, and civic engagement, but less research is dedicated to the dynamic interplay of all three.

CIVIC LITERACY THROUGH CIVIC EDUCATION

Civic education entails increasing a citizen's comprehension (knowledge dimension), skills (ability dimension), and aptitudes (affective dimension) to engage in politics and political systems.[84] For democracy, the goal is to produce a citizenry more engaged and effective at self-government.[85]

An essential pillar in the civic education dynamic is civic literacy or political knowledge. A certain level of basic knowledge of and skills in politics seems necessary to enable a citizen to participate and be effective in (self-)government.[86] Three findings stand out in the area of civic literacy:

1. Additional levels of education, if not additional civic courses, improves civic literacy;
2. Civic literacy is low and has seen no significant change at an aggregate level for over the last half decade; and
3. There is a pronounced civics gap.

First, scholars have long known that increased educational levels result in increased civic literacy.[87] Second, two seminal studies of civic literacy, one at the collegiate level (Delli Carpini and Keeter) and one at the high school level (Niemi and Junn), establish that—contrary to popular belief that political knowledge has declined—civic literacy has not significantly changed in over half a century.[88] These fundamental findings have withstood repeated tests over time. However, current research on civic literacy has been producing a major revision in this literature. The belief since the mid-1900s that taking additional courses specifically in civics has no effect on civic knowledge has been called into question. In the 1960s, Langton and Jennings popularized this conclusion, offering as explanation the redundancy theory. They argued that additional civic courses are just redundant, no better than attempts to add more water to an already saturated sponge.[89] If their argument is correct, the low civic literacy of Americans for over half a century, which has shown no real change in overall levels even as the number of civic courses declined from three to one civic course in public schools, means Americans have a very low saturation ceiling, so low in fact that any additional civic courses are redundant.[90]

While the redundancy theory was the conventional scientific understanding for the twentieth century, research over the last few decades have called it into question. Delli Carpini and Keeter as well as Niemi and Junn find evidence that additional instruction in civics can result in higher levels of civic literacy. While the increase is not much—only about 2% for twelfth graders who have completed a civic course over those who have not—there is growth from a civic course.[91] Similarly, Gooch and I have also consistently found a course in civics has a significant impact on civic literacy, at least in the short term. Through a pretest and posttest of college students in American government courses taught at our universities, we consistently find that—regardless of teacher—one college civic course typically raises our students' civic literacy scores from percentages in the mid-40s to just passing in the low 60s. We may be disappointed that the posttest scores are not higher, but our findings consistently demonstrate that an additional civic course matters.[92]

As pointed out previously, civics coverage in secondary school has declined from a norm of three courses to just one today. Likely, the scholarly popularity of the redundancy theory contributed to this civics decline. However, today there is some resurgence in states in the minimal requirements of civics in high schools.[93] Still, the norm of requiring one civic course at most in secondary schools and the lack of a collegiate requirement for most states today means Americans' exposure to civics is not as rigorous as it was with the 1960s three-course sequence. During this time of declining civics coverage, Niemi and Junn found through studies of the high school level and Delli Carpini and Keeter as well as Gooch and I have found at the collegiate level that civic literacy is improved in statistically significant ways by specific courses in civics. Given the consistency of these more recent studies, the civic literacy literature is overdue in declaring the redundancy theory inadequate.

Drawing on a corollary argument in Langton and Jennings, as well as Niemi and Junn's discussion of the importance of exposure, Gooch and I suggest the exposure theory in place of the redundancy theory as a better explanation of the impact of civic courses on civic literacy. After comparing the civic literacy of Caucasians and African Americans and finding a racial civics gap, Langton and Jennings suggest that individuals with the least exposure to civics benefit the most from additional civic courses.[94] First, it should be noted that research today continues to find a civics gap. This civics gap in political knowledge persists not just between African Americans and Caucasians but also Latinos. Such gaps between races seem to carry over in the area of civic engagement as well.[95] Second, it seems fair to conclude Langton and Jennings did not give the civics gap finding enough weight. If additional civic courses matter for some groups, they likely matter for all. There must be some intervening variable causing the difference. The exposure theory is an improvement over the redundancy theory because it not only asks *how much* one is exposed to civics. It also asks *how often* one is exposed to the materials and puts the emphasis on the latter as opposed to the former. It does not assume redundancy starts instantaneously or quickly but is derivative of how much exposure and repetition occurs over time.

The exposure theory acknowledges that the benefits of more civic courses may result in a declining impact on civic literacy at an increasing rate, particularly if they are taken one after another repeatedly. However, that effect depends on *how often* or the spacing between these courses in one's education and life, as well as how much other factors (like the media) promote and reinforce such education. When civic courses are spaced apart, the exposure theory posits an additional civic course will have a more positive impact on political literacy. While redundancy assumes additional courses have no effect, the exposure theory posits a more complex relationship. Additional civic courses do not mean there is no impact on civic knowledge, just that as exposure increases the impact gets smaller and smaller. There may even be a saturation or redundancy point, especially if the same content is repeated in each additional civic course in rapid succession. However, there has yet to be an empirical study that adequately tests how civic course spacing and the varying of subjects covered (e.g., state politics as opposed to just more national politics) in each additional civic course affects civic literacy. The growth in political literacy may continue with additional courses, although at a decreasing rate, and may even hit a saturation point where no further growth is possible.

Simply put, an exploration of the civic literacy literature shows that a number of issues need further exploration. Scholars need to test and develop a better understanding of how additional courses in civics affect civic literacy (test the exposure theory), and we need to continue to explore if the affect varies by demographic groups (test for the civics gap). Maybe Langton and Jennings were seeing redundancy because three civic courses is the saturation point for most Americans. However, maybe it was because the courses were too similar in coverage. What if the first course is American government and the second state and local government? What affect does that have on civic literacy? Is it different by demographic group? For assessment purposes and to enhance its legitimacy in the curriculum, the discipline of political science needs to know what the added value of each additional civic course is in public schools and colleges. Scholarship also needs to establish if the added value decreases at an increasing rate and how quickly. Is the decline rapid or slow for each additional course? Then, how does the sequence and spacing of civic courses affect civic literacy?[96] If too far apart, how much civic literacy is lost? If too close together, does redundancy make additional courses inconsequential? Finally, how does pedagogy affect civic literacy? Much of the SoTL research has explained how pedagogy can affect civic engagement. The focus has been less on how pedagogies affect civic literacy, which is something education has been studying for a long time.

THE NEED FOR MULTIDISCIPLINARY RESEARCH OF CIVIC ENGAGEMENT

Like civic literacy, civic engagement is an essential pillar in the civic education dynamic. Also like civic literacy, it needs a comprehensive definition that encompasses the diverse activities that signify civic engagement. Since the introduction of this book rigorously defines civic engagement, here it is only necessary to raise some tensions and challenges that exist between civic engagement and civic literacy when it comes to civic education.[97] In the following text, it is argued that in the future interdisciplinary research on civic education is needed. Scholars of various disciplines have already made significant contributions to the civic literacy or the civic engagement literatures.

However, future work needs to promote the interplay of these two literatures more, to investigate the tensions and challenges between civic and/or political engagement and civic literacy.

To highlight some tensions between civic engagement and civic literacy, it is first worthwhile to note David Campbell's important point that scholars need to distinguish between civic engagement and political engagement. As he explains, civic engagement is more "duty-driven" and may incorporate political engagement activities. Political engagement, thus, is a subset or one type of the former and reflects more of a "political motivation." Political engagement typically entails either promoting a particular policy or defending a personal political interest or right.[98] As scholars gained a better understanding of civic and political engagement, new questions have emerged. Does civic education as currently practiced promote civic engagement, political engagement, or both? How does pedagogy affect each or both? As will be explained next, SoTL research (often from psychologists and sociologists, not political scientists) is just beginning to explore such issues.

Too often, scholars miss such tensions by conflating civic and political engagement. Peter Levine, a sociologist, gives an operationalized definition of civic engagement that includes the following variables: community participation, political engagement, and political voice.[99] While conceptions like Levine's that embed political engagement in civic engagement are generally functional, such definitions may create conceptual problems that hamper scholarly advancements in our knowledge of civic education. For example, one finding by psychologists is that some civic engagement—most notably volunteering in the community—does not necessarily yield any increase in political knowledge or engagement.[100] How are scholars who conflate civic and political engagement likely to account for this if they treat the two terms interchangeably? By using the terms interchangeably, one would create the conceptual problem of having the same variable on both sides of the equation, as the dependent and an independent variable. Simply put, current scholarship has not adequately modeled or explained the complicated civic education process, particularly the relationships between civic literacy and civic and political engagement. In our work, Gooch and I have made significant revisions and increased the complexity of each civic education model used in our studies of how one course in American government can affect political knowledge and civic engagement.

Being late to the SoTL movement, political science needs to engage in interdisciplinary work as we investigate the relationship between civic literacy and civic and political engagement. For one, it is by no means original to argue that social studies is a collaborative, interdisciplinary endeavor. For example, Ahmad claims, "Material from other social sciences, such as history, economics, psychology, political sociology, and anthropology, provide insight on … citizenship education. Therefore, ideally, citizenship education has to be interdisciplinary and multidisciplinary; it must borrow materials from all social sciences."[101] What needs to be added to Ahmad's observation is that—since political science is late to the SoTL movement—we should not reinvent the wheel but work with and build on the decades of civics research of our sister academic disciplines (education, history, psychology, and sociology). We need to bring our unique perspective and expertise in politics to give new eyes to what these disciplines have already discovered and know. Then, interdisciplinary research is needed to enhance the scholarly knowledge of civic engagement because a number of the areas of focus in the civic engagement literature—areas like political socialization, civic identity formation, and social capital production—are all inherently interdisciplinary literatures. As is demonstrated next, psychologists and sociologists have made contributions to these research areas that are just as significant as those of political scientists.

INTERPLAY OF POLITICAL SOCIALIZATION, CIVIC IDENTITY, AND SOCIAL CAPITAL

For one example of the need for interdisciplinary research, consider the political socialization literature, which has recently seen a resurgence with the twenty-first century. In the mid-1900s, this research established the important role socialization plays in the likelihood that children grow up to become politically active and engaged citizens. Political socialization research has long established how factors like family, school through peers, religion, and political discussion (among others) influence civic engagement. David Campbell provides a good overview of political socialization research. He notes the early research from scholars like David Easton and Jack Dennis focused on preadolescence as the critical age for civic education. Campbell also explains that later research (like Jennings and Neimi) argued adolescence is the key time for the development of civic and political attitudes. He then explains that political socialization research is seeing a revival in interest, particularly for how the environment plays an important role in influencing civic engagement by citizens.[102] More accurately, Lonnie Sherrod et al. argue that the 1960s and 1970s saw "*waves of attention*" or "surges of research on civic engagement or political socialization." They conclude that the 1990s represented another wave that has resulted in the coming of age in the field of youth civic engagement.[103]

It is no coincidence that this revival in interest comes at the same time that a widespread public concern about a civic crisis emerged in the country. Such concern helped produce at the beginning of this century the coming of age of political socialization research. The political socialization literature now boasts achievements such as the *Handbook of Research on Civic Engagement in Youth* (*HRCEY*) in 2010. This book pulls together psychologists, sociologists, and political scientists in a study of youth political development and engagement. It epitomizes the potential interdisciplinary research can have for civic engagement. As just one example, in 2007 psychologists McIntosh et al. explain how cognitive developmental theory is an alternative to political science's traditional political socialization argument and highlights many limitations in the latter.[104] These psychologists have enhanced our political socialization literature by giving a much denser understanding of the process. They encourage us to question if family and schools are as powerful of incubators of political activity and engagement as the political socialization posits. Instead, McIntosh et al. emphasize civic engagement is more complex, not just the result of cognitive and affective dynamics; the process is also behavioral and tied to the public and political sphere. Their point is civic and political engagement develops not as an individual process in one family or school, but as a social process occurring through diverse youth collaborations, whether it is physically and voluntarily in group environments or verbally through collective political discussions. It is not just any family or school that promotes political socialization. It is highly dependent on the type of society, the values and makeup of society, and the likelihood of it creating routinely important cognitive developmental opportunities at the right times for youth political engagement to develop and become behavioral.[105]

Similar to this, Conover and Searing explain how psychologists have made political scientists more cognizant of the need to understand "how students develop a sense of citizenship (civic identities and understandings), political tolerance, and the ability to deliberate." Through cross-disciplinary research, they argue political scientists can advance our understanding of the reinforcing patterns of behavior of civicness, that is, "in the case of students, the question becomes are they developing lifelong patterns of political discussion, staying informed, and being tolerant in the ways that can sustain a full practice of citizenship?"[106] The literature on civic identity shows a reciprocal relationship between civic identity formation and civic participation and engagement. Thus, political socialization, a traditionally political science and sociology literature, becomes intertwined with civic identity formation, largely a research focus of psychologists. In fact, the psychologist Heather Malin goes so far as to suggest the civic woes in America today are fundamentally a result of the youth civic identity crisis.[107] The point is political science has much to learn from psychology on political identity formation. Yet, sociologists and political scientists likely have something to contribute to psychologists on how these individual identities morph through socialization into group identities that make political and civic activities and engagement possible and common.

It is also important to note an important advancement in civic education and engagement research occurred in the 1990s and early 2000s through interdisciplinary work. Political scientists and sociologists came together to advance research on social capital. Putnam is up front in acknowledging his debt to sociology for his social capital arguments.[108] Since his publication of *Bowling Alone*, social capital has been one of the leading research areas for both political science and sociology. In fact, Ben Fine notes Putnam became the most cited scholar across the social sciences in the 1990s and only globalism seemed to receive more attention as a research focus.[109] Social capital is likely to have a central place in investigations of civic engagement in the future, as it shows how norms like reciprocity and trust, as well as bridging and bonding social capital, are all ingredients of a healthy civic ecology.[110]

Through interdisciplinary research among psychologists, sociologists, and political scientists, there is good reason to expect the next few decades will produce major breakthroughs in our academic understanding of how the interplay of political socialization, civic identity formation, and social capital production all affect civic education and engagement. While not dealing with youth civic engagement per se, a promising example of a fruitful synthesis worth mimicking in the future is Nick Hopkins's work on how minority Muslim religious group identities, which are usually seen as undermining social cohesion, can achieve civic integration in the proper social capital environments.[111] Also, there is Ahnlee and Hyunhee's article exploring how the "situational cultural identity" of young Korean Americans represents an intersection of cultural identity and social capital.[112] Such works are not found in political science journals or even through the traditional JSTOR search methods of political scientists. Yet, such social psychology offers a promising convergence of social capital with identity investigations. Overall, these examples suggest the benefits political scientists can reap by lowering the barriers dividing us from our social science colleagues.

CONCLUSION

In conclusion, political science should follow the strategy of influential and effective interest groups; political scientists need to be the information experts on civic education as well as a point of first contact on such subjects if our discipline is to emerge as a central force in the fight for enhanced civic education and engagement in the twenty-first century. Having emerged from our disciplinary cocoon, political science is well-poised to become the information expert in the teaching and understanding of the civic education and engagement processes. Through interdisciplinary research into the interplay of civic literacy, political socialization, identity formation, and social capital production, political science can be a primary resource to government and community agencies interested in addressing the civic education crisis. By seeking to be a part of all government and community organizations' discussions of civic education and engagement, the discipline can do something it largely avoided for much of the twentieth century: it can be a driving force promoting a more vibrant civic ecology in the twenty-first century.

However, like powerful interest groups, political scientists should not pursue this goal alone. Interdisciplinary research should be leveraged to promote cross-disciplinary advocacy of civic education and engagement. Sometimes, the social sciences undermine our voice by competing with each other. When it comes to promoting the revival of civic education and engagement in the United States, political science needs to exercise our coalition building skills and renew alliances with our fellow social studies disciplines to promote civics. The coalition building should branch out from there to other like-minded entities (including civics teachers, state and federal government agencies, think tanks, and nonprofits organizations.), as we build an issue network advocating enhanced civic education at all levels—primary, secondary, and collegiate. ∎

ENDNOTES

1. James Farr, "The Science of Politics—as Civic Education—Then and Now," *PS: Political Science & Politics* 37, no. 1 (2004): p. 39.

2. Elinor Ostrom, "Civic Education for the Next Century: A Task Force to Initiate Professional Activity," *PS: Political Science & Politics* 29, no. 4 (1996); APSA, "Task Force to Set Agenda for Civic Education Program," *PS: Political Science & Politics* 30, no. 4 (1997); APSA, "Apsa Task Force on Civic Education in the 21st Century: Expanded Articulation Statement: A Call for Reactions and Contributions," *PS: Political Science & Politics* 31, no. 3 (1998).

3. Michael X. Delli Carpini and Scott Keeter, *What Americans Know About Politics and Why It Matters* (New Haven, CT: Yale University Press, 1996); Richard G. Niemi and Jane Junn, *Civic Education: What Makes Students Learn?* (New Haven, CT: Yale University Press, 1998). For more recent studies of civic literacy, see Richard G. Niemi and Julia Smith, "Enrollments in High School Government Classes: Are We Short-Changing Both Citizenship and Political Science Training?," *PS: Political Science & Politics* 34, no. 2 (2001); Henry Milner, *Civic Literacy: How Informed Citizens Make Democracy Work* (London: University Press of New England, 2002); ISI, "The Coming Crisis in Citizenship" (Willimington, DE: Intercollegiate Studies Institute's National Civic Literacy Board, 2006); ISI, "Failing Our Students, Failing America: Holding Colleges Accountable for Teaching America's History and Institutions" (Willmington, DE: Intercollegiate Studies Institute's National Civic Literacy Board, 2007); ISI, "Our Fading Heritage: Americans Fail a Basic Test on Their History and Institutions" (Wilmington, DE: Intercollegiate Studies Institute's National Civic Literacy Board, 2008); Donald M. Gooch and Michael T. Rogers, "A Natural Disaster of Civic Proportions: College Students in the Natural State Falls Short of the Naturalization Benchmark," *Midsouth Political Science Review* 13, no. 1 (2012); Donald M. Gooch and Michael T. Rogers, "Dude, Where's the Civic Engagement? The Paradoxical Effect of Civic Educaon on the Probablity of Civic Participation," in *Civic Education in the Twenty-First Century: A Multidimensional Approach*, ed. Michael T. Rogers and Donald M. Gooch (Lanham, MD: Lexington Books, 2015).

4. See Robert Putnam, *Making Democracy Work: Civic Traditions in Modern Italy* (Princeton, NJ: Princeton University Press, 1993); Robert Putnam, "Bowling Alone: America's Declining Social Capital," *Journal of Democracy* 6, no. 1 (June 1995); Robert Putnam, "Tuning in, Tuning Out: The Strange Disappearance of Social Capital in America," *PS: Political Science & Politics* 28, no. 4 (Dec. 1995); Robert Putnam, *Bowling Alone: The Collapse and Revival of the American Community* (New York: Simon and Schuster, 2000); Robert Putnam, "Community-Based Social Capital and Education Performance," in *Making Good Citizens: Education and Civil Society*, ed. Diane Ravitch and Joseph P. Viteritti (New Haven: Yale University Press, 2001).

   For a discussion of works beyond the social capital argument contributing to this dismal portrait of civics at the end the twentieth century, see Michael T. Rogers, "A Civic Education Crisis," *Midsouth Political Science Review* 13, no. 1 (2012).

5. Michael T. Rogers, "A Meta-History of Formal Civic Education: An Episodic History to Be Repeated?" in *Civic Education in the 21st Century: A Multidimensional Inquiry*, ed. Michael T. Rogers and Donald M. Gooch (Lanham, MD: Lexington Books, 2015). For an explanation of what I mean by meta-history (versus micro-history), see 4–5.

6. Michael X. Delli Carpini and Scott Keeter, *What Americans Know About Politics and Why It Matters* (New Haven, CT: Yale University Press, 1996); Richard G. Niemi and Jane Junn, *Civic Education: What Makes Students Learn?* (New Haven: Yale University Press, 1998); Stephen Macedo et al., *Democracy at Risk: How Political Choices Undermine Citizen Participation, and What We Can Do About It* (Washington, DC: Brookings Institution Press, 2005); Robert Putnam, "Bowling Alone: America's Declining Social Capital," *Journal of Democracy* 6, no. 1 (1995); Robert Putnam, *Bowling Alone: The Collapse and Revival of the American Community* (New York: Simon and Schuster, 2000).

7. For my explanation of the difference between informal and formal civic education, see Rogers, "A Civic Education Crisis," 2–5.

8. For evidence of this, see Claire Snyder, "Should Political Scientists Have a Civic Mission? An Overview of the Historical Evidence," *PS: Political Science & Politics* 34, no. 2 (2001); Hindy Lauer Schacter, "Civic Education: Three Early American Political Science Association Committees and Their Relevance for Our Times," *PS: Political Science & Politics* 31, no. 3 (1998). For a more diverse perspective on the founding of APSA and the *American Political Science Review*, see the "Thematic Issue on the Evolution of Political Science, in Recognition of the Centennial of the *Review*" *American Political Science Review* 100, no. 4 (November 2006). In particular, see John G. Gunnell, "The Founding of the American Political Science Association: Discipline, Profession, Political Theory, and Politics," *American Political Science Review* 100, no. 4 (2006).

9. Iftikhar Ahmad, "Teaching Government in the Social Studies: Political Scientists' Contributions to Citizenship Education," *The Social Studies* 97, no. 1 (2006): 8.

10. Richard M. Battistoni, "Should Political Scienctists Care About Civic Education?" *Perspective on Politics* 11, no. 4 (2013): p. 1138.

11. Rogers, "A Meta-History of Formal Civic Education: An Episodic History to Be Repeated?" 16–18.

12. For a good introduction to the origins of political science, see Gunnell, "The Founding of the American Political Science Association: Discipline, Profession, Political Theory, and Politics."

13. Snyder, "Should Political Scientists Have a Civic Mission? An Overview of the Historical Evidence," 303–4.

14. Ahmad, "Teaching Government in the Social Studies: Political Scientists' Contributions to Citizenship Education," 9.

15. Both of these programs were by nature civically-oriented, see James Farr, "The Science of Politics—as Civic Education—Then and Now," *PS: Political Science & Politics* 37, no. 1 (2004): 37.

16. He also notes the more negative side of this—that it was done within the backdrop of racism, sexism, and Northern superiority over the Southern states. See ibid., 38.

17. Sheilah Mann, "Political Scientists Examine Civics Standards: An Introduction," *PS: Political Science & Politics* 29, no. 1 (1996): 48.

18. Ahmad, "Teaching Government in the Social Studies: Political Scientists' Contributions to Citizenship Education," 11.

19. Mann, "Political Scientists Examine Civics Standards: An Introduction," 48.

20. Schacter, "Civic Education: Three Early American Political Science Association Committees and Their Relevance for Our Times," 631–32.

21. Stephen Leonard, "'Pure Futility and Waste': Academic Political Science and Civic Education," *PS: Political Science & Politics* 32, no. 4 (1999): 750.

22. Ibid., 749. The APSA's interest in political science being recognized as a legitimate, scientific profession of the academy is also a pronounced feature of Gunnell, "The Founding of the American Political Science Association: Discipline, Profession, Political Theory, and Politics."

23. Rogers, "A Meta-History of Formal Civic Education: An Episodic History to Be Repeated?" 18–21.

24. Leonard, "'Pure Futility and Waste': Academic Political Science and Civic Education."

25. To be exact, the conventional view that arises is that civic courses do not increase civic literacy but additional education in general does. The work that popularizes this norm is K. Langton and M. K. Jennings, "Political Socialization and the High School Civics Curriculum in the United States," *American Political Science Review* 62(1968). However, research over the last few decades has increasingly called this view into question. See Don Gooch and Michael T. Rogers, "A Natural Disaster of Civic Proportions: College Students in the Natural State Falls Short of the Naturalization Benchmark," *Midsouth Political Science Review* 13, no. 1 (2012); Michael Delli Carpini and Scott Keeter, *What Americans Know About Politics and Why It Matters* (New Haven: Yale University Press, 1996); Richard G. Niemi and Jane Junn, *Civic Education: What Makes Students Learn* (New Haven: Yale University Press, 1998).

26. Richard G. Niemi and Julia Smith, "Enrollment in High School Government Classes: Are We Short-Changing Citizenship and Political Science Training?" *PS: Political Science & Politics* 34, no. 2 (2001), p. 282 (TABLE 1).

27. APSA Committee on Instruction in Political Science, "The Study of Civics," *The American Political Science Review* 16, no. 1 (1922): 118.

28. Ibid.

29. For an alternative, but no less scathing formulation of political science's minimalist and problematic traditional approach to civic education, see Ahmad, "Teaching Government in the Social Studies: Political Scientists' Contributions to Citizenship Education."

30. Gunnell has written extensively on the origins and history of political science, particularly the transition from the German statism paradigm dominant during the origin of the distinct academic discipline to its adoption of the new pluralism in the 1920s and 1930s. In particular, see John G. Gunnell, "The Real Revolution in Political Science," *PS: Political Science & Politics* 37, no. 1 (2004). See also John G. Gunnell, "Political Science on the Cusp: Recovering a Discipline's Past," *The American Political Science Review* 99, no. 4 (2005); Gunnell, "The Founding of the American Political Science Association: Discipline, Profession, Political Theory, and Politics." For other discussions of this transition in the discipline of political science, see John S. Dryzek, "Revolutions without Enemies: Key Transformations in Political Science," *American Political Science Review* 100, no. 4 (2006); Bernard Crick, *The American Science of Politics: Its Origins and Conditions* (Berkeley: University of California Press, 1967).

31. Gunnell, "Political Science on the Cusp: Recovering a Discipline's Past," 598.

32. Robert Maranto, "It Can Work: The Surprisingly Positive Prospects for Effective Civic Education," in *Civic Education in the Twenty-First Century: A Multidimensional Inquiry*, ed. Michael T. Rogers and Donald M. Gooch (Lanham: Lexington Books, 2015); Jeffrey D. Hilmer, "The Irony of Civic Education in the United States," in *Civic Education in the Twenty-First Century: A Multidimensional Inquiry*, ed. Michael T. Rogers and Donald M. Gooch (Lanham: Lexington Books, 2015).

33. Gary Bugh, "Models of Civic Education in America," in *Civic Education in the Twenty-First Century: A Multidimensional Inquiry*, ed. Michael T. Rogers and Donald M. Gooch (Lanham: Lexington Books, 2015).

34. Rogers, "A Meta-History of Formal Civic Education: An Episodic History to Be Repeated?." As an alternative discussion of the politicization of civic education, see the symposium discussion in the April 2004 edition of *PS: Political Science & Politics*. In particular, see Joel Westheimer, "Introduction—the Politics of Civic Education," *PS: Political Science & Politics* 37, no. 2 (2004); E. Wayne Ross, "Negotiating the Politics of Citizenship Education," *PS: Political Science & Politics* 37, no. 2 (2004).

35. Leonard, "'Pure Futility and Waste': Academic Political Science and Civic Education." See also Anne Colby et al., *Educating Citizens: Preparing America's Undergraduates for Lives of Moral and Civic Responsibility* (San Francisco: The Carnegie

Foundation for the Advancement of Teaching, 2003); Snyder, "Should Political Scientists Have a Civic Mission? An Overview of the Historical Evidence."

36. Leonard, "'Pure Futility and Waste': Academic Political Science and Civic Education," 751.

37. For example, Leonard explains the next committee after the 1930 one to address civic education is the 1951 APSA Committee for the Advancement of Teaching. He argues it was the first to do so in over two decades and last for many years after, and its conclusions were an endorsement of the status quo, not a revival in the civic mission of the discipline. See ibid., 753.

38. She draws this conclusion based on the APSA report of the Committee on Pre-Collegiate Education. See Mann, "Political Scientists Examine Civics Standards: An Introduction," 48–49. See also, John Ishiyama, Marijke Breuning, and Linda Lopez, "A Century of Continuity and (Little) Change in the Undergraduate Political Science Curriculum," *American Political Science Review* 100, no. 4 (2006): 662.

39. Ahmad, "Teaching Government in the Social Studies: Political Scientists' Contributions to Citizenship Education," 11.

40. Stephen Earl Bennett, "The Past Need Not Be Prologue: Why Pessimissism About Civic Education Is Premature," *PS: Political Science & Politics* 32, no. 4 (1999).

41. Niemi and Smith, "Enrollments in High School Government Classes: Are We Short-Changing Both Citizenship and Political Science Training?" 281.

42. Langton and Jennings, "Political Socialization and the High School Civics Curriculum in the United States."

43. Ahmad, "Teaching Government in the Social Studies: Political Scientists' Contributions to Citizenship Education," 12.

44. Mary A. Hepburn, "Improving Political Science Education in the Schools: College School Connections," *PS* 20, no. 3 (1987): 691.

45. Ibid., 691–92.

46. Ibid., 692.

47. Ibid., 692–96. She is not alone in lamenting teacher training. For example, see Bruce Cole, "American Amnesia," in *Civic Education and the Future of American Citizenship*, ed. Elizabeth Kaufer Busch and Jonathan W. White (Lanham: Lexington Books, 2013).

48. Mann, "Political Scientists Examine Civics Standards: An Introduction," 47. Mann is not the only author to claim such obstacles to civic education and engagement in political science. Macedo et al. acknowledge the diversity of views in the discipline as well, see Stephen Macedo et al., *Democracy at Risk: How Political Choices Undermine Citizen Participation, and What We Can Do About It* (Washington, DC: Brookings Institution Press, 2005), 16. For the lack of reward incentives for such activities, see Susan Hunter and Richard A. Brisbin Jr., "Civic Education and Political Science: A Survey of Practices," *PS: Political Science & Politics* 36, no. 4 (2003); Ishiyama, Marijke, and Lopez, "A Century of Continuity and (Little) Change in the Undergraduate Political Science Curriculum."

49. Hepburn, "Improving Political Science Education in the Schools: College School Connections," 696.

50. APSA Committee on Education 1991–1993, "Apsa Guidelines for Teacher Training: Recommendations for Certifying Precollegiate Teachers of Civics, Government, and Social Studies," *PS: Political Science & Politics* 27, no. 2 (1994).

51. Ostrom, "Civic Education for the Next Century: A Task Force to Initiate Professional Activity."

52. See Putnam, "Bowling Alone: America's Declining Social Capital"; Robert Putnam, "Tuning in, Tuning Out: The Strange Disappearance of Social Capital in America," *PS: Political Science & Politics* 28, no. 4 (Dec. 1995). For discussion of the perceived civic education crisis among scholars and media, see Rogers, "Introduction: A Tocqueville-Inspired Assessment of America's Twenty-First Century Civic Ecology"; Rogers, "A Civic Education Crisis."

53. Niemi and Smith, "Enrollments in High School Government Classes: Are We Short-Changing Both Citizenship and Political Science Training?"; Kenneth Stroupe Jr. and Larry Sabato, "Politics: The Missing Link of Responsible Education," University of Virginia Center for Politics, http://www.centerforpolitics.org/downloads/civicengagement-stroupe-final.pdf; Rogers, "A Civic Education Crisis." For state civic mandates at the collegiate level, see Karen Kedrowski, "Civid Education by Mandate: A State-by-State Analysis," *PS: Political Science & Politics* 36, no. 2 (2003).

54. Niemi and Smith, "Enrollments in High School Government Classes: Are We Short-Changing Both Citizenship and Political Science Training?" 281–82.

55. For a critical discussions of the way political scientists teach civics, see Hindy Lauer Schachter, "Civic Education: Three Early American Political Science Association Committees and Their Relevance for Our Times," *PS: Political Science & Politics* 31, no. 3 (1998): 634. For a good summary of political science education in the history of the discipline, see Ishiyama, Breuning, and Lopez, "A Century of Continuity and (Little) Change in the Undergraduate Political Science Curriculum."

For works questioning teacher training and quality, see Keith C. Barton, "Expanding Prospective Teachers' Images of Self, Students, and Democracy," in *Making Civics Count: Citizenship Education for a New Generation*, ed. David E. Campbell, Meira Levinson, and Frederick M. Hess (Cambridge, MA: Harvard Education Press, 2012); Pamela Johnson Conover and Donald D. Searing, "A Political Socialization Perpsective," in *Rediscovering the Democratic Purposes of Education*, ed. Lorraine M. McDonnell, P. Michael Timpane, and Roger Benjamin (Lawrence: University of Kansas Press, 2000); Sandra Day O'Connor, "The Democratic Purpose of Education: From the Founders to Horace Mann to Today," in *Teaching America: The Case for Civic Education*, ed. David Feith (Lanham, MD: Rowman & Littlefield Education, 2011); Eugene Hickok, "Civic Literacy and No Child Left Behind," in *Teaching America: The Case for Civic Education*, ed. David Feith (Lanham, MD: Rowman & Littlefield Education, 2011); Bennett, "The Past Need Not Be Prologue: Why Pessimissism About Civic Education Is Premature."

For works criticizing the quality of textbooks, see Wilfred M. McClay, "Memory and Sacrifice in the Formation of Civic Consciousness," in *Civic Education and the Future of American Citizenship*, ed. Elizabeth Kaufer Busch and Jonathan W. White (Lanham, MD: Lexington Books, 2013); Cole, "American Amnesia." Most of these are simply discipline specific arguments reflective of the general thesis of Diane Ravitch, *The Language Police: How Pressure Groups Restrict What Students Learn* (New York: Alfred A. Knopf, 2004).

56. Rogers, "A Meta-History of Formal Civic Education: An Episodic History to Be Repeated?" 23–25.

57. Richard M. Battistoni, "Should Political Scienctists Care About Civic Education?," *Perspective on Politics* 11, no. 4 (2013): 1137.

58. Thomas Ehrlich, "Civic Education: Lessons Learned," *PS: Political Science & Politics* 32, no. 2 (1999); Tobi Walker, "Service as a Pathway to Political Participation: What Research Tells Us," *Applied Development Science* 6, no. 4 (2002); James Youniss, "How to Enrich Civic Education and Sustain Democracy," in *Making Civics Count: Citizenship Education for a New Generation*, ed. David E. Campbell, Meira Levinson, and Frederick M. Hess (Cambridge: Harvard Education Press, 2012).

59. J. Cherie Strachan and Elizabeth A. Bennion, "Consortium for Inter-Campus SoTL Research National Survey of Student Leaders: Arkansas Tech University Report," (2015), 383. For a similar summary, see Battistoni, "Should Political Scienctists Care About Civic Education?"

60. As of January 2017, APSA replaced the section as the sponsor of the journal.

61. Strachan and Bennion, "Consortium for Inter-Campus SoTL Research National Survey of Student Leaders: Arkansas Tech University Report," 383. (Italics added to original for emphasis)

62. The University of Central Florida consistently comes up as a top preference for SoTL resources and information through simple Google searches and it conveniently lists journals by discipline, which is why I chose it for this analysis of the SoTL history of academic disciplines for social studies.

63. If the criteria is the journal *solely* publishes SoTL research, political science only has one journal as this eliminates *PS* and *Perspectives on Politics* from our discipline's list.

64. "About the Organization," Society for History Education, Inc., http://www.societyforhistoryeducation.org/about.html.

65. HistorySOTL, "About the Society," HistorySOTL, http://www.indiana.edu/~histsotl/blog/?page_id=6.

66. "*Teaching of Psychology*: Offical Journal of the Society for the Teaching of Psychology," Society for the Teaching of Psychology, http://teachpsych.org/top/index.php.

67. ASA, "Journals Print Advertising," American Sociological Association, http://www.asanet.org/journals/print_advertising.cfm.

68. Barry Checkoway, "Renewing the Civic Missions of the American Research University," *The Journal of Higher Education* 72, no. 1 (2001).

69. "Planning Our Future: The Report of the American Politcial Science Association's Strategic Planning Committee," *PS: Political Science & Politics* 33, no. 4 (2000): 880; APSA, "About Apsa," American Political Science Association, http://www.apsanet.org/ABOUT/About-APSA.

70. See Ostrom, "Civic Education for the Next Century: A Task Force to Initiate Professional Activity"; Lief Carter and Jean Elshtain, "Task Force on Civic Education Statement of Purpose," *PS: Political Science & Politics* 30, no. 4 (1997); "Task Force to Set Agenda for Civic Education Program," *PS: Political Science & Politics* 30, no. 4 (1997). For a work summarizing and questioning its accomplishments, see Melvin J. Dubnick, "Nurturing Civic Lives: Developmental Perspectives on Civic Education: Introduction," *PS: Political Science & Politics* 36, no. 2 (2003).

71. Macedo et al., *Democracy at Risk: How Political Choices Undermine Citizen Participation, and What We Can Do About It*, vii.

72. Farr, "The Science of Politics—as Civic Education—Then and Now," 37.

73. Ishiyama, Breuning, and Lopez, "A Century of Continuity and (Little) Change in the Undergraduate Political Science Curriculum," 663.

74. See particularly Plato's *Republic* in, *Plato: The Collected Dialogues*, eds. Edith Hamilton and Cairns Huntington seventy-first edition, volume seventy-one, Bollingen Series (Princeton, NJ: Princeton University Press,1961).

For further discussion of educational relativism, see Rogers, "A Meta-History of Formal Civic Education: An Episodic History to Be Repeated?" 5–6. See also Amy Gutmann, *Democratic Education*, second edition (Princeton, NJ: Princeton University Press, 1999); Checkoway, "Renewing the Civic Missions of the American Research University."

75. See Aristotle, *The Politics*, trans. Carnes Lord (Chicago: The University of Chicago Press, 1984); Aristotle, *Nicomachean Ethics*, trans. Terence Irwin (Indianapolis, IN: Hackett Publishing Company, Inc., 1985).

76. For works most directly addressing this interplay, see William A. Galston, "Civic Knowlege, Civic Education, and Civic Engagement: A Summary of Recent Research," *International Journal of Public Administration* 30, no. 6 (2007); William A. Galston, "Civic Education and Political Participation," *PS: Political Science & Politics* 37, no. April (2004). For more empirical study of this interplay, see Gooch and Rogers, "Dude, Where's the Civic Engagement? The Paradoxical Effect of Civic Educaon on the Probablity of Civic Participation."

77. For Rousseau, see Jean-Jacques Rousseau, *Emile or on Education*, trans. Allan Bloom (New York: Basic Books, Inc., 1979); Jean-Jacques Rousseau, "*On the Social Contract*," in *Jean-Jacques Rousseau: The Basic Political Writings* (Indianapolis, IN: Hackett Publishing Company, 1987). For Tocqueville, see Alexis de Tocqueville, *Democracy in America*, volume two (New York: Random House, Inc., 1990). For Mill, see John Stuart Mill, *On Liberty*, ed. Currin V. Shields (Upper Saddle River, NJ: Prentice Hall, Inc., 1997).

78. By formal civic curriculum, I mean both Plato and Aristotle map out a specific curriculum, one readily integrated into a school curriculum, for those involved in politics. For further discussion on the difference between formal civic education and informal civic education, see Rogers, "A Civic Education Crisis."

79. For Plato's rigorous education of the guardian class, see particularly books V–VII of the *Republic* in Hamilton and Huntington, eds., *Plato: The Collected Dialogues*. For Aristotle's treatment of education, see Book VIII in Aristotle, *The Politics*. See also Aristotle, *Nicomachean Ethics*.

80. Rousseau, "On the Social Contract."

81. See the second book of volume II, particularly chapter VII on the "Relation of Civil to Political Associations." In it, Tocqueville talks about how the "great associations" of politics educate the common man in the principle of association and then man carries this principle over into civic life and uses it to achieve numerous goods through small civil associations. Thus, Tocqueville argues participation in political and civil associations educate men in politics and reinforce that education on the grand and smaller scale. For more on this, see de Tocqueville, *Democracy in America*, (vol. II) 115–20.

82. In particular, see Mill's discussion of the educational effects "Of the Liberty of Thought and Discussion" in Chapter II, as well as his discussion of "Individuality" in Chapter III of Mill, *On Liberty*.

83. Gooch and I found the former is the case in Gooch and Rogers, "Dude, Where's the Civic Engagement? The Paradoxical Effect of Civic Educaon on the Probablity of Civic Participation." For arguments supporting the latter claim, see Youniss, "How to Enrich Civic Education and Sustain Democracy," 127; Walker, "Service as a Pathway to Political Participation: What Research Tells Us."

84. Gooch and I provide an endogenous model of this complex relationship and even update it based on our own empirical work. See Gooch and Rogers, "Dude, Where's the Civic Engagement? The Paradoxical Effect of Civic Educatioon on the Probablity of Civic Participation," 301–02, and 26–32. See also Gooch's extended discussion of the models of civic education in Donald M. Gooch, "Conclusion: The Dimensions of Civic Education in the Twenty-First Century," in *Civic Education in the Twenty-First Century: A Multidimensional Inquiry*, ed. Michael T. Rogers and Donald M. Gooch (Lanham, MD: Lexington Books, 2015).

85. For other formulations and definitions of civic education, see Elizabeth Kaufer Busch and Jonathan W. White, "Introduction," in *Civic Education and the Future of American Citizenship*, ed. Elizabeth Kaufer Busch and Jonathan W. White (Lanham, MD: Lexington Books, 2013), 5; David E. Campbell, "Introduction," in *Making Civics Count: Citizenship Education for a New Generation*, ed. David E. Campbell, Meira Levinson, and Frederick M. Hess (Cambridge, MA: Harvard Education Press, 2012), 1. See also the statement on civic education on behalf of the Center for Civic education by Margaret Stimmann Branson, "The Role of Civic Education."

    Among all these explanations, there are comprehensive and wide-ranging ones like that provided in the *Stanford Encyclopedia of Philosophy*. It recognizes that communities, groups, families, schools and other entities can all contribute to and provide civic education. It explains, "In its broadest definition, 'civic education' means all the processes that affect people's beliefs, commitments, capabilities, and actions as members or prospective members of communities." In fact, civic education need not even be an intentional action of these entities. See Jack Crittenden and Peter Levine, "Civic Education," in *Stanford Encyclopedia of Philosophy*, ed. Edward N. Zalta (Stanford, 2013). Still, most often schools are seen as the essential medium for civic education. For an explanation of the role schools are to play in civic education, see "Citizenship Education: Educating Students to Be Competent and Responsible Citizens and Leaders," *The Progress of Education Reform* 11, no. 5 (2010), http://www.ecs.org/clearinghouse/87/95/8795.pdf.

86. Putnam (among others) notes this in his seminal work Putnam, *Bowling Alone: The Collapse and Revival of the American Community*, 35. For further discussion of civic literacy and a comparison of our literacy to other countries, see Milner, *Civic Literacy: How Informed Citizens Make Democracy Work*.

87. Langton and Jennings, "Political Socialization and the High School Civics Curriculum in the United States"; Delli Carpini and Keeter, *What Americans Know About Politics and Why It Matters*; Niemi and Junn, *Civic Education: What Makes Students Learn?*

88. Delli Carpini and Keeter, *What Americans Know About Politics and Why It Matters*; Niemi and Junn, *Civic Education: What Makes Students Learn?* See also, Milner, *Civic Literacy: How Informed Citizens Make Democracy Work*; Richard G. Niemi, "What Students Know About Civics and Government," in *Making Civics Count: Citizenship Education for a New Generation*, ed. David E. Campbell, Meira Levinson, and Frederick M. Hess (Cambridge, MA: Harvard Education Press, 2012).

89. Langton and Jennings, "Political Socialization and the High School Civics Curriculum in the United States." For a more recent study with this view, see Conover and Searing, "A Political Socialization Perpesctive."

90. Of course, Langton and Jennings were researching civic literacy in the 1960s, when the norm was a three semester civics regiment in many public schools. See Langton and Jennings, "Political Socialization and the High School Civics

Curriculum in the United States." Today, only about three-quarters of high school students have had a civic course and that is typically only for one semester. See Niemi and Smith, "Enrollments in High School Government Classes: Are We Short-Changing Both Citizenship and Political Science Training?"; Bob Graham and Chris Hand, "A Failure of Leadership: The Duty of Politicians and Universities to Salvage Citizenship," in *Teaching America: The Case for Civic Education*, ed. David Feith (Lanham, MD: Rowman & Littlefield Education, 2011), 64; Bob Graham and Chris Hand, *America, the Owner's Manual: Making Government Work for You* (Washington, DC: CQ Press, 2010), 22; O'Connor, "The Democratic Purpose of Education: From the Founders to Horace Mann to Today," 6.

91. See Niemi and Junn, *Civic Education: What Makes Students Learn*; Delli Carpini and Keeter, *What Americans Know About Politics and Why It Matters*; Niemi and Smith, "Enrollments in High School Government Classes: Are We Short-Changing Both Citizenship and Political Science Training?"; Norman Nie and Sunshine D. Hillygus, "Education and Democratic Citizenship," in *Making Good Citizens: Education and Civil Society*, ed. Diane Ravitch and Joseph P. Viteritti (New Haven, CT: Yale University Press, 2001).

92. Gooch and Rogers, "A Natural Disaster of Civic Proportions: College Students in the Natural State Falls Short of the Naturalization Benchmark"; Gooch and Rogers, "Dude, Where's the Civic Engagement? The Paradoxical Effect of Civic Educaon on the Probablity of Civic Participation."

93. For more discussion of the coverage of government in high schools and college, see Rogers, "A Civic Education Crisis." See also Kedrowski, "Civid Education by Mandate: A State-by-State Analysis"; Rogers, "A Civic Education Crisis."

94. Langton and Jennings, "Political Socialization and the High School Civics Curriculum in the United States," 857-65.

95. Peter Levine, "Education for a Civil Society," in *Making Civics Count: Citizenship Education for a New Generation*, ed. David E. Campbell, Meira Levinson, and Frederick M. Hess (Cambridge, MA: Harvard Education Press, 2012), 40-43; Meira Levinson, *No Citizen Left Behind* (Cambridge, MA: Harvard University Press, 2012); Meira Levinson, "The Civic Empowerment Gap: Defining the Problem and Locating Solutions," in *Handbook of Research on Civic Engagement in Youth*, ed. Lonnie Sherrod, Judith Torney-Purta, and Constance A. Flanagan (Hoboken, NJ: John Wiley and Sons, 2010); Ahmad, "Teaching Government in the Social Studies: Political Scientists' Contributions to Citizenship Education," 13.

As just an introduction to the civic engagement gap literature, see Laura Wray-Lake and Daniel Hart, "Growing Social Inequalities in Youth Civic Engagement? Evidence from the National Election Study," *PS: Political Science & Politics* 45, no. 3 (2012); Rebecca Jacobsen, Erica Frankenberg, and Sarah Winchell Lenhoff, "Diverse Schools in a Democractic Soceity: New Ways of Understanding How School Demographics Affect Civic and Political Learning," *American Educational Research Journal* 49, no. 5 (2012); Lisa Garcia Bedolla and Luis Ricardo Fraga, "Latino Education, Civic Engagement, and the Public Good," *Review of Research in Education* 36(2012).

96. For example, does it matter that students in Arkansas typically have their civic course in ninth grade when most states require it in eleventh or twelfth? Do they have lower civic literacy in general than other graduating seniors? Do they benefit more from a civic course in college? Is it better to stack them (twelfth grade in high school and freshmen year in college) or does it not matter?

97. The core of a definition of civic (and political) engagement is individual or collective action that is intended to benefit the community or political society. Possibly Thomas Ehrlich defines civic engagement best, writing it "means working to make a difference in the civic life of our communities and developing the combination of knowledge, skills, values, and motivations to make that difference. It means promoting the quality of life in a community, through both political and nonpolitical processes," see Ehrlich, ed. *Civic Responsibility and Higher Education*, vi. In contrast, Colby et al. "define *political engagement* as including activities intended to influence social and political institutions, beliefs, and practices and to affect processes and policies relating to community welfare, whether that community is local, state, national, or international," see Colby et al., *Educating Citizens: Preparing America's Undergraduates for Lives of Moral and Civic Responsibility*, 18.

For an alternative conceptualization, there is an externalities formulation in Levine, *The Future of Democracy: Developing the Next Generation of American Citizens* 5 & 7. Additionally, the explanation of civic engagement from a social capital perspective in Putnam, *Making Democracy Work: Civic Traditions in Modern Italy*; Putnam, *Bowling Alone: The Collapse and Revival of the American Community*. Some additional sources are Sherrod L. R., J. Torney-Purta, and C. Flanagan, eds., *Handbook of Research on Civic Engagement* (Hoboken: Jon Wiley & Sons, Inc., 2010); Richard P. Adler and Judy Goggin, "What Do We Mean by 'Civic Engagement'?" *Journal of Transformative Education* 3, no. 3 (July 2005); and Theda Skocpol and Morris P. Fiorina, eds., *Civic Engagement in American Democracy* (Washington, DC: Brookings Insitution Press, 1999). Finally, the American Psychological Association's offers the following on their website: "Civic engagement is the following: individual and collective actions designed to identify and address issues of public concern." See Michael Delli Carpini, "Civic Engagement," American Psychological Assocation, http://www.apa.org/education/undergrad/civic-engagement.aspx.

98. David E. Campbell, *Why We Vote: How Schools and Communities Shape Our Civic Life* (Princeton, NJ: Princeton University Press, 2006), 6 and 16. For a similar discussion on the importance of differentiating civic and political engagement, see Cliff Zukin et al., *A New Engagement?* (New York: Oxford University Press, 2006), 51–52.

99. Peter Levine, The Future of Democracy: Developing the Next Generation of American Citizens (Tufts, 2007), 1–2.

100. Again, for an illustrative example see Youniss, "How to Enrich Civic Education and Sustain Democracy."

101. Ahmad, "Teaching Government in the Social Studies: Political Scientists' Contributions to Citizenship Education," 13.

102. Campbell, *Why We Vote: How Schools and Communities Shape Our Civic Life*, 96–101, 43. For more on the history of the political socialization literature, see also Molly W. Andolina et al., "Habits from Home, Lessons from School: Influences on Youth Civic Engagement," *PS: Political Science & Politics* 36, no. 2 (2003); Conover and Searing, "A Political Socialization Perpesctive."

103. Lonnie R. Sherrod, Judith Torney-Purta, and Constance Flanagan, "Research on the Development of Citizenship: A Field Comes to Age," in *Handbook of Research on Civic Engagement in Youth*, ed. Lonnie R. Sherrod, Judith Torney-Purta, and Constance Flanagan (Hoboken: Jon Wiley & Sons, Inc., 2010), 2.

104. Hugh McIntosh, Danil Hart, and James Youniss, "The Influence of Family Political Discussion on Youth Civic Development: Which Parent Qualities Matter?" *PS: Political Science & Politics* 40, no. 3 (2007).

105. Hugh McIntosh and James Youniss, "Toward a Political Theory of Political Socialization of Youth," in *Handbook of Research on Civic Engagement in Youth*, ed. Lonnie R. Sherrod, Judith Torney-Purta, and Constance Flanagan (Hoboken, NJ: Jon Wiley & Sons, Inc., 2010).

106. Conover and Searing, "A Political Socialization Perpesctive," 93–94.

107. Heather Malin, "America as a Philosophy: Implications for the Development of American Identity among Today's Youth," *Applied Development Science* 15, no. 2 (2011).

108. Putnam, *Making Democracy Work: Civic Traditions in Modern Italy*; Putnam, *Bowling Alone: The Collapse and Revival of the American Community*, 19–22. For additional discussion of the history of social capital, see James Farr, "Social Capital: A Conceptual History," *Political Theory* 32(2004); Ben Fine, "Eleven Hypotheses on the Conceptual History of Social Capital: A Response to James Farr," *Political Theory* 35, no. 1 (2007).

109. Fine, "Eleven Hypotheses on the Conceptual History of Social Capital: A Response to James Farr," 50, 52.

110. Putnam, *Making Democracy Work: Civic Traditions in Modern Italy*; Putnam, *Bowling Alone: The Collapse and Revival of the American Community*.

111. Nick Hopkins, "Religion and Social Capital: Identity Matters," *Journal of Community & Applied Social Psychology* 21(2011).

112. Jang Ahnlee and Kim Hyunhee, "Cultural Identity, Social Capital, and Social Control of Young Korean Americans: Extending the Theory of Intercultural Pulic Relations," *Journal of Public Relations Research* 25, no. 3 (2013).

SECTION II

Civic Engagement Education:
Purpose and Practice

Introduction

ELIZABETH C. MATTO

As demonstrated in the previous section, it is by teaching civic and political engagement that we prepare students to be lifelong participatory citizens. Out of the scholarship of engagement has emerged a pedagogical toolbox of evidence-based techniques for enhancing students' civic knowledge, skills, and attitudes. In *Teaching Civic Engagement: From Student to Active Citizen* (2013), contributors offered political scientists a range of models of civic engagement pedagogy, from a variety of subdisciplines, that suited diverse teaching styles, students, and institutions. Although political science should play a central role in university civic education and engagement initiatives, teaching civic engagement should not be restricted to political science classrooms. Advancing the scholarship of teaching civic engagement requires educators of all disciplines to embrace the value of civic learning and demonstrate how such pedagogy can be included in a breadth of classrooms. This section of the text takes this step, extending the range of civic learning models beyond political science to include disciplines such as English, civil engineering, and the arts. As the scholarship then moves forward, the pedagogical toolbox grows.

To be sure, the rigor and creativity of civic engagement research continues to advance in political science. The American Political Science Association's Teaching and Learning Conference as well as panels organized by the political science education section at the association's annual meeting offer venues to share and disseminate some of this research. In addition, the *Journal of Political Science Education* and *PS: Political Science & Politics* publish peer-reviewed research on the scholarship of teaching political science, deepening our theoretical understanding and advancing the evidence-based pedagogy. Similarly, this text builds on the research offered in *Teaching Civic Engagement: From Student to Active Citizen* and advances our understanding of how to meaningfully integrate civic learning into political science classrooms. Although much of this work is focused on higher education, the task of effectively preparing college students to be informed and engaged citizens is made much easier if a strong foundation is laid in elementary, middle, and high schools. Given that this stage of education is interdisciplinary by nature, teaching civic engagement effectively from kindergarten through high school also lays the important groundwork necessary to teach civic engagement to students of all disciplines when they get to college.

As demonstrated in *Teaching Civic Engagement: From Student to Active Citizen*, classroom activities and civic education programs in middle and high school can make a positive impact on the knowledge, skills, and dispositions that facilitate future civic engagement. For instance, O'Shaughnessy found that incorporating campaign and election activities into coursework enhanced students' willingness to do such work in the future.[1] Owen's research concluded that students in civic education programs with active-learning elements were most inclined to participate in elections.[2]

Owen and Riddle build on and advance this research in this text by considering the effects of both teacher training and classroom environment on students' civic learning. Using survey data from a study of Indiana high school students and their teachers, they find that students whose teachers had completed the We the People professional-development program gained more knowledge of the US Constitution, Bill of Rights, government institutions, and race and politics than did other students. This research points to the importance of training teachers to teach civic engagement, a conclusion that is applicable at all levels of education and all disciplines.

Owen and Riddle also find that an open classroom facilitates civic learning. This conclusion aligns with others offered in this text that the climate for civic teaching and learning, whether it is classroom climate or the climate of the campus as a whole, plays an important role in fostering students' civic knowledge, skills, and attitudes. Healy's chapter amplifies this theme. In his multi-method research on Illinois high schools, Healy identifies common elements for sustained, systemic commitments to students' civic development. Strong civic mission statements, shared dedication to civic learning among school leaders, and innovative civic learning practices all contribute to a climate for civic learning. Again, these are lessons that are applicable to all levels of education and all types of disciplines.

The importance of innovative teaching in the field of civic engagement certainly extends to college classrooms. Given the importance placed not only on instilling knowledge but also teaching the skills of citizenship, it is critical that educators devise effective methods of teaching that utilize the tools their students are using. In *Teaching Civic Engagement: From Student to Active Citizen*, VanVechten and Chadha laid that groundwork in their research on their social networking project. Through content analysis of online discussions held in Introduction to American Politics on campuses around the country, they found that such a venue can be a productive method for preparing students to be active citizens.[3] Woodall and Lennon's chapter presented in this section picks up this theme by focusing their attention on the effectiveness of using Twitter in the classroom to promote civic engagement. Using an experimental design as well as focus groups, their preliminary results show that treatment classes utilizing Twitter had statistically higher levels of political knowledge and engagement as well as gender differences in how participants use Twitter. As not only our students but our public officials make more frequent use of such modes of communication, it is critical that we continue to find meaningful ways to integrate these into our instruction and that we rigorously study their effects.

As shown in *Teaching Civic Engagement: From Student to Active Citizen*, political science classrooms have been successful venues for teaching civic engagement through community-based research, either by focusing on local government[4] or by working with community partners.[5] As an academic discipline, urban studies is rooted in addressing the evolving challenges faced by cities and urban landscapes and is a field that has naturally attracted academics and practitioners from a number of disciplines, including political science. The very nature of urban studies lends itself to extending learning beyond the classroom and conceptualizing civic learning in an interdisciplinary way. Such experiential learning is exemplified by research presented in this section by Mixon. Her research on three urban studies courses at Elmhurst College offers evidence of how interdisciplinary urban studies programs with a focus on active and participatory learning increase civic orientations among students. As the author writes, "the study of cities is the study of citizenship."

Efforts to teach civic skills are not exclusive to social scientists, nor should they be. Although it may not come as naturally as to those in the social sciences, educators in the humanities and the sciences have found ways to incorporate meaningful civic learning into their classrooms, exposing students of a range of disciplines to instructional techniques that promise to enhance their civic knowledge, skills, and attitudes. Frequently, these techniques center around service-learning and project-based learning, modes of instruction well-known and rigorously studied by political scientists.[6] This section offers models of how educators in English, the arts, and civil engineering have woven civic learning into their instruction and, thereby, have broadened the range of classrooms teaching civic engagement.

In his chapter, Suarez describes how integrating civic learning into first-year English composition courses has fostered a commitment to civic engagement among his students at SUNY Cortland. Through service- and problem-based learning efforts rooted in the surrounding community, students are offered opportunities to practice the skills of civil discourse, critical thinking, and relationship building. Suarez's experiences also allow him to comment on the agility necessary among instructors to ensure that the service-learning experiences are meeting learning objectives. His chapter provides a marvelous example of how these evidence-based methods of civic instruction can be incorporated into required courses in large public institutions and, thereby, reach a broad range of students from a variety of disciplines.

The chapter by Devereaux also offers a model of how civic engagement can be woven into the study of the arts. Premised on the notion that the arts are alternately demonized and idealized in American politics, Devereaux holds that arts education ought to include an education in civic engagement for students to acquire an understanding of the governmental process and an ability to interact with it. Using her own coursework as an example, Devereaux offers guidelines for integrating civic engagement education into the collegiate-level training of artists (of all disciplines), arts managers, arts policy practitioners, and those in related fields. True to the interdisciplinary focus of this text, the chapter holds that the arts are an integral component of daily life and that civic engagement is an effective approach for establishing their role in the community.

Finally, although the sciences often are resistant to incorporating civic and political engagement into their coursework, the prominence of the field in contemporary politics offers marvelous opportunities to expose students in the sciences to civic learning. Research presented in this section by Kulkarni and Coleman offers an example of how such instruction was integrated into an undergraduate environmental engineering course. In carefully constructed experiences directly tied to the curriculum, students step outside of the classroom and lab spaces and engage in hands-on learning via service and project-based learning in local K–12 classrooms. These exercises not only deepen appreciation of concepts of environmental engineering but apply these concepts to community needs. Kulkarni and Coleman's research demonstrates that, although it may be challenging to students, such experiential civic learning offers an opportunity to foster important skills such as leadership and communication that will be useful to them not only as engineers but as citizens.

The purpose of teaching civic engagement in the classroom, and even extending that learning outside the classroom, is to prepare students to be informed and engaged democratic citizens. Teaching civic engagement is a shared responsibility, however, and requires a collective effort to develop, test, and disseminate effective practices for such teaching. Over the years, political scientists have developed a set of evidence-based best practices to impart civic knowledge, skills, and attitudes. To be sure, the discipline's civic engagement research and practice serve as a model not only for political scientists but for other disciplines. Although the discipline can play a lead role, the mission of teaching civic engagement is incomplete if it is reserved to political science classrooms.

The chapters in this section offer models of how disciplines beyond political science—the humanities and the sciences—have taken up the call and integrated teaching civic engagement into their classrooms. Just as the research presented in *Teaching Civic Engagement: From Student to Active Citizen* encourages and facilitates civic engagement pedagogy among political scientists, the chapters presented in this section extend that invitation to educators of all disciplines. If we are to have a peaceful and thriving democracy, it requires a civically educated populace. This is the work of all educators of all disciplines—to let every classroom serve as a laboratory for democracy. ∎

ENDNOTES

1. Betty O'Shaughnessy, "High School Students as Election Judges and Campaign Workers: Does the Experience Stick?" in *Teaching Civic Engagement: From Student to Active Citizen*, eds. Alison Rios Millett McCartney, Elizabeth A. Bennion, and Dick Simpson (Washington, DC: American Political Science Association, 2013), chapter 19.

2. Diana Owen, "The Influence of Civic Education on Electoral Engagement and Voting," in *Teaching Civic Engagement: From Student to Active Citizen*, eds. Alison Rios Millett McCartney, Elizabeth A. Bennion, and Dick Simpson (Washington, DC: American Political Science Association, 2013), chapter 20.

3. Renee Bukovchik VanVechten and Anita Chadha, "How Students Talk to Each Other: An Academic Social Networking Project," in *Teaching Civic Engagement: From Student to Active Citizen*, eds. Alison Rios Millett McCartney, Elizabeth A. Bennion, and Dick Simpson (Washington, DC: American Political Science Association, 2013), chapter 11.

4. Shannon Jenkins, "Using Best Practices Research and Experience with Local Governments to Increase Political Engagement," in *Teaching Civic Engagement: From Student to Active Citizen*, eds. Alison Rios Millett McCartney, Elizabeth A. Bennion, and Dick Simpson (Washington, DC: American Political Science Association, 2013), chapter 7.

5. Michelle Lorenzi, "From Active Service to Civic and Political Engagement: Fighting the Problem of Poverty," *Teaching Civic Engagement: From Student to Active Citizen*, eds. Alison Rios Millett McCartney, Elizabeth A. Bennion, and Dick Simpson (Washington, DC: American Political Science Association, 2013), chapter 8.

6. For definitions of service-learning and project-based learning, see Alison McCartney, "Introduction: Higher Education, Civic Engagement Pedagogy, and Political Science Education," in *Teaching Civic Engagement: From Student to Active Citizen*, eds. Alison Rios Millett McCartney, Elizabeth A. Bennion, and Dick Simpson (Washington, DC: American Political Science Association, 2013).

Active Learning and the Acquisition of Political Knowledge in High School

8

Diana Owen and G. Isaac W. Riddle

This study assesses the effectiveness of high school civic education in conveying political knowledge, which is an important precursor to political engagement. Specifically, it addresses this question: is political knowledge acquisition related to the type of classroom civic education a student receives? Using data from a 2014–2015 study of Indiana high school students and their teachers, we find that students whose teachers had gone through the We the People professional development program gained more knowledge of the US Constitution, Bill of Rights, government institutions, and race and politics than did other students. In addition, students who take civics as an elective course gain more knowledge than students who take it as a required class. We also find that an open classroom is conducive to students' civic learning.

High school civics instruction offers the opportunity to impart core political knowledge and establish habits for acquiring political information for the long term. Understanding the conditions under which political knowledge is successfully acquired is essential for fostering democratic engagement. Classroom civics instruction offers the opportunity to impart political knowledge to young people in a structured environment. In particular, civic education in junior high and high school can impart lasting democratic citizenship orientations. Exposure to basic information about government and democratic processes in adolescence provides a foundation for the further acquisition of political knowledge and greater development of civic skills in adulthood.

However, the civics curriculum varies markedly across schools. Class content and instructional methods can differ even among schools in the same county or state. People who receive high-quality civics instruction that includes active and innovative teaching methods are more likely to gain political knowledge and consequently become active citizens than people whose civic education experience is less robust or absent.[1] These variations correspond to different types and levels of democratic citizenship in practice. The disparity in the quality of civic education available to privileged and disadvantaged groups further contributes to the participation gap in American politics.

This study assesses the effectiveness of high school civic education in conveying political knowledge and addresses the general research questions: is political knowledge acquisition related to the type of classroom civic education a student receives? Specifically, how does the political knowledge gain of students who have taken civics classes that use the We the People: The Citizen and Constitution (WTP) instructional program compare to that of students who have taken standard American government classes?

WTP is a curriculum intervention that has involved more than 28 million students and 75,000 teachers in all 50 states and the District of Columbia since 1987. The WTP program is grounded in the foundations and institutions of American government and is distinctive for its emphasis on constitutional principles, the Bill of Rights, and Supreme Court cases and their relevance to current issues and debates. Students take part in a range of learning activities, such as group projects, debates, and student speeches, culminating in simulated congressional hearings. WTP middle and high school classes have the opportunity to participate in statewide competitions based on the congressional hearings. States send representatives to the National Finals in Washington, DC, that are held each spring.[2] The comparison group for this research consists of students in American government, constitutional government, political studies, and advanced placement (AP) government classes. These classes were taught using a standard lecture format and did not include the learning activities, such as simulated congressional hearings, that are central to the WTP curriculum.

This study examines the knowledge levels of students who take civics as an elective versus a required class as well as those who earned AP credit and those who did not. We anticipate that students who take civics as an elective and AP students may have higher levels of knowledge at the outset and may be more motivated to learn about politics and government than students taking a required class or a non-AP course. This research also explores whether an open classroom climate, where students feel that they can express themselves freely in a respectful environment, is related to knowledge gain. Further, we probe the extent to which particular pedagogies—such as lecture– and current-event–based approaches—are conducive to students' knowledge gain. We find evidence that teacher professional development and classroom climate are relevant to the acquisition of political knowledge.

We employ student knowledge assessment data from an original study we fielded in high schools across the state of Indiana during the 2014 fall semester comparing teachers of WTP and a control group of teachers who taught civics using primarily a lecture format. WTP is a widely adopted civics curriculum that features active learning elements, including a simulated congressional hearing. We find that students whose teachers had gone through the WTP professional development program gained more knowledge of the US Constitution, Bill of Rights, government institutions, and race and politics than did other students. In addition, students who take civics as an elective course gain more knowledge than students who take it as a required class. We also find that an open classroom is conducive to students' civic learning.

CIVIC EDUCATION AND THE ACQUISITION OF POLITICAL KNOWLEDGE

Knowledge forms the foundation for citizens' engagement in political life.[3] A strong knowledge base facilitates individuals' development of political attitudes that are predicated on more than just emotion and fosters comprehension of how their own interests fit into a complex political system. People possessing greater civic knowledge tend to be supportive of democratic values, such as liberty, equality, and political tolerance.[4] Further, knowledge is directly related to participation. People who possess sufficient political knowledge tend to be more politically efficacious as they have the confidence and ability to stake a position in the marketplace of political ideas and to actively engage in governmental and civic affairs.[5]

Political knowledge encompasses a vast amount of information pertinent to government and political life. Delli Carpini and Keeter define political knowledge as "the range of factual information about politics that is stored in long-term memory."[6] Decades of research confirm that the public has a relatively low level of political knowledge and that knowledge levels have remained fairly stable over time.[7] About half of the public is somewhat knowledgeable about the core institutions, such as the presidency, Congress, and the judiciary, and procedures of government, such as how a bill becomes law, although knowledge of the Constitution and Bill of Rights is less robust.[8] In sum, the average American citizen is poorly informed but not uninformed.[9] Individuals who are very informed about one aspect of politics tend to be knowledgeable in other areas.[10]

Researchers across a variety of fields have identified three major antecedents of knowledge acquisition—ability, motivation, and opportunity.[11] These traits can be fostered in the high school civics classroom. Grade point average (GPA), while imperfect, is a widely used measure of students' ability.[12] However, ability and motivation are traits intrinsic to the individual. Ability refers to a person's cognitive skills and capacity for learning. People develop different levels of proficiency in retaining and processing information. Civics teachers can recognize and tap into students' ability in a way that stimulates political learning. For example, they can relate theoretical concepts to students' role in real-world events, such as election campaigns. Motivation represents people's desire to learn and a willingness to engage with and process information. Students' level of interest in political and civic life as well as their capacity for engagement varies based on multiple factors, including those related to home and family life and their social networks. In school, motivation may be linked to teachers' encouragement, class climate, or the instructor's pedagogic style. Dynamic learning pedagogies may inspire students to learn more than standard lecture formats. An engaging discussion of current events may stimulate learning more than listening to a teacher's lecture. Opportunity takes into account the availability of information to the student and the manner in which it is presented, such as through a lecture or classroom activity. It encompasses factors that can be largely outside the control of the individual, such as the amount of exposure to a message, the number of arguments it contains, and the presence of distractions that can hinder comprehension.[13] Under the right circumstances, high school civics classes have the potential to offer significant intentional exposure to political information within a structured environment that is conducive to learning.

The classroom is a unique setting where young people can gain knowledge, establish autonomy in their ideas, and develop confidence in their ability to be political actors.[14] Civics classes can stimulate interest in political affairs, create a lasting sense of civic duty, and encourage an orientation toward political life that compels people to be attentive to politics over the long haul.[15] Knowledge gained through civics instruction can serve as a foundation for seeking further information. Events, such as an election campaign, public policy controversy, a discussion of politics, or a media report, may invigorate recall of relevant political facts that were learned in class. Thus, civic education may be responsible for positioning people to encounter and be receptive to information about the political world long after they leave the classroom.

Civic education varies greatly across, and even within, schools. Civics offerings range from dedicated social studies/American government classes to brief sections of a history class. Coursework can extend from a couple of weeks to a full year or more. Civics classes often are conducted using a standard lecture/textbook approach. Some schools offer civics programs that employ active pedagogies designed to impart civic dispositions and skills that encourage students to take part in the polity. Active learning approaches engage students with the civics curriculum in a way that stimulates reading, writing, discussion, and engagement in problem solving. They can invite enthusiasm for civics by "involving students in doing things and thinking about what they are doing."[16] Research has demonstrated that active approaches in conjunction with lecture and textbook learning will be more conducive to students' knowledge acquisition than static instructional methods that rely on rote learning of facts.[17]

Our study examines the relationship of particular types of civics instruction to the acquisition of political knowledge among high school students. We take into account approaches that rely heavily on textbook reading, lecture, and discussion of current events as well as innovative methods, such as classroom activities that include debates and simulated hearings. More time spent on civic education utilizing traditional instructional approaches—textbook and lecture-based instruction—can enhance political knowledge.[18] Textbooks convey discrete facts about political institutions, actors, and processes. This information can be reinforced and contextualized through lectures and is often the basis for testing and evaluation. However, there is some indication that textbook facts may be forgotten soon after the test is taken. Therefore, we present evidence that students can better retain this information when it is presented in conjunction with current events or a learning activity.[19]

Classroom-based activities can expand a young person's capacity to gain knowledge about politics, especially when interactive, student-centered methods are combined with lecture and textbook instruction. Innovative methods include discussion of current events, simulations of democratic processes and procedures, and service-learning. The WTP program employs simulated congressional hearings and encourages both independent and group work to develop students' research, analytic, and public speaking skills. Students who take part in programs that integrate problem solving, collaborative thinking, and cross-disciplinary approaches in their curricula may develop a greater sense of their own agency as civic actors.[20] Innovative methods that augment and deepen textbook learning, particularly in the hands of skilled teachers, can increase knowledge.[21]

The integration of current events into classroom discussions is positively related to conveying political knowledge to students.[22] Current events can bolster civic knowledge by providing new and timely information to students, as opposed to other classroom approaches that may present redundant material in a dry format.[23] Instruction incorporating current events is most effective when it involves discussion that is tailored to students' interests and does not avoid controversial topics.[24] The 2005 California Survey of Civic Education reported that 61% of students in classes that continuously discussed current events were interested in politics compared to 32% in classes that did not.[25] However, a current-events–centric curriculum may not be sufficient to promote knowledge gain, especially of facts about institutions and processes. Discussion of current events requires context and reinforcement through lectures and educational materials like textbooks, readings, videos, and online resources. Vercellotti and Matto found that students who read political articles and discussed them at home had higher levels of internal political efficacy compared to those who discussed the articles only in class.[26] Hess suggests that classroom discussion of controversial issues should be carefully considered in terms of public policy rather than being a quick response to the day's headlines, which is more like Shea and Harward's explanation of "drive-by" civic participation.[27]

Simulations, such as role playing, elections, mock trials, and simulated congressional hearings, can be effective in increasing knowledge and fostering the development of political attitudes.[28] Yet such simulations of civic activities are often limited to select programs, such as AP classes, or omitted due to strict curriculum guidelines and time constraints.[29] Community-based activities, like attending meetings, service-learning, and field trips, can demonstrate to students how they can participate in politics, provide information that becomes especially relevant later in life, and activate their political knowledge. Still, community-based activities do not always contribute to the acquisition of political knowledge, especially when the curriculum is not linked directly to the experience.[30]

Research has demonstrated that maintenance of an open classroom climate, where students feel comfortable expressing their ideas and their opinions are treated with respect, significantly improves acquisition of political knowledge, development of political efficacy, and voting intent.[31] In fact, an open class climate can lead to high levels of voting behavior, especially among high-need students.[32] Adolescents' political knowledge and appreciation of political conflict can improve in an open classroom environment, which also can compensate partially for disadvantages accruing to low socioeconomic status.[33] Conversely, closed classroom environments, where students are discouraged from actively engaging in discussions, may alienate students from politics. One early empirical study of classroom climate found that discussing controversial topics in a closed classroom environment had an especially negative effect on young black students.[34] However, education that provides experiences that sharpen political capabilities can promote individuals' overall political development.[35] Student racial and socioeconomic diversity in an open classroom climate has been found to increase political knowledge and intention to vote.[36]

HYPOTHESES

We expect to find that students whose civic education involved active learning elements and took place in an open classroom climate will exhibit superior knowledge gain. Teachers who received WTP professional development and taught the WTP curriculum were matched with civics teachers in their schools who did not teach WTP. The WTP teachers also taught civics classes that did not employ the WTP curriculum. Our research team conducted classroom ethnographies in all but one of the schools. We observed that the WTP teachers employed active learning approaches and fostered an open class climate regardless of whether they were teaching a WTP class or not. We also found that the majority of teachers without WTP professional development experience employed more standard, lecture-focused approaches to teaching civics and were less likely to incorporate active learning into the classroom. Thus, we test the following hypotheses:

H_1: Students who took a class with a We the People teacher gained more political knowledge than students taking a class with a non-We the People teacher.

H_2: Students in We the People classes gained more civic knowledge than students in other civics classes.

Our classroom observations indicate that the WTP teachers in our study incorporated active learning approaches and encouraged an open class climate more often than non-WTP teachers. However, the extent to which teachers used active learning techniques and fostered an open classroom environment varied, even among the WTP teachers. We test the following hypotheses related to active learning and classroom climate:

H_3: Students whose civics class incorporated active learning approaches have higher civic knowledge scores than students whose class did not involve active learning.

H_6: Students whose civics class was conducted in an open classroom environment have higher civic knowledge scores than students whose civics class took place in a closed classroom environment.

DATA

Pre- and postsurvey data on students' political knowledge, civic dispositions, civic skills, political media use, civics classroom climate, and civics classroom pedagogies were collected for students in civics, social studies, and American government classes at multiple school sites across the state of Indiana in the fall semester of 2014. Schools with teachers who had gone through a WTP professional development program and instructed classes using the WTP curriculum were recruited to take part in the study. Civics instructors who had not received the WTP professional development constitute a comparison group. Twenty-one teachers from 12 high schools took part in the study. In three of the schools, there is only one instructor who teaches all of the civics classes. The WTP teachers taught other civics/social studies classes in addition to their WTP class with one exception. The schools vary in size, location (urban/suburban/rural), and type (neighborhood/selective enrollment/technical; public/private). The student samples per school range in size from 39 to 169, with a mean of 85 students.

Teachers completed a baseline survey in September 2014 prior to the administration of the student surveys. The comparison group teachers were matched to the extent possible with the WTP teachers based on their educational background and years of experience. The WTP and comparison group teachers in the study are highly comparable on these indicators. The average number of years teaching civics—20—is identical for each group, and ranges from 5 to 36 for the WTP teachers and 7 to 34 for the comparison group teachers. For educational background, 27% of the WTP teachers have bachelor's degrees and 73% have advanced degrees (master's/law degree), while 33% of the comparison group teachers hold bachelor's degrees and 67% have master's degrees. All of the teachers in the study had participated in professional development of some type. The WTP teachers took part in five- to seven-day WTP summer institutes that conveyed the content knowledge and specialized skills required of instructors in the program. These teachers also had follow-up services, including one-day seminars and engagement in a network of WTP instructors.[37]

Teachers administered pretests to students online near the beginning (early September) and posttests at the end (late December) of the fall semester 2014 during class periods. There are no confounding factors in the study because the WTP teachers had no contact with the comparison group students, and the tests were administered to all students during the same time period in each school. Close contact with teachers was maintained by the researchers throughout the study in an effort to minimize sample attrition. All teachers were provided with a stipend for participating in the study, and there was no teacher attrition. Students who were absent could make up the test on another day. Thirty-eight students dropped out of the study, for an overall student attrition rate of 3.6%. There is no evidence of differential attrition for the comparison or intervention groups or for particular schools.

Complete pretest/posttest data were collected on 1,015 students. In total, 663 students were in classes taught by WTP teachers; 386 of these students were enrolled in the WTP program and 277 took a traditional civics class. There were 351 students who took civics with non-WTP teachers. The vast majority of students (84%) took civics as a required class; 58% of students took WTP as a required class and 42% took it as an elective. In this group, 399 (32%) of the students were enrolled in an AP class. About half of the AP students took WTP for AP credit. There are no statistically significant differences in the gender composition of the students in the comparison and intervention groups. The majority of students in the sample are white. However, the comparison group has a greater percentage of black students than the WTP teacher groups, which have more Asian American/Pacific Islander students. All groups have approximately the same percentage of Latino students. As for class standing, 87% of the students in the sample were seniors in high school, and the rest were mostly juniors.

MEASURES

POLITICAL KNOWLEDGE

Political knowledge is the dependent variable in the analysis. This study employs 48 political knowledge items that were included in both the pretest, which established a baseline, and the posttest. The pretest knowledge measures are treated as covariates in the analysis. The knowledge survey items were constructed after consulting prior research, civics inventories, grade-appropriate civics tests, and state civic education rubrics, including the Indiana rubric. We reviewed content areas with the participating teachers at an orientation meeting held in Indianapolis prior to administering the pretest to ensure that the questions covered material that would be presented in class. The survey items consisted of both original questions and those that have been previously tested and have known reliability. The test used primarily multiple-choice questions with three open-ended items. Each item was coded 1 for a correct answer and 0 for an incorrect answer. There is a debate in the literature about the treatment of the "don't know" responses to political knowledge questions.[38] We combined the "don't know" response with those indicating an incorrect answer. Additive indexes representing five dimensions of political knowledge were constructed: US constitutional principles, the Bill of Rights, US government institutions, political parties and elections, and race and politics. The internal consistency for each measure is greater than .50 (Cronbach's alpha) and increased for each variable over the course of the study. (See the Appendix for knowledge index reliabilities.)

Students were surveyed about their understanding of principles, thinkers, and key events related to the inception of the US Constitution. This measure consists of 12 items (range 0–12). Participants were asked about the nature of a constitutional form of government, classical Republicanism, and the federalist elements of American government. The survey also covered items on checks and balances in the Supreme Court Justice nominating process and the Constitutional Amendment process as well as the debate at the 1787 Constitutional Convention and the purpose of a bicameral legislature. Students interpreted a quotation from John Locke about the rule of law and an excerpt from the Declaration of Independence outlining unalienable rights and protections against tyranny.

The survey contains five questions that gauge students' knowledge of the Bill of Rights. Respondents were asked questions about the Establishment Clause of the First Amendment, the purpose of the Bill of Rights, and the historical circumstances surrounding the ratification of the Fourteenth Amendment. They also interpreted a quotation from correspondence between Thomas Jefferson and John Jay about freedom of the press. The additive index representing knowledge of the Bill of Rights ranges from 0 to 5.

Knowledge of the three branches of government was ascertained by a 14-item index (range 0–14). Students answered questions about the constitutional authorities of the president, presidential succession, and the executive's role in foreign policy. They were asked about checks on presidential power as outlined in the War Powers Act and the legislative requirements to overturn a presidential veto. The survey includes open-ended questions about the number of senators in the US Congress, the term of office of members of the House of Representatives, and the number of Supreme Court Justices. Respondents were surveyed about the role of the House as a voice of the people, the fate of most bills introduced in the House of Representatives, and historical uses of the filibuster by Southern senators in the 1950s and 1960s. They were asked about the concept of judicial review as set out in *Marbury v. Madison* and the implications of the Supreme Court case of *United States v. Nixon*.

Twelve items tested students on their understanding of the role of American political parties and elections (index range 0–12). Students were asked about the philosophical role of political parties according to James Madison in *Federalist 10* as well as the current role of parties in American politics, state voter requirements, the notion of proportional representation, the Electoral College, parties' role in nominating presidential candidates, and the impact of third parties. Participants were asked the definition of a political action committee (PAC), the influence of PACs on parties, and the outcome of the Supreme Court case *Citizens United v. Federal Election Commission*. This dimension also covers muckraking and television's role in elections.

A five-item additive index (range 0–5) taps students' knowledge of race and politics. Respondents were surveyed on their knowledge of the Supreme Court case of *Brown v. Board of Education*, the definitions of affirmative action and multiculturalism, and Dr. Martin Luther King Jr.'s call for nonviolent protests. Students interpreted a quotation about America as a melting pot from Israel Zangwill to gauge comprehension of the concept of assimilation.

CLASS TYPE

The questionnaire includes dichotomous items indicating whether or not a student had taken a WTP class or an AP class. In total, 48% of students took neither a WTP nor an AP class, 31% took either WTP or AP, and 21% took WTP for AP credit. The study also ascertained whether the students had taken civics as a required (84%) or an elective (16%) class.

CLASSROOM CLIMATE

Classroom climate indicates the amount of freedom students feel they have to express themselves during instructional periods. The measure gauges students' perception of the openness of their classroom to student input, voicing opinions, discussion about political ideas, teacher-student disagreements, and student-student disagreements. We constructed an index consisting of seven four-point Likert-scale items scored in the direction of an open classroom. These items were adapted from prior works, especially the *IEA Civic Education Study*.[39] The classroom climate index ranges from 0 to 29 and has a reliability of .887 (Cronbach's α).

INSTRUCTIONAL METHODS

The survey includes five items that account for the type of instruction respondents experienced in their civics class. Students were asked to what extent their instruction was based on lecture, textbook, or current events-based learning and whether or not classroom and community-related activities were part of respondents' civic education. Classroom activities include simulated hearings, moot court, debates, and other forms of active classroom pedagogies. Community-related activities take into account actions that involve students beyond the classroom, such as contacting public officials, attending community meetings, and service-learning. Each of these survey items is measured on a four-point scale indicating if respondents' civics instruction never/rarely (1) or always (4) included the approach.

GRADE POINT AVERAGE

Studies have shown that grade point average (GPA) is positively associated with factual knowledge gain from traditional social studies classes.[40] We include GPA as a control variable in our analysis. In cases where students have earned AP credit, their GPA can be higher than 4.0. GPA in this study has been normalized and is measured on a four-point unweighted scale to achieve consistency across schools.

DEMOGRAPHICS

Controls for students' gender and race are included in the analysis. Gender is coded 1 for female and 2 for male. Race categories consist of white, black/African American, Latino, Asian American/Pacific Islander, and multiracial.

ANALYSIS AND FINDINGS

Students participating in this study, much like the wider American population, are not highly knowledgeable about politics, nor are they uninformed. Rather, students have low to moderate levels of knowledge. None of the students in the study received a perfect score on the knowledge pretest or posttest. However, the study participants' knowledge of government and politics increased as a result of taking a civics class. As table 8.1 indicates, students' average scores for

Table 8.1 Knowledge Pretest/Posttest Mean Difference Scores				
MEASURE	**PRETEST**	**POSTTEST**	**x̄ DIFFERENCE**	**SIGNIFICANCE**
Constitutional Principles	6.29	6.32	.03	n.s.
Bill of Rights	2.91	3.15	.24	.00
Government Institutions	7.94	9.05	1.11	.00
Political Parties and Elections	5.28	5.86	.58	.00
Race and Politics	2.62	2.88	.26	.00
n = 1,015				

the entire sample improved significantly from the pretest to the posttest for every knowledge dimension except constitutional principles. The subsequent analyses will demonstrate that there is substantial variation in knowledge gain within each dimension based on teacher professional development, class type, instructional methods, and classroom climate.

To determine the effects of WTP teacher professional development and class type (WTP and non-WTP) on students' acquisition of the five dimensions of political knowledge, we estimated a hierarchical linear model using analysis of covariance (ANCOVA). A random factor representing the schools in the sample accounts for clustering of students within schools. A three category teacher/class type measure is a fixed factor in the model. There are three categories of teacher/class type:

1. teacher with WTP professional development/WTP class
2. teacher with WTP teacher professional development/non-WTP class
3. comparison group (non-WTP teacher/non-WTP class)

The two WTP teacher professional-development categories and the comparison-group scores on the knowledge indicators were not equivalent at baseline. A statistical adjustment was made, with pretest knowledge scores entered as covariates. Students' GPAs also were included as covariates.[41]

We report the unadjusted posttest mean knowledge scores and standard deviations as well as the estimated mean outcomes and the standard errors for the WTP professional development teacher groups and the comparison group. We also present the difference of means between the comparison group and the two WTP professional development teacher groups along with the related significance tests. Post hoc analyses with a Bonferroni adjustment were performed to establish statistical significance. We computed the Benjamini-Hochberg correction for multiple comparisons to counter inflated estimates of statistical significance. The effect size estimated using Hedge's g is computed for each knowledge dimension and is reported in the last column of table 8.2. Hedge's g is computed for the control group and the WTP professional development teachers/WTP class intervention, as the difference of means between these groups is largest in most instances.[42] A score of .2 is considered a weak effect, .5 is a moderate effect, and .8 or greater is a large effect.[43]

After adjusting for the baseline knowledge scores and GPA, there are statistically significant differences ($p \leq .05$) in the posttest scores based on teacher professional development and class type for four of the five dimensions of knowledge: the US Constitution, Bill of Rights, parties and elections, and race and politics (see table 8.2). There are no significant differences based on teacher/class type for knowledge of US government institutions. This result is likely due to the fact that students came to the course with a greater knowledge of US government institutions than other topic areas so their knowledge gain would be smaller. In addition, the non-WTP classes focused heavily on government institutions and spent less time on the Constitution and other topics.

The impact of WTP professional development and the WTP curriculum is greatest for knowledge of the Constitution. The findings generally support H_1 as students taught by teachers with WTP professional development had significantly higher adjusted mean scores than students in the comparison group for the four knowledge measures. There is more qualified support for H_2. Students enrolled in the WTP class had the highest scores in the study for knowledge of the Constitution. The differences in the adjusted means between the WTP professional development teacher/WTP class group and both the comparison and WTP professional development teacher/non-WTP class groups are statistically significant ($p \leq .00$). However, WTP students' scores are very similar to those of students taking a traditional civics class with a WTP professional development teacher for knowledge of the Bill of Rights and race. Teachers who have had WTP professional development do not "reinvent the wheel" when they are teaching a traditional civics class. Instead, they employ similar instructional strategies even when they are not teaching the WTP curriculum. WTP students scored lower than students taking traditional civics with a WTP professional development teacher on knowledge of parties and elections. The WTP curriculum focuses heavily on the foundational documents and places somewhat less emphasis on topics like parties and elections. The effect size is highest for the four knowledge measures and falls into the low-moderate to moderate range.[44] Knowledge of the Constitution has the largest effect size followed by race, Bill of Rights, and parties and elections.

Some explanations for these basic differences in knowledge level between the WTP and non-WTP students were revealed on further analysis of student data. Knowledge of the US Constitution and the Bill of Rights was lowest for the comparison group and highest for students who took the WTP class. We expect WTP students to gain constitutional knowledge because the WTP curriculum focuses heavily on this content. Further, teacher training and skills are established factors that contribute to enhanced student learning. In particular, programs that integrate knowledge and practice are especially effective.[45] All of the teachers in the study have taken part in at least one training program related to US government and social studies. The WTP teachers participated in summer institutes and other training opportunities that conveyed the content material and specialized skills required of instructors in the program. WTP teachers are encouraged to use active learning strategies, such as student-led group work, as they prepare their students for the culminating activity of the simulated congressional hearing. Five of the WTP teachers in the study also taught non-WTP classes. We assume that aspects of the content and pedagogy they employ when teaching their WTP classes would carry over to their other civics courses, which helps to explain the more pronounced knowledge gain for students of WTP teachers compared to the control group of students whose teachers did not have WTP professional development.

Table 8.2 Estimated Impacts of WTP Teacher Professional Development and Class Type on Political Knowledge

	n	Unadjusted $\bar{x}$	SD	Adjusted $\bar{x}$	SE	$\bar{x}$ Difference	p	Effect Size
CONSTITUTION								
Comparison	352	5.13	2.43	5.72	.15			
Non-WTP Class	277	6.72	2.51	6.48	.16	.76	.01*	.40
WTP Class	386	7.10	2.58	6.74	.11	1.02	.00*	
BILL OF RIGHTS								
Comparison	351	2.46	1.42	2.84	.09			
Non-WTP Class	277	3.41	1.41	3.32	.10	.47	.01*	.35
WTP Class	386	3.59	1.35	3.33	.07	.49	.00*	
GOVERNMENT INSTITUTIONS								
Comparison	351	7.81	3.24	9.12	.17			
Non-WTP Class	277	9.68	2.87	8.95	.19	-.17	1.00	.04
WTP Class	386	9.72	3.02	9.01	.13	-.11	1.00	
PARTIES AND ELECTIONS								
Comparison	351	4.91	2.40	5.23	.15			
Non-WTP Class	277	6.47	2.50	6.22	.16	.93	.00*	.33
WTP Class	386	6.27	2.56	6.03	.11	.75	.00*	
RACE								
Control	351	2.39	1.23	2.56	.08			
Non-WTP Class	277	3.13	1.30	2.99	.09	.43	.01*	.38
WTP Class	386	3.15	1.31	3.05	.06	.49	.00*	

*The estimated impact is statistically significant at p≤.05 after applying the Benjamini-Hochberg correction for multiple comparisons.

We now examine the bivariate relationship between students' knowledge scores on the posttest and class type, teacher type, instructional methods, class climate, and demographics (see table 8.3). As the foregoing analysis of knowledge gain indicates, taking a WTP class, having a WTP teacher as the instructor, taking civics as an elective, and taking an AP class are all positively associated with political knowledge. The second strongest set of correlations is for taking civics with a WTP teacher. The relationship is statistically significant for all of the knowledge dimensions and is especially strong for constitutional principles and Bill of Rights. Taking civics as an elective class is significantly correlated with all of the knowledge indicators. WTP students have a stronger grasp of knowledge of constitutional principles and the Bill of Rights than non-WTP students, which is in keeping with the program's content focus. The correlation between taking an AP class and knowledge of government institutions and political parties and elections is higher than for taking a WTP class. It may be the case that the content of the AP class focuses more heavily on these topics whereas the WTP curriculum concentrates more on the Constitution.

There is a strong relationship between classroom environment and students' knowledge levels. Classes in which students were encouraged to express themselves and felt that their opinions were respected by the teacher and their colleagues were more conducive to the acquisition of knowledge. Class climate is positively related to all of the dimensions of political knowledge. The association between class climate and knowledge is stronger than for any of the instructional approach measures that we included in this analysis.

Classes with a prominent lecture component contribute favorably to the acquisition of political knowledge. The incorporation of current events into the curriculum also is positively associated with knowledge gain. The correlations, however, are not especially strong. The relationship

Table 8.3 Correlations (Pearson's R) Between Posttest Knowledge Indexes and Class Type, Teacher Type, GPA, Class Climate, Instructional Approach, and Demographics

	CONSTITUTIONAL PRINCIPLES	BILL OF RIGHTS	GOVERNMENT INSTITUTIONS	RACE	POLITICAL PARTIES
WTP Class	.232[a]	.205[a]	.137[a]	.161[a]	.107[a]
AP Class	.172[a]	.177[a]	.181[a]	.148[a]	.211[a]
Elective Class	.350[a]	.239[a]	.211[a]	.260[a]	.222[a]
WTP Teacher	.333[a]	.311[a]	.269[a]	.269[a]	.244[a]
Class Climate	.322[a]	.301[a]	.307[a]	.264[a]	.291[a]
Lecture	.081[a]	.065[b]	.100[a]	.079[a]	.090[a]
Textbook	.017	.016	-.054	-.044	-.030
Current Events	.057[a]	.067[b]	.095[a]	.048	.063[b]
Class Activities	.008	.017	.015	.018	-.002
Community Activities	-.046[b]	-.003	-.082[a]	-.082[a]	-.080[a]
Gender	.067[b]	.069[b]	.071[b]	.034	.062[b]
White	.138[a]	.171[a]	.218[a]	.151[a]	.226[a]
Black	-.170[a]	-.153[a]	-.205[a]	-.162[a]	-.201[a]
Latino	-.067[b]	-.130[a]	-.109[a]	-.083[a]	-.101[a]
Asian American	.071[b]	.080[a]	.056	.058	.018
Multiracial	-.056	-.072[b]	-.092[a]	-.042	-.086[a]
Pretest Knowledge	.687[a]	.603[a]	.712[a]	.584[a]	.641[a]
GPA	.445[a]	.411[a]	.478[a]	.367[a]	.416[a]

n = 1,015
[a]p ≤ .01; [b]p ≤ .05

between lecture and all of the knowledge dimensions is statistically significant. The correlation with current events is significant for every knowledge dimension except political parties and elections. The finding of a connection between lecture and current events approaches and political knowledge acquisition corroborates prior research results.[46]

There is a negative relationship between classes that incorporate community activities and political knowledge. A focus on community activities is more likely to promote learning about public policy issues than the type of knowledge represented in this study. These types of activities often emphasize community concerns and current practices as opposed to knowledge of governmental principles and institutions. There is no relationship between knowledge and a civics class that relies heavily on textbook learning. It is our assumption that textbook reading will not contribute significantly to students' acquisition of political knowledge when it is a centerpiece of the curriculum. However, it is likely that textbook assignments in conjunction with other approaches, such as instruction using current events to stimulate discussion, can be effective in conveying information.[47] Contrary to our expectations, there is no relationship between any of the knowledge measures and classroom activities. It may be the case that activities such as classroom debates and simulations contribute more to the development of civic dispositions and skills, such as contacting officials and participating in town meetings, than to the acquisition of knowledge.

Prior research indicates that levels of political knowledge based on gender and race are influenced by resources, opportunities, and motivation that are afforded to particular groups.[48] Female students traditionally have scored lower on political knowledge tests than male students. One explanation is that female students are socialized to nonpolitical roles and are less motivated to learn about politics, which they perceive to be a male-dominated field.[49] However, there is evidence that gender differences in political knowledge are diminishing as societal norms have been shifting in favor of greater female political engagement.[50] Further, female students show a greater aptitude toward political knowledge that requires reasoning skills, and not the mere statement of fact, than male students.[51] Female students in our study reflect this evolving trend as they score higher on all of the knowledge measures with the exception of race and politics, where there is no gender difference.

Racial differences in political knowledge have persistently demonstrated that whites have greater factual knowledge of politics than members of minority groups.[52] For blacks and Latinos, especially, these disparities have been attributed to socioeconomic inequities, lack of resources, and low quality or a complete lack of civic education.[53] Less research has focused on Asian American students, but findings indicate that levels of political knowledge may be higher for some Asian ethnic groups, such as Chinese and Korean Americans, than for blacks and Latinos.[54] In keeping with prior research, we find positive, statistically significant relationships for white students and all of the knowledge indicators. The relationship is strongest for knowledge of government institutions and political parties. The coefficients for Asian American students are positive and significant for knowledge of constitutional principles, the Bill of Rights, and government institutions but are nonsignificant for racial politics and political parties. Negative correlations exist for black, Latino, and multiracial students on all of the measures. The coefficients are higher for black students than Latino students.

We also correlated pretest knowledge and GPA with the posttest knowledge measures to establish the strength of their relationship as we will be incorporating these measures as controls in the subsequent analysis. There is a substantial correspondence between pretest and posttest knowledge on the five dimensions. The relationship is strongest for knowledge of government institutions and weakest for race and politics. As one might expect, GPA is a strong correlate of all of the indexes of political knowledge. The correspondence between GPA and knowledge is higher for dimensions that deal with the principles, foundations, and institutions of government than for race and politics.

The bivariate correlations provide some preliminary support for our hypotheses that teacher professional development, class type, classroom climate, and instructional methods are related to students' political knowledge levels. We now employ multiple ordinary least squares regression (OLS) analysis to determine if these relationships hold up after statistical controls are introduced. OLS is an effective method for distinguishing the impact of educational interventions when pretest/posttest data are available. Using the student as the unit of analysis, we are able to control for individual differences that are accounted for by students' a priori knowledge and GPA.[55] The regression coefficients for the independent variables directly related to the intervention represent their estimated effect on the posttest knowledge dependent variables holding pretest knowledge and GPA constant.

Separate models are presented for each of the five knowledge domains with the dependent variable in each equation being the knowledge posttest score. The independent variables are entered in blocks containing three categories of variables—covariates, class type and teacher professional development indicators, and classroom climate/instruction variables. The covariates or controls are the students' pretest knowledge scores and GPA, which are likely to influence students' knowledge scores outside of the civics class intervention. Students' pretest scores provide a knowledge baseline. The bivariate analysis has established strong correspondences between pretest knowledge and GPA and posttest knowledge. Pretest knowledge and GPA are collinear, but we include both indicators in the block as they are conceptually distinct. The second block contains the WTP, AP, and elective class dummy variables as well as the WTP/non-WTP teacher professional development indicator. There is evidence of multicollinearity in block two, especially between the WTP teacher and WTP class variables. Classroom climate and the five instructional methods variables are entered in the third block. There is slight collinearity between current events and class climate. We report the proportion of variance explained by each block (R^2 block) as an indicator of the collective relationship between the variables in the block and the dependent variable. The individual regression coefficients can be unstable as a result of the multicollinearity within blocks. We did not include the demographic variables in the final OLS regression analyses as they were not statistically significant in the multivariate models.

As anticipated, the block of control variables explains the highest proportion of variation in the dependent variables. Pretest knowledge is the strongest predictor of posttest knowledge in all of the equations as was the case in the bivariate analysis (see table 8.4). The largest coefficient is associated with knowledge of government institutions (.629) followed by constitutional principles (.585) and political parties (.537). The relationship is somewhat less robust for knowledge of race and politics (.493) and the Bill of Rights (.473). The coefficients for GPA are significant for all five knowledge dimensions, but they are substantially smaller than for pretest knowledge due to multicollinearity. GPA has a moderately strong correlation with each of the pretest knowledge scores.

The block of class and teacher variables is statistically significant in all but the government institutions equation. The findings introducing controls for prior civic knowledge and GPA provide support for our hypothesis that teacher professional development contributes to knowledge gain among high school students. Studying civics or social studies with a WTP teacher is the strongest predictor in this category, as the students of WTP teachers scored higher than the comparison group students on all but knowledge of political parties. Students who took an elective civics or social studies course performed better on the knowledge posttest than those whose class was required. Taking civics as an elective is positively associated with knowledge gain for constitutional principles, Bill of Rights, race, and political parties. AP civics is only significant for knowledge of political parties, which is a topic that is emphasized in the AP class to a greater extent than in the WTP classes that focus more on the US Constitution. Taking a WTP class is nonsignificant for all of the equations. The WTP teacher and WTP class variables are collinear, which explains the nonsignificant coefficients for the WTP class variable in the multivariate analysis.

Table 8.4 OLS Regression of Posttest Knowledge Indexes on Class Type, Teacher Type, Class Climate, Instructional Approach, and Demographics

	CONSTITUTIONAL PRINCIPLES	BILL OF RIGHTS	GOVERNMENT INSTITUTIONS	RACE	POLITICAL PARTIES
Pretest Knowledge	.585[a]	.473[a]	.629[a]	.493[a]	.537[a]
GPA	.054[b]	.133[a]	.127[a]	.094[a]	.122[a]
R² Block	.484[a]	.380[a]	.530[a]	.363[a]	.439[a]
WTP Class	.020	.005	.009	.046	.054
AP Class	.028	.031	.028	.013	.111[a]
Elective Class	.114[a]	.063[b]	.014	.095[a]	.104[a]
WTP Teacher	.072[a]	.076[a]	.065[b]	.090[a]	.022
R² Block	.022[a]	.018[a]	.002	.021[a]	.022[a]
Class Climate	.108[a]	.100[a]	.210[a]	.094[a]	.093[a]
Lecture	.020	-.016	-.015	-.037	.006
Textbook	-.019	-.027	.028	.008	-.024
Current Events	.016	.006	-.060[b]	.017	.017
Class Activities	.001	.032	.006	-.018	-.048
Community Activities	.073[a]	.009	.057[b]	.053	.108[a]
R² Block	.013[a]	.009[b]	.014[a]	.032[a]	.014[a]
R Square	.519[a]	.407[a]	.547[a]	.394[a]	.475[a]

Beta coefficients are reported
n = 1015
[a]p≤.01; [b]p≤.05

The final block of variables, which accounts for classroom climate and instructional approaches, is statistically significant in each of the five knowledge equations. An open class climate is a stronger predictor of knowledge than any of the teaching approaches we examined in this study; the relationship is statistically significant for all of the equations. Classes conducted in an atmosphere that encourages civil discussion and opinion sharing are more successful in conveying information than closed classrooms. The coefficient for government institutions (.210) is more than double the size of the association for any of the other types of knowledge—constitutional principles (.108), Bill of Rights (.100), race (.094), and parties (.093). We find qualified support for the hypothesis that active learning approaches correspond to greater knowledge acquisition. Incorporating community activities into the curriculum can enhance knowledge gain related to constitutional principles, government institutions, and political parties. This finding is in keeping with our contention that activities that make a connection between classroom learning and real-world experience can reinforce knowledge. However, we find no relationship between classroom-based activities and knowledge. Standard lecture, textbook, and current events-based approaches are not significantly related to any of the knowledge dimensions, with one exception. There is a weak negative association between current events and knowledge of government institutions. As noted previously, we found some weak, statistically significant relationships between lecture and current events in the bivariate analysis, but these relationships did not hold up in the multivariate model.

CONCLUSION

Our research builds on prior studies demonstrating that classes involving lecture and current events material are successful in conveying core knowledge of democratic principles, government institutions, and political processes.[56] We find some evidence, especially in the bivariate analysis, to support this contention. However, the strongest takeaway from our research is that an open class climate is more conducive to students' acquisition of political knowledge than any particular classroom pedagogical approach. Students who are encouraged to engage with the course material through respectful discussions are not only likely to better process and retain information, they also can develop essential political skills and dispositions for democratic engagement, such as expressing opinions at town meetings.

Students of WTP teachers, regardless of whether or not they took a WTP class, perform better on tests of political knowledge than other students, especially in specific knowledge domains associated with the WTP curriculum. Further, students who choose to be in a civics class will outperform students who take civics because it is required. It stands to reason that a self-selecting group will have a higher level of motivation to perform than those who are in the class because it is a graduation requirement. The ethnographic research that accompanied this study found that the level and creativity of instruction in elective classes often exceeded that of required civics classes. Students in elective classes engaged in independent research and took part in class activities, such as debates, more often than students in required classes.

Students in AP classes scored higher on the civic knowledge test than their counterparts taking civics for standard credit. AP students are primed to perform well on exams testing their knowledge of government and politics, and so their superior scores on the indicators in this study are to be expected. They also came to the class with higher baseline knowledge than other students. As the multivariate analysis demonstrates, knowledge gained from taking the AP class is significant only for the political parties domain.

In sum, political knowledge is a precursor to political engagement. People who understand the basics of American government and how political processes work are more likely to feel politically efficacious and to take part in politics.[57] Effective middle and high school civic education can instill knowledge that forms a foundation for political engagement over the life course.[58] Students who have experienced programs employing an innovative curriculum taught by well-trained teachers will exhibit higher levels of knowledge than their peers and, as a consequence, may be more inclined to become active political participants as they enter the electorate. In particular, teachers who cultivate an open class environment where students' voices are heard and respected can contribute to creating a more engaged citizenry. ■

ENDNOTES

1. Diana Owen, "Political Socialization in the 21st Century: Recommendations for Researchers," at The Future of Civic Education in the 21st Century Conference, cosponsored by the Center for Civic Education and the Bundeszentrale fur politische Bildung, James Madison's Montpelier, September 21–26, 2008; Diana Owen, "The Influence of Civic Education on Electoral Engagement and Voting," in *Teaching Civic Engagement: From Student to Active Citizen*, eds. Alison Rios Millett McCartney, Elizabeth Bennion, and Richard Simpson (Washington, DC: American Political Science Association, 2013).

2. See http://www.civiced.org/programs/wtp.

3. See Richard G. Niemi and Jane Junn, *Civic Education: What Makes Students Learn* (New Haven, CT: Yale University Press, 1998); William Galston, "Political Knowledge, Political Engagement, and Civic Education," *Annual Review of Political Science* (2001): 217–34; Henry Milner, *The Internet Generation* (Lebanon, NH: Tufts University Press, 2010); David E. Campbell, *Why We Vote: How Schools and Communities Shape Our Civic Life* (Princeton, NJ: Princeton University Press, 2006).

4. Stephen E. Finkel and Howard Ernst, "Civic Education in Post-Apartheid South Africa: Alternative Paths to the Development of Political Knowledge and Democratic Values," *Political Psychology* (2005): 333–64; William Galston, "Civic Education and Political Participation," *PS: Political Science & Politics* (2004): 263–66; Richard Brody, "Secondary Education and Political Attitudes: Examining the Effects on Political Tolerance of the We the People . . . Curriculum" (Calabasas, CA: Center for Civic Education, 1994); James Youniss, "Civic Education: What Schools Can Do to Encourage Civic Identity and Action," *Applied Developmental Science* (2011): 98–103.

5. Galston, "Civic Education and Political Participation," 2004; Michael X. Delli Carpini and Scott Keeter, *What Ameri-*

cans Know About Politics and Why It Matters (New Haven, CT: Yale University Press, 1996); Michael McDevitt and Steven Chaffee, "Closing Gaps in Political Communication and Knowledge Effects of a School Intervention," *Communication Research* (2000): 259–92; Patrick C. Meirick and Daniel B. Wackman, "Kids Voting and Political Knowledge: Narrowing Gaps, Informing Votes, " *Social Science Quarterly* (2004): 1161–77; Campaign for the Civic Mission of Schools, "Guardian of Democracy: The Civic Mission of Schools," Research Report, The Leonore Annenberg Institute for Civics of the Annenberg Public Policy Center at the University of Pennsylvania and the Campaign for the Civic Mission of Schools, Accessed January 11, 2015, http://www.cms-ca.org/guardianofdemocracy_report_final.pdf.

6.   Delli Carpini and Keeter, *What Americans Know,* 1996, 10–11.

7.   Stephen Earl Bennett, "'Know-Nothings' Revisited: The Meaning of Political Ignorance Today," *Social Science Quarterly* (1988): 476–90; Stephen Earl Bennett, "Trends in American Political Information, 1967–1987," *American Politics Quarterly* (1989): 422–35; Russell W. Neuman, *The Paradox of Mass Politics* (Cambridge, MA: Harvard University Press, 1986); Eric R. A. N. Smith, *The Unchanging American Voter* (Berkeley: University of California Press, 1989; Michael X. Delli Carpini, "An Overview of the State of Citizens' Knowledge About Politics," in *Communicating Politics: Engaging the Public in Democratic Life*, eds. Michael S. McKinney, Lynda L. Kaid, Dianne G. Bystrom, and Diana B. Carlin (New York: Peter Lang, 2005), 27–40; William A. Galston and Mark H. Lopez, "Civic Education in the United States," in *Civic Engagement and the Baby Boomer Generation*, eds. Laura B. Wilson and Sharon P. Simson, (New York: The Haworth Press, 2006), 3–19; Jeffrey Friedman and Shterna Friedman, *Political Knowledge* (New York: Routledge, 2013).

8.   Delli Carpini and Keeter, *What Americans Know*, 1996; Pew Research Center, for the People & the Press, "Political Knowledge Update," Research Report (Washington, DC, March 31, 2011), Accessed December 20, 2014, http://pewresearch.org/pubs/1944/political-news-quiz-iq-congress-control-obesity-energy-facebook.

9.   Delli Carpini, "An Overview of the State of Citizens' Knowledge," 2005.

10. Delli Carpini and Keeter, *What Americans Know*, 1996.

11. Delli Carpini and Keeter, *What Americans Know*, 1996; Kirk Hallahan, "Enhancing Motivation, Opportunity, and Ability to Process Public Relations Messages," *Public Relations Review* (2000): 463–80; Jason Barabas, Jennifer Jerit, William Pollock, and Carlisle Rainey, "The Question(s) of Political Knowledge," *American Political Science Review* (2014): 840–55.

12. Pui-Wa Lei, Dina Bassiri, and E. Matthew Schultz, "Alternatives to the Grade Point Average of Academic Achievement in College," ACTRR No. 2001-4 (Iowa City, IA: ACT, Inc., 2001).

13. Richard E. Petty and John T. Cacioppo, *Communication and Persuasion* (NewYork: Springer-Verlag, 1986); Shelly Chaiken, "The Heuristic Model of Persuasion," in *Social Influence: The Ontario Symposium*, volume five, eds. Mark P. Zanna, James M. Olson, and C. Peter Herman (Hillsdale, NJ: Lawrence Erlbaum Associates, 1987), 13–39; Deborah J. MacInnis, Christine M. Moorman, and Bernard J. Jaworski, "Enhancing and Measuring Consumers' Motivation, Opportunity, and Ability to Process Brand Information from Ads," *Journal of Marketing* (1991): 32–53; Hallahan, "Enhancing Motivation, Opportunity, and Ability," 463–80.

14. Lee H. Ehman, "An Analysis of the Relationships of Selected Educational Variables with the Political Socialization of High School Students," *American Educational Research Journal* (1969): 559–80; William Morgan and Matthew Streb, "Building Citizenship: How Student Voice in Service-Learning Develops," *Social Science Quarterly* (2001): 154–69.

15. Owen, "The Influence of Civic Education," 2013.

16. Charles C. Bonwell and James A. Eison, *Active Learning: Creating Excitement in the Classroom*, ASHE-ERIC Higher Education Report No. 1, School of Education and Human Development (Washington, DC: The George Washington University, 1991), iii.

17. See Becci Burchett Gauna and Michelle Paul, "Civic Education Training Promotes Active Learning with Real-World Outcomes," *SPACE: Student Perspectives about Civic Engagement* (2016): Article 4.

18. Niemi and Junn, *Civic Education* 1998; Diana Owen, Suzanne Soule, and Rebecca Chalif, "Civic Education and Knowledge of Politics and Government," paper prepared for presentation at the Annual Meeting of the American Political Science Association, Seattle, Washington, 2011.

19. Michael Winerip, "Teaching Beyond the Test, to Make Room Again for Current Events," *The New York Times*, May 22, Accessed December 23, 2014 http://www.nytimes.com/2011/05/23/nyregion/teaching-beyond-test-with-eye-on-current-events.html.

20. Herbert Atherton, "We the People...Project Citizen," in *Education for Civic Engagement in Democracy: Service-Learning and Other Promising Practices*, eds. Sheilah Mann and John Patrick (Bloomington, IN: Indiana University Press, 2000); Kenneth Tolo, "An Assessment of We the People: Project Citizen: Promoting Citizenship in Classrooms and Communities," [#161], Lyndon B. Johnson School of Public Affairs, University of Texas at Austin, 1998, Accessed January 6, 2015, http://new.civiced.org/resources/research/researchevaluation.

21. Steven E. Finkel, "Can Democracy Be Taught?" *Journal of Democracy* (2003): 137–51; Judith Torney-Purta, Rainer Lehmann, Hans Oswald, and Wolfram Schulz, *Citizenship and Education in Twenty-Eight Countries: Civic Knowledge and Engagement at Age Fourteen* (Amsterdam: International Association for the Evaluation of Educational Achievement, 2001); Judith Torney-Purta, "The School's Role in Developing Civic Engagement: A Study of Adolescents in Twenty-Eight Countries," *Applied Developmental Science* (2002): 203–12; Joel Westheimer and Joseph Kahne, "What Kind of Citizen? The Politics of Educating for Democracy," *American Educational Research Journal* (2004): 237–69; Judith Tor-

ney-Purta, Jo-Ann Amadeo, and Wendy K. Richardson, "Civic Service Among Youth in Chile, Denmark, England, and the United States: A Psychological Perspective," in *Civic Service Worldwide: Impacts and Inquiry*, eds. Amanda Moore McBride and Michael Sherraden (Armonk, NY: M. E. Sharpe, 2007), 95–132.

22. Niemi and Junn, *Civic Education*, 1998.

23. Galston, "Political Knowledge, Political Engagement, and Civic Education"; Diana Hess, *Controversy in the Classroom: The Democratic Power of Discussion* (New York: Routledge, 2009); Diana E. Hess and Paula McAvoy, *The Political Classroom* (New York: Routledge, 2015).

24. Niemi and Junn, *Civic Education*, 1998.

25. California Campaign for the Civic Mission of Schools, "The California Survey of Civic Education," Research Report (Constitutional Rights Foundation, 2005), Accessed January 11, 2015, http://www.cms-ca.org/civic_survey_final.pdf.

26. Tim Vercellotti and Elizabeth Matto, "The Kitchen-Table Connection: The Effects of Political Discussion on Youth Knowledge and Efficacy," CIRCLE Working Paper #72, 2010, Accessed December 23, 2014, http://www.civicyouth.org/wp-content/uploads/2010/09/WP_72_Vercellotti_Matto.pdf.

27. Hess, *Controversy in the Classroom*, 2009.

28. Niemi and Junn, *Civic Education*, 1998; Leming Robert, "We the People...The Citizen and the Constitution" (Calabasas, CA: The Center for Civic Education, 1996); Brody, "Secondary Education and Political Attitudes," 1994; Joseph Kahne and Ellen Middaugh, "High Quality Civic Education: What Is It and Who Gets It?" *Social Education*(2008): 34–9; Joseph Middaugh, Ellen Middaugh, and Chris Evans, *The Civic Potential of Video Games* (Boston: Massachusetts Institute of Technology Press, 2009).

29. Joseph Kahne and Ellen Middaugh, "Democracy for Some: The Civic Opportunity Gap in High Schools." CIRCLE Working Paper 59, 2008, Accessed August 6, 2011, http://www.civicyouth.org/PopUps/WorkingPapers/WP-59Kahne.pdf; Torney-Purta, "The School's Role in Developing Civic Engagement,"2002.

30. James Youniss and Miranda Yates, *Community Service and Social Responsibility in Youth* (Chicago: University of Chicago Press, 1997).

31. David E. Campbell, "Sticking Together: Classroom Diversity and Civic Education," *American Politics Research* (2007): 57–78; David E. Campbell, "Voice in the Classroom: How an Open Classroom Climate Fosters Political Engagement Among Adolescents," *Political Behavior* (2008): 437–54; Jason Gainous and Allison M. Martens, "The Effectiveness of Civic Education: Are 'Good' Teachers Actually Good for 'All' Students?" *American Politics Research* (2012): 232–66.

32. Campbell, "Voice in the Classroom," 2008.

33. Ibid.

34. Ehman, "An Analysis of the Relationships of Selected Educational Variables," 1969.

35. Elizabeth Beaumont, "Promoting Political Agency, Addressing Political Inequality: A Multilevel Model of Internal Political Efficacy," *The Journal of Politics* (2011): 216–31; Adam Voight and Judith Torney-Purta, "A Typology of Youth Civic Engagement in Urban Middle Schools," *Applied Developmental Science* (2013): 198–212.

36. Campbell, "Sticking Together," 2007; Campbell, "Voice in the Classroom," 2008; Orit Ichilov, "Civic Knowledge of High School Students in Israel: Personal and Contextual Determinants," *Political Psychology* (2007): 417–40.

37. Information about the teacher professional-development program is available at http://jmlresearch.org/.

38. See Robert C. Luskin and John G. Bullock, "'Don't Know' Means 'Don't Know': DK Responses and the Public's Level of Political Knowledge," *The Journal of Politics* (2011): 547–57.

39. Torney-Purta et al., "Civic Service Among Youth," 2001; Campbell, "Voice in the Classroom: How an Open Classroom Environment Facilitates Adolescents' Civic Learning," CIRCLE Working Paper 28. Research Report. (The Center for Information and Research on Civic Learning and Engagement, 2005), Accessed January 11, 2015, http://files.eric.ed.gov/fulltext/ED491131.pdf.

40. Carol S. Botsch and Robert E. Botsch, "Audiences and Outcomes in Online and Traditional American Government Classes: A Comparative Two-year Case Study," *PS: Political Science & Politics* (2001): 135–41; Leonard Champney and Paul Edleman, "Assessing Student Learning Outcomes in United States Government Courses," *PS: Political Science & Politics* (2010): 127–31.

41. G. David Garson, "Testing Statistical Assumptions" (Statistical Association Publishing, 2012) http://www.statisticalassociates.com/assumptions.pdf.

42. Joseph A. Durlak, "How to Select, Calculate, and Interpret Effect Sizes," *Journal of Pediatric Psychology* (2009): 917–28.

43. David M. Lane, *Online Statistics Education: An Interactive Multimedia Course of Study* (Houston, TX: Rice University, 2016).

44. Jacob Cohen, *Statistical Power Analysis for the Social Sciences* (Mahwah, NJ: Lawrence Erlbaum Associates, 1988); Lane, *Online Statistics Education*, 2016.

45. Lawrence Ingvarson, Marion Meiers, and Adrian Beavis, "Factors Affecting the Impact of Professional Development Programs on Teachers' Knowledge, Practice, Student Outcomes & Efficacy," Research Report (Australian Council for Educational Research, 2005), Accessed January 11, 2015, http://research.acer.edu.au/professional_dev/1; Torney-Purta, "The School's Role in Developing Civic Engagement," 2002; Campbell, "Voice in the Classroom," 2005.

46. Niemi and Junn, *Civic Education*, 1998; Owen, Soule, and Chalif, "Civic Education and Knowledge," 2011.

47. Owen, Soule, and Chalif, "Civic Education and Knowledge," 2011.

48. Delli Carpini and Keeter, *What Americans Know*, 1996.
49. Marta Fraile, "Do Women Know Less About Politics Than Men? The Gender Gap in Political Knowledge in Europe," *Social Politics: International Studies in Gender, State & Society* (2014): 261–89; Elizabeth Frazer and Kenneth Macdonald, "Sex Differences in Political Knowledge in Britain," *Political Studies* (2003): 67–83; Kate Kenski and Kathleen Hall Jamieson, "The Gender Gap in Political Knowledge: Are Women Less Knowledgeable Than Men About Politics," in *Everything You Think You Know About Politics... and Why You're Wrong*, ed. Kathleen Hall Jamieson, 83–89 (New York: Basic Books, 2000); Mary-Kate Lizotte and Andrew H. Sidman, "Explaining the Gender Gap in Political Knowledge," *Politics & Gender* (2009): 127–51; Jeffery J. Mondak and Mary R. Anderson, "The Knowledge Gap: A Reexamination of Gender-Based Differences in Political Knowledge," *The Journal of Politics* (2004): 492–512.
50. Ichilov, "Civic Knowledge of High School Students," 2007; Torney-Purta et al., "Civic Service Among Youth," 2001.
51. Mónica Ferrín Pereira, Marta Fraile, and Martiño Rubal, "Young and Gapped? Political Knowledge of Girls and Boys in Europe," *Political Research Quarterly* (2014): 63–76.
52. Marisa Abrajano and R. Michael Alvarez, *New Faces, New Voices: The Hispanic Electorate in America* (Princeton, NJ: Princeton University Press, 2010); Marisa Abrajano, "Reexamining the 'Racial Gap' in Political Knowledge," *The Journal of Politics* (2014): 44–54. Appendix can be found online here: http://www.journals.uchicago.edu/doi/full/10.1086/678767#rf1.
53. Delli Carpini and Keeter, *What Americans Know*, 1996; Sidney Verba, Kay Lehman Schlozman, Henry Brady, and Norman H. Nie, "Race, Ethnicity and Political Resources: Participation in the United States," *British Journal of Political Science* (1993): 453–97.
54. Janelle Wong, S. Karthick Ramakrishnan, Taeku Lee, and Jane Junn, *Asian American Political Participation: Emerging Constituents and Their Political Identities* (New York: Russell Sage Foundation, 2011).
55. Roddy Theobald and Scott Freeman, "Is It the Intervention or the Students? Using Linear Regression to Control for Student Characteristics in Undergraduate STEM Education Research," *CBE Life Sciences Education* (2014): 41–8.
56. Niemi and Junn, *Civic Education*, 1998.
57. Delli Carpini and Keeter, *What Americans Know*, 1996.
58. Owen, Soule, and Chalif, "Civic Education and Knowledge," 2011.

APPENDIX 8.1

Knowledge Measures Reliabilities (Cronbach's α)		
MEASURE	**WAVE 1 α**	**WAVE 2 α**
Constitutional Principles	.605	.655
Bill of Rights	.555	.619
Government Institutions	.735	.775
Political Parties and Elections	.612	.654
Race and Politics	.504	.578

Essential School Supports for Civic Learning

9

Shawn P. Healy

This chapter summarizes previous research on essential school supports for students' civic development in the context of high schools. Through analysis of 2013 Illinois Five Essentials survey data, school mission and vision statements, student handbooks, school-wide civic assessments, and structured interviews with 25 teachers and administrators at Illinois high schools recognized for their strong civic learning programs, common elements for sustained, systemic commitments to students' civic development were deduced.

Schools with sustained, systemic commitments to students' civic development have strong civic mission statements and shared leadership in their pursuit. They boast challenging curriculum with traditional and innovative civic learning practices woven across grade levels and subject areas. They also leverage reciprocal relationships with parents and the surrounding community, where all parties view one another as vital resources. Although the selected schools have room for improvement in the areas of civic-oriented staff development and a school climate that nurtures students' civic development, these indicators are vital to sustaining and systematizing school-based civic learning.

Finally, this chapter draws parallels from findings at the high school level for translation to higher education. Challenges are acknowledged, but opportunities abound, as colleges and universities have an important civic mission that must ultimately form a P–20 continuum as we prepare students for careers and informed, effective participation in our democracy.

Generational declines in both political knowledge and engagement are widely documented, along with their deleterious implications for representative democracy.[1] Civic participation is premised on the early acquisition of related knowledge, skills, attitudes, and behaviors, a process long known as political socialization. The process itself is complex and a product of multiple influences, including parents, peers, socioeconomic status, and schools. These sources considered, our public schools (prekindergarten through college, P–20) stand alone as the institution over which we have the most control from a public policy standpoint and thus remain our best hope to reverse the tides of civic apathy and disengagement.[2]

The influence of schools was long dismissed in the field of political science, but recent research accounts for a dramatic reversal. During the past decade and a half, political scientists and educational researchers have examined the impact of school-based civic learning and engagement opportunities, and identified mostly positive results. As Peter Levine writes, "Schools are not the only venues for civic development, but they are vital."[3]

Although the literature to date clearly delineates the power of incorporating civic learning opportunities across the curriculum using both traditional and interactive pedagogical approaches, findings are mostly obtuse and lack a descriptive sense of how sound approaches to civic learning translate in practice. Moreover, the literature largely ignores the broader context of essential school or institutional supports for students' civic development.

This chapter draws from my previous research on high schools' civic learning programs and related organizational culture,[4] and attempts to apply it to our larger educational system with specific translation to institutions of higher learning. My research is positioned within the larger framework of essential school or institutional supports for student learning.[5]

The framework begins with the notion that leadership and vision undergird an educational institution's ability to incubate student learning. Powerful curriculum, combined with an ongoing commitment to staff development, follows. Student learning thrives within a positive academic climate, and educational institutions benefit from a reciprocal relationship with their surrounding community where both view one another as valuable resources and key stakeholders. This framework is anchored in measures of student achievement in subject areas outside of civic learning, namely reading and math. My hypothesis tests the extent to which it can be transferred to civics.

Channeling the findings of the Campaign for the Civic Mission of Schools' *No Excuses* report,[6] my hypothesis builds off of the dependent variable, namely schools with sustainable, systemic approaches to civic learning. Independent variables that will be tested, in turn, include a "strategically designed curriculum" that incorporates promising civic learning practices; "a vision for the importance of civic learning and effective leadership to see it through"; staff development practices that support civic learning, including hiring, evaluation, and professional development; a strong, reciprocal relationship with parents and the surrounding community; and a school climate that "...nurture[s] and model[s] civic dispositions."

The *Illinois Civic Blueprint*[7] sets forth a process by which Illinois high schools complete an assessment of their civic education offerings, along with the organizational culture undergirding them, in pursuit of recognition as an "Illinois Democracy School." Interested schools assess the degree to which students are exposed to promising civic learning practices articulated in across the formal curriculum, extracurricular opportunities, and the day-to-day governance of the school as a whole. Data are gathered from multiple stakeholders, including students, teachers, school administrators, parents, and community partners.

Applicants also complete a qualitative summary of current activities and evidence for assessment in the aforementioned civic learning practices and organizational culture. Finally, applicants develop future plans to demonstrate their schools' continued commitment to the civic development of their students, consider opportunities to better leverage the reciprocal relationship between the school and the local community, and are subsequently eligible for supplementary funding from the Robert R. McCormick Foundation. "Since 2006, [54] Illinois high schools have successfully completed a [school-wide civic assessment] and have been subsequently recognized as Democracy Schools" by the Illinois Civic Mission Coalition.[8]

My hypothesis from previous research on Democracy Schools reads as follows:

Schools with sustainable, systemic approaches to civic learning have these common elements:

1. A strategically designed curriculum that incorporates promising civic learning practices
2. A vision for the importance of civic learning and effective leadership to see it through
3. Staff development practices that support civic learning, including hiring, evaluation, and professional development
4. A strong, reciprocal relationship with parents and the surrounding community
5. A school climate that models and nurtures civic dispositions

To test this five-part hypothesis, six Illinois Democracy Schools were selected that represent the network's geographic and demographic diversity. Selected Democracy Schools were paired with another Illinois high school using a "compare schools" tool on the Illinois Interactive Report Card website.[9] Comparison schools have similar student populations, standardized test performance, financial resources, and attendance and graduation rates. These high schools have not yet pursued recognition as Illinois Democracy Schools, and thus their commitment to civic learning is largely unknown.

Data were drawn from teacher and student responses to the 2013 "Five Essentials" Survey administered to teachers, students, and parents at every public school in Illinois. The survey identifies schools' strengths and weaknesses through a series of questions and follow-up analysis. It operationalizes the essential supports framework for school improvement that encompasses "ambitious instruction," "effective leaders," "collaborative teachers," "involved families," and a "supportive environment."

The University of Chicago Consortium on School Research converts the raw survey data into useful information for school leaders. Ultimately, schools are able to compare their performance across time and also to compare themselves both inside and outside their district. Through descriptive comparisons of results from schools with publically recognized commitments to civic learning with comparable schools lacking this distinction, I assessed discernible differences in these schools' broader supports for student learning.

These findings were supplemented with qualitative data gleaned from the Democary Schools. First, the Democracy School applications of the six high schools selected were analyzed for data on the extent to which (a) promising civic learning practices predominate across the curriculum, and (b) these opportunities are available to students throughout their four-year high school experience.

Next, I engaged in a content analysis of school vision and mission statements along with school policies articulated in student handbooks. The vision and mission statements were evaluated on the extent to which civic learning is articulated, be it overt, implicit, or altogether missing. The same gradations were used for student handbooks in search of civic learning goals in schools' expectations of students' academic performance, behavior, and personal development.

Finally, I conducted semistructured interviews of select school personnel, namely members of the Democracy School application team, including an administrator (the principal or the assistant principal specializing in instruction), the social studies department chair, and at least one other member of the social studies department. Across the six high schools I conducted 25 interviews in all from November 5, 2013, through December 26, 2013. I interviewed four principals, two assistant principals, six social studies department Chairs, and 13 social studies teachers. The survey questions are addressed, in part, in the section that follows.

The interviews lasted 30 to 45 minutes, and I immediately transcribed these recorded conversations. Then, I coded the responses to each of the questions, and the aggregated responses, tied to direct quotations, are discussed, in turn, in the next section.

FINDINGS FROM ILLINOIS HIGH SCHOOLS

In my 2014 study of selected Illinois Democracy Schools,[10] I found at least partial evidence of five common elements that encompassed students' learning experiences and the organizational cultures of these schools supporting them.

The first element, a strategically designed curriculum with promising civic learning practices woven throughout, was universally present. Drawing on data from school-wide civic assessment instruments at selected Illinois Democracy Schools, along with quantitative data from the Illinois "Five Essentials" survey (measures five components found critical for school success: "effective leaders," "collaborative teachers," "involved families," a "supportive environment," and "ambitious instruction") specific to these schools and their paired comparisons (similar in terms of student demographics and per pupil expenditures), the Democracy Schools use a mix of promising civic learning practices in the social studies, and often across the curriculum. Students experience these opportunities at strategic junctures throughout their four-year high school careers.

Structured interviews with administrators and faculty at these selected schools reveal an impressive mix of home-grown civic learning practices supplemented by resources from outside providers in the greater community. An example of the latter is the county clerk serving the community surrounding one of our selected Democracy Schools who works with the school to train students as election judges. The teacher who leads this program called this clerk a "tremendous asset." In the late 1990s, he reports, the clerk

> Opened her staff to us for everything we want. To bring trainers to campus. So we do all of our election judge training on campus on our late arrival mornings. So it's convenient for our kids' schedules, it's convenient for our clerk. They get tons of election judges out of it when they need them.

Finally, interviews demonstrated that the arrival of Common Core standards and perennial standardized testing pressures need not further narrow the curriculum. Subjects were asked, "Given testing pressures and a mandated standard curriculum, how does your school find time to offer students civic learning opportunities, too?"

Responses were coded based on whether civic learning predominates, a balance exists between civic learning and the standard curriculum, or the standard curriculum predominates (see figure 9.1). These codes are not based on an established ratio, but instead on the general sentiments of the interviewees' responses. Instead of further marginalizing civic learning, it may be a lever by which the larger educational mission of the school is pursued.

For example, one assistant principal for instruction I interviewed claimed that the school's embrace of critical-thinking skills from the get-go (the school opened in 2008) led to a complementary balance between civic learning and the standard curriculum. She suggested,

> It's not either or. For some schools, it's a real challenge to have that conversation. Probably because we were new and we had an opportunity to build a new school, we really looked to what's important and looked at successful communities and schools, and much of what we see now is that kids really do need to be part of the larger community to be successful.

The second common element, a vision for the importance of civic learning and effective school leadership to see it through, was also omnipresent. An analysis of school vision and/or mission statements at selected Illinois high schools revealed the overt or implicit capture of civic goals.

Student handbooks at these same schools address students' behavioral and personal development goals from a civic angle too, again

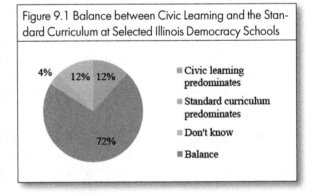

Figure 9.1 Balance between Civic Learning and the Standard Curriculum at Selected Illinois Democracy Schools

4% 12% 12%

72%

- Civic learning predominates
- Standard curriculum predominates
- Don't know
- Balance

either explicitly or subtly. Some handbooks do not address civic learning goals from an academic perspective, but all six schools weave promising civic learning practices throughout the social studies during students' four-year experience, and frequently across the curriculum.

For example, at one selected Democracy School with explicit civic learning goals, the foremost goal for students under curriculum is "…becoming contributing, responsible citizens of our society." To achieve this goal, not only are the social sciences emphasized, but so is "action learning," "respecting of individual differences," and maintenance of a "positive learning environment."

Under "Development, Growth, and Creativity," students' educational experiences are to provide them with the "resources necessary to relate to others as well as a larger society." Through experience, students should "develop values, awareness, interests, concerns, and...recognition of the obligation and value of service."

Students are also to learn the "changeable nature of the world," along with the processes to affect change. This entails understanding of the interaction of social, political, and economic forces, and "...respect for...government, tradition, customs, and (the) heritage of this country and for all of the citizens who have contributed to its development."

Civic learning is often required at selected Illinois Democracy Schools (as of the 2016–2017 school year, it is now a high school graduation requirement in the State of Illinois), and, at a minimum, encouraged. In pursuing it, teachers enjoy the respect of their principal and peers and have autonomy to innovate when it comes to curriculum, instruction, and classroom materials.

Moreover, administrators at these schools are strongly supportive of their civic missions. For example, a question posed to teachers in the 2013 Illinois Five Essentials survey asks how well the principal at their school "communicates a clear vision." More than half of teachers at selected Democracy Schools (51.7%, see figure 9.2) rate their principals as highly effective at communicating a clear vision. By comparison, a little more than one third of their colleagues at comparison schools say the same.

One response from a principal interviewed at a selected Democracy School reflects a complete embrace of the school's civic mission and leadership to this end:

> Fifteen percent of the seniors last year were undocumented. Ninety-four percent of my student body is either an immigrant themselves or their parents immigrated. They all came here for a reason, and that reason was a better life, and shot at the middle class.
>
> And I think it is part of my job to ensure that not only they are academically and socially-emotionally prepared to do that work, but also make sure that they understand that ... democracy is everybody's job. Freedom ain't free. We all serve. You either serve badly through ignorance, or you serve appropriately by being prepared. So we just want ... awareness ... on their radar ... so that later in life they will understand that if you have, you give back.

Administrators at selected Illinois high schools find a way to balance standardized test pressures and national standards with high-quality civic learning opportunities. Rather than further marginalizing the social studies and civics specifically, teachers and administrators alike see civic learning as a vehicle to meet standards and elevate test scores. They understand that civic learning opportunities

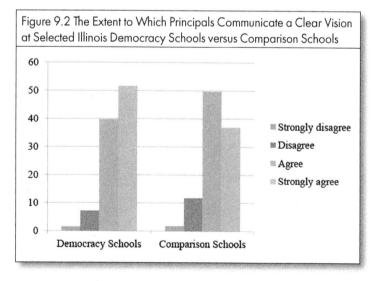

Figure 9.2 The Extent to Which Principals Communicate a Clear Vision at Selected Illinois Democracy Schools versus Comparison Schools

■ Strongly disagree
■ Disagree
▨ Agree
▨ Strongly agree

lead to desirable dispositions beyond voting, like paying attention in class, working hard, and following the news.[11]

Finally, based on interviews with administrators at selected Illinois Democracy Schools, with the exception of one, they enjoy strong or adequate support for civic learning from district leadership.

For example, one principal circled the "… plethora of … resources and financial support …" provided by the district for students' civic development. Specifically, she highlighted the district's community service requirement, which is not mandated by state law. She continued, "It's not something I would say is the norm in public high schools, but the community, the school board, and the administration feel it is an extremely crucial part of a student being able to function in today's society."

According to the principal at the one urban school among the selected Democracy Schools in this study, district level support is "never direct," and to take advantage of available resources "you have to be clever." She attributed her school's success in attracting district-level support to having spent eight years in the district office downtown. This allowed her to develop deep connections with the social science department and when opportunities in the civic learning space surface, "they call." She also credited "brilliant" staff hires "… who have really powerful connections in the world of civic … engagement and they bring that with them."

The third common element that sustains and institutionalizes school-based civic learning is staff development. This includes hiring teachers with civic learning in mind, supporting them through a meaningful mentoring program, and providing ongoing opportunities for civic learning-focused professional development.

Data from the Illinois Five Essentials survey and interviews with teachers and administrators at selected high schools demonstrated that most of them recruit staff with civic learning goals in mind. A couple of principals suggested the opposite; however, both contended that civic learning commitments are a byproduct of the other credentials they seek in prospective faculty members. Moreover, teachers at selected schools proved more likely than their colleagues at comparison schools to have influence on the hiring process of prospective peers (see figure 9.3).

Turning to mentoring, veteran teachers at selected Illinois high schools are more likely to invite younger colleagues into their classrooms to observe and provide feedback. Moreover, teachers' ongoing professional development at Democracy Schools receives greater personal interest from their principals than those at comparison schools (see figure 9.4).

As the literature reveals, teachers are powerful sources of learning for one another.[12] Here, too, teachers at selected Democracy Schools outperformed their peers at comparison schools on various measures of collegiality and peer learning, including conversations about student learning and curriculum development. While peer observations for the purpose of providing feedback are more common in selected Democracy Schools, observations to generate ideas for one's own classroom are rare in both cohorts and stand as an area for future growth. Overall, teachers at these schools inspire one another and collectively create innovative civic learning opportunities for their students.

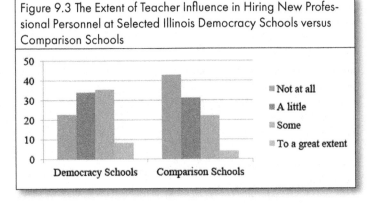

Figure 9.3 The Extent of Teacher Influence in Hiring New Professional Personnel at Selected Illinois Democracy Schools versus Comparison Schools

Teachers at selected Illinois Democracy Schools meet more frequently with their peers to review student assessment data, work on instructional strategies, and develop related materials. Most point to weekly collaborative opportunities. The Professional Learning Community (PLC) model is the vehicle through which much of this collaboration takes place.[13]

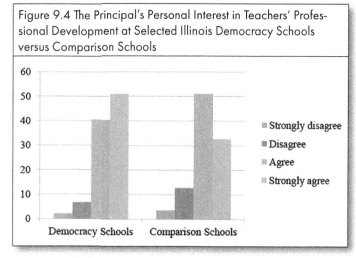

Figure 9.4 The Principal's Personal Interest in Teachers' Professional Development at Selected Illinois Democracy Schools versus Comparison Schools

The fourth common element at schools with sustained, systemic approaches to civic learning is a reciprocal and mutually beneficial relationship with the surrounding community. This group includes parents, professionals recruited to speak in classrooms, and service organizations. Selected Illinois Democracy Schools frequently invite community members to address students (see figure 9.5), and community partners regularly call on students to serve on both civic and political projects.

Selected Democracy Schools also have adequate-to-strong protocols to ensure that all stakeholders' voices are considered in school governance. Although they differ little from their paired comparisons on a myriad of parental communication measures, they exhibit great strength in this area with the exception of inviting parents into classrooms to observe their instructional program.

For example, one principal creates task forces composed of "…parents, teachers, students, [and] community members…if [they] want to have a fundamental change in the way that [they] teach…" He elaborated, "There would be a set of meetings to first, teach people about the topic, and then secondly, to find out what their opinions are." He considered this protocol critical and hired a "parent-community coordinator" whose "…fundamental job is to work on this."

Lastly, although selected schools do not universally benefit from a single, dedicated staff member who is responsible for building and nurturing community partnerships, all take this responsibility seriously and often spread the labor across administration and faculty members alike. The universal presence of common element four therefore is confirmed.

School climate is the fifth and final common element. In the context of civic learning, school climate should model and nurture civic dispositions for and among students. Selected Illinois Democracy Schools demonstrated great strength in this area, widely displaying school mission statements and student work reflective of their civic engagement (see figure 9.6).

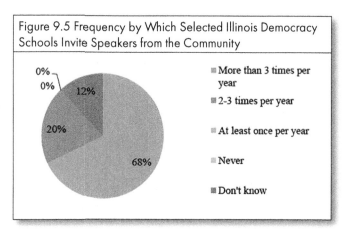

Figure 9.5 Frequency by Which Selected Illinois Democracy Schools Invite Speakers from the Community

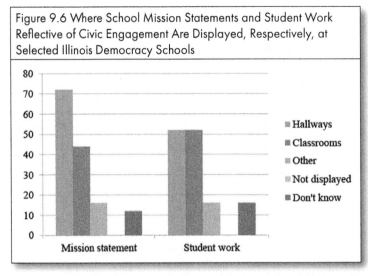

Figure 9.6 Where School Mission Statements and Student Work Reflective of Civic Engagement Are Displayed, Respectively, at Selected Illinois Democracy Schools

One Democracy School displays its mission statement most prominently and thoroughly among the six schools studied. Its assistant principal for instruction contended, "It's all over the place. It's in every classroom, [and] it's in every hallway." She challenged, "You can't walk through a room without seeing the mission." Every year, the school conducts an audit, and the assistant principal reported, "…random kids are selected among our 2,700 and close to 100% can tell you what the vision and mission (statements say), at least in lived reality."

In response to an interview question posed to teachers and administrators at selected Democracy Schools about the degree to which school staff is candid with students about their own civic engagement, 80% of respondents provided answers coded as "somewhat candid." Most prefer to model their engagement more generally, avoiding disclosure of personal ideologies or partisan affiliations. A few teachers are "very candid" in this area, but disclose their beliefs responsibly, and a handful privilege strict neutrality in this delicate area.

More generally, selected Democracy Schools were unanimous in their positive assessments of student-staff relationships, and data from the Illinois Five Essentials student survey supports these claims. For example, the vast majority of students agreed or agreed strongly that teachers treat them with respect at selected Democracy Schools (see figure 9.7). Admittedly, there was little variation with paired comparison schools on this count. In fact, the latter group performed slightly better on this measure.

Students' civic preparedness varied significantly across the selected Illinois Democracy Schools. Teachers and administrators were asked, "To what extent do students at your school graduate with the knowledge, skills, opportunities, and confidence to make a difference in their schools and communities?" Responses were coded on a continuum from "To a great extent" to "Altogether lacking." Although a majority of responses were coded as "To a great extent" and "Above average,"

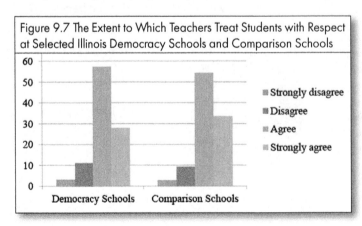

Figure 9.7 The Extent to Which Teachers Treat Students with Respect at Selected Illinois Democracy Schools and Comparison Schools

there was some evidence of a drop-off at schools with more racially and ethnically heterogeneous student populations. All schools must work to ensure equitable civic learning opportunities in terms of both quantity and quality among their entire student bodies. Some schools should even consider employing remedial measures.

Each of the selected Democracy Schools operates sound orientation and mentoring programs for new teachers. However, some schools could do better in integrating training specific to their mission statements.

In sum, the gaps in each of these school climate indicators acknowledged most, but not all, selected Democracy Schools for the most part model and nurture students' civic dispositions.

Drawing from data derived from the 2013 Illinois Five Essentials surveys, Democracy Schools applications, school mission statements, student handbooks, and interviews with teachers and administrators, the first, second, and fourth common elements of schools with sustainable, systemic approaches to civic learning were strongly confirmed to exist in selected Illinois Democracy Schools. These elements include a strategically designed curriculum with promising civic learning practices woven throughout, a vision for the importance of civic learning and effective leadership toward this end, and a strong partnership between schools and the surrounding community. Based on analysis on Illinois Five Essentials survey data, there is some evidence that selected Democracy Schools outperform their paired comparison schools on these measures.

Using the same data sources, the third and fifth elements centering on staff development and school climate are only partially confirmed at selected Democracy Schools. Their variation with comparison schools on these measures is limited on some measures, and interview responses to related questions also present evidence of room for improvement. The inconclusive evidence that emerges on these counts should not diminish their importance, but instead raise the bar for these schools and others to improve their performance.

In sum, selected Illinois Democracy Schools integrate proven civic learning practices across academic disciplines and throughout students' four-year high school tenure. They have civic-oriented mission statements and administrators who support their pursuit, providing autonomy for faculty and staff to take risks and foster students' civic development. Selected Democracy Schools also boast reciprocal relationships with the surrounding community, where the school and community stakeholders view one another as assets. These schools hire, train, and evaluate teachers with civic learning goals in mind, but would benefit from further prioritizing this end. Finally, selected Democracy Schools model and nurture students' civic development through positive school climates, but once more fall short on a few measures. The key is the commitment of these schools to continually improve in their ongoing efforts to fulfill their civic missions.

TRANSFERRING THESE FINDINGS TO HIGHER EDUCATION

The 2012 Crucible Moment report released by the National Task Force on Civic Learning and Democratic Engagement implored "… the higher education community—its constituents and stakeholders—to embrace civic learning and democratic engagement as an undisputed educational priority for all of higher education. …" This requires academic "… environments where education for democracy and civic responsibility is pervasive, not partial; central, not peripheral."[14]

Based on the findings presented previously in a high school setting, administrative buy in is key to building and sustaining institutions' civic missions. In best case scenarios, administrators, in this case university presidents and chancellors, lead on this front. At a minimum, they create space for deans, faculty, and staff to pursue civic ends. Given the specialization within most colleges and universities, institutional leadership on their civic mission is placed at a premium to overcome disciplinary silos. To this end, Campus Compact, discussed at greater length later, supports university presidents in their efforts to create an institution-wide culture that promotes civic learning and democratic engagement.

While political science lends itself naturally to students' civic development, other academic disciplines can and should offer integrative civic learning experiences. The Association of American Colleges and Universities (with funding from the Robert R. McCormick Foundation), convened several Chicago-area colleges and universities to identify "pedagogical approaches…

to better reveal to students the rich civic dimensions of a given subject of study."[15] For example, action projects, oral histories, and internships fit well with arts and humanities curricula, while case-based learning and field work integrate with STEM (science, technology, engineering, and mathematics) courses. Social science courses can embed civic reflection, simulations, and structured volunteer opportunities, and business and preprofessional classes rely primarily on problem-based learning, case studies, and community mapping.

Teachers of political science, and across the academy, would benefit from a broader array of professional development opportunities. Annual attendance at the APSA Teaching and Learning Conference is a luxury for many, so I recommend that a strand be added to state and regional conferences. Moreover, conference sessions should include more hands-on components like demonstrations of classroom practices, moving beyond the mere recitation and discussion of papers. I also encourage APSA and other academic communities to leverage online training opportunities for professional development on teaching and learning.

Perhaps most importantly, I implore college and universities to create space for internal professional development on teaching civic engagement. As discussed earlier, cross-curricular opportunities abound, and resident political scientists have much to offer their peers in this regard, especially when paired with faculty in schools of education with expertise in experiential learning practices like discussion, service-learning, and simulations.

In the high schools I studied with robust community relationships, responsibility for building and sustaining school–community partnerships was the distinct responsibility of one staff member or consciously shared among several faculty members. Given the size and scale of most colleges and universities, community partnerships are arguably most effectively cultivated by centers established for this purpose.

In addition, Campus Compact offers training for faculty and administration on building community partnerships. It also facilitates national partnerships, builds pilot programs, and convenes key stakeholders for purposes of knowledge-sharing and capacity development.

My experiences as a practitioner in and researcher of high schools with strong commitments to students' civic development underline the importance of organizational culture to these ends. Responsibility for an organization's civic mission must not lie merely with an individual faculty member or academic department. It must be prioritized by administration and threaded throughout the curriculum and students' academic journey. The previous supports are critical components of this culture and are nested in the overall climate of the institution.

To this end, the Carnegie Community Engagement Classification,[16] similar to Illinois Democracy Schools in the secondary education space, takes an integrative approach to measuring and strengthening the civic mission of higher education institutions. Two hundred forty US colleges and universities earned this distinction in 2015, 83 for the first time. I encourage many more to apply next time around in 2020.

CONCLUSION

Civic disengagement among our citizenry undermines the health of American democracy at all levels of government, local, state, and national. This problem is particularly acute among our youngest citizens.

At the same time, our nation's schools, from elementary to higher education, have largely abandoned their historic civic mission to the detriment of informed, effective, and lifelong democratic participation. The high schools featured in this chapter represent an alternative path for P–20 institutions to emulate. Although individual civic development is dependent on a number of factors, schools can and must play a fundamental role in reversing these trends. Disengagement is not destiny, and our nation's civic health can and must be resuscitated.

This chapter details civic learning practices and elements of organizational culture at a number of Illinois high schools with deep and sustained commitments to students' civic development.

Not only do these schools leverage promising civic learning practices across the curriculum and student activities, but they see civic learning as central to their mission. School leaders prioritize civic learning and hire faculty, evaluate them, and continuously develop their capacity with these goals in mind. These schools build and sustain reciprocal relationships with the surrounding community and ensure a learning environment that models and nurtures civic engagement for and among students.

Lessons from these exemplary high schools are transferrable to higher education, and there is significant momentum; examples abound of innovative programs and efforts on campuses throughout the country. Promising models must be replicated across academic disciplines and institutions, and colleges and universities should partner with K–12 systems to ensure that civic engagement opportunities are woven throughout students' educational experiences. If successful, trends toward civic apathy and ignorance can be reversed, robust and equitable participation will flourish, and desirable policy outcomes and democratic health should follow. ■

ENDNOTES

1.   Mark Bauerlein, *The Dumbest Generation: How the Digital Age Stupifies Young Americans and Jeopardizes Our Future* (New York: Penguin, 2008); Robert D. Putnam, *Bowling Alone: The Collapse and Revival of American Community* (New York: Simon & Schuster, 2000); Martin P. Wattenberg, *Is Voting for Young People?* (New York: Pearson, 2008).

2.   Shawn P. Healy, "Illinois Democracy Schools: Preparing Students for College, Career, and Civic Life," *The Councilor* 74 (2013): 1–16.

3.   Peter Levine, *The Future of Democracy: Developing the New Generation of American Citizens* (Medford, MA: Tufts University Press, 2007).

4.   Shawn P. Healy, *Essential School Supports for Civic Learning* (Chicago: University of Illinois at Chicago, 2014), http://indigo.uic.edu/bitstream/handle/10027/19362/Healy_Shawn.pdf?sequence=1.

5.   Anthony S. Bryk et al., *Organizing Schools for Improvement: Lessons from Chicago* (Chicago: University of Chicago Press, 2010).

6.   Campaign for the Civic Mission of Schools, *No Excuses: Eleven Schools And Districts That Make Preparing Students for Citizenship a Priority, and How Others Can Do It, Too* (Bethesda, MD: 2010).

7.   Robert R. McCormick Foundation, *Educating for Democracy: Creating a Civic Blueprint for Illinois High Schools* (Chicago), http://documents.mccormickfoundation.org/Civics/programs/democracyschools/resources/EducatingforDemocracy_FINALWholeReport.pdf, accessed December 13, 2016.

8.   Shawn P. Healy, *Civic Mission of Schools* (McCormick Foundation, 2011), http://mccormickfoundation.org/civics/civic-mission-of-schools.

9.   Northern Illinois University, *Illinois Interactive Report Card* (2014) http://iirc.niu.edu/Classic/Default.aspx, accessed June 23, 2014.

10. Shawn P. Healy, *Essential School Supports for Civic Learning* (Chicago: University of Illinois at Chicago, 2014), http://indigo.uic.edu/bitstream/handle/10027/19362/Healy_Shawn.pdf?sequence=1.

11. J. Torney-Purta and B.S. Wilkenfeld, "Paths to 21st Century Competencies Through Civic Education Classrooms: An Analysis of Survey Results from Ninth-Graders," A Technical Assistance Bulletin (Chicago: American Bar Association Division for Public Education, 2009).

12. Bryk, et al., *Organizing Schools*; Geoffrey Caine, and Renate N. Caine, *Strengthening and Enriching Your Professional Learning Community: The Art of Learning Together* (Alexandria, VA: ASCD, 2010); Charlotte Danielson, *Enhancing Professional Practice: A Framework for Teaching*, second edition (Alexandria, VA: ASCD, 2007); Michael Fullan, *The New Meaning of Educational Change*, fourth edition (New York: Teachers College Press, 2007); Diana Hess and John Zola, "Professional Development as a Tool for Improving Civic Education," in *Making Civics Count: Citizenship Education a New Generation*, edited by David E. Campbell, Meira Levinson, and Frederick M. Hess (Cambridge, MA: Harvard University Press, 2012), 183–206.

13. Caine and Caine, *Strengthening and Enriching Your Professional Learning Community*, 2010.

14. The National Task Force on Civic Learning and Democratic Engagement, *A Crucible Moment: College Learning and Democracy's Future* (Washington, DC: Association of American Colleges and Universities, 2012), https://www.aacu.org/crucible.

15. Caryn McTighe Musil, *Civic Prompts: Making Civic Learning Routine Across the Disciplines* (Washington, DC: Association of American Colleges and Universities, 2015), http://www.aacu.org/sites/default/files/files/CLDE/CivicPrompts.pdf.

16. New England Resource Center for Higher Education, *Carnegie Community Engagement Classification* (Boston: University of Massachusetts Boston), http://nerche.org/index.php?option=com_content&view=article&id=341&Itemid=618, accessed January 18, 2016.

Using Twitter to Promote Classroom and Civic Engagement

10

Gina Serignese Woodall and Tara M. Lennon

How can educators harness social media to promote civic engagement? Over three spring semesters, we conducted a nonequivalent control group design experiment in which one class each semester was required to tweet weekly about the course topics and another class was not. In the third year, we also conducted focus groups about students' use of social media to obtain and share political information. Preliminary results of the experiment show that the treatment classes had statistically higher political knowledge and political engagement through Twitter compared to the control classes. Preliminary results also suggest some nuanced gender differences in how participants use Twitter. Compared to other social media, such as Facebook, Twitter leans toward more direct, personal—and often confrontational—communication. While female participants used Twitter for political purposes to a greater extent than male students in our study, the gendered impact of the Twitter requirement is not clear. Our focus group discussions further developed some of our findings regarding the factors that motivate students to follow certain types of political social media accounts. By examining students' motivations and social media behaviors, this chapter contributes to the emerging research on how educators can encourage e-civic engagement habits that foster active citizenship and political knowledge.

C an college students engage in political discussions in only 140 characters? Tweets by young adults often reflect gut reactions, staccato outbursts, selfies, and cute animal pictures. How could these translate into meaningful civic engagement? The answer begins with how students choose to get information. Approximately 45% of youth responded to a 2012 survey that they received the bulk of their news through Twitter and Facebook.[1] Political information is readily available. News sources, interest groups, and political officials at the highest levels post regular tweets. Links to news stories and political analyses are easy to share. While tweets may be brief, the links and real-time dialogue can inform and engage social media users. We believe that meaningful engagement is possible if instructors channel Twitter's informal conversations into more structured political discussions. Accordingly, our project challenges the presumed limits of Twitter as a means for young adults to express thoughtful, evidence-based political views.

We teach political science and require tweets in some of our classes. We use Twitter to connect students to political discussions and as a formative assessment tool (e.g., quick quizzes or lecture "take-away" comments in lieu of attendance). Most of our students are familiar with Twitter but we flip its role in the classroom to our advantage. No longer is it a distraction from our barrage of PowerPoint slides; tweets are part of the class discussion through live Twitter feeds. Student responses to our questions are viewed in real time as well as in re-caps of out-of-class tweets. For those too timid to speak in class, Twitter offers a safe alternative and, in some cases, an entry point to discussion. When students must write original tweets on political topics, they may develop a habit of producing—not just consuming—information. This technology may be one of many paths toward increasing classroom and political engagement. There is a growing body of research that suggests social media, including Twitter, can enhance class discussions and student engagement.[2] Accordingly, we believe that Twitter is a promising format for students to develop the habit of meaningful online political discussions.

Our project focuses on online political engagement, or e-civic engagement, and use of Twitter as a class requirement. We created a survey to ask participants about their traditional political activities, knowledge, interest, and efficacy. Additionally, we conducted focus groups with the experimental group of participants to understand how and why they use social media. The project begins with the premise that our young political science students are online and that many are already interested in politics. Approximately 40% of our participants were political science majors.[3] Our central research question is whether the practice of enhancing in-class political discussions with Twitter impacts students' sense of political efficacy outside of the classroom. Our project aims to measure whether Twitter may increase the number of building blocks of e-civic engagement levels among political science students. Specifically, after tweeting every week about politics for four months, will students increase their political knowledge, interest, efficacy, and their willingness to communicate about politics online, even after class is completed?

RESEARCH DESIGN

To explore the effectiveness of Twitter on students' classroom and political engagement, we first conducted a nonequivalent control group design experiment, with required Twitter use as the treatment. In the spring semesters of 2014, 2015, and 2016, one of the authors of this chapter taught two political theory classes: an introductory political ideologies course required for political science majors and an upper-division elective course, Problems of Democracy. During each semester, students in the treatment class were required to tweet twice weekly about course content, with the total number of tweets worth approximately 11% of their course grade.[4] This requirement complemented but did not replace their participation grade. Students were required to tweet regularly and meet a minimum number of weeks both to avoid a mass set of tweets late in the semester and to develop a habit of tweeting about political information. In addition to student-initiated tweeting outside of class, some class discussions included live Twitter feeds based on instructor-initiated questions and student reactions that were projected for the class to view and discuss. In the control group class, Twitter was not required and not incorporated into class discussions.

Both the treatment and control groups were given pretest questionnaires in the beginning of the semester and posttest questionnaires toward the end of the semester. All questionnaires included measures assessing the students' interest in politics, political efficacy, political participation (offline, online, and online specifically through Twitter), social media use, and political knowledge (see the companion website for copies of the questionnaires). In the pretest, the subjects also provided basic demographic information, academic major(s), and information about their current use of social media. In addition, a brief follow-up questionnaire was e-mailed to both groups three months after classes ended.

We relied on a student sample, which was ideal given our research questions about social media use and classroom engagement.[5] Our university, Arizona State University, is one of the largest universities in the country. We enrolled more than 1,600 political science majors in 2016. During spring semesters 2014 and 2016, we required tweets from students in the in-person Political Ideologies course, and students in the in-person Problems of Democracy course were the control group. In 2015, this was reversed. In addition, in 2016, we included an online Political Ideologies course as a treatment group and a different online section of the same course as its control. Across all three years, the treatment and control groups were similar on a host of factors assessed during the pretests, such as political party, political ideology, and political participation levels offline and online. There were no statistically significant differences between the treatment classes and the control classes for any of these variables. However, the treatment group had slightly more women and lower pretest levels of social media use.[6] Additionally, the 2016 classes differed from the two prior years in that the men reported less interest in politics and the women had lower levels of political knowledge. Accordingly, we controlled for these differences within our regression analyses.

To develop a better understanding of preliminary results from the quantitative analyses, we conducted four focus groups in the spring of 2016 with participants in the current and previous semesters' treatment groups. Each focus group included between five and seven participants, and we asked questions related to social media preference, what they like and dislike about Twitter, why they use it, whether or not they engage in politics via social media, and how they perceive Twitter compared to other platforms. This qualitative component of our project has helped to understand our quantitative findings and to identify new measures and research questions.

Throughout the phases of the research project, we asked whether tweeting about politics and course concepts was associated with higher levels of engagement in the classroom and/or politics in general.[7] We also asked whether Twitter use was associated with any differences in political knowledge or sense of political efficacy, either within or between the groups. Questions regarding classroom engagement were also in the surveys.

TEACHING WITH TWITTER

Our students are already online: during class, out of class, most of their day. We have found that harnessing social media's prevalence as their source for information can work to our advantage in class. In this section, we review how we set up, graded, and coached Twitter use in our classrooms. Reviewing tweets can take time—a downside—but social media, like Twitter, can capture students' attention, compel them to find authoritative sources of political information, connect them to classmates and faculty, and empower them to be coproducers of knowledge.

All students in the treatment class were required to have their own (free) Twitter account and approximately one third reported that they had a Twitter account prior to class. Students could use their existing personal Twitter account or create a Twitter account for the class and other "public purposes." The instructors discussed the privacy benefits of separating the students' private and public Twitter accounts but left the choice to the students. The treatment class had its own Twitter handle (e.g., "@pos210") that students were required to follow and required to tag in their tweets. This system put all of the class-related tweets within one account and kept all of the students' Twitter accounts (and unrelated personal tweets) out of the class's view. There are free applications that automatically retweet all tweets, but we chose to quickly view them and manually retweet, which takes 1–2 seconds per tweet. By using our class handle, every tweet was also downloaded into an Excel file by a free Twitterbot application for future analysis. Within the control group classes, we did not have a class handle nor did we encourage Twitter use in the classroom.

Our Twitter requirement was simple for the students to complete and for us to grade. Tweets received zero, half, or full credit based on whether they "relate to course content." This unstructured approach intentionally matches the convenience and informality of Twitter. While many tweets relate to current political events (e.g., "Putin's fascist rewriting of Crimea's history is familiar—lie, repress, repeat"), others show the student's reflection of personal activities (e.g., "This traffic jam reflects Aristotle's view of the demos"). Students are not graded on the accuracy of their tweets because this is a low-stakes assessment and other assessments capture the mastery of content. For example, during a unit on communism, if a student's tweet relates to communism—even if there is an error in understanding—their tweet "counts" for credit. In case of such errors, the student could delete the tweet and lose credit or leave it as is. We would leave the erroneous tweet visible on the account but not retweet it to classmates. This formative assessment is an effective bellwether of students' understanding of course concepts. We have corrected, during class time, common misunderstandings that students shared in Twitter that may have gone unnoticed until a high-stakes exam.

In addition to out-of-class tweets, students were encouraged to tweet during live, in-class Twitter feeds. We pose a question, project the Twitter feed during class, skim through the real-time tweets, and select a few for general discussion. Sometimes, authors of tweets are called on to further develop the point, leading to better deliberation on the topic. On average, 86% of the class tweeted during a live feed in 2016. That is a high percentage of students who are formulating and expressing opinions about a political topic during class. Students were not required to tweet during live feeds but most still chose to do so. While we do not have the comparative data for our control groups, we are certain that there are far fewer hands raised during our traditional classes. In the non-tweeting control class, we relied on lecture and then devoted about 20–25 minutes of the 75-minute class to a traditional facilitation of questions and answers. Often in such classes, the same 10–15 students participate. During class, it is extremely difficult to get the reserved, maybe self-doubtful student to offer up an idea in front of their peers, even when low-stakes points are attached to their participation. When done outside of class, Twitter allows for quick and convenient dialogue, broad participation, and student practice at "producing knowledge." When Twitter is integrated into class discussion, richer deliberation is also possible.

During class live feeds and throughout the course, we coach our students on good approaches to finding, posting, and commenting or reposting political information. This lesson is an essential part of training college students for e-civic engagement. By showing students basic differences in quality websites with reputable information versus "fake news" sites or sites that do not have evidence to back up arguments, we teach them how to be better citizens. Sometimes, a student will link a tweet to an article with a false claim. Rather than embarrass the student, we use that link to highlight how it is possible to quickly find a reputable article on the same subject. Additionally, we show students what an authoritative tweet looks like (e.g., a cogent connection between a concept learned in class and a link to a current news article) versus a less effective tweet (e.g., a link to a news article that is unrelated to a course concept with no original text by the tweeter). Students then become purveyors of strong tweets that convey insight and information and learn how to identify weak ones that clutter Twitter with uninformed "noise." Students appear to embrace the social aspect of social media and rapidly begin to share authoritative links, repost witty commentary, and develop their own pithy remarks. For example, across all years, approximately 12% of the tweets included links to authoritative news or scholarly articles.[8]

Moreover, in our current political environment following the contentious and historic 2016 presidential election, it is more important now than ever to train students about the difference between productive and destructive tweets and how to, as Danielle Allen suggests, protect oneself in online political discussions.[9] Training students to post productive and authoritative tweets is all the more complicated for educators due to President Trump's Twitter use. President Trump admitted he uses Twitter as a tool to bypass traditional media outlets and bring the truth to the people, which is not something necessarily new for presidents.[10] However, analysts have examined his tweets, particularly since he announced his run for president in June of 2015, and it is clear he uses Twitter in an aggressive way to attack and disparage organizations and people who are critical of him.[11] The president's continued aggressive Twitter use begets additional questions for educators: Will his aggressive and negative approach cause some women to retreat more and prompt some men to feel more comfortable acting aggressively on Twitter? Does it matter whether what we tweet or retweet is factual? What are the implications of this environment for teaching students civic engagement and responsibility? These are important pedagogical questions for all classrooms, not only in political science.

As educators, we also can discuss and warn students about news and social media "echo chambers." In our focus group observations, a student wrote that she prefers Facebook (as opposed to Twitter) because there is a "way to edit newsfeed setting so you can see certain things first." Just as a student can customize Facebook into an echo chamber, they can also limit the accounts that they follow in Twitter. Warning students about only reading information or only following politicians with whom they agree is part of our job. We can guide their approach to consuming information online so that they develop a more authentic understanding for others' political views. Recommending that students follow a variety of accounts and create a more well-rounded Twitterverse is one of the simplest, yet most critical, ways we can help our students become civically responsible.

Finally, in our large classes (100–200 students), Twitter helps to connect students with classmates and with faculty. Students connect with other classmates through their posts; one student noted in his course evaluations that "it made convo between students easier and felt very 21st century." Anecdotally, students have expressed a preference for social media's convenient, real-time dialogue over the learning management systems (LMS) discussion boards. Some students used Twitter to organize working groups. Students can even connect with their friends and family because of the political content of their tweets. A student told us that his family engaged in several dinner conversations about socialism after his dad read his Twitter post about Karl Marx for class. Just as students can learn from each other's questions and comments in class, one student claimed in a course evaluation that "Reading what others in the course have posted on Twitter helped me better understand the concepts being taught."

Using social media in the classroom is also an effective and efficient means for faculty to communicate with students. Compared to discussion boards within traditional LMS, social media platforms are "less clunky," more mobile-friendly, and extremely accessible for students and professors alike. Our students also appear to be less intimidated in approaching professors on social media, since most students are already on it and familiar with it. We have used Twitter to instant-message a student about a computer left in class and make quick class-wide announcements. To the extent that Twitter helps students connect with peers and with faculty in convenient and less formal ways, it may take away the fear or anxiety that some students experience when communicating with others in an academic setting.

Although we are political science instructors with a high proportion of political science majors in our class, we think that Twitter and other social media can be utilized in non-political science classrooms as well. Given the breadth of information online, all types of news articles centered on statistics, history, psychology, the environment, global business, and engineering can "get conversations going" in their classrooms via a tweet. When we have presented our findings to faculty at our institution, we were pleased to learn that professors from a variety of disciplines shared articles via tweets and had students submit assignments through class Facebook pages. As an example, a psychology instructor might tweet about an article on how estrogen levels in women may lead to fear-learning and to post-traumatic stress disorder and then ask students to tweet any issues or problems they see with the described connection between those two variables.[12] Or, instructors might ask students to seek out other articles that note a possible connection between the variables and then be ready to discuss them in class. Overall, we find Twitter helpful in sparking conversation and discussion of concepts and issues in class that may need more explanation. By training students to seek out valid articles, summarize them, and share with their peers, we are training them in the tools of e-civic engagement. Our students are already online, and most of their future participation in political discussions after graduation will likely also be online. Accordingly, we hope to develop informed, deliberative habits.

FINDINGS AND DISCUSSION

Our experiences using social media in our classes has led to increased knowledge about how to engage students in political discussions inside and outside of the classroom. The experimental design has also provided detailed findings regarding the potential of such classroom e-citizenship training for increasing students' civic knowledge, interest, efficacy, and engagement. Students used Twitter to research, tweet, and retweet political news and information. They followed political leaders or news agencies who will continue to post tweets on the students' accounts long after class or at least until the student "unfollows them." Many students shared links to political news stories and academic studies in their tweets and other students followed those links. We are encouraged that the treatment group was using Twitter for political purposes at the end of the semester significantly more than the control group. The treatment group also showed greater average gains in basic political knowledge questions, such as John Boehner's party affiliation or the Republican and Democratic Parties' positions on defense spending. In our increasingly complex online world, where a barrage of information is thrown at consumers every minute of the day, these are positive outcomes of using Twitter in the classroom. At the same time, however, the treatment students' political interest levels increased only slightly and their sense of efficacy decreased slightly over the semester. Finally, the nuanced results related to gender and Twitter use warrant more research. Indeed, our findings led us to think about how to improve our measurements of e-civic engagement for future research. The results section of this chapter is organized as follows: first, we review the encouraging but limited impact of Twitter on classroom engagement. Second, we review the tests related to the building blocks of political engagement: political knowledge, interest, and efficacy. Third, we discuss the results of our regression models for online political engagement measures. Fourth, we discuss questions raised by our focus group findings related to gender. Last, we conclude with suggestions for developing stronger measures of e-civic engagement.

TWITTER USE AND CLASSROOM ENGAGEMENT

Based on the surveys, the tests of our first hypothesis—that students in the treatment group are more engaged in class compared to the students in the control condition—were inconclusive. At the end of the semester, 94% of the students in the treatment group reported that *the class was engaging*, compared to 84% in the control condition (see tables 10.1 and 10.2). However, when we control for other factors, such as pretest levels of social media use, the difference between the groups is not statistically significant.[13] Further, this self-reported, end-of-semester measure is not ideal for assessing student participation.[14]

Comparing levels of classroom engagement between the two conditions is also challenging because of the wide variance in the students' personal habits of classroom engagement. Students in the treatment group reported that they *verbally participated in class* at a higher rate than those in the control group (64% and 46%, respectively). This is encouraging, but with only eight live Twitter feeds each semester, we cannot attribute the higher rate to the Twitter discussions in class. Forty percent of the treatment group also reported that *they participated through Twitter in lieu of verbally participating*, and 38% of the control group reported that they *would have participated more if they could have used Twitter*. While verbal participation in class is ideal, the students who participated through Twitter may be gaining valuable practice expressing their political views in this new "class setting." The high percentage of control group students who were interested in doing so (38%) may reflect a group of students who would have participated more—but did not—in class. In 2016, 86% of the students in attendance on those days tweeted during in-class Twitter feeds, on average. This high percentage makes sense because it is a low-stakes, nonverbal option for participation. In future studies, we plan to assess whether Twitter promotes participation from students who are typically disengaged from class.

Table 10.1 Treatment Posttest: Twitter and Classroom Engagement (2014–2016)

POSTTEST STATEMENTS	STRONGLY AGREE		AGREE		NEITHER AGREE NOR DISAGREE		DISAGREE		STRONGLY DISAGREE	
	N	%	N	%	N	%	N	%	N	%
This class was engaging*	50	41%	65	53%	6	5%	2	2%	0	0%
I participated verbally in class-room discussions*	23	22%	44	42%	22	21%	14	13%	2	2%
Enjoyed using Twitter as part of class	35	19%	60	33%	34	19%	25	14%	27	15%
Twitter enhanced my partici-pation in class	43	23%	56	31%	31	17%	29	16%	24	13%
Twitter enhanced discussions outside of class	15	8%	47	26%	33	19%	49	28%	34	19%
Used Twitter instead of verbal-ly participating	20	12%	45	28%	35	21%	36	22%	27	17%
Using Twitter has increased interest in politics	25	12%	53	26%	43	21%	44	22%	36	18%

*These questions were only included in the 2015 and 2016 questionnaires.

Table 10.2 Control Posttest: Twitter and Classroom Engagement (2015–2016)

POSTTEST STATEMENTS	STRONGLY AGREE		AGREE		NEITHER AGREE NOR DISAGREE		DISAGREE		STRONGLY DISAGREE	
	N	%	N	%	N	%	N	%	N	%
This class was engaging	33	38%	40	46%	11	13%	2	2%	1	1%
I participated verbally in class-room discussions	15	17%	25	29%	30	34%	12	14%	5	6%
I would have participated more during class discussions if I could have done so through social media (e.g., Twitter)	7	14%	12	24%	12	24%	12	24%	7	14%

Responses to the additional questions given to the treatment group about Twitter use in the classroom were also mixed but encouraging. Half (52%) of the subjects in the treatment group reported that they *enjoyed the class Twitter requirement*, with 20% neutral and 29% who did not enjoy the Twitter use. The posttest included five questions regarding the subjects' engagement in the classroom through Twitter. As shown in table 10.1, a similar distribution of students reported that Twitter *enhanced their participation in class* (i.e., 54% agree, 17% neutral, and 29% disagree). Fewer students (34%) reported that it enhanced their discussions outside of class, which suggests that the students were more likely to use it during class through live feeds or otherwise in conjunction with class discussions.

The qualitative feedback in course evaluations was also mixed. Some students liked the new media and demand for concise writing: "I really liked the idea of moving the conversation to Twitter! It made me condense my thoughts and opinions into short and efficient statements." Additionally, students reported that the informal Twitter conversations with classmates helped them to better understand the course material. This result conforms to a study of Twitter that suggested that Twitter helps to connect students through an "online hallway conversation" that is simply easier to use.[15] Still, others were frustrated: "Innovation for innovation's sake is not productive," "I don't like the concept of converting political thoughts and explanations into tweets," and "I felt handicapped on most occasions and when I did use Twit longer to more fully expound on a thought I felt like it was overlooked and the effort wasted." The short length of tweets is particularly challenging for students in an introductory political theory class. We recommend either combining a Twitter requirement with outlets for longer discussions, such as online discussion boards, or using social media without restrictive character limits, such as Facebook, in smaller classes.

TWITTER USE AND POLITICAL KNOWLEDGE, INTEREST, AND EFFICACY

Our project aims to measure how Twitter may increase our students' e-civic engagement levels by developing essential components of such engagement including political knowledge, interest, and efficacy. That is, are they informed and motivated to engage in political discussions, and do they have the skills and confidence required to share ideas and act politically? Some students may feel increasingly ineffective as they learn more about politics, while others act without sufficient knowledge. Students who were required to use Twitter showed modest gains in political interest, stronger gains in political knowledge, and a slight slip in their sense of efficacy.

Our quantitative and qualitative data present mixed results about the treatment group's interest in politics (see tables 10.3a and 10.3b). In our pre- and posttests, the students answered two questions about whether they were "interested about" and /or "regularly follow what is going on in politics and government." The treatment group showed a slight, but insignificant, gain in their interest in politics, from 8.00 to 8.11 on a scale to 10; and the control group showed a slight decline, 8.17 to 8.15. Additionally, in the posttest, 39% of the treatment respondents agreed or strongly agreed that *using Twitter increased [their] interest in politics and/or public policy.* As seen in figure 10.1, our focus groups also reported that one half of the Twitter accounts that they followed after the class ended were related to politics. This focus group included students who indicated that they were not interested in politics at the start of the class. We expected that the participants would primarily use Twitter for social, sports, or entertainment news, and we did not require that students follow any particular accounts. We are encouraged that more than half of their accounts are devoted to politics and political commentary with an additional 10% devoted to general news. Since an important part of citizenship includes being aware and engaged in the civic and political events of the day, the students are fulfilling their duty, albeit via e-civic engagement.

Table 10.3a Treatment Group's Pre- and Posttest Political Knowledge, Interest, and Efficacy (2014–2016)

| MEASURE | QUESTION NUMBER(S) | RANGE OF VALUES | MEAN SCORES | | T | DF | P |
			PRE-TEST	POST-TEST			
Political interest	17 (a & b)	2–10	8.00	8.11	-1.041	238	.299
Political knowledge	5	0–6	4.98	5.16	-2.425	241	.016**
Political efficacy	17 (c,d, & e)	3–15	7.77	7.85	-.460	240	.646

***p≤.01, **p≤.05, *p≤.10

Table 10.3b Control Group's Pre- and Posttest Political Knowledge, Interest, and Efficacy (2014–2016)

| MEASURE | QUESTION NUMBER(S) | RANGE OF VALUES | MEAN SCORES | | T | DF | P |
			PRE-TEST	POST-TEST			
Political interest	17 (a & b)	2–10	8.17	8.15	.287	252	.774
Political knowledge	5	0–6	4.98	5.01	-.378	253	.705
Political efficacy	17 (c,d, & e)	3–15	7.63	7.89	-1.682	252	.094*

***p≤.01, **p≤.05, *p≤.10

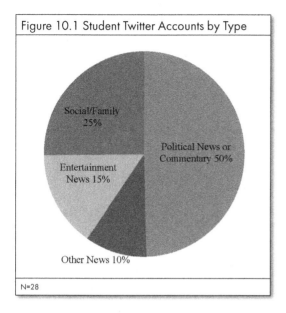

Figure 10.1 Student Twitter Accounts by Type

Social/Family 25%

Political News or Commentary 50%

Entertainment News 15%

Other News 10%

N=28

Students in the treatment group made significant pre- to posttest gains in their political knowledge scores and, per our focus groups, used Twitter to consume political information and expert commentary. As seen in tables 10.3a and 10.3b, the control group started their semesters at the same level of general political knowledge, on average, but did not make the same gains over the semester.

In the focus groups, we asked the students who were required to tweet how they used Twitter for political information. Many of those students explained that they sought out particular tweets from political candidates, organizations, and experts and then reviewed the conversations that followed from those tweets. The students wanted the original source of the information for more accurate context and liked Twitter's convenient interface for that search; it is "better than Google" according to one student. This critical view of the source and context of political information is helpful, even as we and the students recognize the limits of 140-character statements.

Our political efficacy tests produced more perplexing findings. Political efficacy can be understood as both the sense of empowerment and the ability to act in politics, and both the treatment and control groups reported declines in their efficacy since the beginning of class.[16] Our survey questions measured inefficacy as the student's agreement with statements such as "People like me don't have any say about what the government does" and "Public officials don't care much what people like me think." As seen in tables 10.3a and 10.3b, the decline in efficacy (or increase in inefficacy) was slight for the treatment group and significant for the control group. It is not clear why both groups showed this decline. Are the complexities and challenges of effective participation more apparent at the end of our classes, leading to increased political cynicism, which is correlated with higher levels of inefficacy?[17] We do not know for sure. Could the "chaos" of Twitter increase cynicism and inefficacy, as a focus group participant suggested? If so, why did the control group students report a more significant decline in efficacy? The final section of these findings reviews students' reactions to the chaotic Twitterverse within the context of gender. It is clear, however, that the students prefer to read and consume information on Twitter rather than post and produce information. Accordingly, the treatment participants are admittedly more passive consumers of tweets rather than active contributors. It appears that under a deluge of information, few students act. The modal proportion of "reading to tweeting" for the focus group was 90:10. Approximately 60% of the focus group posted devoted 90% or more of their time reading in Twitter. Fifteen percent of participants were more "active" on Twitter, with proportions of reading to tweeting from 75:25 to 50:50. Responses varied as to why some students prefer reading to creating tweets and vice-versa. A student with a 60:40 proportion of reading to tweeting reported that she would respond to an original tweet and engage in a dialogue on Twitter, but she rarely initiated tweets. Still others reported that they "rarely use Twitter except for class." With 32% of the treatment group's students already on Twitter at the start of class, we hope that the Twitter requirement guides them toward political information and encourages them to more actively engage through online posts, even if that engagement is limited to class for some.

TWITTER USE AND POLITICAL ENGAGEMENT

Students in the treatment groups reported significant increases in overall Twitter engagement and political uses of Twitter. Accordingly, our study confirmed our hypothesis that students in the treatment group would be more politically engaged through Twitter than the control group (see tables 10.4 and 10.5). Specifically, only students in the treatment group showed statistically significant increases in all four of the index's political activities: *follow political news, follow political officials, encourage political action,* and *repost other's political content.* Students in both the treatment and control groups showed a statistically significant increase in one of the nonpolitical activities (*follow entertainment news*).

Table 10.4 Treatment Group's Pre- and Posttest Political Interest and Engagement Measures (2014–2016)							
			MEAN SCORES				
MEASURE	QUESTION NUMBER(S)	RANGE OF VALUES	PRE-TEST	POST-TEST	T	DF	P
Twitter engagement index, overall	23 (a–f)	0–6	4.02	4.63	-5.259	119	.000***
Political Twitter use index	23 (a,b,e,f)	0–4	2.55	3.03	-4.942	119	.000***
Twitter, follow political news	23(a)	0–1	.87	.93	-2.169	125	.032**
Twitter, follow political officials	23(b)	0–1	.65	.78	-3.259	121	.001***
Twitter, follow entertainment news	23(c)	0–1	0.83	0.92	-3.626	215	.000***
Twitter, post original tweets	23(d)	0–1	.65	.69	-.897	123	.371
Twitter, encourage political action	23 (e)	0–1	.40	.56	-3.591	123	.000***
Twitter, repost others' political content	23(f)	0–1	.64	.73	-2.235	122	.027**

***p<.01, **p<.05, *p<.10

Table 10.5 Control Group's Pre- and Posttest Political Interest and Engagement Measures (2014–2016)							
			MEAN SCORES				
MEASURE	QUESTION NUMBER(S)	RANGE OF VALUES	PRE-TEST	POST-TEST	T	DF	P
Twitter engagement index, overall	23 (a–f)	0–6	4.18	4.36	-1.381	93	.171
Political Twitter use index	23 (a,b,e,f)	0–4	2.62	2.72	-.791	94	.431
Twitter, follow political news	23(a)	0–1	.82	.89	-1.617	95	.109
Twitter, follow political officials	23(b)	0–1	.69	.75	-1.284	95	.202
Twitter, follow entertainment news	23(c)	0–1	.80	.89	-2.179	96	.032**
Twitter, post original tweets	23(d)	0–1	.73	.76	-.726	95	.470
Twitter, encourage political action	23 (e)	0–1	.42	.44	-.376	95	.708
Twitter, repost others' political content	23(f)	0–1	.70	.65	1.000	96	.320

***p<.01, **p<.05, *p<.10

The Twitter requirement's potential impact through *encouraging political action* tweets and *following political officials* may bode well for e-civic engagement. The statistically significant increase in the treatment students' use of Twitter to *encourage others to take political/social action* is inherently positive for civic action and engagement. In their study of Twitter and political participation, Parmelee and Bichard also found that people who followed political candidates on Twitter were typically more politically engaged online and offline.[18] Our study found the same phenomenon. Students in either the treatment or control group who *follow political figures* have significantly higher reported levels of political engagement: online, offline, and through Twitter.[19] We also found that 90% of our focus group participants follow specific candidates on Twitter or Facebook and are thoughtful about how and why they do so. Some participants said that they followed candidates with whom they disagreed because they liked to "hear from the horse's mouth instead of someone else interpreting what they say," "balance things out," "at least understand their opposition" and even "do a psychoanalysis." This healthy approach to consume political information from multiple sources also can include an awareness of citizens' power in Twitter. A few participants noted that they: "watch [candidates whom they disagree with], but only follow people with similar views," [they] "didn't want to contribute to the success [of that person] because subscribers get people money," and still, another participant said she "goes to see what they are posting, but 'the follow' feels like their way of getting power [so she denies them that power]."

The focus group and treatment group participants' awareness about their e-political power and the treatment group's increases in their intentional political use of Twitter are encouraging, but are these positive indicators associated with the Twitter requirement or with political science courses in general? We predicted and found that, by the end of the semester, students in the treatment group would use Twitter for political purposes more than students in the control condition (see table 10.6).

We also predicted that students in the treatment group would increase their overall engagement on Twitter. We found that students in the treatment group increased their Twitter engagement more than those in the control group, across all three years. As seen in table 10.7, the treatment condition was a statistically significant predictor (p=.026) of increases in the Twitter engagement index; however, the predictive strength of the model is limited (Adjusted R squared=.258). In addition to the Twitter requirement, political interest and prior Twitter use were strong predictors of political engagement via Twitter (p=.005, p=.000, respectively).

In addition, we predicted that students in the treatment group would continue to use Twitter more than those in the control condition. In the summers of 2015 and 2016, we conducted follow-up surveys three months after class had ended. Based on the surveys, similar percentages of control and treatment group students who were already using Twitter at the start of class continued to use it three months after class ended (90% and 85%, respectively). However, of

Table 10.6 Ordinary Least Squares Estimates Predicting Political Use of Twitter, 2014–2016				
	B	**(S.E.)**	**STANDARDIZED COEFFICIENT**	**SIG.**
Condition	.367	.132	.146	.006***
Gender	.292	.142	.115	.041**
Pretest Twitter engagement index	.418	.046	.534	.000***
Political interest	.120	.038	.181	.002***
Politi cal efficacy	-.017	.029	-.032	.552
School year	.058	.070	.044	.409
R²	.421	.954		
***p<.01, **p<.05, *p<.10				

Table 10.7 Ordinary Least Squares Estimates Predicting Overall Twitter Engagement, 2014–2016				
	B	(S.E.)	STANDARDIZED COEFFICIENT	SIGNIFICANCE
Condition	.340	.151	.134	.026**
Gender	.277	.166	.109	.097*
Political interest	.141	.050	.212	.005***
Political efficacy	-.011	.033	-.020	.742
Social media use	-.076	.045	-.129	.094*
Pretest Twitter engagement index	-.411	.053	-.523	.000***
School year	.043	.080	.032	.592
R²	.258	1.084		
***p<.01, **p<.05, *p<.10				

the follow-up respondents who were not on Twitter at the time of the pretest, 47% of the treatment group adopted it and continued to use it three months after class, compared to 16% of the control group. So, when we consider the posttest Ordinary Least Squares results for overall Twitter engagement and the follow-up results about adopting and continuing to use Twitter, our hypothesis that the treatment could spark Twitter use appears to be confirmed. The way in which respondents reported using Twitter for political purposes was also positive but limited. At the follow up, the treatment group reported higher averages of *encouraging political action* and *learning more* after reading something on Twitter or social media compared to students in the control group (.42 vs .31 and .85 vs .59, on 0-1 scales). This difference was also found in the posttest comparisons between the conditions, so we are encouraged to see the trend sustained through the follow up, though limited by the sample size (n=132). These results suggest that requiring Twitter in our classroom and exposing students to political Twitter accounts is associated with them becoming more politically engaged and informed through Twitter. These are positive outcomes for increasing e-civic engagement among our students.

Gender and Twitter Use

Based on focus group data, as well as Jessica Bennett's work,[20] we also examined whether male and female students use and perceive Twitter differently. Through our analyses, we found that gender is a complicated predictor of Twitter use. The unpredictability of female Twitter participation was evident across our models. In the regression model shown in table 10.6, the experimental condition and gender were significant predictors of the Political Use of Twitter Index across at the end of class (p=.006 and .041, respectively).[21] Compared to male students, female students, who composed 30% of the sample, reported lower levels of general social media usage per week and political efficacy at the pretest, yet higher levels of Political Use of Twitter at the posttest.[22] Interestingly, when we apply the Twitter engagement model shown in table 10.7 to only female participants, the experimental condition is no longer a strong predictor.[23] The possible interactive effects suggest that while some female participants in the control and experimental groups are politically engaged on Twitter, many female participants do not respond to the experimental condition and do not increase their overall use of Twitter during the semester.

Another possible explanation for female participants' varying responses to the Twitter requirement is the gendered interaction with Twitter and other social media. While men and women are both online to similar degrees, their choices of and interactions within social media differ. Pew Research Center recently reported that 73% of online men use social media while 80% of online women do, a much smaller gender gap than originally reported just six years ago.[24] Still, women and men appear to prefer different social media platforms. For example, Pinterest, Facebook, and Instagram have a larger female user base, while Reddit, Digg, or Slashdot have a greater share of male users. Gender differences on Twitter, Tumblr, and LinkedIn are not significant.[25] However, we know that there are differences in perceptions and influence of social media. For example, Bennett finds that women and men are more likely to follow men on Twitter and women are more likely (59%) to use "expressive" hashtags (hashtags used to express feelings #mondayssuck, or offer a personal tweet #mybabyisgrowingup) while men (77%) are more likely to use hashtags to be seen and read as a topic that trends (#lingustics, #superbowl, #newdadproblems).[26] Based on this research, we asked our focus group participants whether they

1. follow Twitter accounts mostly authored by men or by women,
2. consider Twitter to be too confrontational; and
3. think posting on Twitter makes themselves vulnerable to attack.

All but three participants across the four focus groups predominantly follow male-authored Twitter accounts. One female student noted that she seeks out female-authored accounts because there are "more men whose voices are out there in politics than women" and she tries to "have an equal amount of female [Twitter accounts]." Another female participant intentionally tries to "search for people in marginalized groups who share similar views [because] [it's] nice to show support that way." A male student reported that he follows mainly male-authored accounts because "the sports world and politics is male dominated." Finally, one male participant noted, "a lot of the accounts [he follows] are non-gendered because it's an organization but when it's a person, most of the accounts are young men."

Additionally, many of the focus group participants reported that they perceive Twitter as confrontational, although male and female students experienced that confrontation differently. For example, one female participant noted that Twitter can be "very hateful, but also a way for other people to get out aggression in a nonviolent way." "It feels like it's a form of therapy," another female participant noted. She continued, "I'd much rather police officers tweet aggression than shoot a victim." This student uses Twitter in an expressive way, much like Bennett discussed. Another female participant noted, "Twitter makes it easier for people to be aggressive because of the anonymity. People get super egos and feel like they can type whatever they want." In contrast, some male participants admitted to being aggressive on social media. A male student noted that "even if you didn't want to cause conflict by posting something, by being on social media you open yourself up to it." Another male participant noted that he often "sees someone saying something stupid and [I'll] attack them." A third noted that he "never starts anything, but if someone attacks me, [I] feel justified in going after them." Still, another male participant noted that he "[has] gone on tirades and tweets at Trump angrily." Here, in the focus group discussions, we see a difference in how some men and women perceive Twitter. The female participants view Twitter as confrontational and feel vulnerable to attack, while men also see it as potentially confrontational but also as an opportunity to defend oneself.

A disturbing example that one of our female participants encountered was when she was tweeted derogatory and lewd comments about her physical appearance and was questioned, "why are all feminists disgusting?" when she tweeted a picture of herself with the hashtag #ThisIsWhatAFeministLooksLike. This same participant said, "Social media effectively changed [her] ideology." When pressed, she recalled how she "grew up conservative, but after social media, she learned about gender, sexuality, and feminism." She continued, "being able to meet people on the Internet and have a certain positive exposure helped [me] figure out [my] own identity and therefore political alignments (sic)." Another student said that a conversation on Twitter "changes [one's] ideas" which is "[cumulative], over time." In this same focus group, another student spoke up and said "people evolve."

Our exploratory hypotheses on gender differences are important because research by Dhavan Shah suggests that "informational" uses of social media (as opposed to expressive) are related to a greater likelihood of increased engagement in political discussion and, thus, civic participation.[27] Additionally, prior research suggested that social and recreational uses of social media were found to either not have a relationship with social capital and political engagement or to have a negative relationship.[28] Our posttests questions related to students' motivations for following certain Twitter accounts reveal the need for additional research. As seen in table 10.8, while a greater proportion of women follow certain Twitter accounts for "self-expressive" purposes, the gender differences are not clear. For example, a similar percentage of male and female students (50% and 52%) follow political experts' and commentators' Twitter accounts for "informational purposes," but women were more likely than men (18% to 9%) to follow those accounts for "guidance" and men were more likely (17% to 8%) to follow them for "entertainment" purposes. To the extent that women engage in social media use for "self-expression" rather than "information," then Shah's research, coupled with our findings, suggests that men may have a "leg up" when it comes to transferring these social media engagement habits to political engagement habits. However, our regression models and the female participants' reported motivations for following certain accounts, such as for "guidance" more than "entertainment," reveal a more nuanced story. Lastly, we are reminded by our focus group discussions that if women are more likely to interpret Twitter as being confrontational, and thus do not tweet as much as they would like for fear of being "trolled," then they may also be less likely to engage in politics, for fear of being verbally attacked or judged for asserting their political views. As educators, we should reflect on the possible gendered impacts of our assignments, the nuances within the perceived gender differences, and guidance for all students' careful and nondiscriminatory e-civic engagement.

Table 10.8 Motivation for Following Twitter Accounts by Gender, 2016

TYPE OF TWITTER ACCOUNT	ENTERTAIN-MENT		GUIDANCE		INFORMATION		SELF-EXPRESSION		SOCIAL UTILITY	
	MALE	FEMALE	MALE	FEMALE	MALE	FEMALE	MALE	FEMALE	MALE	FEMALE
Political officials/ candidates	7%	5%	5%	5%	70%	72%	13%	9%	5%	9%
Experts/ commentators	17%	8%	9%	18%	54%	52%	15%	18%	5%	4%
Political parties	6%	4%	9%	9%	71%	70%	5%	15%	10%	2%

CONCLUSION

In the surveys and focus groups from 2016, we began to explore students' motivations for accessing political information via social media. Some of their insights point to new ways to conceptualize classroom engagement and civic engagement in our digital, highly individualized, yet socially connected world. Twitter offers a forum that is less intimidating than a typical classroom. We have reported that 40% of the students in our treatment group admit that they tweet "in lieu of verbally participating." While a traditional class might need to overlook raised hands in the interest of time management, Twitter provides a forum for broad-level, albeit brief, communication. We are encouraged that 86% of the class participated through live Twitter feeds. This preference for Twitter participation in lieu of verbal participation offers some pedagogical insight into the need to create dynamic classrooms that encourage participation for *all* students, not only the ones who are already confident and advanced in articulating their thoughts.

Our focus group participants have also echoed what Russell Dalton has described as a more individualized form of civic participation.[29] Students seek to customize their social media interface, whether for personal communication or for political information. Faculty can engage students' preference for online information while guiding them out of the online echo-chamber caves. Research into the motivations behind social media use and possible gender differences can assist with this. Articulating informed opinions takes practice. Sometimes the most effective arguments and opinions articulated are concise and cogent, something Twitter forces its users to do. Additionally, faculty can require students to frequently write political statements through tweets rather than passively consume political news. We have suggested a definition of online engagement that includes active participation, such as posting versus just reading tweets.

Given the current political environment, it is imperative that educators continue to guide and model constructive tweeting and online political engagement, more generally. Does Twitter positively affect long-term political engagement? Our results, at best, are inconclusive. The experimental group's level increases in political knowledge and engagement via Twitter were encouraging. Students' higher levels of political engagement through Twitter, both in terms of growth and compared to the control group's posttests, suggest that the Twitter requirement may promote an additional connection to politics more than a typical political science classroom. At the same time, may exposure to politics on Twitter lead to higher levels of political inefficacy? Future research needs to sort this out.

In the end, all tweets are not equal. Just as the voter turnout rate is an incomplete measure of a healthy democracy, the sheer numbers of tweets and followers are alone poor measures of political engagement. Assessing how Twitter fits among other forms of e-civic engagement and whether it can be improved as a form of political engagement will be essential before we recommend it as a best practice in the classroom. If, however, by using Twitter, a student reads a tweet or tweets about Fascism and Star Wars or laments the fact that he should be more civically engaged, and maybe has fun in the process (see figures 10.2 and 10.3), then our duty as educators to increase civic interest and engagement among our students is met. ■

Figure 10.2 Tweet about Fascism and Star Wars

 Andrew Shryock @Shry_Guy · 25 Mar 2014

@asupos210 watching this hitler speech makes me think of star wars, liberty dies....with thunderous applause

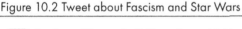

Figure 10.3 Tweet about Civic Engagement

 Adam @frios3523 · Mar 31

I wish I had a more extensive political particiaption repertoire. I mostly complain on social media and vote. @pos346

ENDNOTES

1. Joseph Kahne and Ellen Middaugh, "Digital Media Shapes Youth Participation in Politics," *Phi Delta Kappan* 94 (2012): 52–56.

2. See Alasdair Blair, Steven Curtis, Mark Goodwin, and Sam Shields, "What Feedback Do Students Want?" *Politics* 33 (2013): 66–79; Higher Education Research Institute, "College Freshmen and Online Social Networking Sites," *Higher Education Research Institute Research Brief*, September 2007; Rey Junco, Greg Heiberger, and Eric Loken, "The Effect of Twitter on College Student Engagement and Grades," *Journal of Computer Assisted Learning* 27 (2011): 119–32; and Noeline Wright, "Twittering in Teacher Education: Reflecting on Practicum Experiences," *Open Learning* 25 (2011): 259–65.

3. Of the 870 students who completed pretests between 2014 and 2016, 337 indicated that they were political science majors, with 181 of 443 (41%) in the control condition and 156 of 427 (37%) in the treatment condition.

4. See the companion website for more information.

5. We secured IRB approval from our institution and followed the protocol when using human subjects.

6. Overall, and in both 2015 and 2016, the experimental groups had higher percentages of women and reported fewer "social media days/week" than the control group at the pretest. In the 2014 pretest, the experimental group reported more social media days. In 2014, there were approximately 150 participants, compared to 320 in 2015 and 400 in 2016.

7. We also assessed political engagement in terms of offline political participation, online political participation, and political use of Twitter.

8. A comprehensive content analysis of all tweets from 2014 to 2016 will be conducted in the summer of 2017.

9. Danielle Allen, "Acting Politically in a Digital Age," in *From Voice to Influence in the Digital Age*, ed. Danielle Allen et al. (Chicago: University of Chicago Press, 2015).

10. Tim Molloy, "As President-Elect, Trump Uses YouTube, Twitter to Cut out the Press," November 22, 2017, accessed January 26, 2017, http://www.thewrap.com/donald-trump-uses-youtube-twitter-bypass-disempower-press/.

11. Jasmine C. Lee and Kevin Quealy, "The 305 People, Places, and Things Donald Trump Has Insulted on Twitter: A Complete List," January 20, 2017, accessed January 26, 2017, https://www.nytimes.com/interactive/2016/01/28/upshot/donald-trump-twitter-insults.html.

12. Emory Health Services, "How Estrogen Modulates Fear of Learning," January 18, 2017, accessed January 24, 2017, https://www.sciencedaily.com/releases/2017/01/170118163708.htm.

13. On average, the engagement score of students in the experimental condition was not statistically different from that of the control (p = .653).

14. Future iterations of the study plan to include observations of in-class participation, including counts of students' verbal participation. This would require additional teaching assistant support in classes with over 100 students, but is feasible without support in smaller classes.

15. Blair et al., "What Feedback Do Students Want?" 66–79.

16. Similar to Campbell, Gurin, and Miller's definition. See Angus Campbell, Gerald Gurin, and Warren E. Miller, *The Voter Decides* (New York: Row, Peterson, and Company, 1954).

17. Bruce Pinkleton's and Erica Austin's research exposed a strong relationship between greater levels of cynicism and lower levels of political efficacy. We are interested in exploring an antecedent variable in this relationship: levels of political knowledge. See Bruce E. Pinkleton and Erica W. Austin, "Individual Motivations, Perceived Media Importance, and Political Disaffection," *Political Communication* 18 (2001): 321–34.

18. John H. Parmelee and Shannon L. Bichard, *Politics and the Twitter Revolution: How Tweets Influence the Relationship Between Political Leaders and the Public* (Lanham, MD: Lexington Books, 2012).

19. The average political engagement index's scores for Twitter-using students who "follow political figures" compared to those who use Twitter but do not follow them are, respectively, online political engagement (3.56, 2.20; p<.000), offline political engagement (2.76, 1.53; p<.000), and Twitter engagement (4.71, 2.18, p<.000).

20. Jessica Bennett, "Why Men Are Retweeted More than Women: The Gender Disparity of Influence on Twitter," *The Atlantic*, June 2015, accessed February 15, 2016, http://www.theatlantic.com/magazine/archive/2015/06/why-men-are-retweeted-more-than-women/392099/.

21. Prior Twitter use (p=.000), and political interest (p=.002) were also statistically significant.

22. In the pretests, women reported lower levels of social media use (4.12 vs. 4.62, p=.004) and higher political efficacy (inefficacy 7.49 vs. 7.9, p=.030), on average. In posttests, women reported higher Twitter engagement overall (4.75 vs. 4.17, p=.006) and political use of Twitter (3.08 vs. 2.65, p=.013).

23. For male participants, it remains a strong predictor.

24. Monica Anderson, "Men Catch up with Women on Overall Social Media Use," *Fact Tank. News in the Numbers*, Pew Research Center, 2015, accessed January 23, 2016, http://www.pewresearch.org/fact-tank/2015/08/28/men-catch-up-with-women-on-overall-social-media-use/.

25. Ibid.

26. Bennett, "Why Men are Retweeted More," 2015.

27. Dhavan Shah, Jaeho Cho, William P. Eveland, Jr., and Nojin Kwak, "Information and Expression in a Digital Age: Modeling Internet Effects on Civil Participation," *Communication Research* 32 (2005): 531–65.

28. Dhavan Shah, Nojin Kwak, and R. Lance Holbert, "Connecting and Disconnecting with Civic Life: Patterns of Internet Use and the Production of Social Capital," *Political Communication* 18 (2001): 141–62.

29. Russell Dalton, *Citizen Politics: Public Opinion and Political Parties in Advanced Industrial Democracies*, sixth edition (Irvine, CA: CQ Press, 2013).

All Politics Is Local: Teaching Urban Studies to Suburban Students

11

Constance A. Mixon

Embedded in the name "city," which comes from the Latin "civitas," is a history of citizenship and shared community responsibility. The study of cities is the study of citizenship. This chapter provides evidence that an interdisciplinary urban studies program, with a focus on active and participatory learning, at a private liberal arts college in a wealthy suburb of Chicago, increases civic and political engagement and pluralistic orientations among students. In an increasingly global and urban world, these are critical competencies, values, and skills for our students, citizens, and political leaders.

Urban politics, as Dennis Judd pointed out, has for decades been relegated to the periphery of the political science discipline.[1] While there are many varied explanations for this estrangement, political scientists and policy makers have paid little attention to the politics of cities. They presume, at least in the United States, that democracy and politics trickle down from the federal to state and local governments.[2] Yet, it may be that democracy and politics have the ability to trickle up. In their book, *The Metropolitan Revolution,* Bruce Katz and Jennifer Bradley predict the "inversion of the hierarchy of power in the United States" from federal to urban.[3] This is not a far-fetched proposition, as populations and economic power are now concentrated in urban areas, where more than 80% of Americans live. In the United States, 69% of all jobs are found in the 100 largest metropolitan areas, which are also responsible for 75% of our gross domestic product.[4] By 2050, it is expected that 66% of the world's population will live in urban areas.[5]

In the twenty-first century, cities and their metropolitan regions are leading the charge to address many of our most pressing local, national, and global challenges. As our world becomes more and more urban, interdisciplinary programs of urban studies are poised to lead the inquiry into the central questions of our democracy. As such, postsecondary coursework in urban studies is well positioned at the forefront of preparing citizens for their responsibilities in an increasingly urban and globalizing world.

A great deal has been written about the role of political science in promoting and fostering civic engagement and citizenship. Very little (if any) attention has been paid to the urban subfield, however, much less to the interdisciplinary field of urban studies, which can provide a foundation for fruitful civic action and engagement. Embedded in the name "city," which comes from the Latin "civitas," is a history of citizenship and shared community responsibility. The study of cities is the study of citizenship. Qualitative analyses of course evaluations from three core urban studies courses at Elmhurst College are detailed in this chapter. The results provide preliminary evidence of how an interdisciplinary urban studies program, with a focus on active and participatory learning at a private liberal arts college in the suburbs, increases civic and political engagement and pluralistic orientations among students.

THE ENDURING RELEVANCE OF URBAN STUDIES

The academic field of urban studies began in the 1960s and "reflected the preoccupations of its time." It attracted academics and practitioners from multiple disciplines, including political science, "who felt a personal commitment to the social and political changes that seemed close at hand." Although many of our founding urban studies scholars were political scientists, they were "separated ... from their [political science] peers in other specialties. ... The study of urban politics went in one direction while the rest of the [political science] profession went in another."[6] By the end of the 1960s, urban political scholars were more likely to be found working with peers in other academic disciplines than with other political scientists. Drawing on the strength of scholars in different academic specialties, Michael Danielson pointed out that urban political inquiry had "developed closer intellectual links to other disciplines than most fields of political science."[7]

First-generation urban scholars (from a variety of disciplines) were primarily concerned with the challenges of race relations and inner-city blight and focused on big cities (and their populations) in crisis. This focus mobilized scholars and their students to become active and engaged participants in their communities. While many of the same 1960s and 1970s urban problems exist today, urban studies has adapted to the changing urban landscapes and issues that are more metropolitan and global in scope. Just as cities are continually in the process of building and adapting and changing, the field of urban studies and its curriculum has been built and rebuilt over time. Cities, and it seems urban studies, are always under construction.

Lewis Mumford compared the city to a symphony, where "specialized human aptitudes, specialized instruments, give rise to sonorous results which, neither in volume nor in quality, could be achieved by any single piece."[8] While individual disciplines on their own struggle and grapple with urban issues and the problems of cities, urban scholars collaborating and working across disciplines, with different disciplinary methods, tools, and vocabularies, are tackling some of the largest and most important challenges facing citizens in the twenty-first century. Through unique and coordinated approaches to these challenges, urban studies is giving rise to "sonorous results."

Today's study of the local in a global context requires the interdisciplinary work and methods of urban studies. Different areas of expertise together—under the umbrella of urban studies—have produced agglomerating economies of scale and innovation. "Students learning in this way are able to apply the knowledge gained in one discipline to another different discipline as a way to deepen the learning experience."[9] Gardy and Brinkman provide a useful analogy of the benefits realized through the type of interdisciplinary inquiry and learning that is typical of urban studies:

> Ask someone to tell you the story of the blind men and the elephant, and they'll tell you a tale of six men, each of whom touched a different part of an elephant, unable to see what their hands were resting on. Asked to describe what they had touched, the man who felt the side of the elephant said, "I touched a wall," and the man who felt the elephant's tusk said, "I touched a spear." The six men argued among themselves—was it a snake, a cow, a piece of rope? Only when they worked together, sharing their different ideas and experiences, were they able to discover the truth.[10]

Using the conceptual tools supplied by a variety of disciplines, urban studies scholars and students analyze the city, urban life, and urbanization—locally, nationally, and globally. Students interact with political institutions and the built environment while learning about and applying different perspectives to socioeconomic relations and the cultural frameworks of cities. Like generations before, today's urban scholars and students are active and engaged citizens.

SEGREGATED ENVIRONMENTS: GEOGRAPHY, POLITICS, AND CIVIC ENGAGEMENT

The United States is a highly segregated society. Increasingly, we find ourselves separated and sorted by geography, education, income, demographics, and politics into communities that look, think, and act alike. Many students, especially those who are enrolled at a private liberal arts college located in the suburbs where I teach, come from these segregated environments and are often on the sidelines of politics and urban life. Interdisciplinary urban studies programs that place students on the front lines of urban life, interacting with people of different socioeconomic backgrounds who have different life experiences, ideologies, and worldviews, play an important role in preparing students for active citizenship. This takes on increased importance as our population becomes more and more segregated.

Today, the United States is a majority suburban nation. While the US Census reports that more than 80 % of Americans live in "urban" areas, this definition of *urban* includes cities and their surrounding suburbs. Breaking this down, 26% of Americans describe where they live as urban and 53% describe where they live as suburban.[11] Although many of today's urbanists are fond of narratives centered on declining suburbs and rebounding and revitalized cities, the reality is American suburbs, although changing (increasing poverty, racial diversity, immigration), are holding steady in population, and some are growing. This trend is true for both low- and high-density suburbs. In 2015, suburban counties in the United States had faster population growth than urban counties (see figure 11.1).[12]

Our urban and suburban geographies reflect political and ideological divides in the United States, as witnessed in the 2016 presidential election, when Democrat Hillary Clinton won core cities and Republican Donald Trump won "everywhere else," including suburbs. In a report following the 2016 election, the *Washington Post* argued "geography" was a crucial determining factor of how people vote. Although this may have been news to some, the politics of place is not new to the urban studies literature. Urban sociologists and geographers, for example, have long studied the ways in which place impacts resources, opportunities, and worldviews.

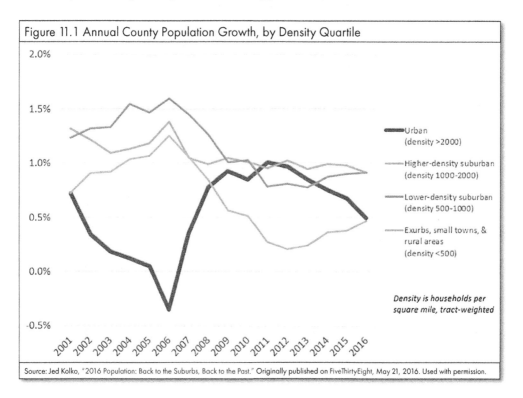

Figure 11.1 Annual County Population Growth, by Density Quartile

Urban (density >2000)

Higher-density suburban (density 1000-2000)

Lower-density suburban (density 500-1000)

Exurbs, small towns, & rural areas (density <500)

Density is households per square mile, tract-weighted

Source: Jed Kolko, "2016 Population: Back to the Suburbs, Back to the Past." Originally published on FiveThirtyEight, May 21, 2016. Used with permission.

Prior to the 2016 election, a Pew Research Center study on political polarization found "that conservatives would rather live in large houses in small towns and rural areas—ideally among people of the same religious faith—while liberals opt for smaller houses and walkable communities in cities, preferably with a mix of different races and ethnicities."[13] Political scientist Michael Thompson published in a leading sociology journal a 2012 article "Suburban Origins of the Tea Party: Spatial Dimensions of the New Conservative Personality" about the geopolitical spatial divide of the United States. In his article, Thompson argues, "suburban/exurban forms of life create an environment for [conservative] ideological identifications." He further explains that "the Tea Party and other grass roots conservative movements and groups have their origins in non-urban space for a reason."[14] Williamson likewise found that suburban residence, as measured by "greater automobile reliance and younger housing stock … are strong predictors of more conservative ideological orientation among individuals."[15]

Richard Florida of CityLab frequently writes and gives talks extolling the virtues of city life and pointing out "that sprawled America is Red America, while Blue America takes on a much more compact geography."[16] Princeton University history professor Kevin Kruse, quoted in a 2012 article in *New Republic* said, "There are certain things in which the physical nature of a city, the fact the people are piled on top of each other, requires some notion of the public good. … Conservative ideology works beautifully in the suburbs, because it makes sense spatially."[17] David A. Graham also addressed American segregation in a 2017 article, "Red State, Blue City," saying, "Americans are in the midst of what's been called 'the Big Sort,' as they flock together with people who share similar socioeconomic profiles and politics."[18]

Americans live in neighborhoods with people who look and act similarly, and have similar political ideologies. People of different races, incomes, and politics are not likely to be our neighbors. We do not go to the same schools or shop in the same places. From one neighborhood or suburb to another, there are significant inequalities that are visible in housing, infrastructure, services, and amenities.

Using statistics from the Census Bureau's 2010–2014 American Community Survey, the Brookings Institution found that most of the largest metropolitan areas in the United States have racial segregation levels between 50 and 70 (with 0 being perfect integration and 100 being complete segregation).[19] Racial and socioeconomic segregation are related. Minorities in the United States are far more likely than white Americans to live in areas of concentrated poverty.[20] This is due, in large part, to our history of structural and institutional racism including discriminatory housing policies like restrictive covenants and redlining, which prevented minorities from living in certain areas of cities and the suburbs.

Racial minorities and economically disadvantaged populations living in segregated areas are also less likely to be civically and politically engaged. In her 2015 book, *Displacing Democracy: Economic Segregation in America*, Amy Widestrom found,

> …segregation in the United States denies low-income citizens the civic and social resources vital for political mobilization and participation. People living in poverty lack the time, money, and skills for active civic engagement, and this is compounded by the fact that residential segregation creates a barren civic environment incapable of supporting a vibrant civic community. Over time, this creates a balance of political power that is dramatically skewed not only toward individuals with greater incomes but toward entire neighborhoods with more economic resources.[21]

Segregation by race, wealth, and ideology has serious and negative implications for our politics and our democracy. Segregation, coupled with political gerrymandering throughout the United States, has made it more difficult to achieve compromise and solve problems through public policy. It has also led to a decrease in civic engagement.

URBAN STUDIES AT A SUBURBAN LIBERAL ARTS COLLEGE

Elmhurst College, where I teach, is a private liberal arts college, located in a suburb just outside of Chicago, with an undergraduate enrollment of 2,840 students at the start of the 2015–2016 academic year. The undergraduate urban studies program at the college was established in the fall of 1969 and was "part of a wave of such programs founded in an era when American cities were experiencing acute social problems."[22] Elmhurst College was "among the first colleges to develop a program in urban studies and has always focused not just on large cities but also on entire metropolitan areas, including suburbs."[23] Preparing students for citizenship is embedded in the program's mission statement, program, and learning goals.

Today, the urban studies program at Elmhurst College enrolls approximately 20 majors and 10 minors on an annual basis and has a strong active and participatory learning orientation. As the major serves other disciplines and fulfills many of the college's general education requirements, two to three core urban studies courses are offered each semester, each with enrollments of between 25 and 30 students per class. On average, at our small college, between 70 and 100 students are enrolled in at least one urban studies course each semester.

Like most interdisciplinary urban studies programs and departments across the United States, majors and minors at Elmhurst College take core courses in urban studies, complemented by a variety of urban-focused courses across different disciplines. Majors choose one of three focus areas for the urban studies major: public service, public administration, or urban planning and sustainability. Within each of these focus areas, students take courses in sociology, political science, business, economics, geography, criminal justice, education, and other disciplines. The common thread of these courses is urban. For example, students can take classes titled Cities; Suburbia; Urban Politics; Urban Economic Geography; Urban Planning; Majority and Minority Relations in Cities; Urban Sustainability; and Urban Education, to name just a few.

Because of the program's interdisciplinary structure, many students complete double majors, most commonly in political science, sociology, history, business, criminal justice, and geography. The urban studies program at Elmhurst College is committed to connecting theory and practice through curriculum and pedagogy. All majors (and most minors) complete a guided experiential learning, internship, or original research project as a capstone of the program. The program has placed approximately 30 student volunteers and interns at nonprofit organizations, community organizations, political campaigns, and governmental offices throughout the Chicago metropolitan area since 2010.

Urban studies students at Elmhurst College benefit from their proximity to the City of Chicago and the larger metropolitan area, which serve as laboratories for curricular, cocurricular, experiential, participatory, and community-based models of teaching and learning. Like all global cities and their metropolitan regions, the Chicago metropolitan region faces significant social, economic, political, and governmental challenges. The most pressing of these challenges is the persistent link between race and poverty because it underlies and penetrates most urban problems like inequality, education, health care, criminal justice, and all the rest. Most Chicagoans live in racially and economically homogeneous neighborhoods. The Chicago metropolitan region is one of the most segregated regions in the United States, with a segregation index of 76—meaning that 76% of Chicago's residents would have to move to achieve full integration.[24] In some neighborhoods on Chicago's south and west sides, which are predominantly black, more than 60% of residents live below the poverty level.[25] Even more troublesome, more than 30% of Chicago's children, regardless of race, are living in poverty.[26] Yet, race matters. In Chicago, blacks are twice as likely to be poor, and there is a growing racial gap in child poverty.[27] In 2011, more than 36% of Hispanic and more than 50% of black children in Chicago were living in poverty.[28] Selected demographics for the City of Chicago, Chicago Metropolitan Region, City of Elmhurst, and Elmhurst College Students are detailed in table 11.1.

Table 11.1 2015 Selected Demographics of City of Chicago, Chicago Metropolitan Region, City of Elmhurst, and Elmhurst College Students

	CITY OF CHICAGO	CHICAGO METRO	CITY OF ELMHURST	ELMHURST COLLEGE STUDENTS
White	32%	53%	84%	67%
Black	31%	16%	1%	5%
Hispanic	29%	22%	8%	17%
Asian	6%	6%	6%	6%
Other	2%	3%	1%	5%
AVERAGE FAMILY INCOME	$48,522	$63,153	$98,789	$86,206.30

Source: Compiled by author with data from the 2015 US Census American Community Survey and Elmhurst College Offices of Institutional Research and Financial Affairs.[29]

In the City of Chicago, there is no majority race or ethnicity. Whites, blacks, and Hispanics each make up about one third of the city's population. Looking at the larger metropolitan area, whites barely represent a 53% majority of the population. This is reflective of changing demographics throughout the United States, which is becoming more racially and ethnically diverse. The US Census Bureau predicts that by 2043, America will be a majority-minority nation.[30] This majority-minority shift will happen even sooner in most of the nation's metropolitan areas as they are already passing minority-majority population thresholds among their younger populations.[31]

While Chicago and its metropolitan region are increasingly multiracial, multiethnic, and multicultural, the same cannot be said for the City of Elmhurst, located just 16 miles west of downtown Chicago and home to Elmhurst College. Originally a farming town and railroad suburb, its population increased in 1871 with the opening of Elmhurst College and an influx of "wealthy refugees" fleeing from the City of Chicago after the Great Chicago Fire.[32] With an average family income of $98,789 in 2015, the City of Elmhurst remains a leafy and historic enclave for wealthy residents seeking single-family homes on large lots, with lots of amenities, in close proximity to the City of Chicago.

Like students at most liberal arts colleges, Elmhurst College students are majority white and wealthier than geographical averages. Elmhurst College students have a reported average annual family income of more than $86,000. The average income in the City of Chicago is $48,522; and, in the larger metropolitan area, it is $63,153. With a hefty annual undergraduate tuition (with room and board) of $46,214 for the 2016–2017 academic year at Elmhurst College, many low- and even middle-class students, who are more likely to be members of underrepresented ethnic and racial groups, experience liberal arts "sticker-shock" and instead decide to enroll in state universities or community colleges. It may also be that colleges like Elmhurst prefer to recruit wealthier students, able to afford its steep tuition. In a 2011 survey of 462 senior college admission officers, 31% of respondents from liberal arts colleges "said they are paying more attention to students' ability to pay."[33] Wealthy students at liberal arts colleges enjoy favored status due, in part, to the fact they "can help schools underwrite the cost of educating low- and middle-income students … tuition-driven schools need to attract enough wealthy applicants to help defray the financial aid costs of other students."[34] Another factor driving the recruitment of wealthier students is these students are more likely to have attended private or selective high schools and are better prepared for college. Academically prepared students are more likely to persist and graduate—all the while paying tuition. They also help to raise the prestige and coveted rankings of the college.

Geography is directly related to wealth. Citizens are constrained in their housing and neighborhood choices by the size of their pocketbooks. Although wealthier residents are returning to certain parts of cities, wealth still tends to be concentrated in suburban communities. This in turn (as detailed earlier) affects worldviews and political ideologies. Although Elmhurst College does not classify students by place of residence, a significant majority of students come from the suburbs of Chicago. To get an estimate of where Elmhurst College students come from, 21 class rosters containing the names and permanent addresses of 556 students enrolled in urban studies and urban politics courses from the fall of 2011 through the spring of 2015 were examined. Each of the 556 students was coded as urban, rural, or suburban, based on their permanent address. Of the students examined, 82% of students were classified as suburban; 9% as urban; and 9% as rural. While this is not a perfect measure of the entire college student population, it does provide evidence supporting the claim that the majority of students attending Elmhurst College come from the suburbs.

During the 2015–2016 academic year, 67% of Elmhurst College undergraduates were white, with Hispanics representing the largest minority group at 17% of the undergraduate population. Asians represented 6%, and only 5% of Elmhurst College undergraduates were black.[35] Elmhurst College is not alone among liberal arts colleges in enrolling smaller proportions of minority students, especially students who are black. For example, only 2% of students at Middlebury College in Vermont are black, and at Colby College in Maine and Carleton College in Minnesota, only 3% of the students are black.[36]

In Illinois, the state board of higher education reported in 2010 (the most recent year available) that white students represented 56% of all college enrollments in the state and 53% of enrollments at independent colleges, like Elmhurst College.[37] At independent colleges in Illinois, blacks represented 15% of the student population. Hispanics represented 9% and Asians 5%.[38] Compared to peer institutions across the state, many of which are located in more rural areas, Elmhurst College, while exceeding state averages in Hispanic enrollments, falls behind when it comes to enrolling black students. In an editorial to *The Baltimore Sun* in 2014, Matthew Gerson, a freshman at Kenyon College, a liberal arts college in Ohio (which is 3% black), made the following salient points:

> Schools like mine have become, in a very real sense, gated communities within gated communities. For small liberal arts colleges, it can be tempting to sweep concerns about a lack of diversity under the carpet by boasting about liberal political leanings of student bodies (a close cousin to the "some of my best friends" argument). Progressivism is all well and good, but it cannot make up for the lack of black voices on campus. The sobering reality is that many white students will graduate from these schools without ever having a policy debate— perhaps even a serious conversation—with an African American student.[39]

Prior to the US Supreme Court case of *Brown v. Board of Education* in 1954, social scientists began to make the argument that "integrated schools … prepare all students, not just the impoverished students of color, to be effective citizens in our pluralistic society, enhance social cohesion, and reinforce democratic values."[40] Parallel arguments have since been made in support for affirmative action programs at institutions of higher education. While administrators at liberal arts colleges may be encouraged to increase student diversity, faculty who care about civic education and diversity have a larger role to play. Lacking a diverse student body at many liberal arts colleges, it is up to faculty to create learning environments that go beyond bringing diverse students together in the same classrooms.

In a study of college students, Brannon and Walton found that "diverse cultural interactions and experiences can improve intergroup attitudes and relationships."[41] Kernahan and Davis found that a course focused on prejudice and racism helped students not only to become more aware of disparities during the term of the course, but also more action-oriented and comfortable with diverse interactions after completing the course.[42] Commenting on the importance of "little interactions" between people of diverse backgrounds after his 2008 election, president Barack Obama said,

America evolves, and sometimes those evolutions are painful. People don't progress in a straight line … progress has to do with the day-to-day interactions of people who are working together and going to church together and teaching their kids to treat everybody equally and fairly. All those little interactions … add up to a more just, more tolerant, society. But that's an ongoing process. It's one that requires each of us, every day, to try to expand our sense of understanding.[43]

PARTICIPATORY ACTIVE LEARNING AND "LITTLE INTERACTIONS" IN URBAN STUDIES

Participatory and active learning engages students in the understanding of facts, ideas, and skills through various tasks, assignments, and activities. Interdisciplinary programs like urban studies are uniquely positioned to advance comprehensive understanding and facilitate the development of "boundary-crossing skills" among our students.[44] "Boundary-crossing skills are … the ability to change perspectives, to synthesize knowledge of different disciplines, and to cope with complexity."[45] Interdisciplinary urban studies programs, by design, integrate theoretical content and intellectual inquiry with application to real-world challenges. In urban studies, theory and application converge across disciplinary boundaries.

Urban studies courses provide students with important knowledge about diverse populations in urban environments and the role of governmental institutions in creating and perpetuating social, economic, and political inequalities. Many students, especially those enrolled at a private liberal arts college located in the suburbs, come from segregated environments. The urban studies curriculum at Elmhurst College is purposefully designed to get our largely suburban students out of the classroom learning about, understanding, experiencing, and witnessing through "little interactions" the challenges (poverty, inequality, racial injustice, crime) facing urban populations.

This study initially hypothesized that core courses in urban studies at a suburban liberal arts college increased civic engagement and pluralistic orientations among enrolled students. To test the hypothesis, this study examined course evaluations from three core urban studies courses taught by the author of this study at Elmhurst College from the spring of 2014 through the spring of 2016: Urban Studies 210 (Cities); Urban Studies 291 (Suburbia); and Political Science 300 (Urban Politics). Each of the three courses examined in this study combines theoretical and practical application of knowledge through a variety of active-learning and hands-on activities, as further detailed in this section. The assignments and activities in each of the three courses are purposefully designed to "engage the learner, promote ownership of the material, advance the development of higher-level cognitive skills, and increase retention better than more passive learning activities."[46] Examples of course assignments and activities are provided on this book's companion website as supplemental materials.

In addition to finding preliminary evidence that core urban studies courses increased civic engagement and pluralistic orientations among enrolled students, this study also found that core urban studies courses increased political engagement. Although increased political engagement was not initially hypothesized, it became clear during the coding of student responses that political engagement was distinctly different from civic engagement. It is important to point out that the courses under study were all courses I taught. I am a political scientist who specializes in urban politics, and I serve as the director of the urban studies program at Elmhurst College.

In 2007, the Carnegie Foundation for the Advancement of Teaching published the results of a national political engagement project (PEP) in the book *Educating for Democracy: Preparing Undergraduates for Responsible Political Engagement*. As a political scientist, I have incorporated (in various ways) the five pedagogical PEP strategies, identified in the book as the best ways to engage students in political learning, into my teaching:

1. political discussion and deliberation;
2. political action and research projects;

3. invited speakers who represent political engagement of various sorts or aspects of policy formulation and implementation;

4. internships or placements in government agencies, nonprofits, and other organizations dealing with political and policy issues; and

5. structured reflection on readings, placements, political action, or other experiences.[47]

Although the urban studies curriculum at Elmhurst College is interdisciplinary, the program includes internships, practical experiences, and a capstone for majors (and most minors) in addition to the three required core courses examined in this chapter. All urban studies majors and minors are required to complete URB 210 (Cities) and URB 291 (Suburbia). Majors are also required to complete POL 300 (Urban Politics). Detailed in table 11.2, each of the three core urban studies courses incorporates four of the five PEP strategies. Internships and placements are stand-alone courses within the program's curriculum.

COURSE NUMBER/ NAME	COURSE CATALOG DESCRIPTION	PEP 1	PEP 2	PEP 3	PEP 4	PEP 5
URB 210: Cities	The history of cities from antiquity to the present. Attention is given to similarities and contrasts in the growth and history of cities. Special emphasis on development of cities in the Western hemisphere.	X	X	X		X
URB 291: Suburbia: People, Problems and Policies	Examines a distinctive form of contemporary life—the suburbs. The history, organizational structures, and values of suburbia. Field trips and guest lecturers provide insight into current ideas for suburban development.	X	X	X		X
POL 300: Urban Politics	This course is an introduction to urban politics in the United States. The course focuses on the problems and achievements of metropolitan areas, including suburbs as well as cities. Socioeconomic issues of race, ethnicity, class, gender, poverty, wealth, and power are highlighted.	X	X	X		X

Table 11.2 Elmhurst College Urban Studies Core Curriculum and PEP Strategies by Course

Each of the three core urban studies courses includes informal political discussion and deliberation. For example, students enrolled in POL 300 debate the pros and cons of urban charter schools, and students enrolled in URB 210 work in small groups and present evidence related to the impact of gentrification on the city and long-term residents. URB 291 students give presentations and lead discussions related to suburban artifacts, making connections to the politics and culture of the time. Each course also includes structured reflection on readings and experiences. URB 291 students complete three essays during the semester, which require them to apply course readings to a contemporary suburban problem. Students enrolled in URB 210 and POL 300 submit short writing assignments, reflecting on different course speakers and applying course readings to speaker topics. A coordinated and planned program of guest speakers is used in each of the three core urban studies courses. Examples of speakers by class are detailed in table 11.3.

Table 11.3 Urban Studies Guest Speakers by Course

COURSE NUMBER/NAME	GUEST SPEAKERS
URB 210: Cities	business CEOs, urban planners, county clerk, mayors, city council representatives and former aldermen, civil rights activists, documentary film producers/writers
URB 291: Suburbia: People, Problems, and Policies	urban planners, environmental lobbyists, suburban mayors, metropolitan planning officials, transportation experts
POL 300: Urban Politics	mayors, county clerk, city council representatives and former aldermen, state legislators, members of Congress, various candidates running for local and national offices, Chicago tourism officials

Guest speakers enhance the learning experience for students and bring the city (and suburbs) into the classroom. For example, three local suburban mayors are graduates of the urban studies program at Elmhurst College. Each regularly visits our URB 291 classes. A local writer and producer of a documentary film about public housing in Chicago also speaks to students enrolled in URB 210 each semester after students have viewed her documentary. Students have also taken field trips to the headquarters of Fortune 500 companies, located in Chicago. In POL 300, we have hosted debates with candidates running for local office and the US Senate. Recently, an immigration attorney addressed students in POL 300 and explained the meaning of "sanctuary cities" under the Trump administration. While the mix of speakers varies by semester and class, outside speakers provide students with practical and alternative viewpoints and expertise.

Political action and research projects are a key component of each core urban studies course at Elmhurst College. As the Chicago metropolitan region serves as a laboratory for our urban curriculum, Chicago is frequently both "the object and venue of study."[48] Students enrolled in URB 210 investigate a neighborhood within the City of Chicago, which requires a personal visit to that neighborhood (project guidelines can be found on the book's companion website). Each student report includes a brief history of the neighborhood; description of the neighborhood at the present time; major problems, strengths, and weaknesses as learned from news accounts; census data; and interviews with residents, elected officials, and business owners. Additionally, students provide analysis and explanation of the changes occurring in the neighborhood while making predictions about the future of the neighborhood. Each student is assigned a different neighborhood, and student presentations at the end of the semester help all students to learn more about the neighborhoods that make up the larger city.

Students enrolled in URB 291 (Suburbia) are required to attend a local suburban government council/board meeting (e.g., city council, park district, library district, school district, and zoning board) and submit an informational memo that describes the suburb, the council/board, and the purpose of the meeting while explaining deliberative processes and outcomes observed (memo directions can be found on the book's companion website). Prior to their attendance, students read the minutes of previous meetings and news reports about pertinent issues facing the government entity. Students are encouraged to participate in these meetings and ask questions.

Students enrolled in POL 300 examine a contemporary urban problem (e.g., poverty, homelessness, hunger, education, crime, pollution, or gentrification) and how that problem is addressed by a nonprofit organization, located within the City of Chicago (project guidelines can be found on the book's companion website). Students research the history and status of the nonprofit while evaluating its structure, focus, programs/projects, funding, effectiveness, and other characteristics. Students are required to visit the offices of the nonprofit organization in Chicago and interview a staff member.

The overarching framework of the participatory and active-learning activities, assignments, and experiences in each of the three core urban studies courses at Elmhurst College pushes students out of traditional and orderly classroom settings and into the complexity and "messiness" of urban life. These experiences provide students with "a unique opportunity to experience the 'messiness' of problem solving and to begin to understand the benefits of uncertainty as part of the process of both learning and social change."[49] While a traditional urban studies curriculum allows students to absorb urban knowledge, the goal of participatory and active urban learning experiences is to engage and involve students in citizenship.

FINDINGS: INCREASED CIVIC AND POLITICAL ENGAGEMENT AND PLURALISTIC ORIENTATIONS

The author of this study taught three different sections of each of the three core urban studies courses from the spring of 2014 through the fall of 2016. A summary of the courses and semesters taught is detailed in table 11.4. Students enrolled in the nine courses studied included political science and urban studies majors and students without preexisting knowledge or interest in urban issues because many students enrolled to satisfy a general education requirement.

Table 11.4 Elmhurst College Core Urban Studies Courses Taught by Author: By Semester	
SEMESTER	**COURSE**
Spring 2014	Political Science 300 (Urban Politics); Urban Studies 291 (Suburbia)
Fall 2014	Urban Studies 210 (Cities)
Spring 2015	Political Science 300 (Urban Politics); Urban Studies 291 (Suburbia)
Fall 2015	Urban Studies 210 (Cities)
Spring 2016	Political Science 300 (Urban Politics); Urban Studies 291 (Suburbia)
Fall 2016	Urban Studies 210 (Cities)

At the end of each semester, students enrolled (and present) in each of the studied course sections completed a standardized Educational Testing Service (ETS) Student Instructional Support (SIR II) survey. The SIR II is designed with a series of structured questions and response scales. In addition to completing the SIR II, students were asked to complete a department/program course evaluation consisting of six open-ended questions (the evaluation can be found on the book's companion website). Both evaluation tools were administered at the beginning of a class period in the final week of each semester. Students were given as much time as needed to complete the evaluations. The instructor was not in the classroom when the evaluations were administered and completed. Both the SIR II and department/program evaluations were collected by students and submitted to the dean of the faculty by a student volunteer. All evaluations were anonymous and returned to the instructor only after final grades for each course had posted.

Student responses to one open-ended question on the department/program evaluation were recorded and coded for this study using thematic analysis: *After taking this course, are you more or less likely to be politically and civically engaged? Explain.* Table 11.5 provides a summary of the open-ended course evaluation and question results.

Of the 225 students enrolled in one of the three core urban studies courses studied from the fall of 2014 through the spring of 2016, 216 students completed the open-ended department/program course evaluation tool. Two hundred fifteen students responded to the question under study (Q1); of the 215 students who provided an answer to Q1, 195 (91%) answered affirmatively that they were more likely to be politically/civically engaged. Only three of the 215 students (1%) responded negatively that they were less likely to be politically/civically engaged. Of the 215, 18 student responses (8%) were judged to be neutral, not increasing or decreasing political/civic engagement.

Thematic analysis, as used in this study, is a "foundational method for qualitative analysis … [and] provides a flexible and useful research tool, which can potentially provide a rich and detailed, yet complex account of data."[50] Fereday and Muir-Cochrane described thematic analysis as "a form of pattern recognition within the data, where emerging themes become the categories for analysis."[51] During reading, recording, and rereading of student response data during the fall of 2016, emerging themes, consistent phrases, words, expressions, and ideas became categories for coding and analysis. Using the techniques of thematic analysis allowed for three distinct and central themes to emerge from the 195 affirmative student responses to the question examined: civic/community engagement (47); pluralistic orientation (49); and political engagement (61). Thirty-eight affirmative student responses did not fit into any of the three central themes, as they were often simply one-sentence responses indicating that students would or would not be more engaged. Thus, they did not merit identification of another theme category.

Table 11. 5 Summary of Urban Studies Open-Ended Course Evaluations: By Semester, Course, Enrollment, Evaluation Tool Completion, and Response Category

Semester	Course	Students Enrolled	Students Completing Evaluation Tool	Students Responding to Q1	Q1: More Likely to be Politically/ Civically Engaged	Q1: Less Likely to Be Politically/ Civically Engaged	Q1: Neutral
Spring 2014	POL 300: Urban Politics	24	23	23	19	1	3
Spring 2015	POL 300: Urban Politics	25	24	24	21	0	3
Spring 2016	POL 300: Urban Politics	31	29	29	28	0	1
Spring 2014	URB 291: Suburbia	26	26	25	20	0	5
Spring 2015	URB 291: Suburbia	24	23	23	20	1	3
Spring 2016	URB 291: Suburbia	22	22	22	21	0	1
Fall 2014	URB 210: Cities	26	25	25	25	0	0
Fall 2015	URB 210: Cities	28	26	26	25	0	1
Fall 2016	URB 210: Cities	19	18	18	16	1	1
TOTALS		**225**	**216**	**215**	**195**	**3**	**18**

The question studied did not provide students with a definition of political or civic engagement. Thus, it was left to students to articulate their understanding and application in their responses. Ehrlich defines civic engagement as citizen behavior "working to make a difference in the civic life of our communities and developing the combination of knowledge, skills, values, and motivation to make that difference."[52] It became clear during the coding of student responses that civic engagement was different from political engagement. Thus, political engagement emerged as its own independent category. For the purposes of this study, affirmative student responses focused on community and service were coded as civic engagement. In many studies, pluralistic orientation is often encompassed under civic engagement. In this study, however, pluralistic orientation was clearly a distinct category of its own, and it differed from the community involvement focus of civic engagement.

Of the 195 students who responded affirmatively that they were more likely to be politically/civically engaged after taking the course, 47 student responses included terms, phrases, and ideas linked to civic engagement and being involved in their communities. The following are representative student responses coded under the theme of increased civic engagement:

- Because of this class, I started a petition to get bicycle lanes in my town. I am not sure it will work—but I am trying.
- Because of the class assignment, I started volunteering with the nonprofit organization I researched. I am tutoring kids in math and feel like I am making a difference.
- I went to a meeting in the Pilsen neighborhood that was about stopping gentrification. I never would have known or cared what gentrification was before this class. I also never would have known where Pilsen was!

- I had to learn about issues in my suburb for this class and attend a school board meeting. I am still looking up and reading the minutes of meetings that happened after I attended just because I am interested.
- I started volunteering at the food bank in DuPage County after I researched and interviewed people at a food bank in Chicago for this class. I wish I could go back to the city because there are so many food deserts there, but it is hard to get there, so I am doing what I can close to my house.

Pluralistic orientation is defined as the "ability to see the world from another's perspective; tolerance for difference; openness to having one's views challenged; ability to work cooperatively with diverse others; and ability to discuss controversial issues."[53] Of the 195 students who responded affirmatively that they were more likely to be politically/civically engaged after taking the course, 49 student responses included terms, phrases, and ideas linked to pluralistic orientations. These pluralistic orientations are an important learning goal for urban studies as "issues of diversity are of critical importance in a world that has become more economically, socially, and culturally interdependent."[54] The following are representative student responses coded under the theme of increased pluralistic orientations:

- I am a Republican. I enjoyed the debates we had in class. I had to take a more liberal position and I learned more. I didn't change my mind, but I can see the other side's points better now.
- Like most people who live in the suburbs I thought poor people in the city were lazy. This class taught me about history and structural racism. Now I understand how where someone is born impacts their life later on.
- I really liked learning about education in Chicago. It's not fair that some students get better schools than others. I am an education major and I hope I can change that someday.
- I'm not black, but I started going to the Black Student Union meetings on campus with a friend from class. Because of this class I try to understand more and talk to people who are different from me.
- I see things I didn't see before this class. Just walking around I notice things like sprawl and gentrification and instead of thinking how cool everything is, I think about the people who used to live in places like Wicker Park and wonder what happened to them.
- I never really talked to people with different political views before this class. I liked that in the class everyone with different opinions could talk.

Political engagement, as defined by the Carnegie Foundation for the Advancement of Teaching, encompasses "political knowledge and understanding; political motivation, including interest in politics and a sense of political efficacy and identity; and a wide array of practical skills of democratic participation."[55] Of the 195 students who responded affirmatively that they were more likely to be politically/civically engaged after taking the course, 61 student responses included terms, phrases, and ideas directly linked to political, rather than civic, engagement. The higher number of affirmative responses categorized in this study as increasing political engagement is likely due to the instructor's primary discipline being political science. Thus, political issues may have been stressed more in each of the studied classes. The following are representative student responses coded under the theme of increased political engagement:

- I am much more aware of politics now. I am paying more attention to local government and political decisions that impact my life.
- Because of this class I think I might want to run for office someday.
- Attending the City Council meeting helped me learn more and pay more attention. I now know the names of the people who represent me and I can make better decisions when I vote.

- I went to a protest march with friends in the class. I don't think we would have done that before this class. I see now that it is important to have your voice heard.
- Because of this class I got to meet an alderman who was running for office in Chicago. I ended up working on his campaign.
- I started working for a candidate who is running for Mayor of my suburb.
- I read more about politics now from both liberal and conservative sources. Before I did not pay attention.

While the responses provided by my students are encouraging and provide some supporting evidence of the positive impact interdisciplinary urban studies courses have on civic and political engagement and pluralistic orientations, more research is needed. Future research might compare student responses across institutions. Similar responses from other students, with other instructors, at other institutions would add to the credibility of this study. I also recommend a more formalized pre- and posttesting of students to assess change over a semester. Testing instruments could be adapted from CIRP Freshman Survey and the Diverse Learning Environments Survey. The findings of this study may also serve as a foundation for future research related to student attitudes, behaviors, and beliefs over time, utilizing interviews and/or focus groups with graduates.

Interdisciplinary urban studies programs offer a multitude of opportunities for active and participatory teaching and learning. The projects and assignments highlighted in this chapter help students to understand the interconnectedness of learning, as they apply what they have learned in different disciplines to the study of cities and metropolitan areas. One of the challenges of interdisciplinary programs, however, is maintaining cohesiveness because "students take courses from a wide range of departments ... with markedly differing methodologies and subject matter."[56] To counter this challenge, it is important to maintain contact with instructors in other disciplines, collaborate, and share course materials. Recognizing this challenge at Elmhurst College has led to the development of an interdisciplinary team-taught course titled "Chicago." Focusing on a central theme of Chicago, instructors from various disciplines, including art, music, history, literature, business, and political science, will work and teach together over one semester during the 2018–2019 academic year.

Planning, coordinating, and implementing the various active and participatory learning experiences detailed in this chapter is also time-consuming. Speaker schedules do not always work with class times, and students frequently have trouble setting up and getting to and from interview and observation locations. This often requires the instructor to spend considerable time helping and coaching students outside of class. The good news is that this gets easier over time. Having taught in and around the Chicago area for nearly 20 years, I have had the opportunity to develop contacts and relationships with leaders of nonprofit organizations, government agencies, and elected officials. This takes time. Instructors new to active and participatory teaching and learning are encouraged to start slowly. It is a building process. It may be that you are only able to line up one speaker for the entire semester or only develop one project for one class. The important thing is to start building a foundation that will grow and flourish over time.

It has been the argument of this chapter that students benefit from an active-learning environment that is typical of interdisciplinary urban studies programs. This requires active teaching. Over the years I have updated, tweaked, and completely redesigned course materials, projects, and assignments, taking into consideration student stumbling blocks and, importantly, student feedback from course evaluations. Active teaching is a continually evolving process that requires educators to continually assess not just what we teach, but how and why we teach.

CONCLUSION

In their responses to whether or not they would be more politically/civically engaged as a result of enrolling in one of the core urban studies courses at Elmhurst College, the largely suburban students of Elmhurst College voiced consistent themes of increased civic and community engagement, pluralistic orientations, and political engagement. In an increasingly global and urban world, these are critical competencies, values, and skills for our students, citizens, and political leaders.

The different lenses, perspectives, and participatory and active-learning experiences in-grained in an interdisciplinary urban studies curriculum are at the heart of a liberal arts education that prepares "students to lead meaningful, considered lives, to flourish in multiple careers, and to be informed, engaged citizens of their communities and the world."[57] Urban-centric curriculum and active-learning pedagogies provide opportunities for students to see the world and cities from varied vantage points and to engage with others who have diverse beliefs and worldviews. As we become more segregated by race, wealth, and ideology, urban coursework provides the skills necessary to counter injustices and take action while negotiating the complicated and con-troversial "messiness" of urban life.

In 1981, Paul Peterson argued, "Every political scientist lives in a city, in a town, or at least in a village; by studying the politics around him, he can—with only modest research resources—gather the rich contextual information necessary for high-quality interpretive analysis, which he then gen-eralizes to the nation as a whole."[58] Since it may be that all politics is local and trickles up, educating generations of citizens for their roles in our democracy may likewise trickle up from the common "little interactions" found in interdisciplinary urban studies and urban politics courses. ∎

ENDNOTES

1. Dennis Judd, "Everything Is Always Going to Hell: Urban Scholars as End-Times Prophets," *Urban Affairs Review* 41 (2005): 119–31.

2. See Paul Peterson, *City Limits* (Chicago: University of Chicago Press, 1981); Dennis Judd, "Everything Is Always Going to Hell"; Joshua Sapotichne, Bryan D. Jones, and Michelle Wolfe, "Is Urban Politics a Black Hole? Analyzing the Boundary Between Political Science and Urban Politics," *Urban Affairs Review* 43 (2007): 76–106.

3. Bruce Katz and Jennifer Bradley, *The Metropolitan Revolution: How Cities and Metros Are Fixing Our Broken Politics and Fragile Economy* (Washington, DC: Brookings Institution Press, 2015), 5.

4. John Rennie Short, "Want the Economy to Grow? We Need to Make Cities More Efficient," *Citymetric* (February 29, 2016), http://www.citymetric.com/business/want-economy-grow-we-need-make-cities-more-efficient-1872.

5. United Nations Report, "World's Population Increasingly Urban with More than Half Living in Urban Areas," July 10, 2014, http://www.un.org/en/development/desa/news/population/world-urbanization-prospects-2014.html.

6. Dennis Judd, "Everything Is Always Going to Hell," 121.

7. Michael N. Danielson and Paul G. Lewis, "City Bound: Political Science and the American Metropolis," *Political Research Quarterly* 49 (1996): 204.

8. Lewis Mumford, *The Culture of Cities* (New York: Harcourt, Brace and Company, 1970), 4.

9. Michelle Appleby, "What Are the Benefits of Interdisciplinary Study?" *OpenLearn* (April 9, 2015), http://www.open.edu/openlearn/education/what-are-the-benefits-interdisciplinary-study.

10. Jennifer Gardy and Fiona Brinkman, "The Benefits of Interdisciplinary Research: Our Experience with Pathogen Bioinformatics," *Science* (January 17, 2003), http://www.sciencemag.org/careers/2003/01/benefits-interdisciplin-ary-research-our-experience-pathogen-bioinformatics.

11. Jed Kolko, "How Suburban Are Big American Cities?" *FiveThirtyEight* (May 21, 2016), https://fivethirtyeight.com/features/how-suburban-are-big-american-cities.

12. Jed Kolko, "2015 U.S. Population Winners: The Suburbs and the Sunbelt," *Citylab* (March 25, 2016), http://www.citylab.com/housing/2016/03/2015-us-population-winners-the-suburbs-and-the-sunbelt/475251.

13. Drew Desilver, "How the Most Ideologically Polarized Americans Live Different Lives," *Pew Research Center* (June 13, 2014), http://www.pewresearch.org/fact-tank/2014/06/13/big-houses-art-museums-and-in-laws-how-the-most-ideo-logically-polarized-americans-live-different-lives/.

14. Michael J. Thompson, "Suburban Origins of the Tea Party: Spatial Dimensions of the New Conservative Personali-ty," *Critical Sociology* (2012): 512.

15. Thad Williamson, "Sprawl, Spatial Location, and Politics: How Ideological Identification Tracks the Built Environ-ment," *American Politics Research* (2008): 903.

16. Richard Florida, "America's Most Sprawling Cities Are Also the Most Republican," *CityLab* (April 10, 2014), http://www.citylab.com/work/2014/04/americas-most-sprawling-cities-are-also-most-republican/8832/.

17. Depillis, "The GOP Can't Afford to Ignore Cities Anymore."
18. David A. Graham, "Red State, Blue City," *CityLab* (February 2, 2017), http://www.citylab.com/politics/2017/02/red-state-blue-city/515514/?utm_source=SFTwitter.
19. William H. Frey, "Census Shows Modest Declines in Black-White Segregation," Brookings Institution (December 8, 2015), https://www.brookings.edu/blog/the-avenue/2015/12/08/census-shows-modest-declines-in-black-white-segregation/.
20. For additional information, see the Working Poor Families Project at http://www.workingpoorfamilies.org.
21. Amy Widestrom, *Displacing Democracy: Economic Segregation in America.* (Philadelphia: University of Pennsylvania Press, 2015).
22. Elmhurst College, "Andrew Prinz, Elmhurst's Urban Legend, Dies," http://www.elmhurst.edu/news/42080037.html.
23. Elmhurst College, Urban Studies, http://www.elmhurst.edu/urban.
24. Tami Luhby, "Chicago: America's Most Segregated City," *CNN Money* (January 5, 2016), http://money.cnn.com/2016/01/05/news/economy/chicago-segregated/.
25. "Poverty Rate Data: Information about Poor and Low Income Residents," US Census (2013), http://www.city-data.com/poverty/poverty-Chicago-Illinois.html#ixzz1BFpArK8f.
26. Steve Bogira, "Chicago's Growing Racial Gap in Child Poverty," *Chicago Reader* (October 4, 2013), http://www.chicagoreader.com/Bleader/archives/2012/10/04/chicagos-growing-racial-gap-in-child-poverty.
27. Luhby, "Chicago: America's Most Segregated City."
28. Bogira, "Chicago's Growing Racial Gap."
29. Elmhurst College Office of Financial Affairs (personal communication February 17, 2017); Elmhurst College Office of Institutional Research (personal communication February 17, 2017); US Census Bureau (2015).
30. US Census Bureau, *US Census Bureau Projections Show a Slower Growing, Older, More Diverse Nation a Half Century from Now* [press release], (December 12, 2012), https://www.census.gov/newsroom/releases/archives/population/cb12-243.html.
31. Nate Berg, "U.S. Metros Are Ground Zero for Majority-Minority Populations," *CityLab* (May 18, 2012), http://www.citylab.com/housing/2012/05/us-metros-are-ground-zero-majority-minority-populations/2043/.
32. Jane S. Teague, "Elmhurst," *The Electronic Encyclopedia of Chicago* (Chicago Historical Society, 2005), http://www.encyclopedia.chicagohistory.org/pages/422.html.
33. Lynn O'Shaughnessy, "Colleges Love Rich Students," *Wealth Management* (November 30, 2011), http://www.wealthmanagement.com/opinions/colleges-love-rich-students.
34. Ibid.
35. Elmhurst College Office of Institutional Research (personal communication February 17, 2017).
36. Matthew Gerson, "Small Liberal Arts Colleges Lack Diversity," *The Baltimore Sun* (October 24, 2014), http://www.baltimoresun.com/news/opinion/oped/bs-ed-liberal-arts-diversity-20141026-story.html.
37. Illinois Board of Higher Education, "Table 1-3: *Race or National Origin of Students Enrolled in Illinois Colleges and Universities by Type of Institution, Fall 2010*," (2010), http://www.ibhe.state.il.us/Data%20Bank/DataBook/2011/Table%20I-3.pdf.
38. Ibid.
39. Gerson, "Small Liberal Arts Colleges Lack Diversity."
40. Marguerite Spencer, Rebecca Reno, John A. Powell, and Andrew Grant-Thomas, "The Benefits of Racial and Economic Integration in our Educational System: Why this Matters for our Democracy" (The Ohio State University: Kirwan Institute for the Study of Race and Ethnicity, 2009): 1–2.
41. Tiffany N. Brannon and Gregory M. Walton, "Enacting Cultural Interests: How Intergroup Contact Reduces Prejudice by Sparking Interest in an Out-Group's Culture," *Psychological Science* (2013): 1,947.
42. Cyndi Kernahan and Tricia Davis, "What Are the Long-Term Effects of Learning about Racism?" *Teaching of Psychology* (2010): 43.
43. President Barack Obama quoted in David Remnick and Barack Obama, *The Bridge: The Life and Rise of Barack Obama* (New York: Alfred A. Knopf, 2010), 584–85.
44. William Henry Newell, "Decision Making in Interdisciplinary Studies," in *Handbook of Decision Making*, ed. Göktug Morçöl (New York: Taylor & Francis, 2007).
45. Elisabeth J. H. Spelt, et al., "Teaching and Learning in Interdisciplinary Higher Education: A Systematic Review," *Educational Psychology Review* (2009): 365–78.
46. Danny Damron and Jonathan Mott, "Creating an Interactive Classroom: Enhancing Student Engagement and Learning in Political Science Courses," *Journal of Political Science Education* (2005): 367.
47. Anne Colby, Elizabeth Beaumont, Thomas Ehrlich, and Josh Corngold, *Educating for Democracy: Preparing Undergraduates for Responsible Political Engagement* (San Francisco: Jossey-Bass, 2007), 5. (http://archive.carnegiefoundation.org/pdfs/elibrary/elibrary_pdf_671.pdf).
48. Thomas F. Gieryn, "City as Truth-Spot: Laboratories and Field-Sites in Urban Studies," *Social Studies of Science* (2006): 6.
49. Thomas C. Henthorn, "Experiencing the City: Experiential Learning in Urban Environments," *Journal of Urban History* (2014): 450.

50. Virginia Braun and Victoria Clarke, "Using Thematic Analysis in Psychology," *Qualitative Research in Psychology* (2006): 4–5.

51. Jennifer Fereday and Eimear Muir-Cochrane, "Demonstrating Rigor Using Thematic Analysis: A Hybrid Approach of Inductive and Deductive Coding and Theme Development," *International Journal of Qualitative Methods* (2006): 3–4.

52. Thomas Ehrlich, *Civic Responsibility and Higher Education* (Phoenix, AZ: Oryx Press, 2000), vi.

53. Mark E. Engberg and Sylvia Hurtado, "Developing Pluralistic Skills and Dispositions in College: Examining Racial/Ethnic Group Differences," *The Journal of Higher Education* (2011): 418.

54. Ibid., 416.

55. See Highlights of Anne Colby, Elizabeth Beaumont, Thomas Ehrlich and Josh Corngold, *Educating for Democracy: Preparing Undergraduates for Responsible Political Engagement* (2007), http://archive.carnegiefoundation.org/pdfs/elibrary/elibrary_pdf_671.pdf.

56. Jill L. Caviglia-Harris and James Hatley, "Interdisciplinary Teaching: Analyzing Consensus and Conflict in Environmental Studies," *International Journal of Sustainability in Higher Education* (2004): 395–403.

57. Marvin Krislov, "The Enduring Relevance of a Liberal-Arts Education," *The Hechinger Report* (December 5, 2013), http://hechingerreport.org/the-enduring-relevance-of-a-liberal-arts-education/.

58. Peterson, *City Limits*, 3.

Promoting Civic Engagement in a Required General Education Course

12

John Suarez

This chapter describes ways in which service-learning and problem-based learning in a learning community helped first-year English composition students begin developing a commitment to civic engagement. Students' basic objective was to demonstrate skills in developing relationships. Those skills are central to coherence, to empathy, and to a commitment to community engagement. The "real-life" character of service-learning nurtured my "academic agility": the ability to replace planned lessons with others that helped students connect service-learning experiences with learning objectives. Students' essays and reflections show the degree to which students demonstrated those skills. In this chapter, I describe ways of addressing the challenges associated with this approach.

My attitude on empathy has changed. Before this class I was very set in my ways, and did not have nearly as much care for the problems of childhood hunger and poverty in general. This class has taught me to not be so hard headed and try to understand people's problems.

I realized that service-learning is a part of class in which we get to experience first-hand the importance of what we research and study in the class room. ... We learn about the issues we study by truly having an impact on those issues, by getting involved, and by making a difference.

—Reflections from two students in a fall 2016 CPN 102 class

The students quoted here were reflecting on their experiences in a service-learning[1] English composition course at SUNY Cortland, a four-year public institution with roughly 6,000 full-time students and 1,000 graduate and part-time students. This class' students helped address a variety of needs in low-income, rural Cortland County, whose 2014 median household income was \$48,357, lower than the national and New York State figures of \$53,657 and \$58,771, respectively. Despite this lower income, the county's rate of children living in poverty was 18.5%, lower than the 21.7% and 22.9% national and state averages.[2]

The service-learning English composition course is offered through SUNY Cortland's Institute for Civic Engagement, a campus office that fosters and facilitates community engagement collaborations. Our motto is "Do Good; Learn Well." Sociology professor Richard Kendrick created our institute in 2003, placing it in the Division of Academic Affairs. The institute's director receives release-time as compensation for institute responsibilities. The institute's Office of Service-Learning, which I coordinate, began in 2005. This position allows me to teach one course/semester; in the fall semesters I teach Writing Studies in the Community I (CPN 102).

My experience with this course during the fall 2015 and 2016 semesters taught me that service-learning instructors who focus on developing students' interest in community engagement should be academically "agile": they should be able to quickly change a class meeting's plan so that they can take advantage of service-learning's unexpected "teachable moments." Those moments arise from students' service-learning experiences; ideally, those moments offer instructors an opportunity to personalize students' learning. The US presidential election provided my 2016 class with many teachable moments for skills in critical thinking, empathy, and civil discourse. In this chapter, I describe lessons (mainly from 2015 and 2016) that I learned regarding the nurturing of students' commitment to community engagement. Those lessons are important for faculty and administrators who are exploring the integration of community-engaged pedagogies into required content-flexible courses such as English composition.

Course Description

SUNY Cortland requires a two-step sequence of English composition courses for full-time undergraduate students who have not "tested-out" of college English through high school advanced-placement courses. Each step in this sequence offers a traditionally taught version of the course and a service-learning version (see table 12.1). Each course meets the college's learning outcomes requirements for its level; the only difference is teaching methodology. The service-learning CPN courses' two sections are taught by a different instructor.

Table 12.1 Course Sequence

	FALL	SPRING
Traditionally Taught	CPN 100	CPN 101
Service Learning	CPN 102	CPN 103

This chapter explores my fall 2015 and 2016 sections of CPN 102. My syllabus lists the learning outcomes of SUNY Cortland's Writing Program, and my assignments list specific writing goals. I e-mail students my writing handbook supplement, "Do Good; Write Well," which helps students reach my course's central learning objective: demonstrating relationship-building skills. Those skills are important in delivering coherent messages (relationships between evidence and claims), which is important for critical thinking. Other relationship-building skills are important in developing empathy. I promote empathy as important for effective communication and for developing a student's commitment to civic engagement.

The Assignment: A Problem/Solution Essay and Presentation

Students in the fall of 2015 and 2016 were given the same major assignments: a personal reaction essay to news articles dealing with that semester's issue (or "theme"), followed by an issue-based problem/solution essay, then an extended definition essay. The problem/solution piece required students to propose a solution to a socioeconomic issue in Cortland County.

In 2015, students' theme was economic *im*mobility. The students' intended audience, the City of Cortland's mayor, helped students tailor their messages to him by answering their questions about the city. During a class meeting, students presented their proposals to the mayor, who then discussed their ideas with them. In 2016, students addressed the issue of childhood hunger in Cortland County; their audience consisted of supervisors from the YWCA's and Cortland Prevention Resources' tutoring/mentoring programs. Although supervisors had not requested students' ideas on childhood hunger, the topic relates to their work, and supervisors do appreciate students' collaboration, so they are happy to partner on assignments such as this. For the service-learning component of this course, 11 of my fall 2016 students volunteered with one of these two mentoring programs, three others volunteered with NYPIRG, one with the college's Health Promotion office, and one with the City of Cortland Police Department.

This problem/solution essay combined three "high impact learning" strategies. Kuh describes "high impact learning" strategies as educational methods that help students achieve "essential learning outcomes" that are crucial to students' success in their careers and in their roles as civically engaged citizens.[3] The three that I combined were learning communities, service-learning, and problem-based learning.[4]

HIGH-IMPACT LEARNING STRATEGIES

Learning Communities

Definitions of "learning community"[5] vary, but the term generally refers to a blending of at least two courses' content around a theme. My course and three others compose the "Learning In Deed" learning community; the other courses are Cortland 101 (COR 101, a first-year experience course), Introduction to Computer Applications (CAP 100), and Introduction to Sociology (SOC 150). The learning community is a "package" because students register for all of the learning community sections of these courses; no other students can register for them.

Kuh identifies the goal of learning communities as fostering cross-disciplinary learning by addressing "'big questions' that matter beyond the classroom."[6] Instructors addressed each semester's theme, and made our courses' content mutually reinforcing. For example,

- The Computer Applications (CAP) instructor assigned readings that described the technology divide between socioeconomic groups, reinforcing the idea that issues such as poverty are complex.
- Our CAP instructor scheduled Excel lessons in time for students to create charts and graphs for the problem/solution essay, and she had students construct minimum-wage budgets in chart form, dramatizing minimum wage's inadequacy.
- The childhood hunger theme related to the sociology course in that the course aims to "familiarize students with the structures of American society, and the social issues it faces," and it helps students develop their critical thinking skills.
- The SOC professor and the CAP instructor designed assignments that examined kinds of civic engagement that contrast with students' views of volunteering, which were limited to tutoring and fund-raising. One assignment dealt with hactivists (people "who [gain] unauthorized access to computer files or networks in order to further social or political ends").[7] The SOC assignment asked students to consider "hactivists" to be a subculture, and a CAP assignment examined the hacktivist group Anonymous, which is relevant because, as CAP instructor Janet Ochs notes, "Anonymous uses an electronic form of civil disobedience to achieve a kind of social change: complete internet freedom."
- Our COR instructor asked students to present a PowerPoint or PowToons Video that explained how their service-learning experiences related to SOC and/or CAP.

Service-Learning

McCartney refers to Bringle and Hatcher's definition of service-learning as

> a credit-bearing, educational experience in which students participate in an organized service activity that meets identified community needs and reflect on the service activity in such a way as to gain further understanding of course content, a broader appreciation of the discipline, and an enhanced sense of civic responsibility.[8]

Reference to reflection is important because, as Wald notes, reflection is "core to professional competency, supporting the active, constructive process of professional identity formation."[9] Powell and Kalina define "constructivist" learning as learning through which "ideas are constructed from experience to have a personal meaning for the student."[10] Through reflection, students "construct" (or create) claims based on their service-learning experiences and course content; students' claims can deal with themselves, community partners, policies, or situations.

To emphasize the importance of reflection, the Institute for Civic Engagement describes service-learning as the DNA double helix, with reflection linking course content with volunteering (see figure 12.1). I integrate service-learning into course content by asking students to apply critical thinking guidelines to evidence that they generate from their service-learning experiences. For example, in an earlier version of this course, a student claimed that her mentee's poor dental hygiene was a characteristic of life in a poor family. During a student/teacher writing conference, we discussed the strength of that assumption. I also incorporate service-learning into course content by having students demonstrate relationships between published data and their service-learning-generated information (the number of apparently underprivileged children, for example).

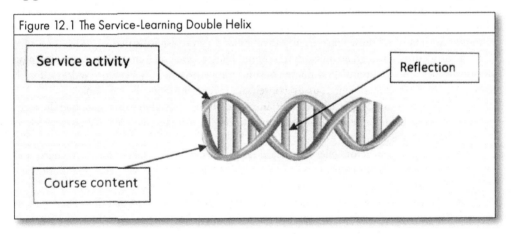

Figure 12.1 The Service-Learning Double Helix

Service activity

Reflection

Course content

My students' dispositions and academic skills ranged from unengaged to self-starters, from weak to strong. They did not know what to expect from a service-learning course. In end-of-semester reflections, for example, eight of the 16 fall 2016 students wrote comments such as, "At the beginning of the semester I really did not know what to expect being in a service-learning group, and honestly the sound of 30 hours of community service kind of scared me." However, the end-of-semester course/teacher evaluations showed that students valued their service-learning experiences. Eleven of the 15 students (one was absent) named service-learning as their "most significant learning experience." One of those 11 said that the community partner (a tutoring program) "allowed me to grow as a person." Another in that group of 11 wrote that "working with the children [let me see] how we could all make a change in their lives." Two others wrote that connecting service-learning to their writing was most significant; a twelfth named the Deliberative Dialog,[11] one named writing skills, and one named the problem/solution essay, which was designed as a kind of problem-based learning assignment.

PROBLEM-BASED LEARNING

Kretchmar's list of problem-based learning's characteristics shows that this approach is appropriate for a writing course because it is process-oriented.[12] In addition, problem-based learning and service-learning share characteristics that can help students develop a commitment to civic engagement: they employ civically engaged, place-based issues in real-life and cross-disciplinary settings that enhance a constructivist pedagogy. Students construct their learning in reflections or class discussion when, based on their service-learning experiences, they make claims about people, policies, or events. Those claims can be thought-provoking observations or contentious perceptions that deserve prompt consideration; because of this, instructors might occasionally want to practice academic agility by replacing planned lessons with others that address students' weak critical thinking.

ACADEMIC AGILITY

To help realize the potential of student-generated lessons in these high-impact strategies, faculty can build "agility" into their plans. That agility is the ability to replace planned lessons with others that help students connect current civic engagement experiences, and the conclusions that students draw from those experiences, with learning objectives. An instructor's academic agility is important because it helps the instructor address students' experience-based concerns and/ or misconceptions. Instructors can develop that agility by electronically saving news articles and other sources (such as podcasts) for use in class, by shifting a discussion's focus to topics raised by students' comments, by adapting existing course materials, and by having classroom activities ready for appropriate occasions.

Saving News Articles. In a class session the year before the fall 2014 class, students were describing their service-learning experiences from the two weeks before that class meeting. One student wondered about her mentee's family: "They're so poor they're on food stamps—So how can they afford a big flat-screen TV?" (I am paraphrasing.). In the meeting that followed, I addressed the issues of definition (the word "poor") and kinds of evidence (anecdotes and statistics) by sharing and discussing selections from a Heritage Foundation (a conservative think tank) document from 2011 that I had stored as a PDF. The article's authors, Rector and Sheffield, wondered how a family could be considered "poor" if it had amenities such as a large TV.[13] We compared that document's claims to readings that we had already discussed, and to other students' experiences. I was not asking students to believe one conception of poverty over another; rather, I was asking them to apply and refine their critical thinking skills.

Shifting Discussion to Student-Raised Topics. A student's comment in another earlier version of CPN 102 led to an unscheduled discussion of connotative meanings.[14] I had asked students to recreate scenes from their service-learning sites so that we could vicariously experience their activities. Three students set up a version of the soup kitchen at which they volunteered. As the class walked through the recreated soup kitchen, one student lifted a box of generic corn flakes, saying, "Oh, Ghetto Flakes!" That day's lesson changed from "skills of observation" to "connotative meanings."

In 2016, I used multidisciplinary teachable moments, as in a conversation that blended a mentee's constant use of social media with the nature and use of information. That conversation led to a computer applications-relevant discussion of "the Internet of things,"[15] especially the idea that devices connected to the Internet—from thermostats to toys[16] to telephones—can be controlled by hackers. As class was about to end, a student showed the class that he had a piece of duct tape over his phone's camera lens, saying "I don't want anyone hacking my phone to see what's going on in my room!" Immediately, many students said, "What?!" "You're kidding!" while taking-out their phones to look at the lenses and saying they will cover their lenses as well.

Keeping Some Classroom Activities Ready to Be Used, as Need Be. As students in a class before fall 2015 were discussing audience analysis, they expressed an "either/or" view of issues, including the supplemental nutrition assistance program. I halted discussion and asked students to meet in the hall. Students who favored the program assembled at one end of the hall; those who opposed it gathered at the other end. As I had hoped, a couple of students asked where they should stand if they "leaned toward" one opinion or the other. I asked them to stand near the appropriate end of the hall, and to stand near one wall or the other, depending on their reasons for liking or disliking the program (so as to separate them from someone who also liked or disliked it, but for a different reason). In this way, students were able to visualize the idea that issues and opinions can be complicated. In helping students acknowledge the complexity of issues, instructors also help students realize that people with opposing points of view might have good reasons for those views. In other words, instructors are helping students to empathize.

DEVELOPING A COMMITMENT TO CIVIC ENGAGEMENT

Empathy

The path toward a commitment to civic engagement includes empathy. Black and Arnold define "empathy" as a cognitive and emotional understanding of another person's reasons for believing and behaving as they do.[17] However, Jacoby points out that students need to understand that they cannot truly understand someone else's life after only a semester's worth of volunteering.[18] To acknowledge Jacoby's concern, I help students develop an empathetic disposition through the use of reflective listening skills and events that include role-play activities and community meetings.

Developing Empathy: Reflective Listening Skills

My students begin revising drafts in a full-class reflective peer review, which is based on the reflective listening skills of asking open-ended questions (OEQs) and paraphrasing the cognitive and emotional content of the person's comments. Reflective listening helps students respect and empathize with other people's ideas nonjudgmentally, especially in tense situations (such as editing sessions).

At this point in an essay's development, I ensure that students are meeting concerns related to clarity and coherence. Classmates ("editors") are forbidden from offering advice; rather, they must apply reflective listening to help the author develop his essay himself. When some students in the 2015 class began to give advice, their classmates reminded them to "Ask OEQs!" There is no correct answer to editors' questions—as long as the author can explain and justify his or her answer.

I reminded students that reflective listening skills are important in their academic and personal lives by having them describe ways in which they use the skills in their service-learning. One poignant example is from a few years ago. The student tutored a child who was usually ready to do homework. One night, though, the child did not want to study, in spite of a big exam. After trying logic ("You need to pass this test to get into 5th grade!"), our tutor decided that using logic was illogical, so she paraphrased the girl's emotion: "You sound sad and upset." After receiving confirmation, she offered to get ice cream from the restaurant in the building. With their snacks, they ate in silence. Later, during conversation, the girl said that her father had been arrested.

This student used reflective listening to learn what was important to her tutee. In doing so, she earned the girl's trust by empathizing with her, thereby strengthening their working relationship.

Developing Empathy: Role-Play Activities and Community Meetings

I use role-play to help students understand hidden barriers that low-income residents face. In 2015, I conducted the Socioeconomic Docudrama role-play during a class meeting. I designed this event, basing it on real people's experiences as reported in news outlets, on interviews with agency supervisors and faculty, and on entries from service-learning students' "logs." Each student reads the dialogue of an individual in this "two-days-in-the-life" of an underprivileged 12-year-old girl. Students receive the script, a data-sheet with statistics about low-income life, and a "Playbill," which includes a prompt that helps students identify their preconceptions of low-income life. After each scene, students write notes regarding the protagonist's strengths and challenges, then we discuss the class' responses.

The role-play in 2016 was an event in SUNY Cortland's Economic Inequality Initiative, which began in November 2014 as an American Democracy Project effort to educate students about economic inequality. It includes faculty, staff, students, and community partners. During its second year, we added an action component for which we recruited community members with diverse economic and political views. To help participants understand the complexity of economic inequality, we scheduled a State of Poverty Simulation and a Deliberative Dialog.

The participants in the two-hour State of Poverty Simulation included the local chairs of both major parties, as well as business, not-for-profit, health care, and education leaders. The simulation is conducted by one of our partners, the Cortland County Community Action Program (CAPCO). It begins with an overview of poverty; it ends with a large-group debrief session. The middle hour (the actual simulation) is split into four 15-minute "weeks" in which people try to survive on slightly more than minimum wage.

To get an idea of the simulation, imagine a bird's-eye view of a large room. Along each of the walls are tables that represent community resources such as a workplace, school, grocery store, utilities company, landlord, pawn shop, police station, Department of Social Services, and a not-for-profit agency. Fifteen CAPCO staff "man" the tables. Each participant receives a "bio": he could be a member of a family, or he could be a young adult or a senior citizen living alone. Each person's goal is to conduct daily business through those four "weeks" by going to the appropriate tables to take care of business. No script, just "live the life."

Neither the simulation nor the dialog had been scheduled when I constructed the course, so I "encouraged" students to participate through extra credit. During a presimulation class meeting, many students said that poor people need to get jobs or work harder. They carried this opinion into the simulation. After participating in that event, however, many students' reflections mirrored this student's comments:

> The State of Poverty Simulation was a complete eye-opener for me. If you talk about an
> issue it seems like something that is distant, but this simulation allowed me to experience this
> issue first hand.... I felt sort of embarrassed that I was not able to help my family [get] their
> necessities.... We couldn't have even gotten food for a week because we had to pay the electric
> bill or the rent, which felt embarrassing. I was ashamed.

These comments dramatize a simulation's power: it provides multisensory situations that foster empathy. My earlier research explains that simulation's effectiveness can come from the human brain's tendency to reconcile two sets of seemingly incompatible operations: it accepts emotion as cognition, and imagined activity as real; working together, these behaviors foster empathy.[19]

The State of Poverty Simulation "primed" its participants for the Deliberative Dialog, which was designed to identify local barriers to economic opportunity for low-income county residents, and to brainstorm ways of addressing those barriers. A Deliberative Dialog is a facilitated event that encourages the civil sharing of diverse ideas around a specific topic. New York Campus Compact's Executive Director, Laurie Worrell, supported training for three dialog facilitators: a SUNY Cortland professional staff member, a student, and an agency partner. Two Broome Community College faculty members conducted the training.

The training helped to make the dialog an event characterized by mutual respect among all 33 participants, which, in turn, helped the student participants (including 11 of my students) observe 13 professionals work across ideological lines to reach a shared goal. We ended our 90-minute session with a dozen action ideas; some CPN students built on ideas from the dialog for their problem-based learning essays. For example, one student wrote, "The dialogue helped my essay in that I heard about failed attempts and ruled out the already attempted solutions as well as ones similar to them. Many of the solutions worked temporarily but are not long term." Another student transformed a community gardens idea into a Soup Kitchen Workshop. The student emphasized the importance of this event by writing,

> Going to the Deliberative Dialog clarified things for me. ... We talked so much [in class] about childhood hunger in Cortland County; however, I never knew just how much of an issue this is and how many people are working every day to put an end to it. [If I hadn't attended the Dialog,] I wouldn't have found out what things people in the community are already doing to help others in their community.

This student seemed to be starting a journey of commitment to civic engagement.

Stages in the Development of a Commitment to Civic Engagement

Students' commitment to civic engagement can begin with a lack of empathy, as shown by one of my students who participated in a mentoring program. The student seemed oblivious to the contrast in the degree of privilege between the tutee and herself:

> A child got hurt, and while I was explaining to their parent what happened, the parent was complaining about having to pay for doctors. After some more conversation, I realized the child lived in a single parent home and the mom just bought a new car and it was a car from 2011. The mother was so happy [yet] most people would be upgrading from the 2011 now.

This student is starting a journey that takes people from a place of little empathy to one of action. Rockquemore and Schaffer identify three stages of thinking and feeling in this journey, beginning with "shock" at the gulf between the person's life experiences and his community partner's life.[20] One of my student's comments about privilege suggests that he is at the shock stage: "I do not take things for granted anymore and I am very grateful for everything I have."

In Rockquemore and Schaffer's second stage, "normalization," the student accepts his community partner's situation as normal for that person.[21] My students demonstrated normalization by expressing an awareness of their community partners' larger social environment. One student wrote that "Because of the events like the State of Poverty Simulation and the Deliberative Dialog, I started to think of others more than I thought of myself."

In stage three, "engagement," students have established personal relationships with community partners, so they want to determine the causes of the conditions in which their community partners are living. This next quote suggests that one of my students was moving through the engagement stage, and into a fourth stage that we can call "commitment":

> [The Dialog] intrigued me because I have never been a part of something that aimed toward helping a community so positively. Everyone in the dialogue had great ideas that I would have never thought of, it surprised me how many solutions there are to improve Cortland.

Another student who is in the commitment stage is the student who, earlier, did not recognize the disparity in privilege:

> [The Simulation] changed my views on how hard it is to be a functioning family of four. ... There were days where I had to miss work or my daughter had to miss school so that the other one could get where they needed to go. Going through this experience shows that this is a tremendous problem and needs a solution immediately.

With commitment comes a sense of effectiveness, which could bring students to a fifth stage: "action." Oceja et al. show that a person who empathizes with a group is more likely to help it, especially when that person thinks of another individual as being a member of that group.[22] My students seemed to empathize with their mentees and, by extension, with their community agencies. One student, a simulation participant who was on this part of the journey, wrote, "I didn't understand how hard it is for some families to go through their day-to-day lives. The sacrifices we had to make in order to still keep our house were scary. My family couldn't buy food sometimes. This was a serious wake-up call for me and we need to find a solution."

This student continued her discussion in a follow-up reflection, writing that the simulation

gave me ideas for my problem/solution essay. When you feel like you are living an issue you are trying to solve, you think of ways to help. I thought to myself, what would I like to have happen to people like me, while in this simulation. I came up with my solution while keeping this experience in mind. I felt sort of embarrassed that I was not able to help my family [get] all their necessities…. My solution would eliminate the stigma on people who go to soup kitchens because it wouldn't be just a soup kitchen, it would have workshops….

With a few exceptions, this class went further along this trajectory than any other service-learning class that I have taught in the last 17 years of teaching through service-learning.

IMPACT ON STUDENTS' WRITING AND DISPOSTIONS TOWARD CIVIC ENGAGEMENT

The goals for this course centered on the idea of *building relationships*. Regarding writing skills, I was especially interested in students' ability to demonstrate relationships between claims and evidence (coherence) and to empathize with audience. For community engagement, I wanted students to take active roles in improving the quality of life for county residents and to continue this habit of engagement after taking my course and graduating college. This chapter focuses on a problem-based learning assignment from a service-learning English composition course; that course was part of a learning community in the fall 2015 and 2016 semesters. The impact that I observed from guiding students through this combination of strategies comes from a comparison of students' grades and from my review of their reflections, their e-mails, and my class notes.

WRITTEN COMMUNICATION

Students in these two years experienced different courses: the 2015 students had many class sessions devoted to the mechanics of writing; they composed two in-class essays, and they had one 30-minute in-class simulation (the Docudrama). In contrast, the 2016 students' mechanics lessons were nestled into critical thinking discussions, the students composed no in-class essays, all students participated in (mostly spontaneous) US presidential election-related discussions, and many joined the two-hour State of Poverty Simulation and/or the 90-minute Deliberative Dialog.

The major assignments, however, were essentially the same for both years. The assignments' grades were based on a rubric. The final grades for the two classes were almost identical: the 15 2015 students' grades averaged 84.1, including a failing grade; the 2016 average was 83.9, excluding a 17th student who dropped the course (failing) at midterm. All but three of the 2016 students participated in the simulation and/or the dialog. One of those three students received a "C-" (the lowest passing grade for this course), one earned a "C," and one earned an "A." The rest of this assessment addresses the fall 2016 course.

Students approached writing as a process. Initially, though, seven students had assumed that we would focus on writing's mechanics. Toward the end of the semester, one student wrote that she adopted one aspect of process: "When I realized how much [writing multiple drafts] helps my writing I began to write multiple drafts in my other classes for writing assignments." Another student wrote that "this course was much different than I expected. … I felt challenged to write so many different drafts." However, she was happy that she and her classmates could "edit our own writing the way *we* wanted to."

The course's focus on process helped students' ability to narrow their essay's topics and to develop coherence. Students narrowed the topic of childhood hunger to solutions that dealt with SUNY Cortland scholarships for local high school athletes, an employment program for high school students, a soup kitchen that provided lessons in budgeting and in buying and cooking healthy foods, and a pregnancy-prevention program.

One student's writing exemplifies the development of a coherence-related skill: integrating source material. She originally included a quote by writing, "The United States is facing a serious problem with childhood hunger today. 'In 2012, nearly 16 million US children, or over one in five, lived in households that were food insecure' (Gunderson and Ziliak, 2014, p. 1)." After reflective peer review, she strengthened coherence: "The United States is facing a serious problem with childhood hunger today. According to Gundersen and Ziliak (2014, p.1), 'In 2012, nearly 16 million US children, or over one in five, lived in households that were food insecure.'"

This same student integrated quotes effectively elsewhere in her essay, synthesizing sources:

> Child hunger is the result of poverty and food insecurity in low-income households. Gundersen and Ziliak (2014, p.1), and Glennon (2016) explain how poverty and low income are predictors of hunger in the community. Gunderson and Ziliak state that "Food insecurity rates remain stubbornly high for a number of reasons" (p.1).

At another point, this student integrated her published source material with her service-learning experience in a way that shows empathy; she begins by referring to a previously cited source:

> Here, Lee is explaining why some of us don't understand how big of a problem food insecurity is in our community. What she is saying is that you don't always know just by looking at a child if they are suffering from hunger. I personally did not realize how many low-income households and hungry children we had in Cortland County until I started my research on child hunger. The Compass [mentoring] program has also opened my eyes to the food insecurity and low-income household rates in Cortland because I've come to realize that the twenty or so kids in the program are only a fraction of the kids in Cortland that live in low-income households.

A COMMITMENT TO CIVIC ENGAGEMENT

Students' end-of-semester reflections offered some insight into their journey toward a commitment to civic engagement. One, for example, addressed critical thinking and empathy:

> My understanding of writing changed in the sense that through this course I have come to realize the importance of the use of reliable sources while writing. But, not only while writing, while speaking to an audience as well, especially while saying things that can potentially offend others. Which is not what I expected to learn in a writing studies course.

Students noted that their volunteering and their participation in the State of Poverty Simulation and/or the Deliberative Dialog helped them develop a sense of effectiveness. A dialog participant wrote, "I got to state my opinion to many different people of many different ages. No one laughed or stated that I was simply a child. ... I felt like I could help society and actually make a difference."

REPLICATING: LIMITATIONS AND SUGGESTIONS

Limitations of this approach include an institution's lack of established community relationships, a lack of time, and students' lack of skills in civil discourse. To successfully replicate or adapt the SUNY Cortland model, faculty (or, ideally, the appropriate office at the institution) should form reciprocal relationships with potential community agency partners. For the students' learning community, the participating faculty should schedule three or four "update" meetings; they should work with their registrar to schedule common meeting times for them and their students, and (for the additional time required for academic agility) plan time for additional preparation. The lack of students' skills in civil discourse should be addressed through the integration of reflective listening skills into at least one of the learning community courses.

LACK OF ESTABLISHED CAMPUS/COMMUNITY PARTNERSHIPS

SUNY Cortland faculty and students are fortunate to have long-running community partnerships.[23] However, every community can probably identify local and/or regional needs that students in different disciplines could address. Community agencies could create a projects "wish list" for students' participation. For example, Cortland County's legislature, businesses, and others are exploring decisions regarding solid waste disposal, glass recycling, and the siting of a new jail. These decisions require research, assessment, and advocacy. Through our Economic Inequality Initiative, we (including students) are planning ways for students from various courses to contribute to these efforts.

A LACK OF TIME

Three time-related challenges are the scheduling of instructor "update" meetings, the lack of a common meeting time for students to reflect on their service-learning experiences in a multidisciplinary setting, and the time needed for academic agility. For fall 2015 and 2016, my learning community colleagues and I planned in person and by e-mail, and we debriefed in person at the end of the semester, identifying changes for the next year. However, due to new responsibilities for three of us in fall 2016, our only course-related communications during that semester dealt with certain students' class participation and grades. The challenge of meeting regularly is difficult to manage, but we are planning to address it, in part, by promptly sharing cross-disciplinary student work (such as the assignments described earlier), especially when that work is submitted electronically.

A second time-related challenge is scheduling an occasion for students to reflect in a multidisciplinary setting. In neither of my 2015 or 2016 classes did students have a common meeting time to reflect with at least two of their learning community instructors present. Scheduling a learning community "lab" is one way to solve that challenge. The learning community's schedule of courses would include a meeting, once each week or once every other week, to allow for multidisciplinary reflections. This approach has the administrative complications of offering students an additional credit hour, and the additional compensation for faculty. An alternative scheduling approach avoids that complication: back-to-back scheduling.

In 2013, a different sociology professor and I scheduled our courses in this way. In the 9:10-to-10:00 time slot, I taught CPN while he had "open time." In the 10:20-to-11:10 slot, he taught SOC while I had open time. This arrangement let us occasionally meet students together for multidisciplinary reflections. Both of these scheduling plans can help address the need for academic agility, a third time-related challenge.

McDonald explains that integrating multiple civic engagement and experiential learning strategies "is more difficult than we think."[24] My experience with this combination of learning strategies reinforces his observation, especially as students' experiences raise teachable moments. In 2016, I did not anticipate the degree of toxicity in the presidential election campaign, nor did I anticipate my students' keen interest in the presidential debates (which had not been confirmed or scheduled when I planned the course). As I walked into class on the morning of the first debate, for example, a couple of students asked, "Mr. Suarez, are you going to watch the debate tonight?!? Can we talk about it in class next time?" Discussion of the debates replaced two class discussions' original plans. The discussions explored critical thinking skills, but detracted from writing's mechanical skills, and threatened productive class discussion.

LACK OF CIVIL DISCOURSE SKILLS

In 2016, I learned that one especially complicated aspect of service-learning during an emotionally charged political climate is the nurturing of civil discourse skills. Learning is motivated, in part, by emotion. As educators, we persuade students to believe and behave in certain ways, so our methods should include an appeal to emotions—not to the exclusion of critical thinking, but as a way of helping students remember, think critically, empathize, and become civically engaged.

Brooke and Harrison emphasize the importance of emotion in civic engagement, writing that emotion effects "attention, perception, memory, and learning, [and it] plays a core part in our social relationships, and forms a foundation for empathy."[25]

Students' written and spoken comments from the State of Poverty Simulation exposed a range of emotions that helped students empathize, including "embarrassed," "felt ashamed," "scared," "frustrated that I couldn't feed my family," "angry that there was no job for when I could work" [due to a lack of child care], and "really upset that I might have to wait 45 days for food stamps."

To avoid counter-productive levels of emotion, we must nurture skills and behaviors that develop interpersonal relationships of mutual respect. To this end, I will avoid discussing the complicated world of "safe places," "safe spaces," and "open spaces." Rather, I will focus on behaviors and skills that develop empathy and mutual respect.

One way of creating such behaviors and skills is through reflective listening habits, which encourage mutual respect and a "willing suspension of disbelief" of opposing viewpoints. Students have not been enculturated to behave this way, so this work must continue across semesters. To help faculty and staff learn and apply such skills (at least in administrative settings), the Institute for Civic Engagement has conducted reflective listening skills workshops, and the dean of the college's School of Arts and Sciences, Dr. Bruce Mattingly, arranges for, and coconducts, "Crucial Conversations" seminars, which provide more extensive workshops.

The importance of the concern for civil discussion was dramatized in my class' discussions of the US presidential election campaign, especially during the class meeting on the morning after the election (I did plan for this discussion); it provided a sobering reminder that tensions can be simmering "below the surface."

Some students made claims about the campaign and the election. When I asked, during the class discussion, for the sources of evidence, students mentioned Fox News, CNN, and MSNBC. I did not ask if students actually went to these sites, or if they accessed the sites through social media. Curiously, only one student mentioned social media, though the *Christian Science Monitor's* Amanda Hoover Staff reports that 88% of 18-year-olds get their news through social media.[26] At one point, two of the class' supporters of Mr. Trump said, basically, that Black Lives Matter (BLM) followers incite violence. One of the students claimed that some violent protesters did not know what one particular protest was about, but that it was a chance to destroy things. Another student said that most violence against blacks is black-on-black violence, and that BLM doesn't care about violence against policemen. I remained quiet, wanting other students to ask for evidence. None did.

Two class meetings later, we launched our final essay, an extended definition assignment in which students created and defined a word that captured some part of their CPN 102 experience. In addition to the assignment instructions, I provided a sample essay that I composed after the post-election discussion (another example of agility). My word, *angstion,* combined "angst" and physical tension: it is an instructor's fear and physical tension when trying to keep tense conversations open, civil, and productive. The word grew from my frustration at not questioning the claims mentioned previously. Within an hour after class, six students e-mailed me a note of thanks for sharing feelings that they also had. At least one of those six supported Mr. Trump.

Obviously, I had not helped all of my students to behave in ways that developed mutual respect for their CPN 102 classmates, but this experience does underscore the need to integrate empathy-related learning across disciplines and across years.

The greater the number of varied experiences that we can offer our students, the greater the chances that they will encounter a life-changing moment in our class. In fall 2016, such a moment might well have arrived for the student whose quote began this chapter. He wrote,

My attitude on empathy has changed. Before this class I was very set in my ways, and did not have nearly as much care for the problems of childhood hunger and poverty in general. This class has taught me to not be so hard headed and try to understand people's problems.

He continued,

There was one situation in my service-learning that really changed my views. In this incident a 16- year-old girl had run away from her parents because of domestic problems. This really made me realize that I cannot judge people until I have walked in their shoes.

This student took at least one step in his journey to a disposition of civic engagement. ■

ENDNOTES

1. Service-learning is a form of experiential learning that uses reflection to combine academic course content with a relevant and meaningful community project. Additional explanation is provided under the Service-Learning section.
2. Seven Valleys Health Coalition, *Cortland Counts: An Assessment of Health and Well-Being In Cortland County* (Cortland, NY: Seven Valleys Health Coalition, 2016), 5.
3. George D. Kuh, *High Impact Learning Practices: What They Are, Who Has Access To Them, And Why They Matter* (Washington, DC: Association of American Colleges and Universities, 2008), 4.
4. Problem-based learning is a form of learning in which students describe and offer a solution to a place-based problem. Additional description is offered under the Problem-Based Learning section.
5. The National Resource Center for Learning Communities at Evergreen State College offers an open-access, peer-reviewed journal, *Learning Communities: Research and Practice*, at http://washingtoncenter.evergreen.edu/. Forms for planning and assessing learning communities are available at the *Teaching Civic Engagement* companion website.
6. Kuh, *High Impact Learning Practices*, 5.
7. *Oxford Living Dictionary*, https://en.oxforddictionaries.com/definition/hacktivist.
8. Alison R. M. McCartney, "Teaching Civic Engagement: Debates, Definitions, Benefits, and Challenges," in *Teaching Civic Engagement: From Student to Active Citizen*, ed. Alison Rios Millet McCartney, Elizabeth A. Bennion, and Dick Simpson (Washington, DC: American Political Science Association, 2013), 15.
9. Hedy S. Wald, "Refining a Definition of Reflection for the Being as well as Doing the Work of a Physician," *Medical Teacher* 37 (2015): 696.
10. Katherine Powell and Cody Kalina, "Cognitive and Social Constructivism: Developing Tools for an Effective Classroom," *Education* 130 (2009): 241.
11. A Deliberative Dialog is a facilitated event that encourages the civil sharing of diverse ideas around a specific topic. This dialog included students, faculty, and community members.
12. Jennifer Kretchmar, "Problem-Based Learning," *Research Starters Education* (2015): n.p.
13. Robert Rector and Rachel Sheffield, "Air Conditioning, Cable TV, and an Xbox: What is Poverty in the United States Today?" *Backgrounder* 2575 (2011): 13.
14. The English Oxford Living Dictionaries define "connotative meaning" as "an idea or feeling which a word invokes for a person in addition to its literal or primary meaning," https://en.oxforddictionaries.com/definition/connotation.
15. The term "the Internet of things," or "the Internet of objects," refers to the Internet connections between electronic devices that allow for remote data collection and/or remote control of objects such as phones, vehicles, and nuclear power plants. Refer to https://www.forbes.com/sites/jacobmorgan/2014/05/13/simple-explanation-internet-things-that-anyone-can-understand/#6cd86ff01d09.
16. Refer to http://wrvo.org/post/banned-germany-kids-doll-labeled-espionage-device.
17. Anthony L. Black and Robert M. Arnold, "'Yes, It's Sad, but What Should I Do?' Moving from Empathy To Action in Discussing Goals of Care," *Journal of Palliative Medicine* 17 (2014): 141.
18. Barbara Jacoby, *Service-Learning Essentials: Questions, Answers, and Lessons Learned* (San Francisco: John Wiley & Sons, 2015), 43.
19. John Suarez, "Empathy, Action, and Intercultural Competence," in *Intercultural Horizons: Intercultural Strategies in Civic Engagement*, volume two, ed. Eliza J. Nash, Nevin C. Brown, and Lavinia Bracci (Newcastle Upon Tyne, UK: Cambridge Scholars Publishing, 2013): 6.
20. Kerry Ann Rockquemore and Regan H. Schaffer, "Toward a Theory of Engagement: A Cognitive Mapping of Service-Learning Experiences," *Michigan Journal of Community Service Learning* 7 (2000): 16.
21. Rockquemore and Schaffer, "A Theory of Engagement," 17.

22. Luis. V. Oceja, Marc W. Heerdink, Eric L. Stocks, Tamara Ambrona, Belén Lopéz-Peréz, and Sergio Salgado, "Empathy, Awareness of Others, and Action: How Feeling Empathy for One-Among-Others Motivates the Helping of Others," *Basic and Applied Social Psychology* 36 (2014): 122.

23. Campus Compact provides resources for developing campus/community partnerships, among other benefits: http://compact.org/.

24. Michael K. McDonald, "Internships, Service-Learning, and Study Abroad: Helping Students Integrate Civic Engagement Learning across Multiple Experiences," in *Teaching Civic Engagement: From Student to Active Citizen,* ed. Alison R. M. McCartney, Elizabeth A. Bennion, and Dick Simpson. (Washington, DC: American Political Science Association, 2013), 371.

25. A. H. Brooke, and Neil A. Harrison, "Neuroimaging and Emotion," in *Stress: Concepts, Cognition, Emotion, and Behavior: Handbook of Stress, volume one,* ed. George Fink (New York, NY: Elsevier, 2016): 219.

26. Amanda H. Staff, "Many Teens Can't Tell Real News From Fake, Study Finds," *Christian Science Monitor* (2016).

Fostering Civic Engagement Through the Arts: A Blueprint

13

CONSTANCE DEVEREAUX

Civic engagement is a core principle in efforts to establish the arts as an integral component of daily life, particularly in the context of community. In defense of the value of arts instruction and participation as part of a core curriculum for K–12 students, and the inclusion of the arts in daily community life, is the argument that the arts help to foster citizenship and promote democratic government. A number of challenges exist, however, for teaching of arts-based civic engagement. They include lack of formal training for instructors in political science fundamentals, definitions of civic engagement in the arts that deemphasize political engagement, overreaching claims about the arts and their effects, and lack of teaching materials that connect the arts to political science basics such as workings of government institutions or the processes of public policy. This chapter addresses these challenges by drawing on examples from courses in arts policy and community engagement taught by the author. Student samples, course assignments, and teaching recommendations are included.

Civic engagement is a core principle in efforts by many arts organizations and agencies to establish the arts as an integral component of daily life, particularly in fostering community participation. Most prominent at the national level are the National Endowment for the Arts (NEA) and the Washington, DC–based advocacy organization, Americans for the Arts (AFTA), both of which are strongly invested in establishing positive societal outcomes from arts participation. State and local arts agencies, community arts organizations, and a number of philanthropic foundations are also highly invested.

Arts instruction and participation can foster the kind of "wisdom and vision"[1] required of citizens in a democratic nation, making them an arguably integral part of core curricula for K–12 students and beyond as well as important for daily community life. For this reason, encouragement and support of the arts was deemed "an appropriate matter of concern to the Federal Government" according to the NEA, which was created in 1965 as the federal government's primary arts agency.[2] Similar reasoning informs state arts agencies and local arts commissions, as well as many educational institutions where arts and arts-related subject matter are taught.

At times dismissed as idle pastime, the arts nonetheless play an important role in US economic policy. Output of creative industries is now calculated in the US GDP. The proliferation of arts districts and the calculation of quality of life to reflect inclusion of the arts are noteworthy developments.[3] As the arts continue to intersect with industry, job descriptions for arts managers and artists employed in nonprofit and public sectors often speak to the desirability of community engagement experience. The need for artists and arts managers who understand the connection of the arts to policy and civic issues has grown over the past several decades. Meanwhile, recurring political efforts over the past several decades have attempted to defund or eliminate federal and state arts agencies as either a waste of taxpayer dollars or a threat to mainstream American culture. These developments are indicators that knowledge of political science fundamentals may be useful for those planning arts-related careers.

This chapter addresses civic engagement in the arts, with guidelines for its integration into collegiate-level training of artists (of all disciplines), arts managers, arts policy practitioners, and those in related fields. The conditions for addressing public concerns, and for working effectively with community groups to bring about change, rely a great deal on governmental systems and institutions to support them. Teaching and learning that includes knowledge of these systems and institutions will help students be more effective in the design and implementation of arts-based civic engagement for future careers. Recognizing, too, that the arts are alternately demonized and idealized in American politics and culture, students studying civic engagement and the arts should be equipped with the degree of fluency in governmental processes and understandings of policy environments needed to negotiate a contested terrain.

The chapter also tackles difficulties stemming from loose and superlative claims about "the arts" that may affect teaching aims and consequent civic-engagement efforts. For example, overreaching statements about *the arts* and their influences should be critically surveyed. While a number of studies claim "strong evidence that the arts enhance civil society,"[4] methodological and definitional problems can lead to "ambitious claims" by arts advocates with little empirical backing.[5] As stated by one arts advocacy trainer, "'Any advocacy is good advocacy' is just not true anymore," suggesting that better preparation and familiarity with existing research are needed.[6] Addressing these difficulties as part of teaching about civic engagement and the arts can better prepare students designing and implementing arts engagement projects both at university and in future careers.

Although the history of the arts demonstrates much engagement by artists in civic life, there are few university courses that specifically address civic engagement skills for students seeking arts leadership and arts management careers or for those entering fields of arts production. Many instructors of art and of arts management lack specific training pertaining to arts policy processes, governmental institutions, or strategies linking civic engagement to civic principles. Significantly, the arts as a specific area of public policy study at the university level is relatively new. These realities may present challenges for teaching if the goal is to provide students with the tools to work successfully on engagement projects with both individuals and governmental entities. While it is not possible to fully flesh out all the areas of competence required of arts managers, one commonly misunderstood concept is important for teaching civic engagement, and that is an understanding of the processes of "public policy" and how they differ from the activities of "advocacy." Knowledge of policy cycles and facility in basic workings of government institutions is also needed. A key assumption for this chapter is that government, through its various actions in enacting policies, passing laws, and providing subsidies, fulfills an important role for the arts in citizens' lives. Therefore, knowledge of government systems; the ability to analyze political behavior; an understanding of theories, practices of politics, and policy processes; and other political science knowledge are all important components of courses connecting civic engagement to the arts. Courses should also provide knowledge of the role of the arts in American society both presently and historically.

The chapter finishes with suggestions for developing a course in arts policy and civic engagement drawing from university-level courses taught by the author. Sample assignments are discussed along with suggested activities; added information on course content and assignments is provided in the online resource repository accompanying this book. Illustrative examples of student outcomes are provided in the form of discussion comments drawn from both residential and online graduate courses in arts policy and in arts-based community collaboration taught at Colorado State University between 2015 and 2016.

A limitation to any study on civic engagement and the arts is construct validity. The difficulty of assessing that participation in or exposure to an art form, or the arts in general, leads to a specified behavior is fraught with difficulties, discussed later. It may not be possible to demonstrate just how or why the arts are important to individuals, to communities, and to society at large, but they have held a demonstrable place of value in all times and all places of human history, if not necessarily for each and every individual. Courses in arts-based civic engagement should make students aware of both the limitations and the desirability of including the arts in civic-engagement efforts and encourage critical reflection on the role the arts play in society. The next section looks at some important challenges that a course in the arts and civic engagement must address.

PERSPECTIVES ON CIVIC ENGAGEMENT AND THE ARTS

Civic education as it pertains to the workings of government is disappointingly absent from required curricula at many universities, particularly from programs training artists, arts advocates, and arts administrators.[7] Courses for artists, arts managers, and arts policy practitioners that address these challenges can both deepen the understanding of the role the arts play in civil society as well as foster civic engagement by individuals practicing in these fields, who in turn may bring about greater civic participation in communities where they work.[8] According to online commentary by a student enrolled in a graduate course, Arts Collaboration and Community Engagement,

> We come from an era where "art and culture are dismissible as nice but not necessary," and we are moving into an era where they are "crucibles for all positive development." ... If we can take advantage of this notion, we can help arts and culture become powerful community changers and enhancers. Besides just being "nice," they become a necessity for positive change.[9]

Bridging the gap between nice and necessary to bring about community change asks more of artists and arts managers than their artistic or project management talent alone. Arts-based civic engagement courses should teach skills for working with community members to assist with problem solving; the creative and critical skills needed to connect the arts to community life, especially in ways that foster continued participation; and the knowledge to make positive influences on policy action. Commenting on the value of understanding policy concepts, a student enrolled in a graduate level arts policy course stated, "Knowledge about policy is important to being a good citizen of your community and world. ... It is a responsibility we have as arts leaders. If we are not aware or educated about what is going on, how can we expect others, who are less engaged, to be?"[10] While knowledge of the fundamentals of policy may not be common in university departments of art or arts management, teaching the history of the arts in the United States provides ample opportunities for making these connections, as is discussed next.

Civic engagement through the arts has a long history in the United States, from engravings in colonial times that were often used to disseminate newsworthy events, to later calls for social action through music, theater, photography, narrative, and other artistic forms. The Arts and Crafts Movement "used creative and material practices to question capitalism [and] industrialization"[11] inspiring socialist experiments in the United States. Throughout the nineteenth and twentieth centuries, artists were actively engaged in labor movements and served in prominent roles in antiwar protests, most notably beginning in the 1960s. Determining whether, and just how, the arts lead to citizen civic engagement, however, depends a great deal on how we understand key terms such as "the arts" and "civic engagement." For example, as one study notes, it is quickly "apparent that when you've read one definition of civic engagement, you've read one definition of civic engagement."[12] Other authors lament the conceptual "stretching" of the term that covers such a wide variety of actions and activities that it muddies the waters of comprehension.[13]

Peter Levine suggests that civic engagement's current popularity has to do with its "generally benign connotations."[14] Thus, it is often seen as a means for "lubricating social life"[15] or the right to "define the public good"[16] rather than a means for questioning or confronting political and social norms to bring about change. The question of self-preservation, therefore, may be an additional complicating factor for defining civic engagement through the arts. Citing the Culture Wars, a period of deep ideological clashes in the United States, as its cause, humanities scholar Mary Rizzo points to a forced "retrenchment in the public humanities away from obviously political topics for fear of retribution, in the form of funding cuts," by legislators of state humanities councils and the National Endowment for the Humanities (NEH).[17] Similar fears have been felt in the arts world with threats to defund the NEA and to eliminate state arts councils. This helps explain why organizations such as the NEA and AFTA may wish to deemphasize the political in their views on civic engagement and the arts.

A case in point is AFTA, which borrows its definition of civic education from the American Psychological Association, describing it as "individual and collective actions designed to identify and address issues of public concern."[18] Citing the work of political scientist Cliff Zukin et al., AFTA's report also notes a "common distinction in the behavioral literature ... between political and civic engagement." The first is "activity aimed at influencing government policy or affecting the selection of public officials," and the latter is "participation aimed at achieving a public good ... through direct hands-on work in cooperation with others, typically in nongovernmental settings."[19] Although poorly documented in scholarly literature, AFTA's influence in arts management and related disciplines means that the definitions they promulgate are likely to influence the way civic engagement is understood, and conducted, in the field.

For the purposes of teaching, definitions that insist on decoupling arts-based civic engagement from government processes and political engagement may be disingenuous given an extensive history in the United States of the arts used for social and political change. It may also mislead students about the important role governments play in arts support through subsidies, policies, and positive laws. Knowledge of political and social action through the arts as well as familiarity with governmental rules, regulations, and norms relating to art production, exhibition, and dissemination are important foundations for arts-based civic engagement efforts by students in both university and in later careers. It is also worthwhile to address how discourses are framed as the result of accepted definitions. In the experience of this author, confusion around terminology is not a trivial concern. As observed by a student enrolled in Arts Collaboration and Community Engagement, "Engaging in the community is tossed around a lot as a buzzword, but I feel that not a lot of people or organizations really understand how to do so, thus training arts professionals in these methods is extremely important."[20] Working effectively with artists, arts managers, arts advocates, and community members whose knowledge, training, and perspectives differ from one's own requires the critical ability to reflect on how discourses, and resulting actions, may be framed around particular understandings of key terms—as are addressed in this chapter. The next section looks more closely at two university-level courses that provide students with some of the skills described.

ARTS POLICY AND CIVIC ENGAGEMENT

Graduate courses designed by this author called "Arts Policy and Advocacy" and "Arts Collaboration and Community Engagement" train students for careers as arts entrepreneurs and arts managers, which often require skills for designing and implementing arts-based civic engagement projects. The courses are taught on a yearly rotation, with students taking the first course as preparation for the second. Students in these courses typically have little or no formal learning experience in the subjects and come with a wide variety of undergraduate training in various art forms such as studio art, dance, and music performance but also related areas such as music therapy, art and music education, culinary arts, history, journalism, creative writing, and other liberal arts subjects. While the courses were not designed or offered for purposes of research into student learning in arts-based civic education, the material examined here can be used to inform curricular design for future courses.

Content of Arts Policy and Advocacy includes the history of arts policy in the United States. The class also covers comparisons of US arts policy to other countries; the operations of policy cycles; the effects of ideologies on arts and culture policy processes; the use of creative expression in civic dialogue and for advocacy purposes; multiculturalism and cultural awareness as they relate to the arts in civil society; persuasive communication strategies for policy and advocacy; and skills for policy research and analysis. The stated objectives for the course include formulating statements about the value of the arts and their role in human society; critical analysis of arts policy positions including ethical issues that may arise; formulating policy briefs for persuasive effect; creating plans for advocacy; developing skills for arts policy research; and applying arts policy knowledge to community action. For purposes of stimulating discussions from a wide range of perspectives, suggested course size is 15–20 students.

The overarching aim of the second course, Arts Collaboration and Community Engagement, is for students to design and implement an arts-based project connected to a community problem defined in collaboration with community members. For purposes of the project, students also define the selected community. Among the types of communities identified by students in this course have been residents in a homeless shelter, survivors of domestic violence, and nonresident university students.

Course material provides students with an array of past and present examples of civic engagement including the following:
- the history of artists' involvement in the US Works Progress Administration,
- creation of public art by artists through the Comprehensive Employment and Training Act (CETA),
- the influences of Paolo Freire and other theorist-activists on Theater of the Oppressed in South America,
- theater interventions for AIDS education, labor actions, and other social/political issues in Africa,
- digital public engagement initiatives, and
- music performances that raise awareness about social and political issues.

In addition to this list, the class also explored many non-arts examples to show the wider range covered by "civic engagement" as a foundation for the role that the arts, artists, and arts managers might play. The term "community engagement" in the course title was not selected by the author but is intended to cover both political and nonpolitical engagements between artists and communities.[21] Because primary research is required as part of the problem-definition phase of designing civic engagement projects, students in this course are required to undergo institutional review board training to learn about their responsibilities in research involving human subjects.

As a result of taking the course, students should be able to do the following:
- make connections between historic movements and the conditions and strategies for current civic engagement efforts,
- use a collaborative process for identifying community problems,
- engage with policy makers in processes required to bring about a successful project,
- anticipate and resolve ethical issues,
- conduct research needed for community engagement, and
- use key terms appropriately in describing and discussing community engagement strategies and issues.[22]

By way of illustrating how students in the two courses accomplish some of these objectives, excerpts from course discussions are provided in this chapter. Students in both residential and online versions of the course participated in asynchronous discussions using *Canvas*, an online learning management system. Online discussion assignments ask students to do directed research on relevant topics and respond to discussion prompts in which they reflect on their own research findings and the comments of other students. To address one set of the challenges identified earlier, namely confusion around terminology, students in both Arts Policy and Advocacy and Arts Collaboration and Community Engagement are asked to consider a variety of definitions they discover on their own through online research and to discuss them in the context of readings and other course material. For example, students in Arts Policy and Advocacy consider usage of the terms "arts policy" and "arts advocacy," which are sometimes conflated in the arts management field, despite seemingly obvious definitional and grammatical differences. Of particular note in completing this assignment is students' reported difficulty in finding adequate information—an ongoing challenge for teaching arts policy and advocacy at the university level. Although scholarly literature exists, there are no textbooks, as such, that teach important fundamentals comparable to textbooks on health policy, educational policy, and the like. Arts policy is also typically absent from introductory-level college textbooks designed for public policy courses. The burden, therefore, is on the instructor—and often the student—to make connections between the arts and more generalized public policy fundamentals.

Commenting on the challenge, one student stated, "I found it difficult to find concrete examples of what arts advocacy and arts policy meant. I was forced to just define policy and advocacy and then put an arts lens on it."[23] Similarly, another student reported, "During this [assignment] I found that it's hard to find specific policy and advocacy definitions related to the arts. So you have to be able to look [at definitions] from an arts policy lens to apply it effectively to the subject you are working on."[24] Responding to peers' posts, a student also commented, "I found it to be very challenging to find decent definitions of arts policy and arts advocacy as well. I agree that we have to look at general definitions for policy and advocacy, and then think of ways that that applies to arts."[25]

Despite the difficulties encountered, lack of readily available instructional materials can provide an opportunity for teaching and learning. Students are actively engaged in constructing their own knowledge and may be more inclined toward critical reflection in their approaches to arts policy and, likewise, to arts-based civic engagement where students encounter similar issues around terminology.

Arts-based civic engagement, for example, has been discussed in terms of building social capital, creating new audiences for arts organizations, and stimulating healthy social activities among participants.[26] Increased political participation is notably described as an outcome. Consider a 2007 report issued by the NEA, *The Arts and Civic Engagement*, which claims that "arts participation builds civic engagement."[27] The report finds, "Americans who experience art or read literature are demonstrably more active in their communities than nonreaders and nonparticipants." The outcomes identified in the report are volunteerism, playing sports, exercising, and engaging in other arts activities (e.g., photography). Whether or not relational activities, such as those described, can be framed in the context of civic engagement may be worthy of discussion in courses connecting civic engagement to the arts. At least one commentator has noted, "Art based in relational encounters can have a superficial effect … of lulling viewers and participants in the notion that they have become politically active, or performed as active members of society."[28] If the aim of civic engagement is to affect individuals' levels of political participation for social and political change, it is clear that not all arts-based civic engagement can be counted as equal.

Students' lack of knowledge about important arts policy events, key individuals, and institutions is also an ongoing teaching challenge. In another assignment, called "Policy Quest," students are given a set of questions to research on important events, organizations, and individuals relating to arts policy. Reflecting on the assignment, one student stated, "The most useful thing I learned was that it helps to read everything. Otherwise you'll find yourself jumping to conclusions that aren't necessarily right. Also, fact checking what you found against other resources helps to ensure the correct answer."[29] Another student "enjoyed being able to search around for credible information to take from and create some basis of knowledge for myself."[30]

An important finding from student responses is that students enrolled in these courses know very little about the history of arts policy in the United States or about relevant government agencies and their functions. In the case of Arts Policy and Advocacy this is significant given that it is a graduate level course for students who hold undergraduate degrees in music, dance, theater performance, studio art, art history, or other arts-related disciplines. This suggests that teaching and learning in this area is rare—or nonexistent—as part of undergraduate study. Pertaining to gaps in knowledge, the comments of the following student are typical:

> The most useful thing I learned was … [about] the National Endowment for the Arts. Previously, I didn't know what it was or how it functioned. It's so crucial for arts policy and the success of the arts in our country. By completing this assignment and jumping into research I was able to quickly digest large topics/events in our nation's history.[31]

Another student similarly reports:

> The most interesting thing I learned as a result of this assignment is the history of the NEA and degree of criticism that it faced throughout the 80's and 90's. … Having knowledge of the NEA's history from its foundation to the many controversies it has faced gives me a better understanding of arts policy in the United States. I feel like I am better equipped to situate current events and issues in an arts policy context now that I know more about the history of the NEA.[32]

Beyond these challenges, courses in arts policy and arts-based civic engagement should wrestle with the difficulties of defining "the arts" for practical purposes, such as just what is included in any discussion about the arts and their impact on civic behavior. "The broader point to be made," according to one study, "is simply that it is crucial to define precisely what are 'the arts'… because different arts activities are likely to lead to a different set of outcomes."[33] As a beginning point, students in the previously described courses consider an enumerative definition provided by the National Endowment for the Arts, which states that "the arts" includes,

> but is not limited to, music (instrumental and vocal), dance, drama, folk art, creative writing, architecture and allied fields, painting, sculpture, photography, graphic and craft arts, industrial design, costume and fashion design, motion pictures, television, radio, tape and sound recording, and the arts related to the presentation, performance, execution, and exhibition of such major art.[34]

Intentionally broad and inclusive, the NEA's definition nonetheless poses practical problems for claims about effects of "the arts" on human behavior. According to AFTA, "Arts and culture promote understanding and action on issues facing our communities and the world."[35] The organization believes, "The arts can and do play a unique role in fostering citizen engagement—by bringing forth new ways to view an increasingly complex world, and providing the creative space in which difficult issues can be addressed and solutions can take form."[36] A report, "Civic Engagement and the Arts: Issues of Conceptualization and Measurement," likewise provides a broad definition of both arts and culture: they "encompasses all the artistic disciplines and the humanities, including the range of folk and cultural expressions … community-based, experimental, and mainstream arts as well as popular culture."[37] The authors find that civic engagement experience may occur in both the process of creating, participating in, or presenting. They claim that the arts "may provide a direct forum to engage in community planning, organizing, and activism."[38] Similarly, the Arts

Policy Roundtable believes, "The Arts provide solutions to many of our most pressing social problems...."[39]

The prior claims rely, in part, on the idea that everything included, no matter how seemingly different, has properties in common and that "the arts" all result in the described outcome. In other words, composing a poem, producing a sound recording, dancing a tango, and fashioning a costume will all lead to increased civic engagement.

While students in the courses described here reflect some of the same tendencies in response to discussion prompts about the purposes and values of the arts, they also consider the merits of more precise definitions. A student in Arts Collaboration and Community Engagement for example, stated, "When people come together for the arts, something powerful is bound to happen. It's such an accessible way for people to communicate ideas, beliefs, and needs within their community."[40] Another student, responding to the first, stated, "The arts seem to manage to get to places and people that other disciplines can't."[41] As a result of this assignment, students not only contemplated on the positive impact they might have in a community but also reflected on the conditions of the field they will enter where knowledge about civic engagement and policy processes may be lacking. A student in Arts Collaboration and Community Engagement, for example, stated, "Communities continue to require help with the various and diverse needs they may have. As arts leaders we are able to seek out these needs and find creative ways to meet them and to solve issues in the community."[42] However, another student commented, "Something that I found troubling, was that so many organizations don't seem to have a grasp of what the real needs of the community really are, and how high the risk of negative impact is."[43]

Importantly, students in both of the described courses were asked to reflect on when, and to what effect delineated categorizations of "the arts" might have value, such as in the case of making decisions in an arts organization or in thinking about policy making. Recognizing some inherent difficulties, a student in Arts Policy and Advocacy stated,

> ...having a definition for art is useful. It would literally be impossible to advocate if there weren't words to describe our cause. I think it may be easier to describe art rather than define it. By describing art we can communicate its importance without restricting it and confining it within walls of limitations. So maybe, after all, we do not need to *define* art, we should begin to *describe* art for policy purposes.[44]

Wrestling with the same issue, another student commented,

> By having a clear definition of art, an organization will better understand its mission. ... Additionally, being able to present a clear definition of art to policy makers could lead to more efficient policy-making. ... However, even if an organization has a well-defined practical definition ... there remains room for disagreement. ... I would argue there is value that comes from the diversity of opinions ... because it allows us to discover new perspectives from which our own views can evolve.[45]

Student responses suggest the importance of considering how terms are used to frame issues and anticipated outcomes as well as the ways that words can either clarify or muddy discourse and the value of questioning accepted claims in a field of study. In sum, increased awareness about the challenges stemming from vague, poorly defined, and contested understandings of key terms relating to arts-based civic engagement will benefit students in not only encouraging active, critical reflection about civic engagement work but also the future roles students may play as artists and arts managers working in communities. In online discussions, students in the courses described are encouraged to develop cogent arguments for advocacy and for more realistic perspectives on the potential benefits of the arts in the civic domain. Discussion assignments stimulate active research by requiring students to find multiple definitions of key terms and to articulate the merits of particular definitions to other students. By combining these discussions of definitions with some of the core, fundamental information addressed in the next section, students will increase their basic knowledge about arts policy issues and about civic engagement combined with the arts. Significantly, however, one student in Arts Policy and Advocacy stated, "I feel like we are definitely just scraping the surface...."[46]

CORE KNOWLEDGE

A basic component of the course Arts Policy and Advocacy is to provide students with fundamental understanding of how policy works in the cycle of phases from problem definition and agenda setting to policy formulation, legitimation, implementation, and evaluation. Course material provides opportunities for students to learn about how individuals in the arts sector can participate in each of these stages, especially as they connect to community engagement. Agenda setting, for example, is an obvious choice where artists and arts managers working with community members can use arts-based projects to raise awareness about social and civic problems. In Arts Collaboration and Community Engagement, students use this knowledge to conceptualize and implement a project. For example, one student discovered that few of her peers knew about the incidence of human trafficking in the United States. She used a poster project to encourage college students to contact legislators about stricter laws. Another student used play-acting techniques to help primary grade students talk to parents, teachers, and administrators about the effects of bullying.

Students in Arts Policy and Advocacy also used knowledge of policy cycles to analyze arts policy actions. One student, for example, examined arts education in her city through the lens of implementation problems with No Child Left Behind. Another student investigated the agenda-setting process leading to creation of local arts districts in her state to understand how advocates could have better prepared community members to advocate for legislative action. Students are encouraged to go beyond the Internet or published research sources to contact policy actors in their communities. The student researching arts districts had an extensive e-mail exchange with the director of her state arts council and was invited to town-hall–style meetings where important issues were discussed. A side benefit of such interaction is networking that can benefit students in job-seeking and in future civic-engagement efforts.

For understanding policy, however, students need awareness of key distinctions in order to be effective participants in arts-based civic engagement, as discussed earlier. These concepts cannot operate in a vacuum. The history of arts-based civic engagement in the United States should be covered and include specific historical projects, programs, and eras of intersection such as The Chautauqua Movement in the nineteenth century, the Culture Wars era, and others, as noted earlier. Current programs and initiatives such as Americans for the Arts' *Animating Democracy* also provide a foundation for students. A more comprehensive course might include use of the arts in US diplomacy in the nineteenth century, in the Cold War era, and post–9/11 strategies using the arts to improve the image of the United States abroad.

But policy also cannot operate independently of ethical considerations. Students must learn about existing ethical standards and which laws and regulations govern the activities in which artists and arts managers might engage. Students in Arts Policy and Advocacy also learn about concepts of justice and fairness as they relate to arts policy issues, and they receive exposure to theories of government that may underlie policy decisions. Exposure to ethical theories helps students contextualize their views and provide the means for articulating their positions on arts policies and civic engagement. Commenting on the problem of unintended outcomes, one student commented,

> In the case of arts policy, it is impossible to conceive, and account for, every single kind of possible outcome associated with an art program. ... Thus, any arts policy will be based at

least partly on inductive reasoning, with some uncertainty associated with its implementation; any policy, therefore, will have some inherent risk that it will not actually *do* what it is intended to do. The goal of the arts manager is to minimize the risk [through careful research].

As a result of exposure to ethical theories and the potential for ethical missteps in the design and implementation of arts-related community projects, students learn that not just any or all arts activities will lead to benefit. Matching arts activities to civic engagement aims—taking care to identify potential risks along with anticipated benefits—is an important component of ensuring ethical considerations are addressed.

SUGGESTED COURSE CONTENT

While recognizing an important result of community engagement is community betterment, the outcome envisioned for student learning is engagement that introduces, develops, or reinforces participation of community members as citizens in the process of community or self-advancement. Courses should encourage participation in activities for identifying, solving, and resolving issues through both informal and formal governmental processes. Achieving these outcomes may include engagement in problem identification, public agenda setting, exploring alternate policy solutions, policy formulation, meeting and negotiating with policy actors or policy makers, publicly oriented critique of existing policy positions, and policy analysis.

Research activities in Arts Policy and Advocacy achieve multiple aims. Students become informed about past arts policy actions and their outcomes but also gain knowledge that can be applied to persuasive advocacy. Students in this course are asked to prepare an arts advocacy brief, addressed to a policy maker, on a particular arts policy issue. Using the same issue, students imagine they are presenting the issue along with policy recommendations in a community town hall meeting. Core competencies for students in arts-based civic engagement courses, therefore, should also include the following:

- Knowledge of historical events and movements for critical evaluation and to inform current arts-based civic engagement strategies. Experience teaching students in Arts Policy and Advocacy at the graduate level revealed a lack of knowledge in this area, including the many ways that the arts have been used, historically, to accomplish societal goals and the ways that the arts have contributed to society-wide controversies that have an impact on arts-based civic engagement.
- Identifying civic engagement opportunities where the arts can play an important role as well as demonstrating the ability to identify ethical issues that might arise in civic engagement efforts.
- The skills and know-how to raise awareness in a community and among policy makers about community problems and potential solutions. The ability to articulate policy positions through persuasive writing and speech requires knowledge of policy processes and familiarity with arts policy issues. Students in Arts Collaboration and Community Engagement perform research to identify community problems and the possibilities for success among a range of arts-based solutions. Students in Arts Policy and Advocacy learn about ways to influence policy decisions using research findings, and they gain practice articulating policy positions in advocacy briefs and mock town hall meetings.

In sum, arts-based civic engagement teaching will benefit from robust instruction that provides knowledge and skills in the areas described earlier. While art creation, exhibition, and participation can be a useful means for fostering civic engagement, designing and implementing effective and ethically based civic engagement projects requires more than a knowledge of art.

CONCLUSION

This chapter introduces some of the inherent challenges for arts-based civic engagement training for students at the university level, with suggestions for overcoming the challenges. Some of the most significant challenges stem from diverse usages of key terminology, vague articulations, and contested concepts. The term "civic engagement" has been applied to a wide variety of behaviors and activities that may bear little resemblance to each other. In the case of arts-based civic engagement, intentional decoupling of activities from political engagement and political science foundations may leave students unprepared to make connections between the arts and governmental institutions that facilitate and support their presence in the community. Other challenges include lack of formal training for instructors in areas such as public policy; lack of knowledge about the operations of policy cycles and advocacy; and the absence of researched and published teaching materials addressing arts policy issues. Exaggerated, and unsubstantiated, claims about the effects of the arts in fostering civic engagement behaviors likewise affects efforts to provide effective training. Nonetheless, recognizing that the arts play an important role in society, there is great potential for the arts as a basis for civic engagement education. The challenges discussed in this chapter can be met and can provide opportunities for active student learning through discussion, critical reflection, and deeper inquiry into the challenges posed. ∎

ENDNOTES

1. National Foundation on the Arts and Humanities Act of 1965 (P.L. 89-209).
2. Ibid.
3. See, for example, Stephen Clift and Paul M. Camic, *Oxford Textbook of Creative Arts, Health, and Wellbeing: International Perspectives on Practice, Policy, and Research* (Oxford: Oxford University Press, 2016).
4. Kelly Leroux and Anna Bernadska, "Impact of the Arts on Individual Contributions to US Civil Society," *Journal of Civil Society* (2014): 144–64.
5. Joshua Guetzkow, "How the Arts Impact Communities: An Introduction to the Literature on Arts Impact Studies," presented at *Taking the Measure of Culture Conference*, 2002. Princeton University.
6. Susan Riley, *A Vocal Advocate: An Arts Advocacy Workbook* (CreateSpace Independent Publishing Platform, 2012).
7. The terms "arts manager" and "arts administrator" are generally seen as meaning the same thing. Use of one or the other is largely a matter of preference. Alternate terms also include "cultural manager" and "cultural administrator."
8. Leroux and Bernadska, "Impact of the Arts."
9. In-course commentary: Student 1, spring 2016, Arts Collaboration and Community Engagement, Colorado State University. For the purposes of this chapter, names and other identifying features of students are not included. The student's quote is a reference to Arlene Goldbard, "Arguments for Cultural Democracy and Community Cultural Development." Grantmakers in the Arts, 2009, http://www.giarts.org/article/arguments-cultural-democracy-and-community-cultural-development.
10. In-course commentary: Student 2, fall 2015, Arts Policy and Advocacy, Colorado State University.
11. Ryan Shin, *Convergence of Contemporary Art, Visual Culture, and Global Civic Engagement* (Hershey, PA: Information Science Reference, 2017), 188.
12. Mary Rizzo, "Finding the Roots of Civic Engagement in the Public Humanities," National Council on Public History, 2014, http://ncph.org/history-at-work/finding-the-roots-of-civic-engagement/.
13. Joakim Ekman and Erik Amna, "Political Participation and Civic Engagement: towards a New Typology," *Human Affairs* (2012): 283–300; Ben Berger, "Political Theory, Political Science, and the End of Civic Engagement," *Perspectives on Politics* (2009): 335–50; Giovanni Sartori, "Concept Misformation in Comparative Politics," *American Political Science Review* (1970): 1,033–53.
14. Peter Levine, *The Future of Democracy: Developing the Next Generation of American Citizens* (Hanover, NH: Tufts University Press, 2007), 1.
15. Robert Putnam, "The Prosperous Community: Social Capital and Public Life," *The American Prospect* (1993): 35–42.
16. David Korten, *Globalizing Civil Society: Reclaiming our Right to Power* (New York: Seven Stories Press, 1998), 30.
17. Rizzo, "Finding the Roots."
18. The report cites Carpini, American Psychological Association, 2008. A search of www.apa.org includes the definition attributed to Micahel Delli Carpini as Public Policy Director of Pew Charitable Trusts. Capelli n.d.
19. Cliff Zukin, Scott Keeter, Molly Andolina, Krista Jenkins, and Michael Delli Carpini, *A New Engagement? Political Participation, Civic Life, and the Changing American Citizen* (New York: Oxford University Press, 2006).
20. In course commentary: Student 4, fall 2016 Arts Collaboration and Community Engagement, Colorado State University.

21. Alison McCartney provides an excellent discussion of the parameters and definitions of civic and political engagement, as well as related terms in Alison Rios Millet McCartney, "Teaching Civic Engagement: Debates, Definitions, Benefits, and Challenges" in *Teaching Civic Engagement: From Student to Active Citizen*, eds. McCartney, Bennon, and Simpson (Washington, DC: American Political Science Association, 2013).

22. A more complete list of objectives for both courses is provided in the online companion to this book.

23. In-course commentary: Student 6, fall 2016, Arts Policy and Advocacy, Colorado State University.

24. Ibid. Student 7.

25. Ibid. Student 8.

26. "The Arts and Civic Engagement," https://www.arts.gov/sites/default/files/CivicEngagement.pdf, accessed April 17, 2017.

27. Ibid.

28. Shin, *Convergence of Contemporary Art*, 189.

29. In-course commentary: Student 7, fall 2016, Arts Policy and Advocacy, Colorado State University.

30. Ibid. Student 9.

31. Ibid. Student 10.

32. Ibid. Student 8.

33. Guetzkow, "How the Arts Impact Communities," 13.

34. National Foundation on the Arts and Humanities Act of 1965.

35. Americans for the Arts. "Social Change."

36. Ibid. "The Arts and Civic Engagement: Strengthening the 21st Century Community."

37. Mark J. Stern and Susan C. Seifert, "Civic Engagement and the Arts: Issues of Conceptualization and Measurement," 2009, http://animatingdemocracy.org/sites/default/files/CE_Arts_SternSeifert.pdf, accessed January 18, 2017.

38. Ibid.

39. Americans for the Arts, "Arts Policy Roundtable."

40. In-course commentary: Student 12, spring 2016, Arts Collaboration and Community Engagement, Colorado State University.

41. Ibid. Student 13.

42. Ibid.

43. In course commentary: Student 5, spring 2016, Arts Collaboration and Community Engagement, Colorado State University.

44. Ibid. Student 14.

45. In-course commentary: Student 16, fall 2016, Arts Policy and Advocacy, Colorado State University.

46. Ibid. Student 9.

Service-Learning in an Environmental Engineering Classroom: Examples, Evaluation, and Recommendations

14

Tara Kulkarni and Kimberly Coleman

Engineering classrooms have started answering the calls of students, professional associations, researchers, and legislators to create active learning spaces. Students are being offered opportunities to engage and learn by stepping outside of textbooks and labs. Group projects, project-based learning, internships, learning communities, active and cooperative learning as well as service-learning are being introduced as pedagogical tools in many educational institutions. Many models exist for implementing such tools; however, most of these examples take place at large and/or well-funded institutions. This chapter examines one framework for implementing service-learning in an environmental engineering classroom at a small collegiate institution. The primary objectives of using the service-learning pedagogy were to deepen learning about classroom concepts and have students apply these concepts in design and/or research and presentations to address a community need. The examples provided here focus specifically on bringing the engineering lessons into K–12 classrooms. The chapter outlines the structure of the course, describes the service-learning projects, presents outputs, and describes our assessment methods. Results of our assessment show that although service-learning proved challenging for students, it also provided an opportunity for them to work on important skills, namely communication and leadership. Finally, we make recommendations based on lessons learned for educators in all disciplines seeking to advance civic engagement learning goals through service-learning pedagogy.

From the first known Signon and Ramsey[1] definition of service-learning as a value-added component of student learning, efforts through entities such as the Campus Compact have greatly succeeded in making service-learning an acceptable pedagogical tool in classrooms across multiple disciplines.[2] In engineering education, service-learning is often analogous to community engagement and experiential learning. The premise is that student learning is complementary to the service students provide to a community partner. It is an opportunity to apply skills and knowledge developed in a classroom to a real-world problem as a true practice of engineering, amplifying their learning and providing service to a community. It is also an opportunity to develop "soft skills" such as communication and leadership that are not part of the traditional engineering curriculum. Bringing together the traditional knowledge and skills of both traditional engineering education and civic engagement education is an important step in creating effective, civically engaged engineers who are capable and experienced in working with their communities in identifying, communicating about, and solving problems.

Engineering is an active discipline. There are plenty of opportunities for active learning in an engineering classroom, with varying levels of efficacy.[3] The service-learning opportunities offered in engineering classrooms range from those provided to first-year undergraduate students in engineering (e.g., Northeastern University[4]), to designing senior-year capstone design projects to be service-learning based, (e.g., South Dakota State University[5]), to entire program curricula based on service-learning principles (e.g., University of Vermont[6]) to a multidisciplinary approach to use engineering principles and solve problems in the community (e.g., the EPICS program founded by Purdue University[7]). Thus, there are a number of studies that provide quantitative research on the beneficial impacts of such service-learning integrations within engineering courses.

However, these examples are from bigger, well-funded schools and programs. The first author has previously documented her experience as a new, small-town, primarily teaching school faculty member—with few local contacts—in establishing a service-learning curriculum in an environmental engineering classroom elsewhere.[8] This chapter builds on that work by providing an example of how engineering faculty at small colleges and universities might structure a successful civic engagement, service-learning course.

We examine one undergraduate senior/junior-year course in environmental engineering at Norwich University in Vermont as a model to integrate service-learning in an engineering classroom. Because the courses included multiple service-learning group projects, it provides several examples of opportunities for such integration. Specifically, the examples highlighted here are ones in which students had to bring their lessons into local K–12 classrooms. Through qualitative analysis of students' reflections, we explore the extent to which students in this engineering class perceived their own personal growth. We also examine students' grades as an indicator of learning outcomes. By comparing service-learning lab grades to traditional lab grades, as well as lab grades to course grades, we investigate any differences in performance between the service-learning and traditional components of the course. Our results indicate that service-learning is a rigorous challenge for engineering students because it exposes them to issues related to working in groups and interacting with communities. We demonstrate that these challenges provide an opportunity for engineering students to develop important professional skills, like leadership and communication.

However, teaching civic engagement through service-learning pedagogy is not always successful. Mismatched teams, partners, and activity types may result in student dissatisfaction and minimize learning. Similarly, projects that are not well-matched to students' knowledge, development stage, and skill level may result in frustration and disengagement.[9] For each project described in this chapter, we include a brief note by the faculty member, providing some details on the final deliverables or outcomes of the projects. We also include an overall reflection by the faculty member on the logistics of planning, scheduling, and coordinating multiple service-learning projects. We conclude this chapter by comparing our findings with existing literature on service-learning and student development to make recommendations for future courses in engineering and other disciplines.

METHODS

We relied on three data sources to assess students' learning as a result of the service-learning course components: faculty self-reflection, quantitative analysis of student grades, and qualitative analysis of students' written reflection assignments. The use of faculty observation, examination of grades, and analysis of written assignments is suitable data for assessing service-learning and civic engagement.[10] The first author of this chapter was also the course instructor and was responsible for one of three lab sections. She was assisted by an adjunct instructor, who covered the remaining two lab sessions. Because reflections on course process and outcomes provide valuable information,[11] we have included the faculty member's perspective on success of the individual service-learning projects within the course descriptions.

We examined students' grades as indicators of learning outcomes. The service-learning component of the course was carried out as part of labs, which ran concurrent with lectures. However, not all of the labs involved service-learning activities. The course was intentionally designed to provide time during labs to work on the service-learning projects, while also maintaining lab time to work on traditional engineering lab topics. In other words, some of the labs were set aside to work on service-learning projects, and some were set aside for more traditional engineering labs. A lab syllabus is provided (see resources on the companion website) for reference and shows that the first series of lab activities laid the foundation for helping students develop and deliver their service-learning project based lab work. All 30 students self-selected the lab sessions they enrolled in based on scheduling availability. For the service-learning lab component, students with the highest grades at midterms were designated team leaders (resulting in nine student leaders for the nine projects). The student leaders could then form their teams (hereafter referred to as the "Norwich team members") with peers in their lab section. Grades for the service-learning labs were distinct from the grades in the traditional labs, and grades for the lecture component were distinct from lab grades (see table 14.1). This division allowed us to run Paired Sample T-Tests in SPSS to compare service-learning lab grades ($n = 30$) to traditional lab grades ($n = 30$). We additionally ran Paired Sample T-Tests to compare overall lab grades (combined service-learning labs and traditional labs) ($n = 30$) with lecture grades ($n = 30$).

Table 14.1 Percent of Final Grades for Distinct Components of an Environmental Engineering Course

COURSE COMPONENT		PERCENT OF FINAL GRADE
Lecture		75%
Lab	SL Labs	15%
	Traditional Labs	10%
Total		100%

In addition, the instructors (the first author and the adjunct instructor) conducted three reflection activities from weeks two to four of the service-learning project period. The prompts included

1. How did you relate to your community partners?
2. How has this experience impacted your individual growth?
3. How does this experience relate back to the course content?

We qualitatively coded the reflections ($n = 90$) in NVivo 11 software (QSR International, Doncaster, Victoria, Australia). The decision to conduct qualitative analysis of the reflection assignments was made retroactively (i.e., the reflection assignment was not designed as part of a research study). Nevertheless, qualitative analysis of the reflection assignments was an appropriate method for evaluating outcomes because reflection provides a rich data source for evaluating course outcomes[12] and because qualitative research is well suited for studying people and social processes such as learning.[13] The coding process involved an iterative approach to data analysis in which we looked for recurrent themes and sought to identify patterns and linkages among them.[14] Because the reflections were assigned at the beginning ($n = 30$), partway through the course ($n = 30$), and at the end of the service-learning experience ($n = 30$) we were able to observe any evolution in students' thoughts and ideas. Our findings are limited due to the small sample size, but we demonstrate important lessons as we seek to advance development of skills for civic engagement for all students in all disciplines.

NORWICH UNIVERSITY

Norwich University, located in Northfield, Vermont, is America's first private military college, established in 1819. It has a current enrollment of approximately 2,800 undergraduate students and an online College of Graduate and Continuing Studies, with an enrollment of approximately 1,200. It was the first private military institution to offer an engineering degree. Its founder, Alden Partridge, was an ardent believer of the place of experiential learning in education and built Norwich on that foundation, training students to be citizen-soldiers. The university is also recognized for several other firsts, such as being the birthplace of the nation's Reserve Officers' Training Corps (ROTC) program and one of the first institutions to accept women and international students. In addition to a promise to offer an education that is "American in character" and "global in perspective," Norwich University is committed to a small class size, as demonstrated by the small course discussed in this chapter.

COURSE BACKGROUND

In fall 2014, 30 junior- and senior-year civil and environmental engineering students, enrolled in the course "CE 421 Environmental Engineering," and participated in nine different service-learning projects, working with 10 different community partners. CE 421 Environmental Engineering is a four-credit, required course for all students enrolled in the civil and environmental engineering degree program. The class met three times a week for 50 minutes each session as well as for a weekly three-hour lab session (CE 421 L1 through L3). The stated overarching course goal was for students to be able

> to define and explain important terms, laws, and principles, related to various environmental media and their relevance in engineering; analyze reactor kinetics and risk assessment problems as a basis for designing treatment technologies for air, water, and land pollution; and determine the environmental impacts of noise pollution.

The stated overarching lab goals were for students to be able to

> perform basic physical and chemical water analyses in the laboratory and in the field, describe the composition of municipal solid waste, use open source environmental models developed by the United States Environmental Protection Agency (USEPA), develop a basic understanding of Geographical Information Systems (GIS) and apply it to prepare basic environmental contamination maps, and research and respond through design and analyses to the needs of a community partner by engaging in a service-learning project.

Because engineers often design technologies for clients and community members from varying backgrounds, the course learning goals also included helping students develop an ability to use questioning to determine the extent of the client's problems, research and help explain potential solutions to clients, recommend the best option for further implementation, and design and implement the final solution. It was also expected that written and oral communication cater to the audience and be modified when addressing a lay audience (e.g., K–12 student groups), as compared to a technical one (e.g., the director of the Vermont Energy Efficiency Program, or "VEEP," who was a community partner on a project not elaborated on in this chapter).

The service-learning projects were part of a four-week lab experience that included activities such as introducing themselves to their community partners, negotiating a scope of work, developing interim deadlines for specific deliverables, and then researching, designing, and developing content to fulfill the needs of their community partners.

The projects ranged from teaching third graders the different components of landfills as a way to increase their understanding of solid waste management, to engineering designs to improve parking lot erosion issues to protect nearby rivers and streams, to energy education and rainwater harvesting. Thus, individual project goals varied somewhat in that some teams were responsible for improving the K–12 student group understanding of an environmental engineering issue (e.g., landfill design for solid waste management), while others helped the K–12 student group perform data sampling and analysis (e.g., water quality testing), and others performed traditional engineering tasks such as surveying and designing infrastructures (rainwater harvesting) including calculations involved in sizing and placement of such units. In each project, the Norwich team members were expected to use the skills from the CE 421 class or lab curriculum to accomplish the goals of their individual projects. They also tried (even though this was not a written expectation) engaging their K–12 student groups through the use of games and model-building type activities. Several of these projects involved elementary through high school students in multiple schools in Vermont. Students used lab time for traveling to their project sites and working on their projects, using additional hours outside lab times as needed. The section that follows documents five of these projects as examples. Two projects focused on waste, and three focused on water. Each description details the roles played by the various participants as well as some of the people and communities with whom the students interacted.

PROJECT DESCRIPTIONS

PROJECT 1: WATER, PLAYGROUND, AND FIFTH GRADERS AT AN ELEMENTARY SCHOOL

Student Participants: Three undergraduate students

K–12 Impact: 21 fifth-grade students

Community Partners: A fifth-grade teacher and an employee of a local nonprofit organization associated with the river network

Project Abstract: The Norwich team members had two main goals in this project:

1. Develop a master plan for a future playground redevelopment scheme (specifically to address issues related to stormwater at the site).
2. Engage a fifth-grade classroom in the process by raising their awareness of stormwater management and introducing them to the engineering design process.

How It Went: The Norwich team members visited the school and the fifth-grade classroom during two weeks of their four-week project. They visited during the three-hour lab session, with an hour spent in travel to and from the elementary school, giving them a two-hour block with the K–12 student team. They involved the fifth graders in determining problem areas of standing water on their playground, explained the consequences of poor stormwater management, and asked for their input in a potential new design. The Norwich team members developed a schematic, using AutoCAD, based on their initial observations and design ideas, took this schematic back to the classroom, and shared it with the fifth graders. Their discussions also included the engineering design process and the iterative approach engineers use in their designs as they work toward an improved solution.

PROJECT 2: ADDRESSING STORMWATER ISSUES AT A MIDDLE AND HIGH SCHOOL

Student Participants: Three undergraduate students

K–12 Students Impacted: 12 high school students, the school, and the local community

Community Partners: One high school teacher

Project Abstract: The objective of this project was to design a parking lot to be used by high school students, teachers, staff, and other visitors at the middle and high school. The Norwich team members worked in conjunction with the junior and senior high school chemistry students. The team members met with the high school students on four separate occasions. During the first meeting, the Norwich team members familiarized themselves with the class and discussed rainwater and rainwater control measures. During the next two meetings, the Norwich team members, high school students, and the high school teacher worked to create a plan for building a student parking lot behind the school with an asphalt surface, access road, and a rainwater collection system to prevent flooding/erosion.

How It Went: This project culminated with a presentation made by the Norwich team members and the high school students to the school's principal, business manager, and other teachers from the high school. The final deliverables for this design project included a graded surface for an asphalt parking lot capable of holding 41 cars, an access road into and out of the parking lot with wooden guardrails, and all necessary safety considerations as well as a rain garden water collection system for storm water runoff. This project, along with its final cost estimate, is under review as a potential future project for the town.

PROJECT 3: RIVER WATER QUALITY AND SEVENTH- AND EIGHTH-GRADE SCIENCE CLASSES AT A MIDDLE SCHOOL

Student Participants: Three undergraduate students

K–12 Students Impacted: 120 across three classes

Community Partners: One seventh-eighth grade science teacher

Project Abstract: This project was unique for the use of Skype by the Norwich team members to communicate with the three classrooms at the middle school. The seventh and eighth graders were working on assessing the quality of water in a river that runs by the school. Their specific interest was in parameters such as nitrates and phosphates and metals such as iron. The Norwich team members visited the school once and helped the school children with sampling protocols, demonstrated the use of various testing equipment, and helped them collect samples. The Norwich team members also analyzed several water quality samples and presented their results to their partners.

How it went: Given the size (40 students in each class) of each of these middle school classrooms, and the short 25-minute class period, Skype was only somewhat effective as a communication medium. The face-to-face visit was especially beneficial in helping the seventh and eighth graders correctly collect water samples and learn how to use the testing equipment (see figure 14.1). The visit also offered the community members more time in small groups with each of the three Norwich team members to better answer questions and help in specific ways. The Norwich team members collected, sampled, and analyzed water quality data and presented their finding to the community partners. The team recommended that Skype would be more effective in smaller class size projects and that a combination of virtual and in-person visits would be a good model for the future.

PROJECT 4: SOLID WASTE MANAGEMENT AND THIRD GRADERS AT AN ELEMENTARY SCHOOL

Student Participants: Four undergraduate students

K–12 Students Impacted: 38 children across two classes

Community Partners: Two third-grade teachers

Project Abstract: The Norwich team members decided to split up into two separate teams to reach two third-grade classrooms and walk the students through the waste management process via games and hands-on activities. The teams focused on the elements of waste products, recycling, and composting. The third graders gained knowledge of the processes waste undergoes from the time it is disposed until the time it enters the landfill and how the waste is handled thereafter. The significance of reducing the percentage of waste that goes into landfills was emphasized as the amount of land available for landfill use is shrinking. The lesson plans were developed as hands-on activities. The activities, to name a few, ranged from a "dumpster dive"— where components disposed in a garbage bag were sorted to determine which ones could be recycled or composted, instead of sending to a landfill—to a Jeopardy-style game. Some of the children, prior to the lessons, had some knowledge on these topics due to sorting their garbage into waste, recycling, and composting piles at the school.

Figure 14.1 Exploring Water Quality Concerns in the River with Middle School Students

This figure shows (clockwise from top right) standing water in the playground area, team members using instruments to conduct field water testing, and a rock specimen that the team found during their visit (photo credit: Norwich team members).

How it went: The Norwich team members (with some help from the two teachers) developed a lesson plan with content and hands-on activities for each of the four weeks they visited the two classrooms. The group started with a background knowledge probe of the students by asking questions, such as "what is waste?," "what is recycling?," and "where does our waste go?," and discussing their answers to these questions. Students then experienced a dumpster dive to better understand how and why waste needs to be sorted. This lesson was followed by an activity of organizing pictures in the correct order to better understand the steps in the process. Landfill components and design came up next with a hands-on S'mores building activity to represent the various layers in a landfill. Finally, the third graders engaged in a competitive Jeopardy-style game to review their understanding and win some prizes (see figure 14.2).

Figure 14.2 Jeopardy-Style Game Screen Created by Norwich Team Members as Part of a Service-Learning Project

Trash, Recycle, or Compost?	What is _____?	Fill in the Blank	True of False
200	200	200	200
400	400	400	400
600	600	600	600
800	800	800	800
1000	1000	1000	1000

PROJECT 5: WASTE AT LOCAL SCHOOLS

Student Participants: Three undergraduate students

K–12 Students Impacted: Local schools and community. There were only four middle school students on this Green Team project, but their dissemination would impact all the three schools in Northfield as well as the local community. For example, the Green Team often cleans up after the town's Labor Day parade.

Community Partners: One local school guidance counselor served as the direct contact.

Project Abstract: The primary purpose of the service-learning project was to meet with the middle school Green Team, a group focused on school sustainability, and assist them with a project that they will eventually present to the school and surrounding community. The Norwich team members met with the Green Team during each week of their four-week project period, during the lab hours, discounting the half-hour travel time. Both the Norwich team and Green Team decided to construct a model landfill. The outcome of the project was a Mason-style jar model landfill (see figure 14.3) built from various craft materials by the members of Green Team, a "Prezi" presentation, and a poster board (see figure 14.4) illustrating the knowledge that the students have gained in regards to waste management. The Green Team is now analyzing the results of their project and presenting these to surrounding schools to create a more environmentally aware community.

How It Went: The Norwich team members were well prepared for this project, having spent a good deal of class time focused on solid waste management-related curriculum. For example, as part of the CE 421 class, students spent three 50-minute sessions learning about the solid waste management and integrated solid waste management concepts in the United States. They learned the basics of landfill design and performed calculations to estimate the quantities of leachate and gases, such as methane, produced in landfills. They also visited local material recovery and composting facilities. They worked with a small group of local school students in the Green Team (about four students). These Green Team members had volunteered to be on this team and work on projects on waste issues with their counselor. The Norwich team members helped the elementary school students build a landfill model and develop a poster and presentation that they could share with the community (see figures 14.3 and 14.4).

Figure 14.3 Landfill Model in a Mason-Style Jar Created by Students as Part of a Service-Learning Partnership

Three students hold a model (in progress) of a landfill using paper waste to represent the solid waste, separated by liners.

Figure 14.4 Poster on Waste Developed by Students as Part of a Service-Learning Partnership

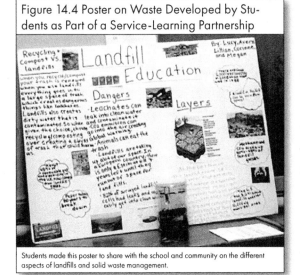

Students made this poster to share with the school and community on the different aspects of landfills and solid waste management.

RESULTS

Quantitative comparison of Norwich students' grades revealed that students earned slightly lower grades in labs than in the lecture component of the course (see table 14.2). Similarly, comparison of the distinct components of the lab grade (service-learning lab grades and traditional lab grades) revealed that students earned slightly lower grades in the service-learning labs than in the traditional labs (also see table 14.2).

Paired Sample T-Tests showed that the difference between the grades for the lecture component of that course and lab component were not statistically significant (see table 14.3). However, there was a significant difference ($p = .026$) between service-learning lab grades and traditional lab grades (also see table 14.3). In other words, students earned significantly lower grades on the service-learning lab assignments than on traditional lab assignments.

Qualitative coding of students reflection provides some potential explanation as to why students earned significantly lower grades in the service-learning component of the course. Two major themes and five subthemes emerged from qualitative coding (see table 14.4).

Table 14.2 Average Grades out of 100 Possible Points for Each of Four Components of an Environmental Engineer Course			
Average Lecture Grade	**Average Lab Grade (combined SL and non-SL grades)**	**Average SL Lab Grade**	**Average Traditional Lab Grade**
85.64	84.33	83.19	86.05

Table 14.3 Paired Sample T-Tests of Components of an Environmental Engineering Course					
COMPARISON GROUPS	**MEAN CHANGE**	**SD**	**T**	**DF**	**SIG (2-TAILED)**
Labs – Lecture	-1.31	7.35	-0.99	30	.329
Traditional Labs – SL Labs	2.86	6.79	2.34	30	.026*
*significant at .05 level					

Table 14.4 Themes that Emerged from Qualitative Coding of Students Reflection Assignments from an Environmental Engineering Course	
MAJOR THEMES	**SUB-THEMES**
Service-learning components were particularly challenging	Team dynamics were challenging
	Project management was challenging
	Communication was challenging
Service learning provided an opportunity to develop "soft skills"	Students developed communication skills
	Students developed leadership skills

The first major theme that emerged was that the service-learning components of the course were particularly challenging for students. Students' reflections revealed that aspects like team dynamics, project management, and communication issues made the service-learning component of the class difficult for students. For example, one student described how dynamics among the students within their project team made the service-learning challenging:

> I know that my service-learning project team has the potential to submit great designs for the school playground, but poor communication between the team lead and the rest of the team is creating turmoil, confusion, and frustration. It has been a challenge to me to know when to step up and when to let the leader lead.

In another example, a student reflected that project management was a difficult aspect of the service-learning:

> I am finding it tough to plan out what needs to be completed each week in order to meet our goal of a presentation to the principal and business manager for the schools. With just a little over a week left, I feel like we still have a lot to do and I will have to portion out the work between the members.

In yet another example, a student commented that communication was challenging:

> One thing that is difficult in the service-learning project is trying to do it with a school that is too far away to travel to every week. Conducting the project over Skype and e-mail is very difficult because it is harder to communicate what exactly you are trying to say through an e-mail. I think that things will be much easier in terms of explanation when we meet with the students this Wednesday.

These themes about challenges with group dynamics, project management, and communication were echoed throughout the reflection assignments that students completed, suggesting that, as a whole, students encountered different challenges and difficulties as they worked on the service-learning component of the course. This may at least partially explain why average grades were lower for the service-learning lab components.

The second major theme that emerged from the qualitative coding was that the service-learning provided an opportunity for students to work on "soft skills." In particular, students discussed improving their communication and leadership skills as a result of the service-learning projects. This is an important finding because it demonstrates that the challenges students faced (communication, project management, issues related to group dynamics) corresponded to the skills they gained. For example, one student reflected that the service-learning project provided an opportunity to practice and develop leadership skills:

> Since I was assigned the leadership role at the beginning of the project, I was in charge of organizing the meetings and keeping my team up to date with what we would be teaching in class. I found that it was difficult to get everyone on the same page at first but as the project has progressed it has become much easier. This project has taught me to listen to everyone's [ideas] and combine them into one idea to produce the best results. Teamwork is a major part of this project, so my ability to lead the team in the right direction has greatly improved.

In a second example, another student echoed that same idea that the service-learning project created a platform on which the student could work on developing a leadership style and skills:

> I have learned that not everybody is self-motivated and it is part of the role of a leader to keep everyone motivated and on track. When I first stepped into this role, I was under the impression that people would come find me in search of information about the weekly tasks. In reality, I have found that if I go directly to them and give them instructions, they are more

likely to follow them because they have been assigned a specific task. I have developed the ability to give instructions to people and keep them accountable for their responsibilities, in the past I have followed a lead by example approach.

Students reflected on improving their communication skills as a result of the service-learning projects. For example, one student wrote about learning to communicate with a diverse audience:

> The greatest skills that I have developed through this project thus far are my ability to communicate to a varying audience, and to interpret the requests of the client. Public speaking has never been the easiest thing for me, and when everyone expects you to know everything about the subject then it is even harder. Being placed in front of a class of fifth graders forced me to develop a plan quickly and to come up with a means to not only present my ideas, but also explain them in a way that could be understood by them. This forced me to be able to adapt to an audience that I was not used to and ensure that the main points were clear enough so they could understand the importance of the project.

In a second example, a student shared similar feelings when reflecting on learning to communicate with K–12 students: "Through this service-learning project, I have learned how to communicate to a younger audience material that may be normally difficult for college students to even comprehend." These themes reoccurred through the students' reflection assignments. Thus, although the service-learning component proved challenging for students, it also provided an opportunity for them to work on important skills, namely communication and leadership. This finding echoes previous work that suggests that civic engagement offers opportunities for students to gain important professional skills.[15]

DISCUSSION

Our results show that students in this environmental engineering course found the service-learning component particularly challenging and indeed earned significantly lower grades on the service-learning portion of the course. Through written reflection activities, students shared some of the difficulties they faced with working on and completing these projects. These ranged from poor communication, especially with regards to the exact nature of project deliverables, the time spent on traveling to and from the project sites (which gave them less time with their community partners), issues with using Skype as a communication tool (which seemed doable with a small group, but not with 40 students at a time), and insufficient preparation from their coursework so far. One explanation for the lower grades is that students in this course were engineering students, and "soft skills," like communication, may not have been emphasized in their previous courses as much as traditional engineering skills, such as math and surveying.

A related explanation for why students encountered difficulty with the service-learning component is that the project may not have been well matched to students' developmental level. Howe et al. describe three "phases," or levels, of service-learning experiences based on students developmental level and past experiences.[16] In phase one, students may be younger and/or less experienced and are thus given less autonomy in the service-learning projects. In this phase, faculty members design the service experience and control many aspects, including communication and relationships with the community partner. As students move through their academic career, they gain more skills that prepare them for more sophisticated service-learning projects in which they assume more autonomous roles. Howe et al. caution that a mismatch between students' developmental and skill level and service-learning phase may result in a negative experience. Sophisticated students in a lower-level course may be bored and thus disengage. Similarly, inexperienced students in a medium- or high-level course may feel in over their heads. These students may become frustrated and discouraged if they cannot satisfactorily complete the service-learning projects. It is possible that the projects in the course discussed in the chapter were too sophisticated for the students in the class, even though the students were juniors and seniors. Specifically, it was the instructor's intention to let the Norwich team members work with their individual community partners to fully flush out the scope of their projects and plan on an effective strategy to work toward their deliverables based on the four-week time constraint. However, not all team members were clear about the scope and did not manage time effectively, resulting in some of the concerns expressed as frustration and discouragement.

To avoid mismatches between student skill level and project complexity, we recommend that faculty interested in teaching service-learning be intentional about designing courses that meet their students where they are. Faculty should consider if students have taken service-learn-ing courses before or if they have worked with community partners in other contexts, such as internships. Faculty may also consider assigning students a skills inventory to have students self-assess where they are in terms communication, team work, project management, and any other skills that may be necessary to complete a given service-learning project. Such assessments can be discussed during in-class debriefs to further explore where students are in with regard to critical skills. Faculty can develop fully flushed out project scopes in working with the community partners themselves and then adjust project goals and expectations to better match their students.

Despite the fact that grades and reflection assignments suggest that students in this course struggled with service-learning, reflections also suggest that the service-learning projects were es-pecially valuable for helping students to develop communication and leadership skills. We posit that the lower grades on the service-learning components were not a reflection of decreased learning or less-engaged learning, but rather were an indication that the students were challenged by the rigorous nature of the service-learning requirements. This does not mean that traditional classroom learning was sacrificed in favor of civic education goals, but rather that the civic engagement goals were as rigorous as the goals related to engineering content. Multiple students chimed in with the thought that these projects had helped improve their communication skills. Explaining complex en-gineering terms and jargon to a lay audience, whether they were K–12 students or members of the community, and practicing these verbal skills was valuable. Some students commented on improved skills as a leader in assigning roles, delegating tasks, and holding team members accountable. Expos-ing students to situations that require these skill sets may prove to be incredibly beneficial, as these are skills that will be important for them as practicing professionals and citizens. Service-learning can be a rigorous academic experience through which students may derive many important learning outcomes. Thus, we encourage other faculty to consider incorporating service-learning components into their courses even though students may struggle.

From the faculty perspective, the logistics of managing nine teams working with eight dif-ferent community partners proved to be a challenge. The primary instructor had developed some relations with these community partners through her own professional consultation and outreach activities, while some partners were recommended through the Norwich Center for Civic En-gagement. While the instructor had a broad project scope developed through discussions with community partners before the start of the semester, interactions between the Norwich student groups and community partners did result in some miscommunication or misunderstandings resulting in uneven scopes for different teams, with variable deliverables, both in terms of quality as well as quantity. The challenge involving travel time and technology also played into a high level of time involvement on the part of students and faculty, despite assistance from the university's Center for Civic Engagement.

However, the instructor believes that the course goals and project goals, specifically the ex-pectation that the Norwich student teams would apply their classroom and lab understanding of environmental engineering concepts to help their community partners, were met. Civic engage-ment is connected deeply with the service mission of the university, and that aspect is well suited to these projects. The projects also helped students developed communication, leadership, and planning skills, even though there was a range in proficiencies. The instructor asserts that offering service-learning projects is a major time commitment on the part of faculty, and although the students may not realize it (as observed in some reflections where the frustrations of the moment are emphasized), their learning of classroom concepts is deepened.

The instructor has since modified this format of service-learning projects and offered a version where various student teams work on different aspects of the same project for a single community partner (2015). A second modification involved a research-based service-learning project where students remained on campus, researching problems posed by their community partners and developing websites to disseminate their research findings. They also created physical and computational models to help visualize the problems and/or the solutions they researched and invited their community partners to campus for a research symposium event, which was well received.

CONCLUSIONS

The contribution of the chapter is threefold: first, it presents a case study of a service-learning environmental engineering course at a small university. It outlines examples of the projects that students engaged in that other faculty may replicate or adapt in their own courses or use one of the modifications that are briefly mentioned in the discussion section. In this class, a small group of university students made a large difference in multiple communities across our small state. Introducing K–12 students to the university and to engineering, as well as involving them in solving some of the environmental problems in their communities, should pay large dividends in the future as these budding members of our next generation take on important professional and citizenship roles to solve local, national, and global challenges. Second, this chapter details an evaluation of students' learning outcomes and illustrates challenges that students encountered as well as gains that they made in terms of new skills developed. Our students gained experience and deepened or expanded their academic knowledge amidst the stresses, frustrations, and joys of meaningful civic engagement learning. Finally, the chapter encourages other faculty to consider service-learning projects and makes recommendations about matching project design to students' skill levels and presents relevant literature to guide faculty. It demonstrates that civic engagement education can be pursued in any discipline, at any type of institution, and in any location. ■

ACKNOWLEDGMENTS

The assistance of contacts and funding provided by Norwich University's Center for Civic Engagement is gratefully acknowledged, as well as the efforts of the coinstructor and the students of this environmental engineering course, and those whose reflections are included in this chapter.

ENDNOTES

1. Sally Berman, *Service Learning: A Guide to Planning, Implementing, and Assessing Student Projects* (Thousand Oaks, CA: Corwin Press, 2006).

2. "Campus Compact: Who We Are," last modified 2016, http://www.compact.org/about/history-mission-vision/.

3. Michael Prince, "Does Active Learning Work? A Review of the Research," *Journal of Engineering Education* 93 (2004).

4. "Northeastern University College of Engineering: Service-Learning," last modified 2012, http://www.coe.neu.edu/experiential-learning/service-learning.

5. Bruce Berdanier, "Year-Long Service Learning Projects in Capstone Design at South Dakota State University," *Conference Proceedings, Capstone Design Conference* (2010).

6. Mandar M. Dewoolkar, Lindsay George, Nancy J. Hayden, and Donna M. Rizzo, "Vertical Integration of Service-Learning into Civil and Environmental Engineering Curricula," *International Journal of Engineering Education*, 56 (2009).

7. "Purdue University: What Is EPICS?" last modified 2017, https://engineering.purdue.edu/EPICSU/About/index.html.

8. Tara Kulkarni, "Service-Learning Projects in Environmental Engineering Courses: Models of Community Engagement Activities," *American Society for Engineering Education Zone 1 Conference* (2014).

9. Carrie Williams Howe, Kimberly Coleman, Kelly Hamshaw, and Katherine Westdijk, "Student Development and Service-Learning: A Three-Phased Model for Course Design," *The International Journal of Research on Service-Learning and Community Engagement* (2014).

10. Sherril Gelmon, Barbara Holland, Amy Driscoll, Amy Spring, and Seanna Kerrigan, *Assessing Service-learning and Civic Engagement: Principles and Techniques* (Campus Compact, Brown University, 2001).

11. Michelle Ortlipp, "Keeping and Using Reflective Journals in the Qualitative Research Process," *The Qualitative Report* 13 (2008).

12. Sarah L. Ash, Patti H. Clayton, and Maxine P. Atkinson, "Integrating Reflection and Assessment to Capture and Improve Student Learning," *Michigan Journal of Community Service Learning* 11 (2005).

13. Joseph Maxwell, *Qualitative Research Design: An Interactive Approach* (Thousand Oaks, CA: Sage Publications, 2012).

14. Corrine Glesne and Alan Peshkin, *Becoming Qualitative Researchers* (White Plains, NY: Longman, 1992).

15. Association of American Colleges & Universities, "A Crucible Moment: College Learning & Democracy's Future" (2012).

16. Howe et al., "Student Development and Service-Learning," 2014.

SECTION III

Connecting Civic Engagement Education Across the Disciplines

Introduction

ELIZABETH A. BENNION

The previous section of this book highlighted a myriad of ways faculty in diverse disciplines are working within those disciplines or across disciplines to integrate civic learning and engagement into the curriculum. This section moves beyond the classroom to explore the ways academic institutions can support civic learning and political engagement across the campus—both inside and outside of the classroom.

One way to promote civic education and engagement across the disciplines and beyond the classroom is to work collaboratively with faculty and staff from multiple disciplines to coordinate interdisciplinary civic education programming that reaches a broad audience. In his chapter, Forren provides a detailed description of a Citizenship and Democracy Week initiative designed to involve students and community members in a multicampus, multievent, and interdisciplinary, civic learning initiative to promote interest and engagement in civic affairs. The initiative moves campuses beyond meeting the legal requirement to recognize Constitution Day toward a weeklong celebration of civic education and engagement. For faculty and staff leaders, the effort has forged closer relationships across departmental and administrative lines, deeper connections to community-based partners, and new opportunities to integrate experiential learning into the curriculum. Program participants report greater interest in civic affairs, a better understanding of politics and government, and increased enthusiasm about future political and civic engagement opportunities. Such initiatives cannot replace a year-round commitment to educating for democracy, but they can make sustained efforts possible.

To offer a wide range of courses across the disciplines and throughout the academic year, faculty must be prepared to offer high-quality civic engagement opportunities. Such preparation requires institutional support for their efforts to infuse hands-on civic learning opportunities into their classrooms. One way to promote the teaching of civic engagement across the disciplines is to develop training programs for faculty across campus who are willing—or eager—to integrate civic engagement opportunities into their courses. Surak, Jensen, McCartney, and Pope consider how to prepare faculty to teach civic engagement. Their chapter explores faculty fellows programs at two of Maryland's regional state universities. The authors describe the faculty training programs offering an honest assessment of the strengths and weakness of each program. The chapter also highlights the fellows' reflections on the type of support required to engage faculty in community-based teaching, including financial, logistical, and programmatic support; opportunities for institution-wide recognition; and a promotion and tenure process that rewards experiential learning pedagogies and the scholarship of engagement.

While it is important to train faculty to deliver high-quality civic learning and engagement opportunities in their classrooms, some campuses are moving beyond a classroom-based learning model toward living-learning communities. Learning communities offer the benefit of shared experiences that extend beyond the classroom. McTague's chapter describes a political engagement learning community at Towson University. He explains how students from a variety of majors live together on one floor of a residence hall while also taking the same section of Introduction to American Government, participating in extracurricular activities and experiential learning requirements designed to promote political engagement, and sharing the same First-Year Experience advisor. This model shows promise with participants reporting greater levels of knowledge about political institutions and current events, as well as increased engagement reading newspapers and discussing public affairs at the end of the semester. This model serves as a starting point for other campuses eager to develop their own living-learning communities. Further iterations might include courses focused on solving community problems as a way to address participants' misgivings about their power to affect change.

Simply taking a US government course, even in the context of a learning community, may not be enough to develop students' identity as community activists or problem solvers. The ability to identify and work collaboratively to solve community problems is the focus of an innovative partnership with local elementary schools highlighted in "Collaborative Civic Engagement: A Multidisciplinary Approach to Teaching Democracy with Elementary and University Students." Crigler, Goodnight, Armstrong, and Ramesh describe a complex, multi-institutional, and multi-disciplinary civic engagement program: the University of Southern California's Penny Harvest. University students, faculty, and staff collaborate with local schools to conduct the effort, a program that encourages elementary school students across the city to discuss issues and learn about resources to address community needs. Children connect with parents, friends, and neighbors as they gather pennies. The process encourages people from different backgrounds and generations to come together to talk and build a community no matter how small a donation they are able to give. Working with coaches to analyze community problems, prioritize pressing issues, design their own service projects, and identify organizations that can best alleviate identified problems gives children the skills they need for long-term civic and political engagement. As the Penny Harvest Project recognizes, it is important for students to be able to engage with community members to identify, define, and solve social problems. A standard classroom assignment will not provide students with the skills they need to become effective civic leaders.

Lifelong civic engagement and leadership requires that citizens are able to engage in unscripted, authentic civic action, as Simeone, Sikora, and Halperin discuss in their chapter, "Unscripted Learning: Cultivating Engaged Catalysts." They describe how the Action Research Center (ARC) at Illinois Wesleyan University provides such opportunities to students through project-based, community-based action research. ARC opens civic engagement opportunities to students from disciplines across the campus providing an opportunity for students to develop multisemester relationships with community organizations and to pursue multiyear projects, beginning as novices and culminating with mastery as students learn to see themselves as "engaged catalysts" for their communities. Students work with local communities to deliberate and to collectively solve real-world problems identified by the community partners.

The important role of nonprofit voluntary associations in community problem solving, civic skill development, and the creation of a robust civil society is well established. Strachan and Bennion continue this theme in their chapter by focusing on the importance of student organizations as a form of civil society and a site for political socialization and civic skill development. They highlight the work of the Consortium for Inter-Campus SoTL Research (CISR), a consortium they established to facilitate cross-campus data collection for civic engagement and pedagogy research. Their chapter focuses on CISR's inaugural project, the National Survey of Student Leaders (NSSL), a survey designed to assess the quality of the civic learning experiences provided by student clubs and organizations. Drawing on the robust literature on the role of voluntary associations and civil society in political socialization, the NSSL provides higher education institutions with the means to assess whether civil society on campus promotes the priorities of the civic engagement movement. The chapter outlines a research-based, accessible, and assessable model for student organizations that promote best practices associated with healthy civic and political socialization.

For student organizations to live up to their potential role in developing civic skills and identities, the university must have institutions in place to support best practices and train student leaders. Civic engagement centers and institutes can serve this function, bridging the divide between academic affairs and student affairs and providing the knowledge, resources, and training required for club advisors, student leaders, and university faculty to offer high-quality civic education and engagement opportunities. Matto and McHugh provide a profile of centers and institutes situated on campuses recognized for their commitment to civic engagement. The authors conclude that what matters most in facilitating widespread civic engagement is that there is an organization (rather than an individual academic department) on campus that focuses on promoting and supporting civic engagement. Their chapter explores the structural features most successful centers share and notes the common resources they provide, including pedagogical resources for faculty, dedicated expert staff, and a faculty reward system. Offering a series of detailed case studies, the authors link readers to useful resources such as syllabi, training modules, and assessments that the centers provide.

Matto and McHugh stress the importance of assessing student learning outcomes, program objectives, and community impact to build on successful practices and replace less successful ones. Bennion picks up this topic in her chapter in which she provides an overview of the most important lessons and resources to consult when designing an assessment plan for civic learning activities. Bennion highlights the importance of backward design: identifying the desired results and determining acceptable evidence before planning a learning experience. The chapter highlights the need to align desired outcomes with learning activities and assessment measures, as well as the importance of distinguishing between broad, ambiguous goals and measurable learning objectives. The chapter provides links to well established rubrics and surveys measuring civic knowledge, skills, and attitudes, as well as innovative new assessment tools in the areas of civic identity, civic agency, and civic mindedness as well as other goals that match campus-defined learning outcomes. Bennion provides readers with the information they need to create civic outcome statements that are specific, measurable, useful, meaningful, and tied to the desired learning outcome. The chapter also provides suggestions for assessing process in ways that help a campus, program, or instructor to distinguish between a flawed design and an implementation problem. This information is important when deciding whether to refine existing civic learning activities or to replace them with new ones.

In "Politics 365: Fostering Campus Climates for Student Political Learning and Engagement," Thomas and Brower argue that the need for evidence-based approaches to civic education and engagement has seldom, if ever, been more important than it is now. The 2016 presidential election season drew attention to global trends where core tenets of democracy (e.g., freedom of the press, free speech, the right to dissent, equal opportunity, respect for minorities, public reason, and the rule of law) are being eroded. The authors stress that American democracy is not just a set of rules for governing. It is also a culture. Democracy is defined by the principles and practices that provide the context for governing. The ability to socialize, collaborate, and govern across partisan differences has broken down due to "entrenched feelings of fear, hatred, entitlement, [and] anger." Thomas and Brower argue that the nation's colleges and universities need to seize this moment to reexamine student civic learning to educate for democratic culture and systems that are "participatory, equitable, educated, informed, and ethically governed." The authors argue that better teaching alone cannot prepare students for public problem solving and policy making. They stress that colleges and universities are "complex organizations with people, systems, norms, traditions, and societal contexts that interact to form the context for student development." To transform adequate numbers of disinterested students into committed political actors, colleges and universities must improve their campus climates for political learning and engagement. The authors present findings from a nine-campus qualitative study of institutional climates to determine which norms, behaviors, attitudes, and structures promote effective and widespread political learning and engagement.

Based on extended campus visits, including focus groups and interviews, the authors developed a "Politics 365" model that identifies five key elements of engaged campus communities. This model is useful for other campuses to consider. As Thomas and Brower emphasize, the most successful campuses recognize that political learning and engagement must be practices modeled year-round in a way that is pervasive across campus and deeply embedded into institutional norms and behaviors. The authors provide specific examples of the norms, structures, activities, and behaviors that characterized positive outliers who are successfully engaging their students in politics and public affairs.

Taken together, the chapters in this section provide a broad overview of the ways campuses can create a supportive environment for effectively developing the knowledge, skills, attitudes, and behaviors required for students to make a meaningful difference in their communities. Such a holistic approach to teaching civic engagement reflects the shared mission of all disciplines to prepare students to be informed and engaged citizens. ■

Partnering with Campus and Community to Promote Civic Engagement: Miami University's Citizenship and Democracy Week

15

JOHN FORREN

How can political scientists work effectively with campus colleagues and community partners to develop and sustain a high-impact civic engagement program? This chapter examines one successful model of grassroots interdisciplinary collaboration—Miami University's annual "Citizenship and Democracy Week"—that offers valuable lessons for faculty members interested in leading such programs at other institutions. As the chapter details, creating and maintaining the annual Miami program—which now involves dozens of separate events each year, staged at multiple community and campus venues—has required the project's leaders to manage a range of significant organizational, logistical, political, and personal challenges. Among the positive results, however, have been closer "town–gown" ties, stronger on-campus relationships across disciplinary lines, deeper integration of curricular and co-curricular programming, and, most important of all, enhanced levels of civic knowledge and interest in politics among its participants.

Reflecting widely shared concerns about the current state of "civic health" in the United States, political scientists in recent years have turned their attention anew to the discipline's long-neglected public role in promoting good citizenship, active community engagement, and deep civic learning.[1] Indeed, as section III of this book illustrates, political scientists working in an array of institutional settings now consider civic and political engagement a meaningful and vital component of their day-to-day professional lives. As veterans of such work can attest, such publicly engaged endeavors can be both deeply rewarding on a personal level and highly effective in promoting the public good.[2] Still, success often requires the effective navigation of a range of political, organizational, and logistical challenges that rarely arise in more traditional venues for professional academic work. Partnering with local community leaders, for instance, may require that a faculty member confront a variety of sticky "town vs. gown" issues while managing notable differences in workstyles, goals, timelines, organizational structures, and standards for measuring success. At the same time, as Meinke has suggested, they may also confront hurdles within their home institutions including tight budgets, skeptical administrators, competing demands on their time, and resistance from colleagues who may not view such work as fitting comfortably within traditional conceptions of the faculty role.[3]

Given such an array of logistical and institutional challenges, how can the civically minded scholar successfully launch and sustain a broad-scale community engagement program? In this chapter, we examine one model for doing so that has been implemented successfully at a midsized public university located in the Midwest. More specifically, what follows is an account of how a small team of faculty and staff at Miami University in Ohio has worked to develop and sustain a university-wide program entitled "Citizenship and Democracy Week"—an annual inter-disciplinary event that incorporates over two dozen separate civic engagement opportunities for students, faculty, staff, and residents of surrounding communities across three campuses. While still young in age and pedigree—it debuted only two years ago, in September 2015—Citizenship and Democracy Week has already yielded significant positive results for the university, for the Week's key organizers and planners, and for the 3,000-plus faculty, staff members, students, and community members who have participated so far in its various programs and events. For the university overall, the Week has produced stronger institutional ties to surrounding off-campus communities, greater coordination among the university's three southwestern Ohio campuses, and enhanced visibility in the region's print and online media. For its faculty and staff leaders, the effort has forged closer relationships across departmental and administrative lines, deeper con-nections to community-based partners, and new opportunities to integrate experiential learning into the curriculum. As for the Week's primary audience—its attendees and participants—post-event surveys suggest that Citizenship and Democracy Week has succeeded quite well, at least in its first two iterations, in boosting participants' levels of interest in civic affairs, their under-standing of politics and government, and, perhaps most important of all, their enthusiasm about engaging themselves directly in political and civic action in the future. In light of such positive effects, the following account is offered both as a description and assessment of Miami's program to date and as a model that might be adapted for use by faculty and staff at other institutions who might wish to explore the development of similar interdisciplinary programs.

THE STRUCTURE AND GOALS OF CITIZENSHIP AND DEMOCRACY WEEK

While Miami's Citizenship and Democracy Week is of recent origin, the roots of the annual program trace back to a long-standing statutory mandate that all federally funded educational institutions commemorate the formal signing of the US Constitution on or near September 17 of each year. Colleges and universities observe this annual "Constitution Day and Citizenship Day" in a variety of ways. In 2012 and 2013, for instance, the commemoration at Miami University Hamilton (MUH)—an open-access commuter campus of about 3,700 students located 15 miles from the university's flagship residential campus in Oxford, Ohio—consisted primarily of two events: a public lunchtime discussion of the US Constitution led by two faculty members and an on-campus voter registration drive sponsored by the MUH Center for Civic Engagement. In 2014, a faculty member in English added a third component to MUH's celebration of September 17: a "Write for Rights" event, inspired by Amnesty International's program of the same name, at which students, faculty, and staff were encouraged to write letters in support of equality and human rights around the world.

These annual "one-off" programs at MUH met both the letter and the spirit of the fed-eral mandate for September 17 while costing little in terms of institutional resources and faculty time. Yet such a small-bore approach to the annual commemoration also represented a significant missed opportunity to engage the campus and surrounding community more deeply in discussion and reflection about government, politics, and citizens' responsibilities in a democracy. Sharing this sense that more could be done, a small group of MUH faculty and staff—led by the organiz-ers of the Constitution and Citizenship Day commemorations discussed earlier—began talking in late 2014 about how future September 17 celebrations on campus might engage a broader segment of the community in the years ahead. Working *ad hoc* at first and without a clearly artic-ulated vision or plan—other than a shared interest in developing something bigger—these initial partners reached out informally to colleagues throughout the campus community for suggestions, feedback, and support. Two key leaders of the emerging effort—the campus' only full-time political scientist and its Director of Civic Engagement—began meeting regularly to flesh out ideas about programming options and themes for a possible multi-day event in early 2015. A third early collaborator—a MUH criminal justice professor who chaired the Department of Justice and Community Studies—pledged key administrative and financial support to any larger effort that might spring from these initial discussions.

By spring 2015, a small interdisciplinary committee of MUH faculty and staff had formed with the purpose of developing a week-long program of coordinated events for the following September. Chaired by the previously mentioned political scientist, this group hashed out the basic goals, themes, and structure of the upcoming commemoration at an early April meeting attended by representatives of five of MUH's academic and administrative units. By consensus, the group opted to "go big" despite the potential obstacles. First, members agreed, the week should include a wide array of diverse participation opportunities—ideally, multiple events each day, held at various locations—all scheduled around two high-profile "anchor" events: a theme-setting keynote address on civic responsibility and action to be delivered on Monday night (by a yet-to-be-determined headlining speaker) and an on-campus federal court naturalization ceremony to be held on Thursday afternoon—Constitution and Citizenship Day itself. (By early April, preliminary arrangements with the US District Court in nearby Cincinnati for hosting a September 17 ceremony at MUH had already been made.) Second, we decided that the week—in line with its basic focus on democratic engagement—should provide meaningful opportunities for participants not only to observe and think about issues of politics and governance but also to *act* as citizens in meaningful ways. (That meant, among other things, that the week's schedule needed to include events beyond the traditional faculty-led, "sage-on-the-stage" lectures on democracy-related themes.) Third, the group agreed that, to ensure maximum impact, the week should be aimed at reaching beyond the Hamilton campus as much as possible and into the surrounding communities—both to engage the campus' immediate neighbors and also to include Miami's other campuses in Oxford and Middletown (each about 15 miles away) as well. Finally, participants agreed that the committee members themselves should each actively seek out ways of incorporating the week's themes and events into their own courses and, more broadly, into other parts of the university's curriculum—both to encourage broad faculty and student participation and expand discussions of the week's themes into a wide range of different settings.

In opting for such an ambitious approach, leaders of the planning effort realized that at least three contextual factors would likely boost their odds for success. For one, the timing for such an effort at Miami seemed especially fortuitous: just months earlier, the university with considerable fanfare had launched a new Hamilton-based interdisciplinary four-year degree program that contained substantial amounts of democratic theory, political science, and community-based experiential learning. The students and faculty involved in that new major, it seemed, would likely be an enthusiastic core audience for a week of themed programming of the type being envisioned. Second, due in part to Miami's somewhat unusual workload policy that effectively rewards faculty members in Hamilton and Middletown for prioritizing service over research in their work, a broad range of faculty colleagues across campus would likely be supportive and willing to lend their time and disciplinary expertise to the effort.[4] Finally, in developing the new week of events, committee members also knew that valuable logistical support as well as programming expertise would be forthcoming from a well-established and well-funded infrastructure for civic and community engagement that was already in place on both regional branch campuses. Both the Center for Civic Engagement in Hamilton and the Office of Community Engagement and Service in Middletown could offer dedicated space, staff support, expertise in cocurricular programming, and, perhaps most importantly, extensive connections to faculty and local community partners as the plan for the September week of events took shape. The director of Hamilton's civic engagement office, as noted earlier, had been involved from the outset in the planning of Citizenship and Democracy Week. Her counterpart on the Middletown campus, while not yet part of the planning group itself in April, had already indicated her enthusiasm for the project and her willingness to support the group's efforts.

The planning committee, in short, would hardly be flying alone in moving forward with an ambitious plan of action. Yet at the same time, the effort needed to overcome several practical roadblocks. Three in particular drew the attention of the planning committee at its April 2015 meeting. First, the planners' intent to stage multiple programs over several days was, at this stage, supported by neither a specific mandate from central administration nor a dedicated budget—both important factors when considering the likely need for broad campus buy-in and the potential for significant costs associated with programming. (In this vein, group leaders were aware that a dedicated campus endowment might be available to fund a keynote address; for other programs, however, sources of funding had to be identified.) Second, the committee faced the challenge of securing the active participation in program events of students beyond the "usual suspects" in political science and the other social sciences—especially on the university's Hamilton and Middletown campuses. (Much like other commuter campuses, Miami's regional campuses enroll large numbers of nontraditional students who, because of competing work responsibilities, family obligations, and other nonacademic commitments, simply cannot take part in many enrichment activities that take place outside of regular class hours.) Further, the committee realized that if Citizenship and Democracy Week were to extend beyond the confines of the MUH campus where all of the initial leaders of the effort were based, then the committee members themselves would need to devote considerable amounts of personal time and energy upfront to the task of "selling" the group's broader vision of the university's September 17 commemoration to various internal and external stakeholders. Taking these challenges into account, each of the organizers committed themselves at the April 2015 meeting to "spreading the word" about the Week within their own personal and professional networks. Beyond that, each agreed to reach out broadly—both within the university itself and to various leaders within the community at large—to seek out additional programming ideas and collaborators who might be interested in joining the effort.

THE 2015 PROGRAM

Having charted their basic course of action in early April, the full planning group met in person only one additional time that year, about two weeks later, to loosely divide responsibilities among its members and devise a specific plan for communicating and coordinating efforts in the months ahead. Planners agreed that the MUH political scientist who chaired the initial effort would continue to coordinate the program and oversee its development; beyond that, he would also take the lead in securing a keynote speaker; recruiting new faculty, staff, and community partners; developing an effective marketing/advertising plan; and serving as the group's liaison to university administrators, faculty, and staff. Other committee members, meanwhile, took primary responsibility for developing and delivering specific parts of the week's program. In that vein, a faculty member from the MUH theater department agreed to create an interactive, improvisational performance on social justice themes that would be presented on Wednesday night in an on-campus studio space. The MUH director of civic engagement similarly volunteered to coordinate a civics-themed faculty development workshop, an on-campus voter registration drive and a September 17 public reading of the US Constitution by community volunteers. A third committee member, representing the Department of Justice and Community Studies, agreed to oversee all of the logistical planning for the on-campus MUH naturalization ceremony, including necessary coordination with US District Court staffers, local elected officials, local law enforcement and security personnel, and campus technology and physical facilities staff. Another member of the group—a junior faculty member in criminal justice—agreed to explore ways in which the week of programs might be incorporated into a one-credit-hour sprint course that would combine experiential learning with selected readings in political and social thought.

All in all, the members of the planning committee—along with over a dozen additional faculty and staff colleagues who joined the effort along the way—collectively devoted hundreds of hours between late spring and early fall of 2015 to the planning and development of Miami's inaugural Citizenship and Democracy Week. The end result was an integrated 24-event program offered over five days in September at various locations on all three of Miami's Ohio campuses as well as at a local high school (pictures and materials from these events can be found on the companion website). Among the major programs offered during the 2015 Week were:

- A two-day visit to the area by social activist and civic engagement scholar Paul Loeb, which included a Monday evening keynote address, interactive faculty development workshops on each of Miami's three Ohio campuses, a lecture to students studying American government at a local high school, and a small group discussion with Miami student leaders of Loeb's seminal work *Soul of a Citizen*;[5]
- A US District Court naturalization ceremony held outdoors on the main quad at Miami's Hamilton campus with participation from senior university administrators, local public officials, a local pipe and drum corps, county board of elections staffers, the Daughters of the American Revolution, and the university's concert choir;
- On-campus public meetings at MUH of a state appeals court and a local elected school board;
- Faculty-hosted screenings of a citizenship-themed documentary—Alexandra Pelosi's *Citizen USA: A 50-State Road Trip* (2011)—at the university's Middletown campus and its Hamilton Downtown Center;
- A "Social Justice Theater" event at MUH during which audience members engaged in improvisational role-playing under the direction of a theater professional;
- A "Write for Rights" session at which community members could choose to compose letters in support of civil rights and equality around the world;
- Week-long voter registration drives held on the Hamilton and Middletown campuses;
- Four different faculty-moderated public discussions on the Hamilton and Middletown campuses (on freedom of speech, immigration policy, community relations, and grass-roots collective action); and
- A week-long opportunity for community members to contribute to a discussion on the meaning of citizenship on a publicly displayed "Democracy Wall" on the Hamilton campus.

Altogether, approximately 1,700 people—including hundreds of people from surrounding communities—took part directly in some element of the inaugural Citizenship and Democracy Week program during its five-day run. Countless others in the local area learned about the week's events via social media and local media coverage—including both a preview article of the Week and a front-page, above-the-fold recap of the Thursday naturalization ceremony in the local daily newspaper. Within the university itself, at least a dozen faculty members incorporated elements of the Week's programming into their courses on American politics, criminal justice, political philosophy, sociology, and civic engagement. More generally, a range of faculty and staff colleagues offered praise to organizers both for Week's interdisciplinary mix of programming and for the positive intellectual "buzz" that it had created on campus. As a senior campus administrator put it in a congratulatory email to organizers, the university's first Citizenship and Democracy Week had been "not only … good for the intellect, it was good for the soul."

THE 2016 PROGRAM

Buoyed by this initial success, the key organizers of the 2015 effort began to plan the follow-up event for 2016 almost immediately. Working this time with the basic conceptual and organizational groundwork for the Week already in place—and with most of the essential collaborative partnerships already established as well—the effort's leaders happily found that much less personal time and energy was needed during the planning stages the second time. Key university administrators and staff members, now more familiar with the basic objectives and look of the Week, readily committed resources, personnel, and organizational support to the 2016 effort. Staffers at the US District Court in Cincinnati and the Ohio court of appeals in Middletown likewise agreed within weeks of the 2015 event to again stage two major programs—the federal court naturalization ceremony and the on-campus appellate court argument—on the Hamilton campus the following year. Local media outlets again pledged to provide both advance publicity and news coverage of Citizenship and Democracy Week in 2016. Perhaps most important, almost all of the key faculty and staff colleagues from throughout the university who collectively had provided such critical (and uncompensated) support to the program in 2015—such as the fine arts professor responsible for "Social Justice Theater," the faculty members in English, criminal justice, and communications who had coordinated various on-campus panel and small group discussions, the civic engagement staffs in Hamilton and Middletown who had led the Week's voter registration drives, and the Oxford-based vocal music professor who agreed to bring the university's concert choir to Hamilton for the naturalization ceremony—readily renewed their personal commitments to the effort for the following year.

With the basic model for the next year already effectively in place by mid-fall of 2015, the planning group over the next few months focused their efforts on improving Citizenship and Democracy Week for 2016 in three specific respects. First, hoping to expand the event's presence specifically on the Oxford campus—where only a handful of events had occurred in 2015—group leaders in late fall reached out to the interim director of that campus' Office of Community Engagement and Service to assist in planning for the following year. She enthusiastically agreed, and over the next several months, she worked with colleagues on the Oxford campus to develop several new engagement opportunities for September 2016. Second, planners hoped to improve both the quality and quantity of the promotional materials (including posters, press releases, and social media postings) used to market the Week's events to various communities in southwestern Ohio. To that end, the chair of the planning group reached out for help from the university's public relations staff, which graciously agreed to lend its professional expertise to the following year's effort. Perhaps most significantly, the planning group also set out to include in the week's programming a greater number and range of opportunities not only for participants to observe government in action and to learn about politics but also to directly *practice* civic skills such as voting, working with others, and deliberating on public issues. Notably, a key impetus for this greater focus on direct political engagement in 2016's Citizenship and Democracy Week was the finding by Miami University researchers—detailed in a National Conference on Citizenship report published the same year—that Ohio's college-aged citizens persistently trail much of the nation in their levels of day-to-day political activism.[6] By providing additional opportunities for hands-on civics "practice," the Week's planners determined, Citizenship and Democracy Week could be used intentionally to instill habits of political action among young people that might pay dividends for civic health in Ohio well into the future.[7]

Held this time over six days (September 12–17), the 2016 Citizenship and Democracy Week included 35 themed events staged on Miami's three Ohio campuses and its Hamilton off-campus Downtown Center. Most of the major elements of the 2015 program were reprised, including a Monday evening address (delivered this time by Dr. Nicholas Longo of Providence College, who spoke on political engagement beyond voting), an on-campus naturalization ceremony, an on-campus state appellate court proceeding, a social justice theater event, a cross-campus voter registration drive, and a range of faculty-led discussions and hands-on civic skills workshops for faculty, staff, and students (pictures of these events can be found on the companion website). Beyond that, a range of new opportunities for direct engagement were offered, included the following:

- Two "Civic Volunteer Fairs" held on the Hamilton and Middletown campuses, at which local nonprofit leaders and candidates for public office described their community-based work and recruited students to join in their efforts;

- A multi-campus "Community Straw Poll" sponsored and conducted by officials from the Butler County (Ohio) Board of Elections, which both provided hands-on experience with actual voting machines and processes and also yielded a data set that was subsequently used for instruction on polling methodology and analysis in a cooperating faculty member's introductory-level course on American politics. (Straw poll participants—over 160 in all—cast simulated votes on the actual November 2016 general election ballot; those results, in turn, were released by the Board of Elections on social media and featured in a local newspaper column.);

- A Wednesday evening deliberative dialogue at the Hamilton Downtown Center—titled "How Do We Get American Politics Back on Track?"—at which a mix of faculty, staff, students, and community members shared their perspectives on contemporary politics in moderated small groups;

- An on-campus evening session of the Hamilton City Council (which was scheduled in lieu of the previous year's on-campus meeting of the local school board);

- A public forum on police–community interactions held on the Middletown campus in cooperation with a local high school's Social Justice Club and the Middletown Police Department;

- A "Freedom Summer App" event, held on the Oxford campus, at which participants used mobile devices and GPS technology to explore, via a specially designed phone application, the experiences of Freedom Summer volunteers who trained on the Miami campus in 1964;

- A public discussion of local government, held on the Oxford campus, with a Cincinnati city council member; and

- An all-day Saturday student "summit" on the Oxford campus, coordinated by a local nonprofit group, which provided hands-on civic skills training as well as opportunities to interact directly with two members of the US Congress.

Altogether, over two dozen Miami faculty and staff members—alongside a comparable number of cooperating partners from governmental agencies, political groups, and local nonprofit organizations—participated directly in the delivery of Citizenship and Democracy Week programming in 2016. Attendance for the various events together again exceeded the 1,700 mark—and once again, feedback from several quarters was quite positive and encouraging of a continuation of the program in the years ahead. Sharing in that positive assessment, almost all of the faculty, staff, administrators, and community partners who played major roles in supporting the 2016 program have since signed on again for 2017. The core leadership of the effort has recommitted as well. Consequently, as of this writing, planning for a third Citizenship and Democracy Week in September 2017 is currently underway.

THE IMPACT OF CITIZENSHIP AND DEMOCRACY WEEK

What has been the impact of this effort so far? Regarding one of the planning committee's original objectives to use the September 17 commemoration as a means of engaging the university and surrounding communities in meaningful reflection and action about politics and civic affairs, there is no doubt that the 2015 and 2016 efforts together reached thousands more students, faculty, staff, and local residents than had the university's previous small-scale observances of Constitution and Citizenship Day. Looking beyond raw attendance numbers, moreover, several considerations suggest that the Week's programming has resonated in a number of less measurable yet still important ways. For instance, several faculty members at the university have intentionally piggybacked on the week's themes by embedding consideration of civic engagement and citizenship issues at appropriate times into their courses. On that front, examples from the first two years include courses in political theory, American politics, constitutional law, sociology, criminal justice, theater, and English. Campus student organizations focused on criminal justice, politics, and pre-law studies have used Citizenship and Democracy Week events as opportunities to advertise their own programming and recruit new members. On-campus voter registration efforts during the week—including those aimed at the newly minted US citizens who participated in the naturalization ceremony held on campus—have netted scores of newly registered voters. Hamilton's daily newspaper, the *Journal-News*, has prominently featured stories on the Week's events and themes both in print and online.

Also worth noting here is the undeniably positive effect that the planning and staging of Citizenship and Democracy Week has had in fostering relationships among its leaders and contributors that transcend traditional disciplinary silos for faculty as well as the broader faculty–staff and town–gown divisions that can hinder effective collaboration in higher education environments.[8] To be sure, some of the collaborative work done in developing and implementing Citizenship and Democracy Week has simply built upon pre-existing professional and personal ties among key players; for instance, the MUH director of civic engagement and the political scientist who has chaired the effort from the outset had previously worked together on a range of other community service projects over several years. Yet in other cases, it was the months-long work on Citizenship and Democracy Week itself that serendipitously provided new opportunities for those involved to strengthen existing interpersonal ties with colleagues and forge new relationships both inside and outside of the university. For instance, the work that has been done jointly on Citizenship and Democracy Week by the civic engagement offices on the Oxford, Middletown, and Hamilton campuses—which generally operate independently of one another at the university—has clearly yielded greater levels of inter-campus cooperation on other projects as well as improved patterns of communication among key staff members. In a similar way, the partnerships developed initially for Citizenship and Democracy Week with county elections officials, local political reporters, and community leaders have already spun off several fruitful byproducts including guest lectures to Miami classes, collaborations on voter registration and recruitment of poll workers, increased sharing of faculty expertise with regional media, and, during the 2016 election season, two jointly sponsored "meet the candidates" events.

Perhaps most importantly, anonymous post-event surveys conducted via Qualtrics (an online survey platform) of student participants following the 2015 and 2016 programs provide at least indirect evidence that Citizenship and Democracy Week has yielded significant educational benefits and positive attitudinal changes among those in its target audience as well. In the 2015 post-program survey, participants were asked to assess the impact of the week's events on their levels of interest in civic affairs and their levels of knowledge about politics.[9] The relevant data are summarized in table 15.1.

Altogether, 95.6% (22 of 23) of survey respondents said that the 2015 Week's events had increased their *level of interest* in politics by either "a little" (30.4%) or "a lot" (65.2%). Likewise, 78.3% (18 of 23 respondents) indicated that the Week's events had increased their *level of knowledge* of politics and community affairs by "a lot."

Five additional questions on the 2015 post-program survey asked participants to report the likely effect of their participation in Citizenship and Democracy Week on their levels of engagement in various forms of civic action in the future. Table 15.2 summarizes that data.

Table 15.1 Participant Self-Reporting of Impact on Interest and Knowledge Levels (2015)					
SURVEY QUESTION	decreased by a lot	decreased by a little	neither decreased nor increased	increased by a little	increased by a lot
My participation in Citizenship and Democracy Week _____ my level of interest in politics and community affairs. (n = 23).	0 (0%)	0 (0%)	1 (4.4%)	7 (30.4%)	15 (65.2%)
My participation in Citizenship and Democracy Week _____ my level of knowledge about politics and community affairs (n = 23).	0 (0%)	0 (0%)	0 (0%)	5 (21.7%)	18 (78.3%)

As table 15.2 shows, almost 70% (16 of 23) of respondents in the 2015 program survey "strongly agree[d]" that their participation had made them more likely than before to vote in future elections. Clear majorities also indicated a greater likelihood in the future to talk with neighbors and friends about politics and community affairs (87%; 20 of 23 respondents), contact elected officials to express their political views (52.2%; 12 of 23 respondents), attend meetings of local governmental agencies (68.2%; 15 of 22 respondents), and follow news and current events about politics and community affairs (86.4%; 19 of 22 respondents). As one anonymous 2015 participant commented on the survey, the Week's events made him/her "much, much more likely to become involved in the community" because "becoming familiar with the processes has made me feel more comfortable becoming involved in the process." Another reported that he/she "learned that you don't have to be well known or famous to make a change. That was huge for me and these events truly changed my outlook on politics for the good."

Table 15.2 Participant Self-Reporting of Impact on Future Participation in Civic Affairs (2015)					
Because of my participation in Citizenship and Democracy Week, I am now more likely to: (n = 23)	*Strongly agree*	*Somewhat agree*	*Neither agree nor disagree*	*Somewhat disagree*	*Strongly disagree*
Vote in future elections (n = 23)	16 (69.6%)	3 (13.0%)	3 (13.0%)	0 (0%)	1 (4.4%)
Contact my elected representatives in government to express by views on public issues (n = 23)	7 (30.4%)	5 (21.8%)	7 (30.4%)	3 (13.0%)	1 (4.4%)
Talk with my neighbors and friends about politics and community affairs (n = 23)*	13 (56.5%)	7 (30.4%)	3 (13.0%)	0 (0%)	0 (0%)
Attend meetings of local governmental agencies (for instance: city council or school board) (n = 22)*	8 (36.4%)	7 (31.8%)	5 (22.7%)	1 (4.6%)	1 (4.6%)
Follow news and current events about politics and community affairs*	15 (68.2%)	4 (18.2%)	2 (9.1%)	0 (0%)	1 (4.6%)
*Aggregate percentages may not equal 100% due to rounding.					

Responses to the 2016 post-event survey largely echoed the same basic themes. Table 15.3 summarizes data provided in response to survey prompts—structured this time in a retrospective pre-test format[10]—that essentially asked participants to compare their levels of knowledge about and interest in American politics and local government before and after the 2016 program.

Table 15.3 Participant Self-Reporting of Levels of Interest in/Knowledge of Politics and Local Government (2016)						
	BEFORE PARTICIPATION IN 2016 C&D WEEK (POOLED RESULTS)			AFTER PARTICIPATION IN 2016 C&D WEEK (POOLED RESULTS)		
GENERALLY SPEAKING, HOW MUCH:	None	A little bit/ some	A lot/a great deal	None	A little bit/ some	A lot/a great deal
Personal knowledge about American politics did/do you have*	1 (2.2%)	28 (60.9%)	17 (37.0%)	0 (0.0%)	18 (39.1%)	28 (60.9%)
Personal knowledge about local government did/do you have	9 (20.0%)	30 (66.7%)	6 (13.3%)	0 (0.0%)	26 (57.8%)	19 (42.2%)
Personal interest in American politics did/do you have	5 (10.4%)	21 (43.8%)	22 (45.8%)	1 (2.1%)	7 (14.9%)	39 (83.0%)
Personal interest in local government did/do you have	9 (20.0%)	26 (57.8%)	10 (22.2%)	1 (2.2%)	22 (48.9%)	22 (48.9%)
*Aggregate percentages may not equal 100% due to rounding.						

Here, too, the survey data provide support for the view that Citizenship and Democracy Week has been effective both in advancing participants' learning about American politics and government and in sparking higher levels of personal interest in those subjects. Regarding levels of civic knowledge, 2016 program participants generally judged their own pre-event levels of understanding to be middling at best: only about one in three (37.0%) claimed "a lot" or "a great deal" of prior knowledge about American politics; even fewer—roughly one in eight (13.3%)—claimed similarly high levels of prior knowledge about local government. Yet these same respondents generally judged their levels of knowledge *after* the event in much more positive ways. More than 60% assessed their own post-event understanding of American politics to fall within the highest two categories ("a lot" or "a great deal") offered in the survey. In the same way, 42.2%—more than three times the pre-event percentage— claimed after Citizenship and Democracy Week to know "a lot" or "a great deal" about local government as well.

The same positive post-event movement can be seen in the general levels of *interest* in politics and local government reported by 2016 participants as well. Even prior to Citizenship and Democracy Week, the vast majority—almost 90% (43 of 48)—harbored at least "a little bit" of interest in American politics; similarly, 80% (36 of 45) of respondents claimed at least "a little bit" of interest in local government as well. Even from those somewhat high baseline levels, however, we see in the post-event response data a clear rise both in the overall number of respondents who claimed to be interested in the subjects at hand and the overall levels of intensity with which those interests were held. Indeed, in the wake of Citizenship and Democracy Week, all but one (97.9%) of the respondents claimed to hold at least "a little bit" of interest in American politics—with 83.0% claiming to hold "a lot" or "a great deal." Quite similarly, all but one (97.8%) reported at least "a little bit" of interest in local government after participating in the Week; among those, half claimed to be interested either "a lot" or "a great deal."

Beyond looking at knowledge and interest levels, the 2016 post-event survey also asked respondents to report whether their participation in Citizenship and Democracy Week had increased the likelihood that they would engage in various forms of civic action in the future. Table 15.4 summarizes that data.

Table 15.4 Participant Self-Reporting of Impact on Future Participation in Civic Affairs (2016)					
BECAUSE OF MY PARTICIPATION IN CITIZENSHIP AND DEMOCRACY WEEK, I AM NOW MORE LIKELY TO:	Strongly agree	Agree	Neither agree nor disagree	Disagree	Strongly disagree
Vote in future elections (n=41)	25 (61.0%)	7 (17.1%)	7 (17.1%)	1 (2.4%)	1 (2.4%)
Contact government officials to express my views on public issues (n=40)	10 (25%)	13 (32.5%)	14 (35.0%)	1 (2.5%)	2 (5.0%)
Talk with my neighbors and friends about politics and community affairs (n=41)	13 (31.7%)	14 (34.1%)	11 (26.8%)	2 (4.9%)	1 (2.4%)
Attend meetings of local governmental agencies (for instance, city council or school board) (n=41)	7 (17.1%)	12 (29.3%)	14 (34.1%)	6 (14.6%)	2 (4.9%)
Keep up with news about politics and community affairs (n=41)	16 (39.0%)	17 (41.5%)	7 (17.1%)	0 (0.0%)	1 (2.4%)
Volunteer to work on a political campaign (n=41)	6 (14.6%)	6 (14.6%)	23 (56.1%)	2 (4.9%)	4 (9.8%)
Join a community non-profit organization (n=41)*	3 (7.3%)	17 (41.5%)	17 (41.5%)	0 (0.0%)	4 (9.8%)
Run for political office myself (n=41)*	3 (7.3%)	6 (14.6%)	16 (39.0%)	8 (19.5%)	8 (19.5%)
*Aggregate percentages may not equal 100% due to rounding.					

Here as well, the views of 2016 program participants largely mirrored those offered by participants from the year before. More than three quarters (78.1% either "strongly agree[d]" or "agree[d]") said that participation in the Week had increased their likelihood of voting in the future. Four out of five (80.5%) reported a greater likelihood of keeping up with news about politics and community affairs. Almost two thirds (65.8%) expressed a greater inclination to talk with neighbors and friends about political and community affairs; at the same time, more than half (57.5%) similarly indicated a greater likelihood that they would contact government officials to express their views. Near majorities expressed greater interest in attending meetings of governmental bodies (46.4%) and joining a community nonprofit organization (48.8%). And quite interestingly, sizeable minorities even expressed greater enthusiasm for the prospect of engaging directly in competitive politics themselves, either by volunteering for a political campaign (29.2%) or by running for office themselves (21.9%).

Finally, the 2016 survey also solicited information from respondents about their general attitudes toward four different modes of political and civic participation. Specifically, respondents were asked to report, regardless of their actual behavior, how important they believed it to be both before and after Citizenship and Democracy Week for people to engage in each of several common modes of civic engagement. Table 15.5 summarizes that data.

In table 15.5 on the following page, we can see clear evidence of positive movement overall in participant attitudes in the wake of Citizenship and Democracy Week. With respect to regular voting, a large majority of respondents reported already holding strong views in favor of this form of participation even before taking part in Miami's 2016 program—perhaps echoing recent poll findings that show Americans generally consider voting to be a central duty of citizenship.[11] Yet even among those already so committed, the Week's events apparently strengthened the intensity of that view at least for some; indeed, after Citizenship and Democracy Week, just over 90% viewed regular voting as "important" or "very important"—up from 73.3% prior to the Week.

Beyond voting, other indicators of positive change in respondents' attitudes about civic engagement emerge from the data as well. Before Citizenship and Democracy Week, 81.8% be-

Table 15.5 Levels of Importance Attached by 2016 Participants to Various Forms of Engagement						
	BEFORE PARTICIPATION IN 2016 C&D WEEK			**AFTER PARTICIPATION IN 2016 C&D WEEK**		
GENERALLY SPEAKING, HOW IMPORTANT DID/DO YOU THINK IT WAS/IS FOR PEOPLE TO:	*Not at all/ not very important*	*Somewhat important*	*Important/very important*	*Not at all/ not very important*	*Somewhat important*	*Important/very important*
*Vote regularly in elections**	3 (6.7%)	9 (20.0%)	33 (73.3%)	2 (4.5%)	2 (4.5%)	40 (90.9%)
Keep up with news about politics and community affairs	8 (18.2%)	13 (29.5%)	23 (52.3%)	0 (0.0%)	5 (11.4%)	39 (88.6%)
Regularly attend meetings of government agencies (for instance, city council meetings, school board meetings, etc.)	24 (53.3%)	14 (31.1%)	7 (15.6%)	3 (6.7%)	20 (44.4%)	22 (48.9%)
Discuss politics and community affairs with their neighbors, family members and friends	16 (37.2%)	11 (25.6%)	16 (37.2%)	3 (7.0%)	11 (25.6%)	29 (67.4%)
*Aggregate percentages may not equal 100% due to rounding.						

lieved that keeping up with political and community news is at least "somewhat important;" just over half (52.3%) thought it "important" or "very important." After the Week, by contrast, 100% agreed that doing so was at least "somewhat important"—and 88.6% rated it as "important" at the least. Furthermore, fewer than half (46.7%) of respondents before Citizenship and Democracy Week viewed it as being at least "somewhat important" for Americans to regularly attend government meetings, and only 15.6% viewed it as "important." After the Week, by contrast, almost half (48.9%) had adopted the latter view. On a similar note, just over six in ten (62.8%) of respondents prior to Citizenship and Democracy Week attached any real importance to discussing politics and community affairs with family, friends, and neighbors. After the Week, by contrast, 93% identified such political activity as now being at least "somewhat important"—and over two-thirds (67.4%) identified such discussions as being "important" or "very important."

Of course, given the methodological caveats that necessarily come with the use of anonymous post-program surveys[12]—as well as the relatively small sample sizes mustered for the two surveys reported previously—we must wait for additional data from future iterations of Citizenship and Democracy Week before drawing more confident conclusions about its educational, attitudinal, and behavioral impact. Still, early indications suggest that the Week's integrated programs of events—which by design serve both a civic education and a civic engagement function—have been effective over its first two years in delivering positive results in both arenas.

CONCLUSIONS

Now only two years old, Miami University's annual Citizenship and Democracy Week is still very much a work in progress. Indeed, as of this writing, planning by a multi-disciplinary group of faculty and staff for the third iteration of the program, to be held in mid-September 2017, is well underway. Still, even at this early point, the history of this distinctive civic engagement effort at Miami already offers a number of practical lessons about organizing and implementing such programs that might usefully inform others who may be thinking about similar initiatives of their own.

One clear lesson of Miami's experience is that civically minded faculty members hoping to launch a broad, interdisciplinary civic engagement program such as Citizenship and Democracy Week need not wait for a specific directive or approval from university administrators before taking action. Neither must they wait for the establishment of a significant dedicated budget or the provision of dedicated administrative or logistical support before getting started. To be sure, the institutional environment must be such that a grassroots initiative by faculty will not be actively stymied or discouraged by adverse university policies, severe resource limitations, or resistance from those in positions of authority. (Indeed, a faculty member would certainly be wise to survey their own unique institutional landscape before tackling such a project to have a clear-eyed view of likely roadblocks as well as possible sources of support.) Further, the ability to draw from assigned accounts or other dedicated sources of institutional support is certainly a "plus" that expands the range of programming ideas that can be pursued. Nonetheless, the Miami experience recounted above suggests that such dedicated support is not a prerequisite to getting a significant multi-event program off the ground; to the contrary, a variety of valuable events—such as voter registration drives, on-campus panel discussions, community-based deliberative dialogues, on-campus sessions of governmental bodies, civic volunteer fairs, "Democracy Wall" dialogues, and theatrical productions—can be staged successfully with relatively little expenditure of tangible institutional resources beyond those (e.g., classroom or meeting space, e-mail, physical facilities support) already available generally to faculty members at most institutions. More important than a large budget or a clear administrative mandate, it seems, is the good will and enthusiasm of like-minded colleagues (both faculty and staff) and community partners who are willing to contribute their own time and talents to the effort.

Another lesson is that broad, interdisciplinary programs such as Citizenship and Democracy Week will likely produce benefits that are broader in scope and impact than one might initially expect. For the organizational leaders of such an effort, the preparatory work itself—which, in Miami's case, has involved extensive interactions among faculty, staff, and community partners situated across multiple disciplines, campuses, and work settings—is quite likely to create a rich web of interpersonal networks that can yield useful new collaborations on teaching, scholarship, and service-related projects in serendipitous ways. For the college or university, such a program can strengthen its ties to its community—while offering for its students a meaningful way to learn more about politics and government, develop personal interests in civic affairs, and foster habits of participation that will hopefully carry far into the future. For the broader community, meanwhile, such a program, if designed properly, can provide a valuable service by linking government and neighborhood groups to civically minded faculty, students, and staff and by providing civic education and engagement opportunities to local residents in a readily accessible way.

Finally, the experience recounted above suggests that a faculty member who ultimately opts to organize a broad, interdisciplinary civic engagement effort like Citizenship and Democracy Week will likely increase their chances of success by keeping at least three very practical tips in mind. First, they should expect that the start-up costs in the first year, especially in terms of their own time and energy, will be quite substantial. Indeed, the faculty entrepreneur in this context will likely confront a range of collective action challenges related to communication, recruitment, and organization that are already quite familiar to most political scientists; accordingly, they should take care to launch such an effort only at a time when their other personal and professional responsibilities allow them to devote significant attention to the task.

Second, they should strive in leading the effort to be as inclusive of diverse faculty, staff, and community perspectives as possible at every stage—even if doing so results in delay, inefficiency, and a degree of "messiness" in the planning and implementation process. As Timothy Meinke observed in his insightful study of interdisciplinary cooperation at Lynchburg College, it is essential to long-term success that leaders of a grassroots interdisciplinary initiative gain and sustain the "buy-in" of their colleagues—especially when no other significant incentives exist for them to commit their time, energy, and resources to the collective effort.[13] Perhaps the best way to earn such investment by colleagues is to ensure that they feel that their ideas and points of view are being genuinely and consistently heard.

Finally, it is essential that leaders of a broad collaborative effort such as Citizenship and Democracy Week take great care to maintain a spirit of genuine interdisciplinarity both at the outset of their work and in later stages as their collective project inevitably evolves. Project leaders must develop and articulate a clear basic vision for the effort to ensure that the resulting program stays on track and retains a certain level of substantive coherence. At the same time, organizers should studiously avoid allowing their own preconceived (and often disciplinary-based) notions of what civic engagement or civic education "looks like" to foreclose experimentation with innovative approaches that may broaden the appeal and impact of the overall program that they coordinate. Simply put, faculty members in theater, English, music, engineering, or other academic fields may have ideas for innovative and engaging programs for the campus and community that would never occur to a political scientist. (Indeed, such was the case with the "Social Justice Theater" event that is now a core part of Miami's Citizenship and Democracy Week.) The same may be said about staff colleagues as well as civic leaders, government officials, and others active "in the field." Remaining open to such new ideas, even as an interdisciplinary program builds upon previous success, is essential to ensuring a continuing freshness in the program over time as well as continued growth in the network of supporting partners who are vital to sustaining the effort. ∎

ENDNOTES

1. See, e.g., John P. Forren and Theresa Conover, *Ohio Civic Health Index Report* (Washington, DC: National Conference on Citizenship 2016); Alison Rios Millett McCartney, Elizabeth A. Bennion, and Dick Simpson eds., *Teaching Civic Engagement: From Student to Active Citizen* (Washington, DC: American Political Science Association, 2013); National Task Force on Civic Learning and Democratic Engagement, *A Crucible Moment: College Learning and Democracy's Future* (Washington, DC: Association of American Colleges and Universities, 2012); National Conference on Citizenship 2009. As detailed in Somit and Tanenhaus (1967) and Schachter (1998), the American Political Science Association focused intently on issues of civic education and engagement during the first quarter-century of its existence. A landmark in the APSA's renewal of interest in such issues was the appointment in 1996 of the Task Force on Civic Education for the Twenty-First Century. See APSA Task Force on Civic Education 1998.

2. Margaret A. Post, Elaine Ward, Nicholas V. Longo, and John Saltmarsh, eds., *Publicly Engaged Scholars: Next-Generation Engagement and the Future of Higher Education* (Sterling, VA: Stylus Publishing, LLC., 2016).

3. In a recent analysis of the civic engagement minor offered at Lynchburg College, Timothy Meinke noted the particular importance of broad faculty and administrative "buy-in" when seeking to institutionalize an interdisciplinary civic engagement program on campus. See Meinke "Learning Objectives and Outcomes of an Interdisciplinary Minor in Civic Engagement," in *Teaching Civic Engagement: From Student to Active Citizen*, ed. Alison Rios Millett McCartney, Elizabeth A. Bennion, and Dick Simpson (Washington, DC: APSA, 2013), 350–52.

4. See Stephen Leonard "'Pure Futility and Waste': Academic Political Science and Civic Education," *PS: Political Science & Politics* 32(4): 749–754, 752. As Leonard pointed out, the general prioritization in American higher education of faculty research productivity over public or professional service creates strong disincentives for faculty across various disciplines to devote their time and energies to long-term civic engagement projects. Assessing the corresponding likelihood of sustaining faculty interest in such projects, he bluntly observed: "If you want to get ahead in academic political science, you don't spend your time engaging in 'civic education.' You spend it doing research. The rewards for excellence in civic education are few, far between, and little coveted; the rewards for publication are many, immediate, and—for so many academics—highly significant."

    Tenured and tenure-track faculty at Miami's regional campuses, by contrast, are encouraged by formal institutional policies regarding promotion and tenure to engage in significant service-related activities. More specifically, the regional campuses since 2008 have maintained a "Service as Second" policy that effectively rewards faculty commitments to service and sets criteria for evaluation of faculty work in public outreach and engagement.

5. Paul Rogat Loeb, *Soul of a Citizen: Living With Conviction in Challenging Times, New and Revised Edition* (New York: St. Martin's Press, 2010).

6. Forren and Conover, *Ohio Civic Health Index Report*.

7. An extensive body of research suggests that exposure by college-aged students to significant opportunities for political discussion, reflection, and action is correlated with greater political understanding, a heightened sense of political efficacy, and heightened expectations for future involvement in political action. See, Anne Colby, Elizabeth Beaumont, Thomas Ehrlich, and John Corngold, *Educating for Democracy: Preparing Undergraduates for Responsible Political Engagement* (San Francisco: Jossey-Bass, 2007).

8. For a thought-provoking critique of traditional concerns about disciplinary silos in higher education, see Jerry A.

Jacobs, *In Defense of Disciplines: Interdisciplinarity and Specialization in the Research University* (Chicago: The University of Chicago Press, 2014), chapters 2–6.

9. Because Citizenship and Democracy Week events are generally open to the public—and because neither personal contact information nor personal identifiers are requested from attendees at events—the author was unable to obtain a verifiably representative sample of attendees for the surveys discussed in this chapter. Rather, the 2015 and 2016 post-event surveys discussed herein were distributed in each case to all Miami University students, aged 18 or older, who were identified by event organizers as having attended one or more Citizenship and Democracy Week events. Per Miami University Institutional Review Board specifications, no personal identifiers were solicited or maintained for respondents, and participation in the surveys was completely voluntarily.

10. The survey instrument used to gather data from 2016 Week participants differed from the 2015 survey both in format and in substantive content. Regarding the former, the 2016 survey employed a "post then pre" (or "retrospective pretest") methodology so as to solicit information about participants' levels of knowledge, interest, and disposition toward political action both before and after their participation in Citizenship and Democracy Week. For useful discussions of the limitations associated with this survey methodology, see Laura Griner Hill and Drew L. Betz, "Revising the Retrospective Pretest." *American Journal of Evaluation* 26(4): 501–517; Theodore Lamb, "The Retrospective Pretest: An Imperfect But Useful Tool." *The Evaluation Exchange* 11(2): 18.

11. For instance, an Associated Press-GfK poll in December 2014 found that about 90% of Americans viewed voting as at least a "somewhat important" civic duty. See Kendall Breitman, "Poll: Americans' Sense of Civic Duty Wanes." *Politico*, December 29, 2014.

12. See note 10 above.

13. See Meinke, "Learning Objectives and Outcomes," 352.

Teaching Faculty to Teach Civic Engagement: Interdisciplinary Models to Facilitate Pedagogical Success

16

SARAH SURAK, CHRISTOPHER JENSEN, ALISON RIOS MILLETT McCARTNEY, AND ALEXANDER POPE

This chapter examines faculty development programming designed to support and encourage the incorporation of civic engagement assignments within normal curricular offerings. By assessing faculty development seminars at two comprehensive institutions, the authors identify the perceived benefits of participants as well as where improvements might be made. The purpose of this chapter is to serve as a model for universities developing programs to support faculty efforts. Through focus groups with participating faculty, the authors find that key factors for success included financial, logistical, and programmatic support as well as the institutionalization of the recognition of efforts in merit, tenure, and promotion processes.

A s many colleges and universities leap into the worthwhile endeavor of civic engagement education, some administrators who make these pledges forget to secure faculty buy-in or to provide the resources faculty need to provide high quality civic education courses. Most of today's faculty were not trained in this type of pedagogy, if they were trained at all in pedagogy. Civic engagement education efforts cannot succeed without sufficient training and support.[1] Faculty development seminars serve as one method to incentivize, encourage, compensate, and reward faculty for designing rigorous and appropriate programming. This chapter assesses the effectiveness of two similar public institutions, Salisbury University and Towson University, in encouraging civic engagement and service-learning (CESL) activities within undergraduate and graduate classrooms.

We begin by providing basic overviews of the universities. We then describe data collected through interviews conducted with faculty who have participated in each of the programs and created or adapted courses as a result. Due to the newness of both programs, we only have a few years of data and participants, limiting our findings. However, as many such programs are also just developing, we believe these findings can help faculty and administrators seeking to develop or advance similar programs at their institutions. Overall, we discovered that the most important benefits of the programs include increased financial, technical, and professional support for faculty; enhanced teaching of traditional course content; and, for some faculty, additional areas for research. Both universities also recorded an increase in civic engagement education options across disciplines. Our findings suggest that specific resources are required to consolidate and sustain existing investments and achieve the goal of providing widespread, regular options for student civic engagement education. Programs need to provide financial and personnel resources to address the logistical barriers of community-based teaching. They also must institutionalize civic engagement education and research through meaningful tenure, promotion, and merit criteria at all decision-making levels. Additional administrative recognition of faculty who invest time and energy into this kind of education is also useful in promoting faculty involvement and maximizing opportunities for student engagement.

INSTITUTIONAL FRAMEWORKS FOR FACULTY DEVELOPMENT AT SALISBURY UNIVERSITY AND TOWSON UNIVERSITY

Salisbury University and Towson University are state-supported, comprehensive universities in the University System of Maryland (not branch campuses of the University of Maryland). Recently, each has undertaken expansion of its civic engagement efforts with a particular focus on faculty development and training. As part of the same state system and pool of students and as similarly classified institutions dependent on state rather than private support, the universities are fairly similar and thus appropriate for comparison. The schools have similar funding levels, institutional structures, student qualifications, faculty workloads, and geographic locations. Simply put, they face similar opportunities and constraints in terms of resources, providing a valuable opportunity for a case study evaluating the effects of different approaches to faculty development on the quantity and quality of civic engagement coursework developed on comparable campuses. We begin this chapter by describing the programmatic efforts and institutional structures supporting civic engagement initiatives to provide a foundation for drawing out lessons learned from these two programs which are applicable to creating or enhancing similar faculty development programs at other institutions.

SALISBURY UNIVERSITY: CIVIC ENGAGEMENT ACROSS THE CURRICULUM

Salisbury University (SU) is a comprehensive public institution on the Eastern Shore of Maryland serving approximately 9,000 students.[2] While offering master's and doctoral programs, SU's educational focus is geared toward its undergraduate population. The average student-to-faculty ratio is 17:1, and faculty teach an average course load of six courses bearing three to four credit hours each year, which must total 24 credit hours.[3] Like many universities today, SU is interested in promoting civic engagement activities on campus. Its mission statement embodies this focus, stating, "Our highest purpose is to empower our students with the knowledge, skills, and core values that contribute to active citizenship, gainful employment, and life-long learning in a democratic society and interdependent world."[4] These civic themes are continued within the university's Values Statement: "The core values of Salisbury University are excellence, student centeredness, learning, community, civic engagement, and diversity."[5]

Salisbury's Institute for Public Affairs and Civic Engagement (PACE) supports these efforts through faculty development programming.[6] Founded in 1999, PACE promotes democratic citizenship cultivation and education through campus-wide public affairs programming and civic engagement offerings. While the Institute's public affairs programming has remained fairly consistent over the years, focusing for the most part on voter registration drives and hosting speakers and community forums, its CESL efforts have taken various forms. Early efforts involved recruiting faculty to teach one-credit-hour special topics civic engagement courses for the Institute as overloads on a voluntary basis. More recently, though, PACE has begun encouraging faculty across the disciplines to incorporate civic engagement within their normal course offerings. The goal is to move from providing special, standalone courses offered on a limited basis to providing a general incorporation of civic engagement activities across a wide range of courses that reach the entire student body. This change increases the ability for students in professional programs with limited elective offerings to experience civic engagement activities as part of their university education.

PACE encourages faculty from across the disciplines to incorporate civic engagement into the classroom through its seminar Civic Engagement Across the Curriculum (CEAC).[7] Over 10 weeks, faculty are provided with the physical and intellectual space, tools, and resources needed to incorporate a civic engagement component into a new or existing course. Successful completion of the seminar involves submitting a revised syllabus, an outline of the assignment prompt, and a course assessment. Faculty who complete these tasks receive a $500 stipend to support research, conference travel, and/or civic engagement activities within their courses. CEAC originated as a program to encourage and support faculty within the Fulton School of Liberal Arts in the incorporation of a civic engagement component as the fourth credit hour of courses. Following a curricular model adopted in 2010, most faculty, rather than incorporate additional classroom or lab time, select from a suite of options designated by the Code of Maryland Regulations (COMAR). These options, referred to as a "one-hour enhancement," allow including civic engagement or service-learning to meet the 45 additional hours of learning for the credit hour.

Now in its fourth iteration (fall 2016), CEAC is open to all university faculty and fulltime instructors. Faculty apply for participation, and seminar member selection attempts to create a broad and diverse cohort with a wide range of disciplines, years of teaching, and prior civic engagement experience. Faculty intending to teach their revised civic engagement course the following spring semester (increasing likelihood of faculty implementation) are given preference. While the four-credit model has not yet spread to all SU programs, the seminar encourages all faculty to make the civic engagement component a substantial portion of course activities and grading (referred to in the seminar literature as the "enhancement").

Each CEAC cohort of six to eight faculty meets for 10 consecutive weeks (nine times in person, one time online) for 75 minutes. Faculty are expected to participate in all weekly meetings and complete all assignments.[8] The first portion of the seminar focuses on defining civic engagement and emphasizing how to differentiate it from other forms of community-based learning, such as students interviewing local elected officials to learn about government versus, for example, a one-day volunteer event to build a house.[9] In this initial portion of the seminar, coordinators also describe the goals of civic engagement within the university setting and how these goals connect to the mission of the university and the institute.

Drawing on literature from secondary and post-secondary research, the seminar then outlines frameworks and theories that underpin civic engagement in the college classroom. Topics such as disciplinary literacy, defining communities of service, identifying relevant community issues, and generating compelling questions serve as starting points for open discussion. While seminar readings are for the most part interdisciplinary, faculty also read articles and share examples of civic engagement within their own fields. Seminar coordinators are quick to acknowledge that faculty are the experts on how civic engagement can and should be deployed within their discipline, not the seminar cocoordinators. Regardless of the discipline, four guiding principles frame the goals for assignment creation: investigating a compelling question tied to one's discipline, incorporating communication with community members outside the classroom, thoughtful planning for or delivery of action items, and encouraging students to move toward the "justice-oriented citizen."[10] Such assignments should include academic rigor, relation to a pressing social issue, and the sharing of enhancement outcomes in a setting beyond the classroom.[11]

CEAC has undergone a good deal of transformation over the past four years. Faculty readings and resources are updated continually. To date, more than 20 faculty members have participated in CEAC from a range of disciplines including economics, geography, and art (see table 16.1). CEAC faculty projects include activities such as Holocaust Remembrance Day events reaching more than 5,000 members of the local community, a student-facilitated informational forum on animal rights legislation debated in the Maryland General Assembly, and support for the establishment of a program in which college students plan and lead philosophical discussions to invoke critical thinking with students in local, underserved elementary schools.[12]

The institute strives for continuous improvement as well as contributions to the larger body of civic engagement literature. The seminar operates in conjunction with a research project

Table 16.1 CEAC Enhanced Courses 2015–2017

DEPARTMENT	LEVEL OF COURSE WITH A REVISED CIVIC ENGAGEMENT COMPONENT	NUMBER OF TIMES OFFERED	NUMBER OF STUDENTS IMPACTED
Art	100	Fall 2015	15
Communication Arts	400	Spring 2015, Spring 2016, Spring 2017	44
Communication Arts	300	Spring 2016, Fall 2016	24
Communication Arts	300	Spring 2017	18
Communication Arts	200 and 400	Spring 2015, Fall 2015, Fall 2016	94
Economics	300	Spring 2016/ Spring 2017	50
Education	400	Spring 2017	22
Education	300	Spring 2015	22
Education	300	-	-
Education	Graduate	Spring 2015	8
English	100	Spring 2015, Fall 2015, Spring 2016	94
English	400 and Graduate	Fall 2016	27
Foreign Language	100	-	-
Foreign Language	300	Spring 2017	14
Geography and Geosciences	400	Fall 2016	15
Health and Sport Sciences	400	Spring 2017	18
History	300	Fall 2015	26
History	200	Fall 2015	25
Philosophy	200	Fall 2015, Fall 2016, Fall 2017	37
Philosophy	300	Fall 2014/ Spring 2017	50
Philosophy	100	Fall 2014, Spring 2015, Fall 2015, Spring 2016, Fall 2016, Spring 2017	158
Political Science	100	Fall 2016, Spring 2015,	68
Political Science	300	Fall 2014, Fall 2016	59
Sociology	300	Fall 2014	29

conducted by the two SU coordinators and approved by the Salisbury University institutional review board (IRB) to assess the usefulness of the seminar as a pedagogical method for promoting course revision.[13] These efforts are funded through the PACE annual budget and supported by a graduate research assistant.

TOWSON UNIVERSITY: OFFICE OF CIVIC ENGAGEMENT

Located eight miles north of Baltimore, Maryland, Towson University (TU) offers students a wide variety of academic programs, coupled with the close-knit community and highly personalized approach of a small college.[14] The current enrollment is approximately 19,000 undergraduates and 3,200 graduates pursuing 64 undergraduate majors, 46 master's programs and four doctoral degree programs.[15] Founded in 1866 as a teacher's college, TU's mission has since expanded to "…foster intellectual inquiry and critical thinking, preparing graduates who will serve as effective, ethical leaders and engaged citizens."[16] Towson University's strong partnerships with public and private organizations provide unique opportunities for research, internships, and jobs. Over two-thirds of courses have fewer than 29 students, with an overall faculty to student ratio of 17:1. Faculty workload for the average instructor is seven to eight three-credit courses per academic year.

In 2007, TU established the Towson University Civic Engagement Advisory Board, including a service-learning subcommittee. The subcommittee's charge was to explore and implement various strategies to increase service-learning as a way to increase civic engagement education across campus. The subcommittee started by identifying faculty at TU involved in service-learning to identify possible advocates and partners, hosting workshops to educate faculty about service-learning, and pinpointing obstacles to service-learning on campus. The obstacles uncovered during the process were insufficient pedagogical and logistical support for the faculty, lack of connections between faculty who were utilizing service-learning pedagogy, and little financial support for their projects. In addition, faculty were concerned about their departments' perceptions of service-learning when it came to promotion, tenure, merit, and workload decisions.

Given the subcommittee's success in service-learning advocacy, the committee received funding the following year from the President's Office to hire a service-learning graduate assistant and launch the Service-Learning Faculty Fellows (SLFF) program and the Service-Learning Grant Program. The Faculty Fellows program was designed to bring interested faculty together to learn and develop service-learning courses and share their experiences, while the grant program helps faculty with funds to support their projects. TU also received a three-year grant to fund an AmeriCorps VISTA service-learning coordinator, whose role included developing resources for faculty and community partners, hosting community service fairs, working with the Service-Learning Subcommittee and Faculty Fellows, and hosting Service-Learning Workshops for TU faculty. These functions were housed in Student Affairs with a partnership with the Office of the Provost. The partnership was fundamental to the success of the program by splitting the costs of the program and bridging a gap between the curricular and cocurricular nature of service-learning.

The Service-Learning Subcommittee also made recommendations on key institutional needs to support faculty, including hiring a fulltime director for the Office of Civic Engagement, which was done in 2013, and a coordinator of community engagement and outreach a year later.[17] The director's responsibilities are to facilitate, coordinate, and develop curricular and cocurricular service-learning and civic engagement initiatives on campus, which include political engagement and environmental initiatives. The primary focus for the coordinator's role is facilitating the Service-Learning Faculty Fellows program and the service-learning grants and assisting the director. In addition, an experienced CESL faculty member works with the SLFF program, attending all meetings and serving as a mentor for new CESL faculty.

The Faculty Fellows program started in 2008 in cooperation with the Division of Academic Affairs to help faculty from a variety of disciplines to incorporate new service-learning components into their courses. Interested faculty members propose a service-learning initiative, explain the significance and expected impact of the project in the community, and describe how the service-learning project seeks to enhance traditional course-learning objectives and advance civic-education learning goals. Faculty apply to the program in the spring prior and must receive approval from their department chair and dean to participate and offer the resulting course.

Monthly meetings provide an opportunity for faculty to gain knowledge about service-learning and develop accompanying course materials and activities. To engage in dialogue on the process, faculty are given materials for each meeting both before and during discussions.[18] Cohorts are kept small—usually about five to eight faculty members—to enable full participation of each person in discussions and allow staff sufficient time to work with each participant. Each Faculty Fellow is awarded a $1,500 stipend (recently increased from $1,000). The faculty's stipend is split between the two terms (fall and spring). It is expected the faculty are teaching the service-learning course during the spring term. A couple of faculty members taught their course during the summer term. In the last three years, only one faculty member did not teach the course, leaving the university prior to the next academic term.[19] Several of the faculty who are participating in the SLFF program were already teaching a course, so the SLFF program assisted them in incorporating a service-learning project in their existing course (see table 16.2). The Office of Civic Engagement offered additional support through Service-Learning Grants and an evaluation[20] to measure the impact of service-learning at Towson University (see table 16.3).[21]

Table 16.2 CESL Enhanced Courses 2015–2017*		
DEPARTMENT	**LEVEL OF COURSE WITH A REVISED CIVIC ENGAGEMENT COMPONENT**	**NUMBER OF STU-DENTS IMPACTED***
Art & Design, Art History, Art Education	400	12
Audiology, Speech Language-Pathology, and Deaf Studies	300	362
Audiology, Speech Language-Pathology, and Deaf Studies	400	8
Biological Sciences	300	3*
Biological Sciences	400	4*
College of Business and Economics	400	70
Early Childhood/Special Education	300	30
Early Childhood/Special Education	400	53
Education	200	356
Educational Technology and Literacy	300	16
Elementary Education/Special Education	400	518
English	400	5
Family Studies & Community Development	300	881
Family Studies & Community Development	400	18
Family Studies & Community Development	500	8
Family Studies & Community Development	600	4*
Geology	400	44
Health Science	400	3*
Health Science	400	22
Health Science	500	2*
History	300	14
Honors College	200	292
Honors College	300	154
Interdisciplinary Arts Infusion	400	51
Interdisciplinary Health Professions	300	304
Interdisciplinary Health Professions	400	35
Mass Communications	400	12
Mathematics	300	32
Metropolitan Studies	400	3*
Nursing	400	122

Table 16.2 CESL Enhanced Courses 2015–2017 (Continued)*

DEPARTMENT	LEVEL OF COURSE WITH A REVISED CIVIC ENGAGEMENT COMPONENT	NUMBER OF STU-DENTS IMPACTED*
Occupational Therapy	300	149
Occupational Therapy	500	14
Occupational Therapy	600	245
Political Science	400	117
Production	400	18
Psychology	400	18
Sociology, Anthropology, and Criminal Justice	300	68
Sociology, Anthropology, and Criminal Justice	400	47
Spanish Translation	400	19
Special Education	400	41
Theatre Arts	400	6

*If 4 or less students are impacted, the students were enrolled in an independent studies course.

Table 16.3 TU Service-Learning (SL) Programs

	FY '13	FY '14	FY '15	FY '16
# of Service-Learning Faculty Fellows	3	7	5	7
# of faculty SL Coordinator worked with 1:1	3	4 not in the FF program	9 not in the FF program	10 not in the FF Program
Service-Learning Grants awarded	11, total of $8,601.36	9, total $7,246.58	9, total $9997.60	18, total of $10,137.03
# of students participating in SL through projects assisted by Civic Engagement department	219	196 130 from Faculty Fellows 66 from SL Grant	256 122 from FF; 135 SL Grants	473 167 from FF; 306 SL Grants
# of community partners involved in SL courses assisted by Civic Engagement department	35	14 (7 faculty fellows; 7 from SL grants)	25 (15 faculty fellows, 10 SL grants)	35 (16 faculty fellows, 19 SL grants)

Note: The program also included 28 Faculty Fellows from FY 2009 to FY 2012. Grants were given to 42 programs totaling $34,084.91. Full data only became available when the director was hired and the office was fully institutionalized.

The Towson University Strategic Plan calls for academic excellence and student success with an emphasis on internships and experiential learning.[22] The design of the Faculty Fellows program reflects the experience of the center addressing the reluctance of faculty to utilize community service in the classroom. A sample agenda of the program may be found on the companion website.

ASSESSING FACULTY DEVELOPMENT PROGRAMMING

As CESL is an increasingly popular component of classroom practice, it is imperative that faculty are not only willing and interested but also prepared to deliver rigorous course content. The success of programs providing this support, though, can only be ascertained through assessment. This chapter undertook program assessment for two reasons. First, Salisbury's PACE and Towson's Office of Civic Engagement seek to support internal efforts of continuous improvement of campus civic engagement education programming. Delivering a faculty development program is a first step toward supporting CESL faculty; external and internal assessment is needed to determine both whether or not a program is meeting its intended goals as well as how further improvement might occur. Second, the researchers seek to contribute to the greater body of knowledge in the field of civic-engagement education. This chapter describes the lessons learned from these assessments in an effort to support the development of similar programs elsewhere.

In surveys and interviews in May 2016, researchers from both universities appraised how faculty perceive the benefits of and areas needing improvement in each campus's professional development programs.[23] To complete this cross-university IRB-approved study, researchers from TU's Office of Civic Engagement traveled to Salisbury University to conduct focus group discussions of faculty trained in PACE's program. Researchers from SU's Institute for Public Affairs and Civic Engagement in turn traveled to Towson University to conduct focus groups of faculty who have completed TU's Faculty Fellows program. Focus groups used common, IRB-approved interview questions. The interviews were facilitated under the assumption that faculty may have different responses to the questions or be more ready to critique strengths and weaknesses of their home programs if they could make confidential comments. Researchers assigned a pseudonym to each focus group participant and recorded notes during each session. Two TU faculty were unable to attend focus groups but answered identical questions in one-on-one interviews over the telephone.[24] Follow-up questions were allowed, and discussions were loosely structured around themes to allow for an organic conversation growing out of participants' viewpoints, experiences, and concerns.[25]

Evaluation of SU Program by TU

At Salisbury University, 12 faculty participated in this study, 10 of whom identified as women and two as men. Of the group, two were full professors, five were associate professors, three were assistant professors. In addition, one adjunct faculty member and one graduate student participated. The participants, spanning all three iterations of the program, represented the following departments: philosophy, art, sociology, communication arts, modern languages, political science, English, and education. Two faculty participated in spring 2014, four had participated in the fall 2014, and six had participated in the fall 2015 semesters. The TU team conducted interviews with two groups of participants in May 2016 at SU and distilled their comments into three overall categories: strengths, areas for improvement, and institutional roadblocks to further development of the program.

CEAC: Benefits of Time, Support, and Knowledge at SU

The strengths of the PACE program generally center around issues of support, time, and knowledge. All faculty members mentioned or concurred that the most valuable component was "talking to other faculty." The time carved out by the program allowed them to have conversations about a wide variety of topics involved in creating and running CESL courses, even if they did not agree on the topic discussed or the methods, while also increasing their knowledge about pedagogy and CESL. These discussion periods allowed faculty to seek out new ideas, see other perspectives on how to reconceptualize CESL, "retool" their approach, and deliver the course content. Discussions also allowed faculty to "troubleshoot" and "brainstorm" teaching possibilities. As part of these group discussions, some participants stressed the beneficial opportunities for workshopping courses or peer review of assignments and syllabi.

The program provided a process that started with an online sharing of materials and continued with in-person discussions that were valuable because these interactions "guided us through the positive and critical feedback." There were also opportunities to talk about constructing and maintaining relationships with their community partners. Further, faculty even had the chance to debate the concept of civic engagement itself, pondering whether that was a useful, political, or "equitable" terminology for what they sought to bring to their students. An unexpected benefit of the cohort model was also learning how civic engagement applied to a wide array of disciplines. Overall, participants felt that they benefitted from "honing pedagogical skills" and being "forced to think about what our goals are and how they fit into the University and overall educational processes of a liberal arts education."

Participants mentioned other kinds of support that they felt were central to the program's success. As a permanent office, PACE provided them with key logistical assistance, especially with community partners, in addition to the actual faculty training program. The continued support through PACE was also noted as "relieving stress" because participants knew whom to talk to and where to get information about other available assistance. The program even ensured that they had lunch or food at some meetings, which helped participants to fit the program into busy schedules. Furthermore, some workshop participants noted that they felt, at times, that they were the only ones doing this kind of teaching and activity, especially in some disciplines. Thus, they perceived a "cheerleading effect" in "seeing the support through the cohort" and via PACE as vital to their success.

Another clear perceived pedagogical benefit of the program was how it enhanced instructors' teaching of traditional course content. Several faculty members felt that the CESL projects in the courses that grew from the program engaged the students more deeply in their learning and pushed them to move beyond abstract concepts. "Students cared more about animal rights through the civic engagement project," stated one faculty member. This sentiment was echoed by another faculty member, who noted, "I can use CE to get students more engaged in the material, beyond philosophical debates." In addition, some participants noted that they "learned the benefits of giving students more freedom in designing projects" and were "impressed by their creativity…in addressing problems."

Faculty also received small grants for participation and had the opportunity to apply for grants to support their CESL activities. One dean also provided awards for civically engaged faculty, public recognition which participants interpreted as an affirmation that some top academic administrators saw this pedagogy as valuable. However, some of these strengths also illuminated areas that needed further improvement and roadblocks to continuing such work.

CEAC: Roadblocks and Areas for Improvement at SU

Assigned readings were one key area of the program that participants agreed needed improvement. The faculty did appreciate being assigned readings, but some faculty thought that literature for service-learning was limited or not relevant to higher education. "We were using K–12 literature," stated one faculty member. This problem could be compounded when all of the faculty had not completed the readings before the seminar, thus limiting the discussion.

Participants also discussed the uncertain impact of their CESL work in promotion, tenure, and departmental evaluation. The faculty did believe that civic engagement could be part of any course and that many deans evaluate their chairs on how much civic engagement is happening in their department. Yet they also stated that while "being involved in local schools is considered as community service, as a pedagogy and [part of] giving opportunities to my students, it is unclear how it would count for me." Another participant explained, "I don't feel the same support from my department and chair and other faculty. There is a disconnect. Some want us to do more, but I don't feel like anyone in the department cares or recognizes the extra civic engagement teaching efforts as much." Another noted that when senior faculty reviewed and provided summary letters of annual reports, the participant could see "the interests of others in the summaries of my work," which did not include much acknowledgement of civic engagement efforts. Given this disconnect, some expressed their "fears" or the fears of others they sought to recruit into CESL or that credit for CESL would "not apply to me as a faculty member on campus." One participant offered a solution: "more positive pressure from the dean to department chairs if this pedagogy and the associated activities are important for the dean and University. [Administrators] can communicate that [goal] for annual reports."

In terms of resources, participants were overall pleased with what PACE offered. The incentives for participating in the program include a $500 stipend for travel. None of the faculty mentioned that they were disappointed with the incentive, but the interviewers heard a clear consensus that more funds should be available given the time investment required by faculty and increasing costs of conference attendance.

Finally, participants stated that what was needed in the program was an opportunity to have follow-up after the course. The faculty thought the program structure was quite beneficial, but they did not have time to process the course and the experiences with other people. The faculty wanted a chance to find out what everyone actually did and share their experiences, successes, and failures. Rather, the faculty felt that they just moved on to the next set of courses. This result is unsurprising, given that the communication and discussion was an enormous benefit of the program as courses were created. They suggested that PACE can improve its program by providing on-going support and resources.

EVALUATION OF TU PROGRAM BY SU

Towson University's Service-Learning Faculty Fellows program (SLFF) alumni participated in focus groups and interviews in May 2016 on the campus of Towson University and by telephone to identify strengths and weaknesses of the program alongside institutional and structural barriers to faculty support of service-learning programming. In total, six faculty members participated in a two-hour focus group, and two participated in individual interviews. Faculty affiliations include the departments of sociology, anthropology and criminal justice, elementary education, family studies and community development, foreign languages, interprofessional health studies, and political science. All participants except for two (associate professor and professor) held the rank of assistant professor at the time of the interview.

The TU faculty described how they enjoyed connecting with like-minded colleagues, were exposed to a wealth of useful resources, felt a greater connection to the community, and found both their teaching perspective and research program augmented in positive ways. Suggestions for program improvement mostly focused on supporting faculty after program completion. Faculty responses to the program were largely positive, but two faculty members did relay how incorporating the results of their service-learning courses within their research portfolios may have impacted their denial of tenure. Both indicated that this broadening of their research portfolios beyond what they were specifically hired to teach resulted in a perceived lack of research cohesion which detracted from other types of scholarly research.

SLFF Program at TU: Benefits: Resources, Community, and Personal Transformation

The faculty as a whole found the provision of technical and knowledge resources one of the most beneficial components of the program. Participants referred on many instances to "the binder," literally a binder containing examples of assignments, models for assessment, and rubrics illustrating the many ways to engage service-learning in the classroom. As one faculty member noted, in providing the material, the coordinators "emphasized that we did not need to reinvent the wheel." Rather than finding this selection limiting, as a suite from which to pick A, B, or C, faculty found the provision of models as opening options or inspiring the use of many forms not necessarily provided in the binder. The binder's usefulness transferred beyond the program as faculty recognized the frequency to which they referred back to resources provided during the seminar.

In addition to the standard resources provided to all participants, faculty also noted the importance of the ability to ask for and receive customized resources depending on their project. One faculty member described how the Office of Civic Engagement provided specific guidance and assistance in determining which activities to select and with which organizations to partner. Initially the faculty member felt overwhelmed by the types of programs with which students could engage the broad topic of institutional racism. The SLFF coordinator provided this faculty member with a long list of potential organizations as a starting point as well as recommendations as to which organizations partnered with university groups in the past. Resource provision does not end at seminar conclusion; faculty members also noted that they find it quite beneficial that they continue to receive e-mails detailing grants, service-learning opportunities, and relevant campus events even after the conclusion of the seminar.

The seminar also provided a space for discussion and the answering of general as well as technical questions. Participants appreciated the feedback from their peers, with one participant describing the meetings as a "support group" and a "nice space to meet and share with like-minded faculty." This strength emerged as both a benefit in networking and in solidarity. Faculty liked the space for discussions with others working in the same area. They benefitted from sharing their projects and their experiences with community connections. One participant noted that syllabus development is usually a "solitary enterprise" and that often trying to innovate might seem "frightening to do on one's own." In reference to the open space for discussion, one faculty member recognized, "This is what I miss about graduate school! We have a space to share ideas and to brainstorm. A space for discussion."

This sense of community was also created through an environment of encouragement from the coordinators as well as fellow participants. This encouragement, though, was placed within a realistic context. One participant said, "I learned that not everyone thinks [CESL] is a good thing. I also learned that we might not get tenure credit for this and therefore each of us individually needed to think about how to package it or sell it to our departments." Another faculty member commented, "I would not have the knowhow or confidence to do so without first having gone through the faculty development course where I learned how to do a reflection assignment."

Faculty identified two forms of transformation resulting from the experience: personal and professional. First, faculty identified how working with partner organizations transformed the way they view themselves as members of their community. The experience created an awareness of the importance of community engagement within their personal lives, and it enhanced the notion of the relationship they as a community member can and should have with their community. As a result, they engage on a personal level with community service organizations, emphasizing that community involvement has become "a way of life, not just part of the job." This benefit was also echoed by another faculty member: "[This program] forces me as a person to think about the role of activism and social change in my own life. That is my central motivation [in both my professional and personal life] in general."

Second, participants noted that they discovered a new way to identify professionally: "Service-learning gives me a home to think about my pedagogy." This transformation was especially beneficial for faculty members new to academia. One stated,

> I'm not new to service-learning but I am new to academia. [The director of the Office of Civic Engagement] and [the coordinator of community engagement and outreach] were instrumental in encouraging the faculty development component and encouraged research support. [The director] helped me find data sets and get connected to other researchers. Without this encouragement, I wouldn't have known how to do this. They were definitely "cheerleaders" in encouraging me in the process.

Most faculty members stated that the program made them more thoughtful and self-conscious of their teaching. This recognition was positive in that they became aware of the need to think about their teaching rather than simply repeating the same tactics used in previous years.

Seminar Drawbacks and Spaces for Improvement at TU

While faculty largely were happy to interact with colleagues outside of their departments, one did identify the difficulty in finding common themes across the experiences:

> All of our courses were different, our community partners were different, and my experience was even more different because I had four partners and not just one partner like most other participants. Other faculty were more involved in organizations and [their class projects were more] hands on. The fact that I was so different made it hard to apply their lessons to my project.

Despite the binder of resources and a space for discussion, faculty did note lingering technical questions in course facilitation when working with partner organizations. A common issue faced by participants was how to hold students accountable (e.g., with time logs) especially when these were not provided by or submitted through partner organizations. Faculty also emphasized a constant struggle with addressing the ever-present issue of students dropping the class well into the semester. Partner organizations also face unique difficulties in working with students completing tasks for credit rather than self-motivated volunteers. Faculty also realized that partner organizations do not necessarily understand the purpose of the course or how service-learning can and should fit within the university curriculum.

Others recognize the need for continued compensation: "$1,000 is nice, but it doesn't approach the additional hours of work required for service-learning courses. I've taught this course twice since and was only compensated for the initial course redevelopment." In addition, faculty identified several technical needs that might be supported by the office. One faculty member stated that they received many requests from faculty and members of the community for descriptions of the program. Faculty also commonly requested technical resources with bureaucratic support such as facilitating MOU (memorandum of understanding) paperwork.

Other common challenges related to the nature of service-learning work: difficulty in coordinating student transportation to site locations, the difficulty of scheduling work around already full student schedules, and lost time due to the closure of campus for snow days. Faculty also struggled with what one termed the "emotional management" of students as they engage with difficult topics and people who have different life stories. Finally, several participants mentioned their interest in continuing engagement with colleagues in both formal and informal ways. Faculty were interested in a 2.0 version of the program where they might assess the material differently after the initial experience. Others mentioned simply wanting to get back together to check in on a regular basis (e.g., each semester or yearly). Another idea was the coordination of an annual resources fair to connect faculty with local agencies.

In addition, faculty identified what one might term institutional roadblocks. These are not impossible to counteract, but also not something that can be addressed simply through changes in the design of a faculty development seminar. The purpose of this chapter is to assess the strengths and spaces for improvement of the two faculty development programs. Still, it is important to identify larger barriers so that efforts can be made to address such issues and ensure success of the development of faculty civic engagement development programs.

A major theme identified by the Towson faculty was the underappreciation of the benefits of classroom-oriented service-learning by university administration. Within the context of a different "binder," that for tenure, faculty noted that there is not actually a standard place within the tenure binder for CESL recognition. This comment led to an interesting discussion as to where tenured or tenure-track faculty should place this information. Is it community service (which should only be 5%–15% of one's time), or is it teaching (which is generally between 65% to 75% of one's time)? Does the scholarship of teaching count as teaching or research (varies between 10% to 25% of time), or not at all? Because of the lack of recognition and consistency, faculty felt the need to further self-promote and push for recognition, something quite time consuming in an ever-busier environment. Some faculty viewed this need to self-promote and advocate as a definite drawback both in terms of program participation specifically and CESL work generally: "It is irrational as an untenured faculty to do a service-learning course and take on the additional risk and work with unknown professional benefits." The same faculty member, in answering the question "What supports do faculty need to deliver civic engagement opportunities to their students?" candidly stated,

> Recognized and rewarded in the tenure and promotion process. That's really it. Supported through programs like the faculty fellows program. It shouldn't be the kind of thing you do when you happen to have your office next door to the program coordinator or once you are safe in your tenure. It should be as recognized as a publication or any of the standard ways we are evaluated. And if people are rewarded and recognized I think they will do it. It is more personally gratifying and rewarding. I think this is the most important thing I do professionally, more so than my research and more so that my service or teaching of other classes.

This comment further illuminates faculty frustrations about the lack of clarity regarding what should be recognized as a publication for the research category and whether scholarship related to student learning outcomes should "count" the same as disciplinary scholarship.

Departmental support was a benefit to some and a barrier to others. One faculty member noted that they had received service awards and recognition from both the university and community, none of which was acknowledged by their own department. Two faculty members noted that their service-learning efforts may have contributed to their not receiving tenure with one specifically identifying that departmental members noted a lack of consistency in their research program in terms of the inclusion of service-learning research. A final concern mentioned by all faculty was that of time. They each recognized the additional time not only to develop the classroom activity but to continue fostering relationships with partner organizations.[26]

LESSONS LEARNED: THE IMPORTANCE OF CESL INSTRUCTOR TRAINING

Mission and values statements from across the country demonstrate that universities have a clear interest in leveraging interactions between students and their larger communities. Many faculty members have shown an interest in integrating civic engagement into their teaching. Universities and faculty perceive civic engagement as an opportunity for faculty to teach content, students to practice skills, and universities to improve the quality of life in their communities. Salisbury and Towson Universities are among those with such interests. Our universities set themselves apart by offering structured faculty development in civic engagement pedagogies that also help to recognize the time, effort, and expertise faculty put into this work.

University faculty are being asked to do more in their positions beyond the traditional teach/publish paradigm. Like Boyer, we believe faculty deserve recognition for their varied activities.[27] Distinctions between teaching, scholarship, and service are increasingly blurred. A faithful approach to faculty development should acknowledge that teaching can be an act of scholarship when it is public, subject to peer review, and available to the scholarly community.[28] Teaching that incorporates civic engagement can also be an act of service to the university and/or community.

As one of the participants in this study noted:

> In a political and economic environment that questions the value of higher education, this kind of work is an answer to the question of the value of higher education. We are providing for our students' real life experience, job skills, the ability to interact with diverse populations. In the end, I really care more about how this impacts students as people. But this *is* the

relevance of a liberal arts education. And we should talk about this specifically as we are asked to justify our existence!

Faculty professional development that both supports course development and incorporates meaningful recognition for tenure and promotion also tells faculty that their work is valued. Further, when that professional development focuses on something intensive like civic engagement, the benefits move beyond the individual faculty member or course. Integrating more civic engagement initiatives more deeply into the fabric of a university sends a message to all university stakeholders and the community writ large that the campus is more than a transient home to young adults. These programs suggest that the campus is an integral part of the community and that the university is a potential partner willing to use its resources to help improve life for everyone.

We have reviewed outcomes in faculty attitudes toward civic engagement pedagogy following their participation in a faculty development program. Though a relatively small sample, faculty participants made it clear that development in civic engagement pedagogy is a cost-effective benefit if properly structured and supported. These benefits include time; collegial, financial, and administrative support; technical, logistical, and financial resources; increased connections to the community; and expanded teaching and research options for both traditional content and CESL. To continue to improve and advance these efforts, we need further research in the following areas:

1. *Critical Mass.* Most efforts to promote civic engagement in college courses have adopted a scattershot approach. Studies that consider a critical mass of faculty and/or courses needed to effectively transform a campus would help institutions to determine how to allocate resources to maximize faculty participation, student learning outcomes, and community impact.

2. *Long-Term Effects on Faculty Engagement.* This study focused on a single moment in time and asked faculty participants to reflect on their civic engagement training. Another useful area of inquiry could track changes in faculty pedagogy over multiple cycles of teaching a CESL course to examine benefits and areas in need of improvement. This type of longitudinal research would shed light on the long-term impact of faculty development with respect to civic engagement pedagogy and research. It would also help to answer questions about productive levels of continued institutional support for faculty who are already trained and engaged in such pedagogies.

3. *Student Outcomes.* The primary purpose of higher education is to impact student knowledge, skills, and attitudes. Further research that addresses student outcomes following participation in courses such as those taught by the faculty in this study would improve our understanding of whether and how these efforts are successful at reaching the target group. We need research on both short-term (post-semester and post-graduation) and long-term impacts on students to understand whether and how we are developing the skills, knowledge, and habits required for lifelong civic activism. This exploration should include factors such as family income and whether or not a student had first-generation college attendance status.

CONCLUSION

The programs reviewed in this chapter demonstrate the potential of faculty development programs to positively impact institutional goals. These goals include fostering critical thinking and students' intellectual development and helping students to gain the knowledge, skills, and values for lifelong citizenship. However, to be successful faculty development programs must include the following:

1. resources and buy-in from administration;
2. a permanent office with permanent, qualified staff who can facilitate grants and logistical support;
3. a well-structured, face-to-face training program (not ad-hoc meetings) based on the study of CESL pedagogical practices and theories; and
4. clear connections between this pedagogy and its related activities and promotion, tenure, merit, and workload criteria and rewards as part of the university's overall goals.[29]

The recommendations from this evaluation for program structure and areas for further research can help institutions use resources more effectively and build a more informed and engaged citizenry. Fostering civic engagement should be a key goal of higher education in all disciplines across the United States. Faculty should be encouraged to continue to develop their instructional practices to help students apply what they learn and become effective citizens. Toward this end, universities should establish stronger programs and practices that both support faculty development and reward faculty effort. We hope to see more of these efforts in the future. ∎

ENDNOTES

1. S. Surak and A. Pope, "Engaging the Educators: Facilitating Civic Engagement through Faculty Development," *Journal of Higher Education Outreach and Engagement*, 20 (2016): 41–62.
2. Salisbury University, " SU At-A-Glance: Salisbury University Analysis, Reporting, and Assessment," Accessed February 6, 2017, http://www.salisbury.edu/uara/profile/home.html.
3. Ibid.
4. Salisbury University, "Salisbury University Mission Statement 2014," Accessed February 6, 2017, http://www.salisbury.edu/about/mission.html.
5. Ibid.
6. Salisbury University, "Salisbury University, Institute for Public Affairs and Civic Engagement: PACE Home," Accessed February 6, 2017, http://www.salisbury.edu/pace/default.html.
7. Salisbury University, "Salisbury University, Institute for Public Affairs and Civic Engagement: Civic Engagement Across the Curriculum (CEAC)," Accessed February 6, 2017, http://www.salisbury.edu/pace/CEAC/welcome1.html.
8. While the Salisbury University CEAC program description uses the term "faculty" to designate cohort membership, fulltime instructors and graduate students may participate in the program as well.
9. The CEAC course pack distributed to participants includes the following definition: "Civic engagement refers to those activities by which individuals become informed participants in their surrounding public and private communities." Kahne and Middaugh explain that civic engagement education "explicitly teaches the knowledge, skills, and values believed necessary for democratic citizenship" [J. Kahne and E. Middaugh, "High Quality Civic Education: What Is It and Who Gets It?" in *Social Studies Today: Research and Practice*, ed. W. Parker (New York: Routledge, 2010), 141–50]. The approach inspires, informs, and shapes learning activities to impact public affairs. Those activities also deepen understanding of how social, political, and economic systems work and how individuals can work effectively within those systems as they develop sustained habits of active democratic citizenship.
10. The justice-oriented citizen model draws from the work of Westheimer and Kahne's 1996 article "What Kind of Citizen: The Politics of Educating for Democracy" in the *American Educational Research Journal*.
11. Faculty are encouraged to design programs where students are interacting with their community beyond the classroom walls. As is good research practice, results of student projects and interventions engaging local communities should be shared with these communities on project conclusion. This may take the form of a public presentation, a written document, or other related materials.
12. For an overview of specific course assignments visit www.salisbury.edu/pace and view the individual pages for each faculty participant.
13. An overview of the inception of this project can be found in Surak and Pope "Engaging the Educators," 41–62.
14. Towson University, "Home Webpage," Accessed February 6, 2017, http://www.towson.edu/index.html.
15. Ibid.
16. Towson University, "Mission & Strategic Plan," Accessed February 6, 2017, http://www.towson.edu/about/mission/index.html.
17. Towson University, "Office of Civic Engagement & Leadership," Accessed February 6, 2017, http://www.towson.edu/studentlife/activities/engagement/civicengagement/index.html.

18. Some of the materials are the *Michigan Journal of Service-Learning Handbook*, worksheets on community-partner agreements, and classroom reflection tips.

19. Due to the sometimes unpredictable nature of course scheduling, we have allowed a faculty fellow to participate in the program but teach the following summer or fall semester. Towson University has never had a faculty fellow return the money. There have been faculty who dropped out/stopped the program. For example, a faculty member stopped because of a death in the family and decided to take a leave of absence from the university. Faculty who have stopped during the year have either not been paid for that semester or returned the following semester to finish the program.

20. Towson University, "Community Service Attitudes Scale," Accessed February 6, 2017, http://www.towson.edu/provost/servicelearning/faculty/documents/attitudesscalearticle.pdf.

21. Towson University, "Service-Learning Grant Opportunity," Accessed February 6, 2017, http://www.towson.edu/provost/servicelearning/faculty/documents/grantapplication.pdf.

22. Towson University, "Mission & Strategic Plan," Access February 6, 2017, http://www.towson.edu/about/mission/index.html.

23. Researchers attempted to solicit information from as many program alumni as possible, and all program alumni received two e-mail solicitations to participate in oral interviews and e-mail surveys.

24. The online survey data provided by three faculty, two from TU and one from SU, echoed the benefits and drawbacks outlined in the focus groups and individual interviews. In the survey, as in the discussions, faculty identified the facilitation of a space for discussion as a valuable component of the development programs. The sense of community developed among the faculty as well as the benefits of networking lasted beyond the facilitation of the program. Drawbacks and difficulties identified by faculty centered on time requirements of the pedagogical practice rather than critiques of the development programs.

25. Questions were approved by both institutions' IRBs. The questions are available on the companion website.

26. The Office of Civic Engagement does provide support in this area, but some of the basic logistics still need to be coordinated by the faculty member, such as ensuring consistency of learning activities for their students with course learning goals.

27. E. L. Boyer, *Scholarship Reconsidered: Priorities of the Professoriate* (Lawrenceville, NJ: Princeton University Press and The Carnegie Foundation for the Advancement of Teaching, 1990).

28. Lee Shulman, "Course Anatomy: The Dissection and Analysis of Knowledge Through Teaching," in *The Course Portfolio: How Faculty Can Examine Their Teaching to Advance Practice and Improve Student Learning*, ed. Pat Hutchings (Sterling, VA: Stylus Publishing) 5–12. See also Ernest Boyer, *Scholarship Reconsidered: Priorities of the Professoriate* (San Francisco: Jossey-Bass, 1997) and Charles E. Glassick, Mary Taylor Huber, and Gene I. Maeroff, *Scholarship Assessed: Evaluation of the Professoriate* (San Francisco: Jossey-Bass, 1997).

29. Towson University is currently reevaluating these criteria and rewards, and Salisbury University is engaged in a full review of general education requirements that may incorporate such measures into the general curriculum.

Politically Themed Residential Learning Communities as Incubators of Interest in Government and Politics

John McTague

This chapter reports findings from the inaugural semester of Towson University's Political Engagement Community, in which students from a variety of majors interested in political engagement live together on one floor of a residence hall while also taking an introductory course on American government. Using the Carnegie Foundation Political Engagement Survey, I find that students report that they are more likely to read about politics in newspapers and discuss public affairs with others after having experienced one semester participating in the Political Engagement Community. They also report higher levels of knowledge about current political issues and how political institutions work, and they have an increased appreciation for the efficacy of working through political parties. In contrast, students also report that solving community problems is less central to their individual sense of self and are more likely to believe that it is difficult to solve problems on campus. While these findings speak to the promise for politically themed residential learning communities to augment other proven methods of promoting civic and political engagement among university students, there is also a clear need for further research to develop best practices to fully appreciate and leverage their potential.

C an residential learning communities serve as incubators of civic and political engagement? While a growing body of research clearly points to the promise of political science education as a gateway to a more engaged citizenry,[1] this chapter explores the potential for partnerships between politically themed residential learning communities and introductory political science courses as a method to cultivate citizenship skills among freshmen students. Learning communities are known to produce positive outcomes in terms of student retention and academic performance.[2] However, to my knowledge, this study represents the first attempt to connect the promise of residential learning communities to outcomes in learning civic and political engagement.

I report the findings from the inaugural semester of Towson University's Political Engagement Community, in which students from various majors interested in political engagement live together on one floor of a residence hall while also taking an introductory course on American government. This program was launched during the fall semester of 2015. Using the Carnegie Foundation Political Engagement Survey's pre- and postsurvey methodology, I find that students report that they are more likely to read about politics in newspapers and discuss public affairs with others after having experienced only one semester participating in the Political Engagement

Community. They also report higher levels of knowledge about current political issues and how political institutions work, and they have an increased appreciation for the efficacy of working through political parties. In contrast, students also report that solving community problems is less central to their individual sense of self, and they are also more likely to believe that it is difficult to solve problems on their home campus.

In this chapter, I briefly review literature assessing the impact of learning communities and theorize how such outcomes might extend to promoting civic and political engagement. Then, I describe the key features of the Political Engagement Community as it was designed and implemented at Towson University. Next, I propose several hypotheses and present the results of the Carnegie Foundation Political Engagement Survey that was administered to those students who participated in the program. I conclude that, although preliminary in nature, the findings reported here speak to the promise for politically themed residential learning communities to augment other proven methods of promoting civic and political engagement among university students.

LEARNING COMMUNITIES AS INCUBATORS OF CIVIC AND POLITICAL ENGAGEMENT

Learning communities are typically defined as "a kind of co-registration or block scheduling that enables students to take courses together."[3] While learning communities can also be, and often are, residential, the only essential feature of a learning community is the construction of a cohort of students taking courses together. The popularity of learning communities has grown in recent decades, leading one pair of authors to characterize it as part of a "national movement" in higher learning.[4] Since the teaching of civic engagement is itself part of a growing national movement among practitioners of higher education,[5] the time seems ripe for making connections between the assessed impact of learning communities and the positive outcomes that we attribute to civic education.

The objectives of learning communities typically revolve around promoting persistence in education and retention of students, higher levels of academic achievement, deeper student involvement in on- and off-campus activities, and greater student satisfaction with their college experience.[6] Retention of students is more likely to occur with those students involved in learning communities in part because learning communities facilitate deeper interaction with both peers and faculty.[7] This outcome is particularly relevant in aiding the transition from high school to college,[8] wherein a learning community can provide students with a smaller peer group in which to integrate into an often much larger university population. Higher rates of retention also result from the ability of learning communities to promote a sense of community among students as they merge both their intellectual pursuits and social pursuits by having more frequent and meaningful interaction with their peers through the linkage of academic and social components of student life.[9] In effect, social and academic activities become merged through the structure of the learning community. Students do not stop learning when their class ends; rather, the learning continues outside of the classroom,[10] particularly in residential learning communities.

The higher levels of retention of students who participate in learning communities is related to several of the other objectives of this pedagogy, namely, its effects on academic achievement, student involvement in extracurricular activities, and student satisfaction. High achieving, involved, and satisfied students are precisely the kinds of students who are more likely to persist in their education until they earn a degree. Student participants in learning communities see higher grade point averages,[11] increased cognitive abilities, and the development of more refined reading and writing skills relative to other students.[12] The effect of having a cohort with whom to work improves study skills[13] and promotes practical competence in the relevant course material.[14] Learning community students are more likely to develop the confidence necessary for social integration on campus,[15] and they are more likely to engage in diversity-related activities, show signs of personal and social development, and engage in active and collaborative learning activities.[16] All of these benefits may be especially relevant for the social and academic transition to college for first-generation students.[17] A great deal of student satisfaction with learning communities derives from their development of closer relationships with faculty and staff, which is also a boon to the professional development of faculty and staff, not just a benefit for students to enjoy.[18] Pedagogical advantages aside, learning communities may yield economic benefits to students by increasing retention in the era of massive student-loan debt.

Drawing lessons from the literature on learning communities and applying them to teaching civic and political engagement, several key takeaways emerge. First, learning communities are inherently flexible in terms of content, which is part of what has led to their emergence as a national movement.[19] Anyone seeking to initiate a learning community focused on civic and political engagement can take the concept and apply it. Thus, learning communities are "important seedbeds for pedagogical innovation"[20] that ought to be leveraged by those interested in promoting civic and political engagement.[21]

Second, the outcomes that we observe from the literature on learning communities overlap to a great extent with the outcomes that we seek to promote in pedagogy focused on civic and political engagement. For instance, one study points out that political knowledge is a strong predictor of later political participation.[22] It follows that the general finding that students in learning communities demonstrate higher levels of academic achievement, including greater practical competence in the subject matter that is the theme of a given community,[23] should carry over to civic and political education. In other words, if we want students to learn about politics and government as a gateway to political participation, then we should consider learning communities as a method of ensuring that they develop that base of political and civic sophistication.

Similarly, the finding that students in learning communities are active learners, deeply engaged in their communities of peers and faculty, and eager for opportunities to use their skills to learn more about both their on- and off-campus communities[24] lends itself to the active and collaborative learning models that characterize so much of civic education. In this sense of overlap in the outcomes and goals of both learning communities and practitioners of civic education, it is fairly surprising that there have not been more examples of politically themed learning communities in recent years. In sum, there are two trains running on parallel tracks in academia. One train is a national movement of learning communities and the other is renewed attention to developing active and engaged citizens through civic engagement education. Perhaps it is time for the passengers on both trains to mix and mingle with one another, and in particular, for those concerned with promoting civic engagement to use the pedagogy of learning communities to help produce the next generation of active, engaged citizens.

PROGRAMMING THE CONTENT OF THE POLITICAL ENGAGEMENT COMMUNITY: SUPPORT FOR EXPERIENTIAL LEARNING

Before proposing and testing hypotheses regarding the effect of a politically themed learning community on civic and political engagement among freshmen students, I will first briefly describe the main features of the Political Engagement Community on which this chapter's empirical analysis is based. One key takeaway from this discussion is that course design can be supported by staff in a way that augments academic learning outcomes and community-building opportunities, while also promoting and facilitating student engagement with both their on- and off-campus communities. All of these outcomes are means of ultimately producing active and engaged citizens.

Through a partnership with Towson University's Office of Civic Engagement and Leadership, Political Science Department, and Housing and Residence Life, the Political Engagement Community was launched in the fall semester of 2015 as an effort to promote civic engagement on campus through the use of a residential learning community directly paired with a course offering of American National Government. The newest of eight residential learning communities at the university, the Political Engagement Community stands alone as the only option at Towson University that offers students living on one floor of residence life the opportunity to all take one select course, American National Government, together and all share the same first-year advisor.[25] I serve in the role of course instructor and first-year advisor, with my first interaction with students occurring during freshmen orientation activities. Students were able to self-select into the community by indicating an interest in political engagement on their housing application forms.[26] A total of 27 students were selected to participate as members of the Political Engagement Community.[27] Of these 27 students, only six indicated an interest in becoming a political science major, with a wide variety of other majors included in the community. A total of 12 different majors, including undecided majors, were present on the first day of orientation. Thus, the Political Engagement Community is not just a home for political science majors but is, in practice, a place for cross-disciplinary learning and interaction.

Programming for the Political Engagement Community is a collaborative effort spanning across one academic department and two separate administrative offices on campus. The political science department has agreed to staff the Political Engagement Community for three years with one professor who serves as both the instructor for American National Government and as the students' First-Year Experience advisor, which includes responsibilities such as general orientation of new students to the transition from high school to college and advising for course selection for the students' second- and third-semester registration. In consultation with the course instructor, the Office of Civic Engagement and Leadership and Housing and Residence Life provide extracurricular programming for residents of the Political Engagement Community that connects to the theme of political engagement. An example of such programming is that students were required to watch one of the presidential primary debates during the fall of 2015 as a group as part of their coursework. The staff of both the Office of Civic Engagement and Leadership and Housing and Residence Life then worked together to provide a venue, refreshments, and structured discussion of the debate. Other programming included providing tickets to guest-speaker events on campus and a day trip to Washington, DC, which included time for informal socializing with their course instructor during lunch. The community also enjoyed a visit from US Congresswoman and candidate for US Senate, Representative Donna Edwards.

Critically, the design of the course required students to engage as active citizens both on and off campus through experiential learning assignments that were supported by the Office of Civic Engagement and Leadership. In addition to using and testing students' knowledge of material from a standard American government textbook,[28] the course mandated two separate "Civic and Political Engagement with Reflection" assignments based on students' experiential learning exercises. Those reflection assignments, in turn, served as potential drafts of excerpts of students' final research papers. The topics for the final research papers were chosen by students on an individual basis but were guided by a theory of American government that they learned in a reading assignment early in the semester.

The theory that guided students in their selection of research topics was based on the article, "Social Construction of Target Populations: Implications for Politics and Policy."[29] Each student had to select a social or demographic group in American society (e.g., military veterans, undocumented immigrant children, Muslims, sex workers, those suffering from mental illness), analyze the stereotypes that surround that group, and then explain how public policy targets that group with either beneficial or punitive treatment. We spent a few class periods dwelling on both the general theory and also applied the theory to two case studies. In one instance, I invited Towson University student activists from the Black Lives Matter movement to speak to the class, which led to discussions of the social construction of race and a lesson on systemic racism. On another occasion, we watched a documentary, *How to Survive a Plague*, which focuses on the activism of ACT-UP and the broader HIV-AIDS community during the 1980s and 1990s. This led to a discussion of the social construction of the LGBT community and how activists can work to change social constructions and thus change public policy from doling out punishment to granting benefits.

In addition to researching scholarly literature on their topics, students were required to somehow interact with their chosen group and write a reflection paper connecting the theory of the assigned article to whatever they learned from their group interaction. One assignment required students to engage with their target population off campus, while the other assignment required students to seek out an experiential learning opportunity related to their research topic on campus. To facilitate these interactions, the Office of Civic Engagement and Leadership provided research support to help students conduct outreach to individuals and organizations that could satisfy their experiential learning assignment. The staff of the Office of Civic Engagement and Leadership also promoted on-campus events such as lectures, panels, and guest speakers that might connect to students' research interests.

The design of the learning community, therefore, encouraged civic engagement by mandating that students perform some ethnographic fieldwork as an experiential learning exercise paired with reflection paper assignments.[30] This is an example of moving beyond the volunteerism model of civic engagement by making the assignments explicitly connected to the students' academic research in their American government course. The support from the Office of Civic Engagement and Leadership was indispensable to coordinating 27 unique paper topics and experiential learning opportunities. Although there are many potential models for making a politically themed residential learning community work,[31] I hope that this description highlights an important point. University staff can and should provide essential logistical support to classroom instructors to facilitate experiential learning opportunities for students that contribute to learning and, ultimately, to more civically and politically engaged student-citizens.

METHODOLOGY AND HYPOTHESES

To assess the impact of the Political Engagement Community on students' learning outcomes, The Carnegie Foundation Political Engagement Survey was administered first during new student orientation and then again two weeks prior to the end of the fall term. This survey instrument has been utilized in the past to gauge the impact of political engagement education on the acquisition of critical citizenship skills.[32] The results reported here focus especially on the influence of the Political Engagement Community on students' reported interest in and knowledge of political affairs and governing institutions.

This focus complements the learning outcomes as explained to students in the course syllabus. First, students were introduced to the learning outcomes of all courses in the political science department and then they were presented with more specific learning outcomes for their section of American National Government. There are four departmental goals. First, on completion of the course, students should "demonstrate substantive knowledge and understanding of the structure and nature of politics and government."[33] Second, students ought to be able to "demonstrate the ability to analyze critically the historical, cultural, and socioeconomic assumptions that underlie politics." Third, we expect an ability to "demonstrate an understanding of the affective meanings of politics in local, national, and international affairs." Finally, students should "acquire skills for learning and life; be able to present articulate and persuasive arguments about politics in written and oral communications."

Immediately following these general departmental course goals, the syllabus identifies six specific learning outcomes of this particular course. The six learning outcomes are presented with the following language:

This section of POSC 103 addresses these learning outcomes through a critical survey of American government and politics and experiential learning activities designed to stimulate curiosity about the power of engaged citizenship. By the end of this course, students who attend class regularly, do all of the assigned readings, study diligently, complete every assignment with care, and engage enthusiastically in the subject matter should be able to do the following:

1. Be able to describe and understand how our system of government is structured and the theory behind that structure.
2. Be able to describe and understand methods of popular participation.
3. Be able to describe and understand the functions and politics of the three branches of government.
4. Be able to describe and understand how policy is produced.
5. Be able to describe and understand the importance of, and limits to, civil liberties in American society.
6. Be able to think and write critically about political issues, leaders and policies, and the system that produces them.

In addition to measuring students' knowledge of political affairs and governing institutions, I report how the Political Engagement Community shaped their sense of self and their perspectives on the efficacy of various methods of political engagement. The method by which I assess changes in interest, knowledge, sense of self, and efficacy is by comparing the mean responses to the presurvey to those of the postsurvey. T-tests were calculated to determine statistical significance of each difference of means. The presurvey had a sample size of 23 students while the postsurvey's sample size is 25. This means that there were just a few students out of the total population of 27 that were absent on the dates the surveys were completed.

The first set of results, reported in tables 17.1 and 17.2, asks students questions about their consumption of political news and their knowledge of politics and government institutions. One question is worded, "Listed below are some ways that people get news and information. In a typical week, on how many days do you do each of the following?" Respondents are offered a choice of answers ranging on a seven-point scale from 0=Zero days per week to 7=Seven days per week. Consistent with the literature reviewed previously, which points to increased engagement as a result of participating in learning communities, I expect that students will report a greater frequency of days in the week in which they follow and discuss political affairs. As with an increased interest in political news, a series of questions queries students on their political knowledge and skills. The question reads, "Please rate your knowledge of the following topics" with a scale ranging from 1=No knowledge to 6=In-depth knowledge. I anticipate an increased level of political knowledge in the postsurvey relative to the presurvey.

Table 17.1 Interest in News about Public Affairs and Politics			
	PRESURVEY	**POSTSURVEY**	**DIFFERENCE**
Read about public affairs/politics in a newspaper	**2.00**	**3.04**	**+1.04***
Read magazines like Newsweek, Time, or U.S. News & World Report	1.55	1.56	+.01
Watch the national news on television	**3.96**	**2.76**	**-1.20***
Watch the local news on television	**3.09**	**1.24**	**-1.85*****
Listen to news on radio	**2.61**	**1.25**	**-1.36***
Read about public affairs/politics on the Internet	4.91	5.17	+.25
Discuss public affairs and politics with others	**3.22**	**4.42**	**+1.20****

Cell entries represent the mean number of days per week that respondents engage in each of the listed behaviors. The presurvey N is 23 and postsurvey N is 25. Statistically significant differences of means are in bold type. p<.01 ***; p<.05 **; p<.10 * (two-tailed tests).

Table 17.2 Political Knowledge and Skills

	PRESURVEY	POSTSURVEY	DIFFERENCE
Current national or international political issues, such as those on the front page of major newspapers	3.70	4.28	+.58
Current local or state political issues, such as those dealt with by city councils or state agencies	2.78	3.34	+.56
Political leaders and their roles	**3.78**	**4.44**	**+.66****
Current economic issues	3.70	3.68	-.02
Organizations that work on social and political problems	3.57	3.52	-.05
Theories about politics and democracy	3.74	4.20	+.46
Political institutions and how they work	**3.61**	**4.36**	**+.75****

Cell entries represent mean ratings of knowledge, which range from 0=No knowledge to 6=In-depth knowledge. The presurvey N is 23 and postsurvey N is 25. Statistically significant differences of means are in bold type. p<.01 ***; p<.05 **; p<.10* (two-tailed tests). The first two rows of results fall just barely shy of the p<.10 level of statistical significance: p<.11, b p<.13.

Moving from political interest and knowledge, table 17.3 reports students' answers to a series of questions asking about how important various characteristics are to their sense of self. Respondents are presented with a visual aid that resembles a "bullseye" with several concentric circles emanating from the center of the circle to the periphery. The question is worded as follows:

> Imagine that the figure below is a diagram of you. The middle circle (6) is made up of characteristics that are very central to your sense of who you are as a person. The next circle (5 or 4) is made up of qualities that are quite central to your sense of self, and the outer circle (3 or 2) includes those that are somewhat important to your sense of self. Qualities that are not part of your sense of identity belong outside the circles (1). If a quality seems good or desirable but isn't an important part of who you are, you should answer "Not central to my sense of self" (1).[34]

I anticipate that involvement in the Political Engagement Community will increase the importance of items related to civic and political engagement to students' sense of self, especially relative to options that are less overtly political in nature. For instance, options such as "Involved in solving community problems," "Politically involved," and "Concerned about government decisions and policies" are more likely to see increased salience to students' self-conceptions than items such as "Guided by spirituality or religious faith" and "Outgoing and sociable."

A final set of results, reported in table 17.4 and table 17.5, speaks to whether student participation in the Political Engagement Community shapes political efficacy and perspectives on the effectiveness of various forms of political action. The first question asks respondents, "Working with others, how hard or easy would it be for you to accomplish these goals?" Answers range from 1=Impossible to get this done, to 6=Easy to get this done. As an empirical matter, I am ambivalent about whether the results will indicate that students view accomplishing political goals as easier or more difficult from the presurvey to the postsurvey.[35] On one hand, it is plausible that students will feel empowered to act politically as a result of the expected increases in political knowledge and skills that I hypothesized in table 17.1 and table 17.2. Others have theorized relationships between engagement in a politically active, high political discourse community and increased levels of political efficacy and agency.[36] On the other hand, it is also possible that students will develop a reasonable and sophisticated view of political action as challenging and will therefore report that it is more difficult to achieve consensus through working with others in civic settings. Indeed, a key lesson of courses in introduction to American government is that the system is designed with multiple checks and balances and that politics is inherently an exercise in navigating conflicting political interests and preferences. For this reason, it is appropriate

Table 17.3 Importance of Each Option to Students' Sense of Self	PRESURVEY	POSTSURVEY	DIFFERENCE
Guided by spirituality/faith	3.09	3.04	-.05
Smart/intellectually capable	**5.13**	**5.48**	**+.35***
Concerned about international issues	4.87	4.68	-.19
Fair, unbiased	5.30	5.24	-.06
Willing to stand up for what is right	5.46	5.48	+.02
Solving community problems	**4.65**	**3.84**	**-.81*****
Creative or imaginative	4.65	4.56	-.09
Politically involved	4.00	4.00	.00
Compassionate/concerned about people	5.30	5.52	+.22
Honest or truthful	5.13	5.36	+.23
Concerned about government decisions and policies	4.87	4.76	-.11
Unconventional, nonconformist	4.00	4.40	+.40
Concerned about justice and human rights	5.39	5.36	-.03
Responsible, someone others can depend on	5.43	5.68	+.25
Outgoing or sociable	5.09	4.92	-.17

Cell entries represent mean ratings of the importance of each option the respondents' sense of self, which ranges from 0=Not central to my sense of self to 6=Very central to my sense of self. The presurvey N is 23 and postsurvey N is 25. Statistically significant differences of means are in bold type. p<.01 ***; p<.05 **; p<.10* (two-tailed tests).

to explicitly employ two-tailed tests of statistical significance of differences of means for these survey items.

A second question asks members of the Political Engagement Community, "There are many ways people try to influence political decisions or outcomes. Here is a list of a few ways. How effective do you think each is in influencing political outcomes?" Several forms of political engagement are listed and students are asked to rank the effectiveness of each form of participation on a scale ranging from 1=Not effective at all to 6=Very effective. As with the previous hypothesis, I am ambivalent as an empirical matter as to whether participants in the learning community will demonstrate feelings of greater empowerment to effectively influence the system for a given item or whether the results will speak to students' sophisticated understanding that the American system of government is inherently designed to make political action challenging.

RESULTS: THE CARNEGIE FOUNDATION POLITICAL ENGAGEMENT SURVEY

The first set of results present the differences in means from the presurvey and postsurvey questions assessing students' political interest, knowledge, and skills. Table 17.1 shows students' reported frequency of consumption of political news. The results show that there are two statistically significant increases and three statistically significant decreases in political news consumption. Prior to participating in the Political Engagement Community, students reported an average of 2.00 days per week reading about public affairs and politics in a newspaper. By the end of the first semester in the learning community, that number increased to a mean of 3.04 days per week, for an increase of one day. Though not a statistically significant difference, there was also a small increase of .25 days reading about public affairs and politics on the Internet. In contrast, three indicators of political news consumption show decreases from the start to the end of the semester. There is a decrease of 1.20 days of watching the national news on television, a decrease of 1.85 days of watching the local news on television, and a decrease of 1.36 days of listening to news on the radio.

Taking these results as a whole, it seems reasonable to conclude that the transition from living at home as a high school student to living in a university residence hall changed the choice of media that students consumed. They spent less time watching television and listening to the radio but spent more time reading newspapers and continued to follow political news on the Internet with regularity, at approximately five days per week. The promising takeaway from these results is that students are spending more time reading to acquire political news rather than watching or listening to what their parents or other family members may have selected, which is an outcome with which we ought to be pleased.

Perhaps the most important finding discovered in table 17.1, however, is in the last row, which demonstrates that students are spending more time discussing public affairs with others in the postsurvey, 4.42 days per week, than they reported in the presurvey, 3.22 days per week. The increase of 1.20 days per week discussing public affairs with others hints at the power of politically themed residential learning communities to take the lessons taught inside the classroom to contexts outside of the classroom, which appears to generally be the case with all manner of learning communities.[37]

Table 17.2 extends the promise of increased political interest as an outcome of a political learning community to indicators of political knowledge. Students may spend more time reading about and discussing public affairs, but do they also know more about what they are discussing? The answer to this question appears to be yes. Students report more in-depth knowledge of political leaders and their roles (+.66), political institutions and how they work (+.75), and although the differences in means fall shy of statistical significance, they also report greater knowledge of current national or international political issues (+.58, p<.11), and current local or state political issues (+.56, p<.13). These results, coupled with those of table 17.1, are very encouraging signs that Political Engagement Community participants have acquired both political know-how and skills, which are gateways to later political participation.[38] These results also speak to the potential of learning communities to increase substantive competence in the subject matter at hand, as has been demonstrated in other studies.[39]

The remaining results present more mixed evidence for the effectiveness of the Political Engagement Community at promoting civic and political engagement. Table 17.3 presents results bearing on the effect of the learning community on students' identities as politically engaged citizens. Out of 15 separate items, only two registered statistically significant differ-

Table 17.4 How Easy Is It to Accomplish Each of the Following Goals?			
	PRESURVEY	POSTSURVEY	DIFFERENCE
Getting potholes in your streets repaired	4.09	4.40	+.31
Solving problems on your campus	**5.09**	**4.46**	**-.63****
Getting the town government to build an addition to the local senior center	3.09	3.34	+.25
Raising awareness of a political issue or problem in your community	4.64	4.70	+.06
Organizing an event to benefit a charity	4.82	4.84	+.02
Starting an after school program for children whose parents work	4.39	4.20	-.19
Changing academic offerings or requirements on your campus	3.45	3.56	+.11
Influencing a state policy or budget decision	2.95	3.08	+.13
Organizing an annual clean-up program for a city park	5.00	4.68	-.32
Influencing the outcome of a local election	3.41	3.60	+.19
Influencing decisions about who teaches on your campus	2.82	3.16	+.34

Cell entries represent mean ratings of how easy it is to accomplish each option, which ranges from 0=Impossible to get this done to 6=Easy to get this done. The presurvey N is 23 and postsurvey N is 25. Statistically significant differences of means are in bold type. p<.01 ***; p<.05 **; p<.10 * (two-tailed tests).

Table 17.5 Perspectives on the Effectiveness of Political Action

	PRESURVEY	POSTSURVEY	DIFFERENCE
Working through political parties	**3.62**	**4.24**	**+.62***
Raising awareness of issues through discussions	4.73	4.28	-.45
Voting in elections	4.45	4.20	-.25
Working with community groups	4.45	4.08	-.37
Personally contacting influential people	4.09	4.04	-.05
Working with issue-oriented or interest groups	4.76	4.96	+.20
Participating in public protests or demonstrations	4.43	4.74	+.31
Working to get attention by the press, radio, and TV	4.77	5.06	+.29
Giving money to a candidate or cause	3.77	3.96	+.19
Becoming informed about issues in order to influence others	5.09	4.92	-.17

Cell entries represent mean ratings of how effective each form of political action is, which ranges from 0=Not effective at all to 6=Very effective. The presurvey N is 23 and postsurvey N is 25. Statistically significant differences of means are in bold type. p<.01 ***; p<.05 **; p<.10* (two-tailed tests).

ences of means, and of those two, one was signed in the opposite direction that we might expect of budding engaged citizens. First, for a positive result, students are more likely in the postsurvey to report that being smart and intellectually capable is more central to their senses of self (+.35). In contrast, there is a large negative result in terms of students' views of solving community problems as being central to their senses of self, with a decrease of .81 from the presurvey to the postsurvey. While I would have expected this result to be signed in the opposite direction, I speculate that this result actually speaks to an increased level of sophistication among students who are newly knowledgeable about how the system actually works, and how difficult it can be to achieve social change.

The results presented in table 17.4 echo this speculation, as the only significant result out of a battery of 11 questions also indicates lower levels of political efficacy in the postsurvey relative to the presurvey. At the end of their first semester in the Political Engagement Community, students were less likely to believe that it is easy to solve problems on their home campus (-.63). Again, this result might speak to a sophisticated sense of how political and social institutions generally tend to privilege the status quo, a theme that we repeatedly discussed and emphasized in class.

A final set of results is presented in table 17.5. This is a 10-question battery assessing students' views of which forms of political action are more or less effective. One statistically significant result stands out: relative to the presurvey, students were more likely to deem working through political parties as an effective means of political action (+.62). It is possible that this result is due to the guest speakers that engaged the community, from a sitting member of Congress (representative Donna Edwards of Maryland) to representatives of both the College Democrats and College Republicans of Towson. It is also plausible that the class emphasis on discussing current events, which was dominated by presidential debates during the period leading up to the first caucus and primary votes being cast, led to students' recognition of political parties as dominant forces in American politics. In any case, this result seems to be further evidence of students' political sophistication and knowledge. We might speculate that their recognition of the effectiveness of working through political parties will ultimately lead to their own participation as political partisans, but that remains to be seen.

DISCUSSION AND CONCLUSION

In sum, the results reported in this chapter are somewhat mixed, but there is also a great deal of promise in thinking about the future of learning communities as incubators of civic and political engagement. It is clear from the findings of The Carnegie Foundation Political Engagement Survey that students in the Political Engagement Community are more interested in consuming news about and discussing public affairs with others. This outcome is unambiguously positive, as political interest is a building block on the path to later political participation. Likewise, the results evaluating students' base of political knowledge showed statistically significant increases virtually across the board. Again, the value of increases in both political interest and political knowledge indicates a foundation of political skills is being laid with students who participated in the Political Engagement Community. Given that these results occurred after only three months of programming, there is much to celebrate in terms of the potential of politically themed learning communities to serve as incubators of active and engaged citizens.

It is, of course, important to qualify that these results are preliminary. We need more research on the role of learning communities in promoting civic and political engagement among university students. Indeed, the program described in this chapter is slated for at least two more years, and there are already changes underway in the content and programming of the community. For instance, in the second year of the Political Engagement Community, we have added a second course for the spring semester that members of the community may select. The course that is proposed for this role is a freshman seminar, which is a curricular requirement for all Towson University freshmen. In addition to serving as the instructor for American National Government and as their first-year advisor, I will also function as the instructor for the freshmen seminar with the special topic focused on the relationship between religion and politics in the United States. It is our hope that adding a second semester linking the residential community to a second course will augment opportunities for building community and make the logistics of extracurricular community programming easier as well. There is also potential for expanding the community into a second year of programming, perhaps with an international focus. The second year of the program overlaps with a presidential election, which presents unique opportunities for students to engage the political world.[40] Regardless of content, a good deal of research focuses on the benefits of having at least two courses linked to a learning community.[41]

Still, even with planned changes, there is enough evidence from the results of the first semester of the program to draw some preliminary conclusions that generalize beyond the case of the Towson University Political Engagement Community. First, there is a great deal of overlap in the goals of practitioners of learning communities and practitioners of civic and political engagement. The pedagogy of learning communities is a perfect tool to add to the pedagogical toolkit for educators interested in promoting civic and political engagement. The literature clearly indicates that students who participate in learning communities are more engaged in their on- and off-campus communities, which is an ideal outcome for promoting active citizenry more generally. Likewise, students who participate in learning communities demonstrate higher academic achievement, and in particular, are more competent in the substantive subject area that characterizes a given learning community. If we wish to promote an active citizenry, learning communities are a great method to promote political knowledge and skills. The results presented in table 17.1 and table 17.2, which highlight increased consumption of media and increased discussion and knowledge of public affairs, exemplify this idea.

A second conclusion from this case study relates to the pedagogy of experiential learning. A learning community is a ripe environment in which to promote experiential learning, which itself is connected to the aforementioned outcome of deeper engagement both on and off campus. The Political Engagement Community at Towson University was able to facilitate multiple experiential learning opportunities, two of which were directly tied to the course content and student research projects. These opportunities benefit students, of course, but they also benefit faculty and staff development, as the logistics of experiential learning were programmed as a team effort connecting faculty and staff at Towson University. Increased collaboration between faculty and staff help to bridge academic silos, which in turn contributes to scholarly and pedagogical innovation and promotes interdisciplinary approaches to problem solving, among other positive outcomes.[42]

A final implication highlights the potential for cross-disciplinary efforts focused on civic engagement. As Meinke demonstrates in his study of interdisciplinary minors in civic engagement, political science does not have a monopoly on promoting civic engagement.[43] In the Towson University Political Engagement Community, there were 12 unique majors represented among the 27 students who participated in the program. The beauty of a learning community with such a diversity of majors is that interdisciplinary learning at least occurs informally through student discussion networks outside of the classroom. There is great potential for politically and civically themed learning communities to facilitate programs such as civic engagement minors, among other possible applications of interdisciplinary learning. Thus, learning communities represent a promising device for promoting the kind of civic renewal that institutions of higher learning ought to be championing as a core mission of higher education,[44] not just for a minority of students who are political science majors.

The pedagogy of learning communities is part of a national movement across American university campuses. Likewise, there is a great deal of energy behind efforts to increase civic and political engagement in higher education. I conclude by advocating for increased use of the pedagogy of interdisciplinary learning communities as a means to serve the end of increased civic and political engagement.

With more politically themed learning communities, we must also develop a body of research establishing and assessing best practices for political learning communities. First, future research must leverage opportunities to test the effects of learning communities on civic engagement against control groups who take similar courses without the addition of a learning community.[45] This would provide a critical test of the independent effects of learning communities on cultivating civic engagement. Likewise, measures of increased political knowledge that go beyond the self-reported assessments contained in the Carnegie Foundation Political Engagement Survey would go a long way toward confirming the students' self-reported increases in knowledge about the workings of government and public affairs. In addition, it would be valuable to develop longitudinal panel data to assess the civic and political engagement of learning community participants through the rest of their undergraduate careers and beyond. While much work remains to be done, this chapter represents an effort to get the conversation started. ■

ENDNOTES

1. Alison Rios Millett McCartney, "Teaching Civic Engagement: Debates, Definitions, Benefits, and Challenges," in *Teaching Civic Engagement: From Student to Active Citizen*, eds. Alison Rios Millett McCartney, Elizabeth A. Bennion, and Dick Simpson (Washington, DC: American Political Science Association, 2013).

2. Julie L. Hotchkiss, Robert E. Moore, and M. Melinda Pitts, "Freshmen Learning Communities, College Performance, and Retention," *Education Economics* 14 (2006): 197–210; Vincent Tinto, "What Have We Learned about the Impact of Learning Communities on Students?" *Assessment Update*, 12 (2000): 12; Chun-Mei Zhao and George D. Kuh, "Adding Value: Learning Communities and Student Engagement," *Research in Higher Education* 45 (2004): 115–38; Stephanie Baker and Norleen Pomerantz, "Impact of Learning Communities on Retention at a Metropolitan University," *Journal of College Student Retention* 2 (2000–2001): 115–26; Teresa Ward and Nannette Evans Commander, "The Power of Student Voices: An Investigation of the Enduring Qualities of Freshmen Learning Communities," *Journal of College Student Retention* 13 (2011–2012): 63–85.

3. Tinto, "What Have We Learned," 1.

4. Jean MacGregor and Barbara Leigh Smith, "Where Are Learning Communities Now? National Leaders Take Stock," *About Campus* (2005): 2–8.

5. See McCartney, Bennion, and Simpson, *Teaching Civic Engagement*.

6. Maureen S. Andrade, "Learning Communities: Examining Positive Outcomes," *Journal of College Student Retention* (2007–2008): 1–20.

7. Gary R. Pike, "The Effects of Residential Learning Communities and Traditional Residential Living Arrangements on Educational Gains during the First Year of College," *Journal of College Student Development* 40 (1999): 269–84; Ward and Commander, Student Voices.

8. Ward and Commander, Student Voices.

9. Faith Gabelnick, et al., *Learning Communities*, (San Francisco: Jossey-Bass, 1990); Zhao and Kuh, "Adding Value."

10. Tinto, "Colleges as Communities".

11. Zhao and Kuh, "Adding Value."

12. Ward and Commander, "Student Voices."

13. Ward and Commander, "Student Voices," 2.

14. Zhao and Kuh, "Adding Value."

15. Hotchkiss, Moore, and Pitts, "Freshman Learning Communities."

16. Pike, "Residential Learning Communities"; Zhao and Kuh, "Adding Value."

17. Karen Kurotsuchi Inkelas, and others, "Living-Learning Programs and First-Generation College Students' Academic and Social Transition to College," *Research in Higher Education* 48 (2007): 403–34.

18. MacGregor and Smith, "Where Are Learning Communities Now?"

19. MacGregor and Smith, "Where Are Learning Communities Now?"

20. MacGregor and Smith, "Where Are Learning Communities Now?" 4.

21. I use the terms "civic" and "political" engagement as either/or options in this discussion to highlight the flexibility of learning communities as potential incubators of either form of engagement. See McCartney, "Debates, Definitions, Benefits, and Challenges," 14, for the distinction between the two terms and a discussion of how both are conceptually distinct from volunteerism.

22. Elizabeth Beaumont and others, "Promoting Political Competence and Engagement in College Students: An Empirical Study," *Journal of Political Science Education* 2 (2006): 249–70. See also Michael X. Delli Carpini and Scott Keeter, *What Americans Know about Politics and Why It Matters* (New Haven, CT: Yale University Press, 1996); Samuel Popkin and Michael Dimock, "Political Knowledge and Citizen Competence," in *Democracy and Citizen Competence*, ed. Steven Elkins (University Park: Pennsylvania State University Press, 1996); Richard G. Niemi and Jane Junn, *Civic Education: What Makes Students Learn* (New Haven, CT: Yale University Press, 1998).

23. Zhao and Kuh, "Adding Value."

24. Ward and Commander, "Student Voices."

25. It is common in the literature on learning communities for the concept to be defined by students taking two or more courses together (Vincent Tinto, "Colleges as Communities," 599–623), even if they are nonresidential models (Zhao and Kuh, "Adding Value"). It is worth pointing out, then, that the model under examination in this chapter is a residential learning community with only one common course shared among student participants.

26. Because students themselves may choose to participate in the Political Engagement Community, it is possible that self-selection effects are present in the analysis that follows. In contrast, I can report anecdotally that many students were unaware that they had selected a residential learning community when they arrived on campus for orientation activities. For some, this may be because they had forgotten that they selected the option on their housing application form. For others, it was clear that their parents or guardians had filled out the housing application forms on their child's behalf. In sum, there was a mix of students who were excited to be part of the community from the first day they arrived, while others seemed to not be entirely sure how they ended up in the community.

27. The average class size for a section of American National Government during the fall 2015 term was 33. At 27, this class was only slightly smaller than average.

28. Students were tested with fill-in-the-blank, multiple-choice, and short-answer questions in the form of quizzes at the start of nine of our class meetings. Quizzes were based on that day's assigned reading and were designed to ensure that students did the reading before coming to class. Quizzes were not announced in advance, so students had to prepare for every class as though there would be a quiz. A representative example of a fill-in-the-blank question was, "_____ refers to a legislature with two chambers."

29. Anne Schneider and Helen Ingram, "Social Construction of Target Populations: Implications for Politics and Policy," *American Political Science Review* 87 (1993): 334–47.

30. Students were told about the experiential component of the course on the first day of classes, not prior to signing up for the learning community.

31. See (Senator) Bob Graham, with Chris Hand, *America, the Owner's Manual: Making Government Work for You* (Washington, DC: CQ Press, 2010), which is an excellent resource for exercises promoting civic leadership.

32. See Elizabeth Beaumont, "Political Learning and Democratic Capacities: Some Challenges and Evidence of Promising Approaches," in *Teaching Civic Engagement: From Student to Active Citizen*, eds. Alison Rios Millett McCartney, Elizabeth A. Bennion, and Dick Simpson (Washington, DC: American Political Science Association, 2013).

33. All quoted material in this and the following paragraph is directly quoted from the syllabus.

34. The question goes on to prompt students to consider a relative ordering of the importance of each option to their self-conceptions. The wording is as follows: "Please think about this figure as you rate these items. Most people will use a variety of answers, rating some qualities as very central and others as less central to their sense of self. To get a good idea of how you will compare and rate the different qualities, please read all items before you go back to rate each of them."

35. As a normative matter, of course, we would like to see increased efficacy.

36. Beaumont, "Political Learning."

37. Tinto, "What Have We Learned?"

38. See Delli Carpini and Keeter, *What Americans Know about Politics*; Popkin and Dimock, "Political Knowledge"; Niemi and Junn, *Civic Education*.

39. See Zhao and Kuh, "Adding Value."

40. Students in the fall 2016 Political Engagement Community partnered with a class of senior political science majors studying presidential elections to put on a voter education drive in the student union the week before the presidential election. Carnegie Foundation Political Engagement surveys were administered to both the freshmen and the seniors. This research is slated for future dissemination.

41. See Zhao and Kuh, "Adding Value."

42. See Steve Kolowich, "Blasting Academic Silos," *Inside Higher Ed*, 2010, accessed on January 12, 2017, https://www.insidehighered.com/news/2010/01/18/silos.

43. Timothy Meinke, "Learning Objectives and Outcomes of an Interdisciplinary Minor in Civic Engagement," in *Teaching Civic Engagement: From Student to Active Citizen*, eds. Alison Rios Millett McCartney, Elizabeth A. Bennion, and Dick Simpson (Washington, DC: American Political Science Association, 2013).

44. National Task Force on Civic Learning and Democratic Engagement, *A Crucible Moment: College Learning and Democracy's Future* (Washington, DC: Association of American Colleges and Universities, 2012) accessed on January 11, 2017, https://www.aacu.org/sites/default/files/files/crucible/Crucible_508F.pdf.

45. Given the distribution of the teaching workload in my department, it would have been impossible for me to teach a second section of American National Government to have a control group.

Collaborative Civic Engagement: A Multidisciplinary Approach to Teaching Democracy with Elementary and University Students

18

ANN N. CRIGLER, GERALD THOMAS GOODNIGHT, STEPHEN ARMSTRONG, AND ADITI RAMESH

Civic engagement has been a hallmark of democratic practice since the beginnings of the American republic. The collaboration of citizens in building communities forms the basis of civic engagement and furnishes ongoing topics of research and teaching for political science. This chapter examines a complex multi-institutional and multidisciplinary pilot project: University of Southern California's Penny Harvest. Our team of scholars and students creates a reflective, experiential learning environment, based in the political science department that fosters civic engagement in both undergraduate and elementary-level students. Political science students work in conjunction with others from across the university and beyond to build an experience that employs philanthropy as a tool for youth to discuss issues and learn about resources that can help to address community needs. At every level, the program practices collaborative civic engagement; as such, it evolves dynamically and organically over time. Stakeholders shift and adopt new approaches as topics, interests, and opportunities change. This chapter discusses the elements of the program, the collaborations and political science initiatives, and the initial evaluations. The five-year effort shares Alexis de Tocqueville's view of civic engagement that collaboration is foundational to American democracy. We follow John Dewey's injunction to match experience to activity in order to cultivate informed citizens. Penny Harvest in Los Angeles strives to assemble a space where everyone can work together successfully.

Famously, Alexis de Tocqueville noted the importance of collaborative citizen engagement in his 1830 travels across the United States.[1] Since that time, many have shared and elaborated his observations.[2] A standard presumption of democratic governance is that, working together, ordinary citizens are able to enlarge circles of debate, gain power, and effect change.[3] Civil rights movements, Occupy, the rise of the Tea Party, and the groundswell of support for outsider candidates in presidential elections furnish recent examples of the mix of turbulent and civil engagements. Certainly, not all members of the public have equal interest, knowledge, or experience in political or civic participation in democracy.[4] The question of how to introduce and cultivate civic participation in local communities, cities, and across the nation raises itself anew for each generation.

In his classic *Democracy and Education*, John Dewey makes the case for education to play a central role in building a strong democracy.[5] He acknowledges that civic engagement is a foundation on which functioning democracies are grounded. He argues that public education is an effective way to instill democratic understanding and practices in youth. To achieve this end, Dewey argues that education should be experiential, related to reflection on the facts and events of situations encountered in a community context. While lesson recitation can promote discipline, discussions can grow judgment. Engaging with community, he argues, thus provides useful opportunities for learning and gaining experience with existing structures and practices.

The social sciences, and political science in particular, have taken Dewey to heart by promulgating civic education and engagement at institutions of higher learning and secondary schools and, to a lesser extent, in elementary schools. This effort has been undertaken through many means, including individual classes, speaker series, interdisciplinary programs, minors and majors, extracurricular efforts, and creation of curricula for secondary educators, to name a few.[6] No matter the format, experience and reflection remain important to democratic learning. Using Tocqueville and Dewey as a foundation, we conceptualize civic engagement as collaborative experiences formed to address issues of importance to members of a community. The collaborative experience relies on communication, leadership, and participation.[7] The process of discussion and decision making in communities prepares students for civic engagement.[8]

This chapter examines a multidisciplinary civic engagement pilot program: the Penny Harvest at the University of Southern California (USC). The effort brings together a multifaceted collaboration among many participants at the university, in the City of Los Angeles, and beyond. Here we present an explanation of the Penny Harvest and the USC pilot program. We further discuss university-based collaborations, define the role of political science courses, discuss evaluations, and conclude with program implications.

The close collaborations among students and teachers of the Penny Harvest community produce an organic and dynamic program that responds to needs and addresses the challenges of communication, continuing participation, and limited resources. The program is not easily replicable in a narrow sense. However, it is readily adaptable to different settings. The elements stressed at USC include a compelling and proven concept, institutional collaborations, undergraduate courses from multiple disciplines, and evaluation with feedback that drives program development.

A CIVIC ENGAGEMENT PILOT PROGRAM: PENNY HARVEST

BACKGROUND

Originally founded in New York City in 1991 by the Common Cents Foundation, Penny Harvest is a school-based service-learning program that civically engages students aged 4–14 to identify and address needs in their neighborhoods and across the globe.[9] The program employs philanthropy to help children discover, express, and analyze the needs of their community; deliberate; and make all philanthropy and service decisions. Since 1991, students in hundreds of schools in New York and other cities have given more than $8 million to support local, national, and international causes of their choosing.

BASIC PROGRAM OVERVIEW

In New York City, the Penny Harvest's goals were to enable children to learn about community and caring for others, to identify issues of concern in the community, to gather pennies to help others address these issues, to discuss and decide on which issues to support through donations of funds and volunteering, and to celebrate and share what they have learned. To achieve these goals, the Common Cents Foundation developed significant procedures and a carefully planned nine-month curriculum that make the program transferable.

In preparation for the school year, principals assign a teacher or school staff person who receives training and serves as a coach for the Penny Harvest. In consultation with the coach and teachers, the principal also selects a group of 15 to 20 student leaders called the "Leadership Roundtable" who lead the school's Penny Harvest under the guidance of the coach.

The Penny Harvest consists of four key phases. First, starting in the fall, children connect with their parents, friends, and neighbors as they go in search of pennies. The penny collection (harvest) encourages neighbors of all types and generations to talk, share, and ultimately coalesce as a stronger community. The emphasis on pennies helps convey that all contributions are welcome, no matter how small, and thus encourages participation by everyone, regardless of their economic status. Second, the "Leadership Roundtable" meets weekly to direct the whole school effort. Children have the power and the freedom to decide how to spend their harvest funds. With guidance from coaches, the children spend time analyzing community problems and figuring out how to represent student priorities. They define their community, deliberate and prioritize the most pressing issues, and then determine which organizations can best alleviate those problems. The children are encouraged to speak directly with the selected organizations, including during site visits, in-school presentations, or telephone interviews with nonprofit organizations. Third, the student leaders plan their own neighborhood service projects, sometimes using their collected pennies to fund these projects and other times volunteering their time. Fourth, after months of intense study and decision making, students present grant checks to their chosen organizations at the year-end Check Presentation Ceremony and pass the baton and their words of wisdom to the new student leaders. Together, these exercises aim to develop skills, knowledge, and experience requisite to become civically and politically active.

CROSS-GENERATIONAL ENGAGEMENT AT USC

In New York, the mature Penny Harvest program has been run by a nonprofit organization, Common Cents, with little direct participation in the day-to-day running of the program in the more than 800 participating schools. In the Los Angeles pilot, university students, faculty, and staff have collaborated with eight local schools to conduct the program. The goals of the USC Penny Harvest program run deeper than its effects on elementary level student participants. They are equally designed to have a lasting impact on both undergraduate student participants and pedagogy at the university.

COLLABORATIONS

The germ of an idea for bringing the Penny Harvest to Los Angeles started with a political scientist's (Crigler's) sabbatical and three desires—to bridge the gap between students' volunteer and political activities; to shift to a more interdisciplinary, problem-based form of pedagogy; and to explore a new area for research. On learning of the successful existence of the Penny Harvest program in New York, it seemed reasonable to try to use political science classes to implement the program in Los Angeles. Discussions with the cofounder and executive director of Common Cents, Teddy Gross, clarified what would be needed to launch the program.

Four faculty members from political science, communications, engineering/education, and public policy began conversations about initiating a collaborative program to implement Penny Harvest as a pilot in Los Angeles. It became clear that to initiate and sustain the program would require commitment from administrators as well as faculty. Meetings with deans, vice provosts, and administrative units around the university yielded some financial support, the go-ahead to develop special topic courses to implement the pilot program, connections with the local schools, and assistance with running the service-learning program. Important to the success of this effort, faculty work on this project is counted toward teaching and research, not just service.

INSTITUTIONAL COLLABORATIONS

Collaborations with the university's Office of Civic Engagement and the Los Angeles Unified School District are both strong examples of institutional collaboration, without which the Penny Harvest pilot would have foundered.

The key university link was with the newly appointed associate senior vice president of the University Relations' Office of Civic Engagement, Craig Keys, who was committed to the university's community outreach and Good Neighbors Campaign. His office agreed to support a dedicated staff person and to fund the licensing fee. In addition, Keys and his staff negotiated agreements with Common Cents, charter and religious schools, and the Los Angeles Unified School District (LAUSD), obtaining buy-in and signatures from all the relevant actors. This was no small feat—apparently, the Penny Harvest agreement with the public schools was the first university-wide memorandum of understanding with LAUSD. The Office of Civic Engagement sent a staff person to Common Cents in New York for training and to build the partnership. On returning, the staff person reached out to key community members to talk about Penny Harvest and to hear about their civic concerns. The staff member and work-study assistants continue to lay the groundwork for the political science class to work in the community schools—establishing agreements with individual principals and coaches; setting up meetings with local leaders including politicians, pastors, and nongovernmental organization (NGO) directors to learn about their civic efforts; managing the day-to-day operations and budgets; and planning and carrying out an annual end-of-year celebration for all the Leadership Roundtable children and their families. The university's support for this function has been essential to the success of the USC Penny Harvest. The university has benefitted as the Penny Harvest works with thousands of families in the neighborhoods surrounding USC's two campuses and can serve as a platform for other university initiatives including classes from multiple disciplines.

Principals of participating charter, religious, and LAUSD public schools commit to provide coach time and access to the whole school. Obviously, their buy in is similarly essential for the success of the USC pilot. The schools have benefitted from the leadership development opportunities for coaches, other faculty, and students as well as from curricular enrichment and expertise offered by USC students and faculty.[10]

MULTIDISCIPLINARY COLLABORATIONS

Multidisciplinary collaborations have occurred since the project's inception, built on the common interest in the civic engagement goals of the USC Penny Harvest pilot. The dynamic needs of the program have led over the five years of the pilot to additional multidisciplinary collaborations with several of USC's professional schools including public policy, communications, business, and education. The collaborations strengthen the communication, leadership, and participation elements of civic engagement. Some are long-lasting, while others are more circumscribed depending on the needs of the program, participant interests, skills, and availability.

Public Policy School. The initial implementation of the program was done through a collaboration of a political science class and an undergraduate public policy school class "Citizenship and Public Ethics." Students from both classes worked together in the elementary schools, sharing experiences with the children. Class meeting times were set to overlap, allowing students to meet together as well as apart, and several of the lecture sessions were held in common so that students could learn about both the Penny Harvest program from its founder and conducting ethical research with children. The collaboration was fruitful and grew stronger as the two classes worked together to create and implement a USC pilot innovation, a "Leadership Academy" held at USC for Leadership Roundtable participants during year two of the pilot. Coordination was facilitated through e-mail and social media and through enrollment of some students in both classes. This collaboration continued until the relevant policy school faculty member left the university.

Communication School. Other cross-university collaborations grew out of a need for improving communications and expanding the pilot. A master's student working on the pilot suggested that we work with the public relations (PR) program in the Annenberg School for Communication at USC. Honing their expertise, the PR class developed a campaign to raise awareness about the Penny Harvest at USC and to raise funds for the elementary schools' penny drives. The PR team presented a detailed plan and timeline for effecting the campaign—a series of media interviews on campus and a fountain penny toss for good luck on move-in day. Unfortunately, the university's facilities management office had other priorities, so that the fountain penny toss fundraiser was not able to go forward. This was somewhat frustrating for students, but was used as an example of how collaborations need to be cultivated to fit with others' goals. It also raised questions about the purpose of civic engagement when others control resources. While it was a fruitful experience for reflection, it was challenging for continuity of engagement.

The Annenberg School for Communication has yielded two more ongoing collaborations: classes in rhetorical inquiry and strategic communication. Concepts about the relation of speaking to deliberation, discussion, and learning were drawn from international projects on argument and language. Pragmatic thinking and interaction outlooks were developed from the International Society for the Study of Argument in Europe, from critical thinking and philosophy at the OSSA University of Windsor in Canada, and from public argumentation and the Japan Debate Association. The strategic communications class contributed valuable communications tools and plans for improving skills across our participants, young and old. For example, principals and teachers in the elementary schools requested simple flyers to describe the Penny Harvest to parents and other members of the community. Students drafted a document with visuals from the local schools that have helped to engage parents, new schools, and other community partners.[11]

The collaborations with the rhetorical communications classes are the deepest and most long-standing. The faculty member was instrumental to the initial creation of the program and his classes cover special topics on civic engagement, philanthropic communications, and communicative cities. The political science and rhetoric classes work together closely through coordination of syllabi, joint class meetings and fieldwork, and partnering on the leadership academy. Faculty and graduate students also collaborate on research and publishing papers. Communications faculty and graduate students took the lead on theorizing how youth can learn to engage civically by learning how to deliberate as individuals in a community. Children working in the Leadership Roundtables expand their circles of belonging (e.g., families, friends) to larger networks in communities of practice (e.g., the roundtable, local communities).[12]

Business School. The business school classes, "Designing and Leading Teams," created a webpage, a Facebook page, and a proposal for sustainable funding. In addition, one of the business students started a café near campus and held a fundraiser for the children's Penny Harvests. The students took initiative and worked effectively in teams while engaging civically.

COMMUNITY COLLABORATIONS

Many individual participants and local leaders have helped Penny Harvest, meeting with the USC classes to advance students' understanding of the complex relationships involved in political and civic activity. For example, Common Cents' Teddy Gross inspired the students to work in nonprofits and civic engagement; an active philanthropist and youth policy expert, Denise McCain Tharnstrom, explained giving circles and the role of youth-oriented nonprofits in California policy making; and a talented Penny Harvest coach, Olga Flores, shared her experiences as a teacher and coach for the Penny Harvest to prepare the university students. Several local community members helped to highlight civic life (positive and negative) in the area. Reverend Msgr. John Moretta, a long-term parish priest who is very dedicated to the community, discussed local actions against a neighboring battery-recycling business accused of poisonous pollution. An award-winning political advocate who grew up in the neighborhood, Lou Calanche, motivated students with the creation of Legacy LA, a community-based nonprofit organization focused on youth development. She also introduced the university students to a local high school student who candidly described some of the challenges with police and gangs growing up in the local community. Many of these collaborations are mutually beneficial, with USC students assisting the presenters to advance their civic missions by analyzing data or volunteering on projects. Each of these community members helped students to reflect on the integral relationships of civic and political actions by sharing their own experiences.

THE ROLE OF POLITICAL SCIENCE CLASSES

The USC Penny Harvest program is directly tied to two upper-level political science seminars initially developed for the rollout of the Penny Harvest Program in 2012–2013: "Civic Engagement and Leadership" taught in the fall and "Youth Participation and Advocacy" held in the spring. The courses are electives open to all undergraduates without prerequisites. In their first five years, classes have been capped at 12 students with a total of 76 undergraduate enrollments.[13] These USC students play a central role in implementing and evaluating the Penny Harvest pilot through their weekly service in local schools, the leadership academy, and their research projects.

Course Structure. Meeting once a week, seminars are highly participatory exchanges in which students discuss readings, share experiences in the schools and in their lives, meet with other faculty and community leaders, and collaborate on team research projects. The class is structured as a safe place where all are encouraged to speak frankly and reflect critically (the syllabi can be found on the companion website).

The learning objectives are to
1. apply theory and practice to reflect on the significance and meaning of youth participation in political and civic life;
2. conduct an original, community-based research project;
3. facilitate youth learning civic skills, leadership, and participation;
4. work collaboratively as well as independently; and
5. present ideas convincingly both orally and in writing.

To meet these learning objectives, there are five assignments. They include
1. reading and participating in class discussion (objectives 1, 2, and 5),
2. working in the elementary schools (1, 3, 4, and 5),
3. creating a Leadership Academy (3, 4, and 5),
4. conducting an original research project (2, 4, and 5), and
5. writing weekly journal reflections (1 and 5).

The syllabi introduce theoretical and empirical readings on themes such as representation, leadership, working with bureaucracy, political socialization, youth advocacy and philanthropy, and deliberation and decision making. Students read materials that are intended to enhance their understanding of these topics, spur development of their original research topics, and consider issues from different viewpoints. The first weeks of the course sensitize students to working with children from diverse backgrounds.[14] In preparation for working in the schools, students complete institutional review board (IRB) certification and required training modules on the ethical practice of research and working with children that are offered through USC's Office for the Protection of Research Subjects. Students also role-play Penny Harvest lessons they will use with the Leadership Roundtable children. These include identifying and articulating community problems; representing diverse interests; deliberating and formulating means for determining group preferences; mobilizing people to take action; understanding and accessing the institutions that can effect change; and working with elected officials. Finally, before the USC students begin their weekly work in the local schools, we take a field trip to a school and its neighborhood to get acclimated and to speak with principals, teachers, a local priest, or directors of NGOs.

Field Work. Based on their schedules and transportation options, USC students are assigned in teams of up to four to participate at a neighborhood elementary school. They attend weekly meetings of the Leadership Roundtables. These sessions, typically lasting an hour, allow undergraduates to facilitate the Penny Harvest curriculum and to assist the schools in moving through the program. The undergraduates write school reports, detailing their experiences and highlighting specific examples of notable comments made by children during each session. They also record the children's progress in the program, note if the coach needs any additional support, and make suggestions for the future. These reports are used to keep track of the progression in each of the schools, to modify the Penny Harvest curriculum, and to improve implementation of the program. They are central to the formative evaluation of the pilot.

For the USC students, the primary goal of the school reports, as with their journals, is to encourage reflection on their collaborative experiences with the children. These are often quite revealing. For example, in 2016, one school report included how the roundtable leaders discussed ways that they engaged civically. Partway through the discussion, one child volunteered that he was not civically engaged, explaining, "I can't pick up trash because I might be shot." This comment engendered the sharing of similar stories, with all but two of the 12 children in the room reporting direct experience with gunfire, gangs, and violence. The coach and the USC undergraduate also shared their stories with the group, creating a remarkable and memorable experience that both adults noted. The lack of a safe community—and how that milieu could inhibit public participation—was not a factor that the undergraduates had considered in their discussions of civic engagement until it was brought up by the children.

Leadership Academy. The Leadership Academy was an idea proposed by the principals of the schools initially participating in the Penny Harvest who hoped that it would encourage their students to start thinking about their own leadership potential and about attending college. All of the Leadership Roundtable elementary school children (60–90) are invited to participate in the bi-annual Leadership Academies that are held on USC's campus. Conducted each semester, the students of the political science seminars in collaboration with other USC classes and organizations plan and execute the day-long Leadership Academy. The undergraduates set goals, write a mission statement detailing what they hope to achieve, carefully plan every step, and write a complete timeline and script. The content changes every semester and covers such topics as deliberation and decision making, four traits of good leaders, effective communication, and building trust and teamwork with the children. Undergraduates do everything to organize the academy, from reserving space on campus to identifying, recruiting, and coordinating other groups on campus to enrich the children's experience (e.g., tour guides, members of sports teams, the marching band, student government leaders, or university administrators). The undergraduates take ownership of the Leadership Academy, and civic engagement becomes a creative outlet. For example, undergraduates made a video to welcome the children from each school. The Leadership Academy is important to the program as a microcosm of civic engagement where multiple participants, undergraduates, children with their coaches, some parents and principals, and university staff and faculty come together to collaborate, communicate, and reflect on what they have learned. While the children are learning about leadership, the collaborating communications classes have held focus groups with the adults to reflect on the meaning of the Penny Harvest experiences for the children and to discuss ways to improve the pilot program.

Student Research Projects. Undergraduates select their own groups (of two to four students) and choose any research topic they wish, with the stipulation that it must relate in some way to civic engagement and the Penny Harvest. In this process, students conduct original, independent research, often for the first time at the university level. This assignment requires training in research ethics and working with human subjects (especially children) as well as preparation in methods and statistical analysis (the syllabi can be found on the companion website). The students' topics have varied, employing quantitative as well as qualitative methods and data. In the past, undergraduates have focused on topics such as eudemonia and hedonia, political socialization of Latino and African American children, youth motivation, the development of self-efficacy, and integrating civic engagement into the common core. Students' research collaborations have produced some of the first evaluations of the program and have been used to make improvements for future years.

Two of the early research papers examined youth motivation and the role of parents in children's socialization, respectively. In the motivation study, 27 fifth-grade students from two schools participating in the USC Penny Harvest were given a survey and asked to draw pictures about what motivates them to be civically active. This project's findings suggested significant connections between the actions of teachers and parents and students' drive to be engaged in their communities. The parent–child socialization study used focus groups and questionnaires to measure roundtable students' parents and their civic attitudes, involvement, and participation with their children. This study found that parents reported seeing significant increases in their children's leadership skills and knowledge of their community. Some parents also said that their children's Penny Harvest involvement had increased their own awareness of community issues. Students presented their findings to USC Penny Harvest administrators who used the information to change their outreach to parents to include visiting back-to-school nights and creating brief flyers to explain the program more clearly to parents.

Journals. As John Dewey and Paolo Freire recommend, the class integrates experience, theory, and reflection in the process of learning.[15] Weekly journals particularly help USC students to process what they are learning about civic engagement. Journal assignments—which may be free-written or respond to prompts such as "Who are you as a person and a civic citizen?"—require students to reflect on their work in the schools, their research, and their own experiences in light of class readings and discussions. Discussions and journals often start with readings and field experiences that students relate to their own personal experiences. Two examples are illustrative. During the week on political socialization, a first-generation Latina college student related her own struggles raising a young daughter as a single parent while trying to complete college. She almost dropped out of school during the semester but stayed, in part, because of the work she was doing with Penny Harvest. The class was teaching her about how she could raise her daughter and how she could engage in the community. Her story was inspirational to all of us (and, in fact, to the wider university community, who invited her to give the student address for the Latino student graduation). During another semester's session on deliberating across differences, students shared their very different perspectives on working in the local schools based on their family backgrounds. One was a daughter of two police officers and the other student was a young man who had grown up close to many gang members. The two came to see the tense relations between police and residents from each other's viewpoints. Their exchanges opened up a space for the entire class to consider questions of justice.

Overall, the goal of these political science classes is to foster some of the same civic skills in undergraduates that are being taught to elementary-level students. The school visits help students gain a better understanding of how to interact effectively with individuals from different cultural backgrounds; the weekly journals and class discussions encourage students to reflect and form opinions on a broad range of issues that affect their communities; the research paper teaches students the process of performing academic research and the importance of collaboration; and the final presentation builds skills of communication. Experiencing the challenges of starting and building a civic engagement program also helps students discover how creative and resilient they can be.

EVALUATIONS

Assessing the effectiveness of the USC Penny Harvest program on student learning is ongoing, but frustratingly challenging and incomplete due to lack of funding, stringent and slow IRB approvals at LAUSD, the need for an independent scholar to conduct the evaluation so that conflicts of interest can be minimized, and difficulties obtaining systematic pre- and posttest measures from comparable sample and control groups.[16] As mentioned earlier, undergraduate research projects have been used to gather some initial evaluations of the program. However, there is an inherent conflict of interest in having the assessments conducted by program participants. The next stage of implementation calls for grant writing to obtain external funding for an independent review.

Much of the evaluation is formative and designed to improve the implementation of the pilot.[17] Due to space limitations, we present a few examples of qualitative discussions and quantitative questionnaire results.

Qualitative. As part of the collaboration with the LAUSD and other schools, we hold four formal meetings with coaches (a two-day summer intensive training, a half-day winter meeting, and sessions during each of the two annual Leadership Academies), as well as several informal, one-on-one contacts to exchange ideas and concerns. The formal sessions are semistructured conversations in which participants (USC students, staff and faculty, elementary school coaches, principals, and occasional parents) share suggestions and expertise. These conversations shape how the program evolves. For example, as mentioned earlier, a principal suggested holding a Leadership Academy at USC that the USC students and staff implemented. The coaches and children liked it and requested that it grow from two hours to all day. A parent was concerned that children were missing school, so coaches and USC student assistants helped children to create drawings and essays that were displayed during parent back-to-school nights.

In another qualitative, formative evaluation example, we asked coaches how they applied Penny Harvest to common core standards. The coaches reported that teachers in LAUSD often did not feel adequately trained in new common core teaching techniques. We invited a professor from USC's education school to work with them to design lesson plans to connect Penny Harvest with common core standards for argument and narrative. In one lesson plan, a coach proposed using a tree analogy to help children understand root causes of problems they observed in the community. Through deliberating about the root causes of the issues, the children are better able to provide evidence of causes, recognize consequences, develop possible action steps, and recommend potential policy changes. These regular discussions among participants tailor the pilot to meet interests, maintain participation, and also to improve performance.

Quantitative. Several questionnaires have been employed to assess the USC Penny Harvest.[18] At the end of the first year, undergraduates asked participating elementary schools' principals and teachers (N=5) to evaluate if student involvement in Penny Harvest had benefitted the children (see table 18.1). Overall, principals and teachers agreed or strongly agreed that Penny Harvest had helped their students. Similar questions asked of university professors and students also

Table 18.1 Impact of Penny Harvest on Elementary and University Students (% Agree or Strongly Agree)		
	ELEMENTARY (N=5)	**UNIVERSITY (N=9)**
Increase understanding of community	100	89
Increase advocacy for people or community	100	78
Increase empathy	100	89
Discover or develop leadership skills	100	78
More able to work cooperatively in group	100	89
More motivated at school	80	67
More able to apply academic skills to real-world situation	80	67
Note: Figures are percentages of respondents (teachers and principals at elementary schools, professors and students at USC) reporting that they agreed or strongly agreed with the statements.		

indicated positive results. The adults consistently agreed that elementary and university students had increased empathy, understanding, and advocacy for community; developed leadership skills; were more motivated at school; and were more able to work cooperatively and apply academic skills to real-world situations.

In subsequent years, using a pre- and post-questionnaire taken the first and last days of the semester, we have started to examine the undergraduate political science students' assessment of their experiences and self-perceptions of their civic engagement. The early numbers are small (N=23) and results from comparisons of means tests show few statistically significant changes over time. Counter to what we initially expected, responses from the last day of class are tending lower than commensurate measures from the first day. We asked students to evaluate "the way you work in comparison to your same-age peers" on a variety of tasks. On a scale of one to four (1 below average, 2 average, 3 above average, 4 far above average), the USC students initially reported being above to far above average (means of 3.48 and 3.00, respectively, on ability to work cooperatively and to shift people to consensus). By the end of term, however, these means had fallen significantly (3.04 (sig. <.015) and 2.65 (sig. <.043), respectively). On further reflection and analyzing the qualitative findings from student journals, the relatively flat or slight decline in self-reports of civic engagement are not all that surprising. Doing this kind of work is demanding and not always immediately rewarding when students are engaged in more than short-term, organized volunteer activities. Reflections from student journals suggest that they have gained a deeper understanding of the responsibilities entailed in civic engagement. As one student wrote:

> Who said that the Penny Harvest program implementation was going to be easy? I don't know, what I do know is that it has been a bumpy road, but the lessons are the best memories I have during the whole year here at USC. Working with the students this semester has been an unforgettable experience and I have learned more from them than them from me.

Another student wrote:

> As much as I would like to think that democratic participation is easy, … when I think about democracy in Dewey's terms, it becomes a laboring process that requires immense care and attention from all of its citizens…. From everything I have learned from this class, I know I'm not there yet, but I am a step closer.

CONCLUSION

Dewey argues that education is best accomplished through experience and reflection that leads to the critical act of public "problem solving."[19] The choice of means and commitments to ends are important elements of civic action. Complementary questions of how a community comes into being, renews itself, and networks across differences call for address, as well. Rather than mourn the absence of the great community, we are moving political science and the university to the task of creating a scene of engagement where the public school becomes a sustainable resource for community development and civic engagement. At the heart of USC's multidisciplinary civic engagement program is a renewal of the intimate connection between the university and the communities on which, over the long term, its flourishing depends.

CHALLENGES AND FUTURE DIRECTIONS: LONGEVITY, SCALABILITY, AND RESEARCH

While the collaborations help to create a foundation for the program, obtaining the financial resources and continued commitment to sustain or grow the program is challenging. In Los Angeles, we have chosen to work intensively with a small number of schools. How do we want to think about scaling the program? Scalability depends on financing and assessment of efficacy. To move forward, we need to conduct more systematic and independent research. This might include comparisons with schools that are not participating in Penny Harvest as well as short-term and long-term assessments of student learning of civic and leadership skills; empathy and other affective measures; and behavioral observations such as performance in school and participation in other civic or political activities.

What makes this program work? An established and proven initial civic engagement program, institutional collaborations, participation by students and faculty from multiple disciplines, and formative evaluations that feed into the development of the program are the essential elements. At every level, the program practices collaborative civic engagement. The program works because it accords all a productive role in creating a space for successful work together. For the children, the program has the attraction of entering a larger world and doing things. For university students, it offers a moment of giving back and reflecting on creating larger spaces in which others can achieve. For faculty, it provides an escape from the corporatization of academe and an opportunity to engage collaboratively.

A top-down autocracy might be easier or more efficient but does not yield the benefit of cultivating elementary and college students in the duties and possibilities of civil society. There may be constructive tensions among participants' goals. Goals change over years, as Penny Harvest members discover new resources and different problems bid for attention. Building a multidisciplinary, collaborative civic engagement program calls for cultivating a common experience that can serve these multiple, sometimes competing, goals and differing expertise. There are many examples: the university's goals of serving the community and bridging town and gown divides sometimes collide with the calls for social justice and empowerment that the undergraduates prefer. Incorporating the educational priorities of the elementary school principals and teachers calls for equal attention and responsiveness to their aspirations. Different disciplinary courses have related but distinct educational goals which require collaborative communication to make them attainable. Reflecting on the tensions and working together enrich the implementation of the program in Los Angeles.

Alfred North Whitehead found the genius of the university in the adventure of the researcher and student. We extend that adventure to the horizon of doing things by assembling a community, endowing it with energy, listening with respect, and angling a contribution (pennies and otherwise). These positive social values of collaborative engagement are important to demonstrate with youth to foster democracy. In times of polarization and conflict at the national level, we feel that this is vital to assure that community engagement endures, expands, and evolves. ∎

ENDNOTES

1. Alexis de Tocqueville, *Democracy in America* (New York: Schocken Books, 1974).
2. Cliff Zukin, Scott Keeter, Molly Andolina, Krista Jenkins, and Michael Delli Carpini, *A New Engagement?* (New York: Oxford University Press, 2006); Robert Putnam, "Bowling Alone: America's Declining Social Capital," *Journal of Democracy* (1995): 65–77.
3. E. E. Schattschneider, *The Semi-Sovereign People* (New York: Holt, Rinehart & Winston, 1960).
4. Sidney Verba, Kay Lehman Schlozman, and Henry Brady, *Voice and Equality: Civic Voluntarism in American Politics* (Cambridge, MA: Harvard University Press, 1995).
5. John Dewey, *Democracy and Education* (New York: Macmillan, 1916).
6. T. Meinke, "Learning Objectives and Outcomes of an Interdisciplinary Minor in Civic Engagement," in *Teaching Civic Engagement: From Student to Active Citizen,* edited by Alison Rios Millett McCartney, Elizabeth A. Bennion, and Dick Simpson, 337–52 (Washington, DC: American Political Science Association, 2013).
7. Barbara Jacoby and Associates, *Building Partnerships for Service-Learning* (New York: Jossey-Bass, 2003).
8. See, for example, David Beetham, "Evaluating New vs. Old Forms of Civic Engagement and Participation," in *Evaluating Democratic Innovations: Curing the Democratic Malaise?* ed. Brigitte Geissel and Kenneth Newton, 56–67 (New York: Routledge, 2012); Harry Boyte, *Everyday Politics* (Philadelphia: University of Pennsylvania Press, 2004); Richard M. Lerner and Peter L. Benson, *Developmental Assets and Asset-Building Communities: Implications for Research, Policy, and Practice* (New York: Kluwer Academic/Plenum Publishers, 2003); Peter Levine, *The Future of Democracy: Developing the Next Generation of American Citizens* (Lebanon, NH: University Press of New England, 2007); Alison Rios Millett McCartney, Elizabeth A. Bennion, and Dick Simpson, *Teaching Civic Engagement: From Student to Active Citizen* (Wash-

ington, DC: American Political Science Association, 2013); M. McDevitt and S. Kiousis, "Education for Deliberative Democracy: The Long-Term Influence of Kids Voting USA," CIRCLE Working Paper 22, *Center for Information and Research on Civic Learning and Engagement* (CIRCLE, 2004).

9. Common Cents Foundation is on hiatus. The New York program is not operating while support is being sought.

10. Several of the principals reported that they use Penny Harvest to differentiate their school from the competition. One school placed three of its Penny Harvest students in LAUSD's gifted program for youth leaders—a first for this school, which is typically performing below average on most metrics.

11. See https://www.dropbox.com/s/s0iz5w005igp9gm/Penny-Harvest-FINAL%20Booklet-2014.pdf?oref=e&n=156579342.

12. G. Thomas Goodnight, Minhee Son, Jin Huang, and Ann Crigler, "Youth, Networks and Civic Engagement: Communities of Belonging and Communities of Practice," in *Speech and Debate as Education for Citizenship*, ed. J. Michael Hogan (University Park: Pennsylvania State University Press, forthcoming).

13. 54% of the students major in political science; 25%, other social science and humanities; 10.5%, communications, journalism, or public relations; 5%, business; 4%, public policy; and 1%, theater.

14. USC students who enroll in the classes come from diverse racial/ethnic backgrounds (11% African American, 1% Native American, 14% Asian American, 26% Hispanic, 47% white, 1% other). But this distribution is different from the ethnic diversity in the five participating LAUSD schools where, between 2013 and 2017, the total student bodies are predominantly Hispanic (1% African American, 0% Native American, 5% Asian American/Filipino/Pacific Islander, 93% Hispanic, 1% white). In addition, according to LAUSD reports, more than 89% of the students in these schools are socioeconomically disadvantaged.

15. Dewey, *Democracy and Education*; Paulo Freire, *Pedagogy of the Oppressed* (New York: Seabury Press, 1970); Paulo Freire, *Pedagogy of Freedom: Ethics, Democracy, and Civic Courage* (Lanham, MD: Rowman & Littlefield, 1998).

16. This project faces challenges similar to those that many school-based programs face in conducting rigorous assessment. We are developing a systematic, multimethod plan for assessment in future iterations. See, for example, Elizabeth A. Bennion, "Assessing Civic and Political Engagement Activities: A Toolkit," in *Teaching Civic Engagement: From Student to Active Citizen*, ed. Alison Rios Millett McCartney, Elizabeth A. Bennion, and Dick Simpson, 407–21 (Washington DC: American Political Science Association, 2013); Shelley Billig and Alan S. Waterman, eds. *Studying Service Learning: Innovations in Education Research Methodology* (Mahwah, NJ: Lawrence Erlbaum Associates, 2003); J. Torney-Purta, C. H. Barber, and B. Wilkenfeld, "Latino Adolescents' Civic Development in the United States: Research Results from the IEA Civic Education Study," *Journal of Youth and Adolescence* (2007): 111–25.

17. See http://evaluationtoolbox.net.au/index.php?option=com_content&view=article&id=24&Itemid=125.

18. Conduct of the questionnaires has met with limited success, often yielding data that are not useable because of problems in data collection with young children and limited resources. Our next step is to seek funding for independent and systematic evaluation.

19. Dewey, *Democracy and Education*.

Unscripted Learning: Cultivating Engaged Catalysts

19

James Simeone, James Sikora, and Deborah Halperin

The Action Research Center at Illinois Wesleyan University provides a model of community-based action research that opens civic engagement opportunities to students from disciplines across the campus. A pedagogy focused on project-based, problem-based, and place-based learning is outlined and four project clusters in the Bloomington–Normal community are charted. This chapter uses student vignettes to illustrate how undergraduate civic engagement capacity can be scaffolded beginning with novices and culminating with mastery. We include formative assessment rubrics that can be used to teach students to see themselves as "engaged catalysts" for their communities.

Civic engagement has long puzzled political observers. People who have grievances to air and who should participate many times do not, while those with few personal interests at stake often participate on a routine basis. As Rogers's chapter in this volume notes, political scientists have been attracted to solving the behavioral puzzle of participation, but they have been less motivated to reinforce it as a norm. One reason is that such normative instruction is considered to be necessarily partisan. But as the editors of *Teaching Civic Engagement* have summarized, "civic engagement pedagogy does not support any particular political party although it is certainly in favor of democracy writ large."[1] The norm of participation generally operates to reinforce liberal democracy as a whole.[2] Teaching "the virtues, knowledge, and skills" that citizens will use to become effective agents of change is justified on many accounts as a necessary component of democratic education.[3]

While political science is once again committing itself to promoting participation, millennial generation students face a different kind of barrier to engagement: a political setting that is arguably more polarized and less civil than the previous generation.[4] Correlated with this setting is the fact that many youth today maintain only a superficial interest in politics, a tendency Harward and Shea believe is only exacerbated by short-term service-learning or volunteer experiences. They theorize that such experiences encourage a horizontal "drive-by" commitment as opposed to "vertical participation" that requires "substantial, prolonged engagement."[5] But, as others have observed, millennials also indicate a strong preference for applying disciplinary learning to real-world problems. They express a desire to engage their communities and to realize "demonstrable results" in civic engagement.[6] This focus on real-world problems dovetails with the contemporary movement on campuses across the country to improve integrative learning in general education programs.[7] Thus, undergraduate educators today have both reason and opportunity to better connect with the current generation of college-aged students, many of whom struggle to find a place and purpose in higher education.[8]

The deep engagement required with community-based action research teaches precisely the set of knowledge, skills, and values needed to cross knowledge domains and foster creative integration. It challenges millennials with unscripted learning opportunities and cultivates the real-world capabilities they seek. In addition, applied learning in the context of long-term relationships can open the door to less cynicism and more realism about the challenges of public work in a pluralistic democracy. In sum, the pedagogical approach discussed here has the potential to move students from disciplinary silos to integrative learning, from the horizontal (private) to the vertical (public and political realms), and from passivity and cynicism about participation and power to interaction and negotiation. Ideally, exposure to meaningful civic activities will overcome the barrier of political polarization, engender trust, and lead to a future of creative political engagement among the dot.com generation—a hope framed and expressed in the landmark work by Zukin et al.[9]

In this chapter, we examine one across-the-curriculum model that teaches civic engagement by focusing on three related learning outcomes: knowledge of place, problem-solving capacity, and the skills of project management. We rely on assessment data compiled by the Action Research Center (ARC) at Illinois Wesleyan University (IWU). We present vignettes of ARC students as they follow projects through the community. Because ARC projects focus on problems particular to a given place and people, they require students to adopt a broad, civic perspective appropriate to students from across the university curriculum. Broad public perspectives often elicit deep self-reflection in students. Learning about a place through immersion in it, following questions and problems defined by community members, and managing projects owned by community partners is by its very nature unscripted and uncertain. But this kind of learning can also lead to enormous personal development and growth, with students emerging from the extended experience as "engaged catalysts." It also requires an improvisational kind of teaching where it is appropriate to use a more formative, less punitive approach to assessment.

We share our assessment rubrics with students throughout their training. Our pedagogical stance is one of coaxing students to recognize their strengths and weakness by comparing their on-going project-management skills with the capacities we highlight in the rubrics. Essential practices such as teamwork, active listening, and prototype building are discussed and practiced in the classroom before being tried in the field. Values like appreciation of diversity and respect for local knowledge are modeled in the premises of exercises in stakeholder analysis and community-asset mapping. Knowledge of public-policy processes, the impact of local governmental forms, and the need for leaders to read organizational culture and political opportunity structures are all taught as part of our pedagogy. Before discussing this pedagogy in detail, we introduce the ARC model and review its structure.

ARC ACROSS THE CURRICULUM

The ARC was founded in 2003 on the IWU campus to bring students, faculty, and community partners together to collaborate on research projects benefiting the public good. Originally funded by a pilot grant from State Farm Insurance, which is headquartered in Bloomington, ARC has become the heart of IWU's commitment to civic engagement in McLean County, the university's wider urban and rural community. In its upper-level classes—seminar, grant-writing class, and internships—together with an introductory class and other fellowships, ARC works with approximately 75 students annually, maintains relationships with more than 90 community partners, and is currently overseeing dozens of projects (see table 19.1). Two full-time staff, a director, and a coordinator help faculty from disciplines as diverse as philosophy, computer science, biology, Hispanic studies, and music forge meaningful long-term relationships with community partners. But ARC staff spend the majority of their time working with students from more than 20 departments on campus to craft experiential learning projects for the seminar and internships

Table 19.1 ARC Community Partners

100 Black Men	Mackinaw River Watershed Partnership
ACLU Central Illinois Chapter	Marcfirst
American Red Cross	McLean County 4-H
Autism Society of McLean County	McLean County Alzheimer's Association
Belle Prairie Township	McLean County Arts Center
Big Brothers/Big Sisters of B/N	McLean County Child Advocacy Network
Bloomington Creativity Center	McLean County Law and Justice Center
Bloomington Farmer's Market	McLean County Master Gardeners
Bloomington Historical Museum	McLean County Wellness Coalition
Bloomington Tool Library	Mennonite Church of Normal
Boys and Girls Club of B/N	Mid-Central Community Action
Calvary United Methodist Church	Milestones Early Learning Center
Central Illinois Small Animal Rescue	Miller Park Zoo
Children's Discovery Museum	Neville House
CHJ Umoja Gardens	Normal Rotary Club
City of Bloomington (multiple offices)	Old House Society of McLean County
Collaborative Solutions Institute	Our Chinese Daughters Foundation
Community Health Clinic	Parklands Foundation
Conexiones Latinas	PATH (Providing Access to Help)
Day Care Center of McLean County	Prairie Rivers
Downtown Business Association	Prairie State Legal Services
East Central Illinois Area on Aging	Prudential Real Estate
Ecology Action Center	Regional Alternative School
Eureka Community Hospital	Rhonda Taylor Law Firm
Founders' Grove Neighborhood Association	Second Presbyterian Church
Friends of the Constitution Trail	Spence Farm Foundation
Friends of the Kickapoo	State Farm
Great Plains Life Foundation	State Representative Dan Brady
Habitat for Humanity of McLean County	The Babyfold
Heartland Head Start	The Immigration Project
Hispanic Families Work Group	The Land Connection
Homes for Hope	The Nature Conservancy
Illinois CASA Foundation	Town of Normal (multiple offices)
Illinois EPA	Unit Five School District
Illinois People's Action	United Way of Mclean County
Illinois Shakespeare Festival	Unity Community Center
Illinois State University	Uptown Normal Farmers' Market
Illinois Stewardship Alliance	Washington School
IWU Peace Garden	West Bloomington Revitalization Project
Kane County Board	Western Avenue Community Center
Lake Bloomington	WJBC
Lamu Center of Preventative Health	YMCA of Bloomington/Normal
Legacy of the Land Farm Coop	YWCA of Bloomington/Normal
LINC Center	

(see table 19.2). Unscripted learning is at the core of what ARC does. The vast majority of ARC projects place students in a community setting to help catalyze and address the unscripted problems citizens face.

ARC projects have four features that distinguish them from traditional academic research or service-learning:

1. the research questions originate with and are refined in collaboration with our community partners, not the academic literature;
2. the projects are coherent parts of larger long-term wholes (two-three years)—much longer than typical service-learning projects;
3. the projects require relationship-building and mutual trust among faculty, students, and community partners; and
4. students spend considerable time as project catalysts who facilitate implementation of collaborative action plan goals.

Table 19.2 Departments at IWU Working with ARC (By Numbers of Student Projects)	
DEPARTMENT PROJECTS	
Sociology	26
Political Science	24
Business Administration	11
Environmental Studies	10
English	7
Accounting and Finance	6
Economics	6
Psychology	6
International Studies	5
Hispanic Studies	5
History	4
Art	3
Educational Studies	3
Biology	3
Physics	2
Computer Science	2
Philosophy	1
Theatre Arts	1
Mathematics	1
German	1
Music	1
Anthropology	1
Nursing	1

ARC'S IMPACT ACROSS THE DISCIPLINES

In 2015, we completed a longitudinal study with a treatment group of ARC students and two control groups (one of political science majors and another of majors from across the curriculum) in which we compared the ARC students' skills, knowledge, and perspective on public work to the randomly selected control-group students.[10]

We surveyed current ARC students and alumni to test the impact of varying degrees of exposure to community-based research—from one to three semesters—and attitudes about future engagement, knowledge of community networks, and stance toward public work. We wanted to know if ARC's pedagogy encouraged our liberal arts students to become more interested in community work and/or more motivated to continue engaging. We also asked whether we had succeeded in educating students about the importance of relationships and social networks in catalyzing public action; and whether the students' experiences led them to modify their commonly inherited baseline view, the individualist "go-it-alone" view of community work.[11] This last query sought to know if we had succeeded in nudging them away from the simplistic "white knight" understanding of their role to the more collaborative and reciprocal stance of the engaged catalyst.

The results of the 2015 study were encouraging. ARC students were different from the two randomly selected, scaled control groups—political science majors and university-wide students enrolled in a lower-level general education course. The ARC students evinced a stronger commitment to community engagement with regard to skills applied and time of involvement, deeper knowledge of how social networks can be tapped to leverage public action, and a positive stance toward the often difficult road to traverse in managing projects owned by community members. Although the differences were not large—as is to be expected given a one-course treatment—they were in the right direction and were strongly reinforced by responses from ARC alumni, many veterans of community-partner relationships that spanned two and three semesters. The number of community-based research skills that our alums reported they routinely used in their current career or engagement work was truly remarkable. We offered a list of 13 skills ranging from talking to community leaders to following an action plan to building a budget. Just over half (53%) indicated between seven and 10 skills (see table 19.3). One-third listed between two and six skills (no one indicated fewer than two). Fifteen percent told us they learned between 11 and 13 different skills. Overall, the civic engagement levels reported by ARC alums almost double the rates reported by IWU alums generally: 61% of ARC alums indicating they volunteer in the community on a regular basis, whereas only 30%–38% of the larger cohort do. While in small part these results may follow from a selection bias—and the pretest of ARC students did indicate a slight bias in favor of community work prior to our pedagogy—the degree of change suggests that the training had a significant impact.[12]

These findings resonate with what students have reported anecdotally over the years about their ARC experiences. Many student evaluations and visiting alumni tell us that their project work

Table 19.3 Alumni Mentions of Civic Engagement Skills Acquired Via ARC	
Skills Acquired	**Frequency of Mention by ARC Alumni Respondents**
How to get involved in the community	72%
Talking to community leaders	67%
Seeing a community for it strengths	67%
Active listening	67%
Working in diverse communities	63%
Following an action plan	55%
Grant writing	42%
Community organizing	41%
Producing reports	36%
Building a budget	36%
Writing a press release	16%
Source: November 2013 survey of ARC alums cited in Simeone and Shaw (2017).	

was the single most transformative experience of their college education. Many also report that seeing results in the community motivated them in ways the classroom experience had not. This suggests that our community-based research pedagogies have the capacity to reach students who for one reason or another have not been accessible by the traditional pen-and-paper approach alone. There are two reasons this finding was not particularly surprising to us and should not be surprising to many veteran college teachers. First, dialogue with many of our underperforming students over the years revealed that many feel that the "golden road" to the professions (law, medical, or accounting school) is not for them. These students often struggle to master college-level academics, yet they care about the community, want to make a difference, and want to develop their civic capacities. Second, assessment of senior capstone research papers in programs across the university at IWU—from political science and history to sociology and religion—indicates a distinct bimodal distribution: while departments succeeded in teaching the basics of research methods with one group of students, about 60% of the whole, they failed to develop the full array of research skills with the rest. Both types of underperforming students, those without a golden-road destination and those not motivated to excel at pen-and-paper research, were nonetheless among the top quintile of college-bound students in the state of Illinois. While lacking the sustained interest needed to excel at the highest levels in book learning, these underperforming students show a latent capacity to learn and apply community-based research skills to real-world problems. Our evidence here is anecdotal, but it is telling: one student related that he had studied social movements enough to want to go out and participate in one. Of course, ARC projects also attract high-performing academic students, but our capacity to reach nontraditional student cohorts such as these underperforming social science majors and students with majors outside the social sciences is perhaps most noteworthy.

As IWU has worked to increase high-impact practices on campus, ARC's project-based pedagogy has become a part of a larger university-wide strategy. Our cross-discipline approach has the benefit of opening the university to more aspects of the community and opening the community to more students. As Nie and Hillygas have shown, there is a remarkable positive relationship between students with high verbal SAT scores and community engagement after college. These have traditionally been the students most interested in civic engagement during and after college. They further discovered that students with high verbal aptitude who later majored in social sciences ended up with the highest engagement scores after college. The same was not true of humanities majors, who often also have high verbal scores. Their most stunning results showed a strong negative relationship between engagement scores and students with high math SAT scores as well as with students majoring in biology, chemistry, physics, and engineering.[13] These students help account for the well-known paradox that Nie, Junn, and Stehlik-Barry attempt to explain, namely that while the percentage of higher education degrees has been increasing in the United States, during the same period individual political engagement has been declining.[14] If, in fact, many students in college have a learned or cognitive disinclination to engage in public work, a cross-discipline approach has obvious tactical advantages.

Setting the engagement goal at the community or public-good level allows a broad problem-solving approach. It targets a civic level of generality that not only fits students from all disciplines but also can be assessed on a university-wide basis. The increasing prominence of interdisciplinary programs on campuses nationwide has already forged the ties across disciplines that make across-the-curriculum civic engagement more possible.[15] Community-based research projects are fit candidates for the kind of culminating, integrative experiences increasingly common in the "signature" work movement within general education programs.[16] Political science and sociology departments may be more able to oversee this kind of university programming because, unlike other departments (e.g., history, economics, and psychology), these disciplines have a history of using internships to enable applied learning. In an era of shrinking budgets at universities across the country, political science as a discipline has an opportunity to lead on campus, and it should put its comparative advantage to use.

While the ARC context—a liberal arts college in a mid-size community[17]—is in some ways unique, this should not limit the applicability of our model, which stresses building civic engagement capacity in students but also features elements of research and service. Institutional civic engagement models exist in an unlimited variety; each combines in its own way the three traditional foci of universities—research, teaching, and service.[18]

ARC's approach is also highly compatible with scaffolding. One message that comes through clearly in the literature on higher education pedagogy is that today's students are asking for more step-by-step training. While this approach is especially needed for discipline-specific skills like research methods and design, it is also true of work across-the-disciplines.[19] Our model, in its ideal form, guides students from what for most is their first unscripted community work as novices to the more intensive associate level (typically in an internship or grant-writing class) to mastery in independent capstone or fellowship projects in which they can apply the full range of skills, knowledge, and perspectives that ARC teaches and demonstrate proficiency in project management.

In sum, university-based civic engagement programs offer a unique opportunity not only for the discipline of political science and its students but for students across the curriculum. They present a chance to improve American civic culture that should not be missed. Students are allowed space to manage and creatively catalyze projects, but they are also provided a safety net as they listen and deliberate to solve real-world problems originally suggested by community partners. As we reach more students, community-based research programs should be able to measure the impact of our gown-sponsored projects on the towns and places in which we live.[20] We turn next to ARC's pedagogy, organized around place, problem, and project, which challenges students and prompts their development as agents of change.

PEDAGOGIES OF PLACE, PROBLEM, AND PROJECT

Citizenship as a general matter occurs in the context of a locale and relies on local knowledge. Place-based learning has had several incarnations on university campuses. One is the town–gown partnership movement, which was spurred by The Carnegie Foundation and the US Department of Housing and Urban Development (HUD) in the 1990s.[21] Traditionally, urban studies and history programs have focused on place as a tool for learning.[22] University-community partnerships are especially common in urban settings. Often, the university acts simply to exert influence on its immediate setting rather than from any larger sense of mission, although the two motives are not mutually exclusive.[23]

Places provide a focus but are also dynamic; long-term relationships among people are the common denominator on both the university and community side. As David Maurrasse noted of Ann Spirn's work with the Mill Creek neighborhood in West Philadelphia, "The relationship may begin by addressing one particular issue, but the continuous collective discussion about the state of the neighborhood leads to other ideas and other strategies. Once the relationships are solidified, numerous avenues can be taken."[24] Town–gown relationships require willingness to trust on both sides. On the one hand, local residents often rightfully have suspicions about the intentions of large institutions, and they have frequently observed their negative impact on the neighborhood.[25] On the other hand, educators need to recognize that not all knowledge comes from a book or a factor analysis. Synthesized knowledge and creative compromise are the result of work done with communities, not on them.

Respect for local knowledge leads directly to opportunities for critical thinking as problem solving forces students and communities to cross knowledge domains in pursuit of solutions. In a Colorado case, ranchers faced off against water engineers; and in Woburn, Massachusetts, popular epidemiology confronted both the courts and the research lab.[26] Interestingly, the crossing of knowledge domains in these cases spurred the academics involved to reconsider their own epistemological assumptions. The Woburn case led a team of epidemiologists at Harvard University to acknowledge that "authorities ... disagree on the level of statistical significance required for intervention in environmental hazard settings."[27] As a result of her community-based work, epidemiologist Beverly Paigen, who worked at the Love Canal toxic waste site, ended up changing her mind on what degree of statistical significance was warranted in environmental impacts on people.[28] Paigen's reaction recalls the adjustments Paul Farmer, Partners in Health founder, made in his clinic's treatment of tuberculosis. Haitian patients told him that the clinic's original method of simply distributing antibiotics was an insufficient treatment of the disease, akin to "*lave men, siye ate* (washing one's hands and then wiping them dry in the dirt)."[29] Farmer listened and changed his protocol to include financial support until the course of medication was complete.[30]

Engaged catalysts also discover that place-based learning is a two-way street. In the Colorado case, the project led some of the local rancher community partners to recognize that they needed to change their ranching practices. Pena argues that "the presence of the outsider, such as a scholarly researcher, can result in the identification of contradictions that may escape the notice of the locals. These contradictions, rooted in the political and economic life of the community, can undermine the collaborative relationship if the locals feel threatened or betrayed by the researcher." However, this new knowledge can also empower the community by pointing to "problems that might destroy the credibility of local knowledge."[31] Farmer, a PhD in anthropology as well as an MD, walked this fine line in his experience with patients' emphasis on Voodoo. He respected Haitian belief systems intrinsically but decided to treat the Voodoo ceremonies instrumentally: they were held because people were sick. Illness and Voodoo were linked in the local imagination, yet "this simple fact has eluded all the many commentaries on Voodoo."[32]

The upshot is that action researchers must balance sensitivity to local ways with commitments to disciplinary knowledge and understanding of the mechanisms of power. Farmer pleads that we not "confuse structural violence with cultural difference."[33] His experience in Haiti takes us back to the paradox of participation: when action is blocked, participants turn to other strategies, perhaps rational only within the setting of structural power in which they function. Pena's and Farmer's experiences suggest that students must be explicit about their own value commitments, about local cultures, and about the power dynamics involved in both.[34] Every place contains a unique structural setting built of culture, institutions, and power. Students must learn to decipher local settings and navigate organizational cultures if they wish to be effective catalysts and change agents.[35]

For ARC students, the pedagogy of place runs parallel to the pedagogies of project and problem. The focus on project-based learning at ARC grew from the desire to meet the challenge of students who were seeking more from existing internships. The project-management focus grew from an effort to teach students with disparate field experiences a common curriculum. One student might be addressing a local housing problem while another looked at an environmental issue, but in seminar they could share and learn simultaneously the processes of interviewing stakeholders, building a collective narrative of a problem or issue, and laying out a best practices study.[36] Students were able to meet weekly to debrief each other and strategize about overcoming gatekeepers and other obstacles. They also learned common tools like action plans, meeting agendas and minutes, and executive summaries.

Problem-based learning was an early focus for ARC. Before 2003, few IWU students were encouraged to look at real-life problems in the local community; they preferred to remain on campus, in the "Bubble" as colloquially called, rather than enter the unfamiliar though nearby urban community. Problem-based learning allows students to "work with classmates to solve complex and authentic problems that help develop content knowledge as well as problem-solving, reasoning, communication, and self-assessment skills."[37] ARC students identify and interview stakeholders and construct complex narratives depicting the problem under study from multiple perspectives. As we placed more academic emphases on community, community partners, and problem-based learning, students began to prefer community learning over the classroom. But questions raised by the partners often sent them back to the library. Students were bridging and integrating the knowledge and skills they learned in the liberal arts classroom with the skills and knowledge required of them to be effective citizens in community-problem collaborations.

In their liberal arts studies at IWU, skills like oral and written communication, literature reviews, critical thinking, information literacy, and other learning all contributed to the students' *individual* learning and general knowledge. In our experience, many were quite comfortable working by themselves, and the high-achieving students were especially inclined not to partner with anyone else, sometimes including their professors. But students quickly changed their approach when they found themselves on collaborative teams of students and nonstudents addressing community-initiated problems that were ill-structured and unscripted. In this context, group and teamwork is prominent. They have to rely on others to deal with the complex, maybe unsolvable, real problems that directly and indirectly affect other citizens. Such problems are open-ended; have multiple solutions and sometimes dead ends; and require collaboration, thinking beyond recall, negotiations between partners, and taking individual risks. Problem-based learning requires interpersonal skills where students lead sometimes and at other times must be a savvy follower. Then there are the typical daily problems of finding the necessary time and scheduling to make a group succeed. These project-management issues usually are not considered initially by students, but other courses, employment demands, and extracurricular activities—to name a few potential conflicts—can make collaborative group work a challenge. The learning curve is steep and unforgiving throughout their team collaborations.

There is much to be learned in these situations. Wilkerson and Gijselaers write that problem-based learning "requires students to be metacognitively aware."[38] That is, students must learn to be conscious of what information they already know about the problem, what information they need to know to solve the problem, and the strategies to use to solve the problem. Being able to articulate such thoughts "helps students become more effective problem-solvers and self-directed learners."[39] Any collaborated effort by multiple stakeholders requires *teamwork*, where, in a truly reciprocal process, all members serve others. Students soon learn that

- they are contributors, not leaders;
- they are expected to accept and seriously consider that others' ideas are equally valid pursuits;
- reaching a consensus takes more time and energy than they are usually prepared for;
- excellence is expected because they are students attending a university seen as privileged in the community;
- positive interactions are the norm;
- conflicts will be resolved constructively;
- they must motivate and support the team members whenever unique situations arise.

These learning outcomes are a lot to ask of undergraduates but are worth specifying.

Teaching undergraduates about problem-based learning in the community moves beyond an explicit syllabus—because life happens and we assist them in confronting and adjusting to the happenings. Our job as instructors is to nudge them to be flexible and tolerate ambiguity. All of these student learning outcomes give them other personal options to consider and ways of looking at the community and themselves anew. Indeed, the importance of personal development, while frequently overlooked in the area of civic engagement, is of central importance to ARC's multiple-pedagogy approach. We match students to projects based on disciplinary preference, but the logic of community-based research takes students on a problem-solving odyssey across many learning domains. Community problems, multifaceted and often the result of the failure of collective action, have no obvious solution—and certainly no simple disciplinary answers. Students pursue solutions by interviewing stakeholders, questioning authorities, interrogating facts, researching best practices, and making their own judgments; the projects evolve under these fluid conditions as students create critical syntheses of local knowledge and expert opinion amid the pressure of impending deadlines. In their journals or other reflective assignments, the students begin to reframe their understanding of where they are living. They begin to see how institutional structures and power as well as their fellow citizens play roles shaping the uniqueness of place.

EXAMPLES OF ARC PROJECT CLUSTERS AND COMMUNITY NETWORKS

To illustrate how ARC pedagogy works, we have assembled a few characteristic action-research vignettes. In practice, ARC operates mainly in four project clusters, one each addressing environmental issues, the City of Bloomington administration, housing, and West Bloomington revitalization (see figure 19.1). Each cluster of projects evolves in its own way over time, and each follows its own rhythm. Some have highly ordered settings, as with the government bureaucracy typical of the city administration, while others are more unstructured and fluid as is routine among the civil society organizations found in the environmental advocacy arena. In addition, some projects live on for years while others die after only one semester. Because community-based research is unscripted, student learning outcomes are unpredictable. Since project outcomes vary sometimes due to factors the students themselves cannot control, we consequently do not grade the projects on outcome alone.[40] Project deliverables are only a part of the grade evaluation, and there are enough pieces of evidence to fairly treat each individual student despite the unscripted nature of the experience. For analytical purposes, we have arrayed the vignettes along the four following features that distinguish action research, as noted previously:

1. project questions originate with the community;
2. projects span multiple years;
3. projects require and build upon community networks and relationship building; and
4. project implementation requires students to act as engaged catalysts.

An example of how ARC students negotiate with community partners to originate research questions appears in the following case of the city's Miller Park Zoo. Although not working with ARC at the time, zoo staff became receptive to a study by biology major Alena Wright after she

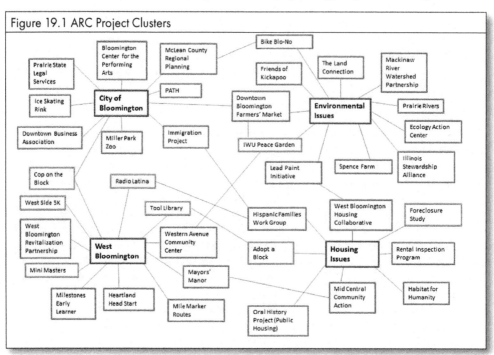

Figure 19.1 ARC Project Clusters

visited briefly as part of a class trip. Alena noticed that the sun bears were exhibiting dysfunctional behavior.[41] She returned to the zoo and persuaded the staff to authorize her to design a study of the bears. Later, as an ARC intern, she extensively observed and tested the bears' cognitive skills to gauge their overall level of curiosity. Her study concluded with several recommended strategies for improving the bears' habitat. In short order, the zoo adopted her study's recommendations as part of a new, cost-effective regime to engage the bears during the daylight hours. Miller Park Zoo is now a receptive ARC community partner.

The length and relational nature of ARC projects (features 2 and 3, noted earlier) is indicated in the following vignette. In the fall of 2005, as part of an environmental regulation course, political science student Jack Ryan began a dialogue with several McLean County farm managers to collect their views on conservation easements. One of his interviews was with the Spence Farm stewards. Jack kept in touch with them, and in the spring of 2006, as part of an ARC internship, he implemented a collaborative action plan to enable the Spence Farm Foundation to move the 1855 Phelps Schoolhouse from a nearby Belle Prairie Township property to their farm as part of their effort to develop Spence Farm as an historic farm site and education center. Jack's "official" project that semester was writing a "Save Our History" grant proposal for Spence Farm to the Illinois Humanities Council. It was not funded. Grant writing benefits from multiple iterations. When Tom Morgan interned with Spence Farm a few years later, he researched and wrote a Specialty Crop Small Grant for the farm through the Illinois Department of Agriculture; Tom relied on the background information Jack had collected about the farm. While Tom's grant was not funded that year, it was resubmitted in substantially the same form and funded the next year. Later, the Spence Farm stewards returned the favor by helping ARC's Peace Garden gain entry into the Legacy of the Land Farm cooperative. As for Tom Morgan, who began college as a biology major, after he graduated he was hired by the US Park Service specifically for his grant-writing skills. Although he served the Park Service with distinction, he was later offered and accepted a scholarship for graduate study in rural sustainability in part due to his experience with Spence Farm and other farms in the area.

Reciprocal action is typical in community-based research because as students follow a problem-solving thread, proposed solutions initiate new projects that then engage further project catalyzing, the fourth feature of ARC projects. Steve Carlyle wrote a pen-and-paper seminar study of food deserts. He followed it with a summer internship where he worked with West Bloomington residents to implement an action plan to address their fresh food access problem. The next fall, Steve wrote and received a $10,000 grant to purchase an Electronic Benefit Transfer machine (which accepts Supplemental Nutrition Assistance Program, or SNAP, benefits) and a token system for the local Farmers' Market. Half of the grant funds were used in $5 tokens, which were distributed to west side residents who live in a food desert but rarely attend the downtown market only a few blocks away.

The success of this project generated interest in food deserts among other environmental studies students. One environmental studies major, Lee Wiseman, used Weir Fellowship money to attend a conference about campus gardens at Lawrence University. The next spring, he presented his findings to the IWU community at the annual Martin Luther King Jr. Teach-In. With the university's president and provost in attendance, Lee challenged the campus to create a garden and grow food to mitigate the west side's food desert. Very soon afterwards, the administrators agreed to support the creation of a garden on campus; in this case, both community and campus were catalyzed by ARC students. The campus "Peace Garden" now hires two summer managers and is the source for many ARC internships annually. Part of the work involves planting, producing, and preparing the garden's produce, half of which is donated to West Bloomington food pantries and half sold at a farmstand that pays the summer managers' salaries. One summer manager, Grace Simmons, was attracted to the Peace Garden through her involvement with the student club that manages it. An international studies major, Grace's interest was also spurred by her high school training as a chef and her interest in global cuisines. As part of an ARC fellowship, she wrote a grant to use the Peace Garden as a field trip destination for teaching elementary school children about sustainability, heirloom seeds, and herbs. Her funded grant "Good Starts for Green Sprouts" introduced local school children to planting and growing four different heirloom varieties of basil (Thai, Italian, lemon, and cinnamon). Given that the school's teachers decided to use the field trips to the garden to meet state requirements for teaching science experiments, environmental studies interns have since built a sustainability education program for the garden using the Next Generation Science Standards as a guide. Student teachers in the educational studies department have presented ARC with a proposal to teach the sustainability program to the schoolchildren and assess its impact as part of their signature work graduation requirement.

The long-term nature of ARC project implementation is one of the great challenges of this kind of work, but it can also lead to the most meaningful results. When a very qualified chief of police was appointed in the city in 2009, the police department suddenly became open to new partnerships. One council member sensed an opening in the spring and asked ARC intern Frank Allegretti to conduct a crime-perception survey in her ward. With the help of a political science professor, Frank wrote the survey. Since he was graduating in the fall, Frank pushed to administer the survey over the summer, motivating a group of dedicated volunteers to pursue the project along with him while he worked two jobs to support himself. In the end, more than 200 residents were contacted in the door-to-door survey. By the fall, Frank had compiled his data, run a multiple-regression analysis, and presented his synthesized findings to the new police chief along with the staff and the council member.

Embedded and sometimes hidden in these unscripted learning vignettes are the ways civic engagement transforms student understanding of how democracy works. Before Tom Morgan interned with Spence Farm, he had written off agriculture as an ally in wilderness preservation. With time, this biology-focused environmentalist came to recognize the common ground he as an ecological holist shared with farmers committed to environmental stewardship, an anthropocentric approach with a different epistemology from his own. Other ARC student projects, not presented in detail here, featured similar transformations. Briefly, economics major Rosie Starceski had a top-down, elitist view of economic development before she engaged the west side community. But after a year of active listening, she convened a housing summit with a representative array of west side stakeholders. The summit initiated an adopt-a-block program that has demonstrated a long-standing impact. Her patient work with stakeholders made the difference between success and yet another noncompliant failure. In another case, accounting major Jonathan Meade had a fact-and-figures view of foreclosures and the banking-industry business before he got involved with the west side. He eventually suggested the prototype of a tool library and catalyzed the institution on the west side. He discovered that bridging social networks can mitigate the powerlessness of financially marginal neighborhoods. In all these cases, the synthesis of local knowledge with disciplinary perspectives produced significant changes in our students' civic attitudes and signature work for the community.

FORMATIVE ASSESSMENT FOR BUILDING CIVIC CAPACITY

For the purposes of student assessment, two features of the variance among ARC projects stand out. The first is the project's community setting, including both the degree of community ownership and the degree of the sponsoring partner's efficacy. The second is the project's developmental stage when students encounter it. Because of these exogenous factors, some students will have an opportunity to move their project through many stages, while others will find their project stalled. For this reason, students should be assessed at "novice," "associate," and "master" levels based not only on their skills but their project's degree of difficulty, ripeness, and ownership. In table 19.4, we present rubrics that specify learning outcomes at these three levels. Program assessment will also be facilitated by such layered tools because regardless of where individual students end, examples of each level can be included in a broader review.

When we talk with students about their ARC experience, they frequently remark on its transformative impact.[42] They reference not any particular skill or set of skills but rather their encounter with overlapping social networks and the importance of their roles as catalysts. It is fitting then to craft an assessment tool that allows a more holistic measurement. Under the approach advocated here, student learning outcomes are grouped under the "observe, judge, act" methodology followed by Paul Farmer after a model first articulated by liberation theology in the 1980s.[43] The rubrics found in table 19.4 feature distinct "observe, judge, act" stances or outlooks on action-research roles. ARC uses a six-step iterative process as part of its civic

Table 19.4 Formative Assessment Rubrics

ARC'S PROJECT-BASED LEARNING RUBRIC

Level/Phase	Observe	Judge	Act
Novice	Active listening	Critical thinking	Project prototype
Proficiency	Journaling, open question asking	Stakeholder analyses	Collaborative action plans
Associate	Active listening	Critical thinking	Project catalyst
Proficiency	Interviewing	Social network leveraging	Teamwork
Master	Active listening	Critical thinking	Project management
Proficiency	Communal narratives	Best practices studies	Implementing, managing, assessing

ARC'S PROBLEM-BASED LEARNING RUBRIC

Level/Phase	Observe	Judge	Act
Novice	Active listening	Critical thinking	Problem/solution definition
Proficiency	Journaling, open question asking	Stakeholder analyses	Collaborative action plans
Associate	Active listening	Critical thinking	Conflict resolution
Proficiency	Interviewing, crafting master narratives	Needs assessments	Network mapping
Master	Active listening	Critical thinking	Project management
Proficiency	Review of statistically significant data	Asset mapping	Grant writing

ARC'S PLACE-BASED LEARNING RUBRIC

Level/Phase	Observe	Judge	Act
Novice	Active listening	Critical thinking	Place exploration
Proficiency	Meet neighbors, activists	Record local knowledge	Community meetings
Associate	Active listening	Critical thinking	Place definition
Proficiency	Meet local officials, non-profit executive directors	Assess local knowledge	Community-setting study (culture, institutions, power)
Master	Active listening	Critical thinking	Place membership
Proficiency	Network mapping	GIS mapping, US Census data, American Fact Finder	Community initiative (e.g., survey, focus groups, workshop)

engagement pedagogy. Whether in the seminar, internships, or grant-writing classes, we ask students to

1. engage the community,
2. find good data,
3. review best practices,
4. layer partnerships,
5. launch a prototype, and
6. review and refine the results.

Step 1 mainly requires active listening to learn how the community partner views the project and its setting. This "observe" stance requires the skills of open question asking, follow-up interviewing, careful notetaking, and narrative writing. Here the point is to arrive at a collaboratively agreed-on narrative of the problem or issue the community faces. Steps 2, 3, and 4, which combine to form the "judge" stance, require students to use critical thinking as they gather data about community assets, determine how best practices can be applied to the setting at hand, and learn to use social networks to connect interested parties. The skills needed to accomplish these steps will vary greatly according to the project but will likely include the use of focus groups, surveys, needs assessments, white papers, asset-based inventories, grant writing, setting studies, comparative policy memos, action plans, stakeholder analyses, and prototype development. The "act" stance begins with Step 5 and continues through Step 6 and successive iterations of the process. Students work in teams on scripted class projects before they are expected to act in the community. The greatest degree of variety in proficiency comes in these final steps as students move from catalyzing an idea for a project to launching a prototype to finally implementing, managing, and assessing revised versions.

Using learning outcomes focused on research stance or role as opposed to content-based outcomes or project deliverables is appropriate in experiential learning because the knowledge domains first envisioned can change radically in what is revised and re-envisioned as projects and problems evolve. Disciplinary frames also evolve; they move from environmental studies to history, Hispanic studies to sociology, or educational studies to music. Students need to become "instant experts" in fields and methods they adopt as required. In the vignettes described earlier, Jack Ryan began with a project framed in environmental studies but ended up with one focused on history. Tom Morgan started in ecology, shifted to agricultural studies, and ended up in environmental policy. Rosie Starceski started in housing and ended up in urban planning. If it is not the project but student interest that evolves, students will be directed to take a methods class in the appropriate discipline before resuming project management. Other students were limited in their mastery because of the nature or timing of the projects they selected. Alena Wright pioneered an ARC connection with the Miller Park Zoo, a connection we (and she) could not develop until after she graduated. Jonathan Meade left his personal signature on the west side with his tool library, which lives on. These and other students achieved a mastery of community-based research by the end of their experiences.

Unscripted learning can be unwieldy. We stress here its transformative potential. We share the rubrics with students strategically to spur their civic capacity. Novices typically have trouble narrowing the scope of their projects. Alena Wright hoped to conduct a study based on a large number of observations but in the end crafted a project that impacted the sun bears' quality of life and initiated a community partnership. We used the project-based rubric to encourage her as she moved from a project prototype to project catalyst (see table 19.4 under the project-based leaning rubric). She responded by narrowing the scope of her personal research project but expanding her overall project's usefulness by listening to the zookeeper's needs. In the end, she was able to see her public work as a small piece of a larger effort and to see that she still had room to grow in mastering project-management skills.

Novices routinely have trouble scaling a social setting that may range from neighbors who live on public assistance to the chief of police. Writing narratives that combine the disparate voices of such stakeholders enables them to see community issues from a broader framework, where solutions can become more apparent. Frank Allegretti, a political science major, focused at first on the police as the locus of power and audience for his crime survey. But repeated visits to West Bloomington where his survey took place led him to frequent interactions with local youth, which Frank discovered he enjoyed immensely. He was encouraged to see the neighborhood he was visiting regularly as a place of unique character and heritage. He began to perceive the neighbors as key stakeholders in his project and to see the crime problem from their perspective, namely that feelings of safety in the area could be greatly increased if the police would engage with youth directly and enforce relatively minor infractions informally. Frank's survey supported this interpretation and he emphasized it in his presentation to the chief. Most remarkably perhaps, Frank learned that he enjoyed working with urban youth, decided to pursue his education certificate, and is now teaching in a large city.

It may seem improbable that undergraduates can reach a master level of civic engagement, but it does happen. Rosie Starceski and Jonathan Meade represent such mastery. They both moved beyond ARC's resources to leverage their own social capital and raised the funds needed to implement their projects. They began with stakeholder narratives and best practice studies that served as catalysts with few moving parts (i.e., housing study and needs assessment) to managing projects requiring knowledge across multiple domains and a high degree of skill (i.e., the adopt-a-block program and the tool library). In each case, they added prototypes new to the ARC portfolio and new to the Bloomington–Normal community. In their evolution, each learned to frame community problems from the perspective of community master narratives that prompted overlapping, layered partnerships and allowed for multiple goals.

The impact of ARC's formative pedagogy is most noticeable on the civic capacities of students who manage projects over several semesters. Students at the novice stage often have meager project-management skills. They will contact a community member via e-mail and wait weeks for a response; they only feel comfortable venturing into the community in large groups; and they attach a single overarching purpose to a project (frequently their own). After two semesters with ARC, they send e-mails but quickly add follow-up telephone calls and office visits; they explore community sites multiple times over the semester and recognize connections between community members, which network mapping makes clear; and they see projects as having multiple goals, can articulate the nuances among various stakeholder views, and have a sense of how local knowledge will frame and shape issues. We encourage them with our rubrics to expand their repertoires of engagement from observation to action. They learn to adopt differentiated scripts as they move from the specialized world of public officials and the professions to general interactions in the public realm in all its diversity of age, income, race, place, and gender.

CONCLUSION

An ARC experience has proven to be a high-impact practice for students from majors across the disciplines at IWU. Unscripted learning in civic engagement leads to better trained, more knowledgeable, more active citizens who can implement traditional classroom learning. Our purpose has been to describe the goals of ARC's project pedagogies, describe how the projects evolve in diverse community settings, and sketch how to use assessment tools designed to minimize whatever problems the variance may entail. The pedagogies and learning goals presented here can be used together or individually. Our project-based, problem-based, and place-based rubrics emphasize skills, knowledge, roles, and perspectives that are widely shared regardless of outcome. Programs that build the civic capacities of students need to be flexible enough to meet the needs of students at all skill levels. Our civic engagement programs must be designed to anticipate the inevitably varied outcomes that occur when students are challenged by unscripted, real-world problems. ■

ENDNOTES

1. Alison Rios Millett McCartney, Elizabeth A. Bennion, and Dick Simpson, eds., *Teaching Civic Engagement: From Student to Active Citizen* (Washington, DC: American Political Science Association, 2013), 5.

2. Voluntarism reinforces liberal democracy mainly when bridging civic society organizations are joined, though bonding organizations can also have this effect. For the argument that voluntarism can undermine democratic trust, see Jason Kaufman, *For the Common Good? American Civil Life and the Golden Age of Fraternity* (New York: Oxford University Press, 2003). The consequences of bridging and bonding civil society are addressed in Robert D. Putnam, *Bowling Alone: The Collapse and Revival of American Community* (New York: Simon & Schuster, 2001).

3. Amy Gutmann, *Democratic Education* (Princeton, NJ: Princeton University Press, 1999), 287.

4. Nolan McCarty, Keith T. Poole, and Howard Rosenthal, *Political Bubbles: Financial Crises and the Failure of American Democracy* (Princeton, NJ: Princeton University Press, 2013), 51; see also Daniel M. Shea, "Nastiness, Name-Calling, and Negativity: The Alleghany College Survey of Civility and Compromise in American Politics" (Center for Political Participation, 2010).

5. Brian M. Harward and Daniel M. Shea, "Higher Education and the Multiple Modes of Engagement," in *Teaching Civic Engagement*, 28.

6. Russell J. Dalton, "The Good News Is, the Bad News Is Wrong: Another View of the Millennial Generation," in *Extensions* (Summer 2015): 12 (Norman, OK: Carl Albert Congressional Research and Studies Center).

7. Paul L. Gaston, *General Education Transformed: How We Can, Why We Must* (Washington, DC: Association of American Colleges and Universities, 2015).

8. AAC&U, *General Education Maps and Markers: Designing Meaningful Pathways to Student Achievement* (Washington, DC: Association of American Colleges and Universities, 2015).

9   Cliff Zukin, Scott Keeter, Molly Andolina, Krista Jenkins, and Michael X. Delli Carpini, *A New Engagement? Political Participation, Civic Life, and the Changing American Citizen* (New York: Oxford University Press, 2006).

10. James Simeone and Gregory M. Shaw, "Do Project Pedagogies Matter?" *Journal of Political Science Education* 13 (2017):75–90.

11. Go-it-alone approaches are consistent with the competitive individualist political culture which is prominent but not hegemonic in the United States. As Verba, Scholzman, and Brady observe, the emphasis they uncovered on "civic gratification" in their survey suggests a strong undercurrent of egalitarianism, "which says something about the peculiar nature of American individualism," 118.

12. Simeone and Shaw, "Do Project Pedagogies Matter?" 87.

13. Norman Nie and D. Sunshine Hillygas, "Education and Democratic Citizenship," in *Making Good Citizens: Education and Civil Society*, ed. Diane Ravitch and Joseph P. Viteritti (New Haven, CT: Yale University Press), 30–57.

14. Norman Nie, Jane Junn, and Kenneth Stehlik-Barry, *Education and Democratic Citizenship in America* (Chicago: University of Chicago Press, 1996), 98–108.

15. Nance Lucas, "The Influence of Integrative and Interdisciplinary Learning on Civic Engagement," in *Civic Engagement in Higher Education: Concepts and Practices*, ed. Barbara Jacoby (San Francisco: Jossey-Bass, 2009), 99–116.

16. Gaston, *General Education Transformed*.

17. Bloomington–Normal ranks 225 out of 381 among metropolitan statistical areas in the United States with more than 50,000 people.

18. Hiram E. Fitzgerald, Angela Allen, and Peggy Roberts count as many as 29 distinct types of engaged scholarship; see "Campus-Community Partnerships: Perspectives on Engaged Scholarship," 5–28 at 12 in *Handbook of Engaged Scholarship: Contemporary Landscapes, Future Directions: Volume 2: Campus-Community Partnerships*, ed. Hiram E. Fitzgerald, Cathy Burack, and Sarena D. Seifer (East Lansing: Michigan State University Press, 2010). While all institutions have unique characteristics, and all experiential-learning programs have to be tailored to fit, there are some constants and continuities. Seminars and internships are standard university courses. Grant-writing courses are becoming more common. Every college or university campus exists in a community, and while creating partnerships takes time, a pilot program can be developed in three to five years. Large universities in rural settings will face more logistical problems, but action research principles, by placing the focus on the community as the source of research questions, will induce a go-slow "do no harm" approach.

19. Gerald Graff, *Clueless in America: How Our Schooling Obscures the Life of the Mind* (New Haven, CT: Yale University Press, 2004).

20. See Randy Stoecker, Mary Beckman, and Bo Hee Min, "Evaluating the Community Impact of Higher Education Civic Engagement," in *Handbook of Engaged Scholarship*, 177–96; Kenneth M. Reardon, "Straight A's? Evaluating the Success of Community/University Development Partnerships," in *Banking & Community* (Boston: Federal Reserve, 2005), 3–10; Alvaro Cortes, "Estimating the Impacts of Urban Universities on Neighborhood Housing Markets: An Empirical Analysis," *Urban Affairs Review* 39 (2004): 342–75.

21. See Jacoby, *Civic Engagement in Higher Education* and *University–Community Partnerships: Universities in Civic Engagement*, ed. Tracy M. Soska and Alice K. Johnson Butterfield (Binghamton, NY: Haworth Social Work Practice Press, 2004.)

22. See Thomas C. Henthorn, "Experiencing the City: Experiential Learning in Urban Environments," *Journal of Urban History* 40 (2014): 450–61.

23. Successful programs, some supported by HUD, some by Campus Compact, some by private groups like the Bonner and Kettering Foundations, have been developed at University of Pennsylvania, Portland State University, Loyola University at Chicago, Berea College, University of Michigan at Flint, and Maricopa Community Colleges, institutions that represent a range of types in the world of American higher learning.

24. David Maurrasse, *Beyond the Campus: How Colleges and Universities Form Partnerships with Their Communities* (New York: Routledge, 2001), 47.

25. Maurrasse, *Beyond the Campus*, 56.

26. Devon Pena and Joe Gallegos, "Local Knowledge and Collaborative Environmental Action Research," in *Building Community: Social Science in Action*, ed. Philip Nyden, Anne Figert, Mark Shibley, and Darryl Burrows (Thousand Oaks, CA: Pine Forge Press, 1997), 85–91; and Phil Brown and Edwin J. Mikkelsen, *No Safe Place: Toxic Waste, Leukemia, and Community Action* (Berkeley: University of California Press, 1997).

27. Brown and Mikkelsen, *No Safe Place*, 133.

28. As Paigen noted: "Before Love Canal, I also needed a 95 percent certainty before I was convinced of a result. But seeing this rigorously applied in a situation where the consequences of an error meant that pregnancies were resulting in miscarriages, stillbirths, and children with medical problems, I realized I was making a value judgment," in Brown and Mikkelsen, *No Safe Place*, 136.

29. Paul Farmer, *Pathologies of Power: Health, Human Rights, and the New War on the Poor* (Berkeley: University of California Press, 2005), 149.

30. As Farmer's biographer Tracy Kidder summed up, "The annals of international health contain many stories of adequately financed projects that failed because 'noncompliant' patients didn't take their medicines." Farmer commented: "The only noncompliant people are the physicians. If the patient doesn't get better, it's your fault. Fix it," in Kidder, *Mountains Beyond Mountains: The Quest of Dr. Paul Farmer, a Man Who Would Cure the World* (New York: Random House, 2004), 36.

31. Pena and Gallegos, "Local Knowledge and Collaborative Environmental Action Research," 89.

32. Kidder, *Mountains Beyond Mountains*, 298.

33. Farmer, *Pathologies of Power*, 48.

34. See Roni Strier, "The Construction of University-Community Partnerships: Entangled Perspectives," *Higher Education* 62 (2011): 81–97.

35. See James Simeone, "Political Culture," in *Political and Civic Leadership: A Reference Handbook*, Vol. 1, ed. Richard Couto (Los Angeles: Sage Publications, 2010), 481–89.

36. Ernest T. Stringer, *Action Research*, second edition (Thousand Oaks, CA: Sage Publications, 1999).

37. Center for Teaching and Learning, "Problem-Based Learning," *Stanford University Newsletter on Teaching* 11 (2001): 1–7 at 1.

38. LuAnn Wilkerson and Wim H. Gijselaers, "Concluding Comments," in *Bringing Problem-based Learning to Higher Education* ed. LuAnn Wilkerson and Wim H. Gijselaers (San Francisco: Jossey-Bass, 1996), 101.

39. Center for Teaching and Learning, "Problem-based Learning," 1.

40. Student grades, whether in the seminar or internship setting, whether tied to an individual or team effort, include narrative (e.g., journals) and process (e.g., stakeholder and setting analyses) pieces.

41. Gender appropriate aliases are used throughout the vignettes to allow for student participants' anonymity.

42. See Simeone and Shaw, "Do Project Pedagogies Matter?" 77–80.

43. Farmer, *Pathologies of Power*, 140.

New Resources for Civic Engagement: The National Survey of Student Leaders, Campus Associational Life, and the Consortium for Inter-Campus SoTL Research

20

J. Cherie Strachan and Elizabeth A. Bennion

Given increasing calls for higher education to promote students' civic and political engagement, the Consortium for Inter-Campus SoTL Research (CISR) was established to facilitate cross-campus data collection for civic engagement and pedagogy research. CISR's inaugural project, the National Survey of Student Leaders (NSSL), is the first effort to rely on scholarly insights about the role associational life plays in political socialization to systematically assess the quality of the learning experiences provided by student clubs and organizations. The NSSL provides higher education institutions with the means to regularly assess whether civil society on campus promotes the priorities of the civic engagement movement. This article relays findings from the first wave of the NSSL while highlighting the types of campus-level data available from this new assessment tool.

Given increasing calls for higher education to promote students' civic and political engagement, the Consortium for Inter-Campus SoTL Research (CISR) was established to facilitate cross-campus data collection for civic engagement and pedagogy research. CISR's inaugural project, the National Survey of Student Leaders (NSSL), is the first effort to rely on scholarly insights about the role that voluntary associations play in political socialization in order to systematically assess the quality of the learning experiences provided by student clubs and organizations. The NSSL provides higher education institutions with the means to regularly assess whether civil society on campus promotes the priorities of the civic engagement movement. This chapter relays findings from the first wave of the NSSL while highlighting the types of campus-level data available from this new assessment tool. The NSSL will contribute to new scholarly insights into whether campus associational life fulfills its potential as a means of preparing students for participation in democracy. Working together, scholars and practitioners nationwide can develop and share best practices in civic education.

This work is essential, as colleges and universities are increasingly called on to promote students' civic engagement and political participation. Efforts to achieve these outcomes have historically focused on coursework, with heavy emphasis on in-class learning supplemented by service-learning projects in the community.[1] Yet, this emphasis on learning experiences tied to coursework, while a key component of the civic engagement movement in higher education, overlooks a key opportunity to cultivate the knowledge, skills, and identities that predict life-long civic and political engagement—that is, students' participation in extracurricular campus clubs and organizations. Political observations, ranging from Alexis de Tocqueville's description of voluntary associations as American "schools of democracy" to contemporary social scientists' well-vetted and longstanding findings, have documented that the best predictor of persistent adult civic and political participation is not formal instruction but civic voluntarism.[2] In short, active and overlapping membership in the myriad voluntary associations that comprise civil society—even when all of these organizations do not serve an overtly political function—is the lynchpin of robust political socialization that sustains long-term civic and political engagement.[3] Further, while the erosion of American civic infrastructure means that fewer Americans have the opportunity to participate in voluntary associations,[4] a rich array of student clubs and organizations has been preserved on college campuses. Significantly, if colleges and universities fail to situate student life at the center of students' civic and political learning, they will overlook the experience that social science research identifies as one of the best ways to promote such engagement.[5]

Not all civic organizations, whether within the collegiate community or not, provide healthy political socialization. Some simply fail to incorporate organizing structures and decision-making practices that teach civic and political skills or that cultivate political interest.[6] Meanwhile, others—with hate groups such as the KKK serving as the most egregious example—promote behaviors and attitudes that undermine democracy.[7] Hence scholarly work on civil society and voluntary associations should inform assessments of the campus version of civil society to promote best practices associated with healthy civic and political socialization.

Higher education scholars celebrate the benefits that accrue to students who are active in campus life[8]—benefits that notably mirror the bridging and bonding social capital that group members acquire through broader civil society.[9] Until now, however, no effort has been made to draw on the social science literature on voluntary associations to identify, assess, and promote best practices in the campus version of civil society. This chapter describes a new assessment tool purposefully designed to offer such insights, the NSSL, which was designed and implemented for the first time in the 2014–2015 academic year by CISR (see Appendix B for more information about CISR.) Rather than report a single finding from this work, the remainder of the chapter grounds each series of items included in the NSSL in the social science literature and describes insights for improving student life that can be garnered from those items. The goal of this work is to increase both scholars' and student affairs staffs' familiarity with a new tool for assessing civic engagement on their campuses.

REDISCOVERING STUDENT GROUPS AS A TACTIC FOR PROMOTING CIVIC LEARNING AND DEMOCRATIC ENGAGEMENT

Given that early levels of civic and political interest and participation help to predict long-term adult engagement, it is increasingly important to identify effective ways to provide college students with meaningful civic education experiences. Professors who respond to such concerns are likely to focus on the substantive content of their courses as a way to shape student awareness of their civic and political obligations. Such efforts make considerable sense, as academics have a great deal of control over their classrooms but often have very little say about what happens elsewhere on campus. Yet, social scientists have long known that participation in civil society (e.g., clubs and voluntary associations) is one of the best predictors of long-term adult civic and political participation—but only when clubs and organizations are structured in ways that build students' civic and political skills, efficacy, and identities.[10] Further, some organizations, such as those that facilitate interaction with diverse others, are much better at cultivating the broad trust in others and inclusive definitions of citizenship required to sustain democracy in a multicultural country like the United States. Other groups may actually undermine these desired outcomes, especially those that primarily facilitate interaction among people who are very similar.[11]

Higher education research regularly identifies participation in student life as an important and highly beneficial college experience.[12] Students who participate make gains in both persistence and academic performance.[13] Astin argued that students' learning and development correspond to the quality and intensity of their involvement, while Kuh et al. emphasized that an engaged student culture and peer norms can reinforce the liberal arts mission.[14] In addition to academic performance, engaged students gain higher levels of personal development,[15] enhanced leadership skills[16] and the ability to maintain mature, intimate relationships,[17] and secure higher post-college income.[18] Wilson went so far as to posit that 70% of what students learn during college results from extracurricular programming.[19] Pace likewise extolled student life, claiming it to be the only college experience predictive of adult success, no matter how "success" is defined.[20] Similar to civil society, much of what students learn in campus life relates to political participation even when groups do not serve an overtly political function. For example, Pascarella, Ethington, and Smart found that campus involvement predicted altruism and broader concern for society, just as Tocqueville argued that such experiences helped Americans learn that self-interest rightly understood is connected to healthy communities.[21]

However, neither higher education scholars nor social scientists who understand the strong connection between associational life and healthy democracy have studied the structure of civil society on their very own campuses. Hence CISR—which was established to facilitate research projects requiring collaborative, cross-campus data collection to assess the effectiveness of civic engagement and political science learning initiatives—conducted the first wave of the NSSL in the 2014–2015 academic year.

A NEW ASSESSMENT TOOL

The NSSL represents the first attempt to rely on social science expertise to systematically assess the quality of the learning experiences provided by student clubs and organizations. With campus-recruiting assistance provided by the CISR, the American Political Science Association (APSA), the National Association of Student Personnel Administrators (NASPA), and the American Democracy Project of the American Association of State Colleges and Universities (AASCU) , the NSSL was administered to student officers representing 5,567 registered student organizations on 36 participating campuses in the spring of 2015. These included community colleges, regional public universities, small liberal arts colleges, and research-intensive universities located in every major region of the continental United States and in one European country.

An initial request to participate and two reminder prompts were e-mailed to the presidents of these student organizations, yielding 1,896 responses in February 2015. For campuses that made additional contact information available, an invitation to participate and two reminder prompts were sent to a secondary contact (typically a vice president or a treasurer) when the president failed to respond. This follow-up effort yielded an additional 297 responses. Of the initial sample of 5,567 student officers, 2,193 answered the questionnaire, for an overall response rate of 39.3% by March 2015. Given that responses to Internet questionnaires tend to be lower than other means of conducting survey research, this response rate was somewhat higher than expected. Introductory e-mails sent by members of each campus' student life staff established the project's credibility with respondents and helped to bolster the response rate.

Student leaders were asked to self-report their own demographic traits as well as the demographic composition, mobilizing capacity, and purpose of their groups to determine whether campus civil society provides adequate opportunities for all members of the student body. Further descriptive information was requested to ascertain if campus groups have adopted the organizational structures, cross-cutting interactions, activity levels, and decision-making procedures recommended by scholars of associational life. This set of questions was newly developed for the NSSL.

Additional questions were modified from established social science instruments, such as the American National Election Study and CIRCLE's Civic and Political Health of the Nation

Survey, to assess student organization leaders' perceptions of bridging and bonding social capital and of the organizational pursuit of civic and political goals. A final series of questions, derived and modified from the same established surveys, measured student leaders' levels of social trust, political interest, anticipated political participation, and efficacy.

The NSSL serves a number of purposes. The NSSL will contribute to new scholarly insights into whether campus associational life fulfills its potential as a means of preparing students for participation in democracy. Just as important, however, the NSSL also provides a new assessment tool for individual campuses. Campuses participating in the NSSL received an in-depth campus report, which established a baseline assessment of each institution's civic infrastructure and offered suggestions for improvement. As the NSSL becomes institutionalized and is administered on a regular schedule, it will provide more higher education institutions with the means to regularly assess whether their version of campus civil society promotes the priorities of recent higher education reform. The ensuing sections of this chapter are intended to increase readers' familiarity with the national-level data from the first wave of the NSSL, along with the types of questions included on this new assessment tool.

DEMOGRAPHIC INFORMATION: MATCHING STUDENT BODY COMPOSITION TO THAT OF STUDENT LEADERS

The NSSL asked student organization officers to provide information about their basic demographic traits. Generally, the proportion of students serving as officers from each demographic group should roughly reflect each group's proportion of the overall student body on the campuses surveyed. When demographic information is reported at the campus level, faculty and administrators should also be able to determine if any particular demographic group is underrepresented in such roles, which could indicate that members of that group have fewer campus leadership opportunities than other types of students. Tables 20.1 to 20.5 in Appendix A report students' class status, gender, age, international status, and racial and ethnic identity across all 36 participating campuses.

Demographic questions were included in the study because they will help to determine whether additional efforts are required to engage certain types of students in leadership opportunities. For example, the high percentage of women (nearly 62%) serving in leadership positions in part reflects the fact that approximately 57% of college students nationwide are women, but it also likely reflects that male students are less likely to seek out extracurricular experiences without encouragement.[22] Given varying enrollment patterns across institutions, campuses participating in the NSSL were encouraged to compare the composition of their student body to campus-level demographic patterns in student life experiences to help determine whether additional efforts are required to engage certain types of students in leadership opportunities. Indeed, several of the 36 campuses participating in the inaugural wave of the NSSL responded to their campus-specific data by establishing new recruiting protocols to improve the diversity of their student leaders. Future waves of the NSSL can help to reveal whether these efforts have been successful.

PURPOSE OF ORGANIZATIONS: FACILITATING POLITICAL AGENDAS

Participation in student life has been linked to increased persistence and improved academic performance, especially among students who are at high risk for dropping out of college.[23] Thus, it is important to have a wide array of different types of groups that will appeal to a diverse student body. Fischer recommended that at least some campus groups should be dedicated to serving members from minority and marginalized groups, as these organizations provide a "safe space" for these students to gather.[24] To mimic the type of public sphere that promotes democracy, a rich array of different kinds of student groups is also required to provide healthy civic and political socialization.[25] Individual organizations provide opportunities for networking, civic skill development, and the development of trust among those similar to oneself, or bonding social capital. Meanwhile, overlapping memberships and activities that cut across groups help to promote interaction with diverse others, help students develop an inclusive definition of citizenship, and cultivate generalized trust in others, or bridging social capital.[26]

Similar to the overall nature of associational life in broader society, many student organizations are likely established to serve recreational interests or professional goals.[27] Intramural sports and career-based professional organizations are both important parts of student life, and coordinating their activities can still provide important skills that readily translate into efforts to influence civic and political outcomes. Yet, at least some organizations on campus should have overtly civic and political agendas to help students learn to connect the organizing skills they gain to the ability to influence public decision making.[28] A series of questions were therefore included in the NSSL to provide insight into the array of groups present on most campuses and to determine if at least some of these groups are providing explicit opportunities for civic and political leadership.

First, student officers were asked to select the category that best described the purpose of their organization. (Some campuses included residence hall associations and varsity sports among their list of registered organizations. Even though these types of campus units are often not categorized as student clubs, they are included here because they provide similar extra-curricular student learning experiences.). In a similar question, the survey asked these student officers to identify their organization's most important function (see tables 20.6 and 20.7 in Appendix A, which provide the full array of responses to these prompts).

Given the long-term trend of college students prioritizing financial security and career success over other potential outcomes from their time in college,[29] it is not surprising that student groups focusing on providing academic and professional experiences are more numerous than any other type of group, as 15.2% of student officials claimed an academic purpose, while another 13% linked their group to a profession. Similarly, 26.6% of student leaders saw their group's most important function to be preparing members for a career. Those hoping that college will trigger active citizens may find these preferences troubling. Moreover, the relatively low number of organizations promoting explicitly political participation, which hovers around 3% in both tables, may add to these concerns. Some may find solace in the number of organizations focused on narrow policy issues (12.8%), on providing opportunities for community service (8.3%), and on bringing attention to an important issue in society (15%). However, these groups' popularity likely reflects the recent trend of college students preferring to address public issues through voluntarism rather than traditional political participation.[30] Hence staff and faculty members may need to encourage students to see the connections between their recreational, professional, and civic interests and the public policies that affect them.

MEMBERSHIP COMPOSITION OF STUDENT GROUPS: PROVIDING SAFE GATHERING SPACES ON CAMPUS
Student officers were also asked to indicate the type of student members their organizations were intended to serve. While most student organizations are intended to attract all types of students on campus, some are created to specifically serve the needs of particular demographic groups on campus. As indicated earlier, robust civil society will include a mix of both types of organizations. For example, institutions with a substantial minority population should be concerned if none of the groups on campus provide that population with a comfort zone. Fischer found that, for minority students, extensive formal ties on campus were linked to higher grades and reduced the likelihood of dropping out by about 83%.[31] Similar findings have indicated that when African American men are socially integrated on campus, they earn higher grades.[32] They are more apt to be socially integrated on HBCU's however, because the student clubs and organizations are more likely to be welcoming and to match their interests. Feelings of alienation and sources of social support affect minority students, especially when they attend colleges with a predominantly white student body.[33] Fischer recommended that minority students in particular should be encouraged during orientation to join extracurricular groups.[34] Further, colleges should ensure that enough

organizations exist to allow these students to feel comfortable joining. While this research specifically addressed the experiences of ethnic minorities and African American men, it stands to reason that members of other historically marginalized groups—such as women or LGBTQ students—are likely to have similar experiences on campus and are likely to benefit if they can join student groups specifically intended to provide them with support on campus.

Table 20.8 in Appendix A reveals that a small percentage of student groups analyzed in the NSSL are intended to serve these types of students on campus. While 6.8% served female members (a result of the popularity of sororities on campus), only 3.9% restricted membership based on racial or ethnic identity, while less than 1% provided a safe gathering space for sexual minorities. These percentages suggest that the 36 participating institutions have an opportunity to make their campuses more welcoming and to increase the persistence and academic performance of the types of students most likely to feel alienated on a typical college campus simply by working to increase the number of campus groups that serve their specific interests.[35]

ORGANIZATIONAL REPRESENTATION IN STUDENT GOVERNMENT ASSOCIATIONS: BOLSTERING POLITICAL CONNECTIONS

On some campuses, student officers from certain types of groups automatically serve as representatives in the student government association. This practice provides student officers with experiences that foster more explicit political socialization, even if their student club or group is not overtly political. Only a minority of campuses (20.5%) implemented this practice (see table 20.9 in Appendix A), suggesting another opportunity for most institutions to help students link their participation in civil society to their ability to wield political influence.

When reported at the campus level, the type of information described in the preceding sections provides insights that can be used for a campus-specific assessment about whether student groups serve a diverse array of student interests, with ample opportunities for participation that provide not only recreational activities, but also more explicit civic and political experiences.

BASIC MEMBERSHIP INFORMATION: IMPROVING THE CAPACITY TO MOBILIZE FOR COLLECTIVE ACTION

Critics of campus life have expressed concern that student groups, reflecting deeper trends in associational life, are becoming "check-book" organizations, meaning that students pay membership dues but have little opportunity to participate in these professionally staffed organizations' decision-making and program implementation.[36] In addition, they fear that student groups increasingly address only narrow interests, with fewer organizations capable of bringing students together in collective action across campus and beyond.[37] This concern differs from the types of members recruited, addressed earlier. For example, student professional associations, such as the Public Relations Student Society of America (PRSSA), are open to all students on campus, but they address very particular sets of issues not likely to mobilize a broad swath of the student body. Responses to specific questions provide information about whether these patterns have taken root on college campuses.

Student officers were asked to report the number of members who regularly participate in organizational activities. Across all 36 campuses, this number ranged from 0 to 550, with an average of 26.1 active members. According to respondents, these active members participated an average of 10.8 hours each month, with estimates ranging from 0 to 160 hours.[38] In comparison, student officers reported that the overall number of members (both active and inactive) ranged from 1 to 1,000, with an average of 67.1 members.[39] Respondents were asked to report the total number of students (beyond members) they thought they could mobilize across the entire campus. This estimate ranged from 0 to 1,000, with an average of 62.5 students.

This type of information will help individual campuses assess whether students are actively engaged in organizational activities and whether at least some student groups are able to mobilize a substantial portion of the student body to engage in collective action in pursuit of an overarching goal or in support of a popular cause. While a small number of students are very actively engaged, most student groups currently appear to lack the capacity to mobilize large groups of students around an important or popular cause. Yet, organizations that provide such capacity in the public sphere—especially when mobilizing ability to cut across larger geographic areas—have historically played an important role in training civic and political leaders.[40] When the infrastructure of student organizations does not provide student leaders the ability to engage in large-scale collective action on issues that they care about, an important opportunity to bolster civic and political organizing skills, as well as political efficacy, has been lost.

ELECTED AND APPOINTED EXECUTIVE POSITIONS: INCREASING FAMILIARITY WITH DEMOCRATIC PROCESSES

Organizations that hold elections and have multiple executive positions provide democratic learning opportunities. The sheer number of civic organizations with elected positions in America's past was celebrated as a way to provide leadership opportunities to a substantial portion of Americans.[41] Even with nearly 90,000 local government units in the United States, few Americans will have the opportunity to experience democratic decision making first-hand by serving as elected officers. At its zenith, American civil society provided this direct learning experience for at least 3% to 5% of the adult population in 1955, whereby they learned "how to run meetings, handle moneys, keep records, and participate in group discussions."[42] This pattern was apparently well-established by the late 1800s, when one observer jokingly described the plethora of official positions available in America's "thousand and one societies" as "the great American safety valve."[43] Student officers were therefore asked to indicate the number of executive positions within their organizations, how frequently they turn over, and whether they are elected or appointed.

Overall, 62.7% of respondents indicated that these executive positions were elected by the full members; 28.8% indicated that they were appointed by group leaders or a faculty advisor; and 8.5% explained that their group relied on a combination of other selection practices, which typically involved a combination of elections and appointments for selected group leaders (see table 20.10 in Appendix A). While a significant majority of officers in campus organizations are elected, shifting even more groups into this category may be a simple way for campuses to improve students' familiarity with the concept and process of democratic elections, along with the responsibilities of serving in an official position.

FEDERATED STRUCTURE: MOBILIZING FOR COLLECTIVE ACTION ACROSS GEOGRAPHIC DISTANCE

Scholars of American associational life have argued that a federated structure (with national, state, and local chapters) provides civic organizations with improved ability to influence policies across geographic boundaries. Such a structure can, for example, influence policies across an entire state or promote similar policies in multiple states, as well as coordinate efforts to shape national policies. This ability bolsters civic and political efficacy, connecting members to persuasive efforts that extend beyond their local communities.[44] It is important to note that these learning experiences readily translate into the ability to wield political influence, even when the organizations providing the lessons are not overtly political. The types of federated voluntary associations that have been praised for providing Americans with civic learning in the past include, for instance, mainline Protestant denominations, veterans associations such as the VFW or the American Legion, and fraternal organizations such as the Independent Order of Odd Fellows or The Benevolent and Protective Order of Elks. These associations provide opportunities to practice skills that civic and political leaders need to possess, like parliamentary procedure, committee work, and persuasive speaking.[45]

Questions in the NSSL are designed to reveal whether student groups typically have a federated structure, as well as whether student delegates from campus chapters actively participate in setting the organizations' policies and priorities at the state and/or national level. As table 20.11 in Appendix A indicates, fewer than 40% of the student organizations included in this study had a federated structure; yet, this is a substantial percentage of campus organizations, which may provide an opportunity for students' civic learning.

Even with a federated structure, however, it is possible that these groups function primarily as "check-book" organizations, with little opportunity for participation. Hence the officers with a federated structure were asked to summarize members' active participation within these groups (see tables 20.12 and 20.13 in Appendix A). A federated structure is linked to higher levels of active engagement, as almost 40% of students in federated organizations coordinated activities with a state chapter several times a semester, while almost 30% did so at the national level. In addition, well over half of the officers serving these federated organizations indicated that student delegates attended state and national conventions, where some had the opportunity to participate in developing organizational policies, deliberating on these proposals using formal parliamentary procedure, and voting to enact or reject them (see table 20.14 in Appendix A).

These questions provide important tools for assessing the degree to which student life offers students opportunities to develop civic and political leadership skills, as a high proportion of organizations with a federated structure on campus would suggest that student members may gain heightened levels of civic and political efficacy. These gains increase if campus chapters not only coordinate activities across geographic boundaries, but also send delegates to state and/or national conventions where they have the opportunity to influence organizational policies and priorities. However, given that these learning experiences often take place in groups without an overt political agenda, faculty and staff advisors should help students recognize the connection between these learning experiences and the ability to resolve public concerns in their communities and to influence political processes.

On-Campus Organizational Activities and Group Decision-Making Styles: Teaching Civic and Political Skills

To serve as a mechanism of political socialization, organizations must meet and undertake activities on a regular basis. Prior studies of civil society have indicated that on average Americans used to attend organizational meetings and functions quite regularly.[46] These activities provided basic civic skills, such as using by-laws and constitutions to structure choices and engaging in deliberative decision making in formal public settings. They also provided civic leaders with the opportunity to cultivate common civic identities by celebrating organizational values and priorities in ceremonies, speeches, and written material. Table 20.15 in Appendix A reveals the extent to which student groups nationwide are engaging in an array of activities ranging from sponsoring educational and social activities to giving speeches and holding meetings. It is troubling to note that about 20% of student officers reported that their organizations rarely if ever undertook several important activities including requiring full-membership votes, coordinating educational events, or giving speeches. Even more student officers reported rarely, if ever, sponsoring fundraising events for themselves (38.2%) or others (41.7%), coordinating social programs (35.7%), or conducting a ceremony or ritual (56.1%). The substantial percentage of student officials indicating that such activities were rarely if ever undertaken represents a lost opportunity for providing civic-skill building experiences.

Simply attending meetings and sponsoring events, however, is not enough to hone civic and political skills and to cultivate civic identity. Scholars have argued that internal organizational dynamics matter a great deal.[47] Groups that mimic formal, deliberative decision-making procedures provide better training in a very important set of civic and political skills. Table 20.16 in Appendix A shows the extent to which student groups nationwide engaged in various types of decision making. Notably, many student officers reported that their groups undertook important activities—such as referring to a constitution or by-laws (31.3%), using formal decision-making rules (64.6%), or negotiating conflict with other members (30.7%)—less than once a year or never.

As these percentages indicate, not all groups on campus will have high activity levels, nor will they all rely heavily on democratic decision making. Some may rely on the advice of a faculty advisor or the decisions of an executive board. Yet, ideally, more campus organizations should provide robust learning experiences by engaging all members in group discussion, deliberation, and decision making. Part of the reason for the limited use of these activities is likely that participation in voluntary associations, which used to be quite common—and quite influential—during childhood and adolescence, is now a missing aspect of youth political socialization.[48] In the past, students were much more likely to arrive on campus already knowing how to coordinate their student groups' activities. Now, many of these basic skills must be taught. Campuses can help to increase these types of beneficial experiences by providing additional mentoring or professional development workshops.

PERCEPTIONS OF ORGANIZATIONAL INFLUENCE: BOLSTERING ORGANIZATIONAL EFFICACY

As scholars have posited, undertaking the types of activities and deliberative decision making described earlier not only builds civic and political skills, but also bolsters self-efficacy or confidence in the ability to successfully use those skills. When members learn that their collective endeavors yield results, they can more easily imagine undertaking similar efforts in the future. Such efficacy is enhanced when their organizational activities stretch across geographic boundaries.[49] Hence, student officers were asked a series of questions in the NSSL intended to measure perceptions of their organizations' influence. Specifically, they were asked to assess whether their organizations had successfully attempted to influence policies on campus, in the local community, or at the state and national levels. They were also asked to assess whether their groups had undertaken successful volunteer efforts and persuasive social values/lifestyle campaigns at each of these levels, as well as whether their efforts required them to coordinate activities with other groups at each of these levels.

The more frequently student officers indicate that their groups influence policies and social values, undertake effective volunteerism, and coordinate efforts with other groups—especially when these activities stretch across geographic boundaries—the more likely members are to feel confident undertaking the same types of activities for civic and political purposes in the future. As tables 20.17 to 20.20 in Appendix A make clear, students saw their organizations as most effective at coordinating collective endeavors and volunteering at the local level, and to a slightly lesser extent influencing others' social values at the local level. This perceived influence dropped when students were asked to estimate how frequently they influenced policymaking. However, many students' personal, professional, and community interests are deeply affected by politics. Virtually every student on campus is affected by public policies that regulate their future professions or affect the community issues they are attempting to resolve via voluntarism, even if students themselves do not see these links. One of the strengths of civic infrastructure has always been the ability to mobilize members of an existing civic or recreational organization when issues directly affect them—a classic example being the American Legion's sponsorship of members' preferred version of the GI Bill after World War II.[50] This feature of civil society is why Robert Putnam—who noted that Americans were no longer forming bowling leagues despite the continued popularity of bowling as a recreational sport—highlighted the trend of all types of associations in his seminal book on civil society *Bowling Alone*.[51]

Intramural sports teams might not care about local politics until budget cuts affect their access to public parks and playing fields. Fraternities and sororities might not care about local politics until zoning and noise ordinances affect their housing options. Student professional associations might not care about state or national politics until regulations affect future job prospects. When these types of issues inevitably arise on campuses, more efforts should be undertaken to help students recognize that the same efforts that make their clubs and organizations effective in other spheres will help them to pursue political outcomes. Student affairs staff need to decide whether to provide additional mentoring, networking, or professional development workshops to connect group members' experiences to explicit civic and political concerns.

BRIDGING AND BONDING SOCIAL CAPITAL: CULTIVATING SUPPORT NETWORKS AND TRUST IN OTHERS

Participating in associational life provides two types of beneficial side effects, often described as bonding and bridging social capital. Both refer to trust in others. Bonding social capital provides members with a strong identity that emerges from participating in a close-knit community.[52] Because members interact regularly, they learn that they can trust and rely upon one another. Moreover, they develop a shared set of values and norms. Obviously, these close relationships are overwhelmingly helpful to the members of such close-knit groups. Even so, social scientists sometimes view bonding social capital with suspicion because it can also encourage the type of in-group prejudice and disdain for others that can undermine willingness to deliberate with those who are different.[53]

Yet, civil society can also produce bridging social capital, which refers to trust in diverse others and which occurs when members of a group are dissimilar from one another. Bridging social capital also develops when groups with different membership composition regularly interact with one another. Members of all the groups learn to trust, respect, and cooperate with those whose values and circumstances are different from their own.[54]

Levels of bonding social capital can be important in helping students transition to and perform well in college. Further, bonding social capital teaches students to cultivate the types of networks that can help them succeed long after they leave campus.[55] Bridging social capital, however, is essential for students not only to learn how to participate in a multicultural society, but also to cultivate inclusive definitions of citizenship that sustain liberal democracy in a diverse nation.[56] Healthy campus civil society should cultivate substantial levels of both—and fortunately the questions posed to student officers in the NSSL indicated that campus organizations are generating high levels of bridging and bonding social capital, as they overwhelming agreed and strongly agreed with all but one of the related items (see tables 20.21 and 20.22 in Appendix A). Only about 50% of members agreed or strongly agreed that members feel obligated to address broad social or political issues, but over 90% indicated that members not only share core values, but that they also respect differing views within the group. If an NSSL campus report revealed that students in a particular setting scored lower on these items than preferred, student affairs staff might decide to provide incentives that promote desired outcomes by, for example, tying funding to activities that bolster trust in others or that require groups with different types of members (such as men and women or those who identify with varying racial, ethnic, or religious groups) to work together.

DIVERSITY IN MEMBERSHIP COMPOSITION: BOLSTERING TRUST IN DIVERSE OTHERS

As noted earlier, a diverse membership is one way that group composition can bolster bridging social capital. Long-standing research on overcoming discrimination has also indicated that ongoing interaction with diverse others, especially in collective endeavors to achieve common goals, is the key to overcoming prejudice toward minority out-groups in society.[57] Thus, group composition in campus civil society can help to bolster levels of bridging social capital, overcome prejudice against minorities, and build inclusive definitions of citizenship.

Yet, these outcomes often do not occur.[58] Some campuses simply lack enough overall diversity in the student body to sustain adequate interactions across demographic difference. On other campuses, students prefer to cluster together with similar others in their on-campus groups. Certain questions in the NSSL were therefore designed to help assess whether student life is helping or hindering campus goals for diversity education and programming.

First, student officers were asked to assess the level of diversity within their groups based on several dimensions of diversity. Student officers perceived their groups to be at least mixed on most demographic traits, with the highest levels of perceived diversity reported for family income, partisanship, and religious affiliation. Further reflecting their awareness of these patterns, student officers were most likely to report wanting a greater mix of members to achieve increased levels of racial, ethnic, and gender diversity, as well as a broader array of academic majors (see tables 20.23 and 20.24 in Appendix A).

Student officers were asked to report if they had at least one active member from specific racial and ethnic groups, as well as from different economic classes. Responses suggest that many student groups have at least some diversity in membership (see tables 20.25 and 20.26 in Appendix A.)

Finally, student officers were asked to indicate whether their organizations promoted diversity by including a statement on diversity in their by-laws, encouraging interactions with diverse others, recruiting diverse members, or requiring participation in diversity workshops or attendance at diversity programming. Officers were most likely to report that they encouraged interaction with diverse others (58%) and least likely to report that they explicitly recruited diverse members (18%) (see table 20.27 in Appendix A). Given the low rates of affirmative responses on several of these items, student affairs staff who want to promote higher levels of diversity within student organizations likely have an array of options for doing so, ranging from providing recruiting assistance to promoting programming and workshops.

REQUESTS FOR ASSISTANCE: IMPROVING LEARNING EXPERIENCES THAT ENHANCE CIVIC LEARNING AND POLITICAL SOCIALIZATION

In addition to the assessment of campus associational life detailed in previous sections, it is important to offer student organization leaders opportunities to provide insights and suggestions of their own. Hence, in the NSSL, student organization officers were asked to indicate whether they would like additional assistance with an array of different group activities.

While student officers requested assistance with a number of different tasks, those at the top of their list were activities—recruiting new (59.5%) and diverse (40.5%) members, planning campus events (45%), and coordinating activities with on-campus (46.6%) and off-campus (38.3%) groups—that would also help their organizations provide more robust civic and political socialization (see table 20.28 in Appendix A). Participating campuses also received verbatim responses to an open-ended question, allowing student officers to explain anything else their institution could do to help make organizations successful. Combined, the closed-ended and open-ended answers provided insight into ways to help student organizations and their executive officers undertake activities that the students themselves believe are important. Offering students the opportunity to provide this input on a regular basis would create a regular feedback loop and would help student affairs staff identify patterns in student needs.

STUDENT OFFICERS' TRUST IN OTHERS POLITICAL INTEREST, ANTICIPATED POLITICAL PARTICIPATION, AND POLITICAL EFFICACY: PREPARING STUDENTS FOR CIVIC AND POLITICAL LEADERSHIP

Finally, while the design of this particular research study cannot provide a direct correlation between all group members' levels of political interest, participation, and efficacy, it does allow for assessment of these attitudes and behaviors among student officers. The well-established connection between participation in civic life and long-term adult civic and political engagement suggests that those serving in executive positions in campus groups should have elevated levels of social trust and political efficacy, while anticipating higher levels of political participation in the future. Several questions are included in the NSSL to determine if such speculation about student leaders is accurate.

Given their likely involvement with their own group and with other groups on campus, one expects student leaders to have higher levels of generalized social trust in others. Trust in other citizens is a prerequisite for a stable, functional democracy.[59] Without it, people are unlikely to respect those who disagree with them enough to engage in democratic, deliberative decision making. They are also unlikely to be willing to enact (or to pay taxes to support) policies that provide benefits to those they deem untrustworthy and therefore undeserving.[60] Thus, it is important for student officers, who are expected to step forward as civic and political leaders, to believe that other people can be trusted, at least most of the time, to contribute fairly to the collective endeavors undertaken by a democratic society. The finding that most student officers (89.4%) agree or strongly agree that most people try to be helpful and that most people (73.3%) can be trusted is reassuring (see table 20.29 in Appendix A).

Similarly, if any students on campus are paying attention to political current events, it is likely to be student officers, who are more broadly connected to public life through their engagement in associational life. Table 20.30 in Appendix A indicates that well over a majority of student leaders are at least somewhat interested in state/local (78.1%), national (83.9%), and international politics (77.6%). Yet, it is problematic that students are least likely to report a strong interest in state/local politics where their organizations are, according to their own responses, capable of achieving the most influence. It is also disconcerting that over 20% of student leaders are completely disinterested in state/local and international politics, while 16% are equally disinterested in national politics. Given this pattern, campuses may need to do more to help students to recognize the way their organizational endeavors are affected by policy outcomes at the campus, local, state, national, and/or global levels. If students, especially student officers, are not making this connection, it seems unlikely that campus civil society is living up to its potential to provide robust political socialization.

Another series of questions in the NSSL was posed in order to measure student officers' levels of internal, external, and collective political efficacy, as even interested students who lack these types of efficacy are unlikely to undertake efforts to influence political decisions. In the aggregate, student officers had fairly high levels of internal and political efficacy (see table 20.31 in Appendix A), with more than half strongly disagreeing or disagreeing with statements claiming that government is too complicated to understand (57.2%) or that it would be difficult to make a real difference in politics (61.4%), and strongly agreeing or agreeing with the claim that they could do as good of a job in public office as others (61.2%). As one might anticipate, these student leaders had even higher levels of collective efficacy, with 94% strongly agreeing or agreeing that working with other citizens is the best way to get things done; that dramatic change can happen when people band together and demand it (88.8%); that politicians respond to citizens' demands for change (82%); and that most people are willing to work together toward a common goal (78.4%). Notably, support for collective efficacy dropped back down to 55% when student officers were asked whether they knew how to work with others to change public policies—suggesting that student leaders' faith in collective action should be bolstered with more specific training on how the public policy process works.

Student officers were also asked to estimate their likelihood of participating in common political acts in the future. Their anticipated future behavior is summarized in table 20.32 in Appendix A. Aside from anticipated voting in national elections (80.2%), student officers were most likely to report being more or very likely to participate in civic acts, such as working with others at the community level (71.8%) or volunteering (70.8%), than they were to anticipate more explicitly political forms of political participation such as persuading others to vote for a preferred candidate (34.2%), attending a rally (28.6%), contacting an elected official (24.7%), or working for a political candidate or party (18.3%). Given the ease of doing so, it is not surprising that student officers were somewhat more likely (49.7%) to anticipate signing a petition about a political issue. While these officers' commitment to civic voluntarism is admirable, many have not made the connection between the skills they are learning as student leaders to the ability to influence political outcomes on issues that they prioritize. Therefore, staff and faculty may need to do more to help students recognize the connection between their organizational activities and the ability to wield influence in the political process.

DISCUSSION: BUILDING ON THE SUCCESS OF STUDENT LIFE

The 2014–2015 NSSL reveals that participation in student life already provides many students with important learning experiences that bolster their civic and political skills. Even if they do not always recognize the ways these experiences prepare them to wield more explicit political influence, many student officers not only gain the ability to do so (if and when they decide that they want to), but also have fairly high levels of trust in others, political interest, and political efficacy.

These learning experiences can be even further improved by recognizing the preeminent role civic voluntarism has played in providing political socialization to generations of Americans and by paying attention to the types of organizational structures, membership composition, and activities that have opened "pathways to democratic citizenship" in our past.[61] The most beneficial voluntary associations in America's history attracted diverse members, promoted their adoption of civic identities, required them to practice democratic decision-making procedures, and channeled their energy into common endeavors with tangible outcomes.[62] Notably, the NSSL identifies room for improvement in each of these aspects of student life. Student affairs staff and faculty mentors should encourage student groups to build their civic muscles by undertaking more relevant activities and by practicing democratic decision making. Staff and faculty should also pay careful attention to the composition of student officers, as well as that of the groups they lead, to ensure diversity goals are adequately addressed. Finally, staff and faculty should promote interaction among groups with diverse membership to cultivate bridging social capital and broad trust in others. Fortunately, the provision of additional training, workshops, and mentoring to promote these desired outcomes should be welcome, as these are precisely the same issues that student leaders prioritized in their requests for assistance.

CONCLUSION: CONTINUING ASSESSMENT OF CIVIC LEARNING AND POLITICAL SOCIALIZATION IN STUDENT LIFE

The in-depth account of the NSSL, along with the accompanying tables in Appendix A, are intended to relay the type of assessment data available to interested administrators and faculty members in future waves of the survey. Several specific recommendations for faculty and staff interested in bolstering civic and political socialization in student organizations are listed as follows:

- Compare the demographic composition of the student body to the composition of student officers. If necessary, implement new recruiting protocols to ensure all types of students seek out leadership opportunities.
- Encourage student officials to make connections between their recreational, professional, and civic interests and the public policies that affect them. Such efforts should at a minimum include never overlooking teachable moments when student groups are negatively affected by policies, but might extend to educational programming and events that encourage students to proactively track relevant policies.
- Make the campus more welcoming, while increasing the persistence and academic performance of students apt to feel marginalized, by helping them to establish new campus organizations that serve their specific demographic groups.
- Encourage officials of established campus groups to consider seeking partners on campuses across the state or country, which could mimic the structure and mobilizing capacity of the federated civic organizations common in America's past.
- Help student officers to tackle public issues of common concern to a broad swathe of the student body on their own campus, and potentially on numerous college campuses.

- Increase familiarity with electoral processes by offering incentives for student organizations that rely on an appointment processes to select leaders to consider selecting officers through a competitive election process. Make sure detailed responsibilities for each position are explained in their organizational by-laws.
- Host professional development workshops where students learn "lost" civic and political skills such as organizing a meeting, consulting by-laws, using parliamentary procedure, drafting internal policies and resolutions, and assigning work to subcommittees. Participation in workshops could be required prior to registering a student organization on campus or could be incentivized with a monetary award.
- Bolster bridging social capital by helping groups to recruit more diverse members, as well as by prioritizing funding for activities that are cosponsored by organizations with demographically distinct memberships.
- Provide ample opportunity for student leaders to provide feedback about the type of help they need, as well as about the types of issues important to them, so that faculty and staff can help the students undertake activities that the students believe are important.
- Attempt to increase students' political interest, anticipated political participation, and political efficacy by sponsoring educational programming and workshops that link their interests to public policies and show them how to influence local, state, and national policy-making processes.
- Participate in future waves of the NSSL to begin the process of formally assessing the quality of political socialization that occurs through participation in campus life.
- Consider seeking Consortium recruiting assistance to implement multi-campus civic engagement research projects on other topics.

In closing, the authors hope that this descriptive approach provides a catalyst for assessing whether the student groups that comprise the campus version of civil society are promoting the civic and political engagement goals embedded in college and university mission statements. Furthermore, it will help student affairs staff, in partnership with faculty and administrators, to identify and promote best practices for democratic engagement whenever possible.

FINAL NOTE

To learn more, see Appendix B, and read more about the importance of multi-campus civic engagement assessment in *PS: Political Science & Politics*; read about Weber State's and the University of Wisconsin Madison's experiences as NSSL-participating campuses; or visit CISR. Joining CISR requires users to provide contact information as well as descriptive information about one's institution, academic unit or department, and interests. Those who take teaching, learning, and assessment seriously and seek like-minded colleagues, whether they work at liberal arts colleges, regional comprehensive universities, community colleges, or research universities, are all eligible to join. ∎

ACKNOWLEDGMENTS

A previous version of this chapter was published in the e-Journal of *Public Affairs*. See J. Cherie and Elizabeth A. Bennion, "New Resources for Civic Engagement: The National Survey of Student Leaders and the Consortium for Inter-Campus SoTL Research." *eJournal of Public Affairs* 5:2 (2016). ISSN 2162-9161.

ENDNOTES

1. J. Cherie Strachan, "Student and Civic Engagement: Cultivating the Skills, Efficacy and Identities that Increase Student Involvement in Learning and in Public Life," in *Handbook of Teaching and Learning in Political Science and International Relations* 2015, ed. John Ishiyama, Will Miller, and Ester Simon (Northampton, MA: Edward Elgar), 60–73.

2. Gabriel A. Almond and Sydney Verba, *The Civic Culture: Political Attitudes and Democracy in Five Nations* (Princeton, NJ: Princeton University Press, 1963); Casey A. Klofstadt, ed., *New Advances in the Study of Civic Voluntarism: Resources, Engagement, and Recruitment* (Philadelphia: Temple University Press, 2016); Robert D. Putnam, *Bowling Alone: The Collapse and Revival of American Community* (New York: Simon & Schuster, 2000); Arthur M. Schlesinger, Sr., "Biography of a Nation of Joiners," *American Historical Review* 50 (1944): 1–25; Theda Skocpol, Marshall Ganz, and Ziad Munson, "A Nation of Organizers: The Institutional Origins of Civic Voluntarism in the United States," *American Political Science Review* 94 (2000): 527–46. Alexis de Tocqueville, *Democracy in America*, ed. Jacob P Mayer and trans. George Lawrence (Garden City, NY: Doubleday, 1969); Sydney Verba, Kay L. Schlozman, and Henry E. Brady, *Voice and Equality: Civic Voluntarism in American Politics* (Cambridge, MA: Harvard University Press, 1995); Mark R. Warren, *Democracy and Association* (Princeton, NJ: Princeton University Press, 2001); Mark R. Warren, *Dry Bones Rattling: Community Building to Revitalize American Democracy* (Princeton, NJ: Princeton University Press, 2001).

3. Michael Edwards, *Civil Society*, third edition (Malden, MA: Polity Press, 2014).

4. Putnam, *Bowling Alone*; Theda Skocpol, *Diminished Democracy: From Membership to Management in American Civil Life* (Norman, OK: University of Oklahoma Press, 2003).

5. Daniel A. McFarland and Reuben J. Thomas, "Bowling Young: How Youth Voluntary Associations Influence Adult Political Participation," *American Sociological Review* 71 (2006): 401–25.

6. Skocpol, *Diminished Democracy*.

7. Morris P. Fiorina, "Extreme Voices: A Dark Side of Civic Engagement," in *Civic Engagement in American Democracy*, eds. Theda Skocpol and Morris P. Fiorina (Washington, DC: Brookings Institution Press, 1999) 395–425; Margaret Levi, "Social and Unsocial Capital: Review of Making Democracy Work," *Politics and Society* 24 (1996): 45–55. See James Sidanius et al., "Ethnic Enclaves and the Dynamics of Social Identity on the College Campus: The Good, the Bad, and the Ugly," *Journal of Personality and Social Psychology* 87 (2004): 96–110 for concerns about certain types of campus organizations. Yet also see Nancy Rosenblum, *Membership and Morals: The personal Uses of Pluralism in America* (Princeton, NJ: Princeton University Press, 1998) for a defense of extending the right of association to all but the most dangerous groups.

8. George D. Kuh, "The Other Curriculum: Out-of-Class Experiences Associated with Student Learning and Personal Development," *The Journal of Higher Education* 66 (1995): 123–155

9. Putnam, *Bowling Alone*; Skocpol, *Diminished Democracy*.

10. Almond and Verba, *The Civic Culture*; Klofstad, *New Advances in the Study of Civic Voluntarism*; Putnam, *Bowling Alone*; Schlesinger, "Biography of a Nation of Joiners"; Skocpol, Gans, and Munson, "A Nation of Organizers"; Tocqueville, *Democracy in America*; Verba, Schlozman, and Brady, *Voice and Equality*; Warren, *Democracy and Association*, *Dry Bones Rattling*.

11. Edwards, *Civil Society*.

12. Kuh, "The Other Curriculum."

13. Ya Rong Huang and Sheue-Mei Chang, "Academic and Co-Curricular Involvement: Their Relationship and the Best Combinations for Student Growth," *Journal of College Student Development* 45 (2004): 391–406; Ernest T. Pascarella and Patrick T. Terenzini, *How College Affects Students: A Third Decade of Research* (San Francisco: Jossey-Bass, 2005).

14. Alexander W. Astin, "Student Involvement: A Developmental Theory for Higher Education," *Journal of College Student Personnel* 25 (1984): 297–308; Alexander W. Astin, *What Matters in College? Four Critical Years Revisited* (San Francisco: Jossey-Bass, 1993); George Kuh, John H. Schuh, and Elizabeth J. Whitt, *Involving Colleges: Successful Approaches to Fostering Student Learning and Personal Development Outside of the Classroom* (San Francisco: Jossey-Bass, 1991).

15. John D. Foubert and Lauren A. Urbanski, "Effects of Involvement in Clubs and Organizations on the Psychosocial Development of First-Year and Senior College Students," *NASPA Journal* 43 (2006): 166–181.

16. John H. Schuh and Megan Laverty, "The Perceived Long-Term Effect of Holding a Significant Student Leadership Position," *Journal of College Student Personnel* 24 (1983): 28–32.

17. Albert B. Hood, *Student Development: Does Participation Affect Growth?* (Bloomington, IN: Association of College Unions International, 1984).

18. C. Robert Pace, *Measuring Outcomes of College: Fifty Years of Findings and Recommendations for the Future* (San Francisco: Jossey-Bass, 1979).

19. Everett Keith Wilson, "The Entering Student: Attitudes and Agents of Change," In *College Peer Groups: Problems and Prospects for Research*, eds. Theodore Mead Newcomb and Everett Keith Wilson (Chicago: Aldine Publishing Company, 1966), 71–106.

20. Pace, *Measuring Outcomes of College*.

21. Ernest T. Pascarella, Corrinna A. Ethington, and John C. Smart, "The Influence of College on Humanitarian-Civic Involvement Values," *Journal of Higher Education* 59 (1988): 412–37; Tocqueville, *Democracy in America*.

22. Linda J. Sax, *The Gender Gap in College: Maximizing the Developmental Potential of Women and Men* (San Francisco: Jossey-Bass, 2008).

23. Pascarella and Terenzini, *How College Affects Students*.

24. Mary J. Fischer, "Settling into Campus Life: Differences by Race/Ethnicity in College Involvement and Outcomes," *Journal of Higher Education* 78 (2007): 125–61.

25. Edwards, *Civil Society*.

26. Putnam, *Bowling Alone*.

27. Ibid.

28. Skocpol, *Diminished Democracy*.

29. Dan Berret and Eric Hoover, "College Freshmen Seek Financial Security amid Emotional Insecurity," *Chronicle of Higher Education* (February 5, 2015) Retrieved from http://chronicle.com.cmich.idm.oclc.org/article/College-Freshmen-Seek/151645/?cid=related-promo; Libby Sander, "Freshmen Survey: This year, Even More Focused on Jobs," *The Chronicle of Higher Education* (January 24, 2013) Retrieved from http://chronicle.com.cmich.idm.oclc.org/article/Freshman-Survey-This-Year/136787/?cid=related-promo.

30. Cliff Zukin, Scott Keeter, Molly Andolina, Krista Jenkins, and Michael X. Delli Carpini, *A New Engagement? Political Participation, Civic Life, and the Changing American Citizen* (New York: Oxford University Press, 2006).

31. Fischer "Settling into Campus Life."

32. Kenneth W. Jackson and L. Alex Swan, "Institutional and Individual Factors Affecting Black Undergraduate Student Performance: Campus Race and Student Gender." *In College in Black and White: African-American Students in Predominantly White and Historically Black Public Universities*, eds. Walter R. Allen, Edgar G. Epps, and Nesha Z. Hanniff (Albany, NY: SUNY Press, 1991), 127–142; James Earl Davis, "College in Black and White: Campus Environment and Academic Achievement of African American Males," *Journal of Negro Education* 63 (1994): 620–33.

33. Jackson and Swan, "Institutional and Individual Factors Affecting Black Undergraduate Student Performance"; Robert Davis, "Social Support Networks and Undergraduate Student Academic Success-Related Outcomes: A Comparison of Black Students on Black and White campuses," In *College in Black and White: African-American Students in Predominantly White and Historically Black Public Universities*, eds. Walter R. Allen, Edgar G. Epps, and Nesha Z. Hanniff (Albany, NY: SUNY Press, 1991), 143–60.

34. Fischer, "Settling into Campus Life."

35. See J. Cherie Strachan and Christopher Owens, "Learning Civic Norms Outside of the Classroom: Diversity and Campus Associational Life," *Journal of Political Science Education* 7 (2011): 464–82 for a more in-depth discussion of diversity and student life.

36. Authur Levine and Jeanette S. Cureton, *When Hope and Fear Collide: A Portrait of Today's College Student* (San Francisco: Jossey-Bass, 1998); Skocpol, *Diminished Democracy*.

37. Levine and Cureton, *When Hope and Fear Collide*.

38. A small number of students claimed that active members participated a full 40 hours a week. While it may not seem likely, it is possible that a small number of students treat participation in student life like a full-time job. Thus, these estimates were included in the average score.

39. Note, however, that 99% of the organizations included in the national sample had 500 or fewer members. The 2% of organizations with membership ranging from 500 to 1,000 were typically national honor societies, in which members are required to meet a minimum GPA requirement, not to actively participate in organizational activities or decision making.

40. Skocpol, *Diminished Democracy*.

41. Schlesinger, "Biography of a Nation of Joiners"; Skocpol, *Diminished Democracy*.

42. Theda Skocpol, "Civil Society in the United States," In *The Oxford Handbook of Civil Society*, ed. Michael Edwards (New York: Oxford University Press, 2011), 115.

43. As cited by Skocpol, "Civil Society in the United States," 114.

44. Skocpol, *Diminished Democracy*.

45. Jeffrey A. Charles, *Service Clubs in American Society: Rotary, Kiwanis, and Lions* (Urbana: University of Illinois Press, 1993); Murray Hausknecht, *The Joiners: A Sociological Description of Voluntary Association Membership in the United States* (New York: Bedminster Press, 1962); Schlesinger, "Biography of a Nation of Joiners"; Skocpol, *Diminished Democracy*; Skocpol, Gans, and Munson, "A Nation of Organizers"; Theda Scocpol, Ziad Munson, Andrew Karch, and Bayliss Camp, "Patriotic Partnerships: Why Great Wars Nourished American Civic Voluntarism," In *Shaped by War and Trade: International Influences on American Political Development*, eds. Ira Katznelson and Martin Shefter (Princeton, NJ: Princeton University Press, 2002), 134–80.

46. Almond and Verba, *The Civic Culture*; Putnam, *Bowling Alone*; Schlesinger, "Biography of a Nation of Joiners"; Skocpol, *Diminished Democracy*.

47. Skocpol, *Diminished Democracy*.

48. CIRCLE: The Center for Information & Research on Civic Learning & Engagement, "Understanding a Diverse Generation: Youth Civic Engagement in the United States," 2011. Retrieved from http://www.civicyouth.org/wp-content/uploads/2011/11/CIRCLE_cluster_report2010.pdf; McFarland and Thomas.

49. Skocpol, *Diminished Democracy*.

50. Michael J. Bennet, *When Dreams Came True: The GI Bill and the Making of Modern America* (Washington, DC: Brasseys, 1996); Theda Skocpol, "The GI Bill and the US Social Policy, Past and Future." *Social Philosophy and Policy* 14 (1997): 95–115.

51. Putnam, *Bowling Alone*.

52. David E. Campbell, *Why We Vote: How Schools and Communities Shape our Civic Life* (Princeton, NJ: Princeton University Press, 2006); Putnam, *Bowling Alone*.

53. Fiorina, "Extreme Voices"; Margaret Levi, "Social and Unsocial Capital: Review of *Making Democracy Work*," *Politics and Society* 24 (1996): 45–55; Strachan and Owens, "Learning Civic Norms Outside of the Classroom"; Jan van Deth and Sonja Zmerli, "Introduction: Civicness, Equality, and Democracy—A 'Dark Side' of Social Capital?" *American Behavioral Scientist* 53 (2010): 631–39.

54. Putnam, *Bowling Alone*; Robert Putnam, "E Pluribus Unum: Diversity and Community in the Twenty-First Century," *Scandinavian Political Studies*, 30(2007): 37–174.

55. Kuh, Schuh, and Whitt, *Involving Colleges*.

56. Putnam, "E Pluribus Unum."

57. Gordon Allport, *The Nature of Prejudice* (Reading, MA: Addison-Wesley, 1954).

58. Strachan and Owens, "Learning Civic Norms Outside of the Classroom."

59. Putnam, *Bowling Alone*.

60. Bo Rothstein, *The Quality of Government: Corruption, Social Trust, and Inequality in International Perspective* (Chicago: University of Chicago Press, 2011); Eric Uslaner, *The Moral Foundations of Trust* (New York: Cambridge University Press, 2002).

61. Skocpol, *Diminished Democracy*, 98.

62. Skocpol, *Diminished Democracy*.

Appendix A[1]

Table 20.1 Student Officers' Class Status

	PERCENTAGE*
Freshman	1.1
Sophomore	10.3
Junior	25.0
Senior	50.2
Graduate	13.1

N = 2,131
*Column may not sum to 100.0% due to rounding.

Table 20.2 Student Officers' Gender

	PERCENTAGE*
Male	38.1
Female	61.6
Other	0.4

N = 2,177
*Column may not sum to 100.0% due to rounding.

Table 20.3 Student Officers' Age

	PERCENTAGE*
Traditional (18–24)	84.6
Non-Traditional (Over 24)	15.4

N = 2,193
*Column may not sum to 100.0% due to rounding.
The average age of student officers in the national sample was 22.4 and ranged from a low of 18 to a high of 59.

Table 20.4 Student Officers with International Status

	PERCENTAGE*
American	93.1
International	6.9

N = 216
*Column may not sum to 100.0% due to rounding.

1. The varying numbers of respondents reported in these tables reflects missing data from unanswered questions. While the overall response rate was N = 2,193, some respondents failed to answer every item included in the on-line questionnaire.

Table 20.5 Student Officers' Racial/Ethnic Identity

	PERCENTAGE*
White/Non-Hispanic	70.2
Black/African American	7.0
Hispanic or Latino	7.1
Asian or Asian American	9.6
Native American	0.3
Pacific Islander	0.3
Multi-Racial or Ethnic	3.4
Other	2.0

N = 2,156
*Column may not sum to 100.0% due to rounding.

Table 20.6 Organizations' Purpose

	PERCENTAGE*
Honors Society (e.g., Pi Sigma Alpha)	4.7
Academic (ex: Spanish Club, Sociology Club)	15.2
Residence Halls Council (e.g., groups that set policies in residence halls)	1.0
Intramural Sports (e.g., Soccer Club, Intramural Basketball)	4.1
Varsity Sports (e.g., university or college athletic teams)	1.2
Greek Fraternity or Sorority (e.g., Delta, Sigma Tau)	8.3
Cultural/Ethnic (e.g., Black Student Union)	7.0
GLBTQ (e.g., Gay-Straight Alliance)	1.0
Religious/Spiritual (e.g., Campus Bible Fellowship, Muslim Student Association, Hillel)	5.7
Service (e.g., Alternative Spring Breaks, Habitat for Humanity)	8.3
Professional (e.g., Public Relations Student Society of America)	13.0
Political (e.g., College Democrats, Young Republicans, Young Americans for Freedom)	2.9
Special Interest (e.g., Students for Life, Environmental Club)	12.8
Other	14.7

N = 2,051
*Column may not sum to 100.0% due to rounding.

Table 20.7 Organizations' Most Important Function

	PERCENTAGE*
Help student to be successful in class	13.1
Help students prepare for a career or internship	26.6
Provide a religious or spiritual community	6.3
Sponsor social activities (dances, movies, etc.)	10.7
Provide opportunities to play a sport	7.2
Encourage volunteering in the community	12.6
Encourage political participation	2.2
Celebrate a common heritage of ethnic identity	6.3
Bring attention to an important issue in society	15.0

N = 1,629
*Column may not sum to 100.0% due to rounding.

Table 20.8 Organizations' Intended Student Members

	PERCENTAGE*
All Students	72.9
Male Students	4.8
Female Students	6.8
GLBTQ Students	0.8
Students who identify with a specific racial, ethnic, or cultural group	3.9
Other	10.9

N = 2,057
*Column may not sum to 100.0% due to rounding.

Table 20.9 Student Government Association Participation

	PERCENTAGE*
Yes	20.5
No	79.5

N = 2,052
*Column may not sum to 100.0% due to rounding.

Table 20.10 Number of Executive Positions and Annual Turnover Rate

Position	Groups with Position (N = 1,853)	Groups with Annual Turnover (N ranges from 1,801 to 582)
1	97.8	87.0
2	95.0	90.0
3	90.6	91.9
4	81.0	93.5
5	59.1	95.0
6	42.5	96.3

Table 20.11 Organizations with Federated Structures

	PERCENTAGE*
Affiliated with a State Organization	3.0
Affiliated with a National Organization	26.7
Affiliated with Both	9.2
Not linked to a State/National Organization	61.1

N = 1,845
*Column may not sum to 100.0% due to rounding.

Table 20.12 Students Coordinating Activities with State Chapters

	PERCENTAGE*
A Few Times a Semester	37.9
Once a Semester	23.0
Once a Year	18.7
Less than Once a Year	20.4

N = 235
Column may not sum to 100.0% due to rounding.

Table 20.13 Students Coordinating Activities with National Chapters

	PERCENTAGE*
A Few Times a Semester	27.3
Once a Semester	19.4
Once a Year	28.8
Less than Once a Year	24.5

N = 670
*Column may not sum to 100.0% due to rounding.

Table 20.14 Delegate Activities at State and National Conventions

	PERCENTAGE*	N
Delegates help to develop policy for the entire organization	54.4	447
Delegates participate in deliberation at convention meetings	65.5	446
Delegates use parliamentary procedure at convention meetings	51.5	447
Delegates have the opportunity to vote on policy positions at convention meetings	57.8	446

*Column may not sum to 100.0% due to rounding.

Table 20.15 Frequency of Organizational Activities

	LESS THAN 1X/YEAR OR NEVER	1X/YEAR	1X/SEMESTER	2X/SEMESTER	1X/MONTH	2X/MONTH	1/WEEK OR MORE	N
Held a meeting open to all members	3.7	1.8	5.3	7.5	18.5	22.4	40.8	1738
Required the membership to cast a vote	23.8	29.2	17.7	8.0	7.6	7.2	6.5	1731
Held a meeting of the executive board	10.0	3.3	7.7	8.6	18.9	18.6	32.9	1724
Assigned important tasks to a committee or subcommittee	17.7	4.5	10.5	9.2	18.1	19.6	20.3	1717
Sponsored or co-sponsored an educational event or program	21.8	9.1	23.7	17.9	17.6	6.9	2.9	1718
Sponsored or co-sponsored a social activity	35.7	9.2	20.1	14.6	12.3	5.5	2.7	1724
Sponsored or co-sponsored a fundraising event for charity	41.7	13.6	21.7	11.1	7.6	2.9	1.3	1715
Sponsored or co-sponsored a fundraising event for the group	38.2	13.1	23.8	12.9	7.6	3.4	1.0	1719
Held a ceremonial ritual or event	56.1	18.9	13.7	6.1	3.4	1.1	0.7	1728
Gave speeches that explain the group's values and priorities	23.9	17.7	28.1	12.2	9.3	4.7	4.0	1727
Distributed materials that explain the group's values and priorities	23.6	17.3	28.8	13.7	8.2	5.0	3.4	1727

Table 20.16 Frequency of Democratic Decision-Making Practices

	LESS THAN 1X/ YEAR OR NEVER	1X/ YEAR	1X/SEMESTER	2X/SEMESTER	1X/MONTH	2X/MONTH	1/WEEK OR MORE	N
Referring to constitution or by-laws to guide decision-making	31.3	19.5	18.3	8.2	7.4	7.0	8.3	1,705
Engaging the full membership in deliberations	19.0	12.2	15.8	9.0	14.7	13.4	15.8	1,699
Relying on the group's executive board	8.7	3.7	7.5	6.0	15.6	17.8	40.9	1,690
Using formal rules to guide discussions	64.6	4.9	5.5	3.2	5.9	5.4	10.6	1,685
Negotiating compromise among members who disagree	30.7	7.8	11.3	8.7	14.1	12.5	14.9	1,698
Relying on a faculty advisor	28.2	9.6	14.2	10.2	15.0	11.4	11.5	1,703

Table 20.17 Groups Influencing Policies

	A FEW TIMES/SEMESTER	1X/SEMESTER	1X/YEAR	LESS THAN 1X/YEAR	N
On your campus	16.2	14.7	14.8	54.3	1,552
In your town or community	5.2	11.1	11.6	72.0	1,545
In your state or across the country	4.0	7.1	7.7	81.2	1,540
In more than one country or across the globe	3.0	3.4	4.5	89.0	1,520

Table 20.18 Groups Undertaking Effective Volunteerism

	A FEW TIMES/ SEMESTER	1X/ SEMESTER	1X/YEAR	LESS THAN 1X/YEAR	N
On your campus	39.3	23.1	13.9	23.7	1,553
In your town or community	32.6	24.5	14.6	28.3	1,549
In your state or across the country	9.3	12.2	13.2	65.4	1,545
In more than one country or across the globe	3.8	4.2	8.2	83.8	1,540

Table 20.19 Groups Coordinating Activities with Other Groups

	A FEW TIMES/ SEMESTER	1X/SEMESTER	1X/YEAR	LESS THAN 1X/YEAR	N
On your campus	39.7	27.6	16.7	16.0	1,477
In your town or community	21.9	23.4	16.3	38.4	1,467
In your state or across the country	7.8	12.5	12.6	67.1	1,470
In more than one country or across the globe	2.6	3.6	6.4	87.4	1,448

Table 20.20 Groups Influencing Others' Social Values and Life-Style Choices

	A FEW TIMES/ SEMESTER	1X/SEMESTER	1X/ YEAR	LESS THAN 1X/ YEAR	N
On your campus	31.3	15.1	9.5	44.0	1,474
In your town or community	15.8	13.5	8.4	62.4	1,470
In your state or across the country	7.6	6.3	7.7	78.5	1,470
In more than one country or across the globe	3.8	2.9	4.3	89.0	1,468

Table 20.21 Indicators of Bonding Social Capital

	STRONGLY DISAGREE	DISAGREE	AGREE	STRONGLY AGREE	N
Members have a tight bond with one another.	1.4	14.5	52.0	29.7	1,653
Members feel obligated to help one another.	2.1	13.8	57.6	26.5	1,650
Members trust each other a lot more than they do others.	3.5	28.9	48.7	18.8	1,648
Members almost always agree with each other about important issues.	4.1	32.7	52.7	10.5	1,650
Members share important core values.	1.3	6.3	60.7	31.7	1,649

Table 20.22 Indicators of Bridging Social Capital

	STRONGLY DISAGREE	DISAGREE	AGREE	STRONGLY AGREE	N
Members regularly interact with other student groups.	33.8	14.5	52.0	29.7	1,653
Members regularly interact with community groups off campus.	6.7	33.1	46.3	13.9	1,645
Members feel obligated to address broad social or political issues.	11.1	38.2	35.3	15.5	1,646
Members share a respect for differing views within the group.	0.8	2.9	54.5	41.8	1,648

Table 20.23 Student Officers' Estimated Levels of Diversity in Group Composition

	PRETTY MUCH THE SAME	MIXED	VERY DIFFERENT	N
Academic Major	33.6	41.6	24.7	1,645
Race/Ethnicity	31.2	55.7	13.1	1,645
Gender	26.7	63.7	9.6	1,645
Family's Income	6.1	74.4	19.5	1,628
Religious Affiliation	14.5	67.4	18.1	1,622
Political Party or Ideology	13.3	70.7	16.0	1,627

Table 20.24 Student Officers Desiring "Greater Mix" of Diversity

	PERCENTAGE	N
Academic Major	38.7	1,655
Race/Ethnicity	51.7	1,655
Gender	40.7	1,655
Family's Income	17.2	1,655
Religious Affiliation	16.7	1,655
Political Party or Ideology	17.5	1,655

Table 20.25 Student Officers Claiming to Have at Least One Member from Each Ethnic Group

	PERCENTAGE	N
White/Non-Hispanic	93.3	1,602
Hispanic	60.6	1,568
Black or African American	63.7	1,571
Asian or Asian American	60.1	1,577
Native American	13.2	1,525
Pacific Islander	12.7	1,525
Middle Eastern	31.8	1,521
Multi-Racial or Ethnic	54.5	1,541

Table 20.26 Student Officers Claiming to Have at Least One Member from Each Economic Class

	PERCENTAGE	N
Disadvantaged	49.0	1,598
Middle Class	85.1	1,609
Wealthy	64.7	1,602

Table 20.27 Formal Promotion of Diversity within Organizations

	PERCENTAGE	N
A statement on diversity is included in our by-laws or constitution.	42.1	1,497
Members are strongly encouraged or required to interact with diverse others.	58.0	1,490
Members with diverse backgrounds are explicitly recruited.	18.0	1,490
Members are strongly encouraged or required to attend diversity training or workshops.	21.8	1,493
Members are strongly encouraged or required to attend diversity events and programs.	31.7	1,483

Table 20.28 Student Officers' Requests for Assistance

	PERCENTAGE	N
Giving speeches	21.0	1,474
Running executive board meetings	20.5	1,475
Running meetings of the full membership	24.7	1,475
Using parliamentary procedure	12.5	1,475
Helping members to resolve conflicts	17.8	1,475
Seeking help from a faculty adviser/mentor	20.3	1,475
Recruiting new members	59.5	1,475
Attracting members from diverse backgrounds	40.5	1,475
Planning an event on campus	45.0	1,474
Coordinating activities with other campus groups	46.6	1,474
Coordinating activities with groups off campus	38.3	1,474

Table 20.29 Student Officers' Trust in Others

	STRONGLY DISAGREE	DISAGREE	AGREE	STRONGLY AGREE	N
Thinking about human nature in general, most people can be trusted.	2.4	24.3	63.8	9.5	1,508
Most people will take advantage of you if given the chance.	5.7	62.3	28.2	3.8	1,507
Most people try to be helpful when they can.	0.5	10.1	72.4	17.0	1,509

Table 20.30 Student Officers' Political Interest

	NOT AT ALL INTERESTED	SOMEWHAT INTERESTED	STRONGLY INTERESTED	N
State and Local Politics	22.0	54.9	23.2	1,516
National Politics	16.1	48.2	35.7	1,514
International Politics	22.3	52.1	25.5	1,515

Table 20.31 Student Officers' Levels of Political Efficacy

	STRONGLY DISAGREE	DISAGREE	AGREE	STRONGLY AGREE	N
INTERNAL EFFICACY					
People like me don't have a say about what government does.	21.9	52.8	21.5	3.8	1,435
Sometimes politics and government can seem so complicated that a person like me can't really understand what is going on.	20.9	36.3	37.2	5.7	1,428
I feel that I could do as good a job in public office as most other people.	8.5	30.2	45.5	15.7	1,432
EXTERNAL EFFICACY					
Public officers don't care much what people like me think.	7.8	51.0	34.8	6.4	1,428
It would be difficult for someone like me to make a real difference in politics or government.	12.4	49.0	32.6	6.0	1,430
COLLECTIVE EFFICACY					
Politicians respond to citizens if enough people demand change.	3.0	14.9	60.8	21.2	1,427
Most people are willing to work together toward a common goal.	2.4	19.1	66.0	12.4	1,430
If you want to get things done as a citizen, working with others is the best way.	0.8	5.3	56.2	37.8	1,428
Dramatic change can occur in this country if people band together and demand it.	1.1	10.0	54.1	34.7	1,424
I know how to work with others to change public policies.	6.1	38.6	44.3	11.0	1,420

Table 20.32 Student Officers' Likelihood of Participating in Political Acts

	NOT AT ALL LIKELY	SOMEWHAT LIKELY	MORE LIKELY	VERY LIKELY	N
Work with others to solve community problems	4.0	24.2	35.3	36.5	1,489
Volunteer regularly for civic organizations	6.4	22.8	33.6	37.2	1,484
Vote in national elections	7.4	12.4	19.1	61.1	1,482
Vote in local elections	10.2	18.3	23.9	47.5	1,485
Persuade others to vote for a candidate	38.0	27.8	16.1	18.1	1,484
Work for or donate money to a candidate or party	58.7	23.0	9.9	8.4	1,481
Contact an elected official	46.1	29.2	13.1	11.6	1,485
Attend a political rally or protest	45.6	25.7	15.1	13.5	1,484
Sign a petition about a political issue	16.9	33.5	26.5	23.2	1,485

Appendix B

A NEW ASSESSMENT COMMUNITY: THE CONSORTIUM FOR INTER-CAMPUS SOTL RESEARCH

Consortium for Inter-Campus SoTL Research (CISR) was launched to facilitate research and assessment projects requiring collaborative, cross-campus data collection to assess the effectiveness of classroom pedagogy and campus-wide civic engagement initiatives. The coauthors worked to establish CISR because they both believe that more systematic, multi-campus data collection will help to identify the effective teaching practices and programming efforts that generalize beyond a single campus setting. Many of the teacher-scholars who are most interested in conducting SoTL research do not have the time or the resources to coordinate multi-campus efforts—which not only prevents large-N surveys from being undertaken, but also limits the selection of cases in qualitative work and subjects in experimental designs.

CISR's structure is intended to ease these constraints on multi-campus research and assessment projects by building a network of academics and administrators interested in helping to implement collaborative research. When members join CISR, they receive updates about upcoming peer-reviewed, advisory board-approved projects, with the option of participating in data collection. Those who opt in and facilitate a particular project will at minimum receive a summary report specific to their own campus, along with broader national trends that can be used as a point of comparison in internal assessment. Whenever possible, principle investigators are encouraged to share raw campus-level data for use in participating members' own scholarly or administrative work. In some cases, a principle investigator may seek coauthors and agree to provide full access to the database produced by a project. CISR members can also respond to calls for proposals and submit an original project for review by the advisory board, which will give extra consideration to members who have participated in previous projects.

The consortium, which currently has over 200 member campuses, is intended to provide those who join with access to more students, classes, and campuses—which should not only improve civic engagement assessment projects, but also provide improved SoTL findings worthy of publication. One of CISR's primary goals is to make it easier for teacher-scholars at colleges with heavy teaching loads to participate in cutting-edge SoTL research. In addition to recruiting participating campuses for member-initiated research projects, CISR will continue to coordinate future waves of the NSSL.

Civic Engagement Centers and Institutes: Promising Routes for Teaching Lessons in Citizenship to Students of All Disciplines

21

Elizabeth C. Matto and Mary McHugh

More and more frequently, colleges and universities are turning to civic engagement centers and institutes to facilitate civic engagement education. These stand-alone units are woven into the campus culture and accessible to faculty and students of all disciplines. In this chapter, we identify a number of centers and institutes situated on campuses recognized for their commitment to civic engagement, explore the structural features they share, and link readers to a number of useful resources such as syllabi and assessments. Occasionally, faculty members who would like to include civic engagement opportunities in their courses are hesitant to do so. Challenges such as finding the appropriate projects and contacts and integrating activities into the classroom create obstacles that faculty might find daunting and time-consuming. This chapter serves then as a useful guide for faculty of all disciplines and administrators who want to create or advance civic engagement education and encourages readers to better utilize the civic engagement centers and institutes that exist on their own campuses.[1]

The responsibility of educating college students to be active and engaged citizens is a shared responsibility that must extend beyond an individual discipline and reach all students. A college or university's commitment to civic engagement education often is embedded in the structure and culture of the campus via civic engagement centers and institutes. Centers and institutes are a promising route for institutionalizing civic engagement education, linking curricular and co-curricular civic learning opportunities, and serving as an important resource for students and faculty of all disciplines. As such, we believe that there is much to be gained by those faculty on diverse campuses and from a range of disciplines who are interested in facilitating the civic engagement of their students by highlighting such centers and the resources they offer.

As Welch and Saltmarsh point out, a number of centers and institutes cropped up on campuses in the 1980s and 1990s to serve as clearinghouses and organizational resources for the growing number of service and experiential learning initiatives that were taking place.[2] As campuses in recent years have responded to the call to more vigorously prepare students to be active citizens, they have turned to these centers and institutes to facilitate students' civic engagement education.[3] These centers and institutes then can serve both as models of civic engagement education and a fount of resources.

One of the most common questions asked about teaching civic engagement is how to begin. Faculty members who might have an idea for an activity or just a desire to get their students involved can find logistical issues daunting. Teaching loads, other university commitments, and family life can mean that a professor has little time to devote to setting up and running civic engagement activities. The time and commitment needed to learn how to teach civic engagement is another challenge that faculty face. While we have learned the material to teach in our disciplines, the topic of civic engagement usually is not part of our training and takes other types of knowledge, practice, and skill.

A civic engagement center, institute, or office can be a launching pad for a professor interested in this work or even for those faculty members already doing projects that they might want to expand or enhance. These centers contain a variety of resources (sometimes untapped) for faculty on our campuses. The staffs of these centers have community connections, experience, and contacts. They often have organizations willing to work with faculty on projects and sometimes even projects ready to go that would help a faculty member save time and energy. Staff members of such centers are usually able to tailor the needs of a faculty member to the opportunities that exist in the community. They also are able to help with solving logistical issues such as liability and transportation and offer suggestions to faculty on how to make these projects go smoothly. Oftentimes, civic engagement centers are able to provide assessment and reflection tools and syllabi samples that can save a faculty member from "re-creating the wheel." Some centers offer faculty development workshops and have grant funds available for training and conference attendance. In short, civic engagement centers and institutes should be able to support and guide faculty through the process, provide pathways to successful outcomes for these projects, and thereby allay some of the concerns that beginners have about getting and staying involved in civic engagement activities.

This chapter identifies a broad range of centers and institutes of civic engagement and, more importantly, discusses the structures and practices that make them useful for faculty across multiple disciplines. As we have learned in researching this subject, there is limited information available on the universe of centers and institutes on all types of campuses around the country that are doing this type of work. In this chapter, we offer a description of this universe. We provide a sense of the number of such centers and institutes that exist on campuses recognized for exemplary civic engagement efforts, the type of centers and institutes that different campuses foster, and the nature of the work these centers and institutes undertake. In addition, we describe their common features while zeroing in on a few that have an interdisciplinary appeal. By shining a light on these centers and institutes and linking readers to the numerous resources they offer, such as syllabi and assessments, this chapter serves as a "one-stop-shop" for teacher-scholars who are considering pursuing this work but are wondering how to go about it effectively. Moreover, this chapter might spur readers to utilize and even strengthen the civic engagement centers and institutes that already exist on their own campuses or help them leverage the resources required to establish one.

IDENTIFYING CIVIC ENGAGEMENT CENTERS AND INSTITUTES

Before commencing with the study of civic engagement centers and institutes, it was necessary to devise a systematic method for identifying them. Although we each came into this project with an awareness of centers and institutes of civic engagement around the country, we also were mindful that there was plenty we did not know and wanted to be sure we accounted for the full range of civic engagement initiatives pursued at institutions of higher education of all types—large and small, public and private—and from all regions of the nation.

Assuming that high-quality civic engagement centers and institutes would be found on campuses that have demonstrated a commitment to civic engagement, we began by identifying these colleges and universities. The Carnegie Foundation for the Advancement of Teaching invites colleges and universities with "an institutional focus on community engagement" to apply for classification as a community engagement institution and requires schools to provide evidence of "curricular engagement" and "outreach and partnership" to be classified as such. In composing our sample of institutions of higher education committed to civic engagement, we began with the 360 Community Engagement Classified Institutions for 2010 and 2015.[4]

To construct a sample of a manageable size but one that represented the full range of schools dedicated to civic engagement, we narrowed the list of schools holding a Carnegie classification by selecting those colleges and universities that fell into at least two of the following four categories:

- Presidential Honor Roll: An initiative of the Corporation for National and Community Service, the President's Higher Education Community Service Honor Roll, "recognizes institutions of higher education that support exemplary community service programs and raise the visibility of effective practices in campus community partnerships."[5] A total of 375 colleges and universities were cited on the most recent honor roll and were included in our sample selection.
- American Democracy Project/The Democracy Commitment: An initiative of the American Association of State Colleges and Universities, the American Democracy Project is a network of state colleges and universities whose goal is to "produce college university graduates who are committed to being informed, engaged members of their communities."[6] Modeled after the American Democracy Project and with a similar aim, the Democracy Commitment's network is composed of community colleges (associate's colleges). Our sample selection included the 256 American Democracy Project schools as well as the 93 Democracy Commitment schools.
- National Campaign: The National Campaign for Political and Civic Engagement is a consortium of colleges and universities based at Harvard University's Institute of Politics whose mission is to develop "civic minded and politically engaged students."[7] The 27 current members of the National Campaign were included in our sample selection.
- Campus Compact: A national coalition of 1,100 schools, Campus Compact's mission is to advance "the public purposes of colleges and universities by deepening their ability to improve community life and to educate students for civic and social responsibility."[8] The Campus Compact schools also were included in our sample selection.

This selection process took place in the summer and fall of 2016 and resulted in a total of 77 colleges and universities in our sample. Table 21.1 lists the schools we studied as well as the categories in which each school falls. It bears emphasizing that we are quite certain that there are plenty more colleges and universities that are doing exemplary work in the area of civic engagement. We devised this selection method to compose a manageable list of schools to consider for this research.

As expected, colleges and universities that have been recognized for their active support of civic engagement come in all shapes and sizes, are of all types, and are located in all regions of the country, from Keene State College in New Hampshire to the California State University in Chico. Of the schools under consideration,

- 17 were private and 60 were public
  - 29 doctoral universities
  - 37 master's colleges and universities
  - 6 baccalaureate colleges
  - 5 associate's colleges
- With student populations as small as fewer than 2,000 students and as large as approximately 70,000.

For many of the colleges and universities under study, their commitment to civic engagement was explicit in their mission statements or core values. Of the 77 schools we studied, 35 of them explicitly reference the term "civic" or "citizen" in either their mission or vision statements. For example, Central Connecticut State University's mission statement reads,

Table 21.1 Civically Engaged Collges and Universities

SCHOOL NAME	STATE	SELECTION CATEGORIES*	TYPE	PUBLIC OR PRIVATE	STUDENT POPULATION**
Allegheny College	PA	C/NC/CC	Baccalaureate College–Arts and Sciences Focus	Private	2,100
Appalachian State University	NC	C/ADP/CC	Master's College & University–Larger Programs	Public	18,295
Arizona State University	AZ	C/HR/NC/CC	Doctoral University–Highest Research Activity	Public	69,551
Auburn University	AL	C/HR/CC	Doctoral University–Higher Research Activity	Public	27,287
Ball State University	IN	C/HR/CC	Doctoral University-Higher Research Activity	Public	21,000
Bergen Community College	NJ	C/HR/CC	Associate's College–High Transfer-High Traditional	Public	17,000
Bristol Community College	MA	C/HR/CC	Associate's College–High Transfer-High Traditional	Public	11,954
California State University, Channel Islands	CA	C/HR/ADP/CC	Master's College & University–Small Programs	Public	6,167
California State University, Chico	CA	C/HR/ADP/CC	Master's College & University–Larger Programs	Public	16,140
California State University, Fresno	CA	C/HR/ADP/CC	Doctoral University–Moderate Research Activity	Public	24,400
California State University, Fullerton	CA	C/HR/ADP/CC	Doctoral University–Moderate Research Activity	Public	38,948
California State University, Monterey Bay	CA	C/HR/ADP/CC	Master's College & University–Medium Programs	Public	7,000
California State University, San Bernardino	CA	C/HR/CC	Master's College & University–Larger Programs	Public	20,767
California State University, Stanislaus	CA	C/HR/ADP	Master's College & University–Larger Programs	Public	9,282

Table 21.1 Civically Engaged Collges and Universities Continued

SCHOOL NAME	STATE	SELECTION CATEGORIES*	TYPE	PUBLIC OR PRIVATE	STUDENT POPULATION**
Central Connecticut State University	CT	C/HR/ADP/CC	Master's College & University–Larger Programs	Public	12,086
Chandler-Gilbert Community College	AZ	C/HR/TDC	Associate's College-High Transfer-Mixed Traditional/Non-Traditional	Public	19,040
Cleveland State University	OH	C/HR/ADP/CC	Doctoral University–Higher Research Activity	Public	17,730
Drexel University	PA	C/HR/CC	Doctoral University–Higher Research Activity	Private	26,359
Elizabethtown College	PA	C/HR/CC	Baccalaureate College–Art and Sciences Focus	Private	1,800
Elon University	NC	C/HR/NC/CC	Master's College & University–Medium Programs	Private	6,631
Florida Gulf Coast University	FL	C/HR/ADP/CC	Master's College & University–Larger Programs	Public	14,846
Georgetown University	DC	C/HR/NC/CC	Doctoral University–Highest Research Activity	Private	3,759
Georgia College & State University	GA	C/HR/ADP/CC	Master's Colleges & Universities–Larger Programs	Public	6,600
Gettysburg College	PA	C/HR/CC	Baccalaureate College–Arts and Sciences Focus	Private	2,632
Indiana State University	IN	C/HR/ADP/CC	Doctoral University–Moderate Research Activity	Public	13,584
Indiana University–Purdue University, Indianapolis	IN	C/HR/ADP/CC	Doctoral University–Higher Research Activity	Public	29,804
James Madison University	VA	C/ADP/CC	Master's College & University–Larger Programs	Public	21,227
Keene State College	NH	C/HR/ADP/CC	Master's College & University–Small Programs	Public	5,500

Table 21.1 Civically Engaged Collges and Universities Continued

SCHOOL NAME	STATE	SELECTION CATEGORIES*	TYPE	PUBLIC OR PRIVATE	STUDENT POPULATION**
Louisiana State University	LA	C/HR/NC/CC	Doctoral University–Highest Research Activity	Public	31,527
Mercer University	GA	C/HR/CC	Doctoral University–Moderate Research Activity	Private	8,603
Mesa Community College	AZ	C/HR/TDC/CC	Associate's College–High Transfer-Mixed Traditional/Non-Traditional	Public	21,491
Metropolitan State University	MN	C/HR/ADP/CC	Master's College & University–Larger Programs	Public	11,506
Middle Tennessee State University	TN	C/HR/ADP/CC	Doctoral University–Moderate Research Activity	Public	18,295
Millersville University	PA	C/HR/ADP/CC	Master's College & University–Larger Programs	Public	8,075
Missouri State University	MO	C/HR/ADP/CC	Master's College & University–Larger Programs	Public	22,273
Mount Wachusett Community College	MA	C/HR/TDC/CC	Associate's College–Mixed Transfer/Vocational & Technical–High Traditional	Public	10,371
North Carolina Agricultural and Technical State University	NC	C/ADP/CC	Doctoral University–Higher Research Activity	Public	10,725
North Carolina Central University	NC	C/HR/ADP/CC	Master's College & University–Larger Programs	Public	8,155
Northern Michigan University	MI	C/HR/ADP/CC	Master's College & University–Medium Programs	Public	8,303
Rutgers University, Newark	NJ	C/HR/CC	Doctoral University–Higher Research Activity	Public	11,314
Saint Mary's College of California	CA	C/HR/TDC/CC	Master's College & University–Larger Programs	Private	4,030

Table 21.1 Civically Engaged Collges and Universities Continued

SCHOOL NAME	STATE	SELECTION CATEGORIES*	TYPE	PUBLIC OR PRIVATE	STUDENT POPULATION**
San Francisco State University	CA	C/HR/ADP	Doctoral University–Moderate Research Activity	Public	30,256
State University of New York at Geneseo	NY	C/HR/ADP/CC	Master's College & University–Small Programs	Public	5,699
State University of New York at Oswego	NY	C/HR/ADP/CC	Master's College & University–Larger Programs	Public	8,000
State University of New York, Cortland	NY	C/HR/ADP/CC	Master's College & University–Larger Program	Public	6,926
Stonehill College	MA	C/HR/NC/CC	Baccalaureate Colleges–Arts & Sciences Focus	Private	2,400
Swarthmore College	PA	C/HR/CC	Baccalaureate College–Arts & Sciences Focus	Private	1,581
Tennessee State University	TN	C/ADP/NC/CC	Doctoral University–Moderate Research Activity	Public	9,027
Towson University	MD	C/HR/ADP/CC	Master's College & University–Larger Programs	Public	22,284
Tufts University	MA	C/HR/CC	Doctoral University–Highest Research Activity	Private	11,767
Tulane University	LA	C/HR/CC	Doctoral University–Highest Research Activity	Private	13,449
University of Alaska, Anchorage	AK	C/HR/ADP/CC	Master's College & University–Larger Programs	Public	18,116
University of Central Florida	FL	C/ADP/CC	Doctoral University–Highest Research Activity	Public	63,000
University of Central Oklahoma	OK	C/ADP/CC	Master's College & University–Larger Programs	Public	16,428
University of Kansas	KS	C/HR/NC/CC	Doctoral University–Highest Research Activity	Public	27,983

Table 21.1 Civically Engaged Collges and Universities Continued

SCHOOL NAME	STATE	SELECTION CATEGORIES*	TYPE	PUBLIC OR PRIVATE	STUDENT POPULATION**
University of Missouri, St. Louis	MO	C/ADP/CC	Doctoral University–Higher Research Activity	Public	16,989
University of Nebraska at Omaha	NB	C/HR/ADP/CC	Doctoral University–Moderate Research Activity	Public	15,627
University of North Carolina at Greensboro	NC	C/HR/ADP/CC	Doctoral University–Higher Research Activity	Public	19,400
University of North Carolina, Wilmington	NC	C/HR/ADP/CC	Master's College & University–Larger Programs	Public	15,800
University of North Florida	FL	C/ADP/CC	Master's College & University–Larger Programs	Public	15,839
University of Northern Iowa	IA	C/HR/ADP/CC	Master's College & University–Larger Programs	Public	11,981
University of Pennsylvania	PA	C/HR/CC	Doctoral University–Highest Research Activity	Private	24,876
University of Redlands	CA	C/HR/CC	Master's College & University–Larger Programs	Private	5,333
University of Southern California	CA	C/HR/NC	Doctoral University–Highest Research Activity	Private	43,000
University of Texas	TX	C/HR/NC/CC	Doctoral University–Highest Research Activity	Public	50,950
University of Wisconsin, Parkside	WI	C/HR/ADP/CC	Baccalaureate College–Arts & Sciences Focus	Public	4,557
Utah Valley University	UT	C/HR/ADP/CC	Master's College & University–Small Programs	Public	34,978
Wagner College	NY	C/HR/CC	Master's College & University–Medium Programs	Private	1,750
Wake Forest University	NC	C/HR/CC	Doctoral University–Higher Research Activity	Private	7,669

Table 21.1 Civically Engaged Collges and Universities Continued

SCHOOL NAME	STATE	SELECTION CATEGORIES*	TYPE	PUBLIC OR PRIVATE	STUDENT POPULATION**
Weber State University	UT	C/HR/ADP/CC	Master's College & University–Larger Programs	Public	26,000
West Chester University of PA	PA	C/HR/ADP/CC	Master's College & University–Larger Programs	Public	16,606
Western Carolina University	NC	C/HR/ADP/CC	Master's College & University–Larger Program	Public	10,805
Western Illinois University	IL	C/HR/ADP/CC	Master's College & University–Larger Program	Public	11,094
Western Washington University	WA	C/HR/ADP/CC	Master's College & University–Larger Program	Public	15,332
Winona State University	MN	C/HR/ADP/CC	Master's College & University–Medium Programs	Public	8,486
Winthrop University	SC	C/HR/ADP/CC	Master's College & University–Larger Programs	Public	4,974
Wright State University	OH	C/HR/ADP/CC	Doctoral University–Moderate Research Activity	Public	17,775

Note: Classifications from Indiana University Center for Postsecondary Research (2016). Carnegie Classifications 2015 public data file, http://carnegieclassifications.iu.edu/downloads/CCIHE2015-PublicDataFile.xlsx, June 16, 2016.
* This column represents in which selection categories the school belongs: C=Carnegie Classications, HR=Presidential Honor Roll, ADP/TDC=American Democracy Project or The Democracy Commitment, NC=National Campaign, CC=Campus Compact.
** This information was gathered from campuses' websites and reporting varied between "total" population and "undergraduate" population.

Central Connecticut State University is a community of learners dedicated to teaching and scholarship that emphasizes development and application of knowledge and ideas through research and outreach activities, and prepares students to be thoughtful, responsible and successful citizens.[9]

California State University, Chico's mention of civic engagement in its expression of values reflects a multifaceted conception of civic education,

We seek the purposeful integration of liberal and applied learning and the provision of full access and equal opportunity for all our students to the knowledge, skills, and habits that form the basis for life-long learning, civic engagement, and enlightened service in a diverse society and global community.[10]

Even without explicit mention, other schools' commitment to civic engagement and fostering citizenship is evident in their mission statements. For example, Mercer University's mission statement makes is clear that they seek to foster a sense of public service in their student body: "Mercer University's mission is to teach, to learn, to create, to discover, to inspire, to empower and to serve."[11] Ball State University's vision statement reflects a similar purpose:

Ball State University aspires to be the model of the most student-centered and community-engaged of the twenty-first century public research universities, transforming entrepreneurial learners into impactful leaders—committed to improving quality of life.[12]

Of course, an institution's mission statement is not sufficient evidence of its commitment to preparing its students to be active citizens. What matters is the manner in which the mission is embodied in the structure and culture of the campus, and one way institutions might actualize their commitment to civic engagement is via well-structured and properly resourced centers and institutes. In an effort then to identify and better understand civic engagement centers and institutes, we began with this list of 77 campuses. Our initial goal was to identify centers and institutes on these campuses and capture a sense of their purpose.

We went about this task by visiting each school's website and, using the website's search engine, typed in the search term "civic engagement" to locate any bodies on campus dedicated to such work. We then viewed the webpages dedicated to these efforts to determine whether the unit was still in operation and fit the parameters of our search. In some instances, we found that the civic engagement initiative that resulted from the search was a one-time or short-lived campus effort or an umbrella term used to group together all of the campus units dedicated to civic engagement. We eliminated those results from consideration and instead focused on centers and institutes—stand-alone units that had their own staff, their own budget, and their own purpose or mission. The search process we utilized also generated a number of offices and schools dedicated to civic engagement, and we have included them in our study to capture the full range of such structures on college campuses today. It is worth mentioning that our research was restricted to the information found on each school's website. Clearly, this method has its shortcomings—what is posted on a website may not always be current. Given that the overall purpose of this chapter is to describe the universe of centers and institutes in higher education, we believe that it is nonetheless a suitable approach.

The initial questions we addressed were these: how many of these schools have centers and institutes (or similar units), how many do each have, and what is the nature of their work? The answers to some of these questions can be found in table 21.2. We found that of the 77 colleges and universities under consideration, 68 of them had centers or institutes (or similar structures) dedicated to civic engagement on their campuses. Of those schools that had centers or institutes, most had only one office while four of the campuses held as many as three centers or institutes dedicated to civic engagement: Arizona State University, Georgetown University, the University of Pennsylvania, and the University of Southern California.

Table 21.2 Civic Engagement Centers and Institutes

SCHOOL NAME	TYPE	PUBLIC OR PRIVATE	CENTER/INSTITUTE	CENTER/INSTITUTE	CENTER/INSTITUTE
Allegheny College	Baccalaureate College – Arts and Sciences Focus	Private	Office for Civic Engagement	The Center for Political Participation	
Appalachian State University	Master's Colleges & Universities – Larger Programs	Public	Civic Engagement Program		
Arizona State University	Doctoral University – Highest Research Activity	Public	The College of Public Service and Community Solutions	Morrison Institute for Public Policy	Congressman Ed Pastor Center for Politics and Public Service
Auburn University	Doctoral University – Higher Research Activity	Public	The Community and Civic Engagement Initiative	David Mathews Center	
Ball State University	Doctoral University – Higher Research Activity	Public	Bowen Center for Public Affairs	Office of Community Engagement	
Bergen Community College	Associate's College – High Transfer – High Traditional	Public			
Bristol Community College	Associate's College – High Transfer – High Traditional	Public	Center for Civic Engagement		
California State University, Channel Islands	Master's Colleges & Universities – Small Programs	Public	Center for Community Engagement	Center for Multicultural Engagement	
California State University, Chico	Master's College & University – Larger Programs	Public	Office of Civic Engagement		
California State University, Fresno	Doctoral Universities – Moderate Research Activity	Public	Jan and Bud Richter Center for Community Engagement and Service-Learning		
California State University, Fullerton	Doctoral University – Moderate Research Activity	Public	The Center for Public Policy	Center for Internships & Civic Engagement	
California State University, Monterey Bay	Master's Colleges & Universities – Medium Programs	Public	Service Learning Institute		
California State University, San Bernardino	Master's Colleges & Universities – Larger Programs	Public	Office of Community Engagement		

Table 21.2 Civic Engagement Centers and Institutes Continued

SCHOOL NAME	TYPE	PUBLIC OR PRIVATE	CENTER/INSTITUTE	CENTER/INSTITUTE	CENTER/INSTITUTE
California State University, Stanislaus	Master's Colleges & Universities–Larger Programs	Public	Office of Service-Learning		
Central Connecticut State University	Master's College & University–Larger Programs	Public	The Office of Community Engagement	Center for Public Policy and Social Research	
Chandler-Gilbert Community College	Associate's Colleges–High Transfer–Mixed Traditional/Nontraditional	Public	Service Learning/Office of Student Life and Leadership	Center for Civic Participation	
Cleveland State University	Doctoral Univerisities–Higher Research Activity	Public	Office of Civic Engagement		
Drexel University	Doctoral University–Higher Research Activity	Private	Lindy Center for Civic Engagement		
Elizabethtown College	Baccalaureate College–Arts and Sciences Focus	Private	Center for Community & Civic Engagement		
Elon University	Master's College & University–Medium Programs	Private	Kernodle Center for Service Learning and Community Engagement	Institute of Politics and Public Affairs	
Florida Gulf Coast University	Master's College & University–Larger Programs	Public	Office of Service-Learning and Civic Engagement		
Georgetown University	Doctoral University–Highest Research Activity	Private	Office of Community Engagement	Institute of Politics and Public Service	Baker Center for Leadership and Governance
Georgia College & State University	Master's Colleges & Universities–Larger Programs	Public	Office of ENGAGE		
Gettysburg College	Baccalaureate College–Arts and Sciences Focus	Private	Center for Public Service	Fielding Center for Presidential Leadership Study	
Indiana State University	Doctoral Univerisities–Moderate Research Activity	Public	Center for Community Engagement		
Indiana University–Purdue University, Indianapolis	Doctoral Univerisities–Higher Research Activity	Public	Center for Service and Learning		

Table 21.2 Civic Engagement Centers and Institutes Continued

SCHOOL NAME	TYPE	PUBLIC OR PRIVATE	CENTER/INSTITUTE	CENTER/INSTITUTE	CENTER/INSTITUTE
James Madison University	Master's Colleges & Universities–Larger Programs	Public			
Keene State College	Master's College & University–Small Programs	Public	Community Service at KSC		
Louisiana State University	Doctoral University–Highest Research Activity	Public	Center for Community Engagement, Learning, & Leadership		
Mercer University	Doctoral University–Moderate Research Activity	Private	Office of Service-Learning		
Mesa Community College	Associate's College–High Transfer–Mixed Traditional/Non-Traditional	Public	Center for Community and Civic Engagement		
Metropolitan State University	Master's College & University–Larger Programs	Public	The Institute for Community Engagement and Scholarship (ICES)		
Middle Tennessee State University	Doctoral Universities–Moderate Research Activity	Public	MTSU American Democracy Project		
Millersville University	Master's Colleges & Universities–Larger Programs	Public	Walker Center for Civic Responsibility and Leadership		
Missouri State University	Master's Colleges & Universities–Larger Programs	Public	Center for Community Engagement		
Mount Wachusett Community College	Associate's Colleges–Mixed Transfer/Vocational & Technical–High Traditional	Public	Center for Civic Learning and Community Engagement		
North Carolina Agricultural and Technical State University	Doctoral Universities–Higher Research Activity	Public			
North Carolina Central University	Master's Colleges & Universities–Larger Programs	Public			
Northern Michigan University	Master's Colleges & Universities–Medium Programs	Public			

Table 21.2 Civic Engagement Centers and Institutes Continued

SCHOOL NAME	TYPE	PUBLIC OR PRIVATE	CENTER/INSTITUTE	CENTER/INSTITUTE	CENTER/INSTITUTE
Rutgers University, Newark	Doctoral Universities–Higher Research Activity	Public			
Saint Mary's College of California	Master's Colleges & Universities–Larger Programs	Private	Catholic Institute for Lasallian Social Action		
San Francisco State University	Doctoral Universities–Moderate Research Activity	Public	Institute for Civic and Community Engagement		
State University of New York at Geneseo	Master's Colleges & Universities–Small Programs	Public			
State University of New York at Oswego	Master's Colleges & Universities–Larger Programs	Public			
State University of New York, Cortland	Master's Colleges & Universities–Larger Program	Public	Institute for Civic Engagement		
Stonehill College	Baccalaureate Colleges–Arts & Sciences Focus	Private	The Martin Institute for Law and Society	Office of Community-Based Learning	
Swarthmore College	Baccalaureate Colleges–Arts & Sciences Focus	Private	Lang Center for Civic and Social Responsibility		
Tennessee State University	Doctoral Universities–Moderate Research Activity	Public	Center for Service Learning & Civic Engagement		
Towson University	Master's College & University–Larger Programs	Public	Office of Civic Engagement & Leadership		
Tufts University	Doctoral University–Highest Research Activity	Private	Tisch College of Citizenship and Public Service		
Tulane University	Doctoral University–Highest Research Activity	Private	Center for Public Service		
University of Alaska, Anchorage	Master's Colleges & Universities–Larger Programs	Public	Center for Community Engagement & Learning	Dialogues for Public Life	
University of Central Florida	Doctoral Universities–Highest Research Activity	Public	Burnett Honors College Research & Civic Engagment	Lou Frey Institute	

Table 21.2 Civic Engagement Centers and Institutes Continued

SCHOOL NAME	TYPE	PUBLIC OR PRIVATE	CENTER/INSTITUTE	CENTER/INSTITUTE	CENTER/INSTITUTE
University of Central Oklahoma	Master's Colleges & Universities–Larger Programs	Public	Center for Civic Engagement American Democracy Project	Volunteer and Service Learning Center	
University of Kansas	Doctoral University–Highest Research Activity	Public	Dole Institute of Politics	Center for Civic and Social Responsibility	
University of Missouri, St. Louis	Doctoral Universities–Higher Research Activity	Public	The Center for Teaching and Learning		
University of Nebraska at Omaha	Doctoral Universities–Moderate Research Activity	Public	Office of Civic & Social Responsibility	Barbara Weitz Community Engagement Center	
University of North Carolina at Greensboro	Doctoral Universities–Higher Research Activity	Public	Office of Leadership and Service-Learning	Institute for Community & Political Engagement	
University of North Carolina Wilmington	Master's Colleges & Universities–Larger Programs	Public			
University of North Florida	Master's Colleges & Universities–Larger Programs	Public	The Center for Community-Based Learning	The American Democracy Project at UNF	
University of Northern Iowa	Master's Colleges & Universities–Larger Programs	Public	The University of Northern Iowa American Democracy Project		
University of Pennsylvania	Doctoral Universities–Highest Research Activity	Private	The Netter Center for Community Partnership	Civic House	The Penn Project for Civic Engagement
University of Redlands	Master's Colleges & Universities–Larger Programs	Private	The Office of Community Service Learning		
University of Southern California	Doctoral University–Highest Research Activity	Private	Center for Religion and Civic Culture	Center for Diversity and Democracy	Jesse Unruhe Institute of Politics
University of Texas	Doctoral Universities–Highest Research Activity	Public	Annette Strauss Institute for Civic Life	The Longhorn Center for Community Engagement	
University of Wisconsin, Parkside	Baccalaureate Colleges–Arts & Sciences Focus	Public	Continuing Education and Community Engagement		
Utah Valley University	Master's Colleges & Universities–Small Programs	Public	Volunteer & Service-Learning Center	The Office of Engaged Learning	

Table 21.2 Civic Engagement Centers and Institutes Continued

SCHOOL NAME	TYPE	PUBLIC OR PRIVATE	CENTER/INSTITUTE	CENTER/INSTITUTE	CENTER/INSTITUTE
Wagner College	Master's College & University–Medium Programs	Private	Center for Leadership and Community Engagement		
Wake Forest University	Doctoral University–Higher Research Activity	Private	Civic Learning and Democratic Engagement		
Weber State University	Master's College & University–Larger Programs	Public	Walker Institute of Politics and Public Service	Center for Community Engaged Learning	
West Chester University of PA	Master's Colleges & Universities–Larger Programs	Public	The Office of Service-Learning and Volunteer Programs		
Western Carolina University	Master's Colleges & Universities–Larger Program	Public	Center for Service Learning	Public Policy Institute	
Western Illinois University	Master's Colleges & Universities–Larger Program	Public	Volunteer Services	Center for Study of Civic Engagement	
Western Washington University	Master's Colleges & Universities–Larger Program	Public	Center for Service-Learning		
Winona State University	Master's College & University–Medium Programs	Public	Community Engagement		
Winthrop University	Master's College & University–Larger Programs	Public	Center for Career and Civic Engagement		
Wright State University	Doctoral Universities–Moderate Research Activity	Public	Center for Service-Learning and Civic Engagement		

Of these 68 schools, we identified a total of 46 centers and 16 institutes. In addition, our search produced 33 offices or initiatives dedicated to civic engagement and three colleges or schools.

- Of the 46 centers, 21 are at doctoral universities with two of these campuses housing more than one center. Of the remaining centers, 16 are at master's colleges, five at baccalaureate colleges, and four of the centers can be found at associate's colleges.
- Of the 16 institutes we identified, eight are located at doctoral universities and seven on campuses classified as master's colleges or universities. Only one of the institutes is located at a baccalaureate college, and there are no institutes at the associate's colleges in our sample.
- Most of the 33 civic engagement offices we identified are at master's colleges, 17 offices in all. Twelve of the total of offices are at doctoral universities.
- Of the three colleges/schools dedicated to civic engagement that we identified, all three are located at doctoral universities.

After we accounted for the number of centers and institutes dedicated to civic engagement in existence on these campuses, our goal was to get a sense of the sort of work that they did. Specifically, we considered the extent to which centers and institutes' work was focused on civic engagement in general or political engagement specifically. As McCartney asserts in *Teaching Civic Engagement: From Student to Active Citizen*, the term "civic engagement" is a "larger, more encompassing term" and relates to

> an individual's activities, … that focus on developing knowledge about the community and its political system, identifying and seeking solutions to community problems, pursuing goals to benefit the community, and participating in constructive deliberation among community members about the community's political system and community issues, problems, or solutions.[13]

Although it emanates from civic engagement, political engagement is defined as "explicitly politically oriented activities that seek a direct impact on political issues, systems, relationships, and structures."[14]

Using these definitions as a guide, we classified those centers and institutes whose efforts are mainly community-centered as having a civic engagement focus. As we will explain, many of the centers and institutes categorized in this way are focused on service-learning—a pedagogy that links community-centered work to a course and includes such components as readings, reflection, and assignments.[15] Those centers that are less focused on raising awareness about community problems and engaging in problem solving and more concerned with directly affecting political change are classified as having a political focus. Centers with public policy as a focal point, for example, are categorized this way. In a handful of cases, centers and institutes further both civic and political engagement.

As seen in table 21.3, the vast majority of the centers and institutes we identified are concerned mainly with civic engagement. For example, the mission of Appalachian State University's Civic Engagement Program is centered in its surrounding community with the intention to foster mutually beneficial learning, involvement, and benefits:

> Civic engagement encompasses actions wherein individuals participate in activities of personal and public concern that are both individually life enriching and socially beneficial to the community. As with any community-based learning, the participation and leadership of the community is paramount.[16]

Rooted in this understanding, Appalachian State University's Civic Engagement Program's work involves civic engagement education through a combination of service-learning activities,

Table 21.3 Types of Centers and Institutes

POLITICAL ENGAGEMENT	CIVIC ENGAGEMENT	CIVIC & POLITICAL ENGAGEMENT
Annette Strauss Institute for Civic Life (University of Texas)	Center for Civic and Social Responsibility (University of Kansas)	Office of Civic Engagement (California State University, Chico)
Baker Center for Leadership and Governance (Georgetown University)	Center for Civic Engagement (Bristol Community College)	Office of Civic Engagement & Leadership (Towson University)
Center for Civic Engagement American Democracy Project (University of Central Oklahoma)	Center for Civic Learning and Community Engagement (Mount Wachusett Community College)	The Center for Political Participation (Allegheny College)
Center for Public Policy and Social Research (Central Connecticut State University)	Center for Community & Civic Engagement (Elizabethtown College)	Tisch College of Citizenship and Public Service (Tufts University)
Center for Study of Civic Engagement (Western Illinois University)	Center for Community and Civic Engagement (Mesa Community College)	
Congressman Ed Pastor Center for Politics and Public Service (Arizona State University)	Center for Community Engaged Learning (Weber State University)	
Dole Institute of Politics (University of Kansas)	Center for Community Engagement (California State University, Channel Islands)	
Fielding Center for Presidential Leadership Study (Gettysburg College)	Center for Community Engagement (Indiana State University)	
Institute of Politics and Public Service (Georgetown University)	Center for Community Engagement (Missouri State University)	
Jesse Unruhe Institute of Politics (University of Southern California)	Center for Community Engagement & Learning (University of Alaska, Anchorage)	
Lou Frey Institute (University of Central Florida)	Center for Community Engagement, Learning, & Leadership (Louisiana State University)	
Morrison Institute for Public Policy (Arizona State University)	Center for Diversity and Democracy (University of Southern California)	
Public Policy Institute (Western Carolina University)	Center for Internships & Civic Engagement (California State University, Fullerton)	
The Center for Public Policy (California State University, Fullerton)	Center for Leadership & Community Engagement (Wagner College)	
The Martin Institute for Law and Society (Stonehill College)	Center for Multicultural Engagement (California State University, Channel Islands)	

Table 21.3 Types of Centers and Institutes Continued

POLITICAL ENGAGEMENT	CIVIC ENGAGEMENT	CIVIC & POLITICAL ENGAGEMENT
The Penn Project for Civic Engagement (University of Pennsylvania)	Center for Public Service (Gettysburg College)	
Walker Center for Civic Responsibility and Leadership (Millersville University)	Center for Public Service (Tulane University)	
Walker Institute of Politics and Public Service (Weber State University)	Center for Service and Learning (Indiana University–Purdue University, Indianapolis)	
	Center for Service Learning (Western Carolina University)	
	Center for Service Learning & Civic Engagement (Tennessee State University)	
	Center for Service-Learning (Western Washington University)	
	Center for Service-Learning and Civic Engagement (Wright State University)	
	Civic Engagement Program (Appalachian State University)	
	Civic House (University of Pennsylvania)	
	Community Engagement (Winona State University)	
	Community Service at KSC (Keene State College)	
	Continuing Education and Community Engagement (University of Wisconsin, Parkside)	
	David Mathews Center (Auburn University)	
	Dialogues for Public Life (University of Alaska, Anchorage)	
	Institute for Civic and Community Engagement (San Francisco State University)	
	Institute for Civic Engagement (State University of New York, Cortland)	
	Jan and Bud Richter Center for Community Engagement and Service-Learning (California State University, Fresno)	
	Kernodle Center for Service Learning and Community Engagement (Elon University)	
	Lang Center for Civic and Social Responsibility (Swarthmore College)	
	Lindy Center for Civic Engagement (Drexel University)	

Table 21.3 Types of Centers and Institutes Continued

CIVIC ENGAGEMENT

MTSU American Democracy Project (Middle Tennessee State University)	The Center for Community-Based Learning (University of North Florida)
Office for Civic Engagement (Allegheny College)	The Center for Teaching and Learning (University of Missouri, St. Louis)
Office of Civic & Social Responsibility (University of Nebraska at Omaha)	The College of Public Service and Community Solutions (Arizona State University)
Office of Civic Engagement (Cleveland State University)	The Community and Civic Engagement Initiative (Auburn University)
Office of Community Engagement (Ball State University)	The Institute for Community & Economic Engagement (University of North Carolina at Greensboro)
Office of Community Engagement (California State University, San Bernardino)	The Institute for Community Engagement and Scholarship (Metropolitan State University)
Office of Community Engagement (Georgetown University)	The Longhorn Center for Community Engagement (University of Texas)
Office of Community-Based Learning (Stonehill College)	The Netter Center for Community Partnership (University of Pennsylvania)
Office of ENGAGE (Georgia College & State University)	The Office of Community Engagement (Central Connecticut State University)
Office of Leadership and Service-Learning (University of North Carolina at Greensboro)	The Office of Community Service Learning (University of Redlands)
Office of Service-Learning (California State University, Stanislaus)	The Office of Engaged Learning (Utah Valley University)
Office of Service Learning (Mercer University)	The Office of Service-Learning and Volunteer Programs (West Chester University of PA)
Office of Service-Learning and Civic Engagement (Florida Gulf Coast University)	The University of Northern Iowa American Democracy Project (University of Northern Iowa)
Service Learning Institute (California State University, Monterey Bay)	Volunteer & Service-Learning Center (Utah Valley University)
Service Learning/Office of Student Life and Leadership (Chandler-Gilbert Community College)	Volunteer and Service Learning Center (University of Central Oklahoma)
The American Democracy Project at UNF (University of North Florida)	Volunteer Services (Western Illinois University)

community-based research (research conducted collaboratively between scholars and community partners), service-based internships, and engaged scholarship (research conducted by scholars and practitioners).

The Center for Community-Based Learning at the University of North Florida also emphasizes the collaborative relationship with community as a core component of its efforts. Moreover, the center aims to integrate such civic engagement learning throughout the campus through the "institutionalization of community-based learning; preparing faculty, organizationally and pedagogically, for the demands of community-based teaching and learning; and establishing quality partnerships with community organizations."[17] Students access such learning via community-based "immersions" and instruction, apprenticeships and internships, and community-based research.[18]

Although fewer in number, some of the centers and institutes we identified focus less on community-engaged awareness and action and more on political outcomes. Some of these centers' political focus is a function of the role of public policy in their missions. For example, Central Connecticut State University's Center for Public Policy and Social Research is meant to serve as a policy and research resource for elected officials, nonprofit organizations, and the public at large. These efforts also are meant to offer applied research opportunities for faculty and students. Similarly, the goals of the Public Policy Institute at Western Carolina University include "*To help students* to become active participants in their communities" and "*To improve public policy in the region* by conducting rigorous research on major issues and making it available and understandable to a practitioner audience," and "*To exercise policy leadership* in the region" (emphasis in original).[19] Just as political engagement is rooted in civic engagement, these efforts certainly are rooted in the needs of the community and the problems facing it. Still, the policy focus suggests a heightened interest not only in influencing the political process but also teaching students how to affect political change.

Less focused on policy, we identified other centers and institutes with more of a focus on political rather than civic engagement. Primarily through credit-bearing internships, the Walker Institute of Politics and Public Service at Weber State University, for example, aims to prepare students for a life of public service. The University of Kansas's Dole Institute is meant to be "a forum for discussion of political and economic issues, fostering public service leadership and encouraging participation in the political process...."[20]

Finally, we identified a few centers and institutes that convey an equal emphasis on political and civic engagement, involving students in raising awareness and devising solutions to community problems and engaging them in the work of affecting the political process. A good example is the Office of Civic Engagement and Leadership at Towson University. The office promotes political engagement by playing an active role in voter registration efforts and disseminating voter information around campus while also facilitating service-learning opportunities across campus.

COMMON COMPONENTS

The 77 schools and the centers they house possess a variety of attributes that make each one unique in their approach to teaching civic engagement. These centers have a variety of resources that can help students understand how to connect service to citizenship in creative ways.

As we have discussed previously, the purpose of this chapter is not to evaluate centers. Instead, we seek to provide examples for faculty and administrators who are considering pursuing or increasing this sort of work but are wondering how to go about it effectively. This next section of this chapter will highlight several centers and institutes with links to the numerous resources they offer.

In our review of these centers, we found several common attributes. We have separated them into three categories that we will explain next:

- pedagogical resources available to faculty
- dedicated, expert staff
- faculty reward systems

PEDAGOGICAL RESOURCES

The availability of pedagogical resources is important because if we want to "do" civic engagement, having an effective center allows for a faculty member to focus on the project without becoming overwhelmed by the logistics. Handbooks, guides, samples of syllabi, assignments, and projects are all areas that can be helpful for both first-time users who want their students to be involved in civic engagement but might not be sure where to start and for veteran faculty who might want to revamp a course. Here are examples of centers that have these resources:

- Appalachian State University's Academic Civic Engagement Center (assignments and syllabi examples)
- Elizabethtown College's Center for Community and Civic Engagement (faculty handbook and forms)
- Louisiana State University's Center for Community Engagement, Learning and Leadership (syllabi, handbook, best practices)
- San Francisco State University's Institute for Civic and Community Engagement (library, workshops, videos, forms)
- Stonehill College's Office of Community-Based Learning (handbook, training examples)
- University of Missouri St. Louis's Center for Teaching and Learning (faculty guide, syllabi examples, project examples)
- University of Texas at Austin's Longhorn Center for Community Engagement (course development, checklists, other resources)

As Bennion explains in Chapter 27 of *Teaching Civic Engagement: From Student to Active Citizen*, assessment is a critical component in civic engagement education.[21] Assessing student learning outcomes, program objectives, and community impact helps instructors and institutions to build on successful practices and replace practices that are not working with more fruitful approaches. Tools for assessment and reflection are among other pedagogical resources that can be found in these centers. Access to these tools can ease the burden on faculty who might not have the expertise in these two critical areas.

Examples of assessment and reflection tools can be found here:

- Georgia College's ENGAGE program (assessment toolbox)
- Mercer University's Office of Service Learning (reflection resources, faculty guides)
- Towson University's Office of Leadership and Service-Learning (student surveys, community and faculty feedback forms)
- Utah Valley University's Volunteer and Service-Learning Center (reflection guide)
- Weber State University's Center for Community Engaged Learning (toolkit)

STRUCTURE AND STAFF

The structure of a center is also important. Where the center appears on the organizational chart of a college makes a difference because its mission, budget, and priorities could vary depending on where it is situated and who it reports to on campus (e.g., academic affairs versus student life). Also, the number and expertise of the staff of the center is worth considering. For example, are there faculty attached to the center, how many permanent members, how many VISTA, graduate students, or other temporary employees work in the center? As Welch and Saltmarsh note in their study of campus centers,

A typical community engagement center exists in an environment of campus wide commitment to community engagement and is structured as a central coordinating office reporting to academic affairs with a budget from institutional funds. The director of the center has a graduate degree and is most often professionally aligned with academic affairs; however, the disciplinary background of the administrator varies considerably.[22]

The sustainability and success of the projects, the courses, and the stability of the community partnerships can be affected by the quality, the skill, and the dedication of the staff. Administrators who are being asked to support these initiatives and faculty who want to create them should be mindful of the institutional structure of a center and consider the resources (budget, staff, space) needed to be an effective one.

FACULTY DEVELOPMENT AND REWARDS

A third common feature of centers and institutes is the availability and the distribution of faculty rewards. Incorporating civic engagement into a class can be a major undertaking for a faculty member. Many centers offer workshops and seminars to support course development and allow faculty to meet and share ideas. As advocates for civic engagement, we hope that our faculty colleagues would consider the work of civic engagement as part of their responsibilities as educators. However, we know that this is not always the case. Understandably, tenure and promotion concerns can sway a junior faculty member away from civic engagement work if it does not clearly fit into their campus tenure processes. In times of tight budgets, tenured faculty are less willing to use limited travel funds on nondisciplined-based conferences that might not generate the scholarship they need for advancement. Centers and institutes that sponsor recognitions and awards, offer mechanisms for consideration of civic engagement for promotion and tenure, and provide avenues for research and publishing opportunities make participation in civic engagement more acceptable and inviting to skeptical or overstretched faculty.[23] Here are some examples of centers that offer faculty development opportunities and rewards:

- Ball State University Office of Community Engagement (publishing, conferences, grants)
- Cleveland State University Office of Civic Engagement (grants, showcases)
- Drexel University's Lindy Center for Civic Engagement (development grants)
- Missouri State University's Center for Community Engagement (stipends, promotion, rank, and tenure guidelines)
- Tufts University's Tisch College of Citizenship and Public Service's Faculty Fellow program (faculty fellow program, research support)
- University of North Carolina Greensboro's Office of Leadership and Service-Learning (promotion, rank, and tenure guidelines)
- University of Pennsylvania's Netter Center (academic summit)
- Western Washington University Center for Service-Learning (innovative teaching showcase)

CASE STUDIES

Although the purpose of this chapter is not to evaluate the quality of these centers and institutes, we do want to highlight a few that serve as examples of interdisciplinary programs dedicated to civic engagement. We believe that these centers serve as models for faculty who are interested in either launching such efforts on their campus or enhancing their current initiatives. We are confident that there are more (and we will continue to update those on the book's companion website).

Our first example is a center in a large public university. The Center for Service and Learning at Indiana University–Purdue University Indianapolis is a resource for extensive materials regarding course development, research and assessment, and publishing opportunities. Funding is available to faculty and staff in the forms of three categories of grants (course development, dissemination, and program/department level). Other forms of professional development are available that include showcases and roundtable discussions offered on a regular basis to engage faculty across the disciplines in conversation about engagement. Because of the myriad of resources that this center offers, anyone who might be interested in creating a center or institute should start here.

A second example is Auburn University's Community and Civic Engagement Initiative. This initiative is housed in its College of Liberal Arts and has a strong interdisciplinary emphasis. As stated on its webpage,

> The goals of the Community and Civic Engagement Initiative are to continue this Auburn tradition of service and scholarship, to further collaboration among the diverse disciplines in the College of Liberal Arts, to highlight the unique outreach activities initiated by our faculty and students, to provide a context for the creation of shared knowledge between Auburn University and its multiple community partners, to advance community-engaged scholarship, and to provide students with the skills to become effective local and global citizens.[24]

Faculty members who are interested in civic engagement or service-learning have many dedicated resources available to them through the Auburn Initiative. In addition to pedagogical resources (e.g., sample syllabi and travel funds), the initiative hosts an annual Academy for Civic Engagement that is a "3-day workshop for faculty in the arts and humanities who are interested in incorporating civic engagement/service-learning practices into their courses, outreach scholarship, and P & T documentation."[25] Faculty also apply to be "Engaged Scholars" and, if selected, are awarded a three-year appointment to work on strengthening faculty and student engagement in the local community. The Auburn Initiative can be an example for schools that might want to consider a more interdisciplinary approach to civic engagement.

A third model is The Office of Civic Engagement at California State University, Chico. The Office of Civic Engagement focuses on building a curriculum of civic engagement across the various academic divisions on their campus.[26] Faculty members who participate in civic engagement activities receive support from this office in a variety of ways. Faculty resources include a downloadable packet of information, the ability to enroll in a Civic Learning Institute (a foundational workshop to develop ideas for potential projects), civic engagement readings, Faculty Learning Communities (a higher level of support and resources for those faculty who completed the Civic Learning Institute and are intent on implementing and pursuing a civically engaged curriculum), exercises for creating a civic curriculum, and other helpful tools. This office has a strong attachment to political science as its director also teaches in the political science department. This center could be an example for political scientists or other social scientists who might want to get more involved in campus-wide civic engagement activities.

Elon University has been a leader in higher education in experiential learning, and it should not be surprising that we include it here as another model for civic engagement centers. It does its work in civic engagement in many centers including The Center for Public Affairs and The Kernodle Center for Service Learning and Community Engagement.

As the Center for Public Affairs' mission states,

> The Center for Public Affairs fosters academic engagement that combines learning with "real world" practice for students to be informed global citizens and leaders motivated by concern for the common good. It is comprehensive in its approach, responding to Elon University's broader mission of teaching, research, and public service. The Center conducts its activities in a collaborative, nonpartisan manner and is focused on meeting the needs of students while enhancing the quality of community life and public discourse. With experiential education as its primary objective, the Center sponsors policy studies, policy relevant research projects, conferences, lecture series, and special speakers.[27]

The Kernodle Center for Service Learning and Community Engagement complements the work of the Center for Public Affairs and offers a multitude of faculty resources, including professional-development fellowship programs, training, course assistance, and funding for travel and conferences. Although the Kernodle Center's main focus is service-learning and volunteerism, it is linked to the Center for Public Affairs through civic engagement activities. This is a good model for schools looking to develop programmatic and community collaboration between political engagement and service-learning centers.

A final example is Tulane University's Center for Public Service. It is highlighted here because of the emphasis it places on its public-service curriculum and collaboration with community partners. As a result of recent disasters in Louisiana, Tulane University has rededicated itself to community engagement. Tulane University has a public-service graduation requirement that is administered by the Center for Public Service. In addition, community partners may apply to be "fellows" to participate in an experiential learning and leadership institute "with scholars and researchers in a program intended to increase their capacity and that of their communities to address complex social problems through experiential education partnerships."[28] Faculty can apply for Community-Based Participatory Research grants to collaborate with community partners to advance research on civic agendas. Additional faculty resources offered by the Center for Public Service include syllabi examples, trainings for reflection and assessment and course coordinators, additional grant opportunities, faculty awards, and travel and conference funding. The center also oversees a faculty-scholar program. Each semester, a faculty member is recognized as a faculty scholar and assists the center with creating new projects and leading workshops and seminars for other faculty. This is a good example of a center that intentionally collaborates with community partners on all facets of the curriculum. Faculty members or schools who want to expand their community relationships and create projects for their students to affect policy change could use this center as a model for this sort of civic engagement work.

CONCLUSION

As we have shown, a number of the centers and institutes that we identified on civically engaged campuses are interdisciplinary in nature—offering opportunities for students from all majors and disciplines. We also have found that, although many are primarily focused on either civic engagement or political engagement, a number of these units offer a mixture of more than one facet of engagement or demonstrate a "crossover" to other types of engagement. We encourage such crossover and argue that mixing political learning with service-learning is not as daunting as it might seem. For example, as one would expect, service-learning centers are dedicated primarily to providing service to the community. However, depending on school policy, these centers also can be platforms on which political (but nonpartisan) engagement activities might be built. Such service-oriented centers are usually conduits to the community and can provide avenues and structures for service experiences that could easily translate to political experiences. A service project dedicated to serving the needs of the homeless population, for example, might also consider the political institutions and processes that might be utilized to address homelessness.

Although we do see the participation and influence of political scientists in some of these programs, it should reassure us that civic engagement is not only a responsibility of political science departments. It does surprise us, however, that political scientists are not necessarily leading the way in these centers or institutes. This void might provide an opportunity for political scientists to become more involved in their campuses' civic engagement centers and institutes to bring their expertise (especially in their knowledge of structures and processes of government) to help their colleagues in other disciplines meet their civic engagement goals more effectively.

As we reflect on our research, we realize and appreciate that the type of engagement promoted in these centers and even the names that these units go by are not the most important factors in promoting civic engagement. We have found that what matters is that there is an organization (not an individual department) on campus that is focused on promoting and supporting the important work of civic engagement. In future research efforts, we hope to explore these centers further to measure their success and evaluate their impact on campuses. We end with a final suggestion. Given the many benefits that we have shown that a center or institute can offer, we suggest that faculty consult the centers on their own campuses. If there is no such center on campus, using the many examples we have listed in this chapter, faculty should consider working with their administration to create one. Faculty and administrators also can consult this guide for ways to improve existing centers and expand faculty participation, thus bringing civic engagement learning opportunities to their entire student bodies. Again, while our research remains in progress, we suggest that well-structured, properly resourced civic engagement centers can increase an institution's ability to achieve its civic engagement mission. ∎

ENDNOTES

1. The authors wish to acknowledge Brendan L. Keating for his assistance in preparing this manuscript.
2. Marshall Welch and John Saltmarsh, "Current Practices and Infrastructures for Campus Centers of Community Engagement," *Journal of Higher Education Outreach and Engagement*, 17 (4): 25–28.
3. For a review of the history of community and civic engagement centers and the research on them, see Welch and Saltmarsh, "Current Practices," 25–28.
4. For more information about the Carnegie Foundation for the Advancement of Teaching, see https://www.carnegiefoundation.org/; New England Resource Center for Higher Education, http://nerche.org/index.php?option=com_content&view=article&id=341&Itemid=618.
5. President's Higher Education Community Service Honor Roll, http://www.nationalservice.gov/special-initiatives/presidents-higher-education-community-service-honor-roll/2014-presidents-higher.
6. American Democracy Project, http://www.aascu.org/programs/ADP/.
7. National Campaign for Political and Civic Engagement, http://iop.harvard.edu/get-involved/national-campaign.
8. Campus Compact, http://compact.org/who-we-are/mission-and-vision/.
9. Central Connecticut State University, http://www.ccsu.edu/about/mission/.
10. California State University, Chico, http://www.csuchico.edu/vpaa/wasc/value/index.html.
11. Mercer University, https://about.mercer.edu/mission/.
12. Ball State University, http://centennialcommitment.bsu.edu/.
13. Alison McCartney, 2013. "Teaching Civic Engagement: Debates, Definitions, Benefits, and Challenges," in *Teaching Civic Engagement: From Student to Active Citizen*, eds. Alison Rios Millett McCartney, Elizabeth A. Bennion, and Dick Simpson (Washington, DC: American Political Science Association, 2013), 14.
14. McCartney, "Teaching Civic Engagement," 14.
15. McCartney, "Teaching Civic Engagement," 15.
16. Appalachian State University's Civic Engagement Program, https://engagement.appstate.edu.
17. University of North Florida, Center for Community-Based Learning, https://www.unf.edu/ccbl.
18. University of North Florida, Center for Community-Based Learning, https://www.unf.edu/ccbl/CBTL_for_Students.aspx.
19. Western Carolina University's Public Policy Institute, http://www.wcu.edu/engage/regional-development/public-policy-institute.
20. The University of Kansas's Dole Institute of Politics, http://doleinstitute.org/visit/about/mission.
21. Elizabeth A. Bennion, "Moving Assessment Forward: Teaching Civic Engagement and Beyond," in *Teaching Civic Engagement: From Student to Active Citizen*, eds. Alison Rios Millett McCartney, Elizabeth A. Bennion, and Dick Simpson (Washington, DC: American Political Science Association, 2013).
22. Welch and Saltmarsh, 34.
23. For more on faculty development and rewards, see research by Kelly Ann O'Meara.
24. Auburn University's The Community and Civic Engagement Initiative, http://www.cla.auburn.edu/cla/cce/resources-for-faculty.
25. Ibid.
26. California State University, Chico, The Office of Civic Engagement, http://www.csuchico.edu/civic/index.shtml.
27. Elon University, The Center for Public Affairs, http://www.elon.edu/e-web/students/ippa/public_affairs/about.xhtml.
28. Tulane Univeristy, http://www2.tulane.edu/cps/community/experiential-education-and-leadership-institute.cfm.

Moving Forward with Assessment: Important Tips and Resources

ELIZABETH A. BENNION

This chapter provides an overview of the most important lessons to remember and resources to consult when designing an assessment plan for civic learning activities. It highlights the importance of backward design: identifying the desired results and determining acceptable evidence before planning a learning experience. The author stresses the importance of aligning desired outcomes with learning activities and assessment measures, as well as the importance of distinguishing between broad, ambiguous goals and measurable learning objectives. The chapter provides links to rubrics and surveys measuring civic knowledge, skills, and attitudes and provides readers with the information they need to create civic outcome statements that are specific, measurable, useful, and meaningful. The chapter functions as a "top-10 list" for assessing civic learning outcomes: work backward, know your goals, create measurable learning objectives, operationalize your objectives, keep it simple, map your plan, develop a rubric, assess both outcomes and process, learn from others, and close the feedback loop. Each of the tips will help a campus, program, or instructor measure the effectiveness of current civic education efforts and improve these efforts in the future.

Teaching Civic Engagement Across the Disciplines focuses on a range of ways that campuses promote civic learning and engagement. Courses, curriculum, learning communities, faculty training programs, student leadership development, well-resourced centers or institutes, and campus-wide engagement initiatives are all important ways to promote desirable civic learning outcomes. Student learning, collaborative relationships with community partners, and positive community impact are all desired outcomes of community-based approaches to civic education. However, simply creating courses, programs, events, or centers is not enough to guarantee success or to determine whether positive outcomes have occurred. Assessment is required to determine whether specific courses, programs, and campus units are meeting their civic learning and engagement goals. Careful assessment allows a campus to document the success of civic engagement initiatives and to revise strategies and activities to be more effective in the future.

The 2013 text *Teaching Civic Engagement: From Student to Active Citizen* provides a series of chapters on assessment designed to move civic educators toward rigorous assessment of course, activity, and program outcomes.[1] The book includes a toolkit describing a wide range of qualitative, quantitative, and mixed-methods assessment strategies that range from simple headcounts to randomized multicampus field experiments.[2] It offers tips for successfully utilizing each method and provides answers to frequently asked questions. The APSA-published book also provides some "best practice" advice regarding the importance of pretests, direct measures, cross-campus research, longitudinal analysis, and benchmarking.[3]

This current volume takes a step back, focusing on how to articulate measurable civic outcomes to assess. This chapter focuses on creating (or identifying) assessment tools that provide meaningful feedback that facilitates improved civic outcomes. It provides an overview of the most important lessons to remember and resources to consult when designing an assessment plan for civic learning activities. The chapter stresses the importance of backward design and explains how to align desired outcomes with learning activities and assessment measures. It provides readers with the information they need to create specific, measurable, operationalized civic outcome statements. The chapter also provides advice for assessing the actions taken to achieve the learning outcomes. Finally, the chapter provides links to well-established rubrics and surveys measuring civic knowledge, skills, and attitudes, as well as innovative new assessment tools. Well-designed, goal-driven, meaningful assessment tools provide an opportunity to maximize the effectiveness of campus and community engagement efforts.

ASSESSMENT 101: A TOP 10 LIST

This chapter highlights 10 important tips to consider when developing your assessment plan. These tips are

1. Work backward
2. Know your goals
3. Create measurable learning objectives
4. Operationalize your objectives
5. Keep it simple
6. Map your plan
7. Develop a rubric
8. Assess both outcomes and process
9. Learn from others
10. Close the feedback loop

In summarizing these best practices, the chapter highlights key points to consider and resources to consult when developing a plan to assess civic learning outcomes. Of particular importance are links to a wide range of existing tools for assessing civic learning outcomes.

WORK BACKWARD: START WITH YOUR DESIRED OUTCOMES

Civic engagement initiatives take many forms. These include, but are not limited to, service-learning, community-based learning, community-based research, and other forms of civic education. The list of possibilities for promoting civic knowledge and skills is almost endless. Different disciplines use different terminology and focus on a wide variety of skills including capacity building, community service, economic development initiatives, mentoring, needs analysis, patents, public outreach, social entrepreneurship, philanthropy, sponsorships, training and technical assistance, translational research, and workforce development.[4] All of these activities are amenable to meaningful and useful assessment as long as participants define their goals and articulate measurable objectives connected to each learning activity.

The key to a successful assessment strategy is to start with the desired outcomes. Instructors, department chairs, deans, program directors, and others involved in civic engagement pedagogy and research should start by identifying the desired results. A good assessment tool provides valuable feedback whether one is designing a single activity, course module, complete course, or academic program. Developers should ask: What do we hope to accomplish? What would "success" look like? These are questions to answer before selecting or designing an assessment plan. The next step is determining acceptable evidence. What evidence is easily available? Easy to collect? Possible to gather? The defined outcome should determine what evidence is collected. Finally, it is time to plan the learning experience and instructional approach. To assure proper alignment between the activity, desired outcome, and assessment methods, plan the experience after identifying the desired outcomes and most relevant (and accessible) evidence. For example, an instructor of a service-learning course should determine what key knowledge, skills, or attitudes a student will acquire, deepen, and display through completing the activity. By specifying what students should know—and what they should be able to do—after completing the activity, the instructor can design a module, unit, assignment, or activity to develop the desired knowledge and skills. Instructors should consider cognitive, affective, and kinesthetic outcomes. What will students know, believe, or do after the learning experience?[5]

Taking a "backward design" approach to course, program, and activity development ensures proper alignment between civic engagement activities, desired outcomes, and assessment methods. As noted earlier, this approach requires that desired outcomes be measurable. It is important to distinguish between broad goals (i.e., ambiguous general statements) and measurable outcomes. Breaking a goal into measurable objectives (or learning outcomes) is required to assess whether the activities undertaken advance the advertised broader goal.

KNOW YOUR GOALS: DETERMINE WHAT TYPE OF LEARNING YOU WANT TO TAKE PLACE

Goals express intended learning outcomes in broad global language, expressing the general habits of mind, intellectual capacities, and personal qualities the learner will exhibit after completing a course or curriculum. A campus goal may be to produce citizens who display a strong sense of "civic identity,"[6] "civic agency,"[7] or "civic mindedness"[8] upon graduation. To determine whether students are civic minded, the campus first has to determine what a civic-minded graduate looks like. What are the specific learning objectives and outcomes that a civic-minded graduate displays? A team at Indiana University Purdue University Indianapolis (IUPUI) decided that a civic-minded graduate, at a minimum, displays a strong sense of civic identity, is an active participant in society to address social issues, works with diverse others, understands how social issues are addressed in society, and displays an orientation to social change. Accordingly, they define the civic-minded graduate (CMG) as "a person who has completed a course of study and has the capacity and desire to work with others to achieve the common good."[9]

One cannot observe "civic-mindedness." Assessing whether graduates have achieved it requires an assessment tool that breaks the concept into its component parts and creates specific objectives operationalized in ways that make them both observable and measurable. First, the IUPUI team constructed a conceptual model of civic-mindedness, providing a Venn diagram illustrating the overlap between educational experiences, identity, and civic experiences. Next, the team specified the knowledge, skills, dispositions, and behavioral intentions exhibited by a CMG. Finally, the team created three assessment tools for measuring the CMG construct: a quantitative self-report measure, a qualitative narrative-based measure, and an interview rubric and protocol. The CMG scale, CMG narrative prompt, CMG narrative rubric, CMG interview protocol, and CMG interview rubric are all available online. Rubrics measure the extent to which a graduate demonstrates civic-mindedness. Categories range from novice, to apprentice, to proficient, to distinguished. Rubrics are useful for systematic assessment of learning outcomes. Rubrics require clearly stated learning objectives and a clear understanding of what it means to master each objective.

CREATE MEASURABLE LEARNING OBJECTIVES: USE ACTIVE VERBS TO SPECIFY WHAT LEARNERS WILL DO

To move beyond vague goals to produce measurable civic learning objectives, those who are designing the civic learning activities should first describe what participants should be able to do. In the case of student learning objectives, the outcome statement should specify what knowledge, skills, and attitudes successful learners will exhibit following instruction. Do not focus on the activity (e.g.,

"My plan is to talk about ..."), instead focus on the resulting cognitive, affective, or kinesthetic outcomes (e.g., "After this session, students will be able to ..."). A clear civic learning objective will connect content and assessment, guide selection of learning activities that will best achieve the desired outcomes, give learners a clear picture of what to expect and what is expected of them, and form the basis for evaluating teachers, learners, activities, and/or curriculum effectiveness.[10]

Before writing learning objectives, decide what type of learning is desired. Two useful approaches to categorizing types of learning are described by Bloom et al.[11] and Fink.[12] Bloom's Cognitive Taxonomy includes six types of cognitive processes, arranged as a hierarchy. The lowest level, knowledge, is primarily content-oriented. It consists of three subcategories: knowledge of specifics, knowledge of ways and means of dealing with specifics, and knowledge of universals and abstractions in a field. Observation and recall of information; knowledge of dates, events, and places; knowledge of major ideas; and mastery of subject matter all fit into this category. Other categories include comprehension, application, analysis, synthesis, and evaluation.[13]

Comprehension includes abilities such as understanding information, grasping meaning, interpreting facts, and translating knowledge into new contexts. Application includes the ability to use methods, concepts, and theories in new situations, or solve problems using required skills and knowledge. Analysis refers to the ability to recognize the organizational structure of a work of music, art, or writing and to break down material into its component parts. Analytic skills include the ability to recognize unstated assumptions and logical fallacies in reasoning, to distinguish between facts and inferences, and to evaluate the relevance of data. Synthesis requires an ability to use old ideas to create new ones, to generalize from given facts, and to relate knowledge from several areas. Meanwhile, evaluation includes the ability to assess the value of theories, verify the value of evidence, and make choices based on reasoned argument. Bloom's model assumes that acquisition of these skills is cumulative; that is, students master one level of skills before taking on the next.[14]

Another popular taxonomy is L. Dee Fink's taxonomy of significant learning. Fink's taxonomy involves both cognitive and emotional dimensions. Fink stresses that significant learning "requires that there be some kind of lasting change that is important in terms of the learner's life."[15] Fink's first three categories, foundational knowledge, application, and integration, correspond to Bloom's six stages. An additional three categories focus on more emotion-based outcomes: the human dimension (recognizing human significance), caring (developing new feelings or interests), and learning how to learn (developing one's own path to knowledge). Rather than hierarchical, Fink concludes that learning is most significant when it spans across categories.

Both Bloom and Fink provide a solid framework for determining appropriate learning outcomes and finding suitable verbs that clearly express key learning objectives. For example, Bloom's taxonomy might generate the following list of active verbs (and many more)[16]:

- *Knowledge* (recall and understanding): associate, compare, contrast, define, describe, differentiate, distinguish, label, list, name, paraphrase, provide examples, recognize, repeat, restate, review, show, state, summarize, tell
- *Application*: calculate, demonstrate, draw, employ, estimate, illustrate, locate, measure, operate, perform, prescribe, record, set up, sketch, solve, trace, use
- *Problem-Solving* (analyzing, synthesizing, evaluating): advocate, analyze, assess, challenge, compose, conclude, construct, create, critique, debate, decide, defend, derive, design, evaluate, formulate, infer, judge, organize, plan, propose, rank, recommend, select, suggest.

Fink's addition of the human dimension (i.e., what learners should know about themselves and about interacting with others) and the caring dimension (i.e., what changes in learners' feelings, interests, and values are important) are particularly relevant to civic learning goals. Most instructors and institutions believe that knowledge-based civic education is not enough (on its own) to produce engaged citizens. Knowledge, skills, and values are all important in creating citizens with the capacity and desire to make a meaningful difference in their communities.

Active verbs addressing the human dimension focus on learners' interpersonal relationships, self-authorship (i.e., the ability to create and take responsibility for one's own life), leadership skills, cultural sensitivity, teamwork skills, citizenship commitments, and environmental ethics. Verb options include collaborate, communicate, cooperate, empathize, inspire, interact, lead, mediate, mobilize, motivate, negotiate, nurture, reconcile, resolve, and respect. Action verbs might also include compound verbs such as: critically reflect, interact with, respond sensitively, resolve conflict, serve as a role model, suspend judgment, and take responsibility.[17]

Fink's "caring" dimension includes not only a learner's attitudes about learning (i.e., wanting to master the material, desiring to achieve high standards, and developing a keen interest in the subject), but also a commitment to "live right" (to take care of one's health and well-being, or to live by a certain code). Useful verbs include discover, explore, express, pledge, revitalize, share, and value. Compound verbs might include be ready to, commit to, decide to, get excited about, recognize the value of, renew interest in, and take time to. Well-written learning objectives use precise terms that focus on the students rather than the curriculum. The use of active verbs keeps programs, teachers, and learners focused on what students will be able to do when they complete the learning experience.

OPERATIONALIZE YOUR OBJECTIVES: EXPLAIN HOW STUDENTS WILL DEMONSTRATE LEARNING

To make learning objectives measurable, rely on active verbs, noting what students should be able to demonstrate or produce over time. In addition to using active verbs, operationalize the statements to specify where and how students will exhibit the selected behaviors.

Some scholars are critical of those who write verb-driven outcome statements by "defaulting to Bloom's six-stage taxonomy" and the placement of "sometimes formless lumps of verbs" under each state. Clifford Adelman advocates operational verbs, grouped according to their "governing functions."[18] Adelmen has created a long and detailed list of verbs fitting 17 separate categories. Here are some of the most useful from a civic learning perspective:

- Verbs describing student acquisition and preparation of tools, materials, and texts of various types: access, acquire, collect, accumulate, extract, gather, locate, obtain, retrieve
- Verbs describing what students do when they "inquire": examine, experiment, explore, hypothesize, investigate, research, test
- Verbs that describe forms of deliberative activity in which students engage: argue, challenge, debate, defend, justify, resolve, dispute, advocate, persuade
- Verbs that describe the various ways in which students utilize the materials of learning: apply, carry out, conduct, demonstrate, employ, implement, perform, produce, use
- Verbs related to the modes of communication that indicate what students do in groups: collaborate, contribute, negotiate, provide feedback
- Verbs that describe what students do in various forms of "making": build, compose, construct, craft, create, design, develop, generate, model, shape, simulate
- Verbs that describe various executive functions students perform: operate, administer, control, coordinate, engage, lead, maintain, manage, navigate, optimize, plan.

Adelman provides lists of verbs that represent a wide range of functions including adapting, accumulating, administering, advocating, analyzing, applying, arranging, assimilating, auditing, building, calculating, categorizing, citing, collaborating, elaborating, inquiring, and reporting data. Adelman encourages faculty to work backward from the assignment they present every day to think about what they are asking students to do. This strategy may be a good way to clarify and document learning outcomes for existing classes and programs. The key, then, is to remove or revise assignments that do not develop the knowledge, skills, or values desired. When designing assignments and instructional techniques, keep in mind that different teaching and learning strategies are suited to different types of learning.[19]

Operationalization is key to creating assignments and activities that measure civic learning in observable (and assessable) ways. To operationalize something is to express or define it in terms of the operations used to determine or prove it. Active ("operationalized") verbs that tell what learners will be able to do are a good first step. Avoiding vague verbs (e.g., "know" and "understand") in favor of active verbs (e.g., identify, explain, translate, construct, solve, analyze, compose, compile, design) focuses attention on what learners will know and be able to do by the end of the course or program. These general learning objectives are content-free. The statements do not include the methods by which the learning will take place or the procedures through which students will demonstrate each objective. This approach keeps the list of learning objectives manageable and allows course, curriculum, and program designers to develop applicable outcomes for different courses, units, and activities. It also allows for flexibility in the instructional strategy, a procedure for accomplishing the objective, and a method of documenting accomplishment. The best assessment plans for individual courses, programs, and activities go further to specify exactly how students will demonstrate each learning outcome. Will students demonstrate knowledge and skills through critical analysis of specific case studies, an original computer presentation, an oral presentation, a reflective essay, a research paper, a client-ready needs analysis, or a five-page action plan? Specifying this level of detail in the learning outcomes statements is helpful in matching learning objectives and content to specific assessment tools.

Whether you are designing a new course or program or revising an old one, knowing what you want participants to learn—and at what level that learning will take place—is key. Equipped with a wide range of action verbs and suitable instructional strategies (see again endote 19), you are ready to create (or enhance) your learning objectives, learning activities, and assessment plan.

Keep It Simple: Do Not Try to Assess Everything at Once

Instructors, program managers, and departments sometimes feel overwhelmed at the thought of creating an assessment plan. Keep in mind that the best assessment plans provide educators with useful and meaningful information to guide future practice. It is acceptable, even desirable, to focus on a few high-priority learning outcomes, areas in which assessors are seeking significant improvement. No instructor, department, or campus can assess all the learning that takes place on a college campus (or within the broader community). Focus on major goals and work to develop learning outcome statements tied directly to those goals. Focus on working SMART, rather than assessing every conceivable learning outcome.[20] The SMART strategy to learning objectives focuses on creating objectives that are specific, measurable, attainable, relevant, and targeted. Objectives should be realistic. They should be attainable for the target audience with the scheduled time and specified conditions. They should also be results-oriented and targeted to the learner and the desired level of learning.

In the area of civic education and engagement, you must determine what knowledge, skills, values, or behaviors are most important, or most directly related to the course, curriculum, program, or activities for which the assessment is taking place. One area to assess is *civic knowledge*. The type of knowledge you assess as "civic knowledge" is dependent, in part, on your disciplinary perspective.[21] Political scientists may emphasize knowledge of the legislative process, how a bill becomes a law, or the role interest groups and lobbyists play in shaping public policy. Public administration programs might emphasize knowledge of government agencies, nonprofit organizations, or bureaucratic decision-making processes. Meanwhile, art courses might develop students' understandings of the importance of the First Amendment in protecting artistic expression, the role of art in social and political debates, and the ways in which art can strengthen communities and address social problems.[22] Disciplines have diverse conceptual frameworks for understanding "citizenship" and delineating civic skills.[23]

Knowledge is dynamic, changing, socially constructed, and "implicated with power."[24] For this reason, civic knowledge includes familiarity with key historical struggles, campaigns, and social movements, in addition to knowledge about fundamental principles and central arguments about democracy over time and the ability to describe the main civic intellectual debates within a discipline.[25] Civic knowledge also includes an understanding that "knowledge is actionable" and when individuals join together to "co-create knowledge" it empowers them to make positive changes in the world around them.[26]

Alternatively, one must determine to focus on *civic skills*. Effective engagement requires a variety of skills. These include civic discourse and dialogue,[27] including dialogue across difference.[28] Mary Kirlin identified four major categories of civic skills: organization, communication, collective decision making, and critical thinking.[29] Examples include organizing and persuading others to take action, navigating the political system, consensus building toward the common good, listening to diverse perspectives, and forming positions on public issues.

A third area for assessment involves *civic identity*. The term civic identity describes the aspect of identity that leads a person to take public action to solve community problems.[30] People with a strong civic identity view themselves as active participants in society and share a strong commitment to work with others to promote the public good. Numerous studies point to civic identity as an important factor inspiring civic engagement.[31] A sense of civic identity, when combined with relevant knowledge and skills and motivation, explains why people engage in politics and public action.[32] Civic identity includes both intellectual and ethical components (e.g., critical thinking skills and empathy for others). While these skills and dispositions may seem difficult to measure, tools are available. For example, students' participation in organized groups during adolescence[33] and during college[34] contribute to formation of lifelong civic identity and engagement. Rubrics for measuring critical thinking and empathy are highlighted later in this chapter. Strachan and Bennion present an assessment tool for measuring the degree to which student organizations develop civic skills and identity in their chapter, "New Resources for Civic Engagement: The National Survey of Student Leaders, Campus Associational Life, and the Consortium for Inter-Campus SoTL Research."

To return to an earlier theme, the key is to start by determining your goals. No person or program can measure everything a student learns or administer all existing civic learning assessments. An extracurricular leadership program may focus exclusively on assessing the development civic identity among students. Meanwhile, an introductory survey course might focus on assessing civic knowledge, while a 200-level civic engagement workshop might focus on assessing civic skills. Start simple. Assess. Evaluate. Revise. Repeat.

MAP YOUR PLAN: CHART YOUR GOALS, OUTCOMES, AND ACTIVITIES

Individual departments or instructors can work together to determine what knowledge, skills, and attitudes to assess. First, identify a civic goal related to your course, activity, or program. Next, create learning outcomes statements linked to each goal.[35] These include a general learning objective as well as a list of representative learning outcomes stated in performance terms that clarify the acceptable evidence for attaining the stated objective.

A basic worksheet can be useful in crafting a solid plan. As you plan, consider the audience for your assessment data. How will you use the results of your assessments? Where will you share your assessment findings? The answers to these questions may shape the kinds of goals you set or outcomes you measure. Civic outcomes assessment experts Kristin Norris and H. Anne Weiss suggest a simple chart[36] that looks like the one in figure 22.1. Civic outcomes that are specific, measurable, and operationalized provide useful and meaningful assessment that allows course, program, or activity developers to improve the experience (and outcomes) for future participants. Assessment measures may be qualitative or quantitative, direct or indirect. The key is that outcome statements allow for one or more methods of data collection and measurement tied to the desired learning outcome.

Figure 22.1 Sample Chart

GOAL(S)	OBJECTIVE/OUTCOME(S)	ACTIVITY	WHAT EVIDENCE (DATA, ARTIFACT) WILL YOU COLLECT OF THAT LEARNING?	HOW WILL YOU ASSESS (MEASURE) THAT ARTIFACT/EVIDENCE?	How will you USE the results of this assessment?
					How or Where will you SHARE/ disseminate these findings?

NOTES:

DEVELOP A RUBRIC: CREATE A COHERENT CRITERIA FOR EVALUATION

Rubrics provide a valuable way to assess civic learning outcomes. A rubric is "a coherent set of criteria for students' work that includes descriptions of levels of performance quality on the criteria."[37] Rubrics require coherent sets of criteria and descriptions of levels of performance for these criteria. Assessing performance using a rubric, evaluators match the performance to the description. Effective rubrics have appropriate criteria and well-written descriptions of performance at various levels of mastery.

The purpose of rubrics is to assess performance. For some performances, you observe a student in the process of doing something (e.g., discussing an issue). For other performances, you observe the work product (e.g., a written report). A rubric recognizes that learners do not all achieve the same level of proficiency toward all learning objectives and allows evaluators to determine where students are excelling and when they require additional help and development.

Rubrics have several benefits.[38] First, they help teachers teach. Rubrics refocus instructors on learning rather on than task completion. To write or select rubrics, educators need to focus on the criteria used to assess learning outcomes. Focusing on *learning* rather than on *teaching* helps improve instruction. Rubrics also help students learn. The criteria and performance-level descriptions in rubrics help students understand what the desired performance is and what it looks like. In addition, rubrics also help coordinate instruction and assessment. Ideally, students get rubrics in advance and use them repeatedly, for different tasks, and over time. Students do the work, get feedback, revise their work or do another similar task, and continue to practice until they achieve the desired learning outcomes. Both instructors and students receive valuable feedback that allows them to improve future performance.

A helpful example is the civic-minded graduate rubric described earlier in this chapter. When assessing graduates' personal narratives, evaluators consider whether a learner has achieved each desired learning outcome at the novice, apprentice, proficient, or distinguished level. For example, an apprentice in the category "Active Participant in Society to Address Social Issues" describes some involvement in the community through occasional or periodic service activity, describes previous service experience, and identifies ways to take individual action (e.g., tutoring, cleaning environment). In contrast, a "distinguished" graduate demonstrates a sustained involvement over time through direct service, projects, or advocacy efforts; personal involvement in a variety of service activities that has led to more depth of engagement; the ability to develop new ideas and serve as a catalyst for change; and the ability to convene or lead others in addressing social issues or participating in group activities.

"Unscripted Learning: Cultivating Engaged Catalysts" in this book provides another good example of a civic learning rubric. Simeone, Sikora, and Halperin provide useful rubrics for assessing Action Research Center (ARC) interns to determine whether they have achieved desired learning outcomes at the novice, associate, or master level. ARC provides project-based, problem-based, and place-based rubrics highlighting the skills, knowledge, roles, and perspectives required to become an Agent of Change. Importantly, ARC uses the rubrics to assess students' demonstrated ability to "observe," "judge," and "act," regardless of the project outcome. As the authors note, programs that build the civic capacities of students must be flexible enough to meet the needs of students at all skill levels and must anticipate the varied outcomes that occur when students face challenging, unscripted, real-world problems.

ARC learning outcomes focus on a research stance or role as opposed to content-based outcomes or project deliverables. The ARC team notes that this approach is appropriate in experiential learning because "the knowledge domains first envisioned can change radically as projects and problems evolve."[39] Disciplinary frames also evolve as students become "instant experts" in fields and methods they adopt as required. The ARC rubric also illustrates the important role that rubrics can play in student learning. Mentors discuss rubrics with students to inspire, inform, and increase their civic capacity.

Assess Both Outcomes and Process: Distinguish between Theory and Implementation

When assessing the effectiveness of interventions designed to further civic knowledge, skills, and dispositions, it is useful to assess process. Assessing process is an important, but often overlooked, part of an assessment plan. It is important to know whether the program activities took place as planned and how well activities were implemented. Were the activities high quality? How well was the program implemented? The quality of the program components are important to consider when determining if a program or curriculum succeeded or failed to achieve the desired civic outcomes. If an intervention is designed poorly, or is not carried out as intended by the developers of the protocol, the intervention should not be blamed for learners' failure to achieve the desired outcomes. Also consider how external factors, beyond organizer or participant control, influenced curriculum or program delivery and impact. Finally, document whether the intervention actually reached the target audience. If not, seeking evidence of change in this population is misguided. Information about process—including deviations from planned activities and best practices—is important when deciding whether to refine existing civic learning activities, better train people to deliver existing activities, or replace current approaches to teaching civic engagement with new ones.

Learn from Others: Use Existing Assessment Tools

Creating your own assessment tools may seem like a daunting task, but there is no need to start from scratch. In fact, there are very good reasons to rely on existing assessment tools. Using existing assessment surveys, rubrics, and other tools has several advantages. First, tools developed by universities and national organizations reflect many hours of careful thought and design. Why "reinvent the wheel" when you can benefit from the efforts and collective wisdom of others? Second, the instruments have already been tested and revised. These instruments have been used and refined based on feedback from respondents and evaluators. Third, some tools allow for useful comparisons of campus results to national results or peer-institutions. Whether instructors use existing tools exclusively, modify them to fit local campus needs, or combine them with home-grown assessment tools, a review of available tools is valuable. At the very least, such tools provide useful frameworks, wording options, and ideas for building your own assessment instruments. At best, these provide you with a ready-to-use tool to assess a wide variety of civic learning outcomes on your campus.

Existing Assessments Measuring Civic Learning Outcomes among College Students

There are many examples of assessment tools designed to assess civic learning outcomes at the course-level and campus-level. The Bonner Foundation Network Wiki, the IUPUI Center for Service and Learning website, and the National Service-Learning Clearinghouse website provide useful sample materials. The Center for Information and Research on Civic Learning and Engagement (CIRCLE) provides a set of survey measures of civic engagement that can be used without permission (though consultation with CIRCLE staff is available). The Teaching Civic Engagement website provides links to other assessment materials, including the American National Election Study (ANES) website, which provides high-quality survey data on voting, public opinion, and political participation that is useful for comparison purposes when studying student political behavior. In addition, the Educational Testing Service (ETS) published a research report in 2015 "Assessing Civic Competency and Engagement in Higher Education: Research Background, Frameworks, and Directions for Next-Generation Assessment." The report, available free online, provides useful tables summarizing terms and definitions, assessment frameworks, item formats, and existing assessments related to civic competency and engagement. The next section features descriptions of several of the most useful assessment instruments for college campuses and provides links to free, online versions of each instrument.[40]

- **AAC&U Civic Engagement Value Rubric**: a rubric for judging written material designed to measure diversity of communities and cultures, analysis of knowledge, civic identity and commitment, civic communication, civic action and reflection, and civic context/structures. The Civic Engagement Value Rubric is one of 16 valid assessment of learning and undergraduate education (VALUE) rubrics available as a free download from the Association of American Colleges and Universities (AAC&U) website. The site lists rubrics sorted by learning objectives within the broad categories of intellectual skills, personal and social responsibility, and integrative and applied learning.
- **AASCU Campus and Community Civic Health Matrix**: a rubric for assessing the civic health of a community. The rubric assesses political engagement, public work, volunteering and giving, group participation, online engagement, social trust, civic knowledge and agency, and social connectedness. A copy of the rubric is available free, online. Additional information about the Civic Health Initiative is available on the American Association of State Colleges and Universities (AASCU) website.
- **Activism Orientation Scale**: a survey measuring activism orientation. This 35-item Likert-type survey measures two aspects of activism orientation: low-risk/conventional activism and high-risk activism. Respondents answer each question by circling how likely it is that they will engage in each of the listed activities in the future. Response options range from extremely unlikely to extremely likely. The survey's creators at the University of Notre Dame provide a formatted ready-to-administer survey free, online.
- **Civic Literacy Exam**: a survey measuring civic literacy or knowledge of critical facts and concepts related to US history, government, and economics. The survey's sponsor, the Intercollegiate Studies Institute (ISI) National Civic Literacy Board, provides a free version of the 2008 survey, online.
- **College Senior Survey**: a survey measuring academic, civic, and diversity outcomes along with a comprehensive set of college experiences. Activities from campaigns to demonstrations to volunteering are included, as are questions about awareness of global events and political agency. The survey also includes an eight-item subscale of civic values. The Higher Education Research Institute (HERI) at University of California, Los Angeles provides direct links to the paper version and the web version of the 2016 survey.
- **Diverse Learning Environments (DLE) Survey**: a web-based survey measuring student perceptions regarding institutional climate, campus practices, and student learning

outcomes. Diverse student populations are at the center of the survey, which studies issues including social mobility and intergroup relationships.[41] Measures of institutional climate, campus practices, and student learning outcomes include civic actions, social action, and pluralistic orientation, as well as important civic values (social agency), skills (perspective-taking, negotiation, cooperation), and knowledge. A copy of the complete 2017 survey instrument is available online.

- **National Civic and Political Health Survey** (CPHS): a survey measuring 19 indicators of civic engagement divided into three main categories: civic activities, electoral activities, and political voice activities (e.g., contacting elected officials). The Center for Information and Research on Civic Learning and Engagement administers the survey to young people ages from 15 to 25 and adults over age 26 in the continental United States. College students are not the target audience, but the survey design makes it possible to compare college and noncollege youth. Data is collected using yes/no and Likert-type telephone and web interviews. The 2006 report includes complete wording for all survey items. CIRCLE also provides a pen-and-paper Civic Engagement Quiz, available free, online.

- **National Survey of Student Engagement** (NSSE): a 14-item topical module on civic engagement measures students' self-perceptions of their conflict resolution skills and examines student engagement in campus, local, state, national, and global issues. This survey-based module complements the core NSSE survey questions regarding service-learning, community service, and campus engagement. Campuses administer the survey to first-year and senior-year college students. A facsimile of the core NSSE survey and a copy of the module are both available free, online.

- **Political and Social Involvement Scale**: a survey measuring the importance students place on volunteering, promoting racial understanding, and influencing political structures. The 11-item Likert-type survey is administered by the Center of Inquiry as part of the Wabash National Study of Liberal Arts Education, a large-scale longitudinal study to investigate critical factors that affect the outcomes of liberal arts education. Free copies of all survey instruments, including the Political and Social Involvement Scale are available online.

Other assessment instruments of potential interest to campuses, especially those seeking measures of political engagement, include the Carnegie Foundation Political Engagement Project (PEP) survey,[42] the National Youth Civic Engagement Index Project, the Youth and Participatory Politics Survey, and the Socially Responsible Leadership Scale. Information about these surveys and how to obtain copies of these (nonpublished) surveys, are included in the notes sections for this chapter.[43]

CLOSE THE FEEDBACK LOOP: USE ASSESSMENT TO IMPROVE FUTURE LEARNING EXPERIENCES

Campuses committed to graduating informed and engaged citizens should commit to regular assessment—and constant improvement—of their civic learning outcomes Whether you opt to pay to administer a national survey, use existing instruments as a model to create your own, or develop your own learning outcomes using the planning worksheet in this chapter, it is critical that your assessment tools align with your learning activities and that your learning activities are designed to achieve stated learning objectives stemming from your civic learning goals. Ultimately, assessment should be both useful and meaningful. It should provide educators with the feedback they need to adjust learning activities, refine learning objectives, and improve student learning. The tools provided in this chapter offer educators of all disciplines the support necessary to incorporate this essential component into their coursework, ensuring that their civic engagement efforts are effective. In this way, the methods developed and furthered by political science can benefit civic engagement efforts across all disciplines and advance the common cause of preparing our students to be active and informed citizens. ■

ENDNOTES

1. Alison Rios Millett McCartney, Elizabeth A. Bennion, and Dick Simpson, *Teaching Civic Engagement: From Student to Active Citizen* (Washington, DC: American Political Science Association, 2013), 405–48.

2. Elizabeth A. Bennion, "Assessing Civic and Political Engagement Activities: A Toolkit," in *Teaching Civic Engagement: From Student to Active Citizen*, ed. Alison Rios Millett McCartney, Elizabeth A. Bennion, and Dick Simpson (Washington, DC: American Political Science Association, 2013), 407–22.

3. Elizabeth A. Bennion, "Moving Assessment Forward: Teaching Civic Engagement and Beyond," in *Teaching Civic Engagement: From Student to Active Citizen*, ed. Alison Rios Millett McCartney, Elizabeth A. Bennion, and Dick Simpson (Washington, DC: American Political Science Association, 2013), 437–48.

4. The civic engagement pedagogies listed here represent some of the experiential learning strategies best suited for teaching civic and political engagement. For a discussion of a full range of approaches to experiential education in the disciplines of political science and international relations see Elizabeth A. Bennion, "Experiential Education in Political Science and International Relations," in *Handbook on Teaching and Learning in Political Science and International Relations*, ed. John Ishiyama, et al. (Northampton, MA: Edward Elgar, 2015), 351–68.

5. For more information about backward design see, Grant Wiggins and Jay McTighe "Backward Design," in *Understanding Design*, expanded second edition (Upper Saddle River, NJ: Pearson Education, Inc., 2006), 13–34.

6. Lee Knefelkamp describes people with a mature sense of civic identity as "Those fully engaged, fully human citizens of their communities. They see their role in life as contributing to the long-term greater good. And perhaps most importantly, they have the courage to act." Lee Knefelkamp, "Civic Identity: Locating Self in Community," *Diversity & Democracy* 11 (2008): 3.

7. Harry Boyte stresses the importance of creating students who see themselves as agents of change. The concept of "civic agency" focuses on the "capacity of human communities and groups to act cooperatively and collectively on common problems across their differences" and emphasizes "not only individual action, but also the collective capacity to act on common challenges across difference." Harry Boyte, "Building Civic Agency: The Public Work Approach," openDemocracy, November 21, 2007, accessed April 23, 2017.

8. Bringle and Steinberg define civic-mindedness as "a person's inclination or disposition to be knowledgeable of and involved in the community, and to have a commitment to act upon a sense of responsibility as a member of that community." Robert G. Bringle and Kathryn S. Steinberg, "Educating for Informed Community Involvement," *American Journal of Community Psychology* 46 (2010): 429.

9. Center for Service and Learning at Indiana University Purdue University Indianapolis, http://csl.iupui.edu/teaching-research/opportunities/civic-learning/graduate.shtml

10. "Effective Use of Performance Objectives for Learning and Assessment," *Teacher & Educational Development*, University of New Mexico School of Medicine, 2005.

11. Benjamin S. Bloom, Max D. Engelhart, Edward J. Furst, Walker H. Hill, and David R. Krathwohl, eds., *Taxonomy of Educational Objectives, Handbook I: The Cognitive Domain* (New York: David McKay Co, Inc., 1956).

12. L. Dee Fink, *Creating Significant Learning Experiences: An Integrated Approach to Designing College Courses* (San Francisco, CA: John Wiley & Sons, Inc., 2003).

13. For more information about using Bloom or Fink's typologies to write effective learning objectives see Margaret J. Naume, "Writing Effective Learning Objectives," *Case Research Journal* 33 (2013): 165–71.

14. A group of education specialists developed a revised version of Bloom's Taxonomy that separated the cognitive processes or skills from content type. See Lorin W. Anderson and David R. Krathwohl et al., *A Taxonomy for Learning, Teaching, and Assessing: A Revision of Bloom's Taxonomy of Educational Objectives*, Abridged Edition (New York: Longman, 2001). Anderson and Krathwohl identify three types of content in Bloom's original hierarchy: "factual," "procedural," and "conceptual," and add a fourth type, "metacognitive knowledge." Metacognitive knowledge involves awareness of and knowledge about one's own processes of acquiring knowledge and understanding. The metacognitive dimension recognizes that in order to solve everyday problems people need to know how to seek out and evaluate information.

15. Fink, *Creating Significant Learning Experiences*, 30.

16. Useful charts matching Bloom's and Fink's taxonomies to a wide range of active verbs, objects, and sample learning objectives is available at https://www.mtsac.edu/felt/docs/EffectiveUseofLearningObjectives.pdf. Source: "Effective Use of Performance Objectives for Learning and Assessment (For Use With Fink's and Bloom's Taxonomies)," *Teacher & Educational Development*, University of New Mexico School of Medicine, 2005.

17. "Effective Use of Performance Objectives for Learning and Assessment," *Teacher & Educational Development*, University of New Mexico School of Medicine, 2005.

18. Clifford Adelman, "To Imagine a Verb: The Language and Syntax of Learning Outcomes Statements," National Institute for Learning Outcomes Assessment, Occasional Paper #24, February 2015, accessed April 1, 2017, http://learningoutcomesassessment.org/documents/OccasionalPaper24.pdf

19. Within Bloom's framework, knowing and comprehending can be developed through presentation, question-and-answer, small group discussion, self-awareness exercises, review sessions, independent study, and web-based instruction. Applying can be practiced through hands-on activities including labs, demonstrations, case studies, simulations,

role-playing, guided practice with feedback, and role-modeling. Analyzing can be observed in question-and-answer sessions, brainstorming, case studies, problem-solving exercises, trouble-shooting, role-playing, and article discussion. Synthesizing is required for case studies, writing, concept mapping, theory and model building, developing research questions, and direct contact with patients, clients, and other key stakeholders. Finally, evaluating can be practiced through case studies, critical reviews, self- and group-assessment, reflective writing, and direct contact with coalition partners, clients, and other key stakeholders in a service-learning environment. In addition, all levels can be further developed and demonstrated through teaching others.

20. The SMART framework is used (usually without attribution) by authors, centers, businesses, universities, and others publishing in the area of learning outcomes assessment. The acronym traces back to a November 1981 issue of *Management Review* paper by George T. Doran, "There's a S.M.A.R.T. Way to Write Management's Goals and Objectives."

21. Julie A. Hatcher, "Assessing Civic Knowledge and Engagement" *New Directions for Institutional Research* 149 (2011): 81–92.

22. See Constance DeVereaux, "Fostering Civic Engagement through the Arts: A Blueprint," this volume.

23. Richard M. Battistoni, *Civic Engagement across the Curriculum: A Resource Book for Service-Learning Faculty in All Disciplines* (Providence, RI: Campus Compact, 2002).

24. Hatcher, "Assessing Civic Knowledge," 84.

25. Caryn McTighe Musil, "Educating Students for Personal and Social Responsibility: The Civic Learning Spiral," in *Civic Engagement in Higher Education: Concepts and Practices*, ed. Barbara Jacoby (San Francisco: Jossey-Bass, 2009), 49–68.

26. Nicholas V. Longo and Marguerite S. Shaffer, "Leadership Education and the Revitalization of Public Life," in *Civic Engagement in Higher Education: Concepts and Practices*, ed. Barbara Jacoby (San Francisco: Jossey-Bass, 2009), 154–73.

27. Cheryl Keen, "Measuring Dialogue across Difference as a Civic Skill," *Journal of College and Character* 11 (2010): 1–8.

28. Cheryl Keen and Kelly Hall, "Post-Graduation Service and Civic Outcomes for High Financial Need Students of a Multi-Campus, Co-Curricular Service-Learning College Program," *Journal of College and Character* 10 (2008), 1–15.

29. Mary Kirlin, "The Role of Civic Skills in Fostering Civic Engagement," CIRCLE Working Paper 6, Center for Information and Research on Civic Learning and Engagement, University of Maryland, 2003.

30. Another framework is to focus separately on civic knowledge, skills, values, and collective action. Caryn McTighe Musil provides a "Framework for Twenty-first Century Civic Learning and Democratic Engagement" in the AAC&U publication *Civic Prompts* https://www.aacu.org/sites/default/files/files/CLDE/CivicPrompts.pdf. See Table 1 (page 5) for a useful delineation of the elements of this comprehensive approach designed to foster civic knowledge, skills, values, and collective action.

31. Consult the book's bibliography for more information about studies of civic identity including Colby and Damon, 1992; Parks Daloz, Keen, Keen, and Daloz Parks, 1996; Colby and Sullivan, 2009; Knefelkamp, 2008; Youniss, McLellan, and Yates, 1997.

32. Anne Colby and William M. Sullivan, "Strengthening the Foundations of Student's Excellence, Integrity, and Social Contribution," *Liberal Education* 95 (2009): 22–29.

33. James Youniss, Jeffrey A. McLellan, and Miranda Yates, "What We Know About Engendering Civic Identity," *American Behavioral Scientist* 40 (1997): 620–31.

34. Terrell L. Strayhorn, "How College Students' Engagement Affects Personal and Social Learning Outcomes." *Journal of College and Character* 10 (2008): 1–16.

35. There is no consistent language usage within the assessment literature. Some experts (especially those working in K–12 settings) describe learning goals as specific and measurable (similar to the way learning objectives are defined by most assessment experts working in higher education). Similarly, some assessment experts use the terms *learning objectives* and *learning outcomes statements* as synonyms, while others distinguish between *goals* (expressing intended outcomes in broad, global language), *learning objectives* (using precise terms that focus on what students will know and be able to do), and *learning outcomes* (focusing on what students will be able to demonstrate and how they will demonstrate the achievement of key learning objectives).

36. H. Anne Weiss and Kristin E. Norris, "The Matrix: A Planning Tool for Assessing Civic Learning or Development during College" [PowerPoint slides], retrieved from http://indianacampuscompact.org/assessment-resources/.

37. Susan M. Brookhart, *How to Create and Use Rubrics for Formative Assessment and Grading*, ASCD Member Book (Alexandria, VA: ASCD, 2013), accessed April 23, 2017, http://www.ascd.org/publications/books/112001/chapters/What-Are-Rubrics-and-Why-Are-They-Important%C2%A2.aspx.

38. For more information about rubrics see Brookhart, "How to Create and Use Rubrics."

39. See Simeone, Sikora, and Halperin, "Unscripted Learning: Cultivating Engaged Catalysts," this volume.

40. This section does not include the Civic-Minded Graduate assessments developed at Indiana University Purdue University Indianapolis because those links and descriptions for the CMG scale, CMG narrative prompt, CMG narrative rubric, CMG interview protocol, and CMG interview rubric were provided earlier in this chapter.

41. https://www.heri.ucla.edu/dleoverview.php.

42. For an overview key assessment instruments and survey findings from the PEP project see Elizabeth Beaumont, "Political Learning and Democratic Capacities: Some Challenges and Evidence of Promising Approaches," in *Teaching Civic Engagement: From Student to Active Citizen*, ed. Alison Rios Millett McCartney, Elizabeth A. Bennion, and Dick

Simpson (Washington, DC: American Political Science Association, 2013), 41–55. The chapter includes survey scales, items, questions, and response options regarding political understanding, political motivation, civic and political skills, civic identity, and civic and political involvement.

43. Other assessment instruments of interest to campuses, especially those seeking measures of political engagement, include the Political Engagement Project (PEP) survey, an extensive college student survey measuring civic knowledge, skills, values, volunteerism, interest, motivation, efficacy, and involvement. The complete survey is not available to the public, but the authors provide (partial) survey scales and results in *Educating for Democracy: Preparing Undergraduates for Responsible Political Engagement*. Another good model for measuring political engagement includes the National Youth Civic Engagement Index Project, a telephone survey of individuals (not only college students) age 15 and older measuring cognitive engagement in politics, civic activity, political engagement, and indicators of public voice. Results of this study are documented in the book *A New Civic Engagement: Political Participation, Civic Life, and the Changing American Citizen*. The MacArthur Foundation Research Network's Youth and Participatory Politics Survey measures politics-driven, interest-driven, and friendship-driven dimensions of online participatory civic/political cultures as well as democratic habits, skills, and commitments. A copy of the 2011 data can be requested by agreeing to the terms of use online. A final well-known assessment tool is the Socially Responsible Leadership Scale, a survey measuring eight dimensions (the 8 C's) of The Social Change Model of Leadership including consciousness of self, congruence, commitment, collaboration, common purpose, controversy with civility, citizenship, and change. Persons interested in obtaining a copy of the survey instrument must contact the National Clearinghouse of Leadership Programs.

Politics 365: Fostering Campus Climates for Student Political Learning and Engagement

23

Nancy Thomas and Margaret Brower

All college level teaching for political knowledge and engagement happens in the context of a campus climate, a combination of the norms, behaviors, attitudes, structures, and external influences that shape the student experience. In this chapter, the authors argue for attention to improving the campus environment as a means to increasing the pervasiveness and effectiveness of student development for civic engagement, political activism, and social action. This chapter reviews the findings from a nine-campus qualitative study of institutional climates for political learning and engagement in democracy, and the essential role faculty members, particularly political science professors, play in fostering a robust climate for learning for democracy.

Over the last 20 years, colleges and universities have exponentially increased their commitment to providing students with a wide range of civic experiences, from community service to nonprofit leadership education. Unfortunately, that commitment has fallen short of educating students across disciplines for the participation needed to ensure the future and health of democracy. By "democracy" we not only are referencing a form of government, but also a culture, a set of principles and practices that provide the context for shared governance in the United States. The 2016 presidential election season and outcome may have awakened the academy to ongoing global challenges to democratic principles: freedom of the press and speech, the right to dissent, equal opportunity, respect for new populations, public reason, and the rule of law. It may also have drawn attention to challenges in democratic culture: the declining ability of Americans to live and work together due to entrenched feelings of fear, hatred, entitlement, anger, and, what University of Wisconsin political scientist Kathy Cramer calls, the *politics of resentment*.[1] In these unsettled political times, colleges and universities need to seize this teachable moment, reexamine student civic learning, and educate for democratic culture and systems that are participatory, equitable, educated and informed, and ethically governed.

Earlier chapters in this book focus on teaching practices that effectively increase students' civic and political knowledge, agency, and interest. Indeed, in our previous chapter, "The Politically Engaged Classroom" in this volume, we suggested that quality classroom discussions, characterized by norms of free expression, skilled facilitation, attentiveness to the discussion process, and high standards for multiple, evidence-based viewpoints, contribute to a broader, vibrant campus learning environment for political engagement. Yet, will better teaching alone prepare students for public problem solving and policy making, particularly among students who are not already politically attentive? We do not think so. Like societies, colleges and universities are complex organizations with people, systems, norms, traditions, and societal contexts that interact to form the context for student development. Change to any one of these characteristics alone, including improved teaching, is unlikely to transform adequate numbers of disinterested students into committed political actors. Instead, institutions need to assess and improve their campus climates for political learning and engagement as a means to improving effectiveness and pervasiveness.

In this chapter, we present findings from our nine-campus qualitative study of institutional climates—specifically our analysis of the norms, behaviors, attitudes, and structures—for political learning and engagement in democracy.[2] We also provide evidence of the essential role faculty members, particularly political science professors, have as an integral part of fostering a robust climate for political learning. We conclude by making the case that colleges and universities should be viewed as a collection of minipublics in which people with diverse social identities, ideologies, perspectives, and interests associate, coalesce, discuss problems, and share authority in decision making.

METHODS

In 2014 and 2015, a team of researchers at Tufts University's Institute for Democracy and Higher Education visited nine colleges and universities nationwide to conduct studies of their campus climates for political learning and engagement in democracy. The nine campuses were selected based on their geographic locations, size, institutional type, students served, and results from the National Study of Learning, Voting, and Engagement (NSLVE). Launched in 2013, NSLVE is both a service to US colleges and universities—providing participating institutions with their aggregate student voter registration and voting rates—and a large database of individual student records. The database is created through a merging of student enrollment and publicly available voting records from federal elections. Colleges and universities must opt into the study. Currently, more than 1,000 US colleges and universities nationwide participate in NSLVE. In addition to representing all 50 states, the participating NSLVE institutions reflect a proportionate number of four-year public and private research and masters-granting institutions and liberal arts colleges, as well as and more than 300 community colleges.

The NSLVE database was created by combining college student enrollment lists with publicly available voting records. NSLVE data currently includes voting records from 2012 and 2014. (Data from 2016 will be available in the summer 2017.) Student-level data includes the institution attended, age on the date of the election, and in many cases, demographic data and class level. Half of the students in the database have identified a field of study. And for about half of the student records, the database also includes voting method (e.g., in person, by mail).

Adding institution-level data collected by the US Department of Education's Integrated Postsecondary Education Data Systems (IPEDs) and civic conditions surrounding each institution, we used quantitative methods to identify indicators for voting. In February 2014, the NSLVE database represented 219 colleges and universities. In March 2015, 473 colleges and universities had joined the study. And in September 2016, the number of NSLVE institution was 696 colleges and universities. We then calculated for each institution both a predicted and an actual voting rate from the 2012 presidential election. From this list, we focused on colleges and universities with voting rates between five and 20 percentage points higher than predicted ("positive outliers"), as well as lists of institutions with voting at rates seven or greater percent points lower than predicted ("negative outliers"). We sought diversity in institutional type, the student populations served, and geographic location; we selected seven institutions with voting rates that were higher than predicted and two with rates lower than predicted. From 2014 to 2016, we visited the following nine institutions, seven positive outliers and two negative outliers, identified by pseudonyms:[3]

- **Northeast State College:** Four-year public located in a suburb of a large city in the Northeast; enrollment of approximately 4,000; residual 13.3 percentage points **above** the predicted voting rate
- **Eastern Liberal Arts College:** Four-year private located in a small city in the East; enrollment of approximately 2,200; residual 5.5 percentage points **above** the predicted voting rate
- **Midwest Community College:** Two-year public located in a mid-sized city in the Midwest; enrollment of approximately 19,500; residual 7.9 percentage points **above** the predicted voting rate
- **Southwest Urban University:** Four-year public located in a large city in the Southwest; enrollment of approximately 13,000; residual 5.2 percentage points **above** the predicted voting rate
- **Southeast Public University:** Four-year public located in a suburb of a midsized city in the Southeast; enrollment of approximately 5,500; residual 10.2 percentage points **above** the predicted voting rate
- **Midwest Public University:** Four-year public located in a suburb of a large city in the Midwest; enrollment of approximately 16,500; residual 9.5 percentage points **above** the predicted voting rate
- **West Coast Community College:** Two-year public located in a small city in the West; enrollment of approximately 19,000; residual 8.8 percentage points **above** the predicted voting rate
- **Northeast Rural State College:** Four-year public located in a rural town the Northeast; enrollment of approximately 6,000; residual 11.9 percentage points **below** the predicted voting rate
- **Southwest Liberal Arts College:** Four-year private located in a large city in the Southwest; enrollment of approximately 2,100; residual 11.5 percentage points **below** the predicted voting rate

A team of three to four researchers visited each campus for several days and collected data via interviews and focus groups. We visited these institutions between national elections to avoid having to distinguish between situational election-related activities and embedded norms and practices. To ensure our sample was diverse and representative of the campus, participants were selected to represent students and faculty members from different disciplines, racial backgrounds, genders, leadership and authority positions, and years of experiences on the campus. Ultimately, the research team interviewed 59 people and conducted 65 focus groups of students and faculty, in total involving nearly 500 people. All of the interviews and focus groups were recorded, transcribed, coded, and analyzed.[4]

RESULTS

The college experience provides an ideal opportunity for students to develop knowledge and interest in political affairs and public policy and to learn and practice democratic skills. The positive outlier institutions, when analyzed for this study, manifested remarkable consistency in the political attributes of their campus climates. We share five specific *attributes* in this chapter. People on these campuses experienced strong *social cohesion*, as they repeatedly pointed to strong interpersonal relationships between faculty and students, institutional concern for student well-being, peer-to-peer support, as well as local community support for the institution and students. Social cohesion emerged as a complimentary feature of compositional *diversity* in the student population, as well as a strong commitment on the part of the institution to promote social mobility and equal opportunity as an aim of the college student experience. Engaging in a diversity of perspectives among students then allowed for political discussions to flourish, especially around policy questions and political issues. These types of *pervasive habits of political discussion* both in and beyond the classroom were common to all of the positive outlier campuses. We also found that attitudes toward *students as colleagues* mattered, and at the positive outlier institutions, students had authentic decision-making authority on campus and were told their voices mattered. Finally, support for *student political actions*, during and between elections, mattered. At the negative outlier institutions, most of these attributes either did not exist or were problematic. Our analysis of the negative outlier institutions provides a deeper understanding of how attributes of a campus can result in different levels of student political learning and engagement.

SOCIAL COHESION

On the positive outlier campuses we visited, students developed trusting relationships with their professors and with each other, which we identify as a "social cohesion" attribute. Social cohesion was not an outcome that happened serendipitously. Rather, social cohesion was carefully cultivated by the institution through traditions, events, expectations of faculty, and messaging to students.

At Southeast Public University, students were welcomed at convocation with faculty in full robes and much fanfare; similarly, graduation was a community affair, with thousands of people from the local community attending, bringing lawn chairs and picnics to celebrate the 600 or so students receiving degrees. During orientation, students learn about R.U.O.K., a program advertised on most doorways and even a highway billboard. Students learn that they share responsibility for each other's living and learning experiences. Students who are experiencing emotional, physical, or academic distress can be identified to the institution's counselling center through a hotline. Serving a predominantly low-income population, the institution has set aside dormitory rooms in case a student becomes homeless. The students and faculty also jointly support a food pantry at this university. Students can obtain canned goods, diapers, toiletries, and other essentials from a room that is stocked entirely from faculty and community donations. We regularly heard statements like, "this place takes care of me" and "we take care of each other here."

One administrator explained that students receive a strong "student-first, student-focused" message. Faculty, we were told, chose Southeast Public University because faculty and staff "really care about teaching, and they really care about students."

At many of the other positive outlier institutions, students are advised on the first day to take advantage of faculty office hours and to reach out to individual faculty. At these institutions, faculty and staff were expected to reach out to and encourage students, not just when a situation called for an intervention, but as a daily part of faculty life. The expectation regarding taking the initiative to connect began with faculty establishing flexible office hours and going the extra mile to help students. At Midwest Community College, one student shared the nature of her relationship with a particular professor, "I've spent a lot of time with my professors. And the professors at [Midwest Community College] are one of the best, that's very undeniable. I think all of you that know, you have to know one particular professor that has changed your life." Another student from this same college shared his experience with another professor, saying, "He opened up a lot of opportunities for me. And I think I'm very proud to say that I am the way I am today and the way I do things. It's mainly because of him." Students also appreciated their professors for maintaining an open-door policy, for being willing to work with them on assignments, and for being open to discussing not just the course materials but also, as one student explained, "any and every thing under the sun." At the positive outlier institutions, students view these relationships as powerful opportunities for networking and mentorship, but the relationships also build trust among students of faculty and loyalty to the institution more broadly. A student summarized, "Faculty is what makes this campus. I love the people here."

Administrative structures also matter. Most of the positive outlier institutions, particularly the public community colleges and four-year publics, support pipeline programs for nontraditional students (single parents, veterans, individuals who were formerly incarcerated, people with mental and physical disabilities, and undocumented students) and offer personal and academic support when they arrive. Both faculty members and students at West Coast Community College spoke highly of the institution's equal opportunity (EO) department. Described as unique to this college and "probably one of the most resourceful and supportive departments of probably all of the community colleges in [the system,]" the EO department oversees pipeline programs in addition to paying for faculty childcare and books. A student told us, "I was kind of one of those people. Like they said, EOPS, they really helped me out. I had no idea what I was doing when I got here. I was scared and intimidated, and I felt like I didn't belong, I wasn't smart enough. ... But they really made me feel like I belong."

Similarly, peer relationships were strong at the positive outlier institutions. At Eastern Liberal Arts College, students pointed to an ethos of cooperation and support. One student told us, "It's not really competitive. We challenge each other, but it's not like a competition where you're trying to always be better than someone else. It's really, like we said earlier, supporting and support of one another's accomplishments and successes." At West Coast Community College, students pointed to the EO program as a place where nontraditional students met and provided support to each other.

The combination of structures to ensure student well-being, faculty and staff attitudes that students come first, and the emphasis on shared responsibility for peer learning, health, and happiness contributed to an overall campus climate that valued community, associations, and collaboration.

DIVERSITY AS REALIZED PRACTICE

At the positive outlier institutions, diversity was viewed as an educational asset both in the classroom and beyond, but at the negative outlier institutions, students experienced diversity differently. Of the nine institutions we visited, students from diverse racial/ethnic backgrounds accounted for 40% of the student populations, and on average 28% of the students were Pell grant recipients. But at the positive outlier institutions, diversity was viewed as more than something the institution "had." Rather, it was institutionalized as part of student learning priorities, academic programs, and institutional identity. Diversity was understood as a social perspective through which students learned. Compositional diversity also challenged the patterns in public life, where Americans sort into social and economic groups and find themselves with others who share their views and values.[5] At these institutions, the breaking down of exclusionary or discriminatory practices was viewed as part of the institution's democratic mission.

At the campuses we visited, social group representation improved the quality of the educational programming. For example, Eastern Liberal Arts College lacked compositional racial/ethnic diversity, but the institution nonetheless identified social justice as a core outcome of student learning there. To achieve that goal, 100% of the students studied abroad at some point over their time as undergraduates. And prior to any study abroad experience, students studied the cultures, histories, and values of that nation or community. This learning experience included training in intercultural norms and relationships. An administrator shared:

> I think it's the students. I think it's the faculty, and I think it's the staff, too. I mean, I'm just going to throw out some examples to you. Our Chaplain is openly a lesbian and that, at some institutions around America, would not set well with a lot of people but that's [the college]. We're cool with it. We have a tennis coach who has one arm, and he has been incredibly successful. He's an amazing athlete, but I think a lot of schools may have been like, ugh, you know what I mean. But that's not [the college]. [The College] is accepting of this difference and really looking past labels and disabilities.

Even at diverse institutions, professors might teach a homogeneous group of students (drawn to a class, for example, by the subject matter). In those cases, the professors played devil's advocate to introduce perspectives missing from the room. Institutional leaders on the positive outlier institutions often developed programs and practices according to the diversity of their student body. On one positive outlier institution, the president requested a scatter plot diagram showing the addresses of the students so that the university could match internships with home addresses. On a few case-study campuses, administrators and faculty specifically recruited a diverse group of students to select speakers and plan events. Students took this role very seriously and asked their peers to vote democratically to ensure a cultural event represented all of the students attending the university. At another institution, a dean played the role of checking proposals for events or activities by students, asking students to identify whether that event would appeal to some students more than others, and why, and then having the students rethink their choices, if needed. At these positive outlier institutions, these were intentional and structural approaches to ensuring that inclusion shaped programs and practices.

Faculty took seriously their role as educators of diverse student populations. At Midwest Community College, a small group of faculty members (led by a political science and an English professor) launched a grassroots effort out of concern that the faculty was predominantly white and straight, and the students increasingly diverse by race, sexual orientation, and gender. They spent a year studying diversity and working with outside diversity trainers. At the end of a year, the group self-identified as "Agents of Change" and loosely affiliated with the institution's faculty development center. Their work became more formal—meeting six times a year, bringing in speakers and trainers. They bring in one trainer annually—someone who assesses where the institution is regarding diversity—developing a plan of action for the following year, and then returning to check progress. These faculty members placed "Agents of Change" stickers on their office doors to signal to students that they were trained and open to talking candidly about diversity. Now, more than 80 faculty members have joined the group. We were told in a focus group that no committee or task force is convened on campus now without someone asking, "Wait, how many Agents of Change are in this group?"

Attention to and value for the ways in which their students differed by race, ethnicity, ideology, age, income, and sexuality established an inclusive culture of politics at these positive outlier institutions. Students, faculty, and administrators all adopted an inclusive orientation to politics as they thought critically about power dynamics, privileges, and disadvantages interwoven into the structures of the institution. It was this attention to these structures that appeared to foster and cultivate the attribute, diversity as realized practice.

PERVASIVE POLITICAL DISCUSSIONS

Pervasive political discussions emerged as an important finding for all the positive outlier campuses. As reported in our previous chapter "The Politically Engaged Classroom," the classroom was an important venue for political discussions, and professors required students to support their opinions with evidence. Professors also set the right tone of respect and listening. And in the classroom, the facilitation skills of the professor made a difference. Some of the critical ingredients for a skillfully moderated discussion included professors playing devil's advocate to elicit unpopular or unrepresented perspectives. A student told us, "And I love, I love that. I love it whenever I can learn and someone can learn from both the students and the professors themselves." Students felt respected for their ideas and respected their peers and professors in return. A faculty member at Eastern Liberal Arts College said:

> I feel as faculty we have to be very intentional about introducing those perspectives because otherwise you can have a conversation that you sort of know what everyone's going to say or where they're leaning and it requires either a faculty member or a student in the class to, you'll occasionally hear someone say, well I'll play devil's advocate you know?

On these campuses, students were prepared to engage in discussions. We were surprised to learn that of the seven high outlier campuses we visited, several taught the arts of discussion in first-year English classes, and at least one had developed a first-year experience in intergroup relations. In one of these classes, the students examined one political issue, such as healthcare in the United States, for the entire semester. In the other, they used current events, covering many topics over the term. In these classes, students learned to frame issues, identify many perspectives, discuss, deliberate, and write about the issues, and, in some cases, debate or advocate for a particular stance. In some cases, students wrote mock letters to elected officials. In others, they also learned to lead discussions and manage any conflict that might occur.

Engaging in dialogue was also embedded in other student experiences. A student at Eastern Liberal Arts College told us, "We are constantly schooled in how to have discussions with people." There, students frequently participate in open forums and fish bowl conversations (a small group discussion that others observe). Institution-wide, students receive training in privilege and power disparities and in conflict resolution (separate programs), experiences that are required of students before they can study abroad. The president taught a first-year course on the First Amendment and free speech. Students, faculty, and administrators mentioned the importance of the college's "community principles" and that they are discussed and revised regularly.

Other institutions embedded discussion into the student experience as well. At Southeast Public University, students received training on intercultural and intergroup relations before going into the community to engage in service. Students working in area high school book clubs were trained to facilitate book discussions. At Southwest Urban University, the student government ran workshops year-round on facilitating dialogues and managing conflict as part of student leadership programs that they managed for leaders of student clubs and new student government leaders. Both Midwest Community College and Southwest Urban University worked with the Kettering Foundation to teach students to organize and facilitate National Issue Forums on topics of national and local concern.

Free expression was identified at all of the positive outlier institutions as a strong normative value for discussions alongside values of respect and civility. A public statement at Southeast Public University reads:

> While the First Amendment does give you the right to free speech, it does not entitle you to harass, intimidate, or bully others. So before you post nasty comments about someone else, review the law and remember what your mother said, "If you don't have anything nice to say, don't say anything at all."

Similarly, the provost at Eastern Liberal Arts College said, "There are no codes other than our community principles, and those include respect and inclusion." Students, not faculty or staff, were identified as the primary enforcers against degrading speech aimed at one social group. As one student at Eastern Liberal Arts College explained, "I just feel like people here … will not tolerate certain things … you can't go around wearing KKK masks here … that's not going to work."

Nationally, critics argue colleges and universities are places of liberal indoctrination, but we saw no evidence of that, even at the most liberal-leaning institutions we visited. As public institutions, several of the institutions we visited were subject to visits and protests by outside groups with conservative political views, particularly on abortion, and those groups visit the campus at least annually. An administrator at Northeast State College told us this story:

> [We] have, every year a group, a religious group that comes on campus and … students are always questioning why I let them do it … but I said look, it's their First Amendment right to do that, and I said, you can choose not to listen to this. … So it's always, every year they show up, and they do it, and it's always this kind of give and take, I'm answering questions about First Amendment rights, and the whole bit. I think that's probably one of the best examples of, you know, the freedom that people should have.

Although students may protest or express frustration about an unpopular speaker, administrations and faculty saw a value in, as one faculty member explained, inviting speakers who "go against the grain." However, disruptive hecklers were asked to leave because these institutions valued having exposure to different perspectives, even if they disagreed with them. Both faculty and staff confirmed what one president told us:

> I had Newt Gingrich here, I had Karl Rove less than a year after the '08 election, I think, and you know there were people who tried to shout him down and prevent him from speaking. I think there was a powerful lesson to be had in my throwing those people out of the auditorium who were trying to prevent him from speaking.

Many of the institutions we visited supported physical spaces for political expression. Midwest Public University reserved a hall in a heavily trafficked area for political posters and tables. Southwest Urban University identified a wall where members of the campus community recorded experiences showing their privilege. West Coast Community College, Midwest Community College, and Northeast State College established free speech zones. Southeast Public University also supported a free speech zone, but no one knew where it was located. In one student focus group, when asked where the free speech zone was located, a student responded, "I think it's all campus." And on many of these campuses, students could point to lounges or other common areas where political conversations were common. These walls, zones, and common areas were not the only places on campus where people could express their political views. They were simply places where students, faculty, and staff could spark political conversation or find other people interested in a particular political topic. Reflecting a theme we heard at all of the positive outlier institutions, a faculty member at Southwest Urban University told us, "Anywhere on campus is a safe space to speak about politics."

Political discussions were the most pervasive feature of the politically engaged institutions we visited, but it was important that these discussions take place in an environment that valued free expression and dissenting viewpoints.

STUDENTS AS COLLEAGUES WITH SHARED RESPONSIBILITY

At the politically engaged institutions we visited, students had real decision-making authority. Governance in higher education usually entails a system in which administrators and trustees or governing boards make management and financial decisions, and the faculty controls academic/curricular decisions. Ideally, it is often argued, the faculty, administration, and trustees share responsibility for decision making and the institution's future.[6] Yet shared governance has been criticized as outdated and unresponsive to the current fiscal concerns and the needs of new populations of students from disadvantaged backgrounds or underrepresented groups.[7]

At the politically engaged institutions we visited, students shared decision-making responsibilities within a more collaborative, horizontal decision-making structure. The locus of authority still rested with institutional leaders and faculty, but students played significant formal and informal roles.

Colleges and universities are notorious for their committees, and the committee structure lent itself well to student involvement. We saw examples of students working with the president to create a local wind farm near campus and students working with faculty, local experts, and government authorities to draft antifracking policies. When issues regarding the campus climate for different groups of students arose, the institutional leaders turned to the students to administer a climate survey to faculty and staff and to develop appropriate policies for improving those campus conditions. When students raised concerns about sexual assault on campus, students formed a committee to develop antiharassment and discrimination institutional policy. A student at Southeast Public University explained:

> I'm pretty sure everybody has sat on a board, a task force, a committee, if something's not working they're going to pull [students] together and it's normally student-focused. … [They will say] we see that it doesn't work, what can we do to make it better, and they'll implement those changes. And there's at least a student sitting on just about every committee that affects students. [If the] outcome will affect students, students sit on it.

By respecting student viewpoints, the administration built trust and commitment among students which would then serve the administration well when faced with an institution-wide conflict. And for institutions serving large numbers of historically marginalized groups of students, including their voice in decision making can prevent mistakes. An administrator from the Midwest Public University explained, "I don't pick carpet without student input. I don't paint a wall color without, 'Hey, which color do you like?' Not that I ask 150 people, but we have infrastructures and advisory boards where we live off of student input." At these positive outlier institutions, student perspectives, opinions, and voices were central to decision making.

Committee structures were not the only way institutions shared power with students. At Northeast State College, students operated a building that houses the cafeteria, the bookstore, student common areas, classrooms, and office spaces. The student government association managed the 450 or so students employed there each semester. An administrator explained how students shared this responsibility stating,

> No administrators have the keys. [Students] staff it completely with just students. They hire students from their own student body to run the student center and create the budget and events and the hours of the student center from 4PM until 2AM. You know, it's really on their terms and that in and of itself is political engagement.

Similarly, at Southwest Urban University, students were responsible for event planning. Because the standing committee responsible for events consisted of representation by students of all backgrounds, the events generally appealed to diverse groups of students. One student leader said,

> You'll find that a lot of the active students here are very interested in catering to every demographic type you can find, be it racial, religion, you know, being smart, educational. We're not looking for the most popular or most likely to be successful. We want everyone to be successful. We like to give everyone opportunities and open their eyes to things they never knew before which, once you give someone the chance to speak, an opportunity, you'd be surprised at what they can say.

Similarly, at both Eastern Liberal Arts College and Midwest Public University, the student government managed a large pool of money that was available to other student groups for competitive minigrants for community innovation.

Sometimes students were not handed power; they seized it. At Southwest Urban University, students wanted more say in institutional choices, so they formed a group they called the Empower Party and laid out a platform with a goal of not only shared decision making but more equitable and inclusive decision making. At Eastern Liberal Arts College, the student government was accused of being unresponsive to the entire student body, so they convened a group, rewrote the student government constitution, and then put it to a vote among the entire student body. At Southwest Urban University, a student told us that the student government was "a positive outlet for us to express our opinion" and a place "where stuff actually gets done."

The student government at Southwest Urban University exemplifies this ideal of seized authority. They wear suits or business attire to school every day because, as they explained, one never knows when the media or a political leader will be on campus. When Nelson Mandela lay on his deathbed, students decided to hold a candlelight vigil in his honor. One group bought candles and started notifying others on social media. Another group contacted the media to say that political leaders would be there, holding candles. A third group contacted political leaders and told them to come and hold candles because the media would be there. Both the politicians and the media joined the vigil, which was then reported on national news. At most institutions, students would be reticent to bypass institutional offices of public relations by contacting the media and inviting them to campus. At this institution, the student leaders had both the media and politicians among their contacts on their phones.

Finally, students actively shaped institutional policy, sometimes through protest but also through visible advocacy and campus-community organizing. We were actually on one campus when the students began a protest over the termination of a faculty member. The president left his office and met with the protesters to explain the process for hiring and firing decisions. The students left satisfied, assured that the process had now (as a result of the protest) been transparent. On several of the other positive outlier campuses, when students protest, the administrations respond by authorizing them to study the subject and draft an institutional policy for consideration. Students on these campuses wrote or influenced institutional policies concerning sexual harassment, student conduct codes, gender-neutral bathrooms, location of cameras on campus, inclusion of sexual orientation to the nondiscrimination policy, installation of more bike racks on campus, revision of food choices in the cafeteria, permission for nude modeling in art classes, procurement of a particular water pump, establishment of a food pantry on campus, including negotiating with local groceries for donations, changes in amount undocumented workers are paid, construction of a meditation room on campus, revision of maternity and paternity leave policies, and budget decisions.

The majority of students and faculty in our focus groups expressed satisfaction with how their voice and interests were received. One student at Southeast Public University explained,

> We learn how to express our voice at our university and are encouraged to stand up for our rights. If you are used to talking to your chancellor and then your governor and so forth then it has the ripple effect so I think [my campus] is a really good starting point for understanding how a democracy is supposed to work.

A faculty member from Southwest Urban University echoed a similar sentiment, stating, "From a social change standpoint, it's like [students] challenge the status quo. They're not afraid to challenge the status quo." Student leaders there had a reputation as the movers and shakers. One student explained, "Our student government president, he is very influential to the administration. He has built a very good connection with them. ... If the students come to him, he can really get it done."

In contrast, the institutional leaders and the faculty members we met at the negative outlier institutions were skeptical of the role of students in governance beyond the usual nonvoting membership on large committees or boards. At Northeast Rural State College, student leaders were mainly selected by the president or because they knew another student on the committee. At Southwest Liberal Arts College, faculty alone selected students to work with the first-year experience, overruling student and administrator efforts to democratize the process. Interestingly, on one of the two campuses, the division between the faculty and the administration was so difficult that they often clashed over institutional decisions publicly. Both institutions held onto a lot of centralized control of the institution, at Southwest, by the faculty and at Northeast Rural, by the administration.

POLITICAL ACTION

We define political action to include voting, campaigning, running for office, attending a town meeting, lobbying, and other forms of engagement with government as well as activism such as community organizing, public deliberation, and protest. At the positive outlier institutions, students acted out of interest for a political issue both within and beyond formal government structures. Engaging in activism was a frequent political action. Students utilized protests, demonstrations, and sit-ins to bring attention to national and local political problems. At West Coast Community College, there was a small population of homeless students enrolled in the college. One of the students, who had been formerly homeless, was determined to make the campus a more supportive environment for these students. He and others working with him experienced political barriers, but ultimately they negotiated these politics to achieve an institutional change. A student recounts the experience:

> Well, just to point out how active the students have been [here]. We have had a student by the [name.] He has been fighting I think for over a year to provide shower access for homeless students. I think the first time he was shot down. His idea was shot down and the whole proposition was shot down. But because of his activeness in campaigning and talking to students and the [state] student community college student senate, it's finally been passed in [West Coast Community College] so now homeless students can have a shower in the gym…

This example illustrates how students attending these institutions learn critical political skills, navigating, negotiating, and confronting institutional structures. In this case, the institutional change occurred as a result of visible campaigning with other students around this issue in connection to activism at the student senate level.

At Midwest Public University, students often engaged in visual demonstrations to express political issues such as racism, intolerance, and oppression. For example, students organized together to display pieces of red papers with descriptions of their experienced oppression and taped these pieces of paper to the glass of a walking bridge between academic buildings. Hundreds of students participated in this demonstration; a student explains the event, "That's Wall of Intolerance…where you write down about moments of oppression…on the walkway bridge… we had over, uh, over a thousand people participate, which for a commuter campus is not bad."

At this institution, students also organized a "Day of Silence." During this day students did not speak until the end of the day. At the end of the day there was an open mic organized for students to then speak out about issues that typically silence others. The positive outlier institutions leverage activism as a political tool for achieving institutional changes, for demonstrating political issues, and for creating coalitions or support groups around issues that were marginalized particular groups on campus and nationwide.

At most of the positive outlier institutions, election seasons were characterized by gatherings, celebrations, discussions, high emotions, and excitement. Voter registration involved many faculty and students. At Southwest Urban University, faculty members told us that there is not one week over the course of a year (not just election season) when he is not asked, "Are you registered to vote?" At Southeast Public University, all clubs and sororities/fraternities can fulfil part of their student government imposed community service requirement by tabling to register voters. At Southwest Urban University, students recruited nonpartisan representatives from the local community such as the League of Women Voters and others to serve as advisors to Walk-2Vote. A student described it:

> So one day, we had a rally essentially where we told students, "We're excited about the fact that we can vote early" and "You should take advantage of that opportunity." … We had, it was like a big pep rally [in the main common area of the campus.] We had food there, and we told students, "these are where your voting locations are." We told them what the calendar was to vote. SGA gave out little pom poms and American flags and little stickers and stuff like … We had guest speakers, and then afterwards, anybody who wanted to could walk down and cast an early vote.

Others agreed. One student added, "We put flyers everywhere. We chalked up the sidewalks, Walk2Vote, Walk2Vote. …"

Similarly, a student at Midwest Community College reported:

> There was a lot of political talk during the presidential—during the 2012 election. You could
> sit in the library and listen to people talk. And they're like, have you voted yet? Did you
> go across the street and vote yet. ... Everyone was, like, way hyped about it. The [school
> newspaper] did a lot on it, but not where you would think the school, I mean, it never felt like
> the school was into one party over another.

On nearly all of the positive outlier campuses, the political science faculty played a significant role in increasing interest in elections and in influencing the political climate on campus beyond an election season. During election seasons, they participated in voter mobilization drives. They hosted voter education sessions and advised the student Democrats and Republicans on registering voters or on hosting political debates. Faculty invited political speakers to campus, both liberal and conservative. They used class time to encourage students to register to vote. A PIRG (Public Interest Research Group) representative at Northeast State College told us that the faculty were amenable to "give her the spotlight," meaning class time, to pass out voter registration forms, to help students fill out the forms, to solicit volunteers for lobbying on behalf of the institution's financial needs at the state capital, or to let students know about food drives and other community work.

Faculty political engagement goes beyond the election season. At Midwest Community College, the faculty promotion and tenure requirements include a mandate that faculty engage with the local community, including serving on local commissions, running for an elected position, and working with the local city to tackle sticky public issues, particularly about racial divides and disparities. These faculty members worked annually to organize a march in the city to draw attention to racial divides in the community.

At these positive outlier institutions, faculty, particularly political science faculty, worked with students across disciplines by partnering with faculty members to offer interdisciplinary experiences, hosting speakers and panels on political issues, partnering with offices such as the interfaith chaplain to teach democratic skills of deliberation, advising student governments, and working with centers for teaching and learning (faculty development centers) on discussion-based pedagogies. In these and other ways, individual faculty members played a significant role in fostering the kind of campus climate conducive to political learning for all students.

RECOMMENDATIONS

We share these findings, which we call "Politics 365," to emphasize that pervasive political learning and engagement is not something connected to a single structure, one individual, the work of one department, or even an event, like an election. It is something that is practiced and modeled year round and is deeply embedded into institutional norms, behaviors, and, as several participants on the positive outlier campuses told us, "the way things are done around here." We offer these Politics 365 characteristics—social cohesion, diversity, pervasive political discussions, students as colleagues, and excitement around elections, and other political efforts—as a composite, a complex and intersecting set of norms, structures, activities, and behaviors. We suspect that no single characteristic will work in isolation. All of these findings suggest a need for additional study, such as controlled experiments and targeted interventions.

These qualitative case studies are valuable because they offer examples against which other professors and institutions can compare their own practices. But we cannot and do not claim causation—that if you do these things, your students will vote. We used voting rates as a sampling tool to identify places where students might be engaging politically at higher levels, but, as with any case study research, generalizability requires more study.

Campus climates reflect widely shared sets of norms, patterns of behaviors, and attitudes as well as structures and programs that manifest or reinforce those institutional attributes. Together, these attributes represent values and practices that are widely accepted and shared. This does not mean that everyone thinks or acts the same way, nor does it mean that the institution faces no conflicts or tensions. At the positive outlier institutions we visited, dissenting perspectives were welcome and managed constructively.

Fostering the kinds of learning environments described in this chapter will require a combination of institutional, collective, and individual action. Institutional leaders can initiate an assessment of the institution's political climate through a campus-wide reflection effort using dialogues or focus groups.[8] They can review written policies and procedures, particularly those concerning the intersection between free expression and inclusion and the role of academic freedom on campus. Based on the results of these assessments, institutional leaders can channel financial resources to efforts by individuals and groups, such as departments, student organizations, or the faculty development center.

Groups of faculty, however, need not wait for institutional approval. Grass-roots efforts involving faculty, such as the Agents of Change initiative described earlier, may be more effective than top-down action. Faculty may want to consider surveying faculty on their perceptions about the political landscape for teaching and whether that landscape has changed during and since the 2016 presidential election.[9] A tool for these discussions is the institution's NSLVE report, which provides individual colleges and universities tailored student voting data.

Action can and should be at the individual level, and there, it is a matter of making a personal commitment to making some changes. Our findings suggest that professors have a special role in the lives of students and are critical to in- and beyond-the-classroom experiences and that political science professors play a unique role in creating campus-wide conditions for political learning and engagement. In the classroom, professors can work with the teachable moments in public life—elections, policy debates, data, and events. Students can learn the arts of discussion, critical inquiry, collective reasoning, and compromise. Beyond the classroom, professors play a significant role in creating the levels of trust and cohesion essential to conditions for political discourse and engagement. One place to do that is through advising. Another is through disciplinary clubs (e.g., the Political Science Club, the International House), which are ideal structures for talking about political issues that may be extraneous to a particular course but are nonetheless important for students to examine.

Professors of political science, government, American studies, justice studies, ethnic studies, international studies, and other related fields are on the front line of policy debates on college campuses and often in the United States. By nature of the courses taught and the scope of these fields, politically charged discussions are central to their teaching. This experience needs to be shared with other disciplines, particularly those where the faculty members are less skilled at facilitating difficult dialogues or less informed about social change movements, structural inequalities and power dynamics underlying public issues, sources of information, and knowledge of political systems. Sharing expertise can be formal (team teaching, workshops for other faculty) or informal (brown bags, interdisciplinary coalitions of professors). Other chapters in this book provide additional valuable approaches to teaching democratic principles, practices, and issues. The goal should be to make student political learning more pervasive on campus and to shift institutional priorities and practices toward this type of learning and engagement. ∎

ENDNOTES

1. Katherine J. Cramer, *The Politics of Resentment: Rural Consciousness in Wisconsin and the Rise of Scott Walker* (Chicago: University of Chicago Press, 2016).

2. Our previous chapter, "The Politically Engaged Classroom," examined classroom pedagogy and the role of discussion-based teaching. It was written earlier when we had only examined five of the nine institutions we visited. This current chapter is based on the analysis from the data from all nine institutions.
3. The first four institutions were selected using the February 2014 model (N=219) and the fifth institution was selected using the March 2015 model (N=468). For the last four institutions, we used a model from September 2015 (N=679). For all institutions, we rounded the enrollment numbers to preserve their anonymity.
4. For a more comprehensive review of the research methods, see "The Politically Engaged Classroom."
5. Bill Bishop, *The Big Sort: Why the Clustering of Like-Minded America Is Tearing Us Apart* (New York: First Mariner Books, 2009).
6. William G. Bowen and Eugene M. Tobin, *Locus of Authority: The Evolution of Faculty Roles in the Governance of Higher Education* (Princeton, NJ: Princeton University Press, 2015).
7. Ibid.
8. The Institute for Democracy and Higher Education is happy to share a rubric developed as a result of these case studies, discussion guides on the NSLVE voting report, and/or the interview guides from these qualitative case studies. Contact IDHE@Tufts.edu.
9. IDHE has also developed a survey on faculty academic freedom and free expression on campus. Contact IDHE@Tufts.edu.

CONCLUSION

Teaching Engagement Today

Dick Simpson

We have had earlier historical periods in which the teaching of civic engagement in colleges and universities flourished.[1] Today, there is a need to extend that teaching to high schools and community colleges as well. However, the push for civic engagement is usually short-lived and then we return to teaching the basics (reading, writing, and arithmetic) or teaching for the job, not teaching for democracy. There is already some resistance and pushback to the movement for civic engagement today and so we need to take advantage of this opportunity to push our agenda forward as far and as fast as we can before support wanes.

The current effort to teach civic engagement, not only in political science but across disciplines and throughout the university, is a recent phenomenon. For example, our earlier book, *Teaching Civic Engagement: From Student to Active Citizen*, was only published by APSA in 2013, although there were precursors such as the Carnegie Foundation book, *Educating for Democracy: Preparing Undergraduates for Responsible Political Engagement*, as well as national organizations engaged in the effort before that time.[2]

Today, the effort to promote civic engagement is being led by groups like the Association of American Colleges and Universities (AAC&U), the publisher of *A Crucible Moment: College Learning and Democracy's Future*[3] and host of journal articles and conferences; Campus Compact, with its pledge by nearly 500 universities to design a new civic action plan for our campuses;[4] the Carnegie Foundation with its college Community Engagement Certification Program; the Higher Learning Commission with its Quality Improvement Program, including civic engagement for the 1,100 colleges and universities they accredit; and several disciplinary associations like the American Political Science Association with its Teaching and Learning Conference Civic Engagement Tracks, dedicated journals on teaching, and its civic engagement book publications.

There are various other foundations and organizations throughout academia and the educational landscape that promote the civic engagement agenda. At the state level, we are beginning to pass new laws that require teaching civic engagement at the high school level, but there is not much additional funding for the effort from either the national or state governments in a time of general budget cutbacks. It may well be in a time of federal government cutbacks and a focus on private initiatives like charter-school education that the states are a more fruitful place to gain legislation and some funding for civic engagement. It is significant that the Council of State Governments has issued a report summarized in this volume that argues that state legislators should become more involved and supportive of civic education, particularly about state and local government.[5]

In short, the new wave in various forms of civic education has been underway for some time and is beginning to show real results in areas of service-learning (and service-learning centers at colleges), community-oriented research in which community partners help to set the agenda and implement changes, shared civic engagement pedagogies and syllabi for individual courses, and systematic national research on assessment of what actually works to achieve civic engagement goals. Concrete results like vastly higher student voter registration and voting has also been achieved on individual campuses, and regional groups and conferences share best practices. Electronic voter registration, and soon Automatic Voter Registration, will make registering students to vote much easier in future.

Two urgent challenges remain, however. First is the challenge of teaching civic engagement and democracy, not just in individual courses or in the social sciences (which requires intentionality, effort, and careful assessment), but also across the entire university in all disciplines and in the cocurricular activities such as fraternities, clubs, student government and study abroad, speakers, and entertainment programs on campus. We are beginning to ask "how institutions can create environments maximally conducive to student civic learning and development."[6] We are also discovering that teaching civic engagement at all different types of educational institutions including high schools, community colleges, four-year liberal arts colleges, and research universities has very different challenges.[7]

A second challenge, which we had not expected when we began writing this book, is how to teach civic engagement during the Trump presidency. Donald Trump's election has severely divided and polarized the nation. While civic engagement is, in principle, entirely neutral—we want students to vote and participate in policy making and in community groups and organizations whether they are Democrats or Republicans, liberals or conservatives—the time ahead is more likely to be more like the 1960s in its turbulence and activism than recent decades, which, while partisan, were less tumultuous. Conservatives will want to encourage profound changes of policy and direction under President Trump well beyond his first 100 days and controversial cabinet appointments while liberals will turn more radical in their protests against administration policies. In future elections, liberals will try to change the balance of power first to block, and then to defeat, Trump and his congressional and local allies. This is likely to create a pitched battle of public demonstrations and shrill rhetoric inside and outside of government rather than a polite and civil debate of policy. In short, we are advocating more civic engagement in a time of controversy. Because of the increased polarization, it is unlikely that we will be seen as neutral. Rather, our efforts may be portrayed as part of the anti-Trump, rabble-rousing faction.

A RENEWED CIVIC ENGAGEMENT

Despite these challenges, we must press on with renewed civic engagement on our campuses while we have momentum. A lot of the motivation for civic engagement thus far has been because of the low level of political knowledge and political participation, not only in the public but especially among students and youth.[8] Alarm over this state of affairs led to calls for change in this "crucible moment." As the Trump presidency begins, there will be both support for more civil discourse and, at the same time, a call to support and oppose Trump policies. So we are tasked not only with overcoming apathy, which may be less of a problem in the days ahead, but also with encouraging better and more knowledgeable participation and a deeper commitment to the preservation of the institutions and practices of a representative democracy.

The first key to success in promoting more civic engagement will require a clear commitment of the university and higher administration on our local campuses and by academic organizations nationally. Second, we will need an intentional effort to expand the level of civic engagement. If there is a commitment and a plan, the necessary resources are more likely to follow.

At the local level, a beginning point is the mission statement of each college.[9] Usually there is some vague recognition of a goal beyond the neutral transmission of knowledge to some public service or building citizenship. In religious-based colleges or public universities, this commitment is usually even more explicit. If there is an effort to refashion the mission statement to bring it up to the twenty-first century from the language of earlier centuries, then there is an opportunity to advocate for a more explicit commitment to civic learning in the revised statement.

I participated in such a revision of the mission statement at our University of Illinois system, and our campus chancellor has at the same time announced pillars of excellence for our own campus, including a commitment to civic and community engagement. In both the committee and public discussions of our mission, I found almost unanimous support for a commitment to civic learning and incorporated explicit language, which then made possible gaining access to university resources and support by the administration for a much enhanced civic engagement effort. Sometimes the mission of a campus can be made more explicit and particular. For instance, the University of Illinois at Chicago, where I teach, made a commitment to an "urban mission" decades ago that became our "Great Cities Initiative." Along with support for this purpose throughout our university, it allowed the creation of a Great Cities Institute and resources to focus on improving not only the city of Chicago but also large urban centers around the world. It allowed the creation of other research centers and the development of courses such as my "Chicago's Future" course in which the social, economic, political, and governmental trends in a metropolitan region under globalization pressures could be debated by public officials, scholars, and students. All of this is to say that mission statements and commitments matter, especially in gaining support, resources, and focus for civic engagement efforts on each campus.

But mission statements are not self-executing. The next logical step after a generalized statement is a specific university pledge of civic action. The Campus Compact Pledge, which nearly 500 university presidents and chancellors have signed, is a specific promise to do an analysis of existing programs of civic engagement in a template provided by Campus Compact and then, within one year, to draw up a renewed civic action plan.[10]

There have been other coordinated actions among universities and disciplinary organizations as well. One example has been the effort of national social science associations to prevent funding cuts of their research on political topics by the National Science Foundation (NSF) and even on science funding in general by the NSF in response to congressional attacks that are continuing.[11]

In any case, a specific commitment by the highest levels of administration to unified campus efforts to promote various civic engagement goals, like voter registration and voter education, is an important step beyond general platitudes or vague commitments that actually begins to change things at the individual campus and student level. Similar commitments to supporting community organizations and local governments in shaping public policy based on university research can make a huge difference in civic learning in different classes. Nationally, the support and encouragement of disciplinary and academic organizations is also key to getting more high schools and colleges to undertake this effort.

CHALLENGES AT THE DEPARTMENTAL LEVEL

Even if a college has a fine mission statement and commitment at the higher levels of administration, a key to expanding civic engagement is what is taught in individual classes. That is, of course, under the control of individual faculty members and departments. Nonetheless, there are common challenges. Most disciplines value research and "scientific" or objective knowledge. And since previous reform waves, such as the one led by John Dewey and the Progressives, there has been a commitment to objective observation and a scholarship of discovery rather than action. Academics want to be seen as nonpartisan and objective, not as activists.

However, in recent decades many disciplines have begun to pay more attention to teaching, learning styles of students, and assessment of learning and to recognize not only a scholarship of research but also a scholarship of teaching and learning (SoTL).[12] They have been slower to recognize a scholarship of engagement, but there is progress there as well. Thus, we know much more about what works and what does not in our courses and in creating departmental majors, minors, certificate programs, and ladders of courses in civic engagement.

But different disciplines fall at different places on the spectrum as to how much they promote, and their resistance to, teaching civic engagement in their fields. Some professional programs such as teaching, nursing, and urban planning naturally have civic engagement with schools, patients, or community groups as an integral part of their curriculum. As part of their training, they require all their students to have direct contact with and to learn from their interactions with their community.

Other fields of study such as the social sciences, especially political science and public administration, have an obligation to study politics, government, and society so that the introduction of civic learning and civic engagement skills is a natural part of the process. However, even in these fields, developing new ways of incorporating social media and other techniques into courses like political science still need to be developed.[13]

The humanities often take a different approach such as critical literary analysis, abstract art, theoretical philosophy, or historical studies. They can get hung up on trying to decide what civics is or have difficulty in relating their fields to current political or societal problems. Many instructors have incorporated teaching civic engagement and service-learning into their humanities courses but it is by no means the norm in these fields of study.[14]

Despite current examples of the sciences as critical to the discussion and solution of human problems like climate change, often the scientific disciplines are most resistant to incorporating civic learning—even about public policies—into their classes.[15] It is easy to see how biology classes could go beyond teaching about amoebas and various living organisms to teaching about climate change and its effects on living creatures, including humans. But often, scientists claim that political discussions are not "scientific." Some even argue that human interactions are not easily reducible to study by the scientific method, although social scientists obviously disagree. They further say that political opinions should not be taught in science courses and scientists most often do not believe that they have a rightful role as citizens except outside the classroom and beyond the study of science. Attitudes by scientists with the denial by the Trump administration of climate change along with the US withdrawal of the Paris Accords on climate change and proposed cuts to agencies like NSF have caused protests like the March for Science, but this has yet to carry over to teaching civic engagement in most science classes.

For civic engagement to make further advances in the academy, scholars and teachers in each discipline must demonstrate how civic learning can be meaningfully incorporated into these different types of classes and into a ladder of courses that teach different aspects of analysis, philosophy, and action in the public sphere. We cannot simply teach civic engagement in any single class or cocurricular activity but must embed it in a campus culture in which civic engagement is valued.

A start at thinking about how the different disciplines can move forward is contained in *Civic Prompts! Making Civic Learning Routine across the Disciplines* that was developed from an AAC&U and Campus Compact metropolitan regional conference with representatives of different disciplines from a dozen campuses ranging from community colleges to research universities.[16] This brief book, which is available on the AAC&U website, provides a series of questions or prompts that each disciplinary area—professional degree, social sciences, humanities, and the sciences—should ask and answer to move the incorporation of civic engagement into their scholarship and teaching.

To move forward, there must also be leaders in each discipline who advocate for curricular changes. In addition, there have to be rewards for this form of research, teaching, and service in terms of promotion, raises, and recognition at both campus and national levels. This obviously must include full credit for this work in promotion and tenure reviews. While most promotion and tenure forms include information about teaching and some evaluation of that, teaching rarely counts enough to allow promotion and tenure without strong research publication in the scholarship of discovery. And while the forms include service as a category, public service or civic engagement by a faculty member is usually totally discounted in promotion and tenure decisions and very often in giving raises at universities as well. Research is privileged in research universities and teaching is privileged in four-year colleges, community colleges, and high schools. Civic engagement and public service are almost never enough for promotion and tenure in our institutions.

Outstanding members in each discipline are needed to advocate the incorporation of civic learning and teaching for democracy into the curriculum, and these accomplishments need to be recognized and rewarded in promotion, tenure, and salary decisions.

COCURRICULAR CIVIC ENGAGEMENT

Students on our campuses, especially with the heightened tensions and explosive issues of the Trump presidency, will organize many forms of engagement on their own without the intervention of faculty or the administration. Like the 1960s with the civil rights and anti-Vietnam War movements that brought clashes on and off campus, there may be considerable conflict in any pro- and anti-Trump student or faculty efforts, events, marches, and demonstrations.

During at least the next few years, many cocurricular activities may take place outside of university-sanctioned student organizations or activities. We will need to protect the rights of students to engage in nonviolent actions and to continue to provide campus student organizations and activities that promote civic engagement even if they may be controversial at times.

We know from extensive research that students often learn as much from their peers as from lectures in class and this is true of civic engagement as well. The Athenians, especially, thought that democracy was best taught by participation in democratic discussion and participation in the Assembly (and in juries and the executive committee, which were selected by lot) rather than by formal instruction. The deepest and best learning often follows an action/reflection model. We act, we reflect on our actions, and we learn. (This is also called experiential learning.) We need to make the campus a safe place for both speech and action, but we must also provide reflection opportunities and foster opportunities for students to learn from each other.

Even "nonpolitical" student clubs and organizations teach the ability to organize collectively, establish rules, and select leaders. When students join together to volunteer in a community activity, such as at a homeless shelter or to lobby the state legislature for more funding for their university, they learn skills and gain first-hand knowledge of problems that need to be addressed by public policy. These activities outside the classroom (although students may sometimes appropriately receive course credit or extra points on their grade for doing them), can be much more effective than a class lecture on poverty or the legislature.

Having the student affairs officials consciously promoting civic engagement activities is essential to creating a civically engaged campus. Supporting students in their own decision making and public actions provides a base from which they can develop their own knowledge and skills of democracy, and most importantly, a sense of self-confidence and political efficacy that is vital to citizenship.

One very useful step in coordinating and enlarging cocurricular activities is to develop a common civic engagement calendar for each semester of the lectures, programs, and activities in which all students can participate. It should be printed, prominently displayed at the student union and other places that students congregate, and posted on websites. Along with ads on individual events, the dates of civic opportunities should be published in the campus newspaper in both its print and online versions. Finally, social media should be used to promote better attendance and participation at the different events on the civic engagement calendar because students more often rely on social media for information. If everyone knows of campus-wide opportunities, it is easier to do follow up and for different student groups like student government to support one another's efforts. Attendance swells and new events are created to fill any obvious voids. And this sanction of an official posting by the university or college of civic engagement activities is critical to these events flourishing.

Usually the civic engagement calendar begins each fall with Constitution Day on September 17 or a day immediately before or after if the date falls on a weekend. Constitution Day is a federally mandated activity for every university or college that receives federal funding. (It is easy to start one when it is pointed out to college administrators that they could lose federal funding if they do not hold them.) Constitution Day need not be a dull, three-branches-of-government lecture. Instead, it can be a lively discussion of First Amendment rights, constitutional protections for immigrants and noncitizens, excessive use of force by police, or other current issues that spark debate and awareness of the living Constitution and controversies surrounding it.

The civic engagement calendar ends with summer activities such as study abroad, internships, and special programs like the summer study programs some universities offer in Washington, DC. In between Constitution Day and summer semester or vacation are all the speakers, rallies, voter-registration drives, alternative break programs, debate-watch evenings, and the like.

Usually it is best to point the calendar to a culminating event such as Election Day or campus Lobby Day at the state capitol. This makes it easy to provide a structure and to coordinate other events leading to that culmination. The calendar should certainly include any student leadership training programs as well.

CORE CIVIC ENGAGEMENT GROUP

For civic engagement efforts to be effective across campus and across disciplines, there needs to be a small group coordinating activities. This group needs to include any officials charged with implementing the campus civic engagement commitment and others who have access to critical resources necessary for success. At the University of Illinois at Chicago, the Core Civic Engagement Group includes the Office of the Vice Chancellor of Government and Public Affairs, the executive director of the Institute of Policy and Civic Engagement, an official from Student Affairs, the associate director of Student Development Services who directs all student organizations, the director of Illinois Connection (the student and alumni lobbying arm of the university system), myself as a representative from the Department of Political Science (which provides many of the lectures, public programs, and internship program), and a select few undergraduate and graduate student leaders. We had been part of a larger, but still select group, which made the almost-successful bid to house the Obama Presidential Library. So we draw on the civic engagement materials we developed in that effort in our newly coordinated activities.

We meet monthly as a committee to coordinate the civic engagement campus calendar. And since our chancellor has signed the civic engagement pledge with Campus Compact, our committee is also charged with developing the draft of the new civic action plan that will be approved by a higher level committee of deans after public discussion on campus. We will also be the coordinating committee to draft our application for Carnegie Foundation Community Engagement Classification. As of 2015, 361 colleges and universities have earned this classification. In 2018, the University of Illinois at Chicago will apply, and all the reports, documents, and current civic engagement efforts are consciously bent toward meeting the demanding Carnegie Foundation standards.

Our Core Civic Engagement Group also works together to gather the necessary resources for all the different campus civic engagement programs like Constitution Day, National Student Issues Convention, and voter-registration drives. We frequently have to pay for room rentals, speaker honorariums, newspaper advertisements, all-student e-mail notices, and the like. By pooling our resources and seeking funds from other academic units, we are able to pay for these costs and to ensure that the activities are held and properly promoted. In addition in 2016, we ensured that a new polling site for early voting (where more than 1,200 students and faculty voted) was opened for the first time in our university's history. Because of our coordinated voting registration and voting efforts throughout 2016, more than 1,000 students were registered to vote (or changed their registration) and more than 2,400 students voted on campus either early or on Election Day. We also held debate-watch parties for many of the spring and all of the fall presidential campaign debates.

Enlarging civic learning and encouraging civic engagement is not one person's or a single department's task. Our committee's role and our personal role as supporters of civic engagement is to guide and support the efforts of many actors on campus. This effort is most efficiently accomplished if there is a core civic engagement group to provide the coordination.

COLLABORATION BEYOND THE CAMPUS

Many civic engagement efforts take collaboration beyond a single campus and even beyond a university or college system of which our campus may be a part. One type of collaboration is providing a coordinated system of civic learning and engagement from high school through community colleges, colleges, and universities. Hopefully, this work can be extended in appropriate ways to elementary schools as well.

As Shawn Healy from the McCormick Foundation led us in Illinois, one way forward is to build a coalition of "Democracy High Schools" to recognize schools that already do civic education well, provide them with the tools to improve, and discover "best practices" that can be used at any school—public or private.[17] From this base of Democracy High Schools, in Illinois it was possible to create a coalition of schools, college civic engagement educators, students, and state legislators to pass a law that requires that students pass a civic engagement class to graduate from high school after 2017. Then we developed a new curriculum at the state level for such courses. Many states require some type of civics to be taught at the high school level, and research demonstrates that, when it is done well, it does have an effect.[18] Thus, one critical step in our civic learning agenda is to make sure that high schools teach and teach well civic engagement for colleges to build on. (And of course, students who do not go to college will receive their only civics education in high school.)

Colleges have also begun to develop coalitions to advocate for greater state funding for higher education, funding or increasing state scholarships for students, and specific issues such as immigration policies or allowing state universities to use scholar funds for undocumented students. These cross-campus coalitions provide extra opportunities for students to practice democracy beyond the successes or failures of individual issue campaigns to achieve their practical goals.

Beyond civic engagement collaboration around lobbying public officials, coalitions of community colleges, four-year colleges, and research universities have begun to develop in metropolitan regions or statewide to improve civic engagement on each campus and to learn from one another. Campus Compact uses the state as a basis for its local chapters, and they are staffed. But in both metropolitan regions and statewide, conferences on various civic engagement topics are being held around the country.

Nationally, a number of national academic groups loosely collaborate in moving the civic engagement agenda forward. These various national organizations hold conferences for faculty and transmit "best practices" in a variety of newsletters, journals, and electronic formats. Through them, individual faculty find like-minded colleagues to write journal articles and books on these topics, and to do joint civic education efforts across state lines, such as the National Student Issues Convention, which has been held on campuses across several states at the same time each year. Of course, some programs, like Model UN and Mock Trial, are ongoing long-standing events involving hundreds of colleges and universities. Generally speaking, there is much to be gained by having these various individual efforts by different national organizations and groups of schools become more intentional, aware, and collaborative as part of an ecology of civic engagement that fosters success of each.

CAMPUS CLIMATE

Campus climate also affects individual students in both the quality and quantity of their civic engagement.[19] Creating and promoting a civically engaged campus climate has to occur across the campus with the support of the entire campus community, including higher administration. For instance, encouraging political debate and discussion in classes beyond political science affects the level of student voter registration and voting that are concrete measures of civic, and explicitly, political engagement. The earlier study by the Carnegie Foundation as reported in *Educating for Democracy* found that such discussion and deliberation techniques were one of the five key methods to change political efficacy, skills, and action by students without changing their political ideology or indoctrinating them.[20] Some other effective techniques such as providing speakers, internships, and reflection are also likely to proliferate in a campus climate that promotes and supports civic engagement.

A mission statement, a number of faculty who support civic engagement, continual assessment of civic engagement practices on the campus, and a core group to promote civic engagement activities are necessary but not sufficient. Changes in a few courses or even one or two disciplines to promote civic engagement are insufficient unless the overall climate on campus encourages students to be civically, and especially, politically engaged. Accreditation organizations such as the Higher Learning Commission are beginning to recognize and reward civic engagement, but colleges and universities can certainly still be accredited without promoting it.

How can the campus climate be changed? One way is to get the faculty to take ownership of the process and to institute norms such that all classes across disciplines include respectful political discussion—that is, discussion of political topics such as liberal/conservative philosophies, policy issues, and fundamental beliefs like religious and ideological beliefs. Setting up training programs for faculty on diversity issues and facilitating discussions when there are legitimate disagreements provide university recognition of the goal and help to provide the tools necessary for faculty to do a better job teaching. This work can begin as a grassroots effort on the part of concerned faculty or it can be led by administration officials, including department heads.

It is likely that creating a climate that welcomes respectful dissent may become an even more urgent task during the Trump presidency. This is because American politics has become even more polarized after the 2016 presidential election. With Republicans controlling all three branches of the federal government (after the next few Supreme Court appointments) and both political parties tending to become more ideologically extreme (Republicans more conservative and Democrats more liberal), the political and cultural wars will also become more extreme. It is to be expected that some students (and faculty) on our campuses will react very strongly to individual policies and laws that will be enacted and executive orders issued by the Trump administration. So, creating a climate that allows students to be civically and politically engaged takes on a special urgency. It will be especially difficult to get the broad support that the recent efforts to increase voter registration and voter participation by students and youth in a neutral and nonpartisan way has enjoyed in recent years. But civic education is even more important than before.

A RENEWED AGENDA FOR CIVIC ENGAGEMENT

When APSA published our previous book, *Teaching Civic Engagement: From Student to Active Citizen*, four years ago we sought to

- present the case for teaching civic engagement from the publications and experiments of prior years;
- provide examples of how to teach civic engagement successfully for a wide variety of political science classes, from standard American government classes required at many colleges and universities to international relations courses, to scope and methods classes, and various other subfields in the discipline;

- call and provide a template for seriously assessing the effects of those civic engagement courses that use such techniques; and
- articulate a national civic engagement agenda.

In the last four years, there has been amazing forward momentum and progress on each of these four dimensions.

In *Teaching Civic Engagement Across the Disciplines*, we move from teaching better political science courses to teaching civic engagement across the disciplines, university-wide coordinated civic engagement programs and action plans, and a new nationwide action plan across high schools, community colleges, four-year colleges, and research universities to consolidate the gains that have been made and provide the resources for the next leap forward. We also have the goal of providing the guidelines for teaching civic engagement during the Trump presidency that may well prove more challenging than in the 1980s, 1990s, and 2000s when there was broad support and little challenge to teaching civic engagement.

One example of this challenge is the report *Making Citizens* and the series of symposia by the National Association of Scholars with titles such as "Losing the Republic: The Progressive Hijack of Civic Education" and "Wasted Colleges: The New Civics in Colorado."[21] Conservative leaders and organizations are beginning to challenge civic engagement education as a Trojan horse for progressives to brainwash high school and college students. If this becomes a trend in the years ahead, it may undermine what has been broad-based support from politicians, governments, foundations, and academic organizations.

In this book, we have tried to suggest how to adapt to the new cultural and political climate while still moving forward with a civic education agenda.

A REVIEW OF PROGRESS ON OUR PREVIOUS AGENDA

In *Teaching Civic Engagement: From Student to Active Citizen*, we outlined an agenda based on the research and experience of more than 30 authors that we summarize here. We have made the most progress on the following agenda items:

1. APSA should continue to support teaching civic engagement through conferences and publications.
APSA has continued to support teaching civic engagement as have several other national education associations such as the AAC&U, Campus Compact, the Higher Learning Commission, and the Carnegie Foundation, to name just a few. Specifically, APSA, in addition to publishing books such as this one and articles on civic engagement in its journals, has committed to continue to sponsor the Teaching and Learning Conference, include civic engagement panels in its national meetings, create an affinity group on teaching civic engagement within APSA, and maintain a website dedicated to best practices. However, many national disciplinary associations and other groups are not yet as active in their support. Some foundations have provided funding, but it is not a priority for most foundations, even those foundations that have education as a general priority. So there needs to be growing support from national organizations and philanthropic foundations in what is expected to be trying times ahead with reduced federal funding for all educational ventures, except perhaps for charter schools and voucher programs.

2. High schools, colleges, and universities should adopt civic engagement as a goal in their mission statements and promote it across disciplines and across campus.
Some schools at various levels have adopted civic engagement as a critical element in their mission. Ideally, this should be in the mission statement itself and reflected as a commitment in the structure of the campus such as service-learning or civic engagement centers and administrators charged with overseeing fulfillment of this commitment. This is an easy beginning point in the

process of transforming a campus into a civically engaged high school, college, and university, but such a goal cannot be achieved without intentionality and an agreed-upon commitment. Many schools have a commitment to civic engagement in their mission statement already, but others need to adopt amended mission statements and make their commitment real in practice.

3. Universities and colleges that receive federal funding should comply with federal mandates like Constitution Day and promoting student voter registration. Assessment of how well colleges and universities are complying with these mandates should occur at the campus and national levels.

While most universities make some minimal effort to hold programs on Constitution Day and send an e-mail to remind their students to register to vote, these efforts are often perfunctory and unsatisfactory. Constitution Day should become the kickoff for the entire civic engagement campus calendar of events and tackle serious constitutional issues like immigration or excessive use of force by police to engage students in meaningful political discussion and reflection. The day should also be used to register students for student organizations, to vote, and for future civic engagement efforts.

Likewise, if we teach students how to register and make it simple, they will do so in great numbers. They should be given the opportunity to register to vote at the same time they get their student identification cards at orientation, and voter registration drives in election years and in class should be a frequent event. Lobbying for passage of electronic and automatic voter registration should occur in all states that do not have it, which would allow schools to switch from voter registration to voter education and other civic engagement events.

4. Provide more opportunities like Model UN, Mock Trial, Congressional Debate, Model State Legislature, and National Student Issues Convention.

These are existing national programs that are essentially simulations to teach international affairs, national policies, and state government. They are easy to institute and build student skills in democratic government. So it should be easy to expand these programs to other schools even in times of budget cutbacks.

5. There is a duty to provide students with the knowledge, skills, and tools to become informed advocates. One way to do this is to design for cognitive and effective learning along with effective service to the community. As a part of this, reflection needs to be one of the essential tools of teaching civic engagement.

Our previous volume, *Teaching Civic Engagement: From Student to Active Citizen*, other books on civic engagement, and journal articles on the scholarship of teaching and learning (SoTL) during the last four years have provided carefully assessed teaching methods and techniques.[22] They have provided a clear template for teaching courses and undertaking civic engagement across the campus. Based on this information, it is now possible to design courses, programs, and cocurricular activities that have maximum impact and provide students the necessary knowledge, skills, and tools. A part of any effort, however, must include opportunities for reflection by the students, whether these take the form of keeping personal journals of experiences, written class papers, oral reports in class, individual meetings with faculty, or similar reflective opportunities.

6. Multiple courses need to be created to create distinct learning opportunities and a ladder of experiences.

Many of the most effective civic engagement colleges create minors or certificate programs within departments or as interdisciplinary programs. The weight of civic engagement cannot be placed on a single course or on a single department. The new push is to coordinate civic engagement courses and cocurricular events across disciplines. Thinking about building tracks, minors, or certificate programs is one way of providing a path of course and noncurricular activities that can build civic skills, motivation, and knowledge. Assistance in putting together these activities is best achieved if a service-learning or civic engagement center exists or is created on campus.

7. Development of a robust website on teaching and political engagement including assessment techniques.

Since the publication of *Teaching Civic Engagement* in 2013, APSA has dedicated a website to promoting civic engagement and linking to other resources like those of Campus Compact and research like that at Rutgers University and Tufts University. We need to expand offerings on this website, and the authors of the two *Teaching Civic Engagement* books will provide as much material as possible from their work—including syllabi and course assignments—that can be adopted by other teachers as well as assessment tools. We also will offer our readers opportunities to make valuable contributions to the website to ensure that it is a dynamic and relevant resource.

THE PATH AHEAD

As unfinished business, we have other agenda items on which only slight progress has been made in the last four years:

1. The federal government should expand its funding and support for civic engagement.

Even under President Obama's administration, which was, in principle, supportive of civic engagement (after all, Barack Obama began his career as a community organizer), no significant money was available to schools or colleges for this purpose. There was funding for education generally in the stimulus package in 2008 and some conferences and declarations on civic engagement sponsored by the White House, but there was no reliable stream of support for achieving civic engagement goals.

It is likely that the Trump administration will be even less supportive, fearing that civic engagement by students will lead to resistance and demonstrations against the administration and its agenda. Nonetheless, it is important to continue to advocate for federal funding for specific civic engagement efforts.

The states have been no more supportive. Generally speaking, funding for higher education and even elementary and secondary school education has been reduced in the state budget cutbacks since the Great Recession of 2008. However, some specific gains, such as having civics classes required for graduation and revising the social studies curriculum in states to include service-learning and civic engagement, have been achieved in individual states. There needs to be a concerted effort to get state legislatures, governors, and state departments of education to support future civic engagement programs. As the education philosophy of No Child Left Behind is broadened to include other goals than the teaching of reading, writing, and arithmetic (e.g., promoting science, technology, engineering, and mathematics education), we need to make sure that educating for democracy is supported as well.

2. State and local governments should use students as administrators of elections or election judges, and students should be encouraged to work with local government to provide information on best practices.

Very few state and local governments use students (including high school students) to help administer elections and to provide information on improving public policies and programs. It is the job of faculty to help set up such programs, but it is the job of local officials to make many more opportunities available. These efforts to involve students in the political and governmental process make it much more likely that students will become active citizens. In addition, students provide an important resource for cash-strapped local governments in improving government services and functions through their research and work.

3. Civic education should be encouraged at the high school level.

While there has clearly been some progress in increasing civic education at the high school level and some creative programs like the Mikva Challenge in Chicago, generally civic education has suffered as the implementation of new programs like No Child Left Behind have placed so much focus on teaching the basics. As a result, civics has been squeezed out of the curriculum. The one big advance has been in the proliferation of service-learning programs. However, without a clear opportunity for reflection and discussion of the problems like poverty, simply volunteering at homeless shelters, soup kitchens, or literacy programs is not sufficient to bring political awareness and education. Students are much more likely to be willing to volunteer or give money to charities than they are to tackle the underlying causes of the problems they may witness. We need a new national commitment to educating for democracy and the training of effective citizens at the high school level.

It has been very useful to have the National Assessment of Educational Progress tests to monitor the level of knowledge and political action every four years. The fact that these tests are being cut back in 2018 is not a good sign.

4. Faculty should be encouraged to be politically engaged themselves, and disciplinary associations like APSA should adopt a code of ethics that recognizes the benefits of civic engagement. These are particularly controversial recommendations even within disciplines like political science. The dominant opinion in academia is that faculty should not be civically engaged. If they are engaged, they do so on their own time as citizens. Political engagement is not recognized as an academic contribution (even in the area of service). There have always been some scholar-politicians such as president Woodrow Wilson (political science), US senator Paul Douglas (economics), Chicago alderman and mayoral candidate Charles Merriam (political science), or current congressman Bill Foster (nuclear physics). But they are always the exception. More academics serve on local school boards or on boards of directors of not-for-profit organizations providing social services. Some faculty testify before congressional or state legislative bodies about public policies. Additionally, some scholars are "public intellectuals" who use their academic expertise to affect public policy, and others serve as expert witnesses in court cases.

Still, the general belief is that academics should not be politically engaged as academics. Yet, if we expect our students to be civically engaged, then faculty must serve as role models in this type of engagement. Some faculty can then bring firsthand knowledge of politics, government, and public policy into the classroom and their publications. We need to open a space for at least some academics at each university to do this and to be rewarded for doing so if they do it well and with integrity. Teachers and scholars should be encouraged to bring their professional knowledge to the solution of public problems.

5. Civic and political engagement must be rigorously assessed by both quantitative and qualitative methods.
While we have made considerable progress in more rigorously assessing and testing civic engagement classes and course assignments during the last four years, there are still two major problems: first, instructors mostly have anecdotal evidence that whatever they tried, worked; and second, we need new ways to assess not just individual course experiments but also campus-wide civic engagement efforts.[23] In this book, we demonstrate some common assessment practices that produce useful results such as pre- and posttests; paired classes in which a technique is tried in one set of classes but not in the other; and standardized questions that provide a larger data set of responses to determine how effective any particular intervention may be in increasing political knowledge and political efficacy. We need more cross-campus comparisons, and fortunately, research is beginning to be done in this way.[24]

We are beginning to collect information on the actual effect of campus programs in terms of objective indicators such as number of students who register to vote or the number of students who vote.[25] Campus Compact reports and Carnegie Foundation applications for recognition of civic engaged universities should also soon provide us with new data sets of civic engagement efforts at the campus level.

While careful assessment is an important tool and it is important to know what really does work and what does not, there is also the naive hope that if we can simply "prove" that civic engagement contributes to other goals, like improved critical thinking and academic achievement, and that it does not indoctrinate students and change their political ideology, that university administrators and public officials will automatically applaud and speed the adoption of these techniques. It will not be so simple. Many officials will still oppose these innovations, no matter what evidence we produce. We need to know which techniques are most effective, and we can use the evidence to argue for recognition and greater financial resources. It will take more than evidence, however, to win the battle for full recognition of the value of civic education.

6. Increase the support of national organizations and state governments of teaching civic engagement.

This volume has focused on *Teaching Civic Engagement Across the Disciplines* and makes clear that we will not be successful in our broader civic engagement goals by focusing primarily on political science classes. We must consider how civic engagement is taught across the campus and how it is promoted in cocurricular activities within a campus climate that values civic and political engagement.

In this effort, we must have increased support from national organizations and state governments, especially because increased national government support is unlikely in the near future. The coalition of national organizations that have collaborated in the new civic engagement efforts can expand by adding other regional accrediting agencies similar to the Higher Learning Commission and the State Higher Education Officers. The Carnegie Certification process, beginning in 2018 for 2020 designation as a Community Engagement Campus, should be used as an opportunity to motivate efforts at the campus level for greater civic engagement.

7. Train a new generation of civic engagement faculty.

There has been little improvement in the training of graduate students to teach since the Pew Charitable Trusts and AAC&U promoted their Preparing Future Faculty programs beginning in 1993.[26] Although there is a website and some publications from the Preparing Future Faculty program, there is now a renewed need to teach graduate students and new faculty how to use civic engagement techniques in addition to lecture and discussion methods in their classes. We know that to engage students is to keep them and that civic engagement activities, in addition to undergraduate student research projects and similar individualized student-involvement efforts, are a way to accomplish this. But new faculty do not automatically become great teachers. We need to provide better training in teaching and not just in research.

Overall, this 14-point agenda provides a strategy for the years ahead. We cannot all work on each of these efforts but if we each do our part, we can use the new national surge to achieve greater civic engagement. As Jane Mansbridge writes in the first chapter of this book, "Without citizens educated in how our democracy works and prepared to engage in our institutions when they do not work for the people, our democracy cannot survive and thrive in this era of increasingly complex problems." We must work collectively to train the next generation of citizens and leaders in democracy. In this effort, none of us can be "free-riders." We must each do our part. ∎

ENDNOTES

1. Michael Rogers, "The History of Civic Education in Political Science," this volume. See also Michael Rogers and Donald M. Gooch, eds., *Civic Education in the Twenty-First Century* (Latham, MD: Lexington Books, 2015).

2. Alison Rios Millett McCartney, Elizabeth A. Bennion, and Dick Simpson, eds. *Teaching Civic Engagement: From Student to Active Citizen* (Washington, DC: APSA, 2013) and Anne Colby, Elizabeth Beaumont, Thomas Ehrlich, and Josh Corngold, *Educating for Democracy: Preparing Undergraduates for Responsible Political Engagement* (San Francisco: Jossey Bass, 2007).

3. The National Task Force on Civic Learning and Democratic Engagement, *A Crucible Moment: College Learning and Democracy's Future* (Washington, DC: AAC&U, 2012). See also Caryn Musil, *Civic Prompts: Making Civic Learning Routine*

across the Disciplines (Washington, DC: AAC&U, 2015) and Caryn McTighe Musil, "Excerpts of *A Crucible Moment* and *Civic Prompts*," this volume.

4. Andrew Seligsohn and Maggie Grove, "The Essential Role of Campus Planning in Student Civic Engagement," this volume.

5. Katherine Barrett and Richard Greene, "Civic Education: A Key to Trust in Government," this volume.

6. Seligsohn and Grove, "The Essential Role," this volume.

7. See for example, Shawn P. Healy, "Essential School Supports for Civic Learning," this volume and Diana Owen and G. Isaac W. Riddle, "Active Learning and the Acquisition of Political Knowledge in High School," this volume.

8. For information on student voting, see The Center for Information and Research on Civic Learning and Engagement (CIRCLE) at http://civicyouth.org/quick-facts/youth-voting/.

9. See Elizabeth Matto and Mary McHugh, "Civic Engagement Centers and Institutes: Promising Routes for Teaching Lessons in Citizenship to Student of All Disciplines," this volume, for a review of some mission statements that include a commitment to civic and political engagement.

10. See Seligsohn and Grove's chapter in this volume. The Campus Compact Pledge and process is at http://compact.org/actionstatement/.

11. Michael Hitzig, "The Congressional GOP Sharpens Its Knives to Attack Scientific Research," *Los Angeles Times,* April 14, 2017, http://www.latimes.com/business/hiltzik/la-fi-mh-knives-for-scientific-research-20141110-column.html.

12. Ernest Boyer, *Scholarship Reconsidered: Priorities of the Professorate* (San Francisco: Jossey Bass, 2016, Expanded Edition).

13. See, for example, Gina Woodall and Tara Lemon, "Using Twitter to Promote Classroom and Civic Engagement," this volume, on incorporating the use of social media into political science courses.

14. See for example John Suarez, "Promoting Civic Engagement in a Required General Education Course," this volume, on teaching civic engagement in general education English courses and Constance DeVereaux, "Fostering Civic Engagement through the Arts," this volume, on teaching it in the arts.

15. See for example Tara Kulkarni and Kimberly Coleman, "Service-Learning in an Environmental Engineering Classroom: Examples, Evaluation, and Recommendations," this volume, for the teaching of civic engagement in engineering courses.

16. These meetings were held in Chicago during the fall and winter of 2015–2016 and resulted in the publication of Caryn Musil, *Civic Prompts: Making Civic Learning Routine across the Disciplines.*

17. Shawn P. Healy, "Essential School Supports for Civic Learning," this volume.

18. Ibid.

19. Nancy Thomas and Margaret Bower, "The Politically Engaged Classroom," this volume.

20. Colby, et al., *Educating for Democracy.*

21. David Randall, *Making Citizens: How American Universities Teach Civics* (New York: National Association of Scholars, 2017). https://www.nas.org/images/documents/NAS_makingCitizens_fullReport.pdf.

22. Boyer, *Scholarship Reconsidered.*

23. Elizabeth Bennion, "Moving Forward with Assessment," this volume.

24. J. Cherie Strachan and Elizabeth Bennion, "New Resources for Civic Engagement," this volume.

25. Thomas and Bower, "The Politically Engaged Classroom."

26. See the PFF homepage at http://www.preparing-faculty.org/.

Bibliography

AAC&U. *General Education Maps and Markers: Designing Meaningful Pathways to Student Achievement.* Washington, DC: Association of American Colleges and Universities, 2015.

Abrajano, Marisa, and R. Michael Alvarez. *New Faces, New Voices: The Hispanic Electorate in America.* Princeton, NJ: Princeton University Press, 2010.

Abrajano, Marisa. "Reexamining the 'Racial Gap' in Political Knowledge." *The Journal of Politics* 77 (2014): 44–54.

Ackerman, Bruce, and James S. Fishkin. *Deliberation Day.* New Haven, CT: Yale University Press, 2004.

Adelman, Clifford. "To Imagine a Verb: The Language and Syntax of Learning Outcomes Statements." *National Institute for Learning Outcomes Assessment.* Occasional Paper #24, February 2015, accessed April 1, 2017, http://learningoutcomesassessment.org/documents/OccasionalPaper24.pdf.

Adler, Richard P., and Judy Goggin. "What Do We Mean by 'Civic Engagement'?" *Journal of Transformative Education* 3 (July 2005): 236–53.

Ahmad, Iftikhar. "Teaching Government in the Social Studies: Political Scientists' Contributions to Citizenship Education." *The Social Studies* 97 (2006): 8–15.

Ahnlee, Jang, and Kim Hyunhee. "Cultural Identity, Social Capital, and Social Control of Young Korean Americans: Extending the Theory of Intercultural Pulic Relations." *Journal of Public Relations Research* 25 (2013): 225–45.

Allen, Danielle. "Acting Politically in a Digital Age," in *From Voice to Influence in the Digital Age*, ed. Danielle Allen and Jennifer S. Light. Chicago: University of Chicago Press, 2015.

Allport, Gordon. *The Nature of Prejudice.* Reading, MA: Addison-Wesley, 1954.

Almond, Gabriel. A., and Sydney Verba. *The Civic Culture: Political Attitudes and Democracy in Five Nations.* Princeton, NJ: Princeton University Press, 1963.

Amadeo, Jo-Ann, Judith Torney-Purta, Rainer Lehmann, Vera Husfeldt, and Roumiana Nikolova. *Civic Knowledge and Engagement: An IEA Study of Upper Secondary Students in Sixteen Countries.* Amsterdam: International Association for Evaluation of Educational Achievement, 2002. Accessed January 11, 2015, http://www.terpconnect.umd.edu/~jtpurta/UpperSecondary_files/Civics%20Booklet%20JA.pdf.

American Political Science Association. "2016 Call for Editors: APSA Journals." American Political Science Association, http://www.apsanet.org/PUBLICATIONS/Journals/2016-Call-for-Editors.

American Political Science Association. "About APSA." American Political Science Association, http://www.apsanet.org/ABOUT/About-APSA.

American Political Science Association. "Task Force to Set Agenda for Civic Education Program." *PS: Political Science & Politics* 30 (1997): 744.

American Political Science Association Committee on Education 1991–1993. "APSA Guidelines for Teacher Training: Recommendations for Certifying Precollegiate Teachers of Civics, Government, and Social Studies." *PS: Political Science & Politics* 27 (1994): 261–62.

American Political Science Association Committee on Instruction in Political Science. "The Study of Civics." *The American Political Science Review* 16 (1922): 116–25.

American Political Science Association Task Force on Civic Education in the 21st Century. "Expanded Articulation Statement: A Call for Reactions and Contributions." *PS: Political Science & Politics* 31 (1998): 636–38.

American Sociological Association. "Journals Print Advertising." American Sociological Association, http://www.asanet.org/journals/print_advertising.cfm.

Anderson, Lorin W. and David R. Krathwohl, ed. *A Taxonomy for Learning, Teaching, and Assessing: A Revision of Bloom's Taxonomy of Educational Objectives.* Abridged Version. New York: Longman, 2001.

Anderson, Monica. "Men Catch up with Women on Overall Social Media Use." *Fact Tank.* News in the Numbers. Pew Research Center, 2015. Accessed January 23, 2016. http://www.pewresearch.org/fact-tank/2015/08/28/men-catch-up-with-women-on-overall-social-media-use/

Andolina, Molly W., Krista Jenkins, Cliff Zukin, and Scott Keeter. "Habits from Home, Lessons from School: Influences on Youth Civic Engagement." *PS: Political Science & Politics* 36 (2003): 275–80.

Andrade, Maureen S. "Learning Communities: Examining Positive Outcomes." *Journal of College Student Retention* 9 (2007): 1–20.

Andrews, Rhys. "Civic Engagement, Ethnic Heterogeneity, and Social Capital in Urban Areas: Evidence from England." *Urban Affairs Review* 44 (2009): 428–40. doi:10.1177/1078087408321492.

Appleby, Michelle. "What Are the Benefits of Interdisciplinary Study?" *OpenLearn,* April 9, 2015. http://www.open.edu/openlearn/education/what-are-the-benefits-interdisciplinary-study.

Aristotle. *Nicomachean Ethics.* Trans. Terence Irwin. Indianapolis: Hackett Publishing Company, Inc., 1985.

Aristotle. *The Politics.* Trans. Carnes Lord. Chicago: The University of Chicago Press, 1984.

"The Arts and Civic Engagement." National Endowment for the Arts, 2007. Accessed January 12, 2017. https://www.arts.gov/sites/default/files/CivicEngagement.pdf.

"The Arts and Civic Engagement: Strengthening the 21st Century Community." Americans for the Arts, Arts Policy Roundtable. Accessed January 20, 2017. http://www.americansforthearts.org/by-program/reports-and-data/legislation-policy/national-arts-policy-roundtable/2008-the-arts-and-civic-engagement-strengthening-the-21st-century-community.

Ash, Sarah L., Patti H. Clayton, and Maxine P. Atkinson, "Integrating Reflection and Assessment to Capture and Improve Student Learning." *Michigan Journal of Community Service Learning* 11 (2005): 49–60.

Association of American Colleges and Universities. "A Crucible Moment: College Learning and Democracy's Future." Accessed on January 11, 2017. https://www.aacu.org/sites/default/files/files/crucible/Crucible_508F.pdf.

Astin, Alexander W. "Student Involvement: A Developmental Theory for Higher Education." *Journal of College Student Personnel* 25 (1984): 297–308.

Astin, Alexander W. *What Matters in College? Four Critical Years Revisited.* San Francisco: Jossey-Bass, 1993.

Atherton, Herbert. "We the People...Project Citizen," in *Education for Civic Engagement in Democracy: Service Learning and Other Promising Practices,* ed. Sheilah Mann and John J. Patrick. Bloomington, IN: Indiana University Press, 2000.

Atkeson, Lonna Rae, and Ronald B. Rapoport. "The More Things Change the More They Stay the Same: Examining Gender Differences in Political Attitude Expression, 1952–2000." *Public Opinion Quarterly,* 67 (2003): 495–521.

Babcock, Linda, and Sara Laschever. *Women Don't Ask: The High Cost of Avoiding Negotiation—*

And Positive Strategies for Change. Princeton, NJ: Princeton University Press, 2003.

Baker, Stephanie and Norleen Pomerantz. "Impact of Learning Communities on Retention at a Metropolitan University." *Journal of College Student Retention* 2 (2000): 115–26.

Barabas, Jason, Jennifer Jerit, William Pollock, and Carlisle Rainey. "The Question(s) of Political Knowledge." *American Political Science Review* 108 (2014): 840–55.

Barton, Keith C. "Expanding Preservice Teachers' Images of Self, Students, and Democracy," in *Making Civics Count:Citizenship Education for a New Generation*, ed. David E. Campbell, Meira Levinson, and Frederick M. Hess, 161–82. Cambridge, MA: Harvard Education Press, 2012.

Battistoni, Richard M. *Civic Engagement Across the Curriculum: A Resource Book for Service-Learning Faculty in All Disciplines.* Providence, RI: Campus Compact, 2002.

Battistoni, Richard M. "Should Political Scienctists Care About Civic Education?" *Perspectives on Politics* 11(2013): 1135–38.

Beaumont, Elizabeth, Anne Colby, Thomas Ehrlich, and Judith Torney-Purta. "Promoting Political Competence and Engagement in College Students: An Empirical Study." *Journal of Political Science Education* 2 (2006): 249–70.

Beaumont, Elizabeth. "Political Learning and Democratic Capacities: Some Challenges and Evidence of Promising Approaches," in *Teaching Civic Engagement: From Student to Active Citizen*, ed. Alison Rios Millett McCartney, Elizabeth A. Bennion, and Dick Simpson. Washington, DC: American Political Science Association, 2013.

Beaumont, Elizabeth. "Promoting Political Agency, Addressing Political Inequality: A Multilevel Model of Internal Political Efficacy." *The Journal of Politics* 73 (2011): 216–31.

Becker, J., and S. Wright. "Yet Another Dark Side of Chivalry: Benevolent Sexism Undermines and Hostile Sexism Motivates Collective Action for Social Change." *Journal of Personality and Social Psychology* 101 (2011): 62–77.

Bedolla, Lisa Garcia, and Luis Ricardo Fraga. "Latino Education, Civic Engagement, and the Public Good." *Review of Research in Education* 36 (2012): 23–42.

Beetham, David. "Evaluating New vs. Old Forms of Civic Engagement and Participation," in *Evaluating Democratic Innovations: Curing the Democratic Malaise?* ed. Brigitte Geissel and Kenneth Newton, 56–67. New York: Routledge, 2012.

Bennett, Jessica. "Why Men Are Retweeted more than Women: The Gender Disparity of Influene on Twitter." *The Atlantic*, June 2015. Accessed February 15, 2016. http://www.theatlantic.com/magazine/archive/2015/06/why-men-are-retweeted-more-than-women/392099/.

Bennet, Michael J. *When Dreams Came True: The GI Bill and the Making Of Modern America.* Washington, DC: Brasseys, 1996.

Bennett, Stephen Earl. "Comparing Americans' Political Information in 1988 and 1992." *Journal of Politics* 57 (1995): 521–32.

Bennett, Stephen Earl. "'Know-Nothings' Revisited: The Meaning of Political Ignorance Today." *Social Science Quarterly* 69 (1988): 476–90.

Bennett, Stephen Earl. "The Past Need Not Be Prologue: Why Pessimissism About Civic Education Is Premature." *PS: Political Science & Politics* 32 (1999): 755–57.

Bennett, Stephen Earl. "Trends in American Political Information, 1967–1987." *American Politics Quarterly* 17 (1989): 422–35.

Bennett, W. Lance. "Civic Learning in Changing Democracies: Challenges for Citizenship and Civic Education," in *Young Citizens and New Media: Learning for Democratic Participation*, ed. Peter Dahlgren, 59–78. New York: Routledge, 2010.

Bennion, Elizabeth A. "Assessing Civic and Political Engagement Activities: A Toolkit," in *Teaching Civic Engagement: From Student to Active Citizen*, ed. Alison Rios Millett McCartney, Elizabeth A. Bennion, and Dick Simpson, 407–21. Washington DC: American Political Science Association, 2013.

Bennion, Elizabeth A. "Experiential Education in Political Science and International Relations," in *Handbook on Teaching and Learning in Political Science and International Relations*, ed. John Ishiyama, William J. Miller, and Eszter Simon, 351–68. Northampton, MA: Edward Elgar, 2015.

Bennion, Elizabeth, A. "Moving Assessment Forward: Teaching Civic Engagement and Beyond," in *Teaching Civic Engagement: From Student to Active Citizen*, ed. Alison Rios Millett McCartney, Elizabeth A. Bennion, and Dick Simpson. Washington, DC: American Political Science Association, 2013.

Berdanier, Bruce. "Year-Long Service Learning Projects in Capstone Design at South Dakota State University." *Conference Proceedings, Capstone Design Conference*, 2010.

Berg, Nate. "US Metros are Ground Zero for Majority-Minority Populations." *CityLab*. May 18, 2012. http://www.citylab.com/housing/2012/05/us-metros-are-ground-zero-majority-minority-populations/2043/.

Berger, Ben. *Attention Deficit Democracy: The Paradox of Civic Engagement*. Princeton, NJ: Princeton University Press, 2011.

Berger, Ben. "Political Theory, Political Science, and the End of Civic Engagement." *Perspectives on Politics* 7 (2009): 335–50.

Berger, Peter L., and Thomas Luckman. *The Social Construction of Reality: A Treatise in the Sociology of Knowledge*. New York: Doubleday, 1966.

Berman, Sally. *Service Learning: A Guide to Planning, Implementing, and Assessing Student Projects*. Thousand Oaks, CA: Corwin Press, 2006.

Berret, Dan and Eric Hoover. "College Freshmen Seek Financial Security Amid Emotional Insecurity." *Chronicle of Higher Education*, February 5, 2015. Accessed from http://chronicle.com.cmich.idm.oclc.org/article/College-Freshmen-Seek/151645/?cid=related-promo.

Billig, Shelley and Alan S. Waterman, eds. *Studying Service Learning: Innovations in Education Research Methodology*. Mahwah, NJ: Lawrence Erlbaum Associates, 2003.

Bishop, Bill. *The Big Sort: Why the Clustering of Like-Minded America is Tearing Us Apart*. New York: First Mariner Books, 2009.

Black, Anthony. L., and Robert M. Arnold. "'Yes, It's Sad, But What Should I Do?' Moving From Empathy To Action in Discussing Goals of Care," *Journal of Palliative Medicine* 17 (2014): 141–44.

Blair, Alasdair, Steven Curtis, Mark Goodwin, and Sam Shields. "What Feedback Do Students Want?" *Politics* 33 (2013): 66–79.

Bloom, B.S., M. D. Engelhart, E. J. Furst, W. H. Hill, D. R. Krathwohl, eds. *Taxonomy of Educational Objectives, Handbook I: The Cognitive Domain*. New York: David McKay Co, Inc., 1956.

Bogaards, Matthew and Fraziska Deutsch. "Deliberation By, With, and For University Students." *Journal of Political Science Education* 11 (2015): 221–232.

Bogira, Steve. "Chicago's Growing Racial Gap in Child Poverty." *Chicago Reader*, October 4, 2013. http://www.chicagoreader.com/Bleader/archives/2012/10/04/chicagos-growing-racial-gap-in-child-poverty.

Bok, Derek. *Our Underachieving Colleges*. Princeton, NJ: Princeton University Press, 2006.

Bolwerk, Anne, et al. "How Art Changes Your Brain: Differential Effects of Visual Art Production and Cognitive Art Evaluation on Functional Brain Connectivity." PLOS ONE 9 (2014).

Bonwell, Charles C., and James A. Eison. *Active Learning: Creating Excitement in the Classroom*. ASHE-ERIC Higher Education Report No. 1. Washington, DC: The George Washington University, School of Education and Human Development, 1991.

Botsch, Carol S., and Robert E. Botsch. "Audiences and Outcomes In Online and Traditional American Government Classes: A Comparative Two-Year Case Study." *PS: Political Science & Politics* 34 (2001): 135–41.

Bowen, William G. and Eugene M. Tobin. *Locus of Authority: The Evolution of Faculty Roles in the Governance of Higher Education*. Princeton, NJ: Princeton University Press, 2015.

Boyd, Melody L., Jason Martin, and Kathryn Edin. "Pathways to Participation: Class Disparities in Youth Civic Engagement." *City & Community* 15 (2016): 400–22, doi:10.1111/cico.12205.

Boyer, Ernest L. *College: The Undergraduate Experience in America.* Princeton, NJ: Carnegie Foundation for the Advancement of Teaching, 1987.

Boyer, Ernest L. *Scholarship Reconsidered: Priorities of the Professoriate.* Princeton, NJ: Princeton University Press, 1990.

Boyte, Harry. "Building Civic Agency: The Public Work Approach." openDemocracy website. November 21, 2007. Accessed April 23, 2017. https://www.opendemocracy.net/article/building_civic_agency_the_public_work_approach.

Boyte, Harry. "Community Service and Civic Education." *Phi Beta Kappan 72* (1991): 765–67.

Boyte, Harry. *Everyday Politics.* Philadelphia: University of Pennsylvania Press, 2004.

Brannon, Tiffany N., and Gregory M. Walton. "Enacting Cultural Interests: How Intergroup Contact Reduces Prejudice by Sparking Interest in an Out-Group's Culture." *Psychological Science* 24 (2013): 1947–57.

Branson, Margaret Stimmann, and Charles N. Quigley. *The Role of Civic Education.* The Communitarian Network, 1988. Accessed March 20, 2017. http://www2.gwu.edu/~ccps/pop_civ.html.

Braun, Virginia, and Victoria Clarke. "Using Thematic Analysis in Psychology." *Qualitative Research in Psychology* 3 (2006): 77–101. doi:10.1191/1478088706qp063oa.

Breitman, Kendall. "Poll: Americans' Sense of Civic Duty Wanes." *Politico,* December 29, 2014. Accessed January 2, 2017. http://www.politico.com/story/2014/12/americans-civic-duty-poll-113853.

Bringle, Robert G., and Kathryn S. Steinberg. "Educating for Informed Community Involvement." *American Journal of Community Psychology* 46 (2010): 428–41.

Brody, Richard. "Secondary Education and Political Attitudes: Examining the Effects on Political Tolerance of the 'We the People . . .' Curriculum." Calabasas, CA: Center for Civic Education, 1994.

Brooke, A. H., and Neil A. Harrison. "Neuroimaging and Emotion," in *Stress: Concepts, Cognition, Emotion, and Behavior. Handbook of Stress, Volume 1,* ed. George Fink, 251–59. New York: Elsevier, 2016.

Brookhart, Susan M. *How to Create and Use Rubrics for Formative Assessment and Grading.* Alexandria, VA: ASCD, 2013.

Brown, Phil, and Edwin J. Mikkelsen. *No Safe Place: Toxic Waste, Leukemia, and Community Action.* Berkeley: University of California Press, 1997.

Bugh, Gary. "Models of Civic Education in America," in *Civic Education in the Twenty-First Century: A Multidimensional Inquiry,* ed. Michael T. Rogers and Donald M. Gooch, 85–114. Lanham, MD: Lexington Books, 2015.

Busch, Elizabeth Kaufer, and Jonathan W. White. "Introduction," in *Civic Education and the Future of American Citizenship,* ed. Elizabeth Kaufer Busch and Jonathan W. White. Lanham, MD: Lexington Books, 2013.

California Campaign for the Civic Mission of Schools. *The California Survey of Civic Education.* Constitutional Rights Foundation, 2005. Accessed January 11, 2015. http://www.cms-ca.org/civic_survey_final.pdf.

Campaign for the Civic Mission of Schools. *Guardian of Democracy: The Civic Mission of Schools.* Pennsylvania: The Leonore Annenberg Institute for Civics of the Annenberg Public Policy Center at the University of Pennsylvania and the Campaign for the Civic Mission of Schools, 2011. Accessed January 11, 2015. http://www.cms-ca.org/guardianofdemocracy_report_final.pdf.

Campbell, Angus, Gerald Gurin, and Warren E. Miller. *The Voter Decides*. New York: Row, Peterson, and Company, 1954.

Campbell, David E. "Engagement among Adolescents." *Political Behavior* 30 (2008): 437–54.

Campbell, David E. "Introduction," in *Making Civics Count: Citizenship Education for a New Generation*, ed. David E. Campbell, Meira Levinson, and Frederick M. Hess, 1–13. Cambridge, MA: Harvard Education Press, 2012.

Campbell, David E. "Sticking Together: Classroom Diversity and Civic Education." *American Politics Research* 35 (2007): 57–78.

Campbell, David E. "Voice in the Classroom: How an Open Classroom Climate Fosters Political Engagement Among Adolescents." *Political Behavior* 30 (2008): 437–54.

Campbell, David E. *Voice in the Classroom: How an Open Classroom Environment Facilitates Adolescents' Civic Learning*. Maryland: CIRCLE Working Paper 28, The Center for Information and Research on Civic Learning and Engagement, 2005. Accessed January 11, 2015. http://files.eric.ed.gov/fulltext/ED491131.pdf.

Campbell, David E. *Why We Vote: How Schools And Communities Shape Our Civic Life*. Princeton, NJ: Princeton University Press, 2006.

"Campus Compact 30th Anniversary Action Statement of Presidents and Chancellors." *Campus Compact*. 2015. http://compact.org/actionstatement/.

"Campus Compact Overview." *Campus Compact*. 2016. http://compact.org/who-we-are/.

"Campus Compact: Who We Are." *Campus Compact*. Last modified 2016. http://www.compact.org/about/history-mission-vision/.

Carli, Linda L. "Gender Effects on Social Influence," in *Perspectives on Persuasion, Social Influence, and Compliance Gaining*, ed. John S. Seiter and R. H. Gass, 133–48. San Francisco: Jossey-Bass, 2004.

Carnegie Corporation of New York and CIRCLE. *The Civic Mission Of Schools*. New York: Carnegie Corporation of New York and CIRCLE, 2003.

Carter, Lief, and Jean Elshtain. "Task Force on Civic Education Statement of Purpose." *PS: Political Science & Politics* 30 (1997): 745.

Caviglia-Harris, Jill L., and James Hatley. "Interdisciplinary Teaching." *International Journal of Sustainability in Higher Education* 5 (2004): 395–403. doi:10.1108/14676370410561090.

Center for Teaching and Learning. "Problem-Based Learning." *Stanford University Newsletter on Teaching* 11 (2001): 1–7.

Chaiken, Shelly. "The Heuristic Model of Persuasion," in *Social Influence: The Ontario Symposium, Volume 5*, ed. Mark P. Zanna, James M. Olson, and C. Peter Herman, 13–39. Hillsdale, NJ: Lawrence Erlbaum Associates, 1987.

Champney, Leonard, and Paul Edleman. "Assessing Student Learning Outcomes in United States Government Courses." *PS: Political Science & Politics* 43 (2010): 127–31.

Charles, Jeffrey. A. *Service Clubs in American Society: Rotary, Kiwanis, and Lions*. Urbana: University of Illinois Press, 1993.

Checkoway, Barry. "Renewing the Civic Missions of the American Research University." *The Journal of Higher Education* 72 (2001): 125–47.

CIRCLE: The Center for Information & Research on Civic Learning & Engagement. *Understanding A Diverse Generation: Youth Civic Engagement in The United States*. Medford, MA: CIRCLE, 2011. http://www.civicyouth.org/wpcontent/uploads/2011/11/CIRCLE_cluster_report2010.pdf

Cohen, Cathy J., Joseph Kahne, Benjamin Bowyer, Ellen Middaugh, and Jon Rogowski. *Participatory Politics: New Media and Youth Political Action*. Report. New York: McArthur Foundation, 2012.

Cohen, Jacob. *Statistical Power Analysis for the Social Sciences*. Mahwah, NJ: Lawrence Erlbaum Associates, 1988.

Colby, Anne, Elizabeth Beaumont, Thomas Ehrlich, and John Corngold. *Educating for Democracy: Preparing Undergraduates for Responsible Political Engagement.* San Francisco: Jossey-Bass, 2007.

Colby, Anne, Thomas Ehrlich, Elizabeth Beaumont, and Jason Stephens. *Educating Citizens: Preparing America's Undergraduates for Lives of Moral and Civic Responsibility.* San Francisco: The Carnegie Foundation for the Advancement of Teaching, 2003.

Colby, Anne, and William Damon. *Some Do Care: Contemporary Lives of Moral Commitment.* New York: Free Press, 1992.

Colby, Anne, and William M. Sullivan, "Strengthening the Foundations of Student's Excellence, Integrity, and Social Contribution." *Liberal Education* 95 (2009): 22–29.

Cole, Bruce. "American Amnesia," in *Civic Education and the Future of American Citizenship,* ed. Elizabeth Kaufer Busch and Jonathan W. White, 67–77. Lanham, MD: Lexington Books, 2013.

Collins, Allan, and Richard Halverson. *Rethinking Education in the Age of Technology.* New York: Teachers College Press, 2009.

Conover, Pamela Johnson, and Donald D. Searing. "A Political Socialization Perpesctive," in *Rediscovering the Democratic Purposes of Education,* ed. Lorraine M. McDonnell, P. Michael Timpane, and Roger Benjamin, 91–124. Lawrence: University of Kansas Press, 2000.

Cortes, Alvaro. "Estimating the Impacts of Urban Universities on Neighborhood Housing Markets: An Empirical Analysis." *Urban Affairs Review* 39 (2004): 342–75.

Cramer, Katherine J. The Politics of Resentment: Rural Consciousness in Wisconsin and the Rise of Scott Walker. Chicago: University of Chicago, 2016.

"Creating a Great Campus Civic Action Plan." *Campus Compact.* 2016. http://compact.org/resource-posts/creating-a-great-campus-civic-action-plan/.

Crick, Bernard. *The American Science of Politics: Its Origins and Conditions.* Berkeley: University of California Press, 1967.

Crittenden, Jack, and Peter Levine. "Civic Education," in *Stanford Encyclopedia of Philosophy,* ed. Edward N. Zalta. Stanford, CA: Center for the Study of Language and Information, 2013.

Dahlgren, Peter. *Media and Political Engagement.* New York: Cambridge University Press, 2009.

Dalton, Russell J. *Citizen Politics: Public Opinion and Political Parties in Advanced Industrial Democracies,* sixth edition. Irvine, CA: CQ Press, 2013.

Dalton, Russell J. *The Good Citizen: How A Younger Generation Is Reshaping American Politics.* Washington, DC: CQ Press, 2008.

Dalton, Russell J. "The Good News Is, the Bad News Is Wrong: Another View of the Millennial Generation." *Extensions* (2015):10–15.

Damron, Danny, and Jonathan Mott. "Creating an Interactive Classroom: Enhancing Student Engagement and Learning in Political Science Courses." *Journal of Political Science Education* 1 (2005): 367–83. doi:10.1080/15512160500261228.

Danielson, Michael N. and Paul G. Lewis. "City Bound: Political Science and the American Metropolis." *Political Research Quarterly* 49 (1996): 203–20. doi:10.1177/106591299604900113.

Davis, James Earl. "College in Black and White: Campus Environment and Academic Achievement of African American Males." *Journal of Negro Education* 63 (1994): 620–33.

Davis, Robert. "Social Support Networks and Undergraduate Student Academic-Success-Related Outcomes: A Comparison of Black Students on Black and White Campuses," in *College in Black and White: African-American Students in Predominantly White and Historically Black Public Universities,* ed. Walter R. Allen, Edgar G. Epps, and Nesha Z. Hanniff, 143–60. Albany, NY: SUNY Press, 1991.

Delli Carpini, Michael. "An Overview of the State of Citizens' Knowledge About Politics," in *Communicating Politics: Engaging the Public in Democratic Life,* ed. Michael S. McKinney, Lynda L. Kaid, Dianne G. Bystrom, and Diana B. Carlin, 27–40. New York: Peter Lang, 2005.

Delli Carpini, Michael. "Civic Engagement." American Psychological Assocation, http://www.apa.org/education/undergrad/civic-engagement.aspx.

Delli Carpini, Michael, and Scott Keeter. *What Americans Know About Politics and Why It Matters*. New Haven, CT: Yale University Press, 1996.

Depillis, Lydia. "The GOP Can't Afford to Ignore Cities Anymore." *New Republic*. November 11, 2012. https://newrepublic.com/article/110074/republicans-cant-afford-ignore-cities-anymore.

Desilver, Drew. "How the Most Ideologically Polarized Americans Live Different Lives." *Pew Research Center*. Jun. 13, 2014. http://www.pewresearch.org/fact-tank/2014/06/13/big-houses-art-museums-and-in-laws-how-the-most-ideologically-polarized-americans-live-different-lives/.

Dewey, John. *Democracy and Education: An Introduction to the Philosophy of Education*. New York: Macmillan, 1916.

Dewey, John. *Experience and Education*. New York: Touchstone, 1938.

Dewoolkar, Mandar M., Lindsay George, Nancy J. Hayden, and Donna M. Rizzo, "Vertical Integration of Service Learning into Civil and Environmental Engineering Curricula." *International Journal of Engineering Education* 56 (2009): 1257–69.

Doran, George T. "There's a S.M.A.R.T. Way to Write Management's Goals and Objectives." *Management Review*, AMA FORUM 70 (1981): 35–36.

Dougherty, Chrys, Lynn Mellor, and Shuling Jian. 2006. *The Relationship Between Advanced Placement and College Graduation: 2005 AP Study Series, Report 1*. Austin, TX: National Center for Educational Accountability, 2006. Accessed January 5, 2015. http://eric.ed.gov/?id=ED519365.

Drury, Sarah A. Mehltretter. "Deliberation as Communication Instruction: A Study of Climate Change Deliberation in an Introductory Biology Course." *Journal on Excellence in College Teaching* 26 (2015): 51–72.

Drury, Sarah A. Mehltretter et al. "Using Deliberation of Energy Policy as an Educational Tool in a Nonmajors Chemistry Course." *Journal of Chemical Education* 93 (2016): 1879–85.

Dryzek, John S. "Revolutions without Enemies: Key Transformations in Political Science." *American Political Science Review* 100 (2006): 487–92.

Dubnick, Melvin J. "Nurturing Civic Lives: Developmental Perspectives on Civic Education: Introduction." *PS: Political Science & Politics* 36 (2003): 253–55.

Duggan, Maeve. "Demographics of Key Social Networking Platforms." Pew Research Center, Internet Science Technology, August 19, 2015. Accessed February 23, 2016, http://www.pewinternet.org/2015/08/19/the-demographics-of-social-media-users/.

Durlak, Joseph A. "How to Select, Calculate, and Interpret Effect Sizes." *Journal of Pediatric Psychology* 34 (2009): 917–28.

Edwards, Michael. *Civil Society*, third edition. Malden, MA: Polity Press, 2014.

Ehman, Lee H. "An Analysis of the Relationships of Selected Educational Variables with the Political Socialization of High School Students." *American Educational Research Journal* 6 (1969): 559–80.

Ehman, Lee H. "The American School in the Political Socialization Process." *Review of Educational Research* 50 (1980): 99–119.

Ehrlich, Thomas, ed. *Civic Responsibility and Higher Education*. Phoenix: The Oryx Press, 2000.

Ehrlich, Thomas. "Civic Education: Lessons Learned." *PS: Political Science & Politics* 32 (1999): 245–50.

Ekman, Joakimn, and Erik Amna. "Political Participation and Civic Engagement: Towards a New Typology." *Human Affairs* 22 (2012): 283–300.

Elejalde-Ruiz, Alexia. "Chicago Area's Poverty Rate Declined in 2015 as Incomes Rose." *Chicago Tribune*, Sept. 15, 2016. http://www.chicagotribune.com/business/ct-illinois-chicago-census-0915-biz-20160914-story.html.

Ellyson, Stephen L., John F. Dovidio, and Clifford E. Brown. "The Look of Power: Gender Differences in Visual Dominance Behavior," in *Gender, Interaction, and Inequality*, ed. C. L. Ridgeway, 50–80. New York: Springer-Verlag, 1992.

Emory Health Services. "How Estrogen Modulates Fear of Learning." January 18, 2017. Accessed January 24, 2017. https://www.sciencedaily.com/releases/2017/01/170118163708.htm.

Engberg, Mark E. and Sylvia Hurtado. "Developing Pluralistic Skills and Dispositions in College: Examining Racial/Ethnic Group Differences." *The Journal of Higher Education* 82 (2011): 416–43.

Eveland, William P., and Dietram A. Scheufele. "Connecting News Media Use With Gaps in Knowledge and Participation." *Political Communication* 17 (2000): 215–37.

Farmer, Paul. *Pathologies of Power: Health, Human Rights, and the New War on the Poor*. Berkeley: University of California Press, 2005.

Farr, James. "Social Capital: A Conceptual History." *Political Theory* 32 (2004): 6–33.

Farr, James. "The Science of Politics—as Civic Education—Then and Now." *PS: Political Science & Politics* 37 (2004): 37–40.

Fereday, Jennifer, and Eimear Muir-Cochrane. "Demonstrating Rigor Using Thematic Analysis: A Hybrid Approach of Inductive and Deductive Coding and Theme Development." *International Journal of Qualitative Methods* 5 (2006): 80–92.

Fine, Ben. "Eleven Hypotheses on the Conceptual History of Social Capital: A Response to James Farr." *Political Theory* 35 (2007): 47–53.

Fink, L. Dee. *Creating Significant Learning Experiences: An Integrated Approach to Designing College Courses*. San Francisco: John Wiley & Sons, Inc., 2003.

Finkel, Steven E. "Can Democracy be Taught?" *Journal of Democracy* 14 (2003):137–51

Finkel, Steven E., and Howard R. Ernst. "Civic Education in Post-Apartheid South Africa: Alternative Paths to the Development of Political Knowledge and Democratic Values." *Political Psychology* 26 (2005): 333–64.

Fiorina, Morris P. "Extreme Voices: A Dark Side of Civic Engagement," in *Civic Engagement in American Democracy*, ed. Theda Skocpol and Morris P. Fiorina, 395–425. Washington DC: Brookings Institution Press, 1999.

Fischer, Mary J. "Settling into Campus Life: Differences by Race/Ethnicity in College Involvement and Outcomes." *Journal of Higher Education* 78 (2007): 125–61.

Fitzgerald, Hiram E., Angela Allen, and Peggy Roberts. "Campus-Community Partnerships: Perspectives on Engaged Scholarship," in *Handbook of Engaged Scholarship: Contemporary Landscapes, Future Directions: Volume 2: Community-Campus Partnerships*, ed. Hiram E. Fitzgerald, Cathy Burack, and Sarena D. Seifer, 5–28. East Lansing, MI: Michigan State University Press, 2010.

Florida, Richard. "America's Most Sprawling Cities Are Also the Most Republican." *CityLab*. April 10, 2014. http://www.citylab.com/work/2014/04/americas-most-sprawling-cities-are-also-most-republican/8832/.

Forren, John P., and Theresa Conover. *Ohio Civic Health Index Report*. Washington, DC: National Conference on Citizenship, 2016.

Foubert, John D., and Lauren A. Urbanski. "Effects of Involvement in Clubs and Organizations on the Psychosocial Development of First-Year and Senior College Students." *NASPA Journal* 43 (2006), 166–81.

Fraile, Marta. "Do Women Know Less About Politics Than Men? The Gender Gap in Political Knowledge in Europe." *Social Politics: International Studies in Gender, State & Society* 21 (2014): 261–89.

Frazer, Elizabeth, and Kenneth Macdonald. "Sex Differences in Political Knowledge in Britain." *Political Studies* 51 (2003): 67–83.

Freire, Paulo. *Pedagogy of Freedom: Ethics, Democracy, and Civic Courage.* Lanham, MD: Rowman & Littlefield, 1998.

Freire, Paulo. *Pedagogy of the Oppressed.* New York: Seabury Press, 1970.

Frey, William H. "Census Shows Modest Declines in Black-White Segregation." Washington, DC: Brookings Institution, December 8, 2015. https://www.brookings.edu/blog/the-avenue/2015/12/08/census-shows-modest-declines-in-black-white-segregation/.

Friedman, Jeffrey, and Shterna Friedman, eds. *Political Knowledge.* New York: Routledge, 2013.

Gabelnick, Faith, Jean MacGregor, Roberta S. Matthews, and Barbara Leigh Smith. *Learning Communities.* San Francisco: Jossey-Bass, 1990.

Gainous, Jason, and Allison M. Martens. "The Effectiveness of Civic Education: Are 'Good' Teachers Actually Good for 'All' Students?" *American Politics Research* 40 (2012): 232–66.

Galston, William A. "Civic Education and Political Participation." *PS: Political Science & Politics* 37 (2004): 263–66.

Galston, William A. "Civic Knowlege, Civic Education, and Civic Engagement: A Summary of Recent Research." *International Journal of Public Administration* 30 (2007): 623–42.

Galston, William A. "Political Knowledge, Political Engagement, and Civic Education." *Annual Review of Political Science 4* (2001): 217–34.

Galston, William A., and Mark H. Lopez. "Civic Education in the United States," in *Civic Engagement and the Baby Boomer Generation,* ed. Laura B. Wilson and Sharon P. Simson, 3–19. New York: The Haworth Press, 2006.

Gamio, Lazaro, and Dan Keating. "How Trump Redrew the Electoral Map, from Sea to Shining Sea." *Washington Post.* November 9, 2016. https://www.washingtonpost.com/graphics/politics/2016-election/election-results-from-coast-to-coast/.

Gao, Fei, Tian Luo, and Ken Zhang. "Tweeting for Learning: A Critical Analysis of Research on Microblogging in Education published in 2008–2011." *British Journal of Educational Technology* 43 (2012): 783–801.

Gardy, Jennifer, and Fiona Brinkman. "The Benefits of Interdisciplinary Research: Our Experience with Pathogen Bioinformatics." *Science.* January 17, 2003 http://www.sciencemag.org/careers/2003/01/benefits-interdisciplinary-research-our-experience-pathogen-bioinformatics.

Garson, G. David. *Testing Statistical Assumptions.* Asheboro, NC: Statistical Association Publishing, 2012. http://www.statisticalassociates.com/assumptions.pdf.

Gaston, Paul L. *General Education Transformed: How We Can, Why We Must.* Washington, DC: Association of American Colleges and Universities, 2015.

Gauna, Becci Burchett, and Michelle Paul. "Civic Education Training Promotes Active Learning with Real-world Outcomes." *SPACE: Student Perspectives About Civic Engagement.* 2 (2016), Article 4. http://digitalcommons.nl.edu/space/vol2/iss1/4.

Gelmon, Sherril, Barbara Holland, Amy Driscoll, Amy Spring, and Seanna Kerrigan. *Assessing Service-Learning And Civic Engagement: Principles And Techniques.* Providence RI: Campus Compact, Brown University, 2001.

Gerometta, Julia, Hartmut Häussermann, and Giulia Longo. "Social Innovation and Civil Society in Urban Governance: Strategies for an Inclusive City." *Urban Studies* 42 (2005): 2007–2021. doi:10.1080/00420980500279851.

Gerson, Matthew. "Small Liberal Arts Colleges Lack Diversity." *The Baltimore Sun.* Oct. 24, 2014. http://www.baltimoresun.com/news/opinion/oped/bs-ed-liberal-arts-diversity-20141026-story.html.

Gieryn, Thomas F. "City as Truth-Spot: Laboratories and Field-Sites in Urban Studies." *Social Studies of Science* 36 (2006): 5–38. doi:10.1177/0306312705054526.

Gil de Zúñiga, Homero, Aaron Veenstra, Emily Vraga, and Dhavan Shah. "Digital Democracy: Reimagining Pathways to Political Participation." *Journal of Information Technology & Politics* 7 (2010): 36–51.

Glassick, Charles E., Mary Taylor Huber, and Gene I. Maeroff. *Scholarship Assessed: Evaluation of the Professoriate*. San Francisco, CA: Jossey-Bass Inc., 1997.

Glesne, Corrine, and Alan Peshkin. *Becoming Qualitative Researchers*. White Plains, NY: Longman, 1992.

Glick, Peter, and Susan T. Fiske. "An Ambivalent Alliance: Hostile and Benevolent Sexism as Complementary Justifications for Gender Inequality." *American Psychologist* 56 (2001): 109–118.

Goldbard, Arlene. "Arguments for Cultural Democracy and Community Cultural Development." Grantmakers in the Arts, 2009. http://www.giarts.org/article/arguments-cultural-democracy-and-community-cultural-development.

Goodnight, G. Thomas, Minhee Son, Jin Huang, and Ann Crigler. "Youth, Networks & Civic Engagement: Communities of Belonging and Communities of Practice," in *Speech and Debate as Civic Education*, ed. J. Michael Hogan et al. University Park, PA: Pennsylvania State University Press, (forthcoming).

Gooch, Donald M. "Conclusion: The Dimensions of Civic Education in the Twenty-First Century," in *Civic Education in the Twenty-First Century: A Multidimensional Inquiry*, ed. Michael T. Rogers and Donald M. Gooch. Lanham, MD: Lexington Books, 2015.

Gooch, Donald M., and Michael T. Rogers. "A Natural Disaster of Civic Proportions: College Students in the Natural State Falls Short of the Naturalization Benchmark." *Midsouth Political Science Review* 13 (2012): 54–82.

Gooch, Donald M., and Michael T. Rogers. "Dude, Where's the Civic Engagement? The Paradoxical Effect of Civic Educaon on the Probablity of Civic Participation," in *Civic Education in the Twenty-First Century: A Multidimensional Approach*, ed. Michael T. Rogers and Donald M. Gooch, 293–344. Lanham, MD: Lexington Books, 2015.

Graff, Gerald. *Clueless in Academe: How Schooling Obscures the Life of the Mind*. New Haven, CT: Yale University Press, 2004.

Graham, Bob, and Chris Hand. "A Failure of Leadership: The Duty of Politicians and Universities to Salvage Citizenship," in *Teaching America: The Case for Civic Education*, ed. David Feith, 61–68. Lanham, MD: Rowman & Littlefield Education, 2011.

Graham, Bob, and Chris Hand. *America, the Owner's Manual: Making Government Work for You*. Washington, DC: CQ Press, 2010.

Graham, David A. "Red State, Blue City." *CityLab*. Feb. 2, 2017. http://www.citylab.com/politics/2017/02/red-state-blue-city/515514/?utm_source=SFTwitter.

Guetzkow, Joshua. "How the Arts Impact Communities: An introduction to the Literature on Arts Impact Studies." Presented at *Taking the Measure of Culture Conference*. Princeton University, 2002.

Gunnell, John G. "Political Science on the Cusp: Recovering a Discipline's Past." *The American Political Science Review* 99 (2005): 597–609.

Gunnell, John G. "The Founding of the American Political Science Association: Discipline, Profession, Political Theory, and Politics." *American Political Science Review* 100 (2006): 479–86.

Gunnell, John G. "The Real Revolution in Political Science." *PS: Political Science & Politics* 37 (2004): 47–50.

Gurin, Patricia. "Women's Gender Consciousness." *Public Opinion Quarterly* 49 (1985): 143–63.

Gutmann, Amy. *Democratic Education*. Princeton, NJ: Princeton University Press, 1999.

Hallahan, Kirk. "Enhancing Motivation, Opportunity, and Ability to Process Public Relations Messages." *Public Relations Review* 26 (2000): 463–80.

Hamilton, Edith, and Cairns Huntington, eds. *Plato: The Collected Dialogues*. LXXI ed. Vol. LXXI, Bollingen Series. Princeton, NJ: Princeton University Press, 1961.

Hartley, Matthew. "Idealism and Compromise and the Civic Engagement Movement," in *To Serve a Larger Purpose: Engagement for Democracy and the Transformation of Higher Education*, ed. John Saltmarsh and Matthew Hartley. Philadelphia: Temple University Press, 2011.

Harward, Brian M., and Daniel M. Shea. "Higher Education and the Multiple Modes of Engagement," in *Teaching Civic Engagement: From Student to Active Citizen*, ed. Alison Rios Millett McCartney, Elizabeth A. Bennion, and Dick Simpson, 21–40. Washington, DC: American Political Science Association, 2013.

Hatcher, Julie A. "Assessing Civic Knowledge and Engagement." *New Directions for Institutional Research* 149 (2011): 81–92.

Hausknecht, Murray. *The Joiners: A Sociological Description of Voluntary Association Membership in the United States*. New York: Bedminster Press, 1962.

Henthorn, Thomas C. "Experiencing the City: Experiential Learning in Urban Environments." *Journal of Urban History* 40 (2014): 450–61.

Hepburn, Mary A. "Improving Political Science Education in the Schools: College School Connections." *PS: Political Science & Politics* 20 (1987): 691–97.

Hess, Diana E., and Paula McAvoy. *The Political Classroom*. New York: Routledge, 2015.

Hess, Diana. *Controversy in the Classroom: The Democratic Power of Discussion*. New York: Routledge, 2009.

Hickok, Eugene. "Civic Literacy and No Child Left Behind," in *Teaching America: The Case for Civic Education*, ed. David Feith, 51–60. Lanham, MD: Rowman & Littlefield Education, 2011.

Higher Education Research Institute. "College Freshmen and Online Social Networking Sites." *Higher Education Research Institute Research Brief*. September 2007.

Hill, Laura Griner, and Drew L. Betz. "Revising the Retrospective Pretest." *American Journal of Evaluation* 26 (2005): 501–17.

Hilmer, Jeffrey D. "The Irony of Civic Education in the United States," in *Civic Education in the Twenty-First Century: A Multidimensional Inquiry*, ed. Michael T. Rogers and Donald M. Gooch, 61–84. Lanham, MD: Lexington Books, 2015.

HistorySOTL. "About the Society." HistorySoTL, http://www.indiana.edu/~histsotl/blog/?page_id=6.

Holmes, Janet. *Women, Men and Politeness*. New York: Longman, 1995.

Hood, Albert B. *Student Development: Does Participation Affect Growth?* Bloomington, IN: Association of College Unions International, 1984.

Hopkins, Nick. "Religion and Social Capital: Identity Matters." *Journal of Community & Applied Social Psychology* 21 (2011): 528–40.

Hotchkiss, Julie L., Robert E. Moore, and M. Melinda Pitts. "Freshmen Learning Communities, College Performance, and Retention." *Education Economics* 14 (2006): 197–210.

Howard, Amy L. "Engaging the City: Civic Participation and Teaching Urban History." *Journal of Urban History* 36 (2010): 42–55. doi:10.1177/0096144209349883.

Howe, Carrie Williams, Kimberly Coleman, Kelly Hamshaw, and Katherine Westdijk. "Student Development and Service-Learning: A Three-Phased Model for Course Design." *The International Journal of Research on Service-Learning and Community Engagement* (2014): 44–62.

Huang, Ya Rong, and Sheue-Mei Chang, S. "Academic and Co-Curricular Involvement: Their Relationship and the Best Combinations for Student Growth." *Journal of College Student Development* 45 (2004): 391–406.

Hunter, Susan, and Richard A. Brisbin, Jr. "Civic Education and Political Science: A Survey of Practices." *PS: Political Science & Politics* 36 (2003): 759–63.

Hurtado, Sylvia, Mark E. Engberg, Luis Ponjuan, and Lisa Landreman. "Students' Precollege Preparation for Participation in a Diverse Democracy." *Research in Higher Education* 43 (2002): 163–86. doi:10.1023/A:1014467607253.

Ichilov, Orit. "Civic Knowledge of High School Students in Israel: Personal and Contextual Determinants." *Political Psychology* 28 (2007): 417–40.

Illinois Board of Higher Education. "Table 1–3: *Race Or National Origin Of Students Enrolled in Illinois Colleges and Universities by Type of Institution, Fall 2010*." 2010. http://www.ibhe.state.il.us/Data%20Bank/DataBook/2011/Table%20I-3.pdf.

Ingvarson, Lawrence, Marion Meiers, and Adrian Beavis. "Factors Affecting the Impact of Professional Development Programs on Teachers' Knowledge, Practice, Student Outcomes & Efficacy." Research Report. Australian Council for Educational Research, 2005. Accessed January 11, 2015. http://research.acer.edu.au/professional_dev/1.

Inkelas, Karen Kurotsuchi, Zaneeta E Daver, Kristen E. Vogt, and Jeannie Brown. "Living-Learning Programs and First-Generation College Students' Academic and Social Transition to College." *Research in Higher Education* 48 (2007): 403–34.

Ishiyama, John, Marijke Breuning, and Linda Lopez. "A Century of Continuity and (Little) Change in the Undergraduate Political Science Curriculum." *American Political Science Review* 100 (2006): 659–65.

ISI. *Failing Our Students, Failing America: Holding Colleges Accountable for Teaching America's History and Institutions.* Wilmington, DE: Intercollegiate Studies Institute's National Civic Literacy Board, 2007.

ISI. *Our Fading Heritage: Americans Fail a Basic Test on Their History and Institutions.* Wilmington, DE: Intercollegiate Studies Institute's National Civic Literacy Board, 2008.

ISI. *The Coming Crisis in Citizenship.* Willimington, DE: Intercollegiate Studies Institute's National Civic Literacy Board, 2006.

Iyengar, Shanto, and Sean J. Westwood. "Fear and Loathing Across Party Lines: New Evidence on Group Polarization." *American Journal of Political Science* 59 (2015): 690–707. doi:10.1111/ajps.12152.

Jackson, Kenneth W., and L. Alex Swan. "Institutional and Individual Factors Affecting Black Undergraduate Student Performance: Campus Race and Student Gender," in *College in Black and White: African-American Students in Predominantly White and Historically Black Public Universities,* ed. Walter R. Allen, Edgar G. Epps, and Nesha Z. Hanniff. Albany, NY: SUNY Press, 1991.

Jacobs, Jerry A. *In Defense of Disciplines: Interdisciplinarity and Specialization in the Research University.* Chicago: The University of Chicago Press, 2014.

Jacobs, Lawrence. R., Fay Lomax Cook, and Michael X. Delli Carpini. *Talking Together: Public Deliberation and Political Participation in America.* Chicago: The University of Chicago Press, 2009.

Jacobsen, Rebecca, Erica Frankenberg, and Sarah Winchell Lenhoff. "Diverse Schools in a Democractic Soceity: New Ways of Understanding How School Demographics Affect Civic and Political Learning." *American Educational Research Journal* 49 (2012): 812–43.

Jacoby, Barbara, ed. *Civic Engagement in Higher Education: Concepts and Practices.* San Francisco: Jossey-Bass, 2009.

Jacoby, Barbara, et al. *Building Partnerships for Service-Learning.* New York: Jossey-Bass, 2003.

Jacoby, Barbara. *Service-Learning Essentials: Questions, Answers, and Lessons Learned.* San Francisco: John Wiley & Sons, 2015.

Jamieson, Kathleen Hall. "The Challenges Facing Civic Education in the 21st Century." *Daedalius* 142 (2013): 65–83.

Jenkins, Henry. *Confronting the Challenges of Participatory Culture.* Cambridge, MA: MIT Press, 2009.

Jenkins, J. S. "The Mozart Effect." *Journal of the Royal Society of Medicine* 24 (2001): 170–72.

Jenkins, Shannon. "Using Best Practices Research and Experience with Local Governments to Increase Political Engagement," in *Teaching Civic Engagement: From Student to Active Citizen,* ed. Alison Rios Millett McCartney, Elizabeth A. Bennion, and Dick Simpson. Washington, DC: American Political Science Association, 2013.

Johnson, Allen G. *The Gender Knot: Unraveling Our Patriarchal Legacy,* third edition. Philadelphia: Temple University Press, 2014.

Johnson-Hakim, Sharon M., Chris M. Kirk, Rochelle L. Rowley, Ashlee D. Lien, Justin P. Greenleaf, and Charles A. Burdsal. "Exploring Civic Engagement at an Urban Commuter Campus: Pathways and Barriers." *Journal of Prevention & Intervention in the Community* 41

(2013): 279–90. doi:10.1080/10852352.2013.818493.

Jones, Stephanie M., and Suzanne M. Bouffard. "Social and Emotional Learning in Schools: From Programs to Strategies." *Social Policy Report* 26 (2012): 3–22. http://www.srcd.org/sites/default/files/documents/spr_264_final_2.pdf.

Jones, Stephanie M., Suzanne M. Bouffard, and Richard Weissbourd. "Educators' Social and Emotional Skills Vital to Learning." *Phi Delta Kappan*, 94 (2013): 62–65. https://doi.org/10.1177/003172171309400815.

Jordan, Barbara. "Harvard University Commencement Address, June 16." The Barbara Jordan Forum. 2011. http://www.utexas.edu/lbj/barbarajordanforum/quotes.php.

Judd, Dennis. "Everything Is Always Going to Hell: Urban Scholars as End-Times Prophets." *Urban Affairs Review* 41 (2005): 119–31. doi:10.1177/1078087405280197.

Junco, Rey, Greg Heiberger, and Eric Loken. "The Effect of Twitter on College Student Engagement and Grades." *Journal of Computer Assisted Learning* 27 (2011): 119–32.

Kahne, Joseph, and Ellen Middaugh. "Democracy for Some: The Civic Opportunity Gap in High Schools." CIRCLE Working Paper 59: February 2008. Accessed August 6, 2011. http://www.civicyouth.org/PopUps/WorkingPapers/WP59Kahne.pdf.

Kahne, Joseph, and Ellen Middaugh. "Digital Media Shapes Youth Participation in Politics." *Phi Delta Kappan* 94 (2012): 52–56.

Kahne, Joseph, and Ellen Middaugh. "High Quality Civic Education: What Is It and Who Gets It?" *Social Education* 72 (2008): 34–39.

Kahne, Joseph, Ellen Middaugh, and Chris Evans. *The Civic Potential of Video Games.* Boston: MIT Press, 2009.

Kahne, Joseph, Nam-Jin Lee, and Jessica Timpany Feezell. "Digital Media Literacy Education and Online Civic and Political Participation." *International Journal of Communication* 6 (2012): 1–24.

Kann, Mark E. *The Gendering of American Politics: Founding Mothers, Founding Fathers, and Political Patriarchy.* Westport, CT: Greenwood, 1999.

Karpowitz, Christopher F., and Chad Raphael. *Deliberation, Democracy, and Civic Forums: Improving Equality and Publicity.* New York: Cambridge University Press, 2014.

Karpowitz, Christopher F., and Tali Mendelberg. *The Silent Sex: Gender, Deliberation and Institutions.* Princeton, NJ: Princeton University Press, 2014.

Katz, Bruce, and Jennifer Bradley. *The Metropolitan Revolution: How Cities and Metros are Fixing Our Broken Politics and Fragile Economy.* Washington, DC: Brookings Institution Press, 2015.

Kaufman, Jason. *For the Common Good? American Civil Life and the Golden Age of Fraternity.* New York: Oxford University Press, 2003.

Kedrowski, Karen. "Civic Education by Mandate: A State-by-State Analysis." *PS: Political Science and Politics* 36 (2003): 225–27.

Keen, Cheryl. "Measuring Dialogue Across Difference as a Civic Skill." *Journal of College and Character* 11 (2010): 1–8.

Keen, Cheryl, and Kelly Hall. "Post-Graduation Service and Civic Outcomes for High Financial Need Students of a Multi-Campus, Co-Curricular Service-Learning College Program." *Journal of College and Character* 10 (2008), 1–15.

Kenski, Kate, and Kathleen Hall Jamieson. "The Gender Gap in Political Knowledge: Are Women Less Knowledgeable Than Men About Politics," in *Everything You Think You Know About Politics... and Why You're Wrong,* ed. Kathleen Hall Jamieson, 83–89. New York: Basic Books, 2000.

Kenski, Kate, and Natalie Johmini Stroud. "Connections Between Internet Use and Political Efficacy, Knowledge, and Participation." *Journal of Broadcasting & Electronic Media* 50 (2006):173–92.

Kernahan, Cyndi, and Tricia Davis. "What are the Long-Term Effects of Learning about Racism?" *Teaching of Psychology* 37 (2010): 41–5. doi:10.1080/00986280903425748.

Kidder, Tracy. *Mountains Beyond Mountains: The Quest of Dr. Paul Farmer, a Man Who Would Cure the World.* New York: Random House, 2004.

Kirlin, Mary. "The Role of Civic Skills in Fostering Civic Engagement." CIRCLE Working Paper 6. Center for Information and Research on Civic Learning and Engagement, University of Maryland, 2003.

Klofstadt, Casey A., ed. *New Advances in the Study of Civic Voluntarism: Resources, Engagement, and Recruitment.* Philadelphia: Temple University Press, 2016.

Klopfenstein, Kristin, and M. Kathleen Thomas. *The Advanced Placement Performance Advantage: Fact or Fiction?* Texas: University of Texas at Dallas Schools Project, 2005. Accessed January 11, 2005. https://www.aeaweb.org/assa/2005/0108_1015_0302.pdf.

Knefelkamp, Lee L. "Civic Identity: Locating Self in Community." *Diversity & Democracy* 11(2008): 1–3.

Kolko, Jed. "2015 U.S. Population Winners: The Suburbs and the Sunbelt." *Citylab.* March 25, 2016. http://www.citylab.com/housing/2016/03/2015-us-population-winners-the-suburbs-and-the-sunbelt/475251/.

Kolko, Jed. "How Suburban are Big American Cities?" *FiveThirtyEight.* May 21, 2016. https://fivethirtyeight.com/features/how-suburban-are-big-american-cities.

Kolowich, Steve. "Blasting Academic Silos." *Inside Higher Ed.* 2010. Accessed on January 12, 2017. https://www.insidehighered.com/news/2010/01/18/silos.

Korten, David. *Globalizing Civil Society: Reclaiming Our Right to Power.* New York: Seven Stories Press, 1998.

Kretchmar, Jennifer. "Problem-Based Learning." *Research Starters Education* (2015): n.p.

Krislov, Marvin. "The Enduring Relevance of a Liberal-Arts Education." *The Hechinger Report.* December 5, 2013. http://hechingerreport.org/the-enduring-relevance-of-a-liberal-arts-education/.

Kuh, George. D. *High Impact Learning Practices: What They Are, Who Has Access To Them, And Why They Matter.* Washington, DC: Association of American Colleges and Universities, 2008.

Kuh, George D. "The Other Curriculum: Out-of-Class Experiences Associated with Student Learning and Personal Development." *The Journal of Higher Education* 66 (1995): 123–55.

Kuh, George D., and Paul D. Umbach. "College and Character: Insights from the National Survey of Student Engagement." *New Directions for Institutional Research*, 112 (2004): 37–54.

Kuh, George D., Jill Kinzie, John H. Schuh, and Elizabeth J. Whitt, eds. *Student Success in College: Creating Conditions That Matter.* San Francisco: Jossey-Bass, 2005.

Kuh, George D., John H. Schuh, and Elizabeth J. Whitt. *Involving Colleges: Successful Approaches To Fostering Student Learning And Personal Development Outside Of The Classroom.* San Francisco: Jossey-Bass, 1991.

Kulkarni, Tara. "Service-Learning Projects in Environmental Engineering Courses: Models of Community Engagement Activities." American Society for Engineering Education Zone 1 Conference, 2014.

Lakoff, Robin T. *Language and Women's Place.* New York: Harper & Row, 1975.

Lakoff, Robin T. *Talking Power.* New York: Basic Books, 1990.

Lamb, Theodore. "The Retrospective Pretest: An Imperfect But Useful Tool." *The Evaluation Exchange* 11 (2005): 18.

Lane, David M. *Online Statistics Education: An Interactive Multimedia Course of Study.* Houston, TX: Rice University, 2016. http://onlinestatbook.com/2/effect_size/two_means.html.

Lang, Robert E., and Thomas W. Sanchez. "The New Metro Politics: Interpreting Recent Presidential Elections Using a County-Based Regional Typology." *Metropolitan Institute 2006 Election Brief.* Blacksburg, VA: Metropolitan Institute, 2006.

Langton, K., and M. K. Jennings. "Political Socialization and the High School Civics Curriculum in the United States." *American Political Science Review* 62 (1968): 862–67.

Larimer, Christopher, and Karen M. Hempson. "Using Deliberation in the Classroom: A Teaching Pedagogy to Enhance Student Knowledge, Opinion Formation, and Civic Engagement." *Journal of Political Science Education* 8 (2012): 372–88.

Lawless, Jennifer. L., and Richard L. Fox. *Men Rule: The Continued Under-Representation of Women in US Politics*. Washington, DC: Women & Politics Institute, 2012.

Lawless, Jennifer L., and Richard L. Fox. *Not a "Year of the Woman" … and 2036 Doesn't Look So Good Either*. Washington, DC: Brookings Institute, 2014.

Lee, Jasmine C., and Kevin Quealy. "The 305 People, Places, and Things Donald Trump Has Insulted on Twitter: A Complete List." January 20, 2017. Accessed January 26, 2017. https://www.nytimes.com/interactive/2016/01/28/upshot/donald-trump-twitter-insults.html.

Lei, Pui-Wa, Dina Bassiri, and E. Matthew Schultz. *Alternatives to the Grade Point Average of Academic Achievement in College*. ACT Research Report Series No. 2001–4. Iowa City, IA: ACT, Inc., 2001.

Leming, Robert. *We the People...The Citizen and the Constitution*. Calabasas, CA: The Center for Civic Education, 1996.

Leonard, Stephen T. "'Pure Futility and Waste': Academic Political Science and Civic Education." *PS: Political Science & Politics* 32 (1999): 749–54.

Lerner, Richard M., and Peter L. Benson. *Developmental Assets and Asset-Building Communities: Implications for Research, Policy, and Practice*. New York: Kluwer Academic/Plenum Publishers, 2003.

Leroux, Kelly, and Anna Bernadska. "Impact of the Arts on Individual Contributions to US Civil Society." *Journal of Civil Society* 10 (2014): 144–64.

Levi, Margaret. "Social and Unsocial Capital: Review of *Making Democracy Work*." *Politics and Society* 24 (1996): 45–55.

Levine, Arthur, and Jeanette S. Cureton. *When Hope and Fear Collide: A Portrait of Today's College Student*. San Francisco: Jossey-Bass, 1998.

Levine, Peter. "A Public Voice for Youth: The Audience Problem in Digital Media and Civic Education," in *Civic Life Online: Learning How Digital Media Can Engage Youth*, ed. W. Lance Bennett, 119–38. Cambridge, MA: MIT Press, 2008.

Levine, Peter. "Education for a Civil Society," in *Making Civics Count: Citizenship Education for a New Generation*, ed. David E. Campbell, Meira Levinson, and Frederick M. Hess, 37–56. Cambridge, MA: Harvard Education Press, 2012.

Levine, Peter. *The Future of Democracy: Developing the Next Generation of American Citizens*. Lebanon, NH: Tufts University Press, 2007.

Levinson, Meira. *No Citizen Left Behind*. Cambridge, MA: Harvard University Press, 2012.

Levinson, Meira. "The Civic Empowerment Gap: Defining the Problem and Locating Solutions," in *Handbook of Research on Civic Engagement in Youth*, ed. Lonnie Sherrod, Judith Torney-Purta, and Constance A. Flanagan. Hoboken, NJ: John Wiley and Sons, 2010.

Levy, Dena, and Susan Orr. "Balancing the Books: Analyzing the Impact of a Federal Budget Deliberative Simulation on Student Learning and Opinion." *Journal of Political Science Education* 10 (2014): 62–80.

Lewis, Ferdinand. "A Working Guide to the Landscape of Arts for Change." Animating Democracy. 2013. http://animatingdemocracy.org/resource/participatory-art-making-and-civic-engagement.

Lizotte, Mary-Kate, and Andrew H. Sidman. "Explaining the Gender Gap in Political Knowledge." *Politics & Gender* 5 (2009): 127–51.

Loeb, Paul Rogat. *Soul of a Citizen: Living with Conviction in Challenging Times*, New and Revised Edition. New York: St. Martin's Press, 2010.

Longo, Nicholas V. "Deliberative Pedagogy in the Community: Connecting Deliberative

Dialogue, Community Engagement, and Democratic Education." *Journal of Public Deliberation* 9 (2013): 1–18.

Longo, Nicholas V., and Marguerite S. Shaffer. "Leadership Education and the Revitalization of Public Life," in *Civic Engagement in Higher Education: Concepts and Practices*, ed. Barbara Jacoby, 154–73. San Francisco: Jossey-Bass, 2009.

Longo, Nicholos V., and Ross P. Meyer. "College Students and Politics: A Literature Review." College Park, MD: The Center for Information and Research in Civic Learning and Engagement, 2006.

Lorenzi, Michelle. "From Active Service to Civic and Political Engagement: Fighting the Problem of Poverty," in *Teaching Civic Engagement: From Student to Active Citizen*, ed. Alison Rios Millett McCartney, Elizabeth A. Bennion, and Dick Simpson. Washington, DC: American Political Science Association, 2013.

Lucas, Nance. "The Influence of Integrative and Interdisciplinary Learning on Civic Engagement," in *Civic Engagement in Higher Education: Concepts and Practices*, ed. Barbara Jacoby, 99–116. San Francisco: Jossey-Bass, 2009.

Luhby, Tami. "Chicago: America's Most Segregated City." *CNN Money*, January 5, 2016. http://money.cnn.com/2016/01/05/news/economy/chicago-segregated/.

Luskin, Robert C., and John G. Bullock. "'Don't Know' Means 'Don't Know': DK Responses and the Public's Level of Political Knowledge." *The Journal of Politics* 73 (2011): 547–57.

Macedo, Stephen, et al. *Democracy at Risk: How Political Choices Undermine Citizen Participation, and What We Can Do About It*. Washington, DC: Brookings Institution Press, 2005.

MacGregor, Jean, and Barbara Leigh Smith. "Where Are Learning Communities Now? National Leaders Take Stock." *About Campus* May–June (2005): 2–8.

MacInnis, Deborah J., Christine M. Moorman, and Bernard J. Jaworski. "Enhancing and Measuring Consumers' Motivation, Opportunity, and Ability to Process Brand Information from Ads." *Journal of Marketing* 55 (1991): 32–53.

Malin, Heather. "America as a Philosophy: Implications for the Development of American Identity Among Today's Youth." *Applied Development Science* 15 (2011): 54–60.

Mann, Sheilah. "Political Scientists Examine Civics Standards: An Introduction." *PS: Political Science & Politics* 29 (1996): 47–49.

Maranto, Robert. "It Can Work: The Surprisingly Positive Prospects for Effective Civic Education," in *Civic Education in the Twenty-First Century: A Multidimensional Inquiry*, ed. Michael T. Rogers and Donald M. Gooch, 43–60. Lanham, MD: Lexington Books, 2015.

Mattern, Krista D., Emily J. Shaw, and Jessica Marini. *Are AP Students More Likely to Graduate from College on Time?* New York: The College Board, 2013. Accessed January 5, 2015. http://research.collegeboard.org/publications/are-ap-students-more-likely-graduate-college-time.

Maurrasse, David J. *Beyond the Campus: How Colleges and Universities Form Partnerships with Their Communities*. New York: Routledge, 2001.

Maxwell, Joseph. *Qualitative Research Design: An Interactive Approach*. Thousand Oaks, CA: Sage Publications, 2012.

Mayo, Henry. B. *An Introduction to Democratic Theory*. New York: Oxford University Press, 1960.

McCartney, Alison Rios Millett. "Introduction: Higher Education, Civic Engagement Pedagogy, and Political Science Education," in *Teaching Civic Engagement: From Student to Active Citizen*, ed. Alison Rios Millett McCartney, Elizabeth A. Bennion, and Dick Simpson. Washington, DC: American Political Science Association, 2013.

McCartney, Alison Rios Millett. "Teaching Civic Engagement: Debates, Definitions, Benefits, and Challenges," in *Teaching Civic Engagement: From Student to Active Citizen*, ed. Alison Rios Millett McCartney, Elizabeth A. Bennion, and Dick Simpson. Washington, DC: American Political Science Association, 2013.

McCartney, Alison Rios Millett, Elizabeth A. Bennion, and Dick Simpson, eds. *Teaching Civic Engagement: From Student to Active Citizen.* Washington, DC: American Political Science Association, 2013.

McCarty, Nolan, Keith T. Poole, and Howard Rosenthal. *Political Bubbles: Financial Crises and the Failure of American Democracy.* Princeton, NJ: Princeton University Press, 2003.

McCauley, David. "The Impact of Advanced Placement and Dual Enrollment Programs on College Graduation," Applied Research Projects, Texas State University-San Marcos, 2007. Accessed January 5, 2015. https://digital.library.txstate.edu/handle/10877/3597.

McClay, Wilfred M. "Memory and Sacrifice in the Formation of Civic Consciousness," in *Civic Education and the Future of American Citizenship*, ed. Elizabeth Kaufer Busch and Jonathan W. White, 37–47. Lanham, MD: Lexington Books, 2013.

McDevitt, Michael, and Spiro Kiousis. "Education for Deliberative Democracy: The Long-Term Influence of Kids Voting USA." CIRCLE Working Paper 22: September, 2004. Center for Information and Research on Civic Learning and Engagement (CIRCLE).

McDevitt, Michael, and Steven Chaffee. "Closing Gaps in Political Communication and Knowledge Effects of a School Intervention." *Communication Research* 27 (2000): 259–92.

McDonald, Michael K. "Internships, Service-Learning, and Study Abroad: Helping Students Integrate Civic Engagement Learning Across Multiple Experiences," in *Teaching Civic Engagement: From Student to Active Citizen*, ed. Alison Rios Millett McCartney, Elizabeth A. Bennion, and Dick Simpson, 369–83. Washington, DC: American Political Science Association, 2013.

McFarland, Daniel A., and Reuben J. Thomas. "Bowling Young: How Youth Voluntary Associations Influence Adult Political Participation." *American Sociological Review* 71 (2006): 401–25.

McIntosh, Hugh, and James Youniss. "Toward a Political Theory of Political Socialization of Youth," in *Handbook of Research on Civic Engagement in Youth*, ed. Lonnie R. Sherrod, Judith Torney-Purta, and Constance Flanagan. Hoboken, NJ: John Wiley & Sons, Inc., 2010.

McIntosh, Hugh, Danil Hart, and James Youniss. "The Influence of Family Political Discussion on Youth Civic Development: Which Parent Qualities Matter?" *PS: Political Science & Politics* 3 (2007): 495–99.

Meinke, Timothy. "Learning Objectives and Outcomes of an Interdisciplinary Minor in Civic Engagement," in *Teaching Civic Engagement: From Student to Active Citizen*, ed. Alison Rios Millett McCartney, Elizabeth A. Bennion, and Dick Simpson, 337–52. Washington, DC: American Political Science Association, 2013.

Meirick, Patrick C., and Daniel B. Wackman. "Kids Voting and Political Knowledge: Narrowing Gaps, Informing Votes." *Social Science Quarterly* 85 (2004): 1161–77.

Middaugh, Ellen, and Joseph Kahne. "Online Localities: Implications for Democracy and Education." *Yearbook of the National Society for the Study of Education* 108 (2009): 192–218.

Mill, John Stuart. *On Liberty*, ed. Currin V. Shields. Upper Saddle River, NJ: Prentice Hall, Inc., 1997.

Milner, Henry. *The Internet Generation*. Lebanon, NH: Tufts University Press, 2010.

Milner, Henry. *Civic Literacy: How Informed Citizens Make Democracy Work*. London: University Press of New England, 2002.

Mirel, Jeffrey. "Civic Education and Changing Definitions of American Identity." *Educational Review* 54 (2002): 143–52.

Mitchell, Joshua J., Robert. D. Reason, Kevin M. Hemer, and Ashley Finley. "Perceptions of Campus Climates for Civic Learning as Predictors of College Students' Mental Health." *Journal of College and Character* 17 (2016): 40–52. doi:10.1080/2194587X.2015.1125367.

Molloy, Tim. "As President-Elect, Trump Uses YouTube, Twitter to Cut Out the Press." November 22, 2017. Accessed January 26, 2017. http://www.thewrap.com/donald-trump-uses-youtube-twitter-bypass-disempower-press/.

Mondak, Jeffery J., and Mary R. Anderson. "The Knowledge Gap: A Reexamination of Gender-Based Differences in Political Knowledge." *Journal of Politics* 66 (2004): 492–512.

Morgan, William, and Matthew Streb. "Building Citizenship: How Student Voice in Service-Learning Develops." *Social Science Quarterly* 82 (2001): 154–69.

Mumford, Lewis. *The Culture of Cities*. New York: Harcourt, Brace and Company, 1970.

Musil, Caryn McTighe. *Civic Prompts: Making Civic Learning Routine Across the Disciplines*. Washington, DC: Association of American Colleges and Universities, 2015.

Musil, Caryn McTighe. "Educating Students for Personal and Social Responsibility: The Civic Learning Spiral," in *Civic Engagement in Higher Education*, ed. Barbara Jacoby, 49–68. San Francisco: Jossey-Bass, 2009.

Mutz, Diana C. *Hearing the Other Side: Deliberative versus Participatory Democracy*. New York: Cambridge University Press, 2006.

National Commission on Civic Renewal. *A Nation of Spectators: How Civic Disengagement Weakens America and What We Can Do About It*. College Park, MD: National Commission on Civic Renewal, 1998.

National Conference on Citizenship. *America's Civic Health Index: Civic Health in Hard Times*. Washington, DC: National Conference on Citizenship, 2009. Available at http://www.ncoc.net/2gp54.

National Foundation on the Arts and Humanities Act of 1965, Public Law 89–209.

National Task Force on Civic Learning and Democratic Engagement. *A Crucible Moment: College Learning and Democracy's Future*. Washington, DC: Association of American Colleges and Universities, 2012. Available at https://www.aacu.org/sites/default/files/files/crucible/Crucible_508F.pdf.

Naume, Margaret J. "Writing Effective Learning Objectives." *Case Research Journal* 33 (2013): 165–71.

Neuman, W. Russell. *The Paradox of Mass Politics*. Cambridge, MA: Harvard University Press, 1986.

Newell, William Henry. "Decision Making in Interdisciplinary Studies," in *Handbook of Decision Making*, ed. Göktug Morçöl. New York: CRC, 2007.

Nie, Norman, Jane Junn, and Kenneth Stehlik-Barry. *Education and Democratic Citizenship in America*. Chicago: University of Chicago Press, 1996.

Nie, Norman, and Sunshine D. Hillygus. "Education and Democratic Citizenship," in *Making Good Citizens: Education and Civil Society*, ed. Diane Ravitch and Joseph P. Viteritti. New Haven, CT: Yale University Press, 2001.

Niemi, Richard G. "What Students Know About Civics and Government," in *Making Civics Count: Citizenship Education for a New Generation*, ed. David E. Campbell, Meira Levinson, and Frederick M. Hess, 15–35. Cambridge, MA: Harvard Education Press, 2012.

Niemi, Richard G., and Jane Junn. *Civic Education: What Makes Students Learn*. New Haven, CT: Yale University Press, 1998.

Niemi, Richard G., and Julia Smith. "Enrollments in High School Government Classes: Are We Short-Changing Both Citizenship and Political Science Training?" *PS: Political Science & Politics* 34 (2001): 281–87.

"Northeastern University College of Engineering: Service-Learning." Last modified 2012, http://www.coe.neu.edu/experiential-learning/service-learning.

Oceja, Luis. V., Marc W. Heerdink, Eric L. Stocks, Tamara Ambrona, Belén Lopéz-Peréz, and Sergio Salgado. "Empathy, Awareness of Others, and Action: How Feeling Empathy for One-Among-Others Motivates the Helping of Others." *Basic and Applied Social Psychology* 36 (2014): 111–24.

O'Connor, Sandra Day. "The Democratic Purpose of Education: From the Founders to Horace Mann to Today," in *Teaching America: The Case for Civic Education*, ed. David Feith, 3–14. Lanham, MD: Rowman & Littlefield Education, 2011.

Ortlipp, Michelle. "Keeping and Using Reflective Journals in the Qualitative Research Process." *The Qualitative Report* 13 (2008): 695–705.

O'Shaughnessy, Betty. "High School Students as Election Judges and Campaign Workers: Does the Experience Stick?" in *Teaching Civic Engagement: From Student to Active Citizen*, ed. Alison Rios Millett McCartney, Elizabeth A. Bennion, and Dick Simpson. Washington, DC: American Political Science Association, 2013.

O'Shaughnessy, Lynn. "Colleges Love Rich Students." *Wealth Management*, November 30, 2011. http://www.wealthmanagement.com/opinions/colleges-love-rich-students.

Ostrom, Elinor. "Civic Education for the Next Century: A Task Force to Initiate Professional Activity." *PS: Political Science & Politics* 29 (1996): 755–58.

Owen, Diana. "Civic Education and the Making of Citizens in the Digital Age." Paper prepared for presentation at the Annual Meeting of the American Political Science Association, Washington, DC, August 27–31, 2014.

Owen, Diana. "Political Socialization in the 21st Century: Recommendations for Researchers," at the The Future of Civic Education in the 21st Century Conference co-sponsored by the Center for Civic Education and the Bundeszentrale fur politische Bildung, James Madison's Montpelier, September 21–26, 2008.

Owen, Diana. "The Influence of Civic Education on Electoral Engagement and Voting," in *Teaching Civic Engagement: From Student to Active Citizen*, ed. Alison Rios Millet McCartney, Elizabeth A. Bennion, and Dick Simpson. Washington, DC: American Political Science Association, 2013.

Owen, Diana, Suzanne Soule, and Rebecca Chalif. "Civic Education and Knowledge of Politics and Government." Paper prepared for presentation at the Annual Meeting of the American Political Science Association, Seattle, Washington, September 1–4, 2011.

Owen, Diana, et al. "Civic Education and Social Media Use." *Electronic Media & Politics* 1 (2011): 1–28.

Oxford Living Dictionary. "Hacktivist." 2017. https://en.oxforddictionaries.com/definition/hacktivist.

Pace, C. Robert. *Measuring Outcomes of College: Fifty Years of Findings and Recommendations for the Future*. San Francisco: Jossey-Bass, 1979.

Parks Daloz, Laurent A., et al. *Common Fire: Lives of Commitment in a Complex World*. Boston: Beacon Press, 1996.

Parmelee, John H., and Shannon L. Bichard. *Politics and the Twitter Revolution: How Tweets Influence the Relationship Between Political Leaders and the Public*. Lanham, MD: Lexington Books, 2012.

Pascarella, Ernest T., Corrinna A. Ethington, and John C. Smart. "The Influence of College on Humanitarian-Civic Involvement Values." *Journal of Higher Education* 59 (1988): 412–37.

Pascarella, Ernest T., and Patrick T. Terenzini. *How College Affects Students: A Third Decade Of Research*. San Francisco: Jossey-Bass, 2005.

Pasek, Josh, Lauren Feldman, Daniel Romer, and Kathleen Hall Jamieson. "Schools as Incubators of Democratic Participation: Building Long-term Political Efficacy with Civic Education." *Applied Developmental Science* 12 (2008): 26–37.

Pelosi, Alexandra. *Citizen USA: A 50-State Road Trip*. HBO Documentary Films, 2011. DVD.

Pena, Devon, and Joe Gallegos. "Local Knowledge and Collaborative Environmental Action Research," in *Building Community: Social Science in Action*, ed. Philip Nyden, Anne Figert, Mark Shibley, and Darrly Burrows, 85–91. Thousand Oaks, CA: Pine Forge Press, 1997.

Pereira, Mónica Ferrín, Marta Fraile, and Martiño Rubal. "Young and Gapped? Political Knowledge of Girls and Boys in Europe." *Political Research Quarterly* 68 (2014): 63–76.

Peterson, Paul. *City Limits*. Chicago: University of Chicago Press, 1981.

Petty, Richard E., and John T. Cacioppo. *Communication and Persuasion*. New York: Springer-Verlag, 1986.

Pew Research Center for the People & the Press. *Political Knowledge Update*. Research Report. Washington, DC, March 31, 2011. Accessed December 20, 2014. http://pewresearch.org/pubs/1944/political-news-quiz-iq-congress-control-obesity-energy-facebook.

Pew Research Journalism Project. *Digital: News Sources for Americans by Platform*. Online Resource, 2014. Accessed January 15, 2015. http://www.journalism.org/media-indicators/where-americans-get-news.

Pike, Gary R. "The Effects of Residential Learning Communities and Traditional Residential Living Arrangements on Educational Gains During the First Year of College." *Journal of College Student Development* 40 (1999): 269–84.

Pinkleton, B.E., and E.W. Austin. "Individual Motivations, Perceived Media Importance, and Political Disaffection." *Political Communication* 18 (2001): 321–34.

Piscatelli, Jennifer. "Citizenship Education: Educating Students to Be Competent and Responsible Citizens and Leaders." *The Progress of Education Reform* 11 (2010). http://www.ecs.org/clearinghouse/87/95/8795.pdf.

"Planning Our Future: The Report of the American Politcial Science Association's Strategic Planning Committee." *PS: Political Science & Politics* 33 (2000): 877–93.

Pollack, Seth. "Civic Literacy across the Curriculum." *Diversity & Democracy* 14 (2011): 8–9.

Polletta, Franchesca, and Pang Ching Bobby Chen. "Gender and Public Talk: Accounting for Women's Variable Participation in the Public Sphere." *Sociological Theory* 31 (2014): 291–317.

Popkin, Samuel, and Michael Dimock. "Political Knowledge and Citizen Competence," in *Democracy and Citizen Competence*, ed. Steven Elkins. University Park, PA: Penn State University Press, 1996.

Posner, Michael I., and Brenda Patoine. "How Arts Training Improves Attention and Cognition." The Dana Foundation, 2009. Accessed January 5, 2017. http://www.dana.org/Cerebrum/2009/How_Arts_Training_Improves_Attention_and_Cognition.

Post, Margaret A., Elaine Ward, Nicholas V. Longo, and John Saltmarsh, eds. *Publicly Engaged Scholars: Next-Generation Engagement and the Future of Higher Education*. Sterling, VA: Stylus Publishing, LLC, 2016.

Powell, Katherine, and Cody Kalina. "Cognitive and Social Constructivism: Developing Tools for an Effective Classroom." *Education* 130 (2009): 241–50.

President's Commission on Higher Education. *Higher Education for American Democracy, Vol. I, Establishing the Goals*. Washington, DC: Government Printing Office, 1947.

Prince, Michael. "Does Active Learning Work? A Review of the Research." *Journal of Engineering Education* 93 (2004): 223–31.

"Purdue University: What is EPICS?" Last modified 2017, https://engineering.purdue.edu/EPICSU/About/index.html.

Putnam, Robert D. "Bowling Alone: America's Declining Social Capital." *Journal of Democracy* 6 (June 1995): 65–78.

Putnam, Robert D. *Bowling Alone: The Collapse and Revival of American Community*. New York: Simon & Schuster, 2000.

Putnam, Robert D. "Community-Based Social Capital and Education Performance," in *Making Good Citizens: Education and Civil Society*, ed. Diane Ravitch and Joseph P. Viteritti. New Haven, CT: Yale University Press, 2001.

Putnam, Robert D. "E Pluribus Unum: Diversity and Community in the Twenty-First Century." *Scandinavian Political Studies* 30 (2007): 137–74.

Putnam, Robert D. *Making Democracy Work: Civic Traditions in Modern Italy*. Princeton, NJ: Princeton University Press, 1993.

Putnam, Robert D. "The Prosperous Community: Social Capital and Public Life." *The American Prospect* 13 (1993): 35–42.

Putnam, Robert D. "Tuning In, Tuning Out: The Strange Disappearance of Social Capital in America." *PS: Political Science & Politics* 28 (Dec. 1995): 664–83.

Ravitch, Diane. *The Language Police: How Pressure Groups Restrict What Students Learn*. New York: Alfred A. Knopf, 2004.

Reardon, Kenneth M. "Straight A's? Evaluating the Success of Community/University Development Partnerships," in *Banking & Community*. Boston: Federal Reserve, 2005.

Reason, Robert D. "Creating and Assessing Campus Climates that Support Personal and Social Responsibility." *Liberal Education* 99 (2013): 38–43. https://aacu.org/publications-research/periodicals/creating-and-assessing-campus-climates-support-personal-and-social.

Rector, Robert, and Sheffield, Rachel. "Air Conditioning, Cable TV, and an Xbox: What Is Poverty in the United States Today?" *Backgrounder* 2575 (2011):1–23, 18 July.

Remnick, David, and Barack Obama. *The Bridge: The Life and Rise of Barack Obama*. New York: Alfred A. Knopf, 2010.

Rideout, Bruce. E., and Catherine M. Laubach. "EEG Correlates of Enhanced Spatial Performance Following Exposure to Music." *Perceptual Motor Skills* 82 (1996): 427–32.

Rizzo, Mary. "Finding the Roots of Civic Engagement in the Public Humanities." National Council on Public History. 2014. http://ncph.org/history-at-work/finding-the-roots-of-civic-engagement/.

Rockquemore, Kerry Ann, and Regan H. Schaffer. "Toward a Theory of Engagement: A Cognitive Mapping of Service-Learning Experiences." *Michigan Journal of Community Service Learning* 7 (2000): 14–25.

Rogers, Michael T. "A Civic Education Crisis." *Midsouth Political Science Review* 13 (2012): 1–36.

Rogers, Michael T. "A Meta-History of Formal Civic Education: An Episodic History to Be Repeated?" in *Civic Education in the 21st Century: A Multidimensional Inquiry*, ed. Michael T. Rogers and Donald M. Gooch. Lanham, MD: Lexington Books, 2015.

Rogers, Michael T. "Introduction: A Tocqueville-Inspired Assessment of America's Twenty-First Century Civic Ecology," in *Civic Education in the Twenty-First Century: A Multidimensional Inquiry*, ed. Michael T. Rogers and Donald M. Gooch. Lanham, MD: Lexington Books, 2015.

Rose, Barbara. "Poverty in DuPage County," in *Twenty-First Century Chicago*, ed. Dick Simpson, Constance A. Mixon, and Melissa Mourtisen. San Diego, CA: Cognella, 2016.

Rosenblum, Nancy. *Membership and Morals: The Personal Uses of Pluralism in America*. Princeton, NJ: Princeton University Press, 1998.

Ross, E. Wayne. "Negotiating the Politics of Citizenship Education." *PS: Political Science & Politics* 37 (2004): 249–51.

Rothstein, Bo. *The Quality of Government: Corruption, Social Trust, and Inequality in International Perspective*. Chicago: University of Chicago Press, 2011.

Rousseau, Jean-Jacques. *Emile or on Education*. Translated by Allan Bloom. New York: Basic Books, Inc., 1979.

Rousseau, Jean-Jacques. *"On the Social Contract,"* in *Jean-Jacques Rousseau: The Basic Political Writings*. Indianapolis: Hackett Publishing Company, 1987.

Ryder, Andrew J., et al. "Climate for Learning and Students' Openness to Diversity and Challenge: A Critical Role for Faculty." *Journal of Diversity in Higher Education* 9 (2016): 339–52.

Salisbury University. "Salisbury University - About Salisbury University - Salisbury University Mission Statement 2014." Accessed February 6, 2017. http://www.salisbury.edu/about/mission.html.

Salisbury University. "Salisbury University - Institute for Public Affairs and Civic Engagement - Civic Engagement Across the Curriculum (CEAC)." Accessed February 6, 2017. http://www.salisbury.edu/pace/CEAC/welcome1.html.

Salisbury University. "Salisbury University - Institute for Public Affairs and Civic Engagement - Pace Home." Accessed February 6, 2017. http://www.salisbury.edu/pace/default.html.

Salisbury University. "Salisbury University - University Analysis, Reporting, and Assessment - University Analysis, Reporting, & Assessment - SU At-A-Glance." Accessed February 6, 2017. http://www.salisbury.edu/uara/profile/home.html.

Sander, Libby. "Freshmen Survey: This year, Even More Focused on Jobs." *The Chronicle of Higher Education*, January 24, 2003. Retrieved from http://chronicle.com.cmich.idm.oclc.org/article/Freshman-Survey-This-Year/136787/?cid=related-promo.

Sanders, Lynn. "Against Deliberation." *Political Theory* 25 (1997): 347–76.

Sapiro, Virginia. *The Political Integration of Women: Role, Socialization, and Politics*. Chicago: University of Illinois Press, 1983.

Sapotichne, Joshua, Bryan D. Jones, and Michelle Wolfe. "Is Urban Politics a Black Hole? Analyzing the Boundary between Political Science and Urban Politics." *Urban Affairs Review* 43 (2007): 76–106. doi:10.1177/1078087407302901.

Sartori, Giovanni. "Concept Misformation in Comparative Politics." *American Political Science Review* 64 (1970): 1033–53.

Sax, Linda J. *The Gender Gap in College: Maximizing the Developmental Potential of Women and Men*. San Francisco: Jossey-Bass, 2008.

Schachter, Hindy Lauer. "Civic Education: Three Early American Political Science Association Committees and Their Relevance for Our Times." *PS: Political Science & Politics* 31 (1998): 631–35.

Schattschneider, E. E. *The Semi-Sovereign People*. New York: Holt, Rinehart & Winston, 1960.

Schlesinger, Arthur. M., Sr. "Biography of a Nation of Joiners." *American Historical Review 50* (1944): 1–25.

Schneider, Anne, and Helen Ingram. "Social Construction of Target Populations: Implications for Politics and Policy." *American Political Science Review* 87 (1993): 334–47.

Schuh, John H., and Megan Laverty. "The Perceived Long-Term Effect of Holding a Significant Student Leadership Position." *Journal of College Student Personnel* 24 (1983): 28–32.

Scott, Timothy P., Homer Tolson, and Yi-Hsuan Lee. "Assessment of Advanced Placement Participation and University Academic Success in the First Semester: Controlling for Selected High School Academic Abilities." *Journal of College Admission*, January 2010.

Seligsohn, Andrew J. "Colleges and Universities as Exemplars in the Development of Citizens." *Journal of College and Character* 17 (2016): 1–7. http://dx.doi.org/10.1080/2194587X.2015.1125369.

Selya, Benhabib, ed. *Democracy and Difference: Contesting the Boundaries of the Political*. Princeton, NJ: Princeton University Press, 1996.

Seven Valleys Health Coalition. *Cortland Counts: An Assessment of Health and Well-Being in Cortland County*. Cortland, NY: Seven Valleys Health Coalition, 2016.

Shah, Dhavan V., Jaeho Cho, William P. Eveland, Jr., and Nojin Kwak. "Information and Expression in a Digital Age: Modeling Internet Effects on Civil Participation." *Communication Research* 32 (2005): 531–65.

Shah, Dhavan V., Nojin Kwak, and R. Lance Holbert. "Connecting and Disconnecting with Civic Life: Patterns of Internet Use and the Production of Social Capital." *Political Communication* 18 (2001): 141–62.

Shaw, Emily J., Jessica P. Marini, and Krista D. Mattern. "Exploring the Utility of Advanced Placement Participation and Performance in College Admission Decisions." *Educational and Psychological Measurement* 73 (2013): 229–53.

Shea, Daniel M. "Nastiness, Name-Calling, and Negativity: The Alleghany College Survey of Civility and Compromise in American Politics." *Center for Political Participation*, 2010.

Sherrod, Lonnie R., Judith Torney-Purta, and Constance Flanagan, eds. *Handbook of Research on Civic Engagement*. Hoboken, NJ: John Wiley & Sons, Inc., 2010.

Sherrod, Lonnie R., Judith Torney-Purta, and Constance Flanagan. "Research on the Development of Citizenship: A Field Comes to Age," in *Handbook of Research on Civic Engagement in Youth*, ed. Lonnie R. Sherrod, Judith Torney-Purta, and Constance Flanagan. Hoboken, NJ: John Wiley & Sons, Inc., 2010.

Shin, Ryan. *Convergence of Contemporary Art, Visual Culture, and Global Civic Engagement.* Hershey, PA: Information Science Reference, 2017.

Short, John Rennie. "Want the Economy to Grow? We Need to Make Cities More Efficient." *Citymetric,* February. 29, 2016. http://www.citymetric.com/business/want-economy-grow-we-need-make-cities-more-efficient-1872.

Shulman, Lee. *Course Anatomy: The Dissection and Analysis of Knowledge Through Teaching.* Washington, DC: American Association for Higher Education, 1999.

Sidanius, James, Colette van Laar, Shauna Levin, and Stacey Sinclair. "Ethnic Enclaves and the Dynamics of Social Identity on the College Campus: the Good, the Bad, and the Ugly." *Journal of Personality and Social Psychology* 87 (2004): 96–110.

Simeone, James, and Gregory M. Shaw. "Do Project Pedagogies Matter?" *Journal of Political Science Education,* 2016. http://dx.doi.org/10.1080/15512169.2016.1194210.

Simeone, James. "Political Culture," in *Political and Civic Leadership: A Reference Handbook.* Vol. 1, ed. Richard A. Couto, 481–89. Thousand Oaks, CA: Sage Publications, 2010.

Simpson, Dick, Constance A. Mixon, and Melissa Mourtisen, eds. *Twenty-First Century Chicago.* San Diego, CA: Cognella, 2016.

Skocpol, Theda. "Civil Society in the United States," in *The Oxford Handbook of Civil Society,* ed. Michael Edwards. New York: Oxford University Press, 2011.

Skocpol, Theda. *Diminished Democracy: From Membership to Management in American Civil Life.* Norman: University of Oklahoma Press, 2003.

Skocpol, Theda. "The GI Bill and the US Social Policy, Past, and Future." *Social Philosophy and Policy* 14 (1997): 95–115.

Skocpol, Theda, and Morris P. Fiorina, eds. *Civic Engagement in American Democracy.* Washington, DC: Brookings Insitution Press, 1999.

Skocpol, Theda., Marshall Ganz, and Ziad Munson. "A Nation of Organizers: The Institutional Origins of Civic Voluntarism in the United States." *American Political Science Review 94* (2000), 527–46.

Skocpol, Theda., Ziad Munson, Andrew Karch, and Bayliss Camp. "Patriotic Partnerships: Why Great Wars Nourished American Civic Voluntarism," in *Shaped By War And Trade: International Influences On American Political Development,* ed. Ira Katznelson and Martin Shefter, 134–80. Princeton, NJ: Princeton University Press, 2002.

Smith, Aaron. "Civic Engagement in the Digital Age." Pew Internet Project. Pew Research Center, April 25, 2013. Accessed June 6, 2015. http://www.pewinternet.org/2013/04/25/civic-engagement-in-the-digital-age/.

Smith, Aaron, and Joanna Brenner. "Twitter Use 2012." Pew Internet Project. Pew Research Center, May 31, 2012. Accessed June 6, 2015. http://www.pewinternet.org/2012/05/31/twitter-use-2012/.

Smith, Eric R. A. N. *The Unchanging American Voter.* Berkeley: University of California Press, 1989.

Snyder, Claire. "Should Political Scientists Have a Civic Mission? An Overview of the Historical Evidence." *PS: Political Science & Politics* 34 (2001): 301–05.

"Social Change." Americans for the Arts. Accessed January 12, 2017. http://www.americansforthearts.org/by-topic/social-change.

Society for History Education Inc. "About The Organization." http://www.societyforhistoryeducation.org/about.html.

Society for the Teaching of Psychology. "Teaching of Psychology: Official Journal of the Society for the Teaching of Psychology." Society for the Teaching of Psychology. http://teachpsych.org/top/index.php.

Somit, Albert, and Joseph Tanenhaus. *The Development of Political Science: From Burgess to Behavioralism.* Boston: Allyn and Bacon, Inc., 1967.

Soska, Tracy M., and Alice K. Johnson Butterfield, eds. *University-Community Partnerships: Universities in Civic Engagement*. Binghamton, NY: Haworth Social Work Practice Press, 2004.

Spelt, Elisabeth J. H. et al. "Teaching and Learning in Interdisciplinary Higher Education: A Systematic Review." *Educational Psychology Review* 21 (2009): 365–78. doi:10.1007/s10648-009-9113-z.

Spencer, Marguerite L., Rebecca Reno, John A. Powell, and Andrew Grant-Thomas. "The Benefits of Racial and Economic Integration in Our Educational System: Why This Matters for Our Democracy." The Ohio State University: Kirwan Institute for the Study of Race and Ethnicity, 2009.

Staff, Amanda. H. "Many Teens Can't Tell Real News From Fake, Study Finds." *Christian Science Monitor*, 2016.

Stern, Mark J., and Susan C. Seifert. "Civic Engagement and the Arts: Issues of Conceptualization and Measurement." Animating Democracy, 2009. Accessed January 18, 2017. http://animatingdemocracy.org/sites/default/files/CE_Arts_SternSeifert.pdf.

Stiglitz, Joseph E. "8. Inequality and Economic Growth." *Political Quarterly* 86 (2015): 134–55. doi:10.1111/1467-923X.12237.

Stoecker, Randy, Mary Beckman, and Bo Hee Min. "Evaluating the Community Impact of Higher Education Civic Engagement," in *Handbook of Engaged Scholarship: Contemporary Landscapes, Future Directions, Volume 2: Community-Campus Partnerships*, ed. Hiram E Fitzgerald, Cathy Burack, and Sarena D. Seifer, 177–96. East Lansing: Michigan State University Press, 2010.

Strachan, J. Cherie. "Deliberative Democracy," in *American Governance*, ed. S. L. Schechter. New York: Macmillan Reference USA, 2016.

Strachan, J. Cherie. "Student and Civic Engagement: Cultivating the Skills, Efficacy, and Identities that Increase Student Involvement in Learning and in Public Life." in *Handbook of Teaching and Learning in Political Science and International Relations*, ed. John Ishiyama, William J. Miller, and Eszter Simon. Northampton, MA: Edward Elgar, 2015.

Strachan, J. Cherie, and Christopher Owens. "Learning Civic Norms Outside of the Classroom: Diversity and Campus Associational Life." *Journal of Political Science Education* 7 (2011): 464–82.

Strachan, J. Cherie, and Elizabeth A. Bennion. *Consortium for Inter-Campus SoTL Research National Survey of Student Leaders: Arkansas Tech University Report*, 2015.

Strayhorn, T. "How College Students' Engagement Affects Personal and Social Learning Outcomes." *Journal of College and Character* 10 (2008): 1–16.

Strier, Roni. "The Construction of University-Community Partnerships: Entangled Perspectives." *Higher Education* 62 (2011): 81–97.

Stringer, Ernest T. *Action Research*, second edition. Thousand Oaks, CA: Sage Publications, 1999.

Stroupe, Kenneth, Jr., and Larry Sabato. "Politics: The Missing Link of Responsible Education." University of Virginia Center for Politics, 2004. http://www.centerforpolitics.org/downloads/civicengagement-stroupe-final.pdf.

Suarez, John. "Empathy, Action, and Intercultural Competence," in *Intercultural Horizons: Intercultural Strategies in Civic Engagement, volume 2*, ed. Eliza J. Nash, Nevin C. Brown, and Lavinia Bracci, 1–18. Newcastle Upon Tyne, UK: Cambridge Scholars Publishing, 2013.

Surak, Sarah, and Alexander Pope. "Engaging the Educators: Facilitating Civic Engagement through Faculty Development." *Journal of Higher Education Outreach and Engagement* 20 (2016): 41–62.

Teague, Jane S. "Elmhurst." *The Electronic Encyclopedia of Chicago*. Chicago Historical Society, 2005. http://www.encyclopedia.chicagohistory.org/pages/422.html.

Theobald, Roddy, and Scott Freeman. "Is It the Intervention or the Students? Using Linear Regression to Control for Student Characteristics in Undergraduate STEM Education Research." *CBE Life Sciences Education* 13 (2014): 41–48.

Thompson, Michael J. "Suburban Origins of the Tea Party: Spatial Dimensions of the New Conservative Personality." *Critical Sociology* 38 (2012): 511–28. doi:10.1177/0896920511431905.

Tinto, Vincent. "Colleges as Communities: Exploring the Education Character of Student Persistence." *Journal of Higher Education* 68 (1997): 599–623.

Tinto, Vincent. "What Have We Learned about the Impact of Learning Communities on Students?" *Assessment Update* 12 (2000): 1–2, 12.

Tocqueville, Alexis de. *Democracy in America.* New York: Random House, Inc., 1990.

Tocqueville, Alexis de. *Democracy in America,* ed. J. P. Mayer and translated by G. Lawrence. Garden City, NY: Doubleday, 1969 (Original work published 1835–40).

Tolo, Kenneth. "An Assessment of We the People: Project Citizen: Promoting Citizenship in Classrooms and Communities," #161. Lyndon B. Johnson School of Public Affairs, University of Texas at Austin, 1998, Accessed January 6, 2015, http://new.civiced.org/resources/research/researchevaluation.

Torney-Purta, Judith. "The School's Role in Developing Civic Engagement: A Study of Adolescents in Twenty-Eight Countries." *Applied Developmental Science* 6 (2002): 203–12.

Torney-Purta, Judith, and Jo-Ann Amadeo. "The Contribution of International Large Scale Studies in Civic Education and Engagement," in *The Role of International Large Scale Assessments,* ed. M. von Davier, et al., 87–114. New York: Springer, 2012.

Torney-Purta, Judith, C. H. Barber, and B. Wilkenfeld. "Latino Adolescents' Civic Development in the United States: Research Results from the IEA Civic Education Study." *Journal of Youth and Adolescence* 36 (2007): 111–25.

Torney-Purta, Judith, Jo-Ann Amadeo, and Wendy K. Richardson. "Civic Service Among Youth in Chile, Denmark, England, and the United States: A Psychological Perspective," in *Civic Service Worldwide: Impacts and Inquiry,* ed. Amanda Moore McBride and Michael Sherraden, 95–132. Armonk, NY: M.E. Sharpe, 2007.

Torney-Purta, Judith, Rainer Lehmann, Hans Oswald, and Wolfram Schulz. *Citizenship and Education in Twenty-Eight Countries: Civic Knowledge and Engagement at Age Fourteen.* Amsterdam: International Association for the Evaluation of Educational Achievement, 2001.

Towson University. "Course Development Grant Application." Accessed February 6, 2017. http://www.towson.edu/provost/servicelearning/faculty/documents/grantapplication.pdf.

Towson University. "Mission & Strategic Plan." Accessed February 6, 2017. http://www.towson.edu/about/mission/index.html.

Towson University. "Office of Civic Engagement & Leadership." Accessed February 6, 2017. http://www.towson.edu/studentlife/activities/engagement/civicengagement/index.html.

Tucker, M., A. Shiarella, and Anne McCarthy. "Development and Construct Validity of Scores on the Community Service Attitudes Scale." *Journal of Educational and Psychological Measurement* 60 (2000): 286–300.

United Nations. "World's Population Increasingly Urban with More than Half Living in Urban Areas" *United Nations Report,* July 10, 2014. http://www.un.org/en/development/desa/news/population/world-urbanization-prospects-2014.html.

US Census Bureau. "US Census Bureau Projections Show a Slower Growing, Older, More Diverse Nation a Half Century From Now." US Census Bureau Press Release, December 12, 2012. https://www.census.gov/newsroom/releases/archives/population/cb12-243.html.

US Census Bureau. "American Community Survey: 60126," 2015. https://factfinder.census.gov/faces/tableservices/jsf/pages/productview.xhtml?src=CF.

US Census Bureau. "American Community Survey 1-year estimates." 2015. https://censusreporter.org/profiles/31000US16980-chicago-joliet-naperville-il-in-wi-metro-area.

Uslaner, Eric. *The Moral Foundations of Trust.* New York: Cambridge University Press, 2002.

van Deth, Jan W., and Sonja Zmerli. "Introduction: Civicness, Equality and Democracy: A 'Dark Side' of Social Capital?" *American Behavioral Scientist* 53 (2010): 631–39.

Van Vechten, Renee Bukovchik, and Anita Chadha. "How Students Talk to Each Other: An Academic Social Networking Project," in *Teaching Civic Engagement: From Student to Active Citizen*, ed. Alison Rios Millett McCartney, Elizabeth A. Bennion, and Dick Simpson. Washington, DC: American Political Science Association, 2013.

Verba, Sidney, Kay L. Schlozman, and Henry E. Brady. *Voice and Equality: Civic Voluntarism in American Politics*. Cambridge, MA: Harvard University Press, 1995.

Verba, Sidney, Kay L. Schlozman, Henry E. Brady, and Norman H. Nie. "Race, Ethnicity, and Political Resources: Participation in the United States." *British Journal of Political Science* 23 (1993): 453–97.

Vercellotti, Tim, and Elizabeth Matto. "The Kitchen-Table Connection: The Effects of Political Discussion on Youth Knowledge and Efficacy." CIRCLE Working Paper #72, 2010. Accessed December 23, 2014. http://www.civicyouth.org/wp-content/uploads/2010/09/WP_72_Vercellotti_Matto.pdf.

Voight, Adam, and Judith Torney-Purta. "A Typology of Youth Civic Engagement in Urban Middle Schools." *Applied Developmental Science* 17 (2013): 198–212.

Wald, Hedy S. "Refining a Definition of Reflection for the Being as well as Doing the Work of a Physician." *Medical Teacher* 37 (2015): 696–99.

Walker, Tobi. "Service as a Pathway to Political Participation: What Research Tells Us." *Applied Development Science* 6 (2002): 183–88.

Ward, Teresa, and Nannette Evans Commander. "The Power of Student Voices: An Investigation of the Enduring Qualities of Freshmen Learning Communities." *Journal of College Student Retention* 13 (2012): 63–85.

Warren, Mark R. *Democracy and Association*. Princeton, NJ: Princeton University Press, 2001.

Warren, Mark R. *Dry Bones Rattling: Community Building to Revitalize American Democracy*. Princeton, NJ: Princeton University Press, 2001.

Wattenberg, Martin P. *Is Voting for Young People?* third edition. New York: Pearson, 2012.

Wazwaz, Noor. "Its Official: The US is Becoming a Minority-Majority Nation." *US News and World Report*, July 6, 2015.

Weissbourd, Richard, Suzanne M. Bouffard, and Stephanie M. Jones. "School Climate and Moral and Social Development," in *School Climate: Practices for Implementation and Sustainability*, ed. Teri Dary and Terry Pickeral, 30–34. New York: National School Climate Center, 2013. http://www.schoolclimate.org/publications/documents/SchoolClimatePracticeBriefs-2013.pdf.

Welch, Marshall, and John Saltmarsh. "Current Practices and Infrastructures for Campus Centers of Community Engagement." *Journal of Higher Education Outreach and Engagement* 17 (2013): 25–56.

Westheimer, Joel. "Introduction—the Politics of Civic Education." *PS: Political Science & Politics* 37 (2004): 231–35.

Westheimer, Joel, and Joseph Kahne. "What Kind of Citizen? The Politics of Educating for Democracy." *American Educational Research Journal* 41 (2004): 237–69.

Widestrom, Amy. *Displacing Democracy: Economic Segregation in America*. Philadelphia: University of Pennsylvania Press, 2015.

Wiggins, Grant, and Jay McTigue. *Understanding Design. Expanded Second Edition*. Upper Saddle River, NJ: Pearson Education, Inc., 2006.

Wilkerson, LuAnn, and Wim H. Gijselaers. "Concluding Comments," in *Bringing Problem-Based Learning to Higher Education: Theory and Practice*, ed. LuAnn Wilkerson and Wim H. Gijselaers, 101–4. San Francisco: Jossey-Bass, 1996.

Williams, Joan. C., and Rachel Dempsey. *What Works for Women at Work: Four Patterns that Working Women Need to Know*. New York: New York University Press, 2014.

Williamson, Thad. "Sprawl, Spatial Location, and Politics: How Ideological Identification Tracks the Built Environment." *American Politics Research* 36 (2008): 903–33. doi:10.1177/1532673x08318589.

Wilson, Everett Keith. "The Entering Student: Attitudes and Agents of Change," in *College Peer Groups: Problems and Prospects for Research*, ed. Theodore Mead Newcomb and Everett Keith Wilson, 71–106. Chicago: Aldine Publishing Company, 1966.

Winerip, Michael. "Teaching Beyond the Test, to Make Room Again for Current Events." *The New York Times*, May 22, 2011. Accessed December 23, 2014. http://www.nytimes.com/2011/05/23/nyregion/teaching-beyond-test-with-eye-on-current-events.html.

Wolak, Jennifer, and Michael McDevitt. "The Roots of the Gender Gap in Political Knowledge in Adolescence." *Political Behavior* 33 (2011): 505–33.

Wong, Janelle, S. Karthick Ramakrishnan, Taeku Lee, and Jane Junn. *Asian American Political Participation: Emerging Constituents and Their Political Identities*. New York: Russell Sage Foundation, 2011.

Wray-Lake, Laura, and Daniel Hart. "Growing Social Inequalities in Youth Civic Engagement? Evidence from the National Election Study." *PS: Political Science & Politics* 45 (2012): 456–61.

Wright, Noeline. "Twittering in Teacher Education: Reflecting on Practicum Experiences." *Open Learning* 25 (2011): 259–65.

Young, Iris. Marion. *Inclusion and Democracy*. Oxford: Oxford University Press, 2000.

Youniss, James. "Civic Education: What Schools Can Do to Encourage Civic Identity and Action." *Applied Developmental Science* 15 (2011): 98–103.

Youniss, James. "How to Enrich Civic Education and Sustain Democracy," in *Making Civics Count: Citizenship Education for a New Generation*, ed. David E. Campbell, Meira Levinson, and Frederick M. Hess, 115–33. Cambridge, MA: Harvard Education Press, 2012.

Youniss, James, and Miranda Yates. *Community Service and Social Responsibility in Youth*. Chicago: University of Chicago Press, 1997.

Youniss, James, Jeffrey A. McLellan, and Miranda Yates. "What We Know About Engendering Civic Identity." *American Behavioral Scientist* 40 (1997): 620–31.

Zhao, Chun-Mei, and George D. Kuh. "Adding Value: Learning Communities and Student Engagement." *Research in Higher Education* 45 (2004): 115–38.

Zukin, Cliff, et al. *A New Engagement? Political Participation, Civic Life, and the Changing American Citizen*. New York: Oxford University Press, 2006. ∎

About the Authors

STEPHEN ARMSTRONG

Stephen Armstrong is currently a senior at the University of Southern California majoring in political science. He has worked on the Penny Harvest program for more than two years—serving as an assistant coach for the elementary school children, program assistant with the university classes, and student research assistant. Armstrong has also completed both of the undergraduate classes that focus on the Penny Harvest. In addition, Armstrong is an avid musician and composer. He enjoys spending his time repairing and trading old guitars. In the future he hopes to continue his involvement in community service as well as his studies in political science.

KATHERINE BARRETT AND RICHARD GREENE

Katherine Barrett and Richard Greene, a husband-and-wife team, have focused on the field of city and state government through research, analysis, consultation and writing for over twenty five years. They are principals of Barrett and Greene, Inc. They are special project consultants to the Volcker Alliance, senior fellows with the Council of State Governments, senior fellows at the Fels Institute at the University of Pennsylvania, and fellows in the National Academy of Public Administration. They are also management columnists for *Governing Magazine* and senior fellows at the Governing Institute. With underwriting from the Pew Charitable Trusts, they founded, spearheaded, and wrote the Government Performance Project, which was utilized for annual "grading the states" (cities, counties) for a decade, ending in 2008. Barrett and Greene have also served in an advisory capacity to many organizations including the National League of Cities, the Urban Institute, the Governmental Accounting Standards Board, the Association of Government Accountants, the National Association of State Chief Administrators Offices, the Center for a Better South, and others.

ELIZABETH A. BENNION

Elizabeth A. Bennion is a professor of political science at Indiana University South Bend (IUSB). In addition to teaching American politics courses, Bennion is the founding director of IUSB's American Democracy Project and host of WNIT's live weekly television program *Politically Speaking*. In these capacities she moderates political discussions, public issue forums, and candidate debates for local, state, and national candidates. Bennion has won numerous (national, state, and local) awards for her teaching and service, and has published widely in academic books, journals, and newsletters. Her teaching, research, and service all promote civic education and engagement. She is currently working on a national survey of student leaders, a study of youth political ambition, and a multicampus voter registration field experiment. Bennion coedited the previous APSA book *Teaching Civic Engagement: From Student to Active Citizen*. She lives in South Bend with her husband and four children.

Margaret Brower

Margaret Brower is a researcher for the Institute for Democracy and Higher Education at Tisch College, Tufts University. She received her BA in political science and education from Colgate University. She then completed her MA in public policy and higher education at the University of Michigan. Currently, she is pursuing a doctorate degree in political science at the University of Chicago. At the University of Chicago, she continues to design and lead qualitative research studies.

Kimberly Coleman

Kimberly Coleman is a postdoctoral associate at the Rubenstein School of Environment and Natural Resources at the University of Vermont. She is broadly trained in the study of human dimensions of natural resources with particular interest in the intersection of civic engagement and natural resources. Her research ranges from examinations of community involvement in public land management to evaluations of environmentally focused service-learning. She holds a MS in natural resources and a BS in environmental studies, both from the University of Vermont, and a PhD in forest resources and environmental conservation from Virginia Tech.

Ann N. Crigler

Ann N. Crigler is professor of political science with appointments in the Price School of Public Policy and the Annenberg School for Communications at the University of Southern California (USC). She has published numerous books, articles, and essays on political communication, elections, emotions, and political behavior. Her coauthored and edited books include *Common Knowledge: News and the Construction of Political Meaning* (University of Chicago Press, 1992); the award-winning *Crosstalk: Citizens, Candidates and the Media in a Presidential Campaign* (University of Chicago Press, 1996); *The Psychology of Political Communication* (University of Michigan Press, 1996); *Rethinking the Vote: The Politics and Prospects of American Election Reform* (Oxford University Press, 2004); and *The Affect Effect: Dynamics of Emotion in Political Thinking and Behavior* (University of Chicago Press, 2007). Her current research examines the role of social media in US elections, emotions and political decision-making, and youth civic engagement. She and her students are currently working with elementary schools in Los Angeles to conduct research and increase children's civic skills, involvement, and community networks through the USC Penny Harvest.

Constance DeVereaux

Constance DeVereaux is the director of LEAP Institute for the Arts at Colorado State University, which trains graduate and undergraduate students in the skills of arts management, arts policy, and arts-based community engagement. She earned a doctorate degree in philosophy and political science at Claremont Graduate University and an MFA in fiction at Antioch University, Los Angeles. She is a leader in the field of cultural policy and cultural management; her research focuses on cultural identity, cultural citizenship, and the philosophical challenges that arise in arts policy processes. She has authored multiple articles and book chapters on arts and cultural policy including, "Is Art a Fruit or a Vegetable? On Developing a Practice-Based Definition of Art," "Chagrin and the Politics of American Aesthetics," and the coauthored *Narrative, Identity, and the Map of Cultural Policy: Once Upon a Time in a Globalized World.*

John Forren

John Forren is an assistant professor in the department of justice and community studies at Miami University. Forren's research interests are American constitutional law and history, criminal justice, judicial politics, public policy making, and civic engagement. He has written on a range of issues including the development of federal workplace safety standards in Congress; the state of "civic health" in Ohio; the responses of various policymakers to US Supreme Court decisions;

the evolution of First Amendment doctrines in the lower courts; and the policy implications of presidential decision making regarding social service delivery by faith-based groups. His writings and commentary have appeared in the University of Pennsylvania *Journal of Constitutional Law*, *Journal of Markets and Morality*, *PS: Political Science & Politics*, *Publius: The Journal of Federalism*, *Law and History Review*, the *Encyclopedia of Civil Liberties in America*, *Democracy in America*, and *Major Acts of Congress*. He is also coauthor of both the 2013 and 2016 publications of the *Ohio Civic Health Index Report*, published by the National Conference on Citizenship.

GERALD THOMAS GOODNIGHT

Gerald Thomas Goodnight is a professor at the University of Southern California (USC) in the Annenberg School of Communication. Argumentation, deliberation, and the public sphere comprise his primary areas of inquiry. He has directed doctoral studies in communication at USC and Northwestern University, where he directed the Owen L. Coon Debate Society. Having directed 52 dissertations, he has been accorded career awards by the National Communication Association and been named among the five top scholars in argumentation of the last 50 years by the American Forensics Association.

MAGGIE GROVE

Maggie Grove is the Vice President for Strategy and Operations at Campus Compact. For the past 20 years, her work has focused on the development of partnerships between colleges and community-based nonprofits as an independent contractor and as the executive director of Rhode Island Campus Compact. Grove holds a BA from Oberlin College and a master's degree in philanthropic studies from Indiana University.

DEBORAH HALPERIN

Deborah Halperin is the director of the Action Research Center (ARC) at Illinois Wesleyan University in Bloomington, Illinois. ARC facilitates the alignment of university resources with community engagement opportunities. Halperin represents the university on community-wide coalitions addressing housing, health, and civic engagement. She teaches courses in community-based research and grant writing. She also oversees partnerships with local government, community development organizations, and nonprofit agencies. Halperin has over 25 years of experience in nonprofits, a BA in sociology, and an MS in human services administration. In 2015, she presented her vision for Empowering Young People to Get Stuff Done at TEDxNormal.

SHAWN P. HEALY

Shawn P. Healy, the Robert R. McCormick Foundation Democracy Program's civic learning scholar, serves as the Foundation's internal resource for knowledge on civic education and engagement. Healy plays a key role in the Democracy Program's work in the areas of advocacy and public policy, serving as a chair of the Illinois Civic Mission Coalition, and leading the state's Democracy Schools Initiative. Healy recently chaired the Illinois Task Force on Civic Education and led the successful push for a required high school civics course in Illinois. He also led the Illinois Social Science Standards Task Force in 2014–2015. Healy makes regular appearances as a guest speaker and panelist at academic and professional development conferences across the country, is a frequent contributor to local media, and produces original scholarship in the area of political participation and civic education. Before joining the McCormick Foundation, he served as a social studies teacher at West Chicago Community High School and Sheboygan North High School. A 2001 James Madison Fellow from the State of Wisconsin, he holds a MA and PhD from the University of Illinois at Chicago in political science.

CHRISTOPHER JENSEN

Christopher Jensen is the director for the Office of Civic Engagement and Leadership at Towson University. He has worked in higher education for 20 years in the areas of leadership development, community service/service learning, residential life, student activities, orientation, and fraternity and sorority life. Jensen has taught courses on interdisciplinary research and organizational psychology and currently is an adjunct faculty in the Towson University College of Education. He received his BA from the University of Michigan in studies in religion, a MA in student affairs administration from Michigan State University, and a PhD in educational leadership from Oakland University. His dissertation focused on the impact of community service-experiences on students' persistence in college.

TARA KULKARNI

Tara Kulkarni is an assistant professor in the Department of Civil and Environmental Engineering and Construction Management and the director of the Center for Global Resilience and Security at Norwich University. Her research interests are in green infrastructure, sustainable water resources management, and building community resilience through engineering innovation. She has used grants through the National Science Foundation's EPSCoR program and from the US Environmental Protection Agency to research, design, and model green stormwater infrastructure and innovative treatment of nutrients in stormwater and agricultural runoff. She is also heavily involved in K–12 STEM outreach and community engagement. Kulkarni's terminal degree is from Florida State University. Her previous professional experience is in state government and management consulting.

TARA M. LENNON

Tara M. Lennon teaches political theory and oversees the Legislative Internship Program at Arizona State University (ASU). She earned her BA in government and psychology at Wesleyan University in Connecticut and her MA and PhD in political theory and international relations at ASU. Between 2000 and 2011, she evaluated the effectiveness of state agencies and school districts and managed research projects on education funding and academic achievement for the Auditor General's Office, a nonpartisan research branch of the Arizona State Legislature. Since returning to academia, she has conducted research in the science of teaching and learning, earning grants from the Spencer Foundation to explore whether teaching with social media promotes civic engagement and ASU's Center for Education through eXploration to study the impact of teaching with simulations.

JANE MANSBRIDGE

Jane Mansbridge, Charles F. Adams Professor at the Harvard Kennedy School, is the author of *Beyond Adversary Democracy* and *Why We Lost the ERA* [Equal Rights Amendment], and editor/coeditor of the volumes *Beyond Self-Interest*, *Feminism* (with Susan Moller Okin), *Oppositional Consciousness* (with Aldon Morris), *Deliberative Systems* (with John Parkinson), and *Political Negotiation* (with Cathie Jo Martin). She was president of the APSA 2012–2013.

ELIZABETH C. MATTO

Elizabeth C. Matto is an assistant research professor at the Eagleton Institute of Politics and the director of the institute's Center for Youth Political Participation (CYPP). She earned her doctorate in American politics at George Washington University and, prior to her work at Eagleton, taught a variety of courses at Princeton University, Temple University, and George Washington University. As director of CYPP, Matto leads research as well as educational and public service efforts designed to encourage and support the political learning of high school and college students and civic action among young adults. In 2016, she was the recipient of the Craig L. Brians Award for Excellence in Undergraduate Research and Mentorship by the American Political Science Association.

ALISON RIOS MILLETT MCCARTNEY

Alison Rios Millett McCartney is professor of political science and faculty director of the Honors College at Towson University outside of Baltimore, Maryland. She contributed to and coedited another volume on this topic, *Teaching Civic Engagement: From Student to Active Citizen*, with Elizabeth A. Bennion and Dick Simpson in 2013 and has published other work connecting civic engagement education and international relations in the *Journal of Political Science Education*. McCartney is also very involved in undergraduate research and teaching international negotiation simulations. She has received several teaching awards including the University of Maryland System Regents' Award for Mentoring, the Maryland-DC Campus Compact Award for Service-Learning Scholarship, and the Towson University Service-Learning Faculty Member Award. She received her BA from Syracuse University and her masters and PhD from the University of Virginia.

MARY MCHUGH

Mary McHugh is the executive director of the Stevens Service Learning Center and adjunct faculty member in the political science department at Merrimack College in North Andover, Massachusetts. She teaches a variety of classes in US politics and American political institutions. McHugh earned an MA in political science from Boston College, a BA in government and history from Colby College, and is currently working on her dissertation. Her research interests include examining how experiential learning affects and enhances student learning.

JOHN MCTAGUE

John McTague is assistant professor in the department of political science at Towson University. He earned his BA (With Honors) in political science at Rutgers, the State University of New Jersey and completed his PhD in the department of government and politics at University of Maryland, College Park. A practitioner of service-learning pedagogy, McTague teaches courses in American politics, particularly the subjects of religion and politics, race and inequality, political parties, and research methodology. He has made more than 20 research presentations at various professional conferences, and his work has been featured in journals such as *Legislative Studies Quarterly*, *American Politics Research*, and *Political Research Quarterly*.

CONSTANCE A. MIXON

Constance A. Mixon is an associate professor of political science and director of the Urban Studies Program at Elmhurst College. In 2001, she was nominated by her students, and named the Illinois Professor of the Year by the Carnegie Foundation for the Advancement of Teaching. She has also received the APSA's Pi Sigma Alpha National Award for Outstanding Teaching. In addition to publishing several journal articles and book chapters, she is a coeditor of *Twenty-First Century Chicago*, which investigates the social, economic, political, and governmental challenges facing Chicago. Mixon frequently provides political commentary and analysis for local and national media outlets, including the Associated Press, NBC, WGN, FOX, and PBS. She also regularly presents at regional and national conferences on topics related to teaching and civic and political engagement.

CARYN MCTIGHE MUSIL

Caryn McTighe Musil is senior scholar and director of civic learning and democracy initiatives at the Association of American Colleges and Universities (AAC&U), where she had earlier served as senior vice president of the Office of Diversity, Equity, and Global Initiatives for 14 years. Her professional career has been focused on teaching, writing, speaking, and directing national and global projects about civic engagement, diversity, global learning, and democracy. She was the author of *A Crucible Moment: College Learning and Democracy's Future*, written to reflect the national input from multiple constituencies. Musil received her BA from Duke University and her MA and PhD in

English from Northwestern University. She was honored with the 2013 Outstanding Contribution to Higher Education Award from the National Association of Student Personnel Administrators.

DIANA OWEN

Diana Owen is associate professor of political science and teaches in the communication, culture, and technology graduate program, and has served as director of the American Studies Program at Georgetown University. She is the author of multiple books, including *American Government and Politics in the Information Age* (with David Paletz and Timothy Cook, 2012). She is the coeditor of *The Internet and Politics: Citizens, Voters, and Activists* (with Sarah Oates and Rachel Gibson, 2006), *Making a Difference: The Internet and Elections in Comparative Perspective* (with Richard Davis, Stephen Ward, and David Taras, 2009), and *The Internet and Elections in the US, Japan, South Korea, and Taiwan* (with Shoko Kiyohara and Kazahiro Maeshima, 2017). She is the author of numerous journal articles and book chapters in the fields of civic education and engagement, media and politics, political socialization, elections and voting behavior, and political psychology/sociology. She has conducted studies funded by the Pew Charitable Trusts, the Center for Civic Education, and other sources. Her current research explores the relationship between civic education and political engagement over the life course and new media's role in politics.

ALEXANDER POPE

Alexander Pope is assistant professor in the Department of Education Specialties at Salisbury University. He completed his BA in history/philosophy at The Colorado College (2004); his MA in history and in curriculum and instruction at Texas State, San Marcos (2008); and his PhD in social studies education at Teachers College, Columbia University (2013). Pope codirects Salisbury University's Institute for Public Affairs and Civic Engagement (PACE). With his colleague Sarah Surak, he facilitates PACE's Civic Engagement Across the Curriculum (CEAC) program as well as the university's Presidential Citizen Scholars Program. Together they are coordinating a multi-year research project to collect and analyze data on the delivery of a civic engagement component in undergraduate courses. His research investigates, among other things, the way civic engagement experiences influence student and teacher attitudes toward their communities.

ADITI RAMESH

Aditi Ramesh is currently a junior at the University of Southern California, majoring in economics/mathematics. Ramesh has been conducting research under Ann N. Crigler in the department of political science since the beginning of her freshman year and has assisted with a variety of projects. Ramesh hopes to pursue a master's in data science and work at the intersection of big data and humanitarian work. Since freshman year, Ramesh has actively worked with nonprofits in Los Angeles through a pro-bono student consulting organization, Los Angeles Community Impact. Through this, she has served with many clients in the area, from homeless shelters to after-school educational projects.

G. ISAAC W. RIDDLE

G. Isaac W. Riddle is adjunct professor for the communication, culture, and technology program at Georgetown University. He completed his masters in communication, culture, and technology at Georgetown University in 2016. Riddle is a former captain in the United States Marine Corps who served in roles as both an intelligence and reconnaissance officer. He is interested in how citizens are socialized into the political actors they become and how the modern media and technology environment contributes to the formation. This includes how notions of citizenship are changing and what this means for political participation. He is also passionate about civic education and research how it is linked to the acquisition of political knowledge, dispositions, and skills.

MICHAEL T. ROGERS

Michael T. Rogers is an associate professor of political science in the History and Political Science Department at Arkansas Tech University. He received his PhD from the University at Albany–SUNY in 2005. His major subfield is political theory and his minor is American politics. He regularly offers courses in both subfields. His research interests include civic education (literacy and engagement), as well as the history of political thought and democratic theory. He has published manuscripts on civic education and engagement in disciplinary journals and as book chapters in collective volumes. Most recently, he coedited and contributed multiple chapters to *Civic Education in the 21st Century: A Multidimensional Inquiry*, published by Lexington books (2015). Other publications include a piece on criticisms of the Electoral College during the founding ratification debates and a coauthored chapter with Sally Friedman on congressional representation.

ANDREW J. SELIGSOHN

Andrew J. Seligsohn is president of Campus Compact, a national coalition of more than 1,000 colleges and universities dedicated to the public purposes of higher education. He previously served as associate chancellor for Civic Engagement and Strategic Planning at Rutgers University, Camden and director of Civic Engagement Learning at Princeton University. Seligsohn has taught at Rutgers, Princeton, Hartwick College, St. Olaf College, and Macalester College and has authored articles and chapters on student civic learning, institutional engagement, urban politics, constitutional law, and political theory. He holds a BA from Williams College and a PhD in political science from the University of Minnesota.

JAMES SIKORA

James Sikora is professor of sociology at Illinois Wesleyan University. After stints in the Marines, managing Kroger stores, and years as a student, he earned a PhD in sociology at the University of Illinois-Champaign Urbana. An applied researcher, his professor-administrator-consultant career over the last 45 years has focused on bringing students and their learning into the community, whether working with corporations or public-private nonprofit organizations. He served as president of the Illinois Sociological Association and chaired the American Sociological Association's Committee on Teaching. Teaming with James Simeone and Deborah Halperin he developed the Action Research Center for undergraduate students as citizen-scholars and project managers to use to integrate theory, research, and leadership skills for community social change.

JAMES SIMEONE

James Simeone is professor of political science at Illinois Wesleyan University (IWU). His specialization is in American political thought and American political development. He teaches a senior seminar in American exceptionalism. His recent publications include "Reassessing Jacksonian Political Culture: William Leggett's Egalitarianism" in *American Political Thought*. After many years of trial and error with community partners, he cofounded the Action Research Center (ARC) in 2003 with James Sikora. His current ARC projects include a sustainability education program at the campus Peace Garden and an Algebra Project with the Boys and Girls Club of Bloomington-Normal. He oversees the Advocacy Minor at IWU and teaches its core class "Engagement & the City: Millennials and the New Citizenship."

DICK SIMPSON

Dick Simpson has uniquely combined a distinguished academic career with public service in government. He is a former Chicago alderman and candidate for US Congress. He has published widely, been an outstanding teacher, and affected public policy. He began his academic career at the University of Illinois at Chicago (UIC) in 1967 where he has taught for 50 years. At UIC he received the highest awards given for teaching and the American Political Science Association

(APSA) and Pi Sigma Alpha National Award for Outstanding Teaching. He is a former department head (2006–2012), a previous director of the department's Preparing Future Faculty program, and currently a professor of political science at UIC.

STEVEN RATHGEB SMITH

Steven Rathgeb Smith is the executive director of the American Political Science Association. Previously, he was the Louis A. Bantle Chair in Public Administration at the Maxwell School of Citizenship and Public Affairs at Syracuse University. He also taught for many years at the University of Washington where he was the Nancy Bell Evans Professor of Public Affairs at the Evans School of Public Affairs and director of the Nancy Bell Evans Center for Nonprofits and Philanthropy. In addition, he has taught at Georgetown University, Duke University, American University, and Washington University in St. Louis. From 1997 to 2004, he was editor of *Nonprofit and Voluntary Sector Quarterly* and, from 2006 to 2008, president of the Association for Research on Nonprofit Organizations and Voluntary Action. Smith has authored and edited several books including, *Nonprofits for Hire: The Welfare State in the Age of Contracting* (with Michael Lipsky), *Governance and Regulation in the Third Sector: International Perspectives* (coedited with Susan Phillips) and, most recently, *Nonprofits and Advocacy: Engaging Community and Government in an Era of Retrenchment* (The Johns Hopkins University Press, 2014) (coedited with Robert Pekkanen and Yutaka Tsujinaka). He is currently president of the International Society for Third Sector Research.

J. CHERIE STRACHAN

J. Cherie Strachan is director of student and civic engagement for the College of Humanities, Social and Behavioral Sciences, and professor of political science at Central Michigan University. She is the author of *High-Tech Grassroots: The Professionalization of Local Elections*, as well as numerous articles and book chapters. Her recent publications focus on civility in democracy, as well as on college-level civic education interventions. Her applied research, which focuses on facilitating student-led deliberative discussions sessions and on enhancing the political socialization that occurs within campus student organizations, has resulted in ongoing work with the Kettering Foundation. She also codirects the Consortium for Inter-Campus SoTL Research (CISR), which facilitates cross-campus data collection for campus-wide civic engagement initiatives and political science pedagogy research.

JOHN SUAREZ

John Suarez is the coordinator of the Office of Service-Learning at SUNY, Cortland. In 1999, he launched service-learning English composition courses in the college's writing program. He partners with faculty and community agency supervisors on multidisciplinary civic engagement projects. Publications include "Emotion in PBL and SL," in *Engaged Faculty Curriculum, Community-Campus Partnerships for Health* (2015) and "Empathy, Action, and Intercultural Competence: A Neurological Rationale for Simulation's Effectiveness in Developing Intercultural Competence," in *Intercultural Horizons: Intercultural Strategies in Civic Engagement* (2014). Presentations include "Reflective listening in professional settings," United University Professionals meeting, SUNY Cortland, November 2016, and "'Hire' Education, Public Purpose, and Student Employers," Campus Compact Conference, Boston, March 2016. He earned his MS in education and BA in speech and Theater from SUNY, Oneonta.

SARAH SURAK

Sarah Surak holds a joint appointment in the departments of political science and environmental studies at Salisbury University. She earned a Masters of Public Administration from the University of Tennessee, Knoxville (2006) and a PhD in planning, governance, and globalization from Virginia Tech (2012). Surak codirects Salisbury University's Institute for Public Affairs and Civic

Engagement (PACE). With her colleague Alexander Pope, she facilitates PACE's Civic Engagement Across the Curriculum (CEAC) program as well as the university's Presidential Citizen Scholars Program. Together they are coordinating a multi-year research project to collect and analyze data on the delivery of a civic engagement component in undergraduate courses. Her teaching and research interests include civic engagement, environmental policy and political theory, comparative politics, public administration, and modern political and social theory.

NANCY THOMAS

Nancy Thomas directs the Institute for Democracy and Higher Education at Tufts University's Jonathan M. Tisch College of Civic Life, conducting research and providing assistance to colleges and universities to advance student political learning and participation in democracy. The institute's signature initiative, the National Study of Learning, Voting, and Engagement (NSLVE), is a large dataset for research and provides each of the 1,000+ participating colleges and universities with their students' aggregate voting rates. Her work and scholarship center on higher education's democratic mission, college student political learning and engagement, free speech and academic freedom, and deliberative democracy on campuses and in communities. She is the author of multiple book chapters, articles, and the monograph, *Educating for Deliberative Democracy*. She is an associate editor of the *Journal of Public Deliberation* and a senior associate with Everyday Democracy. She received a BA in government from St. Lawrence University, her JD from Case Western Reserve University, and an EdD from the Harvard Graduate School of Education.

GINA SERIGNESE WOODALL

Gina Serignese Woodall is a senior lecturer of political science in the School of Politics and Global Studies at Arizona State University. Woodall's teaching interests include research methods, American government, statistics, and women in politics. Her primary research interests are social media in the political science classroom as well as gender, the media, and negative campaigns; her current work focuses on political science pedagogy, including Twitter in the classroom. She has also coauthored papers on women, the media, and politics. She has coauthored several book chapters and journal articles in *Political Behavior*, *International Journal of Press/Politics*, *Journal of Politics*, *Journal of Women, Politics, and Policy*, and others. ∎

Index

Figures and tables are indicated by an "f" and "t" following page numbers.